# Professional Feature Writing

## Fourth Edition

# Professional Feature Writing

## Fourth Edition

Bruce Garrison
*University of Miami*

**LEA** LAWRENCE ERLBAUM ASSOCIATES, PUBLISHERS
2004    Mahwah, New Jersey                    London

Lawrence Erlbaum Associates, Inc., Publishers
10 Industrial Avenue
Mahwah, New Jersey 07430

Cover art by Thomas P. Calabrese

Cover design by Kathryn Houghtaling Lacey

**Library of Congress Cataloging-in-Publication Data**

Garrison, Bruce, 1950–
    Professional feature writing / Bruce Garrison.—4th ed.
        p.   cm. — (LEA's communication series)

    Includes bibliographical references and index.
ISBN 0-8058-4765-0 (cloth : alk. paper)
ISBN 0-8058-4766-9 (pbk. : alk. paper)
1. Feature writing.   I. Title.   II. Series.
PN4784.F37G37   2003
808'.06607—dc22                                         2003049395
                                                             CIP

Books published by Lawrence Erlbaum Associates are printed on acid-free
paper, and their bindings are chosen for strength and durability.

Printed in the United States of America
10  9  8  7  6  5  4  3  2

# Contents

# About the Author

Dr. Bruce Garrison is a professor in the Journalism Program of the School of Communication at the University of Miami, Coral Gables, FL. He teaches graduate and undergraduate level journalism and mass communication courses. Among them is a class focusing on feature writing. He is a long-time resident of Miami and a Kentucky native.

Garrison has written full-time for daily newspapers, serves as a freelance travel writer, and has taken on freelance assignments for industry magazines. He has worked as a reporter, feature writer, and copy editor for the *Lexington Herald–Leader, Hattiesburg* (MS) *American, Knoxville News–Sentinel, Dallas Morning News, Milwaukee Journal, The Patriot Ledger* of Quincy, MA, *The Miami News,* and *The Miami Herald.* He has supervised and edited nearly 30 special feature writing sections and projects for the daily *Key West Citizen* since 1990.

He has written features for newspaper industry magazines and newsletters, such as *Editor & Publisher, Coach's Corner, Publisher's Auxiliary,* and various annual publications of the Associated Press Managing Editors organization. He is a regular contributor and columnist for *College Media Review,* a publication of the College Media Advisors national organization.

Garrison is author or coauthor of eight other books about journalism and mass communication. His latest work with colleagues Michael B. Salwen and Paul Driscoll is *Online News and the Public* (in press). He has also written *Computer-Assisted Reporting* (2nd ed., 1998), *Successful Strategies for Computer-Assisted Reporting* (1996), *Sports Reporting* (2nd ed., 1993), *Professional News Reporting* (1992), *Advanced Reporting: Skills for the Professional* (1992), *Professional News Writing* (1990), and, coauthored with Michael B. Salwen, *Latin American Journalism* (1991).

## ACKNOWLEDGMENTS

As with the first three editions, I received a lot of help to finish this project. Gratitude is owed to many people who provided assistance, and I want to mention a few of them here. First, I thank Dean Edward Pfister for his assistance in providing the support of the School of Communication at the University of Miami. He has always encouraged me and given me the freedom to work on this project and others like it. I also offer my sincerest thanks to my students, who have always been willing to lend a hand.

Furthermore, my appreciation is offered to these individuals who contributed to this fourth edition:

Colleague Dr. Robert Hosmon, assistant dean in the School of Communication at the University of Miami, for his insightful comments and contributions to the discussion about restaurant and food criticism and for other suggestions for the chapter on reviewing and criticism.

Colleague Alan Prince for his comments and suggestions about travel feature writing.

Dr. Robert A. Logan, director of the Science Journalism Center and associate dean of the School of Journalism of the University of Missouri, for his contribution to the chapter on science and technical feature writing.

Prof. Meenakshi Gigi Durham, School of Journalism and Mass Communication at the University of Iowa, for her helpful comments and suggestions that have been integrated into this new edition.

Thanks are also given to a group of professional freelance writers and editors. These writers and editors offered many good ideas and discussions about their work, which have been incorporated into this fourth edition. Specifically, I want to thank Rama Ramaswami, editor for *Operations & Fulfillment* magazine in Connecticut; Suzy Buckley, staff writer for *Ocean Drive* magazine in Miami Beach; Lesley Abravanel, travel writer, author of Frommer's *South Florida* and *Florida* books, and celebrity and nightlife columnist for *The Miami Herald*; Abby Tegnelia, a staff writer for *Us Weekly* magazine and formerly a staff writer for *New York* magazine; Karen Sloan, a reporter and writer for the *Brunswick News* in Georgia; and Margarita Martin-Hidalgo, a reporter for the *Lakeland Ledger* in Florida.

I also offer thanks to the American Society of Journalists and Authors, Magazine Publishers of America, and the Newsletter and Electronic Publishers Association, for their contributions. Appreciation also goes to those editors and writers who contributed to the first three editions of this book and those whose excellent works are published in this edition with their permission.

My work on the fourth edition could not have been completed without the reliable and thorough assistance of graduate student Paula Nino. I sincerely thank her for her significant contributions to this project.

—*Bruce Garrison*
*Miami, Florida*

# Preface

This book discusses feature writing. Features are a large part of what people seek in their newspapers, magazines, and newsletters, and this book tries to guide motivated writers down the right path. It emphasizes writing values that will strengthen the reader's journalistic practices. The purpose of this fourth edition is the same as that of the original, second, and third editions: to give advanced writers and reporters a thorough look at newspaper, magazine, newsletter, and online feature writing. To fully appreciate its contents, readers need an introduction to writing and reporting for newspapers, magazines, newsletters, and online publications before starting this book.

An advanced student should find it filled with good advice for writing different types of features. The book offers lists of tips, observations, and guidelines for writers. Similarly, lists of sources and story ideas are often offered in each chapter. To accomplish these goals, the book required many sources of information. It is a collection of a wide variety of perspectives and experiences of the author and other experienced writers, editors, publishers, and professors. This volume should be a solid tour of the different forms and approaches to feature writing.

There are several points to note about the book. First, the book is geared to advanced student writers and beginning professionals. Readers should have a foundation in writing basics from beginning writing and reporting classes to get the most from this material. There are no exercises or other classroom activities. Students are expected to practice their feature writing and reporting in the world around them while working on fresh assignments that can lead to publication in their campus news media outlets or in other publications. Second, this book focuses on newspaper, magazine, newsletter, and online publications with emphasis on daily newspapers and consumer magazines.

This latest edition emphasizes three primary aspects of feature writing: introduction and writing skills or basics, article types, and the collegiate and professional writing life. In each chapter, you will learn from the narrative, from the advice of professionals, and by example. In each chapter, there are excerpts and complete articles from some of the nation's leading publications that illustrate points made in the text. Although most of the examples in this edition are new, a handful of the very best examples written by award-winning journalists from the first three editions have been retained.

I have taken much of the material here from 28-plus years of feature writing and reporting classes at three different universities. I also add 6 years of full-time reporting and editing experience at daily newspapers, including 3 years as an entertainment beat writer and music reviewer. I spent more than a year launching and editing an international subscription newsletter, *Money Laundering Alert,* several years of freelance writing for magazines and newspaper travel sections, and a decade of editing special features projects and sections for daily and weekly newspapers in South Florida. I hope you will learn as much from it as I did putting it all together.

This is the fourth edition of *Professional Feature Writing.* The book was first published in 1989 and revised in 1994 and again in 1999. This new edition offers significant changes and improvements. Let me review them for you briefly.

There are updated writing examples from the nation's most outstanding magazines and newspapers. Although I still use several ageless examples, I include in this edition more contemporary illustrations of quality feature writing. I have also improved the organization of the book with some subtle changes from the previous edition.

Second, readers will find updated material on computer-based research tools for writers. I discuss in greater detail online computer-based research tools, especially the World Wide Web. Other references and reference materials have been updated.

Third, I examine online newspapers, magazines, newsletters, and original online publications and the role of feature writing for those electronic publications. These Web- and e-mail-based periodicals provide a growing market for freelance writers and career opportunities for staff writers.

Fourth, there is new content focusing about young writers and veteran editors whose views were not included in earlier editions.

This book was a project well worth doing, especially if it helps someone to get his or her first article published or a more experienced writer to move to the next highest level of his or her writing skills.

—*Bruce Garrison*
*University of Miami*

# PART ONE

# THE BASICS

# CHAPTER ONE

# Feature Writing in the 21st Century

This could be you in just a few years:

Abby Tegnelia graduated from the journalism program at the University of Miami in 1999. After spending the summer backpacking through Europe, she went to New York to find her career as a magazine writer. After earning a master's degree at Columbia a year later, she spent several months looking for work.

She wrote health and medicine features for CBS.healthwatch.com and wound up finding her first magazine staff position as a fact-checker and writer at *New York* magazine and later as a full-time reporter for *Us Weekly* magazine. After graduating, she began her hunt for work in journalism in the Big Apple:

> I finally got some freelance work fact-checking at *New York* magazine. When *Details* magazine needed someone to fact-check the large, in-depth features for its first issue under Fairchild Publications, my supervisor at *New York* recommended me. After about a month, I returned to *New York* and fact-checked on a full-time, freelance basis. I was offered an on-staff reporter position. (Tegnelia, personal communication, September 6, 9, 2002)

> From there, I started writing real estate features and contributing to various staff projects while also fact-checking. "Gotham" is considered the most prestigious section in our magazine, and in September I finally got my first Gotham piece published, the story about yoga self-defense. My next two "Gothams" were about nightclubs after September 11 and the lack of parties during Christmas time. (Tegnelia, personal communication, September 6, 9, 2002)

"My pieces were very New York-y!" the 25-year-old writer from Albuquerque, NM, said when asked to describe her features for *New York* (A. Tegnelia, personal communication, September 6, 9, 2002). "Much of our magazine is very service-y, so much of my work lately has been writing a paragraph here, a paragraph there, on big staff projects."

But her work is never easy, even as a full-time staff member. "We are responsible for pitching all of our own ideas, and getting them printed takes much lobbying and nagging of the editors!" she said.

She has spent considerable time during the past two years writing features about living in the city. Her assignments include real estate stories about apartments and apartment hunting. "I've also done some features for a ballet magazine," she explained.

Then the terror attacks of Tuesday morning, September 11, 2001, roared into her life. Tegnelia lived near Ground Zero in Lower Manhattan. She became part of a team that covered the aftermath of the attacks on the World Trade Center towers for her magazine. Her work not only contributed to the magazine's weekly issues during the following year, but some of her experiences wound up as a chapter in a book, *At Ground Zero: Young Reporters Who Were There Tell Their Stories* (Bull & Erman, 2002):

> On September 11, I was still at home when the towers fell. We don't start work until 10:30. When the subways into and out of Manhattan were closed, I ran toward Ground Zero to start reporting. Most of our reporters live in Brooklyn, so I knew they wouldn't be able to get downtown. On Sept. 13, I was sent to Bellevue Hospital to interview people who had made "missing" posters of their family and friends. My interviews accompanied a portrait grid. Many of my interviews from Sept. 11 made it into our collaborative time-line of events that went through the entire week, using first-person accounts. (Tegnelia, personal communication, September 6, 9, 2002)

> A few weeks later, an editor from Thunder's Mouth Press e-mailed the Columbia J-School listserv, saying he was looking for young reporters to write about their experiences covering September 11. I then told my roommate Amie Parnes. A 4,000-word essay about my experiences reporting was published in the book, which includes 25 essays from 25 reporters. (Tegnelia, personal communication, September 6, 9, 2002)

> Our next two issues were about mourning and getting New York back on its feet. I helped one of our top writers, Jennifer Senior, report a story about loss. I interviewed mayors of small towns who lost a lot of people and priests who gave mass to overflowing churches. I wrote a small piece for the third week's issue called "We Want YOU to help New York."(Tegnelia, personal communication, September 6, 9, 2002)

Abby Tegnelia's feature writing career is moving forward. She moved from *New York* to *Us Weekly* in late 2002 and got her first contract for a long feature piece for *Marie Claire* magazine. She has found her niche writing at a national magazine in one of the world's greatest news towns. But it took a lot for her to get there and will require a lot more work for her to stay.

## GETTING STARTED IN FEATURE WRITING

Like any other beginning feature writer, it will take large amounts of time and effort to succeed as quickly as Abby Tegnelia. You have to ask yourself some tough questions about your abilities. For example, could you write the definitive discussion of cloning procedures and related ethical issues for *U.S. News & World Report*? Or could you write a profile of the hottest new East Coast political leader for *The New Yorker* or *The New Republic*? Can you prepare a compelling article about babies suffering from cancer for *Family Circle*? Or could you write a highly descriptive and entertaining piece about the nightlife on South Beach in Miami Beach for *Ocean Drive*? Could you write a guide to the best mountain hiking trails for *Condé Nast Traveler* or a human interest article about grandchildren in *Modern Maturity*? Could you write a travel feature focusing on finding bargain airfares in the *Chicago Tribune* Sunday edition or maybe a how-to article about installing and using DVD drives in *PC Magazine*?

Is this over your head? Probably. For now, perhaps.

Give yourself time. Find your level. Maybe you could write a short review of the newest Samuel L. Jackson movie in your campus newspaper or even your local newspaper's weekend or entertainment sections. Maybe you could write a humorous column for your campus newspaper or a campus-based World Wide Web site, or perhaps you could prepare a holiday story about foreign students at your school who are experiencing their first Thanksgiving or taking their first final exams. Maybe you can handle a personality sketch of a nearby high school athlete who recently set a school scoring record.

Do these seem to be more reachable goals for you? Possibly. But perhaps not yet. Start by writing about what you know. Feature writing includes all of these possibilities, even those for the top national and international publications, and they are attainable with a lot of hard work and development of your talents.

You may wish to become a feature writer. You like the idea of writing for mass media such as newspapers, magazines, newsletters, and online publications. You may have an interest in writing features or perhaps someone once told you that you could write, saying that you might have what it takes to become a journalist or a novelist. If you want to be a successful professional feature writer, then you have to be willing to sweat. You have to like people and be willing to spend time with them, too. You have to be willing to live with frustration. You have to make personal and professional sacrifices. You have to be willing to work long hours. You have to be willing to take little or no remuneration in the beginning. You have to have a strong desire to publish your writing.

If you are still with me after those admonitions, welcome to the world of feature writing. You might just have what it takes to be a staff or a freelance feature writer. It is important to emphasize the difficulty of being a successful professional writer. Yet for those who do have the drive and talent to succeed, there can be significant personal and professional rewards. Your first byline will be highly satisfying. So will the second, or third, or 400th. The euphoria you feel from this accomplishment at any level, from student newspaper to major international magazine, is equaled by little else in professional writing. And beginners do have a chance at making it. With the right idea at the right time, you can become a published feature writer early in your career.

Professor Myrick E. Land (1993) wrote that success in writing requires intelligence, imagination, talent, and persistence. This volume gives you the basic tools for writing feature stories for newspapers, magazines, newsletters, and online publications. What really motivates you to be a writer? If you can answer that question by the time you finish this book, you might have the foundation for becoming a successful professional feature writer.

## WRITING NONFICTION

You write because you want to pass along facts and other information to others. You write to share what you have learned. You write to tell stories. Readers learn from you. They are entertained. They are thrilled. They are saddened. They become informed. People react to what you have to say in print. At the same time, you have a tremendous responsibility to be accurate, concise, timely, and responsible. You also have to know how to express yourself. This basic communication skill is your starting point in feature writing for the news media. You have to have the interest and you have to have writing ability. At some point in your life, you began to think of yourself as a writing-oriented person. And you wound up with this book, opened to the first few pages of the first chapter, perhaps wondering if you can write features well enough to make a living (or well enough to pass a college writing class).

But knowing you have basic writing interest and ability is not enough, according to Scott Meredith (1987), who managed a New York literary agency:

> To have basic writing ability and no technical knowledge, and to try to earn a living as a writer, is equivalent to finding yourself suddenly endowed with a large amount of steel, lumber, and bricks and, without any knowledge of architecture or building, setting out to earn your living building and selling houses. (p. 3)

## DEFINING FEATURE WRITING

If you take the term literally, a *feature* is a special part of something. Feature articles are often special portions of the periodicals that publish them. They do take many different approaches and forms, of course. Most persons familiar with nonfiction writing for the news media think of the conventional straight news or hard news topics and approaches—police and courts, sports, local government, or business—written to give the who, what, when, where, why, and how. These stories emphasize the important persons, the activities, current events, local and regional orientation, explanation of importance, and nature of the event.

Feature stories go beyond this level to be special. Feature writers often employ some "license" or flexibility and emphasize the unconventional or the different. Feature writers look for the story about someone who is not necessarily a newsmaker. Instead, the story is about something or someone offbeat and entertaining. Feature stories are emotional, and they involve readers. They demand reader reaction because these articles can be serious or light, timely or timeless, funny or sad, joyful or joyless. These articles tell us much about the human condition. All you have to do is pick up a recent copy of your local newspaper or favorite magazine to see the variety of subjects and approaches that are a part of feature article writing.

One professional writer defines feature writing as *creative, subjective* article writing that is designed to *inform* and *entertain* readers. Daniel Williamson's (1975) interpretation emphasizes the four words italicized. These points help to show features are different from straight news or information writing. First, features certainly contain more creative energy than routine nonfiction. Writers and editors take a bit more freedom in their writing style or approaches, selection of sources, and packaging of articles. Second, these articles are often less objective than conventional news writing, offering a particular point of view or the author's personal impressions, perceptions, and opinions (in addition to those of sources). Third, the articles remain informative even if they are more creative and personalized by the writer. The level of reader utility of a story often determines its success with readers. Fourth, the article must entertain the reader while accomplishing all three other goals. The article makes readers satisfied they chose to spend 5 minutes or even an hour reading the article instead of pursuing some other activity. A feature is also less perishable than conventional nonfiction or news writing. Stories often are held for appropriate seasons or for slow news periods at newspapers. And simply because of their less frequent publication schedules, magazines often hold stories for considerable lengths of time prior to publication.

Other professionals compare feature writing to fiction, specifically short stories. The major difference, of course, is that feature writers deal with reality. However, some of the best feature writers incorporate the styles and techniques of fiction writers into their work. Benton Rain Patterson (1986), who has written for newspapers and magazines across the United States, stated the following:

> A feature writer deliberately puts people (characters) into what he writes. He describes them and shows them (description) doing and saying (action, expressed through narrative and quotes) whatever it is that makes the characters worth writing—and reading—about. When he puts those elements into his piece, a writer is *ipso facto* featurizing his subject, handling his material and writing his piece as a feature. (p. 21)

Patterson's (1986) three basic rules for features are straightforward:

1. Put people into the story.
2. Tell a story.
3. Let the reader see and hear for him or herself.

---

## JAMES J. KILPATRICK ON THE CRAFT OF WRITING

[T]he crafts of writing and carpentry are deceptively simple. The carpenter has to begin with a plan; the writer must begin with a thought. There must be at least the germ of an idea. Before the first board is nailed to the second board, or the first word connected to the second word, there has to be some clear notion of where we expect to be when we have finished nailing or writing.

—Red Smith lecture in journalism at the University of Notre Dame
(Kilpatrick, 1985, p. 2)

---

Just about all feature stories have these elements in common and often in large quantity. Good features use people in the story, quoted often about what they do that is so interesting. Feature stories are not written like meeting minutes. Features are not dreary matter-of-fact research reports. They are not lifeless summaries of big events. They are often factual short stories written in active voice. They have a plot. There is a story line. There are characters. There is a beginning, middle, and end. Many writers will say that feature articles fall somewhere between news writing and short story writing.

You will see the major types of feature articles used by magazines, newspapers, newsletters, and online publications later in this volume. You can focus on such story forms as color stories that emphasize descriptive writing, human interest stories, personality sketches and profiles, seasonal feature stories, reviews and critical feature writing, aftermath and follow-up feature stories, the feature series, travel article writing, personal experience stories, how-to-do-it articles, humor writing, and technical and specialized features.

There is a discussion of the tools you need as a feature writer. You learn how to find a good feature idea and how to mold it into a story, how to research story ideas, how to write and edit feature articles, and how to successfully sell feature articles for publication. You also learn professional and ethical standards of professional feature writers. You see these types of stories applied in their major forms: weekly and daily newspapers and general and specialized magazines. The writing strategies and information-gathering approaches for feature writing are discussed in broad terms, but often with particular application to the print media.

## NONFICTION PUBLISHING IN THE NEW CENTURY

There are new writing opportunities today. For example, the online news and electronic publications industry has evolved rapidly. Writing positions have opened at online newspapers, print and electronic magazines, print and electronic newsletters, and online broadcast outlets. In this age of media convergence on the World Wide Web, a growing number of news organizations require staff and freelance writers who can produce feature content involving multimedia, not just print content. News organizations that have taken their publications to the Internet also offer original content on those sites, creating a need for writers and editors.

There were 1,468 morning and evening daily newspapers and 913 Sunday newspapers in the United States in 2001. The vast majority was small, with circulation less than 20,000 copies. There were 7,689 weekly newspapers with an average circulation of 5,857 copies in 2000, including paid and free circulation newspapers. The largest daily newspapers circulate more than 1 million copies daily. These are *The Wall Street Journal* and *USA Today*, both nationally and internationally oriented publications with circulations about 1.7 million each. *The New York Times* and *The Los Angeles Times* are both very large, each with a circulation of more than 1 million copies per weekday (Newspaper Association of America [NAA], 2002).

There are plenty of small newspapers, also. These are often the best markets for beginning feature writers because they have small staffs, limited resources, and welcome contributions from student and freelance writers. Weekly newspapers publish from once every 2 weeks to as many as 3 times a week. Their circulation sizes vary considerably, too. Most weeklies are very small—in the 1,000 to 4,000 copies per issue category—but there are several dozen weeklies each with circulation more than 100,000 copies per issue. It is a large market, when considered all together. The almost 7,700 weeklies in the United States publish almost 71 million copies each week (NAA, 2002).

However, newspapers are experiencing relative hard times. Circulation is flat, even dropping in some markets, but the U.S. population continues to grow. This means fewer people are reading newspapers, preferring to get their information from television or other more immediate sources. Some experts have already labeled newspapers as "irrelevant" (Glaberson, 1993, p. D7). Other authorities think it is an overstatement to call newspapers irrelevant. But the point is well taken: No one seems to know what the future of the newspaper will be for the next generations of writers and editors. Publishers are unsure of content and form in the generations ahead. But for now, there is some optimism, especially if newspapers can adapt and use new technologies, such as the Internet. Some major news and information and telecommunications companies that publish newspapers and other news products are developing such bold changes as electronic versions of their products. This, of course, is not a new idea be-

cause such services have been available for a decade or more. However, these companies are exploring new ways to use computers, telecommunications, and other common consumer technology to deliver news to customers. This not only means personal computers, but such innovations as pocket-sized wireless computer receivers or such things as personalized newspapers printed within the home of subscribers (Gates, 1995). The implications for all writers, not just feature writers, seem to be massive.

There are many more magazines than daily and weekly newspapers. There are as many as 17,800 U.S. periodical titles, according to compilations of the Magazine Publishers of America. This total includes more than 8,100 consumer magazines. In terms of editorial pages, the largest single subject category is culture and humanities. Entertainment and celebrities publications constituted the second-largest number of pages. Other leading categories included food and nutrition pages, sports-hobbies-recreation, wearing apparel, home furnishings, national affairs, and health (Magazine Publishers of America, 2003).

The largest magazines in the country reach older, or retirement age, citizens. *NRTA/AARP Bulletin* and *Modern Maturity* are the two largest periodicals according to independently audited paid circulation figures in 2002. *NRTA/AARP Bulletin* distributes about 21.7 million copies per issue and *Modern Maturity* circulates 17.5 million. *Reader's Digest* and *TV Guide* both publish more than 11.5 million and 8.1 million copies per issue, respectively, and *Better Homes & Gardens* distributes 7.2 million issues each month. *National Geographic* publishes almost 6.6 million copies per month. The top 50 magazines in the United States circulated more than 160 million copies per edition, or an average of about 3.2 million per periodical. The top 113 magazines in the United States in 2000 circulated more than 258 billion pages (Magazine Publishers of America, 2003). Almost two-thirds of the top 100 magazines experienced circulation gains when comparing 2001 and 2000 circulation figures. Although many magazines are dependent upon subscriptions for sales, some sell more single-copy issues than subscription issues. For example, two-thirds of *Cosmopolitan's* three million copies circulation is single-copy sales (Magazine Publishers of America, 2003).

The biggest magazines continue to be very big. However, there are thousands of smaller monthly, bimonthly, and quarterly publications. And some of the smaller national or regional magazines, such as *VeloNews* (competitive cycling; circulation about 48,000) or *Videomaker* (video camera users; 89,000), are comparatively small, but are growing very fast. They are smaller because they reach more specialized audiences, but they offer marvelous opportunities for serious feature writers.

A smart feature writer seeking freelance markets will not overlook newsletter journalism. There are small organization-based newsletters, large public subscription-based newsletters, and lots in between. In this decade, careers are developing in this new and growing field. Newsletters are not all small "mom and pop"-type editorial operations. Commercial business-to-business newsletters have become a major industry with thousands of editions each business day, week, month, or quarter. It may be impossible to estimate the number of newsletters regularly published in the United States. With so many new publications beginning each month and others closing down because funding becomes difficult to find or interests change, the numbers are difficult to estimate. Many newsletters are organizational and not widely circulated. Others are distributed to the public or to private groups free or for sale, but their circulation numbers or simple existence are not regulated or monitored by any national organizations. It is safe to say, however, that there are thousands of such periodicals, and the figure is growing with the recent development of inexpensive production and printing technology. Some are large and some are small.

People who need to communicate something publish these thousands of newsletters. Gale's directory of newsletters, *Newsletters in Print*, lists more than 11,300 newsletters with about 4,000 different key word or subject terms in the United States and Canada (Paré, 2001), but this total does not include many of the smaller circulation newsletters for internal corporate, institutional, organizational, or other proprietary purposes. Other estimates, such as that of the Oxbridge directory, go as high as 21,000 newsletters in the United States (Greenberg, 1992).

For writers, the newspapers, magazines, and newsletters today depend on technology. Because of computers, fax machines, and other modern hardware, you are able to gather information in ways impossible for a generation before you. You are able to work on machines that make preparation of manuscripts much easier than before. Publications are sophisticated in production techniques. This means feature writers on deadline can produce stories faster and closer to printing deadlines and supplement the usual news coverage of an event, whether it be for a daily newspaper, a daily fax newsletter, or a weekly newsmagazine.

Newspaper and magazine group ownership trends have changed the nature of the business. The largest newspaper groups, such as Gannett and Knight-Ridder, have purchased many major and medium-sized dailies. Other companies have gathered up available small dailies and weeklies. Magazines have experienced the same phenomenon, with many ownership changes in the past decade. Companies have bought up independently owned magazines to form new or larger groups. The effect has been less independent management of publications. At times, staff positions have been eliminated to create more profitable operating costs. It has meant a harder time making a living for feature writers in some markets and some specializations. It has also meant greater resources and new ideas. It has meant some publications near failure got a second chance, which has helped writers.

Newspapers are in the midst of significant change. They are using feature material in larger quantities. Because of this, they seek better quality from writers to keep the high demand for their editions. Reacting to television and other electronic media vying for growing entertainment and leisure time of Americans, newspapers are offering material once found only in magazines such as longer in-depth profiles and analyses. Stanford University Professor Emeritus William Rivers (1992) labeled this phenomenon the "magazining of newspapers" (p. 13). Some newspaper feature sections have shown interest in shorter, tightly written pieces with the same "television story" flare of USA Today.

Television, film, and other influences changed newspapers and magazines in the 1960s and 1970s. Newspapers began to develop regional, or zoned, editions and to look at other dissemination techniques. General interest consumer magazines closed when operations became more costly than circulation and advertising revenues could cover. In an effort to segment the general audience, more specialized magazines evolved in the 1960s and 1970s to replace general interest publications. Suddenly, readers interested in health and medicine did not have to depend on newsmagazines or the coffee-table magazines of another era. They, instead, subscribe to Prevention, Vibrant Life, Vim & Vigor, or other similar magazines.

Magazines, like newspapers, have changed as well in the past three decades. In some cases, there have been very difficult times, forcing basic survival decisions by editors and publishers, for magazines, and the problems are not always caused by their choice of content. Magazines such as Psychology Today, Savvy Woman, Fame, Taxi, and Smart were forced to close in the harsh realities of advertising slumps caused by an economic recession in the early 1990s. It has been a case of "too many titles chasing too few ad pages," according to magazine industry consultant George Simpson (Wolk, 1991, p. 2G). Some magazines have survived on sound fiscal management and other rare publications have existed on subscriber and newsstand sales alone. The bimonthly Ms. magazine, for example, did not suffer as much as other publications during the same recession period because it does not accept advertising. It has not depended on advertising since it debuted in 1972.

One key area of growth has been in "alternative newsweekly" publications. These are magazine-like hybrid periodicals that are often published on newsprint in tabloid format. The alternatives are often monthlies or biweeklies and usually serve specific geographic markets such as a metropolitan area. Tennessee's Nashville Scene is one example. New Times draws thousands of readers in the Miami, Denver, Dallas, Houston, San Francisco, Los Angeles, and Phoenix metropolitan markets. Creative Loafing, which is an Atlanta-based alternative, publishes editions in seven cities in the southeastern United States. The San Francisco Bay Guardian circulates about 135,000 copies each issue. The news and feature-based content of alternative publications is often magazine length and magazine quality and offers writing assignment opportunities for both freelance and staff feature writers.

These publications are popular with young adults who seek information and listings about the arts, current events, local nightlife and music, young adult lifestyles, movies and local theater, and other forms of entertainment. However, these publications often do not stop with that—they also offer in-depth features such as profiles and investigative reporting on current issues. The publications often fill a void left by the more mainstream newspapers and lifestyles magazines of their markets. Typical alternative readers tend to be young, between 18 and 45, and they live an active lifestyle. These readers are well educated news readers with a good income (Smith & Davis, 1997).

Sports-oriented magazines have given themselves a new look in recent years. The very traditional *Sporting News* underwent a 5-year multimillion dollar relaunch between 1997 and 2002. The biggest change was toward a magazine look. The publication had been a newspaper tabloid. *Sports Illustrated* also reinvented itself, including a new logo, in 1998. And ESPN, the television sports cable network, started its own magazine, called *ESPN Magazine*, in 1998, to compete against the sports magazine category leaders. In addition, sports magazines oriented to women have been growing in recent years—publishers and advertisers realize that valuable market is still up for grabs.

Women's magazines remain popular and successful at most levels. New titles are announced each year. Although some do not generate the advertising support to continue, others flourish in the era of specialty publications. Two recent new titles will illustrate the point. *More* is a recent bimonthly magazine that is geared toward women ages 45 to 64. *Lucky* magazine is a monthly magazine about shopping that began in 2000. And still another specialty magazine is *Mamm*, a bimonthly magazine that targets women living with cancer, especially those women ages 40 to 55. Breast cancer is the top cause of death for women in that age group. Each publisher has identified a market niche and has filled it with their publication.

One category of magazines showing encouraging growth is magazines geared to children and young teens. These include *Disney Adventures, Sports Illustrated for Kids, Nickelodeon Magazine,* and *Family Life.* Articles focus on indoor and outdoor activities, travel, food, the environment, basic science, television programs, clothing, toys such as video games, and activities designed to enhance quality time with parents. One subset drawing attention is magazines oriented to teenage girls. *Seventeen* is the oldest, with roots back to 1944. Geared to high school females, *Seventeen* has been successful and emulated much over the past 50-plus years. Today, there are dozens of magazines aimed at the same market, but there are many other popular teen publications, which include *YM* and *Twist.*

Time Inc. debuted *Teen People*, a spinoff of its highly successful *People*, in 1998 to attract young readers as well. It includes articles on celebrity teens, but also on noncelebrity teens. Endeavors such as these show the continuing evolution of the magazine market. Writers, as well as editors and publishers, have to keep track of the evolving industry.

Lifestyle publications are popular today. Leading the parade to the newsstand are a collection of specialty books called city and regional magazines.

They continue their 4-decade modern era that began in the 1960s. Their evolution from chamber of commerce publications or urban survival manuals during this time has resulted in a genre of magazines that focus on how we live in cities and their suburbs. They offer high-level and high-quantity service journalism to readers (for more information, see http://www.citymag.org and http://www.citymag.org/links.html). Magazines such as *New York Magazine, Chicago Magazine, Los Angeles Magazine, Washingtonian, Ocean Drive* and *Ocean Drive en Espanol,* or *Boston Magazine* provide alternative voices to local newspapers and television and offer lifestyle feature content focusing on housing, food, entertainment, travel, and other leisure activities. In 2001, there were nearly 100 new city-regional and lifestyle start-ups, more than any other magazine category in nothing less than a difficult and trying economic period (Hynds, 1998; Seemuth, 2002).

Parenting and family publications remain popular, but periodicals emphasizing the skills of parenting and family development have grown in popularity in the past decade. *Parenting, Parentlife, Sesame Street Parents, Parents Magazine* and *Exceptional Parent* are examples of parent-oriented magazines. Family magazines include *Family Life, Family Circle, San Diego Family Magazine,* and *FamilyFun.*

CHAPTER TWO

# A Career as a
# Feature Writer?

Suzy Buckley grew up in suburban Chicago in the late 1980s and early 1990s and didn't imagine herself as a magazine journalist covering the late nights and glitzy celebrities of South Beach and South Florida. She did read a lot of magazines, especially *Vogue* and the now-closed *Taxi*, but she imagined herself as a "rock star" and even played in a garage band in high school. When she was in college at the University of Miami, she majored in public relations and envisioned herself on a somewhat different career track.

"After interning in different permutations of public relations—corporate PR for a bank and not-for-profit PR for a medical research study—I noticed that, although the PR execs might be making the cash, journalists had a lot of power," Buckley (personal communication, September 4, 6, 9, 2002) said.

> I also heard people I worked with complain about how they "almost were journalists" or "once were journalists," as if they had really messed up somewhere along the lines. They told me that it's better to start in journalism and then move over to public relations: Few magazines or newspapers are receptive to public relations professionals who want to switch over to journalism careers. (S. Buckley, personal communication, September 4, 6, 9, 2002)

Buckley, in her late 20s, is one of a small handful of full-time editors for *Ocean Drive* magazine on Miami Beach. *Ocean Drive* is the largest selling local lifestyle magazine in the country and is based in Miami Beach, FL (Seemuth, 2002). Each glossy edition of the magazine named for the art deco hotel-lined street that faces the Atlantic Ocean, about 400 full-size pages in length, is filled with articles about the fast-lane lifestyles of one of the world's most popular destinations. The magazine, in fact, likes to think of itself as an attitude, not just a place.

As *Ocean Drive's* people editor, Buckley writes, assigns, and edits feature articles. She regularly writes monthly nightlife columns such as "Up Late." She also writes stories based on celebrity interviews as well as dining reviews, travel stories, and fashion news. Although the editorial department of the magazine depends greatly on freelance writers, photographers, and other creative contributors, Buckley contributes cover features as well that focus on the glitzy clubs, the beautiful people, hot fashion, both the fine and fun dining of Miami Beach, celebrity parties and debuts, travel to Europe's hotspots, and other aspects of the fabled South Beach 20- and 30-something lifestyle.

> I get a lot of phone calls from public relations professionals who want me to do stories on their clients. If I haven't already talked with the individual, I usually send the calls to voice mail. This frustrates a lot of PR people, but we're a small staff. I simply cannot do my job if I give every single person the chance to pitch their story to me on the phone. I have a voice mail message that describes in detail the way I like to be pitched stories. It's amazing how many people don't listen to it. . . . Besides fielding the outside pitches, I answer a lot of e-mail, meet with the other editors to decide story ideas and receive tons of pitches from people *inside* the office, such as ad sales department execs who want us to give their clients editorial.
>
> Depending on the week of the month, I'll also be interviewing chefs, local entrepreneurs, models, celebrities, nightlife personalities, and real estate professionals . . . just about everyone I need to talk to in which to complete my articles. I record the interviews with a microcassette recorder and then have them transcribed (hopefully by an intern; otherwise I do them myself). I write most of the articles at home, either at night after work or else on days I work from home. (S. Buckley, personal communication, September 11, 2002)

Buckley's schedule is hectic over much of the year, especially during the high winter tourist season. Although she takes a month of unpaid vacation each summer, the rest of the year is a high-octane rush. She is out practically every night at one event or another—all this often following a full day in the office. She interviews pop culture celebrities, attends restaurant and club openings and promotional parties, covers special events such as festivals and conventions, and travels to exotic destinations in search of new features and columns for the magazine.

> I just love the people I'm able to meet and the invitations extended to me. I've been able to sit down with people like Oscar de la Renta and ask them everything I've ever wanted to know. I've been to the best Oscar parties in Los Angeles; I've been driven around in a Cadillac by a personal chauffeur for 6 weeks. . . . I really have to think about everything I've been able to do.
>
> The worst part of my job is the fine line between "work" and "personal life." I'll be having an amazing time with my good friends at a party on a Saturday night and someone I hardly know will *insist* I go to the other side of the room to meet their friend who has started making velvet pillows out of her apartment in Fort Lauderdale (because she'd be "just perfect" for the magazine). "Friends of friends of friends" call me up all day to ask what nightclubs are good on which nights and if I can please get their friends visiting from New York into all the best clubs all weekend.
>
> It's also very hard to write a gossip column, because sometimes doing a "good job" also means hurting people. We have a section of blind gossip and I need to write things such as "a certain coke-addict boutique owner" . . . and really rip a

person apart for something that is rumor/hearsay. I don't use names, but the people and their friends always know who it is. But if I didn't write it, the magazine would find someone else to do it. For better or worse, that's the kind of juicy, sensationalist items our readers just love. (S. Buckley, personal communication, September 11, 2002)

Buckley has developed her career with a solid background in print and broadcast journalism as well as online media. She has done freelance work for the Travel Channel, the TV Food Network, and E! Entertainment Television. Just after finishing her undergraduate work, she spent more than a year working for Cox Interactive Media as entertainment content producer for its SoFla.com Web site and as a feature content producer for the Fort Lauderdale *Sun-Sentinel's* Digital City South Florida. She also wrote features for the newspaper's Lifestyles section.

I went to graduate school to study broadcast journalism. One weekend, while I was home watching "The Gossip Show" on E! Entertainment, I noticed that, while they featured several entertainment journalists from New York and Los Angeles, they didn't have a Miami correspondent. I called up the E! Entertainment studios in Los Angeles and New York to find out why. I told them that I currently wrote the gossip column for a Miami fashion/entertainment/nightlife magazine and that I'd love to become a contributor. To make a long story short, I sent in a reel. They really liked it and ended up hiring me. I was responsible for scouting the Miami gossip, writing and memorizing my segments, finding a location and working with a crew to produce the tape. I FedEx-ed the beta to Los Angeles, where producers edited it and put it on the show. (S. Buckley, personal communication, September 11, 2002)

Buckley often does freelance work and has written on assignment for *Forbes*, *Mademoiselle*, *Seventeen*, *Jalouse*, and the *Robb Report*.

I have read magazines like a maniac my entire life. I've always loved fun things—fashion, restaurants, nightlife, and special events. In college, I dated the photo editor of the university newspaper. I was hanging out in the newsroom one day, waiting for him to finish, when I heard one of the editors complaining that there was "no one" to write about the Bon Jovi concert. She had these two great tickets and no one to go cover the show. I ran up to her and said "I love Bon Jovi! I can write about the show!" I didn't know if I could really write a concert review, but I didn't care. I said I studied writing and would not let her down. I said I'd write the article if she would please give me the tickets.

After that, she asked me to write more and more. I was later asked to be news editor, but was never really into the news. I had a hard time because the passion wasn't there. I felt news stories were very easy to write, but I wasn't interested in the subject matter and didn't enjoy writing what I felt to be "formula, who-what-where-when-why"-type stories. After a year as news editor, I quit and asked if I could just start a new column as restaurant critic. That was a great idea, I have to say. So instead of knocking on the doors of parents' houses whose children had just been murdered, which I had to do once, I just wrote about the best restaurants in town. I used those clips to land bigger and better things. No one knew they were from a school newspaper. (S. Buckley, personal communication, September 11, 2002)

This sort of background and career development is, in many ways, ideal for a feature writer. Every person has a different background and set of experiences that helps them in the writing life. These circumstances and experiences helped Suzy Buckley find her writing career in magazine and celebrity journalism. Unless you know absolutely what you're going to write about, having a varied personal and professional background keeps your writing options open and creates opportunities you might not imagine until they come along. When you're inevitably asked to write about something you know nothing about, you can begin with confidence.

## NATURE OF MAGAZINE FEATURE WRITING

Magazine features are quite different from newspaper features in a number of ways. First, nonstaff members of a magazine often write these articles. Many writers are attracted to the freedom of freelance writing and are able to make good supplemental income as freelance writers. However, it is worth repeating: It is quite difficult to make a substantial career and a living from freelance writing. A good number of individuals do well selling their work to magazines while working another career both in and out of the news media.

There are many opportunities for magazine-oriented, nonfiction writers. As a freelance writer, you can select the subject, the market, and the magazine for which you wish to write. You can specialize if you desire to do so, or you can be a generalist who writes on whatever subject is appealing. You can set your own work schedule for writing and researching articles. A staff writer for a newspaper or a magazine staffer cannot enjoy this luxury most of the time. You can set up an office at home or elsewhere, but you are responsible for whatever costs you incur. The expenses for such things as equipment, furniture, and supplies have to come out of your writer's fees. And, it follows that you are able to live wherever you want as an independent writer. However, there are no guarantees for freelancers and the road to success is difficult to travel.

The magazine industry is still changing. This means the beginning of opportunities for feature article writers, but also the end of other opportunities. For example, one of the real growth areas in the magazine industry over the past 2 decades has been computer consumer publications and computer industry publications.

You have a reasonable chance as an unknown writer to be published by a successful major magazine. However, you do have to work hard on good ideas at the right time. Magazine feature writing is a field with tremendous opportunity. With hundreds of major magazines and thousands more of specialized business publications, you can do much as a magazine feature writer—if you have the drive. Magazines, like newspapers, have their own styles or personalities. Part of this is the look, or graphics of the magazine, but the other major part is the writing style. Magazine writing generally is in essay form with longer, more fully developed paragraphs. Usages are more formalized, also. This subject gets more attention in later chapters.

Despite occasional changes in established publications or the debut of completely new ones, you will find that magazine writing itself tends to be somewhat constant. After all, good writing is good writing. Magazine articles, generally, do tend to be more descriptive and detailed than newspaper writing, but this is partly due to the additional space given to major features in magazines. And, as noted earlier, these articles are a bit more subjective as writers offer their perspectives on the subject.

---

## AMERICA'S LEADING MAGAZINES

Each spring, the American Society of Magazine Editors (ASME; http://asme. magazine.org) presents its National Magazine Awards, known as "Ellies," for editorial excellence in magazine publishing. To be honored signifies that a publication has reached the top of its class. The awards are often referred to as the "Oscars" of the magazine industry.

In 2002, *Newsweek* was named for "general excellence" among the nation's largest magazines (over 2 million circulation). *Entertainment Weekly, Vibe, National Geographic Adventure,* and *Print* magazines also were recognized for general excellence in smaller circulation groups.

The awards were also presented for specific categories. *National Geographic Adventure* was honored for helping readers improve their lives in the personal service category. Other outstanding magazines include *The Atlantic Monthly* (feature writing, reporting, and public interest), *Vogue* (leisure interests), *New York Magazine* (columns and commentary), *The New Yorker* (essays, fiction, and profile writing), and *Harper's Magazine* (reviews, criticism).

*Time* magazine was recognized for its September 11, 2001, single topic issue, whereas *Details* was honored for its design and *Vanity Fair* for its photography.

The Ellies, named after the Alexander Calder Stabile "elephant" that symbolizes the award, were introduced in 1966 by ASME and the graduate journalism program at Columbia University. ASME grew out of, and continues to be affiliated with, the Magazine Publishers of America (http://www.magazine.org).

---

Just remember that, regardless of the writing approach and topic, you will find the magazine industry to be quite different from what it once was. Individuals beginning careers as magazine writers in the postwar 1940s and 1950s found general interest magazines flourishing. Due to the influences of television and other mass media influences on society, leisure time demands are quite different two generations later. To meet this challenge, magazines began to specialize. Your writing challenge is to handle specialized subjects with the authority of an expert. This is still another reason magazine feature writing differs so much from newspaper feature writing.

Magazine feature writers are most often freelance writers. Most magazines maintain very small full-time writing staffs, and most staff members are responsible for postwriting activities such as editing, layout, and other production tasks rather than original writing and reporting. Therefore, magazines depend on freelance writers to submit their work, or they solicit work by known freelance writers.

The traditional staff feature writer position at a magazine will vary, depending on the type of magazine. At a news magazine, for example, the differences between writers and reporters remain great. The functions of writer and information gatherer differ widely for large news organizations such as *Time* or *Newsweek*. Although more and more reporter-originated material is being published, reporters in bureaus around the world still produce information, much of it in memo form, for writers in the main offices in New York to organize and perfect through rewriting. At other types of magazines, the work of reporter and writer is less specialized. Most staffers, especially those at specialized consumer magazines, write and report. At some smaller magazines, writers may also double as editors to help handle material that comes from experts and freelance writers.

The routine at magazines, although deadlines are less frequent, is still similar to that at newspapers for editors and staff writers. The pressure as deadline approaches is intense. Expectations are high. Performance can be no less than top level. Hours are often not within the standard 9-to-5, Monday through Friday, week that beginners might expect from the corporate publishing world.

Because some magazines are organizing into groups under single ownership and, often, single publishers and editors, this could mean a growing emphasis on staff writers and shrinking emphasis on freelancers. In fact, some publications have completely eliminated the need for freelancers by hiring full-time staffs of writers, correspondents, editors, and others, with bureaus around the world or across the country. McGraw-Hill's *BusinessWeek* illustrates this point.

If you do not become a magazine staff writer, your life as a freelance writer for a magazine will be quite different. You are your own boss until you commit to work for a publication on an assignment. Your work will require that you interact with many editors throughout a year, and you will likely be an employee of several bosses at one time.

Small magazines offer the best chance for regular work for beginning feature writers. It is also a different working environment. Writers are less specialized within the scope of the magazine and are asked to produce a greater variety of writing, reporting, editing, and production work. Staff members may be closer at smaller publications because of the need to interact more often. Writers and editors work together more frequently and often exchange duties. Writers become editors. Editors become writers. Publishers become editors and writers. A beginner can learn a variety of feature-writing skills.

## NATURE OF NEWSPAPER FEATURE WRITING

What makes a newspaper feature different from a magazine or newsletter feature? There are a number of answers to that question that go beyond simple frequency or timing of publication. Newspaper features are used throughout the newspaper, but some sections use features more often and very differently from others. The front section, generally containing the spot news of the day from state, national, and international sources, uses features for balance. Features in these sections offer insight into the day's newsmakers and major events. Features are used as sidebars to supplement straight reporting. For example, a story about a truck–van traffic accident that killed nine people might be boosted by a feature sidebar focusing on the one surviving child. The announcement of a nomination of a U.S. Supreme Court justice will often be supplemented by a feature profile of the career of the person seeking the position.

The local section of most daily newspapers will often run features on unusual individuals or events of community interest. Certainly local sidebar features are also used. However, newspapers that have segmented their local news coverage into neighborhood sections frequently fill these sections with features about people, schools, religions, home repair, pets, arts and crafts, parks and recreation, and small businesses.

In lifestyle and living sections, editors devote most of the day's space to a wide variety of feature materials. These stories focus on home how-to-do-it subjects, consumer and shopping ideas, profiles, health and medicine suggestions, child-care news, gardening, cooking and food ideas, and much more. In some newspapers, entertainment news is part of lifestyle coverage, but this category of news creates a different set of feature needs for newspapers. Writers specializing in entertainment provide features on individuals, reviews of their performances, and insight into their creative activities.

Sports sections provide feature content to break the routine of game or event stories. Features also supplement spot sports coverage. Regular readers look for features such as profiles on coaches and players, descriptions of facilities, and in-depth analysis of outstanding strategies and performances. Sports features are less focused on professionals and outstanding amateurs than they were a decade ago. Editors have found that readers want to read features about participation sports, such as jogging and swimming, in addition to the National Football League or Major League Baseball. Editors have also learned that readers would like increased feature coverage of "minor" sports such as soccer, giving writers more opportunities and broader scope for features than in past decades.

Business sections have experienced growth in many daily newspapers in recent years. Even newspapers that do not have separate business sections—such as special tabloids on Mondays—still devote considerable space to business news and features. For writers interested in business, this is an upbeat and opportune time for you. These section editors demand regular features describing new companies, new products, consumerism, successful executives, and trends in the marketplace.

Feature material is also found occasionally on the opinion or editorial pages. It is often in the form of a column or other type of opinion essay, but the same general principles of feature writing have been used to write the feature column. These creative columnists and essayists use satire for humor, or write a profile of an individual, or give how-to-do-it advice on a subject.

Newspapers have outlets for magazine-style writing. The Sunday magazine supplements of major daily newspapers depend a great deal on solid feature essay writing of traditional magazine length each week to build regular readership. Feature subjects are wide ranging in nature. From humor columns to portraits of individuals to accounts of historical events to chronologies of conflicts, these articles are the foundations of Sunday magazines. Sunday magazines also include shorter departmentalized features, such as listings of events, reviews of new restaurants, and summaries of new products on the market.

Newspaper features are usually much shorter in length than magazine features, but this tendency does not hold as firmly as it once did. It is not unusual to find a 5,000-word feature story in a newspaper, even in an era influenced by the brevity and graphics of USA Today. And, of course, magazines often run short feature items, also. However, the majority of newspaper features are short and to the point—500 to 1,000 words. Space does not often provide the chance for depth and development of "characters" in the article. Frequency of publication does, however, provide the opportunity for newspaper features to be timelier than magazine features.

Newspapers depend less on outside material than do magazines, as seen later. Because most newspapers have staffs of writers and reporters available, most sections do not buy much freelance material. Sunday travel sections or pages, however, are an exception because very few newspapers employ full-time travel writers other than a travel editor. Certainly, newspaper feature articles are produced in a shorter deadline framework. There are not too many newspaper feature writers who have not had to research, write, and turn in a complete feature within a few hours. Although this also occurs in magazine feature writing, it is not as likely to happen with monthly or weekly deadlines.

Newspaper feature writers come in two varieties. The most common is the staff writer, an individual who works full time or steady part time for a single publication. Freelance newspaper feature writers often work for local newspapers, but most newspapers do not use their work as often as they use staff-written feature material. Most newspaper staff members work regular schedules. Most work 40 or more hours a week, but some that work on salary find their schedule and demands of the job require more than the conventional week. The work of newspaper feature writers is not limited to a 9-to-5, Monday through Friday, schedule, and the work is also not limited to "scheduled" times. Most top newspaper feature writers, even on a regular work schedule, find they never really stop working even when off duty. If you want to succeed, you must take advantage of the opportunity whenever a good article prospect presents itself. Feature writers for small dailies and weeklies are more oriented to produce finished stories, often at the expense of quality. This makes it a challenge to develop certain skills as a writer, but it also hastens development of the discipline to write fast and to get the job done.

Whether you work general assignment or a beat, the intense nature of newspaper feature writing dictates that you be prepared at all times. With daily, two or three times a week, or even weekly deadlines, a large amount of feature production is expected. You must have an endless stream of strong ideas to develop into stories. You cannot "switch off" your alertness as a feature writer.

There are challenges and rewards that come from working in this environment. The challenge of the newspaper feature writer is to know a great deal about a wide range of subjects in a given community. For specialists on beats at newspapers, the challenge is to know a great deal about a restricted range of subjects, but you carry the burden of responsibility for your entire publication. As a newspaper staff writer, you take advantage of public familiarity with your newspaper. Few communities now have more than one newspaper. If you work for that newspaper or your community weekly, readers and sources will recognize it immediately. This means you have stories come to you, and you might find a higher level of cooperation from sources. You also enjoy the advantage of being known by readers. The community you serve as a feature writer will know your name. If you are good, this can become a major asset in your work as a feature writer. If you are not professional in your work, it becomes the opposite—a liability.

## FEATURE WRITING FOR NEWSLETTERS

Despite a billion-dollar revenue stream and tens of thousands of employees, newsletters have not always been given recognition in the publishing business (Nelson & Danis, 1995). The industry is quite fluid and ripe with opportunities. Some newsletters have grown larger than some newspapers and magazines in terms of circulation and staff size, although most are quite small. The *NIAF*

*News*, for instance, is the newsletter of the National Italian American Foundation. It circulates about 20,000 copies six times a year to individuals interested in their Italian–American heritage. The Washington, DC-based newsletter has found a major market with content that "discusses national and international news concerning Italian Americans" (Paré, 2001, p. 568). The newsletter includes regular features about research, books, member profiles, and a calendar of events. The newsletter is provided to members of the foundation. Newsletters such as the *NIAF News* have existed for as long as newspapers and magazines, but they are enjoying a growing role in mass communication today. Newsletters mean new and growing markets for feature writers. Many newsletters are produced by comparatively small staffs and need both talented staff writers and freelance writers.

Just about everyone reads a newsletter of some sort on a regular basis. Some might even come to you, your business, or your family residence unsolicited. Newsletters are necessary because they, like newspaper and magazines, contain news and information (Greenberg, 1992). Newsletters are highly specialized, reflecting the interests of members of groups, clubs and organizations, institutions, and other entities that need to communicate information. Newsletters give members of organizations information and a sense of belonging. Newsletters sell. They inform. They motivate. "Successful newsletters convey specialized information to narrow markets," wrote newsletter industry executive Goss (1988, p. 1). "The public's demand for specialized information has made the growth of newsletters in the information industry phenomenal" (Goss, 1988, p. 1).

They come and go. A lot of new newsletters begin each year, but an equal number fail because of overoptimism; poor financing; weak reporting, writing, and editing; or all of these factors. However, the majority of newsletters have been in business for several years (Nelson & Danis, 1995). Nevertheless, newsletters today are, with their wide range of specialized subjects, perhaps the single-best potential markets for beginning feature writers. Not only are newsletters available in traditional 8½-inch by 11-inch format, but also by electronic media, such as on the World Wide Web, HTML format e-mail messages, fax machines, computer disks, and CDs.

"Newsletter jobs are not necessarily easier to find than jobs with other news media organizations. (Some newsletter publishers say they never hire people straight out of journalism school)," writes *Criminal Justice Newsletter* editor Craig Fischer (1990, p. 2). "Nevertheless, J-school grads should be aware that newsletters can offer excellent opportunities to practice *bona-fide* journalism, using the same skills as those applied at a newspaper, magazine or wire service job" (Fischer, 1990, p. 2).

Many newsletters are only a few pages and are the effort of just one or two persons. In terms of format and content, most are published on 8½-inch by 11-

inch pages and contain some sort of nameplate, general news and information, feature articles, graphics (both art and photographs), and editorials, and some even contain advertising. They are often photocopied in black and white and stapled before being mailed to readers. They may only be published on a quarterly or monthly basis. These small publications serve an important mass communication need in the contemporary world.

Other newsletters are more substantial. They may have dozens of pages, glossy paper, two-color or even four-color commercial printing, and are distributed two or more times per month, perhaps even weekly. In addition to a publisher and editor, there may be news and feature writers on staff. These newsletters are more commercial and professional in their orientation, circulate more copies, and must make a profit for the publisher. In between, there is a wide range of forms and styles of newsletters.

But what exactly is a newsletter? Newsletters have a number of special characteristics, including publications that are serial in nature, are readily available to the public, have national or broad regional interest but often also have local or community focus, treat specialized interests and topics for readers, and use a variety of formal and informal presentations.

*Newsletters in Print* editor Louise Gagnè (1997) wrote

> Webster's defines a newsletter as "a printed sheet, pamphlet, or small newspaper containing news or information of interest chiefly to a special group." Although accurate, this definition does not do justice to the variety of newsletters available or to their importance in our business and personal lives. Newsletters are an unequaled source of current information; they meet the needs of today's fast-paced society by providing information quickly and in an easily digestible format. Although Webster's provides a concise definition of the term "newsletter," in reality the word is used to describe publications of all kinds, ranging from scientific journals to occasional bulletins that carry commercial product notices. Conversely, publications that are arguably newsletters in format and content call themselves "magazines," "newspapers," or "journals." (p. ix)

In editing *Newsletters in Print*, Gagnè (1997) and her predecessors have used these criteria for listing a newsletter:

- It is a serial publication in North America available to the public (private publications and house organs were excluded in the directory).
- It is of national or broad regional interest.
- It addresses specialized interests and topics and addresses themselves to those who share the interest.
- It uses a variety of formats and presentation styles and typography.

The Newsletter and Electronic Publishers Association (NEPA, http://www. newsletters.org) and its associated Newsletter and Electronic Publishers Foundation (NEPF), both based in Arlington, VA, differentiate between house organ publications and subscription-based newsletters. The NEPF (2002) wrote the following:

> A subscription newsletter is a specialized-information publication that is supported by subscription sales and (usually) does not contain advertising. Successful newsletters convey specialized information to narrow markets—information that isn't available in a daily newspaper or weekly magazine, for instance. There are two distinct types of newsletters. Business-to-business newsletters are written for and paid by a business. A business newsletter specializes in narrow, niche subjects of interest to a limited number of people. It may pertain to a particular industry or government agency, or to a type of government or business function that crosses industry lines. . . . In contrast, consumer newsletters are paid for by an individual. Consumer newsletters are more general, focus on topics such as investment advice, health and travel, and generally have a larger audience. (p. 2)

Subscription newsletters are nearly a century old. The oldest is *The Kiplinger Washington Letter*, which began in 1923. There are several such publications more than a half century old (Wysocki, 1999). Newsletters such as these begin where an informational gap exists. Someone identifies it and the new publication is launched. The beat can be relatively broad in the beginning but will eventually develop into related or spinoff publications that give more information about subdivisions of the topic.

One successful business newsletter, *Communications Daily*, is published by Warren Communications News and focuses on electronic communications. It has since generated several related publications such as *Video Week*, *Audio Week*, and *Public Broadcasting Report* (NEPF, 2002). *Andrew Harper's Hideaway Report*, published by Harper Associates, is a travel-based newsletter for individuals who love to travel (see "Publisher Profile" in Wysocki, 1999, pp. 75–78).

United Communications Group, a newsletter publishing firm headquartered in suburban Washington, DC, is a leading subscription newsletter publishing success story. Founded in 1977 by journalists Bruce Levenson and Ed Peskowitz, the business information company publishes more than 100 specialized newsletters and specialized magazines in a highly diverse group of divisions. These include automotive, computers and technology, energy, health and human services, taxation, government contracting, telecommunications, transportation and delivery systems, defense-military, and financial services-banking.

Writers contributing to newsletters provide an important informational service, especially in a fast-paced information-oriented world. "Because they can be produced so quickly, they are often the first purveyors of important news, such as announcements of medical breakthroughs, results of statistical studies, identification of trends in society, or new shortcuts for professionals," former *Newsletters in Print* editor John Krol (1992, p. xi) explained.

Newsletter writers are most often freelance contributors or staff writers doubling as editors. Most newsletter publishers cannot afford a large full-time staff. Instead, publishers and editors purchase articles or take contributed articles for free from interested people. These outlets, even the ones that cannot pay contributors, can be important starting points for feature writers. Newsletters that succeed are a mix of mostly traditional hard news peppered with features, profiles, humor, and the human element.

A clear advantage is that writers are often working with small organizations and with editors directly. Access is often faster and easier. Opportunities may be greater because they are less competitive than on newspapers and magazines. However, there is a trade-off. Although there may be less competition, newsletters are highly specialized and require feature writers who have an ability to work within the specialization and communicate at the level of the often-sophisticated audience.

Internal newsletters for companies and other types of organizations contain articles that inform and build loyalty to the organization. They can unify readers through the features on employees or members. The news and information keep everyone up to date. External newsletters are often used for sales and publicity purposes. News and feature articles serve customers, potential customers, and members, and tell them about developments such as new products or services. In essence, the types and purposes of feature articles in newsletters may differ somewhat from newspaper and magazine features, but the writing forms and styles will probably not be too different.

Commercial newsletters—those published with subscriber fees only—are, in a sense, the purest forms of journalism. There are no advertising and often no organizational interests to represent or promote. These newsletters are quite expensive, but equally valuable to their subscribers. Anyone willing to spend up to $5,000 per year to subscribe to a particular newsletter demands rare information that cannot be obtained elsewhere and this individual wants it without the sanitized editing that may occur at other publications.

"Newsletters provide more detail, more background, more analysis and more follow up to a story than is required by the average newspaper or magazine reader. Subscribers rely on the newsletter's detailed information to help them do their jobs," offered Patricia Wysocki (1999, p. 3), executive director of NEPA.

The information they offer is very specific. Subscription newsletters provide "information that subscribers seldom can get anywhere else. Some newsletters are considered 'bibles of the industry,' providing need-to-have information without which professionals feel they would lose out to the competition," the NEPF says in its *Newsletter Career Guide* (2002, p. 5).

Individuals writing feature articles for newsletters work under a wide range of circumstances, but the model is much more like that of magazines than newspapers. Newsletters rarely have full-time staff writers and depend a great deal on freelancers or part-time contributors. Larger, well-established newsletters may have small staffs, but these writers probably also have other responsibilities such as editing or other work for the organization the newsletter serves.

Most newsletters, even expensive ones with significant national or international circulation, have small full-time staffs and seek much of their material from outside contributors. Organizations that publish newsletters—companies, associations, country clubs, schools, government departments and agencies, neighborhood groups, and even extended families—may have a single editor who depends on a stable of contributors who have information of interest to readers. This approach to publishing newsletters opens opportunities for beginning and experienced freelance writers, of course.

Full-time journalists working for newsletters are reporters and feature writers just like those at newspapers and magazines. Their audiences may be much more sophisticated and specialized, but they use the same tools and techniques. Newsletter journalists may also be more expert on subjects they cover. The NEPF (2002) noted the following:

> Newsletter journalists cover the same press conferences, congressional hearings, court proceedings, and other events as their colleagues from mass-audience publications. In fact, newsletter journalists often outnumber the other at such events. In Washington, newsletter journalists have the same congressional and White House credentials as those worn by reporters for other types of periodicals. (p. 4)

On the other hand, newsletter feature writers can be, and often are, members of special groups publishing the newsletters. Or they are individuals with a particular specialization or interest. Assignments are obtained by contacting editors and either asking for assignments or proposing article ideas. Much of the time there will be less competition and easier access to editors of these publications. This means it may be easiest for beginners to try writing features for newsletters, rather than newspapers and magazines.

It is also important to note that because of the more independent nature of newsletter reporting and feature writing, there is more flexibility for individual lifestyles. Many writers work out of offices in their homes, using personal computers, modems, fax machines, and overnight mail services. Pay may be per story or per issue, but the additional freedom is worth it for many individuals.

Advancement is also rapid for some persons. A writer may find himself or herself promoted to an assistant editor, associate editor, or editor in chief. Or with experience, you may start your own publication and serve as a writer and editor. It is clear, regardless of the level of work, that opportunities are present in this news and features medium as never before.

## ONLINE FEATURE WRITING

Electronic versions of newspapers, magazines, and newsletters existed prior to the rapid growth of the Internet in the middle and last half of this decade. However, there were few publications that existed solely in their electronic form. Online journalism is growing and will become a force of its own in the near future. It has already become a valid alternative for feature writers. The development of the World Wide Web, with its graphics, scalable fonts, interactivity, sound and video, and overall ease of use compared to earlier online formats, brought digital publications into the homes of millions of readers around the world. The growth of this new medium continues to be rapid and extensive.

Some electronic newspapers, magazines, and newsletters are nothing more than publications "exported" to Web format to extend their distribution. However, there seems to be growth of original publications solely based in their electronic format. In 2003, these publications were most commonly in three forms: Web site pages–documents, electronic mail text and attached documents, and Adobe portable document format (pdf) documents. The main difference is in their format limitations. Text e-mail publications still lack graphics and other multimedia features found on Web sites because of the limitations of some e-mail software, but some e-mail newsletters are using HTML today and this allows for more graphic and visual creativity in presentation. Some are professionally done, but others are crude and homemade in appearance and content. Individuals with the right computer hardware and software can explore these new publications.

There has also been growth of Web-based electronic magazines. These topical online publications are often called "zines" or "e-zines." Most zines did not originate in printed form, but certainly were built on the printed magazine tradition. They are often highly specialized. Zines have been described as "independent publications characterized by idiosyncratic themes, low circulation, irregular frequency, ephemeral duration, and noncommercial orientation" (Rauch, 2002, p. 1). Almost overnight, these energetic periodicals appeared all over the Internet and received a large amount of popular media coverage and attention as the trend of the moment. The World Wide Web created opportunities for this new genre of specialized online news and information in the mid and late 1990s and it has continued into the new century with a steady niche audience appeal. There are thousands of zines on the Internet today and they attract an audience in the millions (Rauch, 2002).

*Slate* (http://www.slate.com), Microsoft's entry into this type of periodical, is more general interest in content. It offers articles about politics, current events, and popular U.S. culture. *Salon* (http://www.salon.com) and FEED Magazine (http://www.feedmagazine.com) are other electronic zine (e-zine) examples. The reputations and credibility of these publications vary and writers must check each as they would check a traditional publication before developing a professional relationship.

E-mail newsletters take advantage of the growing number of individuals with e-mail addresses. Since the mid 1990s, businesses have provided their employees with e-mail addresses. But the growth of commercial online services, such as America Online, with their full access to the Internet, has given millions of others e-mail addresses as well. With this growing market, some specialized newsletter publishers have chosen to use the Internet and e-mail to distribute their content. Some are newsy, informational, and highly local or regional in nature, such as *Muse's News*, a newsletter for songwriters, and *Healthy and Fit*, which offers advice and tips on fitness. Others focus on products and services offered by businesses. Some are organizational in nature, designed for members of specific interest groups. Whatever the purpose of the newsletter, there are hundreds of millions of copies distributed each year.

Another form of online feature writing that has recently become popular is the Weblog or "blog." Weblogs are Web sites offering personal logs and journal-style content. Some Weblogs are single-authored and some are collaborations of groups of interested contributors. These Web sites have attracted quite a following in the past decade and led to the phenomenon of "weblogging" or "blogging." Readers find them appealing because the content changes every day. This highly personal approach to journalism has been used in independent, nonbranded online news sites and has become a feature of some more conventional online news sites as well. The ease of using the software required to create blogs has led to their worldwide growth in popularity (Walker, 2001; Higgins, 2000). Among the more popular Weblogs are Robot Wisdom (http://www.robotwisdom.com), Memepool (http://www.memepool.com), and The Obscure Store and Reading Room (http://www.obscurestore.com).


## TODAY'S MARKETS FOR FEATURE WRITERS

The numerous markets for feature article writers offer many opportunities for good freelancers. Magazines are increasing in number and so are the markets for your work. Although there are fewer dailies than in years past, newspapers emphasize their feature material even more to compete with other soft news sources such as television, radio, and magazines as an information and entertainment source.

Although you might not think much about it, smaller newspapers are the best chance for a beginning writer to find markets for feature articles. Small dailies that do not have large staffs are often responsive to queries or completed manuscripts for timely features. Weekly newspapers, with even smaller staffs, often seek assistance when it does not come to the editor. It is likely that your own journalism school or campus placement service receives telephone calls from time to time from weekly editors seeking part-time or freelance help in covering their neighborhood or community.

Magazines follow the same model of opportunity for writers. Although most magazines seek good writers outside their staffs, many small and specialized publications need quality freelance assistance year-round. This demands that you know about what you write for a specialized magazine.

A beginning feature writer need only look at the latest edition of the *Editor & Publisher International Yearbook*, issued each spring, to find out which newspapers are published in his or her region or area. Similarly, the annual edition of *Writer's Market*, published each fall, gives a complete look at the magazine markets that buy freelance feature work. And, of course, it goes without lengthy explanation that you can simply pull out the local telephone directory yellow pages, especially if you reside in a metropolitan area, to see which publishers maintain offices in your community.

Various specialized subjects have increased their visibility in the past decade. The growing number of separate and larger business sections in newspapers and business magazines means new and more writing opportunities as well. As the Business Press Educational Foundation (n.d.) says, business stories focus on supercomputers, genetic engineering, manufacturing in space, and other unlikely business topics because these activities are financed by businesses and are the work of privately funded laboratories of corporations, not the federal, state, or local governments:

> The results [of these stories in the business press], moreover, promise to have major impact on existing industries and, perhaps, bring entire new industries into existence. It explains why these developments are getting even more diligent attention from the business/industry press than from the mass media. (Business Press Educational Foundation, n.d., p. 1)

There are more than 3,000 business publications in the United States alone, presenting a growing market for writers.

There are other examples. You could make many points about the growth in sports publications, computer publications, and even a rebirth of some general interest publications, such as *Life*, in the past decade. These changes, of course, mean better opportunities for feature writers at present and in the future. And for the beginning feature writer, these publications are probably more accessible than established consumer magazines or daily newspapers.

There are many excellent approaches to feature writing that you will discover. Certain specific features and subjects that are getting inadequate attention or no attention might draw greater readership. Some publications are reexamining how they define and present news in light of dramatically changing markets and readers. Modern readership research has given editors and publishers new insights into more effective ways to serve readers. Features are one of the approaches. Magazines have always had high, if not dominant, feature content, but they are learning new ways to use and present features. Newspapers are becoming more magazine-like in their use of features.

# CHAPTER THREE

# Finding a Good Feature Article Idea

There will be days when a good story idea comes to you easily, and there will be other days when an idea will be difficult to generate. Often, writers must develop workable ideas from circumstances, conditions, and surroundings that are important to their publication's readers. During 2001 and 2002, travel was one of the industries seriously affected by the terrorist attacks on the United States in fall 2001. Security changed. The economy was also changing. Priorities for travel were upended. Travel publications such as *Condé Nast Traveler* published numerous articles about the new conditions for domestic and international travel after September 11, 2001.

Deborah Dunn, associate news editor for *Condé Nast Traveler*, wrote a major article for her magazine that focused on business travel. Focusing on airlines and hotels, she presented readers with the magazine's business travel awards for the year. The article provided lists of top airlines and hotels based on price, value, and services provided in the context of the volatile and unpredictable economy as well as the tightened environment of secure airports. At the heart of her article was a reader survey conducted earlier in the year (Dunn, 2002). The project reflects the best in identifying and executing a good feature story idea.

Dunn, Connie Cho, and her other staff colleagues at *Condé Nast Traveler* (2002) were able to devise the project, distribute the survey questionnaire by mail to 4,000 frequent business traveler readers, collect and analyze about 2,000 responses, and then write a lengthy package of descriptive articles and tables of survey results. To work on such an idea takes planning to make it happen and even more planning to carry it through to publication.

Not all ideas require this much hard work over several months. Some can turn around much more rapidly. However, the process of finding and developing feature story ideas can require patience and organization. It can also require a little serendipity or even luck.

## GETTING STARTED

Do you notice the ordinary and extraordinary things around you? When you drive to work or to school, do you make the extra effort to notice people or places or what is happening during that routine trip? Do you take time to look around when you go someplace new? What do you see? Is it interesting to you? Would it be interesting to others? Do you ever think of these observations as ideas for your writing?

Have you met anyone new today? What does that person do for a living? Has your regular network of friends and acquaintances brought anything different or unique into your life recently? What did you do out of the ordinary this week? Was it fun? Was it informative? Was it significant? Did you learn anything from the experience? Would anyone else be interested?

Any of these questions, if answered in the affirmative, might lead to a very good feature story. Finding feature ideas can be that easy. Some subjects practically announce their potential as a story to an alert writer. Others need the experienced eye and ear of a feature writer to work them into readable and salable articles.

Paying attention to what is going on around her is one of the major ways in which Liz Balmaseda, long-time columnist and feature writer for *The Miami Herald,* comes up with ideas for her award-winning columns and feature articles for the local section of her newspaper. Balmaseda, who won the 1993 Pulitzer Prize for commentary, said the entire city is what gives her ideas. "I look around and see what's going on," Balmaseda (1993, personal communication) explained. "I talk to a lot of people and ask them to tell me what's going on where they work and where they live."

Balmaseda said she also depends on people to call her with column and feature article ideas. As a highly visible columnist for one of the nation's major daily newspapers, she gets large numbers of telephone calls and letters. "People will call me and give me ideas," she said. "And I also talk to people in the newsroom. Reporters around the newsroom are crucial teammates for me. With their help, I look for wrongs—people who have been wronged" (1993, personal communication).

Feature writers have to notice details of things around them. You probably will not have such unusual experiences as Mt. Everest or Antarctic expeditions on which to base your articles. But stories can come from the ordinary, or seemingly ordinary. If you drive the same road to work or school every day, try to vary the route. Look at the scenery with an eye for story possibilities. For example, if you drive past the same house every day, look in the driveway. The old cars that the owner of the house is working on might be more than what they appear. Is there a chance this person restores valuable older cars? Isn't this a story prospect? Why not stop and ask a few questions?

Professor Margaret Davidson believes being a keen observer is what makes the biggest difference between a good writer and an average one, especially in terms of finding news and story ideas. "A good writer is a good observer—of people, surroundings, ideas and trends, and the general flotsam and jetsam of the world around," Davidson (1990, p. 7) explained. "Some people seem to go through life with blinders on. They are so wrapped up in their own comings and goings they are unaware of the ebb and flow around them. But others observe the world in sharp detail with the vision to see everything in perspective, appreciating its true value" (Davidson, 1990, p. 7). Davidson also says this is especially true of college students. "For some of the students—the world seems to be a colorful and fascinating place with an endless supply of worthwhile news stories. But for many others it appears to be very a sterile, boring existence where little that is exciting ever happens" (1990, p. 7).

If you go somewhere new, think even before you leave home about what possibilities for stories and articles exist. If you like the destination, why? Would others like it also? If that new boutique has unusual or new designs, tell others about it—in a feature story.

Meeting someone new and different can be exciting, also. However, don't think about the new acquaintance from a personal perspective. Think about him or her from a writer's professional point of view. Is this person worthy of a feature story? What makes him or her interesting to readers? What has this person done that others would like to know? Perhaps the person is in town for just a few days and really lives in a foreign country—perhaps a relatively unknown small country like Belize in Central America. Wouldn't this be a chance to write about the person, the country, and all the unusual aspects of life in a country that many Americans do not know much about?

Finding story and article ideas are related to natural curiosity. Often, the best ideas occur when writers think like 3- or 4-year-olds, always asking "why?" and "how?" And you have to think about what you do each day—you did something unusual, even something as simple as deciding where to go for spring break or over a long weekend. You could write a story listing your own favorite places. Or compile a list from the information provided by tourism and visitors bureaus. Those might just make a good story.

## IDENTIFYING FEATURE ARTICLE MATERIAL

What makes a great feature article idea—an idea that gets published? Just about everything around you is possible feature material. Use your senses. Look around. Absorb. Notice. Listen. Look. Your job is to take these undeveloped ideas and turn them into something interesting for readers.

People can be the source and subject of some of the best story ideas. Often a powerful story about a successful person's problems helps readers to see the "real" side of that individual. We learn from how he or she has experienced adversity and overcome it, or made the comeback to succeed a second time, lost a loved one, or survived a brush with death. These stories often make wonderful feature articles.

Williamson (1975) says finding a feature story idea should be easy. Those stories seem to jump out and practically scream, "Write me!" Williamson (1975) argued, "A great advantage in being a reporter is that you have a 'license' to find out about all those things you've always been curious about" (p. 70).

The *Dallas Morning News'* Texas Living section, published on Sundays, decided to take a look at a very common human behavior—sleep. The *News*, however, focused on individuals who have difficulty sleeping. It is a sample of the sort of feature that is easy and must be written simply because of the large numbers of people who often cannot sleep well. Staff Writer Steve Steinberg (2002) took a light-hearted approach to the subject when he wrote the Texas Living sleep guide that was a collection of the section cover story and two sidebar features. The package included a link to the newspaper's Web site also, where readers were advised that they could find a "sleep inducing" slide show of vacation photos. Steinberg was highly creative and had fun with his approach to the topic:

> Many of you are not sleeping well.
>
> There is no excuse for this when the Weather Channel and the books of John Grisham are so readily accessible.
>
> Here's the real eye opener: The National Sleep Foundation has found that only 37 percent of adults get at least eight hours of shut-eye on weeknights. And 31 percent say they get less than 7 hours.
>
> Here at the *Dallas Morning News* Sleep Desk, we want to help. But first we must put out heads on the desk and get some sleep.
>
> Ahhh. That helped. Now, why are so many of us having trouble catching up on the snooze?
>
> We may be a little over-stimulated for starters. Dr. John Herman, associate professor of psychiatry at the University of Texas Southwestern Medical Center at Dallas, notes that dark coincided with mammals' rest cycles for eons.
>
> Now we've changed all that. Humans have light, sound, communications, and entertainment around the clock. "This is a base violation of our ongoing physiology," Dr. Herman says.
>
> The Sleep Desk also believes that Carrot Top is somehow at fault, too. But whatever the reason, we desperately need more quality time bonding with our pillows.
>
> So let us help lull you to sleep, dear reader. (Save those nasty cracks, please. We're doing it on purpose today.) We suggest these relaxing options. (Steinberg, 2002, p. 1F)

Steinberg (2002) developed the remaining portions of the story around different approaches to falling asleep. He devoted one section of his cover story to classical music; another discussed reading poetry. Watching movies and television were other solutions. He also developed two useful sidebars. Sidebars are shorter feature stories, often lists or other information, which accompany a main story. Steinberg's approach included a sidebar list of "basic do's and don'ts" for sleeping experts. He also devoted a longer second feature to the causes of sleeplessness that looked at physical and mental disorders that affect sleep and he discussed how diet may affect sleeping patterns. Although the package of features took a light and entertaining approach, it was backed up with experts and authoritative sources about sleeping.

The key is curiosity. Be curious about why people cannot or do not sleep well. Maybe you have not been able to sleep much lately, or a friend is having trouble sleeping. Let these casual observations turn into story prospects. Once you notice things, hear about something appealing, once you meet someone, once you discover something interesting to you, let your journalistic curiosity take over. Satisfy your inquisitiveness by finding out about the subject. How? If you always wanted to learn about sailing, go to interview a local sailor or take lessons at a nearby lake, or go to a nearby sailing club meeting.

Finding the right story idea is also dependent on the publication for which you will write the story. You need to know what sort of material the publication publishes. This is more easily done if you work for the publication, but it can be relatively easy to find out if you take time to research the publication and its market (Bowman, 1997).

You also need to know the basic characteristics of feature ideas. What are they? Traditionally, good feature ideas have eight basic elements, according to Schoenfeld and Diegmueller (1982). Those elements are as follows:

1. Appeal to people—The story has to meet a need of the reader.
2. Facts—A feature that works will contain certain information, or facts, about that subject that will be beneficial to readers in some way.
3. Personalities—Facts are enhanced with personality. A story that can offer some unusual person or personality with facts and appeal will be much stronger.
4. Angle—The right "slant" or theme makes the subject tie together better.
5. Action—Can you make the story come alive? It will if you have some activity in the story. It is relatively simple—people should do something in your story.
6. Uniqueness and universality—The topic should be different and should have broad appeal at the same time.
7. Significance—Timeliness, proximity, prominence, and relevance create significance in a story.
8. Energy increment—The story should stir your readers just as the idea stirred you to write the story. You should show your enthusiasm and sincerity.

Finally, think about the necessity that all feature ideas remain fresh. Just like bread, a feature idea has a certain shelf life and it is up to you as a writer to make certain the idea is developed and published in story form while it is still fresh. The best idea won't work with editors or with readers if it is stale.

## TAKING THE RIGHT STEPS TO IDEA SUCCESS

Nonfiction and fiction writing have a lot of similarities, and many of them are discussed throughout this book. One similarity is the formation of ideas. Successful mystery novelist Elizabeth Peters (1992) says ideas are quite different from the plots she uses in her books. She wrote the following:

> It [the idea] begins with a "one-liner"—a single sentence or visual image, characterized by brevity and vividness. Since an idea is not an avocado, you can't simply go out and get one. In fact, the technique of finding a usable idea is more akin to bird watching than to chasing butterflies: There are ideas all over the place; the trick is to recognize one of the elusive creatures when it flits past. I'm not being whimsical. It is certainly possible to search actively for an idea, but unless you know one when you see one, there is no point in looking. (p. 88)

## SHAPING YOUR STORY IDEAS

Freelance writer Lorene Hanley Duquin (1987) has a four-step plan of attack for shaping story ideas before actually writing the article. She says these steps require "simple brainstorming" by asking yourself the questions and writing down the answers. "It's that information that I mold and shape into a proposal that captures an editor's interest and imagination" (p. 38). Her steps are as follows:

1. Capture the idea—Build an idea file because writers cannot always use ideas when they come along. You can do this with notebooks, file cards, file folders, shoeboxes, and even your word processor. At times, ideas have to wait until a market prospect presents itself, too.
2. Develop the idea—Do some preliminary research to develop that idea into a proposal. Not all ideas are easy to develop, of course, so be prepared to do some work. Think about the idea. Is it too broad or too narrow? Does it have wide enough appeal to your potential readers?
3. Tailor the idea—Shaping the idea to the readers you wish to reach is very important to a successful feature story. Ask yourself questions: What readers will be interested in your article? What has already been done on the subject? What publication will want to publish the article?
4. Test the idea—Duquin says you should be able to answer these questions: Do you really want to write the article? Are you capable of doing the article? How much will the article cost you (in money and time)? What else can you do with the material if an editor does not want it? Are there markets for reprints? Can you do spinoff articles?

For another approach to turning an idea into a workable story, Wisconsin writer Marshall Cook (1986) suggested seven steps:

1. Feed the mind—Try new experiences. Relive old ones through journals and diaries. Read extensively. Talk to people. Do stimulating things.
2. Nurture the idea—Ideas come with a flash of lightning or with the graduate speed of a sunrise. Be ready for an idea to come to you and give it your attention by examining it from all angles.
3. Ignore the idea—After pampering the idea, forget about it for a while. This incubation period helps divert you from pressure of creation on demand. Decide to come back to the idea at an appointed date and time a few days later.
4. Welcome the idea back—When you return to the idea at the appointed hour, be fresh and alert. Be at your most productive period of the day. Write in your regular, yet special, writing place. Be comfortable.
5. Create!—Concentrate on your idea, organize, and get going. Let the ideas flow and worry about style and clarity later. Get something on paper now.
6. Sustain the flow—Regular writing momentum makes a big difference. Successfully developing your idea into an article will depend on continuation of the work.
7. Revise—This involves polishing the original draft into a final product.

## LOOKING AT THE WORLD

You can do stories on an endless list of topics. Start by thinking about your own personal experiences and lifestyle. Stop reading for a moment. Take a piece of paper from your notebook and make a list of possible story ideas. It can be very general. You can refine it later. Compile your list before you read the next paragraph.

Done? Compare your list to the idea categories that follow. If you are a typical college student, it might include such things as cars, music, movies, dancing, clothing styles, housing, food, relationships, dating, classes, grades, fitness and exercise, travel, credit cards and bank accounts, friends, roommates, church, clubs and social groups, part-time jobs, parents–grandparents, and hometowns. Your list probably includes something like those and perhaps more. Your list might be more specific. Not bad for just a few minutes of "brainstorming."

Every one of those categories can be divided into story prospects. You just need to get more specific, that is, give each one a little more focus. You might not realize it, but you are an expert on subjects already and can write about them. If you are interested in fitness and exercise, for instance, do you like to jog? Do you take an aerobics class? If you do, you know more about jogging or aerobics than those persons who do not jog or do aerobics. You've experienced shopping for running and exercise clothes, conditioning, selection of the right foods, and the choice of best places to run, best clubs, and trainers.

Personal expertise can be personal experience also. These can develop into wonderful feature articles for the right publications. How about those categories we called parents–grandparents and hometown? Some writers can turn an ordinary aspect of their lives, such as their family or the home in which they grew up, into a marvelous experience for readers. Suddenly an ordinary part of your life, if reinvestigated, becomes a feature idea, a story prospect, and ultimately an article for a magazine.

Your story ideas can come from a lot of different places. Now, think of your experiences beyond the most immediate personal levels of your life. Professional and personal contacts can be useful, too. Do you belong to a club or business group, or does someone in your family? Sometimes these organizations provide numerous professional and personal contacts that can be used as sources for story ideas or for stories themselves. For example, that neighborhood fitness and exercise club you belong to can become a source spot for stories. You can write how-to-do-it stories, for example, from what you learn about the aerobics classes and other features about fitness, good eating habits, exercise clothing, membership plans and costs, and so forth, about the clubs in your community.

Freelance writer Patricia L. Fry (1997) recommended being prepared for ideas to come at any time. To do this, she is never unprepared to take notes of her observations. "Carry a note pad or tape recorder wherever you go. Start an idea file to keep your notes in, as well as newspaper and magazine clippings. Do this faithfully and you'll always find some fresh ideas to pitch to editors," Fry (1997, p. 40) explained.

Certainly groups will often host programs with instructional and educational value. Speeches and discussions can produce dozens of potential stories, ranging from childcare to income tax preparation. All you need to do is to look through the listings in your local newspaper or the newsletters of organizations in your community for upcoming events that could lead to interesting stories. Think about the subject, not the event itself. The speech or panel discussion might not become an article through the event itself. A speech or panel discussion about "sexual harassment in the workplace" could lead to a feature article about the unique problems some women face in their offices in your community. And that speaker could become a major source for your story about how women should handle such problems and their courses of legal and internal policy action.

Conventions are still another area that might suggest stories for feature writers. National and regional meetings always attract the most active and authoritative persons who are interested in discussing recent developments in their respective specializations. If you are in a metropolitan area or resort region where conventions are frequently held, this source can be very valuable. To keep up with the schedule of conventions, simply make regular contact with your local convention and visitors' office or major convention hotels.

Another set of sources is at local libraries. Every community has a public library. A few minutes spent in browsing through periodicals or new books at the library informs you about the latest treatments of subjects that may interest readers. Larger libraries, such as those at universities and colleges, often offer exhibitions and programs with speakers, even the authors, and other experts who provide material for potential stories. Some larger, more active, commercial bookstores have similar programs.

If your community has a museum, the exhibits and specialists assembled may be useful for story ideas. Both permanent and temporary exhibits offer possibilities for stories, of course, even if the stories are limited to just the fact that these events are occurring. Often, you can go beyond the exhibit itself to generate stories about the artist or event being highlighted. Numerous local, regional, and national markets exist for these features. In most areas, local history makes good story material. This can be a subject area to cultivate for stories, especially if you can find a local historian who is also a good storyteller. Many of your readers will be interested in their community's history, especially if you can explain how and why events, buildings or other landmarks, and people, wound up as they did.

Because house and home are important to just about everyone, writing about these topics is a natural. Numerous "shelter" magazines such as *Better Homes & Gardens* and *Architectural Digest* exist on the subject. Many major newspapers publish home and garden sections on Sundays or in certain seasons of the year.

Just roaming around can generate ideas for stories, too, if you know a good idea when you see it. When was the last time you drove through a neighborhood of your community that you haven't seen for a few months? Or maybe there are parts of your community that you have never visited. The curiosity and inquisitiveness a good feature writer needs should eventually motivate you to take a look at different places and people. In other words, explore and look around.

## COLLEGE CAMPUSES AS SOURCES FOR IDEAS

Where do we get a good feature idea? Everywhere. Well, it seems like it. For starters, people at local colleges or universities can be very good sources. Campuses offer both diversity and expertise. Combine that with relatively easy access and a campus is hard to beat for generating article ideas. If you are a student, think about the story prospects in your own classes. What interesting research is underway in the sciences at your campus? What are your own professors doing? Have you ever thought to ask? Many are working on serious and important projects that are often worthy of a feature or news story. This is particularly true if your campus has a medical school or other health education programs in which human health and human life may be affected by the work that is being done. Even if you are no longer a student, you will find that schools can be rich with story possibilities. You just have to know where to go to start.

Many universities and colleges have public affairs or public relations individuals who can suggest contacts for you on particular subjects. With a telephone call, these persons can suggest story ideas to you based on their knowledge of the current research and service projects on their campus. Some schools publish expert directories that are excellent sources for reporters and writers. Organized by topic, these directories quickly tell you what experts exist in your own backyard. These are free on request and often require only a telephone call to acquire one.

Marshall Swanson (1979), a freelance writer based in Columbia, SC, uses the nearby University of South Carolina campus as a base for many of his feature articles. He suggested these five steps in tracking story ideas:

1. Get to know how things run on campus—Use the public relations people. Get maps and student–staff–faculty telephone directories of large campuses.
2. Subscribe to the student newspaper on campus—Often these publications tell you a great deal about campus goings-on. You can extend this suggestion by reading the campus magazines and faculty–staff publications, also.
3. Get to know the director of the student center—There are many campus events that are coordinated through this office.
4. Establish contact with various deans and chairpersons of departments— Do this in person if possible.
5. Stop off for a visit at the campus research office—Many universities have offices for funded research programs, a campus clearinghouse for funded research. There is often a list produced of this work, or of grants received, that might propose interesting ideas before anyone else gets them.

Swanson also suggested that people on campuses are good prospects for profiles. Both faculty members and students can become story ideas if you ask around to find out who is doing what. Columnist Dennis Hensley (1979) offered the following: "Colleges are the homes of the greatest minds we have in this country and the freelance writer who doesn't tap this source of free information is literally missing the buck—the royalty buck, that is" (p. 34).

## LISTENING TO IDEAS FROM READERS

Many times, readers suggest story ideas. You know you have become established as a writer when readers contact you to pass along their ideas for stories. Although some ideas will not be worthy of a story, or are just not practical given your resources, others will be workable and you should follow up on the suggestions. Never ignore tips from readers. If one tip just will not work, the next one might be ideal. You cannot afford to forget about these suggestions. If you cannot follow up on a tip right away, pass it along to someone who can or, if time permits, write it down for later use. But you must take the time to check out each and every tip. Most reader ideas come in the form of casual conversations. Someone finds out you are a feature writer and wants to pass along the idea, or he or she calls. There are times when someone tries to be a public relations person for a friend or relative and write some sort of announcement or article to start you on your way. If you get a call, or a letter, or someone pulls you aside in an office, listen to the idea even if you are busy and cannot do anything about it right away. Write that idea down for action later. Cook (1986) said, "You [should] scramble for paper and pencil to capture this—You know better than to wait. Write it down now or risk remembering later only that you had a great idea but not what that great idea was" (p. 26).

Tips and other ideas for stories from readers need to be checked out. Occasionally, someone presents an idea to you that seems good, but it might be false, exaggerated, or otherwise problematic. You have to take the time, at the outset, to confirm and verify information before you dig in to begin work. The value of tips cannot be overlooked. Some feature writers make their living off them. Oregon's Gary King, a freelance magazine article writer and book author who specializes in serial crime, finds tips to be his bread and butter. He combines tips with other sources, such as the news media and online computer databases. "At first I got all of my leads for article ideas by following the news—all of it: TV, radio, newspapers, magazines. If I found a particular case that interested me, I would follow up by contacting (either in person, phone, or mail) the primary persons involved," King (personal communication, 1993) explained:

> After a while, however, people began contacting me, particularly those in the law enforcement community whose trust and respect I managed to garner. During the past 2 to 3 years, I learned about the power of the computer, and now make scanning the news wires part of my daily routine. Nothing, however, can fully take the place of the in-person interview. (King, personal communication, 1993)

## GETTING IDEAS FROM OTHER WRITERS

There's absolutely nothing wrong with looking at what other writers and publications are using as sources for ideas. An idea that you see in a west coast magazine or newsletter might not work in an east coast market, but then again, it might. You might be able to adapt it for your own purposes. Start by reading all of your local newspapers, magazines, and newsletters. If you live in a metropolitan area, this might be a chore, but you have to know what is happening locally. This keeps you informed about their potential for publishing when you have an idea, but it also gives you ideas that you can market elsewhere.

Certainly, you should try to read as many out-of-town newspapers, magazines, and newsletters as you can. This is especially true to help you learn markets where you might sell your work, but also to give you new ideas. If your
budget is tight and you cannot always buy subscriptions to newspapers, magazines, and newsletters, then head to your local college or public library, where
you will find many major publications that arrive regularly.

Serious staff and freelance feature writers make this a part of their daily work
habits. "I find that a writer should read everything in order to get article leads.
*The Wall Street Journal* is quite valuable to me for that reason. I often spend several hours a week at the library going through newspapers," said Kansas freelance feature writer Susanna K. Hutcheson (personal communication, 1993).
"Often, just a small item can be a major story or, at the least, a human interest
piece that can be resold a number of times" (Hutcheson, personal communication, 1993).

## USING SPECIALIZED PUBLICATIONS, PROGRAMS

Specialized publications and programs take this concept one step further. Specialized magazines and journals are excellent sources for feature article ideas. If
you write about a particular subject, whether it is gardening, cardiac care, office
equipment, or restaurant food, you need to be in touch with the industries
about which you write. The best way is to read about the concerns, news and
developments, problems, opinions, services, lifestyles, and major issues in publications designed to be read by professionals, the artists, and other experts.

These publications can help you understand the language, contemporary issues, and general concerns of these specialists, as well. *Foodservice Product News*
is an industry monthly produced by Young/Conway Publications Inc., in New
Jersey. Bill Communications in New York publishes *Food Service Director*. Both
are aimed at individuals working in the business of school, factory, and business
food service facilities such as factory or school cafeterias. Readers are most often managers and directors of these locations who are interested in information
about new products, services, promotions by suppliers, special success stories,
and even the law. If part of your work as a student writer for your campus newspaper included covering the university or college dining service, publications
such as these (and several others like them) would seem to be required reading.
In them you could discover what was available, what was happening at other
schools, and whether your own campus "measures up." You would also learn a
lot about the language of the industry (e.g., "steam tables," "nutrient standard
menus," or "ecumenical dining rooms").

Although these sorts of specialized magazines are generally available to
members of organizations or employees of companies clearly involved in the industry, nonmembers can often obtain subscriptions or single copies. Or, of
course, these can usually be obtained by borrowing them or requesting the dis-

cards from members or subscribers you know. But if you are serious about developing story ideas in a specialized area, you have to have access to these publications while they are current.

Research journals are also good regular reading for story ideas. One of the most widely read is the *Journal of the American Medical Association*, which regularly publishes new medical research findings. The journal is a mainstay for health and medicine writers but provides ideas for many general assignment reporters and freelance writers as well. Most journals are published quarterly, but some are monthly and even more frequent. You simply need to familiarize yourself with the existence of these publications by heading to a library or by asking sources you respect for the names of publications they regularly read.

Bulletins and newsletters from organizations are equally valuable. Although these publications often do not offer the depth that a magazine or journal might offer, they still present issues that should suggest stories for you. Regular reading of these topics will make a difference in how you cover your subject.

With the uniqueness of some cable television networks, specialized television programs may be a useful source for story ideas also. With cable television systems growing to more than 100 channels in some communities and 24-hour on-air television and radio broadcasting in many other markets, programs of narrow and specialized nature are getting opportunities to be aired. Talk radio, popular on AM stations in many metropolitan markets, can generate odd and unusual ideas simply by your listening to callers respond to the topic of the day. Shows devoted to local issues or specific concerns such as business or the economy are available and often become good sources for development of stories. Furthermore, public access channels of cable systems provide relatively obscure groups with special interests the time to broadcast. The convenience, for example, of tuning to your local school board meeting or local county government meeting on a cable channel saves time and allows you to pick up concerns of the community.

## WORKING WITH EDITORS' IDEAS

Editors know their markets well. Regardless of whether they are newspaper, magazine, or newsletter editors, these persons are in contact with their readers and other writers, and they probably have had access to research about their publication's readership and reader demographics. You need to know as much as you can about a given publication if you want to write freelance articles for it, and, of course, you need to know your readers and what they want to read if you are a staff member.

You will have countless opportunities to work with your editor on story ideas. Beginning general assignment staff writers at newspapers often start this way and gradually begin to initiate stories on their own as they gain confidence on the job. Magazine and newsletter staffers expect much the same, but because magazines and newsletters may often depend more on freelance material, editors usually only request articles or pass along ideas for articles to experienced writers whom they already know and trust.

Editors work from idea lists, just as you should do. When something interests an editor, he or she usually puts it in some sort of holding spot until planning for a new edition or issue is underway. These idea lists, when stories are assigned or when they are finished, are often called "budgets." Like your own ideas, editors' article ideas come from an equally wide range of possible sources. Editors read extensively. They talk to people. They get tips.

Your part of the system is to complete the legwork. You research and write. But you should not limit yourself to this role when working with an editor on a story idea. You bring into the situation different perspectives, experiences, and orientations. There will be occasions when you have begun to research an assignment and decide the original article idea was not exactly right. So, you refocus the story after discussing this with the editor who assigned the article. You should always share these concerns with your editor and offer to modify his or her suggestions if you have an angle that will make a good idea a better one. And your editor should be willing to listen. Don't change the story without talking to the editor. The editor needs to know what you are doing because your article is just one part of a larger plan for the department, section, or even the entire magazine.

On occasions, you will find a group brainstorming session can generate workable story ideas. You can do this with your supervising editors, with other writers, and even your friends or roommates. Simple conversation around the office or the apartment or dorm floor during a break or after work might do the trick. For freelancers not working in a regular news media environment, writers' clubs and other similar professional organizations can offer the same support.

### An Editor's Idea-Development Tricks

Award-winning trade magazine editor Rama Ramaswami (2002) works with both staff writers and freelance writers to develop story ideas for her magazine on a daily basis. She is editor of *Operations & Fulfillment* (http://www.opsandfulfillment.com), a controlled-circulation monthly trade magazine serving "operations executives at companies selling directly to the customer through a catalog, Web site, or retail store." The magazine covers "everything that the merchant does after a customer places an order, from entering the data to picking, packing, and shipping the item" (About the Magazine, 2002, n.p.). As Ramaswami (personal communication, 2002) stated

*Operations & Fulfillment*, published monthly by Primedia, Inc., is a controlled-circulation magazine that covers everything a company does after a business or an individual customer has placed an order. We offer several channels through which a reader can get information: a print magazine (11 issues a year plus a supplier directory issue), a Web site, an opt-in weekly e-mail newsletter, an annual conference, and occasional seminars.

We cover everything that a retail, catalog, online, or manufacturing business does to get an order to a customer (business or individual) after the customer places it over the phone, online, or by mail. The customer may be located in the U.S. or overseas. Therefore, we deal not with a specific industry but with a function that cuts across all industries, from apparel to groceries to chemicals.

Our goal is to enable operations execs to do their jobs better. Our readers are VPs of distribution, VPs of logistics, directors of customer service, contact center managers, e-commerce managers, etc. These executives want to know how to improve efficiencies, productivity, cost savings, and customer service in their operations, and these are the issues that O&F addresses. In our June 2002 issue, for example, we ran stories on how to prevent rapid agent burnout in call centers, the proper security measures to take when shipping packages overseas, and how best to use the latest warehouse technologies. In September, we published a case study of furnishings retailer Bombay Company's inventory planning, the results of our exclusive benchmark study of retail information systems, and how to ship parcels to exotic international destinations.

Our hallmark is to use a "consumer" rather than a "trade" magazine approach to supply information. We aim to entertain and engage as well as instruct the reader. The editors and creative director work closely together to create a unified product, using attention-grabbing covers, sophisticated graphics, and clever headlines and decks.

Here's how we develop story ideas:

Read—Not just other trade magazines, but anything and everything, from *USA Today* to *Motor Trend* to *Vanity Fair* to online newsletters to business newspapers. You never know what you'll find. For instance, some months ago I was browsing casually through an issue of *Aviation Week* (my son subscribes to it) when I spotted a story about Boeing using the Internet to streamline communications with its dealers. It was a great business-to-business operations case study that we adapted for our readers—our November 2002 cover story is about Harley-Davidson's e-commerce fulfillment model, in which dealers play a central role.

Attend trade shows—Over the years, we've developed a systematic way to "work" these events. At each show, our goal is to find ample material for our print magazine, Web site, weekly newsletter, and other editorial vehicles, as well as possible presenters and topics for our annual conference, the National Conference on Operations & Fulfillment (NCOF).

- Before the show, we look at the brochure to find sessions that pertain to our topics, and assign different editors to cover each one.
- "Covering" means sitting in on the session, taking down notes and quotes as necessary (the quotes make valuable tidbits as well as provide fodder for

our weekly e-mail newsletter), and meeting the presenters afterward, introducing them to our magazine, and asking if they would be available to be interviewed for future stories.

- Another aspect of our trade show coverage is walking the exhibit hall, looking for new companies that might possibly be interested in advertising in the magazine; we pass on these leads to our sales folks. On occasion, the clients of these vendors (i.e., the direct-commerce companies we're interested in) might consent to be interviewed for case studies and other features.

- We pick up tons of "literature" at trade shows, from copies of competitors' magazines (great sources of new story ideas) to university research studies to white papers to media kits. We sift through these when we get home, and usually get several months' worth of material.

Survey our editorial advisory board—About 3 times a year we send out a brief survey to the members of O&F's advisory board. (The people on the board are retail, catalog, or e-commerce operations executives who represent our typical reader—e.g., the VP of logistics for The Borders Group; they're not software vendors or consultants.) The survey asks them to list what their top operational concerns are and what they're doing to deal with these issues, as well as where the execs see their companies heading. Their replies are kept confidential, so they can be totally candid. We use the information only for our own planning purposes and to generate an editorial calendar that is in sync with our readers' needs.

Learn from internal meetings—During monthly powwows that include representatives from the editorial, art, circulation, sales, and conference departments, we discuss the state of the O&F "franchise," directions we're taking, and what's being heard on the street. This doesn't usually generate stories, but does give us the market knowledge we need to make accurate decisions about what to cover and when.

Glean tips from industry experts—We get these all the time from trade shows, interviews, casual e-mail exchanges, reader feedback, and so on.

Use press releases and "found" material—Of course, the amount of PR material we receive is bottomless. A lot of it is trash, but occasionally we'll find something that we can throw in our weekly newsletter (such as event information), or rarely, a nugget that turns into a great story.

## INFORMATION AND COMMUNICATION CENTERS

You can generate ideas by exploring the communication networks of your community. Many institutions and organizations today provide local telephone numbers or toll-free long distance telephone numbers to information lines. These lines are regularly updated reports designed either for the public in general or the news media. When you know you have a subject to write, and you know some of the source organizations and institutions you will use, you should find out if these services exist.

Community bulletin boards exist in just about every place where people regularly congregate. Shopping centers, for example, often have community bulletin boards for wide varieties of goods, services, and other items. You will often find these at larger grocery stores, too. Churches, senior citizen centers, park centers, and other community "living rooms" will be good places to find story ideas. In recent years, some community bulletin boards have become interactive Web sites, chat rooms, newsgroups, or electronic bulletin boards on the Internet. These are public computer sites where basically the same posting practices occur. These virtual communities can be geographic in nature or communities of other types—usually organized by subject interest.

For example, go to the recreation center of a park near you. Dance classes, exercise programs, arts and crafts groups, and other organized activities will be promoted in a variety of ways. And you probably see the article possibilities already. At universities, colleges, and even high schools, campus student centers have a lot going on. Message centers often tell you about lectures, meetings, organizations, programs, and so on. These information centers are not limited to buildings. Bulletin boards often find their way into your home on cable television channels. Community-access channels often run listings of activities that can lead to stories.

Personal computers are now a part of the article idea search process also. Some bulletin boards have found their way onto the Internet as bulletin boards or have moved to other formats such as news groups or chat rooms. A Web site, also, can list useful information similar to bulletin boards. Some community organizations use these sites to distribute information about their activities and they are usually kept current. The important key is to check these sources of information on a regular basis and then double check the information for accuracy before using it in a feature story. Consistent use of these sources eventually pays off with a unique and salable story idea.

## IDEA FILES, CALENDARS, AND DATEBOOKS

Well-organized writers keep an idea file, a calendar, or datebook to plan ahead. Without it, your life as a writer will be filled with scheduling chaos. Idea files can be as simple as scraps of paper with ideas scribbled on them and thrown into a box or file folder. Or they can be more sophisticated and better organized. You can use computer database programs or even work with a word processor to keep a list. Some writers use a card file system for managing their ideas for articles. Others prefer to use calendars or datebooks.

Calendars and datebooks can be quite sophisticated. Perhaps some of the best are called personal information managers. You may already have one. For serious writers, it may be easier to work with two of these. Keep one for personal matters and the other for your writing and professional activities. These can be bound and professionally organized in a notebook format. Also, they can be purchased in fairly expensive computer software packages that allow you to put all your appointments, addresses, notes, to-do lists, and other events into an electronic format. The address section is ideal for compiling a source list in an electronic address book (and you can print them out for your binder that comes with it). Or, calendars and datebooks can be quite simple, such as the pocket-size calendars that are often given away each semester at school bookstores. In short, you have many ways to keep track of upcoming events and activities that might lead to article prospects. Office supply houses, bookstores, and even variety stores sell these tools for your work.

Regardless of what form they take and where you get them, calendars and datebooks are one of the basics of the well-organized writer. You might consider a hybrid form of a calendar-idea list. Some writers like to use file folders, one for each month of the year. Others keep desk books and clip ideas into each appropriate day or week. Some professional writers, using their publication's office or their home workspace, use a large wall calendar for a big picture of upcoming article prospects and deadlines. Find a system that works for you. Try different approaches until something that fits your personal style is found. If you are organized, you will be more efficient and productive in your work.

## YOUR BEST SOURCES FOR STORY IDEAS

- Personal experiences.
- Personal and professional contacts.
- College and university campuses.
- World Wide Web sites, especially those hosted by local community organizations and institutions.
- E-mail distribution lists sponsored by specific interest groups that fit your interests.
- News groups, chat rooms, and Weblogs devoted to specific subjects or topics.
- Meetings and conventions.
- House and home and your own neighborhood.
- Libraries, museums.
- Historians.
- Other publications (newspapers, magazines, newsletters, and online publications).
- Television programs.
- Readers and sources.
- Editors and fellow writers.
- Telephone information recordings.
- Community bulletin boards and communication centers.
- Calendars and datebooks.

Don't forget the seasonal nature of feature writing. Although this is discussed further later, it is important enough to mention here. For example, *Writer's Digest* contributing editor Frank Dickson (1980) wrote two articles for his magazine more than 20 years ago that proposed rather timeless story ideas based on the fall and winter seasons. His point, while listing more than 70 ideas in the articles, is that you must plan ahead as much as 6 months for some stories if you want to sell your work.

## FINDING FEATURE IDEAS ON A BEAT

Staff writers for newspapers, magazines, and newsletters often find themselves on a beat assignment. Although there is considerable freedom being a general assignment staff member who takes any story assignment that comes along, the opportunity to specialize on a beat appeals to many writers. Although a newspaper reporter's beat can be defined as just about any subject—such as health and medicine, transportation, the public zoo, education and the schools, or parks and recreation—magazine and newsletter writer beats are often even more specific and specialized because of the narrow scope of the publication.

For some newspaper, magazine, newsletter, or online publication beat writers, feature stories can be the exception rather than the rule. Many times, beat reporters are bound by the demands of spot news reporting and find little time for features. However, a good feature article can serve several purposes for beat writers. First, they give you a needed diversion from the daily deadline writing. Second, they can build bridges with sources because these stories, if accurate and fair, seldom ruffle feathers. Third, they offer readers a new perspective on a familiar subject.

Let's think about the police beat as an example. A writer covering the police department on a regular basis will have plenty of breaking spot stories for his or her editors without writing feature articles. Yet, some of the most interesting stories take readers behind the scenes. They profile officers with special achievements, highlight special crime prevention programs, or offer depth and insight to an unusual event, such as a shocking crime that has recently occurred, or a crime trend affecting a segment of the community, such as senior citizens. Looking at a different beat, a writer covering education can produce many feature articles about schools, students, programs, teachers, administrators, parental activities, organizations, and the successes and failures of the school system.

Williamson (1975) said beat reporters generate most newspaper features. "Regardless of the reporting specialty you may inherit, feature stories will present an ever-present opportunity to win news sources, educate and inform your readers, and impress your editors with steady, high production" (p. 75).

Magazines, on the other hand, also depend on beat writers, but these people are not always on staff. As already noted, many magazines depend on freelance writers to be their specialists for articles. Or, if you become a specialist on a magazine staff, remember that either way, it is likely that you will be a specialist for a publication quite narrow in its scope. There are few general interest magazines that remain successful. Unless you work for one on them, it is likely you will be covering a specialized area for readers who have a high level of interest in the subject and, it is also quite likely, a high level of knowledge of the subject as well.

## CHOOSING THE RIGHT ANGLE

All feature articles have a particular approach. It really doesn't matter whether your article is written for a magazine, newspaper, or newsletter. It has to have some sort of angle, some major thrust within the subject you have selected. It should also limit itself to one angle or it will have too much direction to it. After you have determined the subject for the article, make a list of all the possible angles of the subject. By exploring your list of options, you begin to get the overall picture and available approaches. Then organize the list. Reorder it. Which one is best? Rank the items on the list according to which you feel are the most appealing and unique to readers. This should help you eliminate some of the less desired approaches. With a practical point of view, determine what angles are within your resources. How much time is needed? Are sources available? Is travel involved? Can you afford the approach within your operating budget? What topics interest you the most? Make second, third, and fourth choices for the story's focus in case your favorite choice does not work out. Always have a backup angle to the idea.

Here's an example of giving some focus to a general idea:

Let's suppose you want to write an article for your local city or regional magazine about running. The process of finding the best angle is similar to a narrowing-down process. What do you want to write about running? Because it is a city or regional magazine, do you write about city trails, street running, or off-street trails on the edge of the city? Do you write about competitive running, local races, or the annual local marathon or 10K race? Do you write about running clubs or teams, shoes, or other equipment? Do you write about the right clothing, training, or trainers? You make these types of decisions many times in conjunction with an editor. As a freelancer, you are on your own. It is a good idea to have this angle set before you pitch the story in a query letter or article proposal.

For this assignment, you decide you want to write about running from a consumer or participation angle. Can you narrow this down further? Probably. You think this through and decide one approach might be the public tracks, park spaces, indoor training tracks, or even new trails built in your metropolitan area in the past few years. However, you still have to go further to determine your final focus. Will you do a user "review" of these facilities? Or will you simply do a descriptive piece with maps that tells readers where they can be found? You decide on the descriptive review. This requires you to walk or run every mile, taking notes along the way about rest stops, traffic, smoothness of the route surface, stops along the way for emergencies, staging or parking areas, and even how busy the tracks or outdoor routes get after work and on weekends. Then you stop some fellow runners and interview them. Other sources, such as officers of local running clubs, members of the college track and cross country teams, and local government officials who oversee recreation and parks, also become part of the story. The purpose of this example is to illustrate that you must keep things specific and focused in your article. Without it, your article will drift without any real beginning, middle, or end, and worse, it will not seem to have any point to it.

Patterson (1986) called an article angle "a frame that contains all the pertinent material. Material not pertinent to the angle is left out of the piece. The angle is also like a clothesline from which the piece's bits of information are hung" (p. 59). He added that a feature article's angle helps structure information around a central idea that gives the reader's mind a clear place to rest.

## TRYING OUT IDEAS BEFORE WRITING

To be fair to yourself and to your potential readers, you must try out the idea before you devote time and resources to it. As noted earlier, freelance writer Duquin (1987) offered a strategy for polishing your story ideas before you sit down to write. She said the approach requires asking questions and writing down the answers. Here is a much closer look at the questions posed earlier:

1. Do you really want to write the article?—You have to consider the motivation level. If it is interesting to you and a worthy subject, you should do it. If you cannot seem to get excited about it, how can you expect your article to show that excitement? How can you expect your readers to be stimulated by what you have written?

2. Are you capable of doing the article?—Some topics are simply beyond a writer's abilities to complete. Because of their technical complexity, the time involved, or the expenses, it might not be workable. Some great article ideas are just out of reach for average writers. Sometimes, a subject requires the sensitiv-

ity or personal experience that you might not have. A mature writer recognizes this and holds the idea until later or gives it up completely.

3. How much will the article cost you?—For both staff writers and free-lancers, you have to consider the resources needed to do a story. For staff writers, you might have a news media organization behind you, but its budget has limitations and priorities that may prevent you from traveling, calling, or otherwise gathering the information you need. Furthermore, this is a serious problem when you are not sure if a publication will pay your expenses. As a freelancer, can you afford to take the chance? Some ideas will be worth the risk; others will not. Finally, there is the consideration of time. If you have the resource backing you need, does this idea merit the time it will require to do it right? Some long magazine pieces require a month or two of full-time research and writing. Other features can be done in a few hours.

4. What else can you do with the material?—What happens to your idea and its development if a targeted publication does not want it? Do you have other publication options? Can this idea become part of another writing project? If you are a staff member, does your publication permit you to market your work to other outlets?

5. Are there markets for reprints?—For freelance writers, this is a concern that may not be so important to staff writers. If you write your article from this idea, can you find second and third outlets for the story in the form of reprints? Some magazines regularly reprint major feature articles. Staff writers might not concern themselves with this because they have less control over distribution of their work. However, some newspaper and magazine groups often exchange the best of their editions through news services and syndicates.

6. Can you do spinoff articles?—For the freelance writer, this is a critical point. To make your work pay off at a level that can sustain you, ideas must generate more than one possible story. Can you take the idea and move into several markets with it? For a staff writer on a regular income, this is a little less important. Yet, from a similar perspective, even a staff writer might consider if the idea would have potential for a series approach or other stories for later issues and editions.

## DEVELOPING AN IDEA INTO AN ARTICLE

Two general steps in developing your idea into a finished manuscript are as follows:

1. Giving the idea an angle—Narrow it down. Cut out unnecessary approaches.
2. Testing the idea for its soundness—Does it seem logical? Does it make sense on its face? Would you want to read this article if someone else had written it? What do people you know think about it?

Once you have satisfied yourself that these steps are completed, then the prewriting and editing process continues with your first efforts to gather and organize materials for your article. These additional three steps are as follows:

1. List the research sources you will need—This subject is covered in depth in chapter 4, but in developing an article idea before the writing stage, you now should consider what research would be necessary. Where do you go?
2. Make a rough outline of the idea as you turn it into an article—You should have some idea of the thrust or angle of the story by now and can begin to list major sections of the article on paper. This will help you understand what needs to be done next.
3. List possible interviews and sources you will need—What persons will be a part of the article? What areas of expertise will they represent? How will you find them? Are they accessible?

# CHAPTER FOUR

# Researching Feature Article Ideas

Each month, the news library at *USA Today* in McLean, VA, receives about 2,500 information requests. The approximately 100 requests per day—the center is open 6 days a week—come from *USA Today* news staff members, the Gannett News Service, the 40,000-employee parent Gannett Company, and the general public from just about everywhere in the world. A total of 17 library staff members provide valued support for writers and editors needing assistance in preparation of daily features and news stories. Staff writers and reporters have access to the Internet, an Intranet restricted to employees only, e-mail, and text and image archives of the newspaper, but librarians provide the more specialized assistance. This is feature writing support at its best. Feature writers and their editors working for top-flight organizations such as Gannett Corporation and its flagship daily newspaper have access to skilled and experienced assistance in a facility that includes a wide range of current reference books and state-of-the-art online databases such as Lexis–Nexis, Factiva, Pacer, AutoTrack XP, Baseline, Courtlink, Dialog, Hoovers, and Periscope (O'Neill, 2002).

*USA Today* reporters and staff writers regularly depend on research to find necessary information for stories. Many will complete their own research for the several dozen feature stories published each day in the newspaper's front News section, or in the Money, Sports, and Life sections as well as for the newspaper's World Wide Web site each day.

Most beginning freelance and staff feature writers, however, do not have access to research centers such as the one at *USA Today*. The usual situation is something between no special library or research center at all to something much smaller. Most freelancers depend on public libraries and other resources such as the Internet and World Wide Web. For most freelance and staff feature writers, research is very much a do-it-yourself proposition. If you need information, you go find it at a library or on a Web site. At daily newspapers and major magazines, assistance from specialists such as those at *USA Today* is always available, but for a large number of writers, research remains a public library or online experience.

Even if it is not at *USA Today*, an enormous library is out there just waiting for you to use it—the Internet and World Wide Web. For much of the information you will need for an article, you will not have to go much farther than your computer. These days, the serious writer who does his or her own research is becoming a computer whiz, weaving his or her way in and out of electronic libraries in a wide range of forms. Mix this with the already looming size and vastness of traditional library collections, and the research process has taken on new meaning when applied to article writing.

Have you found a good idea that you want to develop into a feature article? Do you need to find some basic information about it? Perhaps you need to dig deeper for all there is on a current subject? That's what you learn how to do in this chapter. Focus is on using traditional library resources and employing newer computer-based resources. Brief attention is given to interviewing and observation as significant information gathering tools.

Research is diligent investigation and inquiry into a subject. It is such an important step and professional writers take time to do it. Not only would it be rare to write an article without any research, it borders on foolish. It is a common pitfall for beginners who think they know enough to write an opinion feature or some other type of article with little or no background work. Effective research requires a plan. Freelance writer Gary Stern (1993) advised getting organized before beginning any research. "Before you launch your research, plan your strategy. . . . Do your homework" (Stern, p. 36). Yet, because professional writers must do research for their articles, they often take it for granted. However, they take the time and expense to do the research and are always glad they did.

San Diego, CA, freelance feature writer Andy Rathbone is a believer. He subscribes to the "research first" approach in his work. Rathbone, author of books, magazine articles, and newspaper stories about such wide-ranging topics as computers, food preparation, dining in restaurants, humor, travel, and electronics, says research is one of his first steps in his work. Not only will he spend time on it, he is not afraid to spend considerable money when it is necessary. "When writing computer books, I've spent $300 at the bookstores to grab all the competing books. It's important to know what's been discussed by the competition," Rathbone (personal communication, April 20, 1993 and January 17, 1998) explained. "It's easier to see what approaches work well—and what approaches fail—by seeing it appear on the printed page" (Rathbone, personal communication, April 20, 1993 and January 17, 1998). Rathbone often writes specialty material for beginners who are being introduced to a new subject or product. "I drop by several online services. CompuServe's 'New User' forum, for instance, is a goldmine for finding out the questions that confused computer users are asking. By scanning for some key words, I can trace a subject's history, and perhaps find other angles" (Rathbone, personal communication, April 20, 1993 and January 17, 1998).

Minneapolis feature writer Steve Perlstein agrees with this approach to research. He finds the writing and reporting–researching processes to be inseparable. Perlstein, who has written as a staff member at major daily newspapers as

well as for United Press International, has written two books and numerous national magazine articles. Perlstein (personal communication, May 3, 1993 and
January 15, 1998) commented:

> For me, writing and reporting mesh; one begets the other, and one cannot exist
> without the other. I've always considered myself a natural writer who had to
> learn reporting. Some are the other way around. When I pull in an assignment, I
> first write a list of all the possible sources I can think of from all sides of the issue.
> Unless I can come up with a compelling reason otherwise, I wind up calling ev-
> eryone on this list. And usually, each of these people gives me one or two others
> to call (I always ask), or a book or article I should read for my research.
>
> I regularly use databases from the library and online services to flesh out my
> background knowledge before I call anybody—I've found most sources are expo-
> nentially more forthcoming when you indicate you have at least a rudimentary
> knowledge of what you are asking them. They also are more likely to think you'll
> know if they are lying, so they don't try it as often.

News research—and reporting—are in a new world of computers and database research, as Perlstein's discussion suggests. If computer-based research is
new to you, you might wonder, "Where can I start? What sources can I call on?
Where do I go?" Start with, and master, printed sources. There are still the basic
categories of interview-based resources, but these days, you need to add computer-based sources to the list. This chapter focuses on all three of these areas—
published sources, people sources, and computer databases—because you may
need to employ all of them in working on a feature article. It may be easiest to
start with printed materials in a place with which you are familiar, such as your
campus or local public library. Then you can ease into the more challenging
specialized, online, or other electronic reference materials when you are ready
to do so.

Expect to do some serious work and spend some time on it, no matter what
research resources you use. Some experts say you should expect to spend as
much as 10 hours of research for every 1 hour you spend at your computer
when working on a feature article. Generally, there are two categories of written sources for research: those open and available to you and those which are
not generally available to the public. Although this chapter focuses on discussing public sources, it also gives you some ideas about how to contend with limitations of restricted information that you might need for a story.

## MEDIA LIBRARIES

Most established news organizations have useful libraries. As companies have
seen these grow to potential revenue centers (e.g., some now sell access to their
information to the general public), budgets have grown and so have usable re-

sources. A larger newspaper, magazine, or newsletter will have a staff of professional news librarians and sophisticated computer systems to assist you in your work. In fact, some companies insist on librarians conducting computer searches because that controls costs. However, smaller newspapers, magazines, and newsletters, as well as bureaus of larger news organizations, usually are not as well equipped. As a writer for a smaller publication, you may have to pay for such search expenses yourself. This forces you to be more resourceful in finding information on your own.

If you are fortunate enough to have a news library at your office, information is usually filed two ways—by newsmaker's name and by subject matter—and there are usually two categories: article clippings and still photographs. All news libraries seem to have a standard set of atlases, abstracts, directories, handbooks, encyclopedias, almanacs, and other general reference books. Libraries should update their holdings as often as new editions are published. Later, I suggest some titles to consider acquiring in starting your own desktop reference library. Many writers feel you can never have too many reference books within arm's reach of your favorite writing spot. The standard tools for finding information at full-service libraries are card and online catalogs, as well as book and automated indexes. Specialized news libraries are not often that well organized. When it doubt, get someone to help you.

## PUBLIC AND OTHER PRIVATE LIBRARIES

Both public and private libraries are your next options in conducting research for your article. If you cannot find what you seek at your own organization's news library, then go to your local public library. In many communities, there are also university and college libraries, but these are sometimes restricted. Many state universities and college libraries are open to the general public, but some private schools limit access to faculty, students, staff, and alumni. If you need to use a private library, contact the director of the library for permission to use it.

Public libraries, such as those supported by city or county funds, often contain excellent sources, particularly for local and regional subjects. If you reside in a metropolitan area, then the wealth of library resources should be great. The only restrictions for public libraries are hours of operation and demand on resources. Some special collections are accessible only by advance arrangement, but the reference materials that you need may be available for your use.

Besides your office library, public libraries, and academic facilities, there are three types of special libraries to remember. First, you can often use area historical society libraries. Many communities have these, and in state capitals there may be several that are open to the public. Second, there are museum libraries.

Presidential libraries and topical museums are an example of this type of facility. Third, there are company and corporate libraries. Large corporations, such as those on the Fortune 500 list, maintain these for employees but facilities may be available for your use if you request permission. If you are not permitted on site, it is possible that through the public relations or public affairs department of the company you may reach the company's specialists to get assistance.

Most libraries have open stacks. That is, the shelves are open for you to browse and to find your own materials. However, some libraries do not open their stacks because of theft, incorrect shelving, and other loss of valuable materials. This is a hardship for you because you must list the books you want and request a clerk to get them for you. Needless to say, this takes time. You might want to talk to the director of the library for permission to use the stacks if your research project is complex and you can establish that you will use the privilege with responsibility. Your ability to take advantage of whatever library you use depends on you and one other person: an experienced professional reference librarian who specializes in the subject about which you are writing. Subject specialists are on staff to assist you, so call on them when you need assistance.

Another service to remember is the networking that libraries use to multiply their resources. Many libraries link together in national, state, or regional networks to loan and exchange materials needed by borrowers. These interlibrary loan services may be fee-based and may take time to use, but they can save you a lot of travel expense to find materials not locally available. Finally, check the facility's hours of operation before you leave home. Hours can change and a telephone call may save you valuable time.

## USEFUL REFERENCE BOOKS

Just about all writers need to check facts or find a little bit of information that is not convenient to locate. For example, do you need to know a quick fact for a travel feature, such as the average daily temperature in Toronto and Mexico City during the summer? Go to a reference book. The answers may surprise you: In July there is an average high of 80°F and a low of 58°F in Toronto and a high of 74°F and a low of 54°F in Mexico City, according to *The World Almanac and Book of Facts 2002* (Wiesenfeld, 2002). Or maybe you need to know the top five amusement parks in attendance in the world. They are Tokyo's Disneyland, Florida's Magic Kingdom, California's Disneyland, France's Disneyland, and Florida's EPCOT (Wiesenfeld, 2002). Even a rather common reference book such as this one, available for a few dollars at just about any neighborhood drug store or bookstore, can be a boon when you are researching a quick fact for an article. If you take a step further, you will find your local library's reference section to be one of the most useful sections of any library for any writer. You'll find many types and sources of books and periodicals. A few of the major reference books that are helpful to writers are discussed later.

Although writers need to get their facts straight, many publications employ fact checkers to make sure the information is correct. Staci Bonner (1995), a freelance magazine writer and former research editor for a national entertainment magazine, observed that professional writers would not submit manuscripts with factual errors in them any more than they would submit manuscripts with grammatical or other writing errors. "Publications vary widely in their fact-checking techniques" (Bonner, 1995, p. 37). Bonner pointed to several areas of information that should concern writers: names, numbers, rumors, job titles, ages, dates and times, punctuation, geography, deaths, brand names, chronologies, and quotations.

To begin checking your own facts such as those listed by Bonner (1995), directories are a place to start. These are specialized books that list wide-ranging content such as membership lists and statistics. For example, of particular interest to you as a writer, are city directories. These can be extremely helpful for finding names, addresses, telephone numbers, and building occupants. Writers for newspapers and newsmagazines find them particularly helpful in locating sources. There are directories for several thousand cities in the United States that are published annually by private companies such as Polk Directories in Michigan. Each of these books is different, depending on the company which produced it. They contain traditional white pages (alphabetic listings by last name), but also color pages that list (a) address listings in alphanumeric order, (b) telephone listings in numeric order (often called reverse phone listing), and (c) directories of major buildings and occupants. Some even include directories of government officials, addresses, and telephone numbers.

There are also almanacs. As mentioned previously, some of these basic references are inexpensive and easy to buy. These books are published independently by companies or often cosponsored by news organizations such as the Associated Press or *Time*. They are published annually and list facts and figures on many contemporary items. There are other types of almanacs, too. Some almanacs are more specialized and focus on subjects such as politics, business, agriculture, or an entire state.

Atlases and gazetteers are useful because they include a great deal more information than just maps and geographic data. For starters, you can learn a great deal by simply studying a map of an area. These books often contain statistics and other listings of value to writers. When geography is the subject you need to study, atlases and gazetteers will likely contain the answers. You can use them to verify locations, distances, spellings, population, trade, industry, available natural resources, economic development politics, and distribution systems.

Encyclopedias and yearbooks should not be overlooked either because these books can often give you an authoritative introduction to a subject. Encyclopedias are often thought of as general sets of books that are updated every 1 to 3 years and have a universal application. However, these books are often much more useful as specialized volumes devoted to limited information on subjects such as world history, physical science, and music. Yearbooks are usually supplements that update existing editions of books or series of books such as encyclopedias. One example of a very useful specialized encyclopedia for finding expert sources at the national level for an article is the *Encyclopedia of Associations*. Simply look up the specialty and find the organization or organizations representing that interest. Call the organization's media relations office and you will probably be given names and telephone numbers of individuals who are willing to be interviewed.

Abstracts are valuable because these books take sets of statistics and other data and condense the data into useful form for the user. Abstracts such as *Dissertation Abstracts* or *Psychological Abstracts* also list bibliographic information and offer annotations or summaries of books, articles, theses, or dissertations.

Chronologies are reference books that list events in chronological order over a period of time. Many of these are limited to certain periods of time, such as a decade or century, or are limited to the duration of an historic event, such as the controversial 2000 presidential election, the terrorist attacks on the United States in 2001 and subsequent worldwide war on terrorism, or an event that occurred more than a century ago, such as the Civil War.

Dictionaries are critical to research and writing. Many general dictionaries are available, of course; some within very low price ranges. Yet there are many more expensive dictionaries within particular disciplines, such as law, medicine, or the physical sciences, that can help you when working with technical subjects that require explanation for your readers. If you want to specialize in a subject as a feature writer, consider obtaining a dictionary for that specialty if one exists, even if it is a considerable investment. It may help you through interviews and, even more importantly, prevent errors. For legal sources, a good source is *Black's Law Dictionary*.

Biographical dictionaries are extremely helpful in researching well-known persons. There are different types of biographical dictionaries and many are focused on specific disciplines, so you need to know where to go to find information that concerns the person you are researching. Good examples are *Current Biography, Contemporary Authors,* or *Who's Who*. There are biographical master indexes to these reference books that are kept in most major libraries. Many of these books are updated regularly.

Books of quotations are another category of reference books that are a valued source to writers. When you need an authoritative quote or a familiar quote to make your point, these books are the source to use. The leading example is *Bartlett's Familiar Quotations*.

## USEFUL GOVERNMENT PUBLICATIONS

Tens of thousands of federal, state, and local government publications are created each year and these can help you during research for an article. As has been often said about Washington, DC, most of the time the information you need is there, but you just have to know how and where to find it. This applies to government publications. All branches of government produce publications. These are mostly public documents, although some are classified and unavailable to the public. To help find the information you want, there are indexes, especially at the federal level. General indexes, such as the monthly *Catalog of U.S. Government Publications*, can help. This contains a subject index of new materials that are issued.

Congressional sources provide us with hearings documents on specialized topics such as pending legislation or ongoing concern about medical care, agriculture, and even the routine daily activities of Congress. These documents are available at local libraries that are designated U.S. Government document depository libraries or from the bookstores of the U.S. Government Printing Office (USGPO). USGPO materials are sold, of course, but often at prices lower than what a commercial publisher might charge.

Executive branch sources cover subjects as broad as the various departments that help the White House carry out the laws of the land. The *Federal Register* and *Code of Federal Regulations* are both good sources for orders, proclamations, and regulations that are announced by the White House. A writer interested in the words of the president may check the *Weekly Compilation of Presidential Documents*.

Want to know how U. S. population trends are changing or how many appliances are in a state or county? Use current census data provided by the federal government's Bureau of the Census in the Department of Commerce. There are both lengthy census reports and shorter, more accessible abstracts of census data. The most popular one is the *Statistical Abstract of the United States*, which is published annually. However, there are several other statistical abstract publications produced either annually or at other regular intervals, such as the *City and County Data Book,* produced every 5 years.

For the judicial branch, H. W. Wilson Co.'s *Index to Legal Periodicals* is a good starting point. For court decisions, the West Publishing Company of St. Paul, MN, publishes reports from many federal courts, all state appellate courts, and some state courts in its National Reporter System. This material is also available online at most law school libraries. The published version is often found in county and city libraries, law school libraries, and in some law offices.

In law enforcement, you can find reports by the Federal Bureau of Investigation (such as the *Uniform Crime Report,* issued annually). For other regulations, reports and books are frequently issued by agencies such as the Food and Drug Administration and by the Federal Communications Commission.

At the state level, there are many useful publications and documents. Look for handbooks, directories, guidebooks, and other volumes produced by official and private sources. One good example of an official reference book is the *Blue Book* produced by the state of Wisconsin each year.

Other general reference books include works produced state by state. These books can be excellent regional sources and are published by both public and private sources. These books, such as the *Texas Almanac* and *Florida Almanac,* are published annually or biannually. There are also general indexes of state publications. One such book is the *Monthly Checklist of State Publications,* which is produced by the Library of Congress. Some states, such as Virginia and Kentucky, produce their own similar lists. For most state documents, start with the secretary of state's office. This person is the state's official record keeper.

Local government publications vary in quantity and quality. Most metropolitan areas produce a substantial number of publications and local reference materials. Small cities and towns do not always have the resources to do so. Generally, they cannot afford, and do not have, the space to archive much information except that which is required by law. If you cannot find what you want at a city hall, go to the county or parish as your main regional source. Some private sources can be helpful. For example, the International City Management Association produces the *Municipal Year Book,* which offers statistical data and a summary of activities of American cities.

## USING THE WORLD WIDE WEB

For those who have toiled long hours in libraries searching periodicals and books about a subject, the computer is the best thing that has come along since moveable type. Computer-based research using databases has been available for public use for more than a decade and promises to be the way to do some of your research. The hottest online resource for researchers is the Internet, a worldwide network of computers. It is a series of links of privately owned networks and computer systems. The World Wide Web is a part of that global computer network and uses the Internet to link users to server sites and documents. On the Web, a document is a collection of text information, hypertext, links, and more. Hypertext is a method of linking files or documents to other documents. Links are elements of the document that enhance the document. Links embellish documents through highlighted works, external and internal connections to other documents, tables of data, graphics, sound, and even video. Writers have embraced the World Wide Web as a valuable resource and use it often (Press, 1996a, 1996b).

What makes the World Wide Web appealing to many users is its mix of tools and common base for transfer of information or data. The World Wide Web uses hypertext markup language to transfer information to software known as

Web browsers—the most common ones are Microsoft Internet Explorer and the Netscape Communicator suite with its Navigator browser. Web technology has advanced rapidly. Today's Web browsing includes transfer of text and graphics, audio, and video. And, perhaps most valuable for many journalists, more public and private databases are available.

One of the reasons the World Wide Web has become so popular is its ease of use. For most users, the Web is as simple as using a mouse and clicking on the options on the screen. The downside of all this is simple: users must follow the links and connections made by the developers of pages and sites on the World Wide Web. Although there are a lot of options, there is no complete freedom of movement on the Web unless you know specific addresses of sites and page paths.

Web sites have newspaper-like front pages or magazine-type covers known as home pages; some are known as portals. These are the first pages users see when they arrive at a site on the World Wide Web. Some browsers have default home pages, or locations that users automatically see when first using the browser, but these can be switched very easily. Many home pages use index, homepage, or similar terms in the uniform resource locator (URL) to identify themselves to users. A Web site, in contrast, is the entire set of pages for a particular Web address. A Web page is a single document within a site.

There are billions of pages on the World Wide Web today, so finding useful information on deadline is one of the biggest challenges to feature writers using the Internet. Unless users know a particular location, fast information retrieval is often difficult. However, a number of search and indexing tools have recently evolved on the Web that list resources by topic, search through registered Web sites with key words, or do both.

Five of the leading engines include Google (http://www.google.com), Yahoo! (http://www.yahoo.com), Search.MSN (http://www.search.msn.com), Lycos (http://www.lycos.com), and Alta Vista (http://www.altavista.com) (Nielsen, 2002). Each search engine seeks to be a package of searching services for users, covering general searches, specialty searches, and advanced searches. Another popular search engine is HotBot (http://www.hotbot.com). HotBot has a database of pages large enough to compete with the leading search sites and offers speed, usability, and a wide range of customizable advanced search options that can be saved for later use. AltaVista (http://altavista.com), one of the leading engines, breaks down search results and uses advanced searches based on Boolean operators. Go.com (http://www.go.com), which was once known as Infoseek, is also widely used and growing in popularity.

As with nonelectronic sources, there are many ways to assess the quality of an online information source. Writers look for clues to confirm identities or the reliability of information. They usually confirm information they plan to use with several independent sources. This is especially true when important information is involved. There are safe ways to evaluate and critically analyze the usefulness of information from the World Wide Web (and other online sources). The safest method, like other types of information, is to determine the origins of the information. Who provided it? Who is responsible for it?

One of the most valuable uses of online resources is to locate people or sources. Journalists are rapidly learning that there are many tools available for this reporting task. Although the usefulness, accuracy, and currency of the data provided is uneven, these tools can provide leads for reporters seeking to locate information about individuals—such as full names, addresses, telephone numbers, and e-mail addresses.

These Web-based telephone books permit searching with only a name, for instance. There is a mixture of other features, such as e-mail address searching, business listings searches, reverse number searching, and toll-free number listings that can be searched. Yahoo!, for example, can search for e-mail addresses through Web site archives (such as distribution lists and Usenet Newsgroups). Other e-mail finders include WhoWhere (http://www.whowhere.com) and the Internet Address Finder (http://www.iaf.net). Some Web people-finding services also offer mapping assistance online. One example is infoUSA (http://www.infousa.com). If the individual is found in the database, the site offers an option to create a map to that address.

## OTHER INTERNET RESEARCH RESOURCES

In addition to sending and receiving individual messages on the Internet, e-mail can be used for other purposes helpful to journalists. Perhaps the leading use is distribution lists. One of the two major forms of electronic discussion groups is the distribution list. The other is the newsgroup. Distribution lists are also known as *listservs*—named after one of the software programs used to manage the lists. Distribution lists require a subscription to access the list's information as it is posted. Although it can also be accessed in archive form, the immediate access is through subscription.

Distribution lists are as much a part of the Internet as any of the other utilities. Lists are accessed and read with e-mail. A list manager program distributes information to individual e-mail addresses. A distribution list is a software program that runs on a computer system, typically a mainframe or midrange server. For a searchable index of many lists on the Internet, see http://www.liszt.com.

Another e-mail related resource on the Internet is Usenet *Newsgroups*. Usenet—short for user network—can be accessed by anyone with Internet access. Newsgroups are an electronic space where participants can leave messages, such as comments, questions, and announcements. These groups are similar to the discussion groups found on some commercial online services, although some of those are being moved to Web formats. For a searchable index of newsgroups, see http://www.izwa.co.za/demo/lisztnews.html.

The main difference between a distribution list and a newsgroup is not in the content. Instead, it is the way the information is accessed. Distribution lists are sent to subscribers through e-mail based software on a server. Newsgroups require the user to access them intentionally. The access is achieved through e-mail also, but users must have a service that provides access to the Usenet network. Newsgroups also require a newsreader program. Most e-mail programs offer the feature as a utility built into the program.

There are thousands of newsgroups today. Newsgroups can be used to monitor the "buzz" on a subject. Newsgroups can be used to generate story ideas. They offer access to what people are discussing and talking about, particularly on a breaking story. These electronic places also provide increased diversity in sources and information. They may provide leads for stories. Perhaps most important, newsgroups are places to find possible contacts that may become sources for a story as well.

Chat rooms can also be useful sources of information. These are virtual gathering places on the World Wide Web for persons interested in specific subjects or activities. They are similar to newsgroups in their nature and user culture.

Weblogs or Blogs, a somewhat recent writing phenomenon on the World Wide Web, also provide interesting prospects for research. These are often diary-like and specialized and often highly personalized treatments of subjects and activities.

## USING ONLINE COMMERCIAL SERVICES

One of the fastest growing ways to use databases is through a personal computer from the office or home. In the early days of computer database searching, the effort had to be made from a library or other special facility. With the use of a modem, just about any computer and, therefore, any location, can use a computer database. With news breaking at any time, the instant long-distance reach provided by online computer-based research is increasingly important for feature writers. Online means your computer is linked to a second computer by a telephone line. The link is completed by use of modems in each computer.

Is this confusing? Well, take consolation in the fact that most computer programs that operate modems are very simple and require little programming effort (the most difficult things might be setting up and acquiring accounts and passwords). Almost all computer databases are read-only files that allow you to look at information a record at a time, but not modify the record in any way. You are allowed to copy the information to your own computer and use it later, of course, subject to any copyright restrictions that apply. Almost all services also require a search fee based on time or some other unit charge. These are national commercial services and you pay for the time you are "logged on." These fees are not inexpensive. Some are free, but others run as little as $15 per month with unlimited use to as high as $200 or more per hour for more exclusive systems at corporate, prime usage time rates. Most searches cost just a few dollars, however, and may be well worth the investment in terms of time and other expenses saved. Popular news media database providers are Nexis–Lexis, Dialog, the Wall Street Journal Online and related Dow Jones databases, and Data-Times. However, don't despair over the costs. Most colleges and universities have libraries with access to these and other databases at a completely subsidized, or at least a reduced rate, for students. You should ask about this by checking with your professors or reference librarians.

Another growing tool to access databases is the compact disc or CD. Some are also available on DVD, since DVD discs can store even more information and many databases exceed the capacity of a standard CD. These CD and DVD databases are not online services, but often contain the same information. These permit use for unlimited periods at no additional cost. Libraries often make a one-time purchase of a database, such as a newspaper or magazine over a period of time such as a year, and make the data available to users at no cost. Some of these full-text databases are available for public purchase as well as accessible online. *National Geographic* magazine, for example, markets a collection of CDs that contain back issues of the highly regarded travel and geography magazine. Resources such as this are a popular tool at many university and college libraries. Usually, these are best for high-volume users.

Another good example of an inexpensive CD that is quite useful to writers on a budget is Microsoft's "Bookshelf." This multimedia CD includes a set of reference books that may be used with a word processor. Typical reference books on a Bookshelf CD include a dictionary, world almanac, a concise encyclopedia, world atlas, thesaurus, dictionary of quotations, zip code directory, and a chronology. There are also several more complete encyclopedias available on CD or DVD. Microsoft's "Encarta" is a leading example. Most reference books sets on CD and DVD are updated annually and are available at many libraries.

Most current databases used for literature searches are electronic versions of indexes, which have traditionally been published in hardbound form. The convenience is obvious, if you are willing to pay for the time to do a broad search. Most of the searches your library can do for you are conducted through a central computer located somewhere else. Your library simply links its computer to the computer and requests a particular database for you. The database you request will, of course, depend on the subject of your article. As noted earlier, you can conduct many searches yourself, if you want to learn and want to acquire the additions to your home computer.

The most challenging aspect of computer database use is search strategy. The secret to inexpensive searching is to narrow down the key words that the computer uses to make its search. A key word or series of key words define what the computer searches for in the database. Because most databases are bibliographic—that is, they contain authors, titles, and subjects—you have to have an idea about who the authors are or what correct words might appear in titles. A search of "animals," for example, would work if you wanted to find articles on domestic cats or house cats, but it would generate a lot of information not central to your interests. The search would be even better to request "pets" or "cats" or a specific breed such as "Maine coon cats" if you need to be that narrowly focused.

Some databases, such as the contents of many daily newspapers and major national or specialized magazines, are full text. These databases, when accessed, permit users to look at entire articles as they were published. Naturally, these can be extremely valuable for feature writers searching for previously published, but recent, information.

Many larger libraries are beginning to computerize their card catalogs for easy searching, also. Although some are limited to in-house searching, many libraries are now searchable online. This enables a writer to find material before he or she treks to the library. The scope of these databases may be limited to the last 10 to 15 years, primarily because of the high cost of entering older acquisitions. Yet these databases are helpful in finding the most recent editions of books, or, at least, the most recent acquisitions by libraries. These searches work on the same principle as the database searches: you search for the author, the title, or a subject as key words. Terminals set up in the card catalog room or elsewhere make the work convenient. This would permit searching the catalog of your local or university library through your personal computer from your office or home. Think of the time savings from this convenience alone. You can often obtain the access codes and telephone number from the library. To encourage use of their resources, some libraries provide access to online systems to qualified individuals such as legal local residents, registered students, or alumni. In addition to school users, some public colleges and universities that have placed their catalogs online give connection numbers to the public if their computer systems have the capacity for public inquiries. In recent years, many of the online catalogs have been converted to Web sites or, at least, may be accessed using an Internet tool known as Telnet that is linked with the library's Web site.

Many newspapers, magazines, and newsletters are also getting into the act. Through computers, you can access the articles of most major daily newspapers published since the early 1980s. There are literally thousands of other databases available to check—some larger magazines and magazine groups as well as subscription newsletters are following suit. For example, Time Inc. magazines, such as *Time, Money, Sports Illustrated*, and *Fortune*, have been archived online for several years.

A computer database of periodicals called InfoTrac is now available in many libraries. Like some other databases discussed earlier, it is available on CD-ROM and is regularly updated. It includes newspapers and magazines and is comprehensive in scope. The service includes recent reviews and uses the U.S. Library of Congress subject headings. The service is provided by Information Access Company and encompasses its *Magazine Index*.

## A WRITER'S REFERENCE BOOKSHELF

There are numerous reference books found in newspaper and magazine offices. These are the traditional favorites of reporters, freelance writers, copy editors, and editors. The following is not a comprehensive list, but it can be used in building a personal research library.

### Encyclopedias

Chernow, B. A., & Vallasi, G. A. (Eds.). (1993). *The Columbia encyclopedia* (5th ed.). New York: Columbia University Press.

Gale Research, Inc. (2002, annual). *Encyclopedia of associations* (multiple volumes plus supplements). Detroit, MI: Gale Research Co.

Grolier Educational Corporation. (2001). *Encyclopedia Americana* (international ed., multiple volumes). Danbury, CT: Grolier Incorporated.

Stearns, P. N. (Ed.). (2001). *An encyclopedia of world history: Ancient, medieval, and modern: Chronologically arranged* (6th ed.). Cambridge, England: James Clarke.

World Book, Inc. (2002). *World Book encyclopedia* (multiple volumes). Chicago: World Book, Field Enterprises Educational Corp.

### Atlases

National Geographic Society. (1995). *National Geographic atlas of the world* (2nd rev. ed.). Washington, DC: National Geographic Society.

Rand McNally & Co. (1876 to date, annual). *Commercial atlas and marketing guide*. Chicago: Rand McNally.

Shepherd, W. R. (Ed.). (1980). *Shepherd's historical atlas* (9th ed., revised and updated). Totowa, NJ: Barnes and Noble, Inc.

### Dictionaries

Gove, P. B. (Ed.). (1993). *Webster's third new international dictionary* (unabridged) Springfield, MA: Merriam-Webster.

Guralnik, D. B. (Ed.). (1984). *Webster's new world dictionary of the American language* (2nd college ed.). New York: Simon & Schuster.

Editors of The American Heritage Dictionaries. (2000). *The American heritage dictionary of the English language* (4th ed.). Boston: Houghton Mifflin.

### Directories

*Congressional directory* (new edition each Congress). (n.d.). Washington, DC: U.S. Government Printing Office (Hint: Some congressmen and senators will send you a copy free upon written request).

*Congressional staff directory* (annual). (n.d.). Mount Vernon, VA: Congressional Staff Directory, Ltd.

*Washington information directory* (annual). (n.d.). Washington, DC: Congressional Quarterly Publications, Quadrangle Books.

(City and county directories, R. L. Polk, Bresser, and Cole are among companies that annually produce these directories.)

## Abstracts

*Statistical abstract of the United States* (annual). (n.d.). Washington, DC: U.S. Government Printing Office.
(Various state statistical abstracts are published by public and private publishers.)

## Handbooks

*The official Associated Press almanac* (annual). (n.d.). Washington, DC: Associated Press, Almanac Publishing Co.
*Guinness book of world records* (annual). (n.d.). Stamford, CT: Guinness Media.
*World almanac and book of facts* (annual). (n.d.). New York: Press Publishing Co.
(Various state almanacs are published by public and private publishers.)

## INTERVIEWING: A KEY FORM OF ARTICLE RESEARCH

Certainly an important step in preparing an article is interviewing. After you have done your homework on the subject and learned what you can about it, you still have to consider the special demands of interviews. Each interview, if done well, should have its own preparation effort, customized for the source.

Preparation is the key to interview success, most experienced writers will tell you. Although there are no guarantees, preparation makes it more likely that you will get what you need from the exchange. Professional writer John M. Wilson (1996) pointed to several elements of preparation. First, Wilson said you have to know what you need from the interview. He recommended planning and prioritizing questions that you might ask during the interview. Writers should seek anecdotes during interviews because they are such a vital part of feature writing.

There might be a need for numerous interviews for most feature articles. Some writers interview dozens of individuals for an article. There is a mix of types of sources, too, of course. Some are experts or authorities, and some are eyewitnesses. Some are consumers or users, and some are simply typical "people on the street." You use and choose sources on the basis of need for your article.

Writer Pat H. Broeske is a California-based columnist who strongly believes in doing research and simply digging for information she needs for her assignments that often focus on Hollywood celebrities and the entertainment business. Broeske (1996) offered 15 observations and tactics for "inquiring writers":

- A single interview can make a big difference.
- Don't overlook the obvious source.
- Don't make assumptions.
- Corroborate information gleaned in an interview.
- Streamline your topic.

- Look beyond the obvious.
- Ask your interview subjects whom else they think you should talk to.
- Let others know what you are working on.
- Don't overlook anything you might have in common with your subject.
- If your story involves conflict, put yourself in the midst of it.
- Take advantage of technology.
- Show what you know.
- Look for cues and clues.
- Be patient.
- Before ending an interview, ask this question: "Is there anything I haven't asked you about that you'd like to tell me?"

Geoff Williams (1996), a veteran freelance magazine writer who specializes in interviewing actors and actresses, recommended a moderate amount of preparation, but not too much. He also recommended finding a quiet place to conduct the interview—if this is possible. Even if the interview is done by telephone, he said control is important. Distractions can contribute to bad interviews. Williams said not to be afraid of practicing before a big interview to build confidence and polish approaches.

You should write down or type out your questions in advance, each one based on the research you have done. These question lists can serve as a crutch during the interview. They show the sources that you took the time to prepare for the time you have with them. You must remain flexible during the interview to get into other subjects and concerns beyond what your research told you. There are times when your well-researched questions will wind up only as a jumping off point for an interview.

In most cases, the article you are writing will require that you do some detective work to get the information you need to do the article right. A few subjects will give you the luxury to get by without significant research. Your best bet, regardless, is to know where to go to get the answers when you need to get them before you go into an interview.

## Conducting Interviews

Too many good books are written solely about journalistic interviewing to attempt to tell you everything in part of a single chapter. This discussion focuses on interviewing as part of the overall research and reporting process and offers the advice on how you can use interviews to gather information needed for a feature article. After you have done your preinterview homework, the time arrives to go to the telephone or go to your source in person. Assuming you have found the right sources for your story, the next step is to set up the meeting to talk.

Your interpersonal communication skills are put to the test during an interview. You should try to relax the person you are talking to and make the experience seem less like an interview and more like a conversation between two people who just met. How is this done? If you can, start by chatting about something neutral. Take a moment to get to know the person. Tell the person about yourself. Let them get to know you and become more comfortable with you. You have to judge how much casual conversation is enough. It is obvious that a busy banker is less interested in casual conversation than a relaxed grandfatherly craftsman might be. Remember that you will have different experiences, depending on whether the interview is conducted in person or on the telephone. Although the telephone saves time, you lose the familiarity and depth of detail of being there with the source.

Treat your source as you would like to be treated if you were the source. Dress professionally. Be polite and considerate. Identify yourself. This is especially important if you are conducting an interview by telephone. Explain your purpose and estimate how much time you need. If you plan to use a tape recorder for accuracy and completeness, ask if it matters to the source before you use it. Some state laws require it, especially if it involves a telephone conversation. Remind the source that you are also going to be taking notes during the interview.

Because getting information is your goal, always be certain of the information you are getting during your interview, regardless of whether it is in person or on the telephone. Verify spellings and the meaning of technical terms. Ask a second time if necessary. Follow up the responses with questions designed to clarify, such as "why?" Don't be afraid to show you don't know something.

## GETTING A TOUGH INTERVIEW

It might not seem like a difficult task for the casual observer, but for any reporter from the United States to interview Cuban President Fidel Castro is a nearly impossible assignment to complete. He is generally inaccessible to the news media. Security is extraordinarily tight, especially when Castro is on the road. But persistence, imagination, and luck led to a timely, and exclusive, feature article by two *Miami Herald* reporters who got 10 minutes with Castro for a story that revealed how the long-time world leader had aged and become out-of-touch with the changing Communist world. Reporter Chris Marquis described how he and colleague Mirta Ojito were able to talk with Castro, who was at a meeting with the leaders of the Spanish-speaking nations in Mexico City:

I had placed several formal requests for an interview with Fidel, but as soon as he arrived in Mexico, I feared all bets were off. He moved amid tight security and was plainly taking no chances. A hotel waiter told us Fidel brought his own food, vegetables, and ice with him. The trick, Mirta and I decided, would be getting into the luxury hotel where all the presidents were staying. But the El Camino Hotel was awash in guards and even had sharpshooters on rooftops, and there was no U.S. delegation to help. So we tried the next-best thing: We called the Panamanians to ask for an interview.

OK, they told us, come in. Once there, we chatted up a Chilean security guard. Gee, we said, it would be nice to talk to the president of Chile. Come on, he said, whisking us through metal detectors and past the German shepherds, to the inner garden, where presidents and their aides were meeting in pool-front suites. The Chilean walked off to look for the Chilean press aide, leaving us standing by the pool. Mirta spotted a knot of Cubans standing near a cabana. We started taking baby steps that way, and soon, we were within 20 feet of Room 1114. A maid emerged, carrying an olive drab uniform: Fidel's.

Mirta and I tried to look nonchalant, which was hard as it became increasingly obvious that we represented a major breach of security. Before we knew it, the King of Spain strode by, close enough to touch. Mirta and I were struck dumb. We didn't want to call attention to ourselves, and weren't sure about the protocol: "Hey King?"

Gabriel Garcia Marquez, the famous [Nobel Prize-winning] novelist, zipped past. Alberto Fujimori [president] of Peru was next. We were gambling, risking good interviews for a chance with Fidel. Then he appeared, on the other side of a hedge—tall, green-garbed, looking famous. He was headed straight toward us. "Commandante," I exclaimed. "Where are you from?" he asked. *"The Miami Herald,"* we told him.

Fidel wanted to talk, so we caught our breath and fired away. His gray and white beard made him look old. He had sleep in his eyes. Still, he seemed thoughtful, taking time to ponder the questions we frantically poured forth. As he talked, he seemed smaller, became personable, grabbed our arms to emphasize his words. The anti-Yankee rhetoric and bombast was gone. Like everyone else, he said, he was worried about Cuba. Was this Fidel?

After about 10 minutes, the bodyguard shoved us aside and Fidel ducked into his room. Mirta and I triumphantly walked out the hotel's front door. (Seibel, 1991, p. 1)

(Reprinted with permission of *The Miami Herald*.)

---

These context and verification elements of the interview are quite important, said magazine editorial consultant and former *BusinessWeek* Senior Editor John Campbell. Campbell (1993) believed context should be made clear when questioning a source. This can be done as part of the questioning, such as prefacing a question with a brief factual statement. Verification is equally significant, Campbell said, because "you must understand not just what the interviewee said, but what he really meant to say" (p. 31).

Interviewing in-person on the "street" for an article has its own problems. Many people resist strangers, especially ones with notebooks. Kevin McManus (1992), a reporter for *The Washington Post*, recommended avoiding the outdoors (people prefer indoor situations). He also believed that writers should take time to warm up people and use a tape recorder. He said investing the time and avoiding quick-hit efforts. McManus also recommended that writers find an escort—someone from the neighborhood, the business, or school—and that they use a sign or, in large group situations, use poster board to make a sign to tell people they want to talk. Finally, he said writers should develop a thick skin and not let refusals from strangers to do spot interviews bother them.

Because many interviews in the course of the research process are vital to the article you do, it is often wise to take a tape recorder with you. In fact, some professional writers use two recorders to guard against failure of one of the machines. However, as already noted, be sure your source knows you are taping the interview. At the same time you record, you should continue to take notes as you would normally because your notes will help you in finding quotes on the tape later during the writing process. Hutcheson (personal communication, April 27, 1993), a freelance magazine writer from Wichita, KS, said she depends on her tape recorder for accuracy. "My interviews are taped, as is my practice because it keeps me from misquoting a subject and could help me if I ever had to go to court" (personal communication, April 27, 1993).

John Campbell (1993), who has also served as editorial director for Hearst Business Publishing Group, said interviews are best if you give a little to get a little information. He believed the interview should be kept conversational and not overly rigid and organized. Let the interview flow naturally, he advocated. Talk to your source; don't just question him or her. This helps to establish rapport, allows a chance to test your ideas more effectively, and it gives some feedback to the source to ensure his or her involvement in future requests. This is what he called an informal "payback" for their involvement this time around by letting the source know how he or she has helped you.

Shirley Biagi (1986) agreed with the conversational approach. She recommended that during the interview you should relax and let your source do the talking—simply bite your tongue if you are inclined to talk too much or interrupt before someone finishes answering your question. Biagi also said you should display empathy and concentrate on what your source is saying. She also said it makes a difference if you note gestures and expressions by your source, as well as his or her physical characteristics. It is helpful, of course, during in-person interviews to look around the room when you get the chance—to learn more about the person. Biagi cautioned beginning writers to watch for sudden shifts in direction of the interview. And, she said, be prepared to get away from the questions you developed if something more interesting arises.

Experienced professionals also recommend that you remain firm and in control while using the conversational approach. Be honest and do not pretend to

## BEST SOURCES FOR RESEARCHING FEATURE ARTICLES

1. Recognized authorities and experts such as professors and researchers.
2. Reference books and periodicals, such as the following:
    dictionaries
    encyclopedias
    biographical dictionaries
    atlases, wall maps, and gazetteers
    yearbooks
    almanacs
    books of quotations
    abstracts
    chronologies
    indexes.
3. Databases, such as the following:
    World Wide Web government sites
    online database and publication archive services
    CD and DVD publication archive databases
    other digital and electronic information retrieval systems.
4. Libraries, such as the following:
    your own news organization's library
    public and private libraries
    library telephone reference services.
5. Others with access to experts, such as the following:
    corporate and commercial public relations practitioners.
6. The trained observations of others.
7. Your participant observation experiences.

---

be something you are not. Being prepared through preinterview research is one way to accomplish that. Keep your composure. Relax. This is a natural outgrowth of knowing your material going into the interview. Mixing easy and tough questions will vary the pace and intensity of the interview, also, giving respites to both you and your source, but be sensitive. If you can prepare question lists in advance, keep this in mind as you order the questions (Bottomly, 1991; Ritz, 1993).

Clearly, the telephone is the most convenient method of interviewing. It is indispensable when working on a feature article. Although an in-person interview can yield much richer information and depth of detail, often time or ex-

pense will not permit it. A good feature writer needs to refine his or her telephone interviewing skills. Minneapolis, MN, freelance writer Steve Perlstein
(personal communication, May 3, 1993 and January 15, 1998) offered a tip from
his decade of experience as a journalist:

> I can't stress how important it is to sound *relaxed* on the phone. Remember, inter-
> view subjects either that like you or are intimidated by you because you are writ-
> ing about them—you are in control. Even when someone is hostile, that's be-
> cause they feel they don't have the upper hand and they need to get it. Always
> have your questions written down, so in case someone is short with you, you al-
> ways have something else to move on to without foundering. That contributes
> to your air of knowledge, your control of the interview. Without that, you'll al-
> most never get the information you need.

Pauline Bartel (1992), who has written freelance articles for numerous national magazines, such as the *Saturday Evening Post* and *Mademoiselle,* said organization is the key to efficient use of time for interviews. There is a risk that a
disorganized interviewer can spend too much time on interviews and post-
interview review of notes and tapes. To save time, she recommended setting up
advance appointments, using the telephone as much as possible, tape recording
often, and clustering interviews around the same topic.

Some of the most readable and interesting feature articles are often based on
very difficult interviews to set up and carry out. Freelance writer Toni Wood
(1993), who has written as a staff writer for the *Kansas City Star* and for national
magazines, strongly recommended putting in the effort to get tough interviews.
"Compelling nonfiction is often based on intimate losses, victories or mistakes.
But learning to draw those stories from people is an art. It requires that you ask
tough, personal questions with compassion, patience, persuasion and tenacity"
(Wood, 1993, p. 28). Here is Wood's useful list of 10 recommendations for successfully completing a tough interview:

1. Watch your body language and tone of voice.
2. Start the conversation in neutral territory.
3. Tape recording can be frightening.
4. React to what you hear.
5. Slow down as you move to the sensitive territory.
6. Don't rush to fill gaps in conversation.
7. Pose the most challenging questions with simplicity and be direct.
8. Take time in developing the relationship with the source.
9. There may be source resistance, so be ready and make space for it.
10. Try to keep professional distance and don't meltdown emotionally.

Remember the value of follow-up questions as well. Often a source will give a partial answer to your question or may offer a response that is not completely understandable. Be prepared to ask follow-up questions such as "can you explain that better?" or "give me an example of what you mean" or "I'm not sure I understand. Can you expand a little on what you just said?"

Here's a final tip: When you are winding up the interview, make certain you know how to find your source later if you need to conduct a second, or follow-up, interview. Get a telephone number. It may not always be in the same place as the first interview. Remember to double check critical information before you leave or hang up the telephone.

## OBSERVATION AS RESEARCH

There are times when a portion of an article can be researched simply by going to a location and looking around. You might be writing a piece on flood damage, and a tour of a flooded area can tell you much more than reading books or talking to people who had previously experienced floods. Your own first-hand observation can add much depth of detail and description to your article. Most of the time, you will combine observation with interviewing and other research skills. You do not need to be a detective, but you cannot be oblivious to what is going on, either. If you find yourself dependent on others for detail and description, you must contend with possible distortions of fact. Thus, the more you see for yourself, the richer will be your article. Most people are simply not accustomed to noting detail as detectives do, and you have to train yourself through practice to do it well.

Given that there are certain risks in using observation, Rivers and Harrington (1988, pp. 163–167) recommended these guidelines to avoid the potential pitfalls:

1. Remember the process of distortion—People tend to change what they see to become consistent with their own previous experiences. And there is also distortion of perspective. Point of view can give you a different look at matters from someone else's point of view.
2. Recall emotional states—Your emotional response to a situation can affect what you see and later recall.
3. Concentrate on important details—It is possible to observe too much.
4. Seek other evidence—Consider the perspectives of others.
5. Observe unobtrusively—If people know you are intentionally watching, it may affect their normal behavior. This does not preclude observation that is known to the source, but do not interfere with what you are observing.
6. Become a participant if you can, but only if you want this special point of view—You are certain to distort behavior of those around you if your purpose is known, but often the experience is still worth it for your article.

7. Watch for nonverbal communication such as body language—What a person says is not all that the person communicates.

Author Jacqueline Briskin (1979) recommended one rather unusual technique that may lend a guiding hand to your observational talents. She suggested that when you are out looking around—touring a museum, for example, to research a story—sometimes your camera can help you with your note taking. The pictures don't have to be publishable. Yet the approach makes good sense. The detail contained in a picture might just jog your memory or provide the image for a description needed in your article. In fact, Briskin called her 35 mm camera (or any inexpensive pocketsize instant camera or an inexpensive digital camera, for that matter) her most important research tool. Just consider how a small digital camera might help you capture the color and pageantry of a festival or block party. You might just decide this tool would help you also, especially if you do not plan to write your article right away. In this case a picture might really be worth several thousand descriptive words—in your notebook—and you don't even have to take the film to be processed. The pictures can be stored on your computer until you no longer need them.

## GETTING PERSONALLY INVOLVED

The participant form of journalistic observation is unique because you get involved in the story personally. As a participant, you may actually become part of the story. This can have certain advantages, such as in travel writing when you relate your personal travel experiences to readers. Other approaches are more third person-oriented and do not thrust you as a writer into the middle of the story.

You can accomplish some research for stories by experiencing an activity yourself. Usually this is research that you simply could not find from other sources. Some serious subjects require it, especially if the article subject involves illegal or, at least, questionable activities. Because sources, when confronted with tough questions about illegal or morally and ethically questionable activities, will almost always deny involvement, you get first-hand knowledge by becoming a participant and witness. However, in addition to being potentially dangerous, these stories present ethical problems because there can be no disclosure that you are a writer. Many professionals discourage this because they believe it is a form of deception. However, in some cases it may be necessary. Other professionals feel it is a necessary and legitimate form of information gathering. Ultimately, you and your editors must judge that.

On less serious feature stories, some excellent feature articles can result from do-it-yourself experiences. One student in Florida, when assigned to write a feature story based on participant observation, took a flying lesson and learned the basics of piloting a private plane. Another student took the assignment a step further and actually jumped out of a plane! She was taking parachuting lessons, of course, with a licensed instructor. Both experiences resulted in fine first person feature stories that dependence on another person's descriptions would not produce.

Other stories may be supplemented by participating in one or more activities. A feature article about hospital volunteers might be strengthened if the writer took the time to go through a training program and actually volunteered for a few hours. But the story would not necessarily stand on observation alone. To make the article more complete, you would also interview veteran volunteers, managers of the program, hospital officials, doctors and nurses, patients, and even a beginning volunteer or two. All this would be beyond the library research you started with when the article idea first was chosen.

## A PULITZER PRIZE WINNER EMPHASIZES RESEARCH

Jacqui Banaszynski, senior editor for enterprise for *The Oregonian* in Portland and former feature writer for the *St. Paul Pioneer Press,* is a veteran feature writer and features editor. She won the Pulitzer Prize for feature writing in 1988. She describes her approach to research for her own writing (Banaszynski, personal communication, April 6, 1993):

> Often history-in-the-making catches us by surprise. Only a few of us who covered the meltdown of Three Mile Island had ever studied the innards of a nuclear power plant. Fewer still had first-hand knowledge of volcanoes when we were sent to Washington for the eruption of Mount St. Helens. AIDS remains such a mystery that we struggle to find the questions—to say nothing of the answers. Yet we are expected to write about these subjects with accuracy and authority. Often, we are expected to do that on deadline. So we improvise. We learn to be quick with our pens, quicker with our questions, instant with our analysis. In a few days or a few hours, we cull the pertinent wisdom from experts who have spent lifetimes studying a topic. Unless we settle into a specialized beat and nurture our own expertise, we bounce from story to story armed with little but instinct and moxie. In-depth research is a luxury in the business. Doing your homework—most would call it backgrounding—is a necessity. However rushed the assignment, there are a few basics that will save you embarrassment and mistakes.
>
> Start in the newsroom library, or morgue, then expand your search to the public library. Read everything available in the popular press about your subject. Tap into your newspaper's electronic library and cull some national stories for context. But beware: You are seeking information, not attitude. Don't let background reading shape your point of view. Don't enter an interview looking for a few quotes to drop into an already-written story.
>
> Gather quick tips from other people. Corner an editor or veteran reporter for summaries about your subject. Ask colleagues, friends, and relatives what they

want to know about the subject. Supplement your curiosity with theirs. When I did a profile of North Pole explorer Ann Bancroft, my newsroom curiosity survey revealed a question I would have overlooked: How did she go to the bathroom when it was 70-below? That question led to a wonderful anecdote that gave the story some humor, humanity, and dimension.

If you have time, conduct a few preinterview interviews. Written research will give you background, but it won't give you quotes or character. Glean impressions of your subject first-hand—from boosters, from detractors, and from knowledgeable, but detached, observers. Check their comments against those of your subject.

Since being awarded a Pulitzer Prize, I have been on the receiving end of reporters' notebooks—a vantage point that has underscored some basic journalistic tenets that we too often take for granted. When reporters interview me, I expect them to already have our Pulitzer series "AIDS in the Heartland" and a few other accessible clippings from local newspapers that would include my basic biography. The diligent ones also will have talked to one or more people about me— perhaps an editor or a colleague or one of my story subjects. If they haven't done that legwork, I find myself feeling impatient and a bit insulted. I am not willing to give my time and candor to someone who hasn't shown me courtesy to do their homework. I imagine my interview subjects feel the same way. (Banaszynski, personal communication, April 6, 1993)

# CHAPTER FIVE

# The Writing and Editing Process

Good writing takes a lot of work. It takes strong communication skills and motivation to use them. It takes creative energy and effort.

*Rosebud* is a small literary magazine published out of Cambridge, WI, not far from Madison. It promotes itself as "the magazine for people who enjoy good writing." Available in bookstores around the United States, Canada, and Great Britain or by subscription, *Rosebud* publishes fiction such as short stories, essays, and poetry. Some readers have said it has the flavor of *The New Yorker* or the once-great former *Collier's* magazine. Its editor, Roderick Clark, strives to maintain quality creative writing in the publication:

> Looking out at the market I find that the courageous little magazines who struggle to keep the fresh and independent spirit of American literature alive find themselves constantly at the brink of exhaustion and bankruptcy, while university publications publish work that is arch, bloodless, contrived, and often—simply bad.
>
> Being bad of course, is part of the price of taking risks, and can even be invigorating and refreshing if it is done with imagination, but my feeling is that many "successful" literary magazines, having established a loyal following, take almost no risks at all, publishing work that has exactly the same tone and flavor over and over in order to maintain their established recipe for survival. As a matter of fact, "good work" has come to mean only work that takes no risks and strikes the "high tone" of the rest of the publication. The result is a plethora of literary publications that are more concerned with being taken seriously by their peers and other "literati" than with publishing serious work. (R. Clark, 2002)

Good feature writing has its roots in this type of writing, especially the art of storytelling. Good writing also has a certain foundation on which it is built and a certain polish or finish on which it is sold to the buyer. The late E. B. White (Strunk & White, 1979) made an observation in the writer's little bible, *The Elements of Style*, that is worth noting. His Cornell professor, William Strunk, once said

> The best writers sometimes disregard the rules of rhetoric. When they do so, however, the reader will usually find in the sentence some compensating merit,

attained at the cost of the violation. Unless he is certain of doing as well, he will probably do best to follow the rules. (p. xvi)

Increasingly, feature writers are using the strengths of literary nonfiction. In fact, some experts have noted that a majority of feature-writing Pulitzer Prizes in the past decade have been won by individuals writing stories cast as literary nonfiction (Hart, 1995). They do this by identifying classic story elements in daily life. You can do it also. The elements are relatively simple to list: characters, use of dialogue, use of conflict and tension, and strong organization using scene construction.

Good writing such as that found in articles winning Pulitzers for feature writing is truly difficult to achieve, but with the right desire and right tools, you may be able to do it. Good ideas put on paper (or a computer screen) still need good massaging—good polish, that is—to make them presentable to readers. This chapter presents the basics of effective article-writing style and organization. It offers time-tested suggestions for editing your own manuscript to get it ready for an editor. You investigate the art and craft of article writing. You learn how experts manage their writing and how varied the approaches might be to achieve the same goal of publication. You have to sell your idea and yourself.

Some news media critics feel that writing has deteriorated. Professor Neil Postman (1985) blamed it on television and a video-oriented society. He laments about "the most significant American cultural fact of the second half of the twentieth century: the decline of the Age of Typography and the ascendancy of the Age of Television. This change-over has dramatically and irreversibly shifted the content and meaning of public discourse, since two media so vastly different cannot accommodate the same ideas" (p. 8). Cultural historian Jacques Barzun (1992) agreed, especially about the decline of writing skills within the news media:

The unhappy truth is that the prose of the press, and of broadcast news as well, has fallen below the level of competence that once obtained [sic] and that can reasonably be expected. It is not uniformly bad, but the faults are frequent and of many kinds—blurred meanings; pretentiousness; and irrelevant fiction-style. (p. 3)

## THE ELEMENTS OF GOOD WRITING

Much work goes into good writing. William Zinsser (1980), who has written for newspapers and magazines and authored numerous books, considers good writing a disciplined, rigorous effort that comes from practice. It takes rewriting, what he called "the essence of writing" (p. 4). It takes the same regular, daily schedule that a craftsman might use in making furniture or artwork. Zinsser also explained that writing is a solitary effort of people who do not mind being alone. Yet he also believes writing can be easy and fun.

Lawyers, for example, often write with clutter and complexity in their search for precision necessary in legal documents. Good writers keep it simple while retaining meaning. Zinsser (1980) called clutter the "disease of American writing" (p. 7). He is right. This is especially true for writers for mass audience publications. Because there is no reason for feature articles to be complex or difficult, keep your writing simple. This means you have to translate complicated material, such as medical or other scientific terms, for your readers. "We are a society strangling in unnecessary words, circular constructions, pompous frills and meaningless jargon," Zinsser said (p. 7).

Barzun (1992) was deeply concerned about false meaning in news media writing. He pointed to vogue words and malapropism. Vogue words reduce precision in meaning by giving slangy new meanings to words, keeping better-fitting words out of use. Malapropism is the misuse of often similar but incorrect words. These sorts of writing mistakes, he argued, come from laziness and from ignorance of the language.

Great feature articles include seven basic elements, said Michael Bugeja (1996), magazine writing professor and *Writer's Digest* contributing editor. His seven essential elements are topic, theme, title, viewpoint, voice, moment, and endings. "If you heed these seven basic elements of non-fiction writing, you *will* make your articles better and you will *sell* more," Bugeja argued (p. 22).

There are ways to be successful and avoid such pitfalls in writing. Minneapolis, MN, freelance feature writer Steve Perlstein (personal communication, May 3, 1993; January 15, 1998) believes in simplicity for success:

> Writing style is surely important, but so is keeping your prose simple and straightforward. The great writers never waste words, and their stories are never one word longer than they need to be. Superfluous words—whether they are to pad the word count or to make the piece sound more important—are invariably cut in the editing process anyway. If you write too many words about the same thing over and over again, or just more words than you need, your work winds up looking overblown and tedious, or just plain too long. See what I mean?

A good newspaper, magazine, newsletter, or online publication writer keeps thoughts easy to understand. This is done several ways. First, it is done through word selection. Use the right words, but do not use too many of the right words. Be concise. Be precise in meaning. Use basic subject–verb–object sentence structure. Even if you can find a way to write a sentence with a verb and then the subject, it is likely to be hard to understand and you have wasted your reader's time. If you do that often enough, you lose the reader permanently. A third way to help the reader understand what you are writing is to use correct grammar. Usages do help the communication process. People are accustomed to seeing certain forms of grammar, such as subject–verb agreement and consistent use of tense. Still another way to write in simple English is to keep an eye on sentence length. The longer the sentence, the harder it is to follow. You do not want your reader going through your article and wondering, "What did that mean? Am I crazy? Why can't I figure out what this means?"

## WORD USAGE AND CHANGES IN MEANING

Professor Ernest Brennecke (Wardlow, 1985, p. 24) created the following eight sentences and eight different meanings by changing the location of one word. Read the sentences or say them out loud. Notice how the meaning of each sentence changes as the location of the word *only* changes. Here's a lesson—one you should not forget—about saying precisely what you mean in a sentence:

*Only* I hit him in the eye yesterday.
I *only* hit him in the eye yesterday.
I hit *only* him in the eye yesterday.
I hit him *only* in the eye yesterday.
I hit him in *only* the eye yesterday.
I hit him in the *only* eye yesterday.
I hit him in the eye *only* yesterday.
I hit him in the eye yesterday *only*.

Style is another consideration when you think about good writing. Every writer has a style. Every publication has a style manual. Writing style is much like one's personal appearance. Your appearance reflects your own way of dressing, your mannerisms, and your physical uniqueness. Writing does much of the same thing, but it reveals a bit about our minds, our thinking, our logic, and our expression of those processes. Most experienced writers and writing teachers will tell you that to teach writing, you have to start with basics, no matter whether it is sixth grade theme writing or freshman composition at a Big Ten university. As Zinsser (1980) said, "You have to strip down your writing before you can build it back up" (p. 19).

Oregon freelance nonfiction writer Gary King (personal communication, May 19, 1993) believes in sticking to the fundamentals when he writes his specialty, crime features. King, who has written three books and numerous articles about major crimes, emphasized that writing success is found in the basics:

In writing for the crime magazines, the writer must use correct standard English. Don't use shortcuts, but don't be stiff and too formal, either. Avoid long "travelogue" descriptions of the locale where the crime took place (a mistake that many first-timers make) in the introductory, and get right to the story, usually the discovery of a body. Try to tell the story in chronological order, and emphasize the detective work that leads to the solution of the case. In other words, milk the investigative process for everything you can. Don't pinpoint the guilty person too early in the story, and use active writing constructions wherever possible. There's no reason that nonfiction writing has to be dull. Novices should decide which publication(s) they want to write for, read several copies of the publication, and by all means send off for the magazine's writers' guidelines. (King, personal communication, May 19, 1993)

After mastering cumbersome language, complex sentence structure, and the like, you can begin to build your own style. The late novelist Paul Darcy Boles (1985) called style a "way of saying" and a "way of seeing." He said it is somewhat born into the owner, but it is also borrowed. Many writers become the products of other writers they admire. The process of stealing technique is a rather accepted one in the business of writing—we become a mixture of the styles of writers we read and enjoy the most while we are learning to write.

You do not have to work too hard to develop a style. It is not such a conscious matter of writing as it is an unconscious matter of writing. It evolves and comes through your writing whether you want it to or not. Everyone has a writing style. On the other hand, the business of a style manual is another issue altogether. You will find most, if not all, publications have their own style manuals or have adapted the manuals of other organizations. Magazines such as *U.S. News & World Report* have their own manuals. Newspapers such as *The New York Times* and *Chicago Tribune* have their own. News wire services, such as the Associated Press (AP), have widely-used manuals for writers and editors. The recently enlarged and regularly updated AP stylebook has been used in college journalism classes for several generations of writers. It should occupy a prominent place on any writer's reference bookshelf. In fact, you will find some of these stylebooks are for sale to the public and can be found in any retail bookstore. These books are reference books containing the rules of usage for local and not-so-local matters that are used commonly. The range covers basics such as numbers and names but also more complicated matters such as religious titles, foreign geographic names, and even medical terms. So, even if you are an independent writer, you need to know the style of the publication when you prepare a manuscript for its editor.

Another element of good writing focuses on the audience, or, in the language of communication theorists, the receiver of your message. In communication, there has to be an area of common, or shared, experience. In writing for a newspaper, magazine, newsletter, or online publication, the area of shared experience is reduced because a writer must have a shared experience with thousands of individuals. "The chances soar that a message will go awry when you start factoring more receivers into the equation," said Hart (1990b, p. 3), an editor and writing coach for *The Oregonian* in Portland. You need to consider the following: Who is going to read your article? Do you know? Have you thought about it? How can you find out? There is a high degree of seriousness in those questions. If you do not know the answers, can you honestly write well for that audience? No.

For some publications, it is easy to know who reads each edition. For others, it is difficult to tell without research. A specialized publication, such as an industry magazine or a legal newspaper, has a well-defined audience. However, the general circulation daily or weekly newspaper and some consumer magazines must be researched before you know anything certain about the audience. You want to be careful to write at the level of the audience. If you write too far below it, you will turn off readers. If you write too far above it, you will lose readers as well. In fact, if you miss estimating the audience too much, you will not even get past first base with your editor and you will never reach any readers. You have to have a sense of timing with readers and audiences, too. The right mood, writing style, and sensitivity make an article work. Make the wrong choices and the article works against you. Thus, you have to know when to use humor, when to be serious, when to be gentle, and when to be emotional. Knowing your audience helps you chart the course through these dangerous waters.

Some general points about writing mechanics have already been made. You have read about the value of grammar. In reality, not enough can be said to beginning feature writers about spelling, syntax, and punctuation. In fact, former *Hartford Courant* editor and publisher Bob Eddy (1979) called spelling the curse of the working journalist. For writers, each of these skills is important. If you cannot handle the basic skills such as spelling, you will eventually lose your job. Often writing students dismiss spelling or punctuation as unimportant at the moment because, they say, "It is the idea that matters. I'll learn the rules of spelling later." If a carpenter were to say that about building a house, it would come crashing down. The same goes for your writing. It will cause your plan to fail unless you use the right tools and materials: language, words, spelling, and punctuation. Correct use of words can be helped by regular use of a dictionary, a thesaurus, and other word reference books available at most bookstores. Your shelves should be stocked with at least one dictionary, a thesaurus, and a handful of stylebooks—at least one, but several if you work for a number of publications or use different writing styles. Several good reference books were suggested in the previous chapter. Each of the following points about good writing requires your attention and time. If you learn to manage them, you should find great improvement in your ability to communicate to the world.

Unity is like an anchor for good writing, Zinsser (1980) said. Some might call this concept a matter of consistency in your writing. Whatever you wind up calling it, remember it is a critical element of good writing.

Tense, pronoun point of view, and mood are all indicators of unity in your writing. It is best to maintain a level of consistency in each. Do not mix tenses. Past and present tenses in the same sentence only confuse your reader. Articles that jump around from first to second to third person are equally disconcerting for readers. Mixture of mood can cause perhaps the most serious confusion for a reader who does not know whether to laugh, cry, be sad or happy, or otherwise respond to your message.

Tone is also important in feature writing. Writers establish the mood or texture of their features with use of language. This is the tone of the article. Diction, or word choice, contributes to this characteristic of your writing. "When we select one word over another of equal denotative value, we likely make the selection based on the connotative meaning of the word. And by using that connotation, we effectively establish a mood or texture—the *tone*—of the story," wrote Professor David Brill (1992, p. 32). "In fact, tone is one of the most important elements of writing—and perhaps the most frequently overlooked" (Brill, 1992, p. 32).

---

## FINDING A SATISFACTORY STYLE

William Strunk, Jr., and E. B. White (1979), in their classic *The Elements of Style,* offered cautionary hints to help you find a style that works. Consider these items:

1.  Place yourself in the background.
2.  Write in a way that comes naturally.
3.  Work from a suitable design.
4.  Write with nouns and verbs.
5.  Revise and rewrite.
6.  Do not overwrite.
7.  Do not overstate.
8.  Avoid the use of qualifiers.
9.  Do not affect a breezy manner.
10. Use orthodox spelling.
11. Do not explain too much.
12. Do not construct awkward adverbs.
13. Make sure the reader knows who is speaking.
14. Avoid fancy words.
15. Do not use dialect unless your ear is good.
16. Be clear.
17. Do not inject opinion.
18. Use figures of speech sparingly.
19. Do not take shortcuts at the cost of clarity.
20. Avoid foreign languages.
21. Prefer the standard to the offbeat.

## GIVING AN IDEA FOCUS AND DEPTH

A large portion of chapter 3 was devoted to finding a successful article idea. Although some attention was given to developing the idea and giving it focus and depth, let us return to this in the context of writing. Focus comes throughout the article, but it begins with the lead. A well-chosen lead, or introduction, tells the reader what you mean to achieve in the article. It is up to you to guide the reader through the article, much like a road map, with the theme or idea you introduce in the beginning paragraphs. For a writer, focus is the key. If you can remember this, you will do better as a writer. Your articles will be stronger. The focus must carry through the rest of the article after you have constructed the lead. It carries through the body and dominates the ending also.

Think of the focus as the article's angle. To write a feature article only about appliance repairs leaves so much to write that a series of books could be produced. But to write about a shop that repairs household appliances is another matter. And to center the attention on the 85-year-old owner who does all the work himself redirects the article still again.

You must be disciplined not to fall to the temptation to drift in your writing. Examine each paragraph as a unit. Is it necessary? Does it help get to the point? Then examine each sentence within each paragraph. Does each sentence help maintain the point of the paragraph? Then, finally, examine a word within each sentence. Are all words needed? Do they help the purpose of the individual sentence?

## GETTING AN IDEA DOWN ON PAPER

How do you get the ideas in your mind on paper? Surely, as there are many outlets for your work, there are many approaches to the physical act of writing. Some veteran writers like to labor over a manual typewriter as they have done for years. Others use electric typewriters. But most writers have entered the computer age with a technological leap to powerful personal computers and multifeatured word processors.

There are writers who work in the early morning because they are morning people. They rise and jump at the chance to get their creative juices flowing while they are fresh. Others, it seems, cannot get going until finishing several cups of coffee, a newspaper, the mail, and other activities. These writers seem most comfortable during the afternoon. And, as you have guessed, some writers thrive at night. When all is quiet and the day is almost done, these writers are busy at creating and work through much of the night, only to rest in the morning.

There are writers who use a dictation machine or tape recorder to write, turning over the mundane duties of typing and preparing a manuscript to an assistant. These "idea" writers do not want to be bothered with clerical duties of typing or setting up a printer. Yet, some writers feel much closer to their work when they can do just that—control the typewriter and other effects of the writer's private work environment. Some still prefer to write their manuscripts by hand and do not deal with any machines at all, not even tape recorders.

## DEVELOPING GOOD WRITING HABITS

Each writer needs his or her own "nest" for productive writing. It can be a corner in the bedroom, an office in the basement, or any other secluded location. Freelance newspaper and magazine writer Wendy M. Grossman specializes in computers and paranormal science writing. A member of the Association of British Science Writers and founding editor of Britain's *Skeptic* magazine, she began freelance writing in 1990 from her home outside London in Richmond, Surrey. She was asked to describe her individual writing work habits:

> Other people think I'm disciplined, but I think I'm as disorganized as hell. I have an office in the largest room in my flat, which has a full-sized desk, and a couple of filing cabinets. At the moment it also has three computers and a laser printer. If you're going to review hardware, you need space to put all the boxes in. But really, I can write anywhere, and often do: On planes, in coffee shops, outdoors, in the living room, in bed. For me, a notebook computer is vital—spend 14 hours a day sitting in the same office, and you go mad. I have the office set up with a TV, speakers for the stereo system, and a radio. I have three phone lines (one for the modem and one for the fax). I grew up working in front of the TV, and I find it helps to have some evidence that the outside world is continuing to revolve. I have a second desk which holds the old PC for my half-day-a-week assistant to use. (Grossman, personal communication, May 20, 1993; January 15, 1998)

You can find writers who work in absolute silence to enhance their concentration. Some work in a social environment where other people are present, such as an office. The interaction seems to stimulate and inspire rather than interrupt and retard. Others like to have a stereo playing loudly, or softly, or the television tuned to a program for background noise.

Some writers produce a manuscript in one long and exhausting effort. Others produce it in bits and pieces. Some writers write a manuscript as it is presented, from beginning to end. You will find others who write the middle first, the end, and then the beginning. Some authors research first, then write. Some professionals simultaneously research and write. There also are writers who revise as they write, a sentence at a time. You also can find writers who write many pages and then revise. Some people write in an office at home. Some lease office space to get away from distractions at home. And others, who have full-time jobs doing something else, like to write in their regular work environment.

*Writer's Digest* Senior Editor Thomas Clark said a critical step in getting started as a writer is setting up. "One of the most important commitments you can make to your writing is to *set aside an area where you write*," Clark (1990, pp. 24, 26) explained. "What is essential to your mindset is that your 'office' have an air of exclusivity about it—you're telling yourself that writing is important" (Clark, 1990, pp. 24, 26). Beyond this first step, Clark strongly recommends these other nine tips to establishing yourself in the professional writer frame of mind (Clark, 1990, pp. 24, 26):

- Involve yourself with writing by attending writing classes or conferences.
- Equip yourself with writing tools.
- Read books about writing and other writers.
- Put words on paper.
- Write every day.
- Decide what type of writer you seek to be.
- Think small to build confidence.
- Send out your work after completing it.
- Expect some rejection and analyze the reasons for rejections.

These work styles are as unique as any other personal habits. You have to find what is right for you. Try a variety of combinations to determine what is the most productive and efficient environment for your writing. Then, as Zinsser (1980) has said, stick to it. The habit of writing counts. It is not so important what constitutes the habit, as shown later.

## ORGANIZING ALL THAT INFORMATION

To be organized in your writing means you are more efficient and, likely, more effective and productive. Organizing gives focus by giving each story a dominant element (Sweeney, 1993). Organizing does not come easy to some people. Some writers are naturally disorganized people, so they have to work harder to get to their writing goals. University of Pittsburgh magazine editor David Fryxell believes that. "By getting organized—wresting order out of the chaos of your writing process—you will be liberated to be all that you can be as an author," Fryxell (1990, p. 42) said. "Once you know where a story is going and how you'll get there, it's a lot easier to pay attention to the scenery en route. In other words, by getting organized, you'll write not only faster, but also *better*" (Fryxell, 1990, p. 42).

There are several concerns when organizing the information you have collected for your article. Remember that the organizational approaches vary depending on the style of writing and the medium, but there are several standard ways of organizing yourself before you even start writing. Discussions of both common newspaper and magazine organizational strategies follow.

Different organizational approaches represent the personality of the writer as much as do the space where you work, your typewriter (or computer), and work habits. Probably the most common way to get the mass of information you have collected is to use an outline to get started. Writers who use outlines have different styles of outlining as well. Some write formal sentence outlines and others use simple topical outlines. Others sketch an outline of an article on their computer screen or on paper in their typewriter and fill in the gaps as they sift through the notes of interviews that have been completed. A good procedure for beginners might be the following steps:

1. Think of the main points of the article and make these topics the Roman numerals of your outline. These are also your article's main sections.
2. Next, divide each of the main sections into subsections. What are the major characteristics, or concerns, of each Roman numeral section? There might be just one characteristic or several dozen. List each so you will not forget to include these as you begin to write portions of the manuscript. Letter each of these A, B, and so on.
3. If the article is going to be lengthy, you might want to go beyond the alphabetic listings. If you do extend the outline, these will be details of each subsection and they can be numbered 1, 2, and so forth.
4. On longer articles, or articles with sidebars and boxed inserts such as many magazines use, you should use separate outlines for the sidebars. Often, after writing the main article, you spot a portion of the main article outline that lends itself to a "take out" or "sidebar."

These steps will help you to write and organize and they work well for longer manuscripts. Shorter (less than 1,000 words) articles common in newspapers might not need this sort of rigorous organizational plan, but even shorter pieces benefit if you find yourself confused about what you have before the writing stage.

The newest and more complete full-feature word processors offer outlining tools in addition to all of their other features. This does not mean, of course, that your computer does the outlining for you. However, word-processing software contains features that permit creation of collapsible outlines based on text that you have entered. This way of viewing the words you have written may help you create, organize, and move text more easily. Word-processing software such as Microsoft Word, WordPerfect, and WordPro offer such features and more. However, these can be costly for beginners on a budget. You may wish to use a less expensive package with fewer features. Another convenience of personal computers and word processors is the ease of moving things around. If you use a computer to write, take advantage of the flexibility and ease of organizing and reorganizing your facts even at the outline stage.

Although paper outlines and computers are one approach, there are others. Some experienced writers prefer the standard file card in 3 × 5 or 5 × 7 sizes. This approach works well for shuffling and reordering the information once it is listed on cards. The approach, again, is pretty straightforward:

- List each important point on an individual card.
- Place cards with related information in the same pile as you sort through the deck.
- Order the piles according to the sequence you want the information to flow in the article.
- Sort each individual pile to logically support the general point the pile of cards represents.

Still another approach is to use a notebook. Divide it into sections and place relevant information about each section into the binder. Then you can move material as necessary, page by page, or section by section, until you get it into a sequence that you want to use to write. Another technique some writers use helps them to get "the big picture" of the organizational plan of their article. This approach requires these steps:

1. Write a very rough draft of as much of your manuscript as you can.
2. Take scissors and cut it up, a paragraph at a time.
3. Tape or tack the pieces to a wall or bulletin board.
4. Study the pieces on the wall. Move the pieces as needed to improve the flow and direction of your article.

*The New Yorker* writer and author Ken Auletta has moved from using a pen and a legal pad to using his computer, but he continues to use the same approach to finding organization within his article or book notes. Auletta (1997) said

You gather all this material and what do you do? The answer to that—is to spend a lot of time doing the most laborious indexing. I put it all in an index and stare at it. Then I move it around and try to figure out what the structure is. I master the material of the "trees" of this forest and then step back, sit with it, and try to figure out what is the forest I want to write about. I start with an index and try to wind up with a table of contents. I always find the key thing is to find that lead. We all do that in daily journalism, but I think it is true of the longer form as well. Get the right voice down, the style. Does it make sense? Does it sum up where you want to go? This indexing is the most unpleasant part of everything I do. And yet, it is the most essential single thing you do. (p. 1)

## BASIC STRUCTURE OF FEATURE ARTICLES

Newspaper features employ a variety of leads and organizational plans. You want your article to start well and retain readership for the rest of the article. This part of the chapter discusses approaches to leads, tools to hold the parts together, general organizational techniques used in features, developing and using writing style rules, and point of view.

### Developing the Right Lead

Writing authorities Patricia Kubis and Robert Howland (1985) stated that the lead, or opening paragraph, of a magazine article should achieve three goals:

1. Tell the reader what the article is about.
2. Provide the tone and mood of the article.
3. Catch the reader's attention and entice the reader to go further into the article.

Certainly the lead works with the title of the article and the layout of the first two pages to grab the reader. But the best package of color graphics will not keep a reader unless the author has done a big part in hooking the reader with a strong lead. The lead is crucially important. It can help determine the mood of the article. It should persuade the reader to stay with the article. Here are some of the basic newspaper (as well as magazine and newsletter) leads commonly used for features:

1. Summary lead—This lead gives the traditional five w's and h (who, what, when, where, why, and how) in as few words as possible. Some summary leads focus on one or two of these elements of the story and save the others, which are judged less important, for later in the story.

2. Salient feature lead—This lead focuses on one major characteristic of the story. Instead of several points in a color story about a festival, the salient feature lead emphasizes one point about food, music, or weather, for example.

3. Anecdotal lead—This lead is also called a case-approach lead and *The Wall Street Journal* feature lead. The reason is simple: stories with this lead use a specific representative example or story to illustrate a point about a situation that is discussed in general after the lead of the story. Thus, instead of writing about

the woes of unemployed oil workers in Texas, this approach would describe one person or family in the lead.

4. Quotation lead—Some writers like to open a feature with a quotation. The quotation can be from a person being profiled or an expression of sentiment common at a meeting or concert, but it must catch the gist of the article while being the exact words of a source important to the story.

5. Delayed-suspended interest lead—This lead deliberately holds the big news of the story from the reader to tease the reader further into the story. It is a lead that works well when there is some question of the outcome of a situation, such as an article about a lost memento that is found or an article describing the sudden joy of a big contest prize winner.

6. Question lead—This sort of lead asks a question of the reader, usually in direct address. The key, of course, is to be sure to answer the question in the story, preferably in the top half of the story while the question is still in the reader's mind.

There are still other frequently used approaches to leads. Many writers like to use straight narrative or highly descriptive writing. Some like to employ comparison and contrast for effect. Some use startling statements for impact. You will spot some leads that play on words, using puns as attention grabbers. Also, you might find others with use of direct address as a tool to get to readers who might otherwise find their interest drifting off (Cook, 1991; Garrison, 1990).

Leads should entice readers into the article. Adjunct professor and freelance writer Sally-Jo Bowman (1990) described the work of a good article lead in this interesting manner: "Writing nonfiction articles is like feeding a baby. You warm the little fellow up with a couple of bites of chocolate cake, and when he opens his mushy mouth for more, you cram in some broccoli" (p. 38).

In terms of structure, magazine leads are not bound by the same rules of newspaper lead writing in that most newspaper editors prefer short leads that are supported by subsequent paragraphs. Magazine leads are more flexible and are as often quite long as they are short. Their purposes remain the same, however.

Whatever the lead used, it should be a stirring paragraph. Pulitzer Prize–winning reporter Edna Buchanan said this about her lead-writing philosophy: "My idea of a successful lead is one that might cause a reader, who is having breakfast with his wife, to spit out his coffee, clutch his chest and say, 'My God, Martha! Did you read this?' " (Knight-Ridder, Inc., 1986, p. 5). Leads must be effective and serve the article's purpose.

*Los Angeles Times* Correspondent and Senior Writer Barry Siegel (2002) used a highly descriptive approach to create images in the reader's mind to begin his Pulitzer Prize–winning article about a man tried for negligence that led to the death of his son. The article is the story of the man, the trial, and the judge who presided over the case. The article won the 2002 Pulitzer Prize for feature writing. Here is how the veteran *Times* writer, who started working for the newspaper in 1983, began the well-crafted story:

> SILVER SUMMIT, Utah—He sat in his chambers, unprepared for this. "Just giving you a heads up," his court administrator was saying. "Paul Wayment hasn't reported in yet. They can't find him." Judge Robert Hilder felt uneasy. Wayment was supposed to start his jail sentence this morning.
>
> The 52-year-old judge walked slowly to his Summit County district courtroom. The trial underway passed as a blur. More than once, clerks pulled him off the bench to give him updates on Wayment. Each time, in his chambers, he stared out windows at the jail, hoping to see Paul drive up. At the lunch break, he went into Park City to eat, alone with his thoughts.
>
> He'd sentenced Wayment to jail even though the prosecutor didn't want this distraught father to serve time. Hilder felt he had to. Wayment's negligence caused his young son's death. There must be consequences, the judge ruled.
>
> Now there were—more than he had intended.
>
> On his way back from lunch, Hilder punched off the car radio, wanting to avoid the news. As always, his 6-year-old son's drawings and broken Lego toys covered the floor of his Ford Taurus. At the courthouse, he walked down a hallway that took him past the administrator's glass-walled office. She rose and waved him in. Concern, he saw, strained her face. He approached her door, bracing himself.
>
> Had he driven Wayment to suicide? Hilder believed it possible. Just as he believed it possible that he'd caused his own father's suicide, 20 years before.
>
> Although it includes the Park City ski resorts, Summit County is less the province of people than of rolling pastures and mountain forests. Only about 25,000 live in 1,849 square miles. Only one judge—Hilder—hears criminal cases. Three lawyers comprise the county attorney's criminal division. Two private lawyers on a part-time retainer fill the public defender's role. When they heard of Gage Wayment's death, all of them knew it would come to them. They knew they'd soon have to make their own choices.
>
> The first choice, though, had been Paul Wayment's. (Siegel, 2002)

Siegel next sets the scene that led to the death of the man's 2-year-old child, who had wandered off into the snow-covered mountains, became lost, and succumbed to the unforgiving freezing conditions. He tells readers the compelling story of the pain suffered by the father and the challenge facing the judge, who had lost his own son. Siegel described the classic dilemma in which the judge found himself:

> Hilder had always wanted to be a judge more than a practicing attorney. He was not at core committed to the adversary system, to the role of lawyer as advocate. He was much more interested in the narratives and issues heard in a courtroom. He liked to try to resolve them. He thought he was good at resolving them.
>
> Sentencing, on the other hand, he found hard. There was always that horrible

moment, after he heard the tremendous advocacy, the arguments, the pleas. Suddenly there was silence—and he had to decide. That was hell. That also was what he'd signed up for. (Siegel, 2002)

The story that unfolds is an account of the enormous grief suffered by the father and the difficult decisions facing the judge. Siegel writes about the guilt and pain, and the ultimate act of suicide that the father took to punish himself—even after the judge had issued a 30-day jail sentence. As he does, he tries to tie the storytelling to the scene he sets in his lead.

Soon enough, there came an even greater wave of support for Hilder from lawyers, pundits, hundreds of citizens and—over and over—Wayment's sister Valerie Burke. "I don't believe the 30-day sentence caused Paul to kill himself," she told reporters. "I think the judge was compassionate. Our family understands where the judge was coming from, and we don't blame him at all. He had to do what he felt was right."

Hilder can only shake his head at that phrase, "what he felt was right." He takes comfort from all the support but is no more certain now than before of making correct decisions. This latest experience, above all, has made him look even harder at the role of the judge.

He reflects on what the law accomplishes, what the law can't accomplish. He loves the law but does not worship it. He believes it does not have the answer to everything. In matters full of ambiguity, he suggests, there may be no good solution. "Black and white answers are not always what's needed," he says. "But sometimes they're the only answer."

He says something else as well: "It's not a bad thing to have Paul Wayment's face forever part of my life." (Siegel, 2002)

## Pulling the Various Pieces Together

Another important part of the article is a single sentence or paragraph that gets to the real point of the article. You can create a very strong lead, but few leads truly give focus to a feature article. A lot of writers give different names to that function, but it is a paragraph or sentence that tells readers what is really going on. The article may get off to a great start, but that super lead might not get to the essence of the article. You do that—get to the point of the article—with what is called a *billboard paragraph*, a *nut graf*, or a *summary paragraph*. These statements offer your theme or thesis. This part of the article can be the lead, but it is rare in feature writing. Instead, it usually comes right after the lead is established, or played out. The focus statement is short and to the point. "[W]riters lead in with several paragraphs—frequently anecdotal—then pop in the billboard to sum up the main point, the angle of the story," wrote Wilson (1990, p. 31), a freelance editor with the *Los Angeles Times*. "It's not unusual to follow a billboard with a supporting or amplifying graph, or a quotation for impact and validity" (Wilson, 1990, p. 31).

Transitions are also critical for success in writing, especially in longer pieces. Transitions are often misused and underrated. They link major portions of an article together in an effective way. These can be road maps for longer articles. They tell readers where they have been and where they are going. This might not always be obvious to your readers. Transitions can be a sentence or two, or just a phrase or a few words, often containing the common elements of the two parts being linked (Garrison, 1990).

## Organizing the Article

Story organizational forms are also broad in scope to give you flexibility in fitting the organizational plan to the story. There are variations in approaches, often based on length and not whether the article is written for any particular print medium. There are some differences involving lengthier magazine articles, of course. The body, or middle, of a magazine article is the "meat" of the sandwich. Once the article gets started with a well-conceived lead, the momentum must continue. Linking together the pieces with transitional sentences and paragraphs, this is where you must bring in the material that you promised your reader in the lead.

Regardless of what organizational plan you use for your topic, your conclusion serves a completely different purpose. This is where you clean up, you wrap up, and you tie everything together. In magazine feature writing more than most newspaper or newsletter writing, the conclusion plays a vital role. It is a chance to summarize the major points again for the reader. It is a chance to reveal the delayed or surprise "finish." It is a chance to give the storytelling its closure. Conclusions can be several pages or several sentences. Regardless of the length, the conclusion should not leave the reader hanging in midair by what you have chosen to say. Reach some form of resolution. Close it out, but be careful of writing too much, as some beginning writers will do. Remember that you do get a second chance at the conclusion, if you need it, when you rewrite.

These are the main time-tested story structural approaches of features:

1. Inverted pyramid—This approach might work for some features, but it is best used in straight news writing. This approach is less appropriate for feature material because it is structured by most important to least important priorities. It usually requires a summary lead.
2. Chronological order—This follows sequencing of events. When a feature recounts events or describes a procedure, this approach might be best.

3. Essay—A rather standard approach to all writing, this is found in columns, analyses, reviews, and other personal opinion or subjective writing. The essay format is standardized with an introduction, middle, and conclusion.

There will be many occasions when a combination of these three plans works best for your article. Certainly there will be some subjects that are best handled by one approach or another, but be prepared to mix the best of each of these when the subject calls for it.

### Writing with Style(books)

Although leads and organizational plans are at the top of the list for beginners to learn about feature writing, there are other concerns. Stylebooks contain a wealth of writing rules that make them the top reference book of many writers. Stylebooks include spelling, punctuation, capitalization, other types of grammar, information formatting, writing and reporting advice and policies, and other guidelines. Remember, however, that most major publications maintain their own stylebooks and usages in writing vary from publication to publication. Certainly the differences are distinct when newspaper usages are compared to magazine usages. And there may be a separate set of writing style rules that evolve as online publications mature in the next decade. Two of the most popular stylebooks are those published by Associated Press and United Press International. Get a copy of whatever book is used by the newspaper, magazine, newsletter, or online publication that you write for and use it as you write. You will notice the professional touch it gives your work if you ask questions of your own writing, learn the most common usages, consult it regularly about the usages you do not learn, and apply the usage rules evenly throughout your manuscripts.

### Using the Right Point of View

Another consideration is point of view in your writing. Feature stories for newspapers are most often written in third person, but in some situations, such as personal experience articles, columns, and travel articles, the writing is often in first person. Remember that when you choose to write in first person, you become a significant part of the story. Do you want to be the focus of the article? If so, choose the first person "I." If not, write in third person or even second person.

## WRITING ADVICE FROM A VETERAN EDITOR

Michelle Stacey, *Mademoiselle* magazine managing editor, recommended a sensible approach to writing for beginners. She offered this advice about the writing process (personal communication, October 6, 1988):

First drafts are for putting it all on paper, for getting over the staring-at-a-blank-page stage, for thinking up a wonderful lead that you'll probably hate in the morning. They are not for publication. There's always that dangerous, heady moment when you've finally finished a draft of the piece, when the whole thing sits there in a neat (or not-so-neat) package. You're in the throes of first love. "This is so great," you think. "I may not even need to revise this!" Don't you believe it. That's the moment to dive back in, pencil in hand, and revise, rewrite, reorganize, rethink. But once you've gone through another draft or two and you really know it's close this time—how do you make it into a piece your editor will love, too?

When it comes to final polishing of a story, I like to think in terms of *danger points*. There are three *danger points* in every piece that you write, and there are points every editor looks at and usually ends up having to revise. Save your editor the trouble on these and your stock will rise immediately.

*The lead.* Yes, you have already tinkered with this. You may have gone through two or three different ones. But there's a trick I've had to do as an editor so many times that it's become a basic rule: Look at the second or third paragraph. Chances are your real lead is right there. I can't count the number of times I've had to chop off the first one or two paragraphs of a story—paragraphs that, when you were writing them, made you feel comfortable, buttressed, safe, but that turn out to be completely unnecessary. Beat your editor to the chopping block.

*Transitions.* The most misused and underrated parts of a story, these turning points can be the weak links in the strongest of chains. There is a popular misconception that transitions consist of latching on to a stray word or concept in the last sentence of a section and using that poor stray as a rope to swing, Tarzan-like, to an entirely new section. "Speaking of cows," you write, "Mrs. O'Leary—" This is the sort of lazy writing that has made many a weary editor write "weak trans." in the margin of a piece. Good transitions always have some connection to the main thrust of a piece; they are your opportunity to ask yourself: "Why am I writing this next section? How does this fit in with my overall thesis?" Once you've answered those questions, you can convey the answers to the reader. Transitions remind the reader of where you've been and where you're going; they shouldn't exist in a void. Don't be afraid that you're explaining too much. "Another aspect of municipal disasters that historians tend to ignore is the element of plain bad luck," you write. "Take, for instance, the case of Mrs. O'Leary's cow—"

*Favorite parts.* Those luscious turns of phrase that make your heart beat a little faster every time you read them, those especially creative sentences where you've really found a new way to say something—be suspicious of these. They're probably the worst writing in your story. I know it seems unlikely—and painful—but trust me on this one. Those lovely phrases are more likely to be overwritten, hard to understand, high-falutin', and low in content. The best writing does not go out of its way to be cute or beautiful; it is good because it is clear, informative, and says what needs to be said in the most succinct and effective manner. That is elegant writing—it doesn't draw attention to itself. Go back to every favorite part you have and don't give it any breaks: Is it doing its job in the piece, or is it just serving your ego? Be ruthless.

Now you've got a piece to warm an editor's heart. Is that the last work you'll ever have to do on that story? Don't bet on it—at least if you're writing for a magazine. The nature of magazine writing, with its finely tuned attention to voice and a very specific audience, almost always requires that an author make further revisions. But if you can make your editor say, "This piece is close, really close!" when she reads your story, you've made her day. Trust me on this one. (Stacey, personal communication, October 6, 1988)

## A LOOK AT A PULITZER PRIZE–WINNING ARTICLE

*Miami Herald* Local section columnist and feature writer Liz Balmaseda earned the 1993 Pulitzer Prize for commentary for her columns and feature articles for the newspaper's local section each Wednesday and Saturday. Her articles show a variety of approaches focused on people. Her features, written as fixed-length columns, always seem filled with lots of direct quotations from the people about whom she writes. Balmaseda wrote human-interest feature articles for *The Miami Herald* from 1987 to 1991 after 6 years of news reporting and production for *The Miami Herald* city desk, *Newsweek*, and NBC network news. She began her award-winning column in 1991. Balmaseda (personal communication, June 28, 1993) said 1 of her 10 articles in her Pulitzer-winning package almost did not get written. She was in Haiti on assignment and went with her photographer to a particularly poor part of the island near Port-au-Prince. She explained what led to the story:

> I went to this village while the photographer took some photos and did not plan to write anything. We went behind this old slaughterhouse and saw a strip of little houses. We went to one to meet a family there. I saw that it was a wonderful look at daily life in a poor, poor place. When we went into the house, I did not plan to write anything, but suddenly, on this hot day, it started raining very hard. We were trapped because my photographer could not take his equipment outside. So, I sat there and thought to myself, "this is a blessing." I had been staying in a nice hotel on another part of the island and was suddenly dropped into a life and culture I'd never come into contact with before. It was the real Haitian life and its rhythms.
>
> The man's wife came home soaking wet. The kids from the village were dancing in the rain, but the man protected his kids by keeping them inside. The dynamic of the scene was really incredible. In that moment, I learned what kept life going on that island. In the rain, I saw hope. There was hope in the kids dancing, in the kids catching rain drops with their tongues, in the refreshment they felt from the rain on such a hot and humid day. In it, they saw hope.
>
> I went back to the hotel and thought, "I can't write this. There's no news peg. No press conference. No quotes. No real news." But I thought, what the heck? What's the worst they [her editors back in Miami] can do? So I wrote the story. Of all the stories I did, they [her editors] liked this story best and put it on the front page. They loved it. And that was one of the stories that won the Pulitzer. Some-

thing inside me said to take the risk and write that story. I did it. If you have the
instinctive reaction—if something moves you—then do it. Follow that feeling.

Her story of the man and his family demonstrates a sensitive first-person approach to writing about the political and economic oppression, as well as the in-
domitable spirit, of the people of Haiti. "It is my favorite of all of them,"
Balmaseda (personal communication, June 28, 1993) said. This is her story of
one family in Haiti (Balmaseda, 1992, p. 1A):

PORT-AU-PRINCE, Haiti—Those are the neighbor's children dancing in the
rain, thrusting their faces skyward, trying to catch the raindrops in their mouths,
singing a song that gets lost in the deluge.

Those are not the children of Morales Leger. His children are inside, dry,
pleased nevertheless to witness the downpour on such a suffocating day.

From his house across the alley, he and I watch the neighbor's girls in their eu-
phoric convulsions, drenched, entranced.

Morales, a man of 64, has put out large tin pots to catch the clean rainwater, a
blessing on this humid Feast of the Ascension.

He pulls his young son close to him, kissing his cheek, explaining that "he easily gets the flu."

The sudden storm caught me as we talked in his home. Entirely by chance, I
found myself dropped in the middle of daily life in a squalid shanty strip where a
desperate existence churns on endlessly, even on feast days.

The rain hammered on the tin roof, veiling doorways and windows in misty
curtains. A shower of relief.

To arrive at his house, I crossed the ancient slaughterhouse, walked along the
muck-filled canal where pigs slept. The stench of human and animal and vegetable waste clung to my face like a mask. I took quick, shallow breaths through my
mouth.

A young woman bathed in the pig water, scrubbing her arms with a pink bar
of soap, as if the rosy suds could extinguish the film of God-knows-what-is-
dumped-in-there.

I had passed more than a dozen wooden doorways framing swollen, naked
children. Inside, their mothers and sisters and maybe cousins lounged in a darker
dimension. Because this was a holiday, no one was working. Normally, this place
is alive from 4:30 a.m. with wailing animals and haggling merchants who later
sell the fresh, warm meat at the market.

Then, I slipped into the home of Morales Leger.

Within dim, green walls there are two beds over which gauze mosquito nets
dangle. There is a pink, child-size potty chair where his youngest girl, Philocles, 2,
fidgets, naked.

We talk about his life. He has not worked steadily in years. He was a sergeant
in the military for 26 years, though he says he is not a political man. He left the
service 17 years ago and has worked odd jobs since.

He married a woman much younger, Margareth Coustan, 29. He delivered
their four children in his home, on their matrimonial bed. He writes their names
in my notebook in a spidery hand: Gina, 8, Philomene, 5, Philippe, 3, Philocles, 2.

He lifts the youngest from her chamber pot, slides a piece of cardboard over its seat, and kisses the girl gently.

"My consolation," he whispers, kissing her again.

Then it begins to rain.

I ask him about Haiti, about politics and refugee boats, and the regime du jour. But he shakes his head.

"It is a divine presence that guides us. That is all," he says, offering me a seat in his home.

The rain is powerful and relentless. In a while, his wife arrives, soaked and shivering. She sets down a flat basket of bruised chayotes and mangoes on the kitchen floor.

From what I can understand, she brings back what the market ladies don't sell.

A 25-year-old neighbor named Jonny explains that friends sometimes help her buy food.

"She has many mouths to feed," he says. "She has plenty babies."

And another is on the way. Margareth is five months pregnant.

Why so many babies? I ask.

Morales answers for her.

"They are my security," he says, clutching his chest. "They are my future."

The gray canal outside his window has become a swift river rushing away from the shanty strip, rushing toward the bay, washing the putrid smells, washing the mud off the pigs, cleansing the woman who bathes in the pig water.

After the rain, everything along the alley glistens, and in the distance a rainbow has appeared.

A couple of days later, I watch a storm approach from my hotel balcony high above the capital. The city seems to dissolve gradually into silver sheets of water that sweep inland from the bay, across the slums and markets.

I think of the slaughterhouse and the resilient souls who dwell on its fringe. Probably, they're happily getting wet.

I know I learned something that afternoon at the house of Morales Leger. I learned that neither poverty nor politics can break the Haitian spirit.

I learned that sometimes it can rain on the most putrid of days.

I learned that in this place where hope is too often elusive, the children of Morales Leger, his hope and consolation, are truly his wealth. (Balmaseda, 1992, p. 1A)

(Reprinted with the permission of *The Miami Herald*.)

## THE WRITING PROCESS: HOW ONE WRITER WRITES

Veteran freelance writer Bill Steele (personal communication, May 24, 1993) has written and edited for newspapers and magazines. He has worked with both large and small publications. His own writing habits are well established and he shares them (Steele, personal communication, May 24, 1993):

> I usually begin at the beginning, (i.e., by writing my lead). That's the newspaper background showing. However clever or cutesy it may be (I try to avoid cutesy,

but some publications want it), it has to tell the reader what the article is about; if you don't know that yet you need to do more research, or at least more thinking.

The lead pretty much determines what I have to talk about first, and that helps set up the structure of the article—what some people would call the outline. I seldom do an outline per se, although I may scribble a few sentences that show what comes first, what comes second, and so on. Often the sentences are transitions that show how I'm going to get from one area to the next. I think of the structure from the point of view of a teacher: What does the reader need to know before I introduce this piece of information?

Sometimes I get stuck and have no idea what comes next. In that case, I may pick up some other part of the article and write that—say, some biographical information on the person I interviewed. Thanks to the computer, I can have that floating around until I figure out where it goes, then just paste it in. Sometimes when I'm stuck I just go out for a walk; I'll start out thinking about other things, but after about a mile, the article ideas will come back in and I'll see a way to solve the problem. Then again, often the answers will come to me when I'm in bed trying to go to sleep, which is a nuisance because I have to get up again and write it all down.

I do see writing as a problem-solving process, a sort of engineering job if you will: How do I put this structure together with the materials I've got?

These days I write perforce in front of the computer. That's not much of a change, since I used to write in front of the typewriter. I was never much for writing in longhand; I can go faster on a keyboard, and the only way to keep up with my thoughts in longhand is to write illegibly. The workspace now is sort of L-shaped, with the computer screen in front of me and the disk drives and printer off to the right. I have a swing-arm lamp that illuminates the space on the desk to the right of the keyboard and the keyboard itself without throwing much light on the screen. Notes and stuff I have to look at go on the desk under the lamp—and eventually get piled up to where I spend a lot of time leafing through for the thing I need. The dictionary, thesaurus, White, and a few other basic references sit on the desk just behind that space, and works in progress get stuffed into stacked trays to the left.

I get some of my work done in my head while walking or lying in bed. The majority of the work, really, gets done inside my head; the computer is just the place I put it after it's done. I remember a panel of the comic strip "Shoe" in which someone says, "Why are you staring out the window when you should be working. Start pounding the keyboard." To which Shoe replied, "*Typists* pound keyboards. *Writers* stare out windows." (Steele, personal communication, May 24, 1993)

## USING DIRECT QUOTATIONS

Strong feature articles come alive with liberal use of direct quotations from a variety of people and, occasionally, even documents. People make features work and their words, through your use of direct quotations, give life to your story.

There are some rules about quotations in magazine and newspaper features that you should remember. First of all, in much of your article writing, you will find that quotations help to back up generalizations made about a person, place, or thing. Quotations give the article an element of reality beyond the perspective of the writer. For features, it means you can let someone else speak in the article, using his or her exact words.

*The Miami Herald*'s Balmaseda said she depends a great deal on direct quotations for her articles and columns about people. Balmaseda (personal communication, 1993) explained

> I don't always have a lot to say about a subject. I ask a question and let people say it for me. Sometimes people say it better. Many times, people who never get into the paper say things very beautifully and I feel compelled to use what they say. Quotes give you something to hang the story on. But you also have to recognize that some people don't have something to say and you have to be selective.

Paraphrasing can work as effectively as direct quotations. Sometimes, paraphrases work better. There are occasions when you can state something more efficiently and more meaningfully. This avoids the sense of overquoting and overstating. Full-time freelance writer Hank Nuwer (1992), author of a book on pledging and hazing, believes paraphrases are the desired alternative to bad and inappropriate quotations, also.

*Writer's Digest* columnist Art Spikol (1993) feels direct quotations can add much to nonfiction, if they are used effectively:

> Quotation marks have a power far beyond the space they occupy in print. Use a quotation mark, and the reader infers: *Here's something somebody actually said. Here's a living, breathing individual about to speak to me. Here's something the writer thought was important enough to set off with those funny little apostrophes.* (p. 55)

In addition to quoting one individual at a time, many experienced feature writers use quotations to recreate dialogue to provide for the reader the effect of being there—getting to watch history occur, for example, through the words of the persons who were present. It seems to make the passage move more quickly, too. Here are some helpful guidelines in using quotations in your writing:

1. Make certain it is clear in the flow of your article just who is speaking— This is especially true if you change the person being quoted.
2. Vary your verbs of attribution—At times, you should rely on the standard verb, *said*, but there are other more precise verbs. Most feature writing uses the past tense verb, *said*, instead of the present tense verb, *says*. Re-

member that verbs and verb tenses have specific meaning when used, so take care in selecting just the right word.

3. Vary placement of attribution verbs—It will be necessary to place them at the beginning of a sentence on some occasions; avoid using the verbs only at the end of sentences. Thus, use past tense as your standard tense for attribution.

4. Be careful in using long quotations—If you must use a lengthy quote from a person or text from a document, make certain you have introduced it to the reader to explain what you are doing and why.

5. Dialogue quotations add a great deal—Use them, but be clear who is saying what. And break up long passages of dialogue, if they are necessary, with some description of action by the speakers.

6. Quote exact words and do not change the words in the quotation—Even incorrect grammar will give the reader insight into the personality of the individual speaking.

You must also be very careful to be accurate with direct quotations. Quotations cannot be made up. Most professional journalists do not subscribe to the approach that modifying direct quotations is acceptable. This debate continues because some journalists and writers feel it is not troubling to "clean up" direct quotations to make them more understandable without changing the sense or meaning; others believe writers should not play with reality.

There are some legal limits, too. A writer for *The New Yorker* had a suit filed in federal court against her because a doctor believed he had been libeled by misused and even fabricated quotations in the article based on personal interviews by the writer. Although the case was dismissed on two occasions, it was returned to court a third time and the writer was found to have been wrong in her use of quotations by a jury. But when the jury could not decide a judgment award for the plaintiff—the foreman said it was hopelessly deadlocked on that issue—the judge eventually declared a mistrial. Regardless of the judgment, these matters of honesty and accuracy are serious for feature writers. The safest way to avoid such legal problems is to be accurate and correct and not to fabricate or alter what was said in any deliberate manner (Salant, 1993).

## REWRITING, REWRITING, AND MORE REWRITING

Some writing experts call rewriting an art form. Kubis and Howland (1985) said, "If you are a real writer, you *know* that *rewriting is the name of the game*" (p. 205). Unless you are a particularly gifted writer, you will seldom find that a first draft is sufficient for publication. Most writers find that to finish a manuscript is an achievement of note, but the real work comes in revision.

The best policy is to finish the first draft, then let it sit a while—overnight or longer, if possible. Then read it from top to bottom with a fresh mind and clear head. You can be more critical and make some true improvements in the work. Each time you do this, the manuscript gets better as words are changed or cut, sentences are revised, and passages reorganized. Your goal is to revise until what you have to say flows smoothly. Revise the work until it seems to glide as you read it. Although beginning writers may need more rewrites, as you become more experienced, you will write, revise, and polish to finish an article in three distinct stages.

Rewriting will help you make your thoughts clearer and, at the same time, more efficient. You can use this stage to add information, delete it, or clarify it. Rewriting is a necessary step. Even after that initial surge of creativity in writing the first draft, rewriting makes a significant difference in the quality of your work. Thus, you must make the time to rewrite. It is a part of the writing process. Build it into the article production cycle you use. And remember one key question: If what you have written is not clear to you, how can it be clear to someone else? Rewriting is the answer.

## BORROWING FROM FICTION WRITERS

Some of the best nonfiction writers in the United States also write in a fiction style or use the tools of short story writers and novelists. They may not always realize it, but they use the same techniques. Use of dialogue is but one frequently found example. Countless successful and popular U.S. novelists began as nonfiction writers, of course: for example, Mark Twain, Walt Whitman, Ernest Hemingway, Tom Wolfe, Gay Talese, and Patricia Cornwell. Numerous modern journalists have crossed into fiction and crossed back. There is as much in common with the two approaches as there is not. Four elements in particular—levels of abstraction, storytelling, use of tension, and development of characters—work effectively in many forms of feature writing:

1. Abstraction—Summaries, separate from the specific, seem to be the opposite of what most feature writers use in their writing. Feature writers seldom delve into the theoretical world, right? Without getting overly philosophical, they do. Although an abstract is the essence of something, such as a series of events or a single event, writers often write in the abstract. You do. There are often times when you are general, others when you are specific. Hart (1991e) made this proper observation:

> The best literary writers recognize the importance of varying abstraction levels, depending on the purposes they have in mind. But lots of journalists pay little attention to the degree of abstraction in their writing. Out of habit, they stay at the

same middling abstraction levels all the time. That cruise-control approach robs their writing of both meaning and impact. (p. 1)

Hart (1991e) likes to use a ladder metaphor in referring to levels of abstraction in writing. Think of the bottom of the ladder as the most concrete, or single item, and the top of the ladder as the most general, or everything. And in between, you find varying degrees gradually going from the specific to general as you refer to the item in your article.

2. Storytelling—Humans have always been storytellers, and when typesetting came along, the stories began to be preserved. Journalism, in its most primitive form, began to evolve. Feature writers are storytellers. There are both long and short stories to tell. We tend to tell the short ones. However, think of telling stories as something more than just anything you might write. Stories in the strictest form involve more than what most news and feature writers offer. Some experts say that journalists simply tell the end of a good story. Storytelling involves a dynamic beginning, an unusual setting, and contrast between content and style. Because storytelling involves an entire plot, a good feature writer using storytelling techniques includes the beginning, middle, and then the ending. And the story is often told in this manner, also. Storytelling, in the most traditional manner, is done first-hand. It uses common literary devices such as shifting points of view, irony, dialogue, and surprise endings. Today, it may seem to be a lost art. It was common earlier in this century and remains popular with some magazine and nonfiction book writers (DeSilva, 1990; Hart, 1991d; Wood, 1997).

3. Tension—Another tool used by successful feature writers who borrow from fiction writers is tension, the stretching and straining of human emotions to their limits. Pulitzer Prize-winning feature writer Madeleine Blais (1984) said she likes to build her feature articles around tension involving the central sources, or the characters, in her articles. Without it, she says, her articles would not be worth writing. "Tension offers an element of surprise. It allows the reader to imagine many possible endings to the course of the piece. If there isn't some kind of tension, there's no story" (n.p.). One effective method for creating high levels of tension is foreshadowing, or hinting at things to come through some description in the article. This works because it hooks readers into finding out what will happen later in the narrative (Hart, 1992).

4. Characters—In the preceding paragraph, sources were also described as characters. It is often helpful for feature writers to think of their sources as characters in the overall story they are telling. Naturally, in nonfiction feature writing, the realities of the situation limit what the characters do and do not do. Feature writers develop sources and characters in their articles through description and use of direct quotations. There is little else. Although all sources cannot be developed into characters, it helps in some articles. Sources are distinct. If feature writers could use some of the descriptive techniques that novelists use in

describing their characters, readers would benefit from deeper knowledge of the people in the stories. We should take opportunities, when they come along, to describe people through their words and our observations of their behavior. We also should describe them in terms of their appearance, their possessions, their values, their beliefs, and even how they move, express themselves with their hands, and how they talk (Hart, 1991a, 1991b).

It starts with storytelling skills, some experienced feature writers believe. Joan Ryan, columnist and feature writer for the *San Francisco Chronicle*, emphasized the basic storytelling skill to appeal to readers. Ryan (1997) stated the following:

> When you tell a story to a kid, it doesn't matter what it's about: Galileo or Abraham Lincoln or some kid having a bad day. If it's well told, that kid will sit there slack-jawed listening to you. I think we never outgrow that. I think we always want to be told a good tale. And I don't think it matters what the subject matter is. (p. 1)

Auletta (1997) believed that any time a writer begins a project, he or she should examine the question of how to tell the story:

> You don't want the story to dominate the facts and to shape it in a way that's misleading, but essentially you have to figure out a way to tell a story. One of the things that is critical to story telling is to convey a sense that you are trying to be an anthropologist. That is to say you are going out there and you are trying to capture the essence of what you are reporting on—be it a personality, an organization, or an incident. To do that, you are going there with Colombo-like questions: innocence, don't know the answers. I always keep this aphorism—in mind: "Truth is a liquid, not a solid." (p. 1)

## READABILITY OF WRITING

Regardless of what you use to write your manuscript, good writing must be readable, just as it must be understandable. *Readability* is simply a term that describes how easy something is to read. Writing experts have been studying readability for about 50 years and have devised various rules and formulas for readability. As American Press Institute's Wardlow (1985, p. 15) observed, these tools for measuring readership have different ways of getting to the same points about readable articles:

1. Short is better than long.
2. Simple forms are best.
3. Personal is better than impersonal.

Well-known readability formulas include those created by Rudolph Flesch (1946, 1949) in the 1940s and Robert Gunning (1968) in the 1960s. Flesch found that there is an ideal number of 17 to 19 words per sentence. The ideal number of syllables is 150 per 100 words and an ideal percentage of personal interest words, such as pronouns, is 6% of 100 words. He also said that sentences that have human interest, such as direct address, questions, or quotations should be about 12% of the total. However, Hart (1990e) cautioned the following: "[W]e all need to understand that while readable writing may be simple, it isn't necessarily simplistic" (p. 1).

The late 1980s brought personal computing into writing education. As a result, there are now numerous programs available in secondary and higher education that address writing and readability. Students of writing, as well as writing teachers, now can use computer programs to calculate these readability assessments on the spot. Some grammar and writing checkers are now a part of more sophisticated word processing packages, going well beyond the usual spelling and thesaurus features. Other forms of analysis of writing are also possible, through computers, to determine mechanical and structural writing errors that would reduce readability. Many of these programs are available at low cost through software clearinghouses or local personal computer stores.

## POLISHING AND EDITING MANUSCRIPTS

You can also think of rewriting as a self-editing process, but the process is somewhat different. Rewriting means writing it over and over until it is right. Self-editing is making changes on the existing manuscript without rewriting major portions. The focus here is on self-editing.

There are two ways of looking at manuscript editing. First, you must consider what has to be done on your own part to improve your manuscript. This is an important stage and it is the most significant portion of this discussion. The other, the handling that another person gives your manuscript, also remains vital to the writing process, yet it is out of your control for the most part. But what can you do to improve your article? What is within your control? One editor has an answer. Phil Currie (Wardlow, 1985, p. 45), a Gannett Company news executive, offered this checklist of the most significant problem areas to look for:

1. Dull, wooden phrasing.
2. Poor grammar, spelling, and punctuation.
3. Story organization.
4. Errors of fact or interpretation.
5. Holes in stories, completeness.

6. Clutter.

7. Redundancy.

There are other concerns in tuning a manuscript. You must, as noted before, match a publication's stylebook. You must answer the unanswered questions. You have to check for attribution strengths and weaknesses. Finally, as any copy desk chief will tell you, tightening is always a concern about a manuscript: watch for wordiness.

## WRITING IS GROUNDED IN REPORTING SKILLS

Lucille S. deView (personal communication, May 21, 1993), veteran writing coach for the *Orange County Register,* said feature writers are

> like the dancer grounded in ballet who can switch to tap, jazz, or modern dance—and enjoy performing all of them. The grounding comes from solid reporting skills honed through writing obituaries, doing the police beat, covering sports, any and all tasks that bear down hard on the who, what, where, when, and why.
>
> The joy comes from leaping beyond these vaunted five W's, to write with style and grace. The skilled feature writer borrows techniques from literary masters to infuse stories with a lyrical quality. Within a short span of time, the feature writer may twirl from a scientific breakthrough to the newest discovery in fashions; from explaining the stock market to a how-to piece on cultivating roses. The rewards are great, especially for the writer open to new ideas but blessed with common sense. Some suggestions:
>
> 1. *Do not mistake celebrity or education as the only sources of intelligent discussion, wit, or sagacity.* People whose occupations are humble and names unknown may provide the deepest insights and most compelling quotes. Factory workers go to the symphony; a housemaid becomes an opera star; stevedores publish poetry; homemakers become bank presidents, and more.
>
> 2. *Be unbiased in your writing.* Sexism and racism often take subtle forms and ethnic stereotypes persist unless we are careful to avoid them. Since a majority of women are in the workplace, a writer's vocabulary must keep pace. Use the word "executives," not "businessmen"; "firefighters" instead of "firemen." And do not write "woman doctor"; just say "doctor."
>
> 3. *Don't make racial exceptions.* If you say "the articulate black professor," you imply most are inarticulate. Don't indicate race unless it is relevant to the story. Why mention "the Hispanic bookkeeper" when you would not say "the German bookkeeper"?
>
> 4. *Use the word "disabled," not "handicapped."* People "use" wheelchairs; they are not "confined" to wheelchairs. Use appropriate terminology for specific disabilities. Is the person "hearing impaired" or "deaf"?
>
> 5. *In general, don't call older people senior citizens.* They prefer being called older persons. When so many are active and healthy, it is not appropriate to say a person is "80 (or 90, or more) and still going strong."

6. *Don't portray younger people as always troubled.* See the individual, not the group.

7. *Practice problem-solving journalism.* Explaining the dimensions of a dilemma is helpful to your readers; finding an answer is curative. Seek the solution, test it, and pass it along if it has merit.

8. *Do interviews in person, not on the telephone.* Not seeing the person's raised eyebrows or scowl is a risk—and a lost opportunity for colorful writing.

9. *Make each assignment a learning experience.* See it as an opportunity to enrich your writing and your life. (deView, personal communication, May 21, 1993)

# PART TWO

# TYPES OF ARTICLES

# CHAPTER SIX

# Descriptive and Color Writing

*Dallas Morning News* editorial writer Debra Decker went to the extreme for depth of information, detail, and color for her recent feature package about Islam. She traveled from Texas to Saudi Arabia, Egypt, and Uzbekistan. Decker was part of a group of journalists who visited the Middle East to learn about Islam. The *Dallas Morning News* serves a region of the United States that is heavily Christian, particularly Baptist, so Decker and her editors felt the trip would generate greater understanding of religion and values in the Middle East.

Decker focused a cover story for the newspaper's Sunday Reader section on the roles of women in Islamic countries. To do this, she applied storytelling techniques that included descriptive and color writing to allow readers to imagine the scene and setting for her descriptions of the culture and special lifestyles of Islamic women. Here's how she began her collection of three portraits:

> RIYADH—The iron gate in the white outer wall of the home swung open to a wide front patio, bare except for a small bicycle peeking from the side of the house. Farther on, double doors to the house were ajar and hinted of a welcome refuge from the relentless summer sun.
>
> This could be any upscale neighborhood in America. But it was Riyadh, and I was entering a Saudi home to lunch with Muslim women. The afternoon afforded me a surprising glimpse of them unveiled—physically and intellectually.
>
> The practice of Islam differs among countries. The five basic pillars of the faith are the same. . . . (Decker, 2002, p. 1J)

Decker's approach to the story is simple. She took three separate looks at the role of women in three different countries. She wrote different sections of the two full newspaper pages article on each. She described how these women live and pointed to pride in their culture as well as a generational divide between mothers and daughters. Although the package is well illustrated with color art and photographs provided by the Associated Press, Decker described certain aspects of the way Muslim women live:

> The group of about a dozen Saudi women at one lunch may not have been totally typical—they were relatively well off and were expecting to lunch with six Amer-

ican women journalists—but nonetheless, they and the Saudi home were not what one might expect. In the home, the first object greeting visitors in the entry hall was a 6-foot by 10-foot mirrored fresco of a woman's profile, face thrust up and forward into the home and her hair flowing back in waves. The art indicated the contradictions of Saudi culture—women glorified yet sequestered. (Decker, 2002, p. 1J)

The next passage described how her hosts were dressed:

As for the Saudi women themselves, they were gorgeous, even by Dallas's exacting standards. Most of the women wore glamorous full makeup. Some had on tight low-cut tops and slim-fitting short skirts, backless heels and tasteful but abundant jewelry. Like America, dress did vary. A student was wearing blue jeans and a t-shirt. And a sweet, plain-faced teacher from the eastern provinces kept on her red head scarf during the meals.

Their opinions varied even more than their outfits did. . . . (Decker, 2002, p. 1J)

Some feature stories need to set a scene or establish a mood as their most important objective for readers. Decker's story, through her use of description, does this. We, as readers, cannot be there with her. She shares these observations with her readers to provide a fuller impression of the lives of these Middle Eastern women. If something like this story is your own assignment, your goal may include making the reader "see," "feel," and "touch" the subject of your writing. You want to create mental images of the person, the place, the scenery. You want to present the opportunity for the reader to use his or her "mental senses"—that is, to imagine the smell, sound, feel, the emotion, the physical appearance, and even the taste of the subject.

This is what descriptive and color writing are all about. These types of articles are published often in newspapers, magazines, and newsletters. They are also beginning to appear in features in online formats. This approach to writing can be applied to every feature subject you care to mention, yet the approach is best suited for specific subjects and types of articles. This chapter discusses these approaches and outlines the best ways to use the technique in writing features. This type of writing requires great concentration and highly tuned observational skills on your part. An alert writer will notice the colors, odors, the noise, and other elements of a setting and put the reader in the middle of the action by describing these in depth. You accomplish this by using precise adjectives and adverbs, as well as exact nouns and verbs to convey that right image.

Writers achieve descriptive effects in their articles in a variety of ways with a wide range of writing tools. Some like to focus on their observations and use adjectives, and lots of them, throughout their writing. Others work hard to find the right nouns (for example, *dirge* instead of *song*). This requires a superior command of the English language. Using a broad vocabulary is not enough.

This type of writing also requires timing—you must be able to determine when to go heavily into description and when to back away from the temptation. Some like to let the story be told by the well-chosen words of others in direct quotations.

The primary rule is simple. When you think description helps a story, make certain what you are writing about is distinctive. The description and color should have a purpose. If you can find unique characteristics instead of the ordinary, then the additional color, or atmosphere, you add to a story through detailed descriptive writing usually works. Certainly, the way you write also makes a difference. Choosing words and putting them together also affects the impact description has on your readers. Organization, or order, of the information has a similar impact.

Jack Hart (1990a), an editor and writing coach at *The Oregonian* in Portland, feels description and color add spice to writing. He wrote the following:

> Ordinarily, descriptive color or interesting details brighten news writing, helping draw readers into stories by sparking vivid images in their minds. When used skillfully, such details help motivate readers to make the paper part of their daily routine. But color, like everything else in a story, should serve some larger purpose. Well-chosen details may help to create a mood important to the story. They may serve as evidence for a generalization. Maybe they reveal something about the personality of a key character. Or they introduce an object that will be important to an action line. (p. 3)

## CREATING IMAGES IN THE MIND

As Hart (1990a) noted, detail and color must do something for a feature article when a writer uses them. Ultimately, they should advance the story or contribute to the main theme, he said. A good feature article is enhanced with strong artwork such as photographs or drawings when the artwork and story come together as a unit on the page. Yet, you often have to write as if there is no art with the story; you must write to allow your readers to create images in their minds from reading your article. It does not take much to illustrate this point. Pick up most magazines and you will find at least one article rich in description and detail that give a certain color or atmosphere to the article.

Michael Vitez is a columnist and former reporter for *The Philadelphia Inquirer*. He has worked for newspapers in Virginia, the District of Columbia, and Connecticut before arriving in Philadelphia in 1985. He specializes in general assignment feature writing, which means he writes about a wide range of subjects and people. In recent years, he has specialized in writing about aging, but he has said that his favorite aspect of journalism is storytelling. In the late fall of 1996, Vitez wrote a five-part series of feature stories about terminally ill individuals who seek to die with dignity. With him, photographers April Saul and Ron Cortes documented the stories that were told and the individuals involved in them.

The series was titled "Seeking a Good Death." The first story in the series described the agony of families trying to determine when to let a loved one die. The second story described how families say good-bye to a loved one who is terminally ill. The third story examined the longer lives people live today, but also related longer lives to the longer decline in health experienced by some older persons. Vitez's fourth story looked at issues related to the decision about when to die and whether doctors should help. His fifth story in the set profiled a "long-lived" winner at the end of her life. The set of stories earned the three individuals a 1997 Pulitzer Prize for their abilities in explanatory journalism. "I try to celebrate ordinary people around us by showing how ordinary people sometimes do extraordinary things," Vitez (1998) said. The first story in the series opened this way:

> Patricia Moore read a poem to her husband in the intensive-care unit. She stood beside him wearing a surgical gown, holding the dog-eared book in her latex gloves.
>
> Through her surgical mask came the tender, muffled words of "Knee-deep in June," by James Whitcomb Riley:
> Orchard's where I'd ruther be—
> Needn't fence it in fer me!
> Gene Moore lay before her, unconscious. An IV line entered a vein in his neck and ran through his heart, into the pulmonary artery. It measured blood flow and carried five medicines into his infected body.
>
> A ventilator tube ran like a garden hose down his throat. A feeding tube pushed through his nose and into his stomach.
>
> Bags on his legs inflated and deflated every few minutes to prevent clotting. A catheter drained urine from his bladder. He wore orthotic boots to keep his feet bent so that, should he ever, miraculously, get out of bed, this retired 63-year-old steelworker would be able to stand.
>
> Mrs. Moore stood beside her husband of 44 years, her heart aching with indecision.
>
> Were she and her two sons doing the right thing putting him through this torture? Or should they stop?
>
> Should they tell the doctors to let him die? (Vitez, 1996, p. 1A)

Vitez's story continued with a discussion of the main issue: U.S. medicine is now so effective at keeping people alive that uncounted numbers of life or death decisions are made each year by the patients and their families. "They want control at the end. They want a humane death, a good death," Vitez (1996, p. 1A) wrote, defining the theme of the series. Writing with a feel for the sensitivities of strangers such as was done in the "Seeking a Good Death" series can be achieved by using honed observation, interviewing, and information collating skills. This means using one's senses, in other words, and it does not come automatically to feature writers. It takes considerable effort and experience to write well to convey color and atmosphere in a story, any story. You have to get out and look around. Pay attention to detail. People have to be persuaded to talk, to open up.

Clearly one goal is to provide information to readers through the description and color in feature articles. In this way, color and description do something significant for the article. They are not padding or simply there to impress editors. A contribution of value to the entire piece occurs in the lead to Vitez's article because it sets a scene. It might seem to be stating the obvious, but to get the detail and description needed, writers have to get out of the office. This sort of information can hardly be gathered by telephone. To do it effectively, leave the office. Leave home. Leave town if possible. Writers need to get to the location of people and events to get the right stimulation for this level of detail and description.

Journalist, author, and documentary filmmaker Bill Belleville also used powerful description to take readers with him deep into the waters of a 120-foot deep limestone spring. Writing for the quarterly Florida Humanities Council magazine, *Forum,* Belleville guided readers on a personalized underwater tour where most cannot go on their own:

> I am somewhere inside the vortex of Blue Springs, way past the "Prevent Your Death: Go No Further" sign at 60 feet, and far beyond the muted glow of surface light.
>
> The river that Blue feeds has been gradually warming, and the warm-blooded manatees that winter here have just left. Except for a few snorkelers back up in the shallow run, my dive buddy and I are alone in the spring.
>
> The only illumination down here is portable, hand-held. And like the trail of exhaust bubbles from my regulator, it tethers me to the surface with my own limitations. Scuba tanks, face masks, containers of light—they are all reminders of how unsuited we humans are to immerse ourselves in the most primal and universal element of all.
>
> Here, near the 120-foot-deep bottom of this limestone chasm, I am as aware as I have ever been of the pervasive power and magic of water. All but invisible, it arises from a slot in the rock, flailing me like a rag doll with its energy.
>
> If underground water is the veins and capillaries that sustain our Florida physiography, then I am squarely inside a natural incision, a place where the liquid transports itself to the surface, where science meets myth and culture head on. . . . (Belleville, 2002, p. 8)

Writers must also, as Rivers (1992) argued, make the effort of reading a rewarding experience. Some element of satisfaction should result for readers.

> Success [of your article] pivots almost entirely on whether readers finish a descriptive [article or passage] with the feeling that they have been through a satisfying reading experience. The most evocative descriptives—those fashioned by

writers who have developed and refined a talent for using visual words—are also *viewing* experiences. (Rivers, 1992, pp. 242–243)

Although they were written more than three decades ago, these two short passages from Tom Wolfe's now-classic article in *Esquire* about stock car driver Junior Johnson illustrate that point as they set the scene for the profile:

> Ten o'clock Sunday morning in the hills of North Carolina. Cars, miles of cars, in every direction, millions of cars, pastel cars, aqua green, aqua blue, aqua beige, aqua buff, aqua dawn, aqua dusk, aqua Malacca, Malacca lacquer, Cloud lavender, Assassin pink, Rake-a-Cheek raspberry, Nude Strand coral, Honest Thrill orange, and Baby Fawn Lust cream-colored cars are all going to the stock car races, and that old mothering North Carolina sun keeps exploding off the windshields.
>
> Seventeen thousand people, me included, all of us driving out Route 421, out to the stock car races at the North Wilkesboro Speedway, 17,000 going out to a five-eighths-mile stock car track with a Coca-Cola sign out front. This is not to say there is no preaching and shouting in the South this morning. There is preaching and shouting. Any of us can turn on the old automobile transistor radio and get all we want. (Wolfe, 1966, pp. 105–106)

Not much further into the same article, a different but equally powerful image-provoking passage by Wolfe appears:

> And suddenly my car is stopped still on Sunday morning in the middle of the biggest traffic jam in the history of the world. It goes for ten miles in every direction from the North Wilkesboro Speedway. And right there it dawns on me that as far as this situation is concerned, anyway, all the conventional notions about the South are confined to—the Sunday radio. The South has preaching and shouting, the South has grits, the South has country songs, old mimosa traditions, clay dust, Old Bigots, New Liberals—and all of it, all of that old mental cholesterol, is confined to the Sunday radio. What I was in the middle of—well, it wasn't anything one hears about in panels about the South today. Miles and miles of eye-busting pastel cars on the expressway, which roar right up into the hills, going to the stock car races. Fifteen years of stock car racing, and baseball—and the state of North Carolina alone used to have forty-four professional baseball teams—baseball is all over within the South. We are all in the middle of a wild new thing, the Southern car world, and heading down the road on my way to see a breed such as sports never saw before, Southern stock car drivers, all lined up in these two-ton mothers that go over 175 m.p.h. (Wolfe, 1966, p. 106)

Even if you know very little about the subject, Wolfe's methodical descriptive writing makes it seem as if you are there. After reading this, ask yourself why this article creates such vivid images in your mind. Is it the unusual colors (adjectives) he describes? Is it the emphasis on an action event (driving to the races) you are able to experience? Is it the writer's enthusiasm and excitement (emotions) for the subject? Or it could be the reconstruction of dialogue (direct quotes). In fact, it is probably a little of each of these factors that contributes to Wolfe's success. Wolfe often utilizes what he called the *four techniques of realism* in his writing. In a style that has been labeled *new journalism* by the writers and scholars studying it, these "new journalists" of the 1960s and 1970s often employed these basic steps that Wolfe (Gilder, 1981) described:

1. Scene-by-scene construction of events—Scene-by-scene construction is the most basic of organizational schemes and is different from narrative writing. It is a form of storytelling illustrated by Wolfe's (1966, p. 106) description of the drive on a Sunday morning to the stock car races.
2. Full record of dialogue in the scenes—Magazine writers, with the luxury of more space, can take advantage of this by using longer passages of exact dialogue from sources or between sources and the writer. In this way, however, sources nearly become characters as this type of writing edges toward the fiction form called a short story.
3. Third person point of view—Although this is the norm in most feature writing, this type of writing exhibited by Wolfe shows less involvement by the writer than a first-person point of view would offer.
4. Detailing of descriptive incidentals—Wolfe (Gilder, 1981) calls this sort of writing technique a "social autopsy," the attention the writer pays to minute details of the source's life in characterizing the person.

Whenever you try to create images in your reader's mind, remember you cannot drift from reality. In writing nonfiction, there must still be some information value to the article. You should always ask yourself, "What is the news hook or news peg of the story?" Its focus and current value must be clear to you and to your reader.

## DESCRIPTIVE WRITING AND INTERVIEWING

There will be times when you are assigned to conduct an interview as a basis for an article and find that the piece needs enrichment through description. This makes your challenge as a writer even tougher because you must not only concentrate on the interview by listening to your source's answers, but you must also be concerned with noting details before, during, and after the interview. For example, you should be concerned with your source's body language, or your source's physical responses to your questions, in addition to what the source says. Watch for facial expressions, shifts in seating position, gestures, and other mannerisms. Listen carefully for intonations and other characteristics of speaking.

You can employ techniques of detailed and descriptive writing to set a single impression of an interview for your reader. Often, as you have probably noted, this is not necessarily objective. For magazine writers in particular, this is possible. Many newspapers will permit such "writer's license" in certain types of features such as columns, analyses and interpretive articles, and Sunday magazine features. Remember, however, you still remain objective in your writing by being fair and careful about what you observe. When done well, this becomes an asset for the writer and for the article.

Regardless of the sort of story you are writing, use of description must be built on careful word selection. Remember that you will be serving as the eyes, ears, and other sense organs for your readers. During your interview, take advantage of interruptions to notice things about the room. What is on the desk? How is the room decorated? What objects are on the walls? How is the person you are interviewing dressed? How is his or her hair cut? What sort of food is being served? What color are the interviewee's eyes? Look for characteristics no matter how minute they seem. Look for subtle things such as brand names and positioning of furniture. What do they tell you about your source?

Also remember that you are not the brains of your readers. Leave the conclusions about what you have observed to your readers. You are better off not making judgments about what you describe. Personal conclusions and interpretations are most often not used in newspaper features and many times not desired in magazine article writing unless you are a qualified expert on a subject and can make such comments with authority. Novelist and former *New York Times* syndicated columnist and feature writer Anna Quindlen (1984) said, when covering an event for an atmosphere piece, she writes down everything she sees. "I take down quotes, names on signs and all those things. Just in case it might fit in. And I don't want to trust my memory. Sometimes you remember something red and it's really pink or blue" (n.p.).

## USING THE RIGHT SUPPORTING CAST

As a writer, words are your supporting cast. Like a play or a film, you need the right ones for the right script. You have two basic strategies to writing when it comes to word selection and usage: writing with general, ambiguous words and writing with specific, clear words. Consider, for a moment, the value of the right nouns and verbs and their grammatical assistants, adjectives and adverbs. What exactly are their roles in your script?

Adjectives and adverbs convey distinct impressions. Adjectives express qualities of the nouns they modify. Adjectives can be descriptive, proper (similar to proper nouns), and they can be restrictive. These words tell us more about the noun. Adverbs do much the same thing, except they can also modify adjectives in addition to expressing time, place, manner, degree, or cause. Adverbs limit,

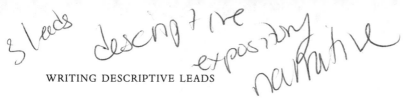

or further define and describe, the verbs with which they are used. In descriptive or color writing, this is perhaps the most important category of words feature writers can use. "Strong modifiers also evoke strong images," Hart (1990d, p. 1), writing coach for *The Oregonian* in Portland, reminded us. "Writers who consistently pick winners look for specific adjectives and adverbs" (Hart, 1990d, p. 1).

Writers most often use verbs to connote movement, action, or an assertion. Verbs are necessary in sentences, performing the expression of action, existence, and occurrence. A writer who does not vary verb usage, or sticks to the same dull verbs all the time, will take much of the life out of the writing. "Our audience naturally focuses on action," Hart (1990c, p. 1) noted. "Journalists sell information about action. And when they lose sight of that simple truth, they lose readers" (Hart, 1990c, p. 1).

Nouns, of course, describe something substantive such as things, concepts, people, places, and objects. There are common nouns, such as generic words (automobile), but writers also use proper nouns (Lexus or Mustang). Abstract nouns describe ideas and qualities (love or loving) and concrete nouns are more definitive objects (bird or sidewalk). Collective nouns describe groups (faculty) whereas mass nouns describe things not usually counted (sand). Take a look at these examples of general and ambiguous usages:

1. *The* small television *was powered by* batteries.
2. *The* community *doesn't have any* pets *like that* cat.

Take a look at these examples of specific and more meaningful usages:

1. Four AAA-sized nickel cadmium *batteries powered the* two-inch black-and-white Panasonic television.
2. *The* secluded cul de sac *doesn't have any* Maine coon cats *like* Felix.

The goal is to emphasize prevailing characteristics of the subject about which you are writing, and, at the same time, convey excitement or other emotions.

## WRITING DESCRIPTIVE LEADS

Descriptive features that convey the color of an event have the important duty of helping to balance the content of a publication. Of the three major types of magazine leads—descriptive, expository, and narrative—only the descriptive lead draws the reader into the article by painting pictures at the outset. The idea of giving features special descriptive content and attention to detail and color is, of course, not a new one. Neither is giving the lead of a story a particularly heavy dose of description as a device to interest readers in the subject a new device of writers.

In fact, University of Wisconsin Professor Willard Bleyer (1913), in his textbook about journalistic writing that was published almost a century ago, said description in the lead of an article is crucial to the success of feature stories.

> A vivid bit of description is sometimes used to advantage at the beginning. If, instead of merely describing and explaining a mechanical process, the writer portrays men actually performing the work involved in the process, he adds greatly to the interest of the article. The effectiveness of an explanation of a new surgical operation can be increased to a marked degree by picturing a surgeon as he performs the operation. (p. 229)

*Chicago* magazine writer Lisa Bertagnoli used a highly descriptive approach in her lead of a sketch about successful divorce lawyer Corri Fetman. She used adjectives and detailed nouns to paint a picture of the attorney. Here's how she began her story:

> When Corri Fetman strides into court, heads turn and mouths drop. Her four-inch heels, patterned stockings, close-fitting suits, and tangle of blonde hair seem the trappings of an *Ally McBe*al extra, not a hard-driving divorce attorney.
> But that's exactly what Fetman is. In her 14 years of practice, she's become known as one of the most aggressive attorneys in a field filled with nothing but. "She allegedly is aggressive; some would say obnoxiously so," says divorce attorney Herbert Glieberman.
> Apparently, that's just what men want. Fetman's aggressiveness has garnered her all-female firm, Chicago Women at Law, Ltd., a client base that is 70 percent male. Fetman herself carries a reputation for being a tough-as-red-lacquered-nails lawyer who poses a formidable challenge in the courtroom. . . . (Bertagnoli, 2002, p. 28)

Tim Clutton-Brock (2002), a freelance writer and professor of animal ecology at the University of Cambridge, used his expertise as a foundation to build the cover-featured article about small mammals known as meerkats for *National Geographic* magazine. Traveling to the Kalahari in South Africa, where the animals live, he wrote a highly descriptive feature for the magazine. He used descriptive language in his lead:

> In the slanting, golden light of a Kalahari evening, Juma, a young male meerkat, stares across the sandy bed of the Nossob River: nothing but the shimmer of hot air and the evening chorus of barking geckos. Six pups, their eyes only recently open, nuzzle at his stomach, hoping to find milk. Juma has been watching over them since dawn, ignoring his own hunger as he scans the sky for eagles and the ridgeline for jackals, snakes, yellow mongooses, and even neighboring meerkats, which would kill the pups if they found their burrow unguarded.

In a large meerkat group, which can have as many as 40 members, six-month old Juma would be too young to baby-sit. But there are only five adults in his small group, so he must take his turn guarding the pups. . . . (Clutton-Brock, 2002, p. 68)

As Clutton-Brock did in his lead, your goal may be to capture the drama, the excitement, and overall emotion of an event and share the experience with readers. Even with a color photograph of a meerkat and two pups on the opposing page, a strong descriptive lead, such as Clutton-Brock uses, grabs the interested reader, explains what is happening, and does not let go. The two elements, artwork and a strong lead, should work together to create the right feel for the article's treatment of the subject.

Myrick Land (1993) said there are numerous options for leads that can employ description and detail. Land listed the anecdote, the narrative series of examples, the first person, the straightforward statement, the surprising statement, the surprising quote, the question, the "you" or direct address, the quotation, the single example, the opinion statement, and the general descriptive leads. Regardless of the type of lead, he said, it should "emerge naturally from the research on your article. An effective lead can be written only if you have shown imagination in selecting a subject, have focused sharply on one aspect of that topic, have been thorough in gathering background information, and have conducted enough well-planned interviews" (p. 85).

Former *New York Times* staff writer Rick Bragg (1998) used detail in an effective manner in his feature stories about the American South. The Pulitzer Prize-winning writer captured the essence of an event or an individual through his insightful observations and his ability to turn those observations into words. He attended the funeral of former Alabama Gov. George Wallace and conveyed the mood and atmosphere in his lead:

The coffin, draped in the blood-red "X" on pure white that is Alabama's state flag, seemed almost too heavy to carry. Eight young, strong-looking Alabama state troopers bore the coffin foot by foot down the massive marble steps of the state Capitol, some of them having to place two hands on the rails of the coffin to steady it between them.

It was not the weight of it—George Wallace was just a small man, withered even more by paralysis and age—but the distance. They carried him some 100 steps. From the rotunda where thousands had viewed his body, down the steep walkway from the Capitol he had once used as a war room to preserve segregation, and off into history. It was eerily quiet, just footsteps on stone.

Just minutes before the troopers carried him off to his funeral and burial in Montgomery, Janel Bell, a 32-year-old black woman, gazed down at the man who had once been shorthand for racism in America, and then, after begging for forgiveness, had won the black vote in his final campaign for governor.

"A servant of the people," Bell said. (p. A20)

## SIX GUIDELINES FOR DESCRIPTIVE WRITING

Journalist Daniel Williamson (1975) suggested six guidelines for descriptive feature writing:

1. Remember that you are, in effect, the eyes, ears, and nose of your readers—Your job is to gather an assortment of material that the readers can analyze and assimilate into an image. In this role, always be aware of any characteristic, however subtle, that would aid readers in coming up with an accurate image.
2. Don't allow your presence as a reporter to influence the subject—Try to blend with the woodwork so that you can observe the subject in a natural state. When it's necessary to conduct an interview, try to put the subject at ease so that he will act more naturally.
3. Gather an abundance of notes—much more than you can use—Then, before writing, sift through your notes to determine which observations most effectively capture the whole subject.
4. In writing, spread description throughout the story—Large "clumps" of description may get in the way of reader flow.
5. A fine line exists between the presence of too much description and the absence of enough description—That fine line is the feature writer's target. If the story is tedious with descriptive detail, chop less important details. If the story doesn't succeed in allowing you to "see" the subject, add more description.
6. Although a writer should, indeed, act as the ears, eyes, and nose for his readers, he should never try to assume the role of their brain by inserting his personal conclusions and interpretations—Often, such conclusion is only a lazy shortcut for good descriptive writing.

Readers thrive on details, especially when the writer is focusing on something unfamiliar to most readers. An article that starts with richness in detail and imagery wins readers from the first sentence to the last. If you do not buy this, just take a look at a piece of fiction on the current bestseller list. Or read a short story by a well-known writer. Good nonfiction writers use this technique as well.

## ADDING COLOR TO WRITING

Color stories are important feature forms. These stories are often used to provide readers with the most descriptive aspects of a news event or other activity. Newspapers use color stories as sidebars to help explain a major news story by providing atmosphere or mood—happy or sad, warm or cold, exciting or dull—for those who could not be there.

Frequently, color stories in newspapers are used with the major news of the day—tragedies such as airline crashes or car accidents or joyful moments such as a papal visit or the opening of a new public facility. Color stories are used to relate the mood of crowds at events such as football games, festivals, parties and other celebrations, parades, concerts, funerals, and memorial services. For example, at a major college football game or the opening day of baseball season, a color story angle might be the activities and reactions of a group of fans that followed the home team on the road several hundred miles to see the big game. It might focus on the team on the sidelines or in the dugout during the game. It might focus on celebrities in the press box or elsewhere in the stadium. It might reflect the party-like atmosphere before the game in the parking lot at the tailgate or tent parties of alumni, season-ticket holders, and other fans. It can focus on the reaction of a single person who might be pivotal to the major story of that day.

Ron Thibodeaux (2001), staff writer for the New Orleans *Times–Picayune*, provided his newspaper's readers with a glimpse into small-town life with a feature story about a supper club in the tiny rural Louisiana town of Chataignier. Here's how used descriptive details and color in combination with the words of the people involved to tell the story of a supper club's role in the town's social life:

CHATAIGNIER —There's never been a bowling alley in this town of 383 people. There used to be a movie theater, with metal folding chairs, but it shut down a long time ago. And one by one, the four bars closed their doors.

So what's a group of buddies to do on boys' night out? In this corner of the rural Cajun prairie, they have supper.

Every Thursday night, Fuzzy, Ironhead, Pinky, T-Don and the other members in good standing with the Chataignier Supper Club gather in the old shed in Darren D'Aubin's yard and kick back.

"There's no more place for us to socialize, there's no more little bars or nothing left around here, so once a week we get together and cook," said Kevin "Ironhead" Richard, 39.

"What's better than good food and good company, you know?" added Pat Duplechain, 54. "There's 16 of us. You eat 15 weeks for free, and the 16th week you furnish a meal for the other 15 people."

Gathering for a meal with friends as a social event is a very Evangeline Parish thing to do, from Ville Platte to the smallest farming communities. Men do it, women do it—even teen-agers, although not as frequently.

A typical menu includes a main course such as deer, duck, crawfish or barbecues, plus salad and dessert. There are few secret recipes in the supper clubs, because most members are none too shy about what makes their recipes the best around.

And usually, it's just called supper. The Chataignier Supper Club trots out its formal name only on those weekends when it enters cooking contests at area festivals for fun and bragging rights.

The guys start showing up after work, each carrying his own beverages in a small ice chest. While one does the cooking, the others sit around on the porch or in the clubhouse where their festival cooking trophies are displayed. They catch up on one anothers' news and swap jokes and stories while knocking back a cold beer or two until the meal is ready. The only ground rules: No religion and no politics.

On one recent Thursday night as D'Aubin kept a pot of crawfish etouffee simmering on the gas stove, the talk ranged from snakes and skunks to the Persian Gulf War to the traffic problems on U.S. 190 to Eunice High School football.

The conversation reflects working men's sensibilities and longtime friends' camaraderie. Roy Fontenot has been with the phone company for 29 years. Don Thibodeaux is a welder. Duplechain is a heating and air conditioning maintenance worker. Fuzzy Quinilty is a farmer and crop duster, as well as an accomplished accordion player. Many of these men, in their late 40s or 50s have lived here all their lives and known one another since their school days.

D'Aubin, a real estate appraiser, is one of the newcomers. A Harahan native, he earned entry when he married Quinilty's daughter.

The group's clubhouse is known to old-timers around Chataignier (*pronounced "shuh–TAN–yuh") as the former cotton gin office from the 1940s and '50s. The men started having supper at Thibodeaux's home in the mid-1980s— until he got married. They bounced from place to place until the D'Aubins bought 13 acres "in the country" abut five years ago. The outbuilding on the property proved to be the perfect meeting place for the weekly supper.

Well, almost perfect.

"It was an old falling-down shed," Duplechain said. "It had trees practically growing through it. Everybody worked together to clean it up. Then somebody brought in an old stove, somebody had an air conditioner, others brought furniture. We got it fixed up pretty nice."

Then there was the matter of the bee hive in the ceiling.

"We treated it. We tried smoking them out," Duplechain said. "I don't know what finally ran them off.

Fontenot remembered. "It was the smell of those burning onions!" he said. (Thibodeaux, 2001)

Rarely does a color story focus on the results of the game or even the principal action of the game. That is likely the purpose of another story by the same reporter or, as preferred by most editors, by a second or even a third reporter. In short, the idea behind this sort of writing is to permit the reader who did not attend to share the event with the writer and others who were there. Color stories take advantage of certain types of sources of information. Color stories almost always have people, your perceptions as an observer, your observations, and a common thread.

These are often reaction stories, but the reaction is often that of the writer. Professor Louis Alexander (1975) said these types of stories are usually written with a point of view or a focus that directs the article. What are you trying to say about the subject? What storyline, or other literary device, are you using? How can you arrange the information to give the event some of the atmosphere it needs? Alexander added that when you successfully answer these questions, you have done your job well. He said

> Overall, because you have all the colors in it [the article] you give the reader a much stronger, more meaningful, more colorful picture—the blacks and the whites, the grays, the blues and peppermint stripes and everything else. You accomplish this by planning your story to make one major point or leave one message and by selecting a story line on which to hang or arrange your materials. (pp. 58–59)

Quintin Ellison, a staff writer for the *Citizen–Times* in Asheville, NC, went outdoors for his descriptive lead to an arts and crafts fair color feature:

> SAPPHIRE—Eleina Butuna of Papua, New Guinea, wandered from booth to booth Sunday afternoon at an arts and crafts fair in southern Jackson County, admiring local artisans' work and enjoying a beautiful autumn day.
>
> While her country is also mountainous, it is hot and dry. Butuna pronounced the tapestry of colors in Western North Carolina—yellows, reds and burnished browns matched as perfectly as any of the quiltmakers' meticulous pieces at the fair in Sapphire—as simply spectacular.
>
> "This is a new experience for me," she said. "I've never seen anything like this."
>
> Most longtime fall foliage observers have described WNC's annual show as quite good this year. More impressive than the color, however, has been the number of visitors. . . . (Ellison, 2001, p. 1A)

Writer John F. Ross (2002), writing for *Smithsonian* magazine, incorporated detail and color into his description of illegally captured and sold animals in Indonesia. Note the description as he recreates the scene—you can almost feel the intense heat and humidity overlaying the chaos of the open-air animal market—in the crowded setting in Jakarta:

> The heat of the tropical sun and the smell of sweating bodies pervade the outdoor Jakarta animal market. Amid a cacophony of parrot chatter, the screams of monkeys and the barking of dogs, Willie Smits, dressed to look like a British oilman, and photographer Viviane Moos elbow their way through the crowd. Smits, a tall man with a demeanor and paunch of a person who doesn't ordinarily care about appearances, calls out in Indonesian, asking if anyone has orangutans for sale. The sea of people parts and a man appears with a red, furry baby orangutan clinging to his waist. It has large black eyes set in a heart-stopping, moon-shaped face.
>
> But then events spin out of control. "It's him," shouts one of the men in the crowd, recognizing Smits. As head of the largest orangutan rescue organization in the world, Smits is hated and feared by people who trade in orangutans and other exotic animals. Although it's illegal to own one of these orangy-red apes on the Southeast Asia islands of Borneo and Sumatra (their last natural refuges) and in many other places, trade in the primate is brisk. An orangutan baby's adorable

looks and similarities to a human infant make them irresistible pets. . . . (Ross, 2002, p. 62)

These stories by Thibodeaux, Ellison, and Ross underline the importance of description in setting scenes and elaborating details for readers. The goal is to allow readers to picture the Louisiana supper club gathering to enjoy a meal or to imagine walking with the animal rescue organization leader into a potentially risky situation in the animal market in Jakarta. The selection of words and scenes must be continuously useful to the reader, or interesting, or both, however. William Rivers (1992) emphasized the following: "One sentence should grow out of another; one paragraph should grow out of another. The middle and end should be as interesting as the beginning. Although a color story has no standard structure, the 'hard news' should usually be somewhere near the beginning" (p. 249). In writing to use color as a tool in your article, several guidelines on detailed content were offered by Patterson (1986):

1. Don't summarize scenes, dialogue, or action. Recreate them.
2. Be specific and avoid vagueness.
3. Show, don't tell. Let the reader see something.
4. Identify the characters and sources completely when they are introduced.
5. Describe the characters and sources in your article.
6. Include important detail to let reader see, but do not show the reader irrelevant objects or insignificant details. These mislead and provide clutter.

Patterson said the following:

There are elements that may be added to a story to make it more interesting, more significant, more memorable: plot (or story line), suspense, conflict, change (whereby one or more characters undergoes a change in understanding, attitude, condition, etc.), and climax. When they are a part of reality, a feature writer should put them into a piece. If they are not a part of the reality, there is no way they can be included. To do so would turn fact into fiction. (p. 20)

You can often take what Patterson said about detailed content and apply it to a major event to enliven it for readers. Quindlen (1984) has a tested and proven successful strategy she uses in writing features. The approach works to portray events, such as the Feast of St. Anthony on Sullivan Street in Manhattan, which she once covered as a feature writer. When she wrote features for *The New York Times'* "About New York" column, she loved to cover such a "quintessential New York event." Quindlen explained the following: "In something like this, where I'm basically going to take the reader and put him on this street, on this day, on this beat, my problem more than anything else is figuring out how to organize and then pick and choose the telling details that are really going to make him feel like he was here with me" (n.p.). She likened covering such an event to painting a picture—she is an artist with words:

If you try to hold up a mirror to an event, if you paint it in broad strokes, you're going to miss on colors, you're going to miss on sights, you're going to miss on all kinds of things. I think if you're going to hold up a mirror and do the painting, the best thing to do is pointillism—a whole bunch of little points. When the reader steps back and looks at it, when they're done, they're not going to see the little points, they're going to see a whole big picture. (Quindlen, 1984, n.p.)

Color writing is a very personal style of writing, Quindlen explained. Each person will gain a different perspective on the same event and will probably write a different story. "Everybody faced with the same event will give you a different viewpoint, a different answer, a different set of people" (Quindlen, 1984, n.p.). And, she added, you have to have confidence in yourself as a writer to write about your own perceptions and reactions to a given situation. "It's the self-confidence that comes from self-confidence in your personality and not so much your skills. I'm just different. I have different perceptions" (Quindlen, 1984, n.p.).

## CREATING MOODS

Good color writing will set a tone for the reader. You can manipulate moods by your choice of words, organizational approach to the information you have and, of course, the subject about which you are writing. Alexander (1975) said that if you can do well writing color, that is, creating a mood for the reader, the rewards are high for both the reader and writer: "When you get your story across, when you convey the color and drama that make other people feel it, you the feature writer gain genuine satisfaction" (p. 59).

---

### BEST SOURCES FOR DESCRIPTIVE AND COLOR WRITING

People and their opinions
Direct quotations
Dialogue
Your own observations
Actions
Environments
Your own perceptions
Your own attitudes and emotions
Your personal experiences
Personal experiences of others

---

As you move into other specific types of feature articles in the next chapters, you get ideas for application of the techniques of descriptive and color writing in these varieties of articles. For example, you see wide possibilities for descriptive writing on seasonal topics and on travel subjects. Some of these types of stories are easy to write and others do not lend themselves to descriptive writing approaches very readily. Writing with heavy emphasis on detail is a valuable tool for feature writers.

## COMING TO YOUR SENSES

Roy Sorrels (1986), a correspondent for *Writer's Digest* magazine and a novelist, offered this exercise for "sensuous writing"—that is, writing with your senses. Here's what he suggested:

> To make your own writing more sensuous, take a series of blind walks. Ask an understanding friend—another writer maybe—to help. Close your eyes and let your companion guide you gently through a few environments. Down a city street, perhaps, past the busy schoolyard, into the park. At first, you will be a bit nervous with your vision cut off, but relax and you'll become more and more aware of all the rich input from your other four senses. Relax into the sounds; notice the surface under your feet—gritty sidewalks, cobblestones, dirt in the park, lush or scraggly grass. Smell the world—can you tell when you pass by the bakery or the fishmonger? With your friend's guidance, touch things in the park—grass, tree trunks, or a worn park bench. Of course, you can do this on your own, just closing your eyes for a few minutes sitting at a sidewalk cafe, or on a bus, or lounging under a tree. (p. 40)

Jonathan Glancey (2002), who used the reactions of his senses in describing a new museum that opened in London for *The Guardian* newspaper, wrote this passage in his feature about the new National Maritime Museum Cornwall in Falmouth:

> The picturesque new building should appeal to both the saltiest old architecture dog as well as the modern-minded: it is a subtle fusion of old materials—oak, slate and granite—and new forms and functions. It reminds me of the Museum of River and Rowing on the Thames at Henley designed by David Chipperfield Architects. It is a decidedly modern building, but one capped with great pitched timber roofs that recall boatyards, boathouses and the traditional construction techniques.
>
> Inside, the collections are displayed under varying conditions of light, both natural and artificial. This ever changing play of light is likely to prove to be one of the new building's most endearing features. There are two main galleries inside the lofty building, one dark, one awash with daylight, and both a haven for old boats roped in from around the world.
>
> The introductory gallery is a black box. The boats on display here are connected to interactive audio–visual links that explain what the boats are, how they

were built, what they did and the conditions under which they sailed. The museum will explain tides and weather as well as the ways of the boats themselves.

The black-box gallery can be transformed into a number of dramatic and intelligently themed experiences at the touch of a button: a storm at sea, a regatta or an estuary smothered in deep fog. Done well, such simulated spatial and sensual experiences really help those who have never put out to sea to understand why boats are designed as they are—to deal with the extraordinary range of conditions they encounter away from the sanctuary of Cornish harbours. Done badly they are best confined to the depths of Davey Jones's locker.

The daylit gallery is hung, rather like the way in which aircraft are from the curved concrete vault of Foster and Partners distinguished American Air Force Museum at Duxford: boats dangle from a waved-like wall lit from above with north light. They range from an old oak Fenland punt, used for collecting reeds and catching eels until the late 1940s, through an 1880s Cornish salmon boat and exotic canoes from Sri Lanka, Canada and the Gilbert Islands, to Waterlily, an early steam launch built in 1866 at Chiswick by John Thornycroft, early racing yachts like the Clyde-built "Fricka" of 1896, and most importantly, perhaps, to Mirror Dinghy 1, a plastic sailing boat from 1963. (p. 12)

Using his senses in a similar manner to create atmosphere of a busy art trading center, United Press International writer Frederick M. Winship (2002) concluded his feature about a wholesale African art market in a storage facility in the middle of Manhattan in New York City:

Some of these more valuable objects may be looted art—stolen from museums and universities or illegally excavated from burial sites, but no one at Chelsea Mini-Storage is asking about provenance, the source or origin of a work of art.

A visit to the African art center toward the rear of the building is a heady sensual experience. The scent of burning stick incense and the smell of exotic foods prepared and sold to traders by female cooks in a backroom kitchen pervade the area, as does the sound of many tribal dialects mixed with French patois and the murmur of Muslim dealers at prayer in a carpeted space reserved for worship.

The stalls, their steel doors pushed out of sight, are bulging with hundreds of wood sculptured gods, goddesses, sacred animals and demons, ritual pouches and food containers, a grand array of human and animal masks, drums and stringed instruments, and a wide variety of textiles. Traders say some of the best things come from poor, remote villages where barter in needed goods is preferred to cash.

"Good trading is built on trust and friendship," a Gambian trader told UPI. "This is more important to many Africans than money."

## ENHANCING WRITING WITH FIGURATIVE LANGUAGE

Many writers who leave lasting images in the minds of their readers know how to use figurative language in an effective manner. Simply put, figurative language is a device that helps readers understand your meaning. Commonly, journalists use concrete words and their modifiers for precision in meaning. Experienced writers also know when to use the two of these forms known as metaphors and similes. Writers often also use allusions and personifications. These are not, of course, the exclusive turfs of fiction writers such as classic poets or short story writers.

Metaphors and similes create impressions in readers by comparing things that are usually not associated. "Combine two previously isolated categories and something mysterious happens. Synapses sizzle. New connections appear. Synergy fashions a new form greater than the sum of the parts," explained *Portland Oregonian* writing coach Jack Hart (1989, p. 1).

Metaphors describe something in terms of something else. They imply comparisons. Similes are more direct comparisons, commonly identified by use of *like* or *as*. The allusion is simply an indirect reference. This occurs most often by using some sort of reference commonly known by writer and readers. Personifications give objects human characteristics.

Tools such as metaphors enhance written communication, but this touch by the writer makes the story more interesting and more appealing to the average reader. As Hart (1989, p. 1) explained, you are not only serving readers when you use figurative language, you are serving yourself. For most writers, such writing is a welcome diversion from the routine. And this might help you remain interested in the art and craft of writing.

Madeleine Blais, a journalism professor at the University of Massachusetts at Amherst, won the Pulitzer Prize for feature writing in 1980 while working as a staff writer for Tropic Magazine, the recently closed Sunday supplement of *The Miami Herald*. She strongly believes in the value of detail, description, and color in feature material. She explained the following (personal communication, October 1, 1988):

> Detail and color in a piece of journalism should work ideally in the same way they function in poetry or in fiction. They should function metaphorically or they should help create a mood. They should contribute to a sense of momentum, not clutter. In the kind of journalism which is only interested in record-keeping, details and color are often used to telegraph the fact that the reporter was an actual witness. In this approach, quotations are also used to prove the presence of the reporter. Thus, quotations are often included that contain little or no information and contribute not a whit to the overall design. Such pieces peter out rather than build and that is why cutting from the bottom makes sense.
>
> Journalism that attempts to be literary narrows the gap between writing that only entertains and writing that only informs. How can you train yourself to know what details to include? First, keep up with your reading of literature. Second, when you are out on a story, use all your senses, not just your ears. I remember once interviewing a woman who wanted more than anything else to rid herself of a bad situation. She kept saying as much, over and over, as she stood in her kitchen, but nothing she said spoke to her pain as insistently and clearly as the

way in which she kept sponging and sponging an already immaculate kitchen counter.

I once wrote a story about a woman who is schizophrenic. It is one thing to say that she lives in a disordered world, another to say: "Two years after Trish's mother died, she wrote her a letter, asking for cigarettes."

Once I wrote a short piece entitled "Monica's Barrel" about a woman who had immigrated from Jamaica and who periodically sent home barrels, big cardboard cylinders with tops made of tin, to the people she had left behind. At first I was going to write that if she had stayed home she would be poor. Upon prodding from my editor I wrote: "In Jamaica Monica's brightest prospect would be a job at the bra and underwear factory making $50 a week in an economy where $5 buys a pound of rice."

Another time I wanted to convey the sense of a beach resort as the epitome of safe haven: "We spend all winter telling the children never to say hello to strangers, yet here the stranger is likely to be a woman with gray hair wearing a belt with whales who happens to be circulating a petition to save St. Joseph's parsonage from being sold to developers."

When in doubt, turn to Strunk and White's *The Elements of Style* before embarking on an important piece: read it, re-read it, memorize and then proceed. (Blais, personal communication, October 1, 1988)

# CHAPTER SEVEN

# The Human-Interest Article

Rick Bragg has established himself as one of American journalism's premier writers in the past decade. He writes about unique people, extraordinary events, natural and man-made disasters, and social conditions and problems. Bragg, who resigned as domestic correspondent for *The New York Times* in 2003, formerly wrote for *Los Angeles Times* magazine and its metro desk. A native of Alabama, he wrote human interest features for his newspaper about the South with a passion and sense of the region that only a native can acquire. He was based in Atlanta, but traveled throughout the nation and the southeast for his newspaper to find the best features for an international audience. He took an issue or an event and wrote about it from the perspective that it became a story of national interest, not just a small town, rural, or regional matter. A group of five of his stories about a variety of people and places that portrayed Southern life in 1995 earned him the 1996 Pulitzer Prize for feature writing.

The package of features was as diverse as the region on which they were based. He wrote about the Oklahoma City federal building terror attack, aging prisoners in Alabama, Mardi Gras in New Orleans, and the man who caught the South Carolina mother who killed her two sons. One of his stories was about an elderly woman who left her life savings to her local university for a scholarship fund. It is a compelling story that collected national attention. His story began with this look at the woman and her modest life (Bragg, 1995a):

> HATTIESBURG, Miss., Aug. 10—Oseola McCarty spent a lifetime making other people look nice. Day after day, for most of her 87 years, she took in bundles of dirty clothes and made them clean and neat for parties she never attended, weddings to which she was never invited, graduations she never saw.
>
> She had quit school in the sixth grade to go to work, never married, never had children and never learned to drive because there was never any place in particular she wanted to go. All she ever had was the work, which she saw as a blessing. Too many other black people in rural Mississippi did not have even that.
>
> She spent almost nothing, living in her old family home, cutting the toes out of shoes if they did not fit right and binding her ragged Bible with Scotch tape to keep Corinthians from falling out. Over the decades, her pay—mostly dollar bills and change—grew to more than $150,000.
>
> "More than I could ever use," Miss McCarty said the other day without a trace

of self-pity. So she is giving her money away, to finance scholarships for black students at the University of Southern Mississippi here in her hometown, where tuition is $2,400 a year.

"I wanted to share my wealth with the children," said Miss McCarty, whose only real regret is that she never went back to school. "I never minded work, but I was always so busy, busy. Maybe I can make it so the children don't have to work like I did."

People in Hattiesburg call her donation the Gift. She made it, in part, in anticipation of her death.

In another feature article, Bragg wrote about the aging prison population in Alabama. How do prisons deal with retirement-age prisoners who are no longer a real threat to society and who have the typical medical problems of the elderly? His story points to the problem with a highly personal approach: He wrote about the men behind bars such as 77-year-old convicted murderer Grant Cooper, who was the focus of his lead (Bragg, 1995b):

HAMILTON, Ala.—Grant Cooper knows he lives in prison, but there are days when he cannot remember why. His crimes flit in and out of his memory like flies through a hole in a screen door, so that sometimes his mind and conscience are blank and clean.

He used to be a drinker and a drifter who had no control over his rage. In 1978, in an argument with a man in a bread line at the Forgotten Man Ministry in Birmingham, Ala., his hand automatically slid into his pants pocket for a knife.

He cut the man so quick and deep that he died before his body slipped to the floor. Mr. Cooper had killed before, in 1936 and in 1954, so the judge gave him life. Back then, before he needed help to go to the bathroom, Mr. Cooper was a dangerous man.

Now he is 77, and since his stroke in 1993 he mostly just lies in his narrow bunk at the Hamilton Prison for the Aged and Infirm, a blue blanket hiding the tubes that run out of his bony body. Sometimes the other inmates put him in a wheelchair and park him in the sun.

"I'm lost," he mumbled. "I'm just lost."

He is a relic of his violent past, but Mr. Cooper, and the special prison that holds him, may represent the future of corrections in a time when judges and other politicians are offering longer, "true-time" sentences, like life without parole, as a way to protect the public from crime.

This small 200-bed prison in the pine-shrouded hills of northwestern Alabama near the Mississippi line is one of only a few in the nation specializing in aged and disabled inmates, but that is expected to change as prison populations turn gradually gray.

While the proportion of older prisoners has risen only slightly in recent years, their numbers have jumped substantially. . . .

Just what is a human-interest article? Certainly Rick Bragg's two examples that are introduced in the passages above illustrate what these types of stories seek to accomplish. This human interest feature has several labels. Some publications just call it a human-interest narrative. Some label it a true-life drama. Former *McCall's* (later renamed *Rosie*) magazine managing editor Don McKinney (1986) says that regardless of what they are called, these articles are stories told by writers about people who have been involved in real dramas and these emotional stories are usually told in narrative form. These articles are quite popular with readers, research shows, and some publications try to balance their editorial content with these sorts of stories appearing with regularity. We see it in the story of the woman who left her entire life's savings to a university and in the elderly prisoners in Alabama.

## WHY WRITE ABOUT PEOPLE?

Names make news—still. This is the primary explanation if you wonder, "Why write about people?" People want to read about their neighbors and neighborhood businesses, especially when unusual events occur involving them. Articles about people, not institutions or other organizations, fill publications such as weekly newspapers and newsletters in small communities. Articles about people are being used more often in larger newspapers, too, to maintain readership. Local magazines can apply the same principle, but, of course, this becomes more difficult for national and general interest magazines. However, magazines that focus on personalities and human-interest, such as *People* or *Parade*, are quite successful in the marketplace.

A newspaper, magazine, newsletter, or online publication that is writing about people only in a personalities–celebrities page or even in the entertainment section is just not doing its job. Readers seek more people-oriented writing in their newspapers, magazines, and newsletters—in all sections and departments. And, it follows, these people should be local people, not just always the meaningless names of people who live a thousand miles away.

So, what makes people so interesting? Human-interest feature writing is sometimes a catchall phrase used in newsrooms and magazine offices to describe a story about people. Whatever the subject, these stories are interesting and popular with readers because they focus on people in unusual and odd situations. Just as all features tend to emphasize the unusual and odd, these articles do so in the most human fashion. People simply want to read about other people. Readers like to see how they "measure up" to others in similar situations. They enjoy seeing how others live, especially the celebrities, personalities, and leaders of our society. And as a human-interest writer, you can bring the lives of these people to your readers.

Human situations, problems, and their solutions are the most popular subjects of writers. Everyday occurrences translate into articles and even books partly because you, as a writer, also have that common experience. Your approaches and ideas often come from that base of experience you have had as a child and an adult, and these experiences, combined with your own values, make you a writer about people. For example, someone's personal mannerisms or other behaviors might spark a story idea. As you begin to write human-interest articles, you might have to depend on suggestions from others, but as you become experienced, these stories become easier to identify.

Lisa Pollak is an award-winning feature writer for *The Sun* in Baltimore. Her features focus on the human-interest dimension of life in Maryland. She writes about Maryland residents and their everyday lives. In 1996, she prepared a story about Major League Baseball umpire John Hirschbeck, his spouse Denise, and the serious health problems of their two sons, John and Michael. The story told about the deadly genetic disease, adrenoleukodystrophy, known as ALD, which both boys carried. The Hirschbecks' sons suffered because their bodies could not produce an enzyme that prevented damage to the brain caused by toxic fatty acids. The Hirschbecks, who were Ohio residents, found a Baltimore specialist who treated ALD.

Pollak learned of the family's troubles and approached the Hirschbecks about telling their story. They agreed, and she explained it all to *The Sun's* readers. She told a story about how the problem was discovered, the efforts to treat it, and the death of John. The story told about the continuing treatment of Michael. And it described the emotions and experiences of these individuals in exquisite, rich details. Here's how Pollak began her story of "The Umpire's Sons" (Pollak, 1996):

How do you survive the death of a child? How do you go on knowing another child shares the same genetic disease? When you've traveled John Hirschbeck's journey, being spit upon is just a footnote.

The boy loves games of chance. He loves slot machines and playing cards and instant-win lottery tickets. He learned at an early age to count coins, and to bet them. He learned in the hospital that money comes in get-well cards.

Michael Hirschbeck learned to play gin in the hospital, too. His father taught him, during the long weeks of waiting, between the chemotherapy and bone marrow transplant and seizures and pneumonia and days when he was too sick to even eat a cup of ice chips. He never asked a lot of questions, even the day his parents told him he had the same disease as his older brother, who was already dying, and that it would take his baby sister's bone marrow to save his life. He was five years old.

"If you want to cry, it's okay," John and Denise Hirschbeck told Michael, and he did, and so did they.

They didn't tell him he was only the 18th child with this disease to have a bone marrow transplant; or that his baby sister was a carrier of the disease; or that the doctors had anguished over whether the sister's tainted marrow would help him.

They didn't tell him it might be too late to save his brother.

That was 1992, the summer Michael learned to watch baseball on television like grown-ups do, patiently and for hours, while recovering from the transplant.

That was the fall he watched the World Series with his father, the American League umpire who stopped working when his sons got sick. People might think the worse thing that ever happened to John Hirschbeck was getting spit on by Orioles second baseman Roberto Alomar during a game last season. But it wasn't, not even close. When the worst thing happened to Hirschbeck, when his children were diagnosed with a deadly neurological illness, he was thankful for baseball. Not just for the season off, or the fund-raiser where famous players sold shirts and signatures to help pay medical bills—but for that simplest of baseball pleasures: games to watch with his son.

In the hospital, the Hirschbecks also played a game called Trouble. In Trouble, you used a die to move colored pegs around a board; when your peg lands on the same space as someone else's, it's trouble.

The game was Michael's favorite.

The object was to get home safe. (p. 1–J)

Writing about the Hirschbeck family helped others to understand how families can cope with medical problems beyond human abilities to solve. And readers learn that these difficulties can occur to the well known in a profession just as well as they occur to ordinary people. Just about everyone benefits from reading, or listening to, a human story such as the portrait of the baseball umpire and his family's struggle with the deadly genetic disease. Pollak did it well. Her storytelling skills earned her the 1997 Pulitzer Prize for feature writing. Human-interest articles should always be based on good stories regardless of whether they are happy or sad stories. It is that simple. These articles are the sort of stories you can curl up with on the sofa and enjoy for a few minutes. Readers react by feeling sad for those involved in tragedy. Readers feel happy because someone has beaten the odds and won a battle against a bigger foe. Sometimes, readers smile because they remember a similar experience they have been through. A human-interest article is often a success because the story that is told is true and involves people in your own town or someone who is just like you, but from a faraway place. Readers find these human-interest articles a change of pace from the normal flow of spot news. Furthermore, these stories serve readers in another way: they offer inspiration and hope for readers who might be experiencing the same troubles or frustrations.

## EMPHASIZING THE HUMAN ELEMENT

A man leaves his child on the roof of his car, drives off to the interstate highway nearby, speeds up to 50 mph, and the baby flies off the car and onto the roadway. Was it a terrible tragedy? No, the baby was not hurt. It is one of those unbelievable people stories. It is a happy-ending story. It is a "boy, was that a stupid thing to do" story. However, it was a story that begged to be told. Chris Reidy, a reporter for *The Boston Globe,* got such an assignment. All the elements were there: a man, his baby, drama, and a crazy mistake. And, oh yes, it was Mother's Day and the husband had to tell his wife about the little problem with their baby. Human-interest such as this can be big news, the major story of the day, in fact. Reidy told of the Murrays' miraculous good fortune in the day's front-page lead story for *The Globe*, with a jump-page sidebar on how people misuse car seats for children, written by another reporter. Here is Reidy's entire story (Reidy, 1992):

MILLBURY—After his 3-month-old son sailed off the roof of his car at 50 m.p.h. and landed unhurt in the middle of an interstate highway in Worcester on Sunday, Michael Murray decided to break the news to his wife gently.

It was, after all, Mother's Day, and Murray, a 27-year-old factory worker, said yesterday he did not want to say right out that he had "messed up" by absent-mindedly driving off while his son was strapped into a car seat that he had left on the sunroof of his bronze 1987 Hyundai.

As her husband sheepishly held Mathew, who was sleeping serenely in white pajamas and sunbonnet, Deanna Murray, 28, recounted the phone call she received from her husband.

" 'Come to the emergency room,' he told me."

A surgical nurse, Deanna Murray was on duty at the Medical Center of Central Massachusetts in Worcester when her husband's call came in. The emergency room is down the hall from her work station.

" 'Just come down here,' that's all he told me," Deanna Murray said, describing the phone call. " 'Mathew has fallen,' he finally said. I ran all the way down the hall."

After learning the full story, Deanna Murray said, "I was in shock. The nurses had to sit me down and hold me. It's a miracle. It really is."

"It's a good thing he didn't tell me on the phone," she said, adding, "Every time I hear the story I could burst into tears."

Deanna Murray heard the story a lot yesterday as the media descended on the Millbury farmhouse where she lives with her husband and two children.

The Murrays obligingly went through the details over and over again, but Deanna Murray balked when a photographer requested that Michael reenact the sequence of events with Mathew posed in his car seat on the top of the car.

"You're not going to put him on the roof again, are you?" Deanna Murray said, the only time she expressed a hint of displeasure with her husband.

As Michael Murray recounted it, things began innocently enough around noon Sunday when he decided to drive Mathew and his 20-month-old sister to the hospital, where Deanna was working the day shift. He wanted to drop off her Mother's Day gifts—a gold necklace bearing the legend "Number One Mom" and a single rose.

After presenting these gifts, Michael Murray carried his two children back to the indoor garage where he parked the car. Murray put his daughter into her car seat but then got into the car with Mathew still on the sunroof.

"The garage was dark," Murray said when asked how he could have forgotten about his son.

Murray then proceeded to drive through the streets of Worcester. Traffic was heavy, he said, but no one beeped at him to indicate that anything was amiss.

As he accelerated onto Interstate 290, the highway that cuts through Worcester, Murray heard a scraping sound on the roof of his car.

"You could hear it slide," Murray said of his son and the car seat. "I looked to where he should have been. Then in the rear view mirror, I saw him sliding down the highway."

Fortunately, the driver following Murray does not believe in tailgating.

"I was coming over Route 290 South about noon," said James Boothby, 67, a retired antiques dealer from Worcester. "I saw something in the air. I thought it was garbage, something somebody had tossed out. Then I thought it was a doll. Then I saw the doll open its mouth. I couldn't believe it. It was a little baby."

At this point, I-290 is three lanes in each direction, and Mathew landed on "the driver's side of the middle lane," Boothby said.

If Boothby had swerved, the Murrays believe their story would have had an unhappy ending. Instead, he came to a stop in the middle lane, halting the flow of traffic. Boothby said he was driving the speed limit—about 50 mph—when he caught sight of Mathew and his car seat.

"It just landed on the road," Boothby said of the car seat. "It bounced a couple times, but it never tipped—It just sat right down."

Murray, who estimated that Mathew was on the roof for a total of about 1 mile, said he stopped his car about "25 to 50 yards" past the point where his son had become airborne.

With his car blocking traffic, Boothby got out to investigate. What he found was a baby uninjured and a car seat undamaged.

"I picked the little fellow up, and he looked all around," Boothby said. "When he started crying, I knew everything was all right—He looked at me as if to say, 'Who are you?' He knew I wasn't daddy or mama. That's when he started to cry."

"Thank God for him," Deanna Murray said of Boothby. "I can't thank him enough."

Commenting on the heavy traffic that had come to a sudden halt behind them, Boothby said, "It's amazing there weren't any fender-benders."

When Michael Murray reached Boothby, he snatched up his son, telling him, "When the police show up, tell them I went to the hospital."

At the hospital, Mathew was deemed to be uninjured, though he was kept overnight for observation. While doctors scanned the son, the father was cited for driving to endanger.

State Trooper Mario Tovar, who issued the citation, said, "I have never seen or heard of anything like this. It was kind of shocking, the whole thing."

"He was a very happy kid, all smiles," Tovar said of Mathew at the hospital. "The doctor gave him a good bill of health. He's a miracle baby. What a Mother's Day gift! The result was one in a million."

Michael Murray noted that "the doctors said that with the shape of the car seat, it actually flew like an airplane."

Murray's car is a hatchback, and its shape may have helped put Mathew into a glide path.

"We're definitely writing to the car seat company," said Deanna Murray.

The seat was identified as a Gerry Guard with Glide, manufactured by Gerry Baby Products of Denver.

When not used as a car seat, it can be converted into a mini rocking chair, hence the word "glide" in the chair's name, said company spokeswoman Stephanie Aragon.

The seat is designed for infants weighing less than 20 pounds, she said.

Said a grateful Deanna Murray: "The Gerry Glider—it certainly lived up to its name." (pp. 1, 18)

(Reprinted with permission of *The Boston Globe*.)

As in this story, the key to telling these stories is the human element. This is a people story. There must be plenty of emotion experienced by the primary characters in the article, as well as emotion experienced by the reader: horror, amusement, excitement, joy, depression, sympathy, sadness, and anger.

Your assignment as a human-interest article writer is to make your readers a vicarious participant in the drama. You react. You hope the baby survived without injury. You root for the child's careless father to make amends with the mother. Your readers' personal involvement in the news draws them further into what you have written and into the publication generally. These articles are most often the odd and unusual stories about people.

Newspapers occasionally publish human-interest articles in sidebar format to accompany other articles on the same subject. Magazines like these articles to contrast with other types of articles, such as travel articles, interview articles, hard-hitting investigations, and regular departments and columns. The time element is of secondary importance in many human-interest articles. In fact, some human-interest subjects are really timeless and could be published anytime. Articles such as any of those sprinkled throughout this chapter are as interesting to read now as they were when they were originally published. Often, the material that forms the story takes years, or even a lifetime, to evolve into the story. Only when the series of events culminates does the writer enter and begin to chronicle it for readers.

Writing human-interest articles requires a unique touch on the part of the writer. You have to have the right frame of mind to find the story and you need the right strategy to handle it. Approach the usual story in a certain way and it is still only a routine news item. If you take that same story and tell it with a human angle, it comes alive and becomes a better overall story, a human-interest story.

Natural disasters and medical problems are common sources of some of the best human-interest articles. Disasters such as tornadoes that strike in the Midwest, earthquakes, and floods are only a few examples of events that nature brings to test human resilience. Medical problems can touch the heart like nothing else, especially those involving suffering children. The stories of children who need transplants of organs, those who are handicapped, and those who

have terminal diseases are always widely read and usually evoke a strong out-
pouring of support and offers to assist the families.

## THE ASSOCIATION–IDENTIFICATION ELEMENT

The successes of regional and city magazines and community sections of major
metropolitan newspapers in recent years have been due, in part, to the fact that
these publications are writing and editing their editorial products for local markets. The appeal to readers is broad, but one strong reason for the local appeal is
the ability of readers to identify with the people, places, and things about which
they read. In the mid-1970s, leading daily newspapers such as the *Philadelphia Inquirer, Orlando Sentinel, Milwaukee Journal-Sentinel,* and *Chicago Tribune* began to
publish specially edited neighborhood sections that are "zoned" or distributed
on a regional level within the larger market that the newspaper serves. These
newspapers hoped they would be better able to write stories about people in the
smaller neighborhoods and communities—the cities within the cities. The
space for these stories became available because smaller advertisers could now
afford to purchase less costly advertising space for their shops and stores. And
editors, guided by their own intuition as well as current market research, decided the best way to fill the sections was with a large amount of human-interest
feature material about the neighborhoods' people, churches, and schools. Most
editors and experts feel the approach is working.

The same applies to the magazine industry, but in a slightly different way.
Regional and city magazines in major metropolitan areas have developed to reflect a lifestyle of young adults in dozens of metropolitan areas such as New
York, Los Angeles, Chicago, Atlanta, Miami, Cincinnati, Indianapolis, Orlando,
and Sacramento over the past 30 years. Yet these magazines filled a void in the
metropolitan market also, providing other outlets for human-interest articles as
well as other forms of reporting about urban and suburban life.

---

## THE ELEMENTS OF A HUMAN-INTEREST ARTICLE

Former *McCall's* (renamed *Rosie*) magazine managing editor Don McKinney
(1986) identified three types of human-interest stories:

1. An extraordinary experience—This type of story involves the natural disaster such as floods, earthquakes, blizzards, hurricanes, fires, and the like.
   Persons who survive these have a story to tell. There is life in jeopardy or
   even death. There is suffering. There is property loss, often priceless and
   precious possessions.
2. A common problem—Men and women who experience a relatively common human problem and succeed in battling it have a good story to tell. It

may be a singular experience or a family experience. The story focuses on how this person dealt with the tension and stress in a situation that readers can easily identify with while reading the article.

3. A national issue—People who suffer because of problems that are on the minds of the citizens of a nation are often heavily in demand and heavily read. This includes health problems such as AIDS.

---

Other types of magazines also depend on human-interest articles to draw readers. General interest personality magazines such as *People* focus on celebrity human-interest writing. *Rosie* and other women's magazines draw heavily on this category of features. *Reader's Digest* has always used these types of features. Columns such as "Life in These United States" are just one example. Small town daily and weekly newspapers have traditionally depended on a large number of human-interest articles in their editions.

You can make your human-interest article easier to enjoy by providing lots of direct quotations from the people about whom you are writing. You can also improve the story by giving the reader detail and description, as discussed in chapter 6, especially when photographs are not used. Direct quotations capture the way the person speaks and, sometimes, how the person thinks. They enliven the human-interest article because quotations allow you to tell the story in the source's own words. Description makes the person come alive in your reader's mind. How is your subject dressed? How is his or her hair styled? What is the person's occupation?

It all comes down to one point—human-interest articles must be written and edited so readers can see some of themselves in the article. You need to write in terms of people and not in terms of numbers or widgets. Readers do not "see" themselves in an article directly, of course, but they can imagine themselves as the principals of your article. Readers can see this person could have been themselves or is somehow like themselves. The events are described in a way that readers can see them occurring in their own homes or in their workplaces. A reader should be able to think or say, "Wow! That could have happened to me!" All of this occurs because of the common purpose, lifestyle, ideas, values, sensations, or characteristics of the human condition between readers and the subject of your article. It is the association and identification element of a human-interest article that permits a reader to think, feel, and even act as he or she imagines the experiences of the person about which you write.

## THE EMOTION ELEMENT

Emotion is a powerful element in any writing. Novelists use it in their work. In nonfiction, it is used to create closer ties between the reader and the story. With emotional elements in the right mix, you might produce one of those articles that readers just cannot put down until it is finished—regardless of the length. Emotion, psychologists tell us, has four general levels: intensity of feeling, level of tension, degree of pleasantness or unpleasantness, and degree of complexity. Emotion is a strong feeling, either general or specific, about a subject. It is manifested in a number of physical and psychological ways. The most common emotions in human experience are joy, anger, fear, and grief.

There are also emotions that we write about that are associated with various physical experiences such as pain, disgust, and delight. Some other emotions are tied to our own appraisals of us. These include feelings of success and failure, pride and shame, and guilt and remorse. Many times, in reading a good human-interest story, you can help readers experience emotions pertaining to other people.

Elinor Brecher writes human interest features for *The Miami Herald*. In 2002, she told the story of two elementary-school age girls suffering from cancer. They became friends. One of the girls received successful treatment and the cancer was gone from her body. But the other girl could not be helped and died shortly after the article was published. It was a story of contrast. It was also an emotional one. Here's her lead (Brecher, 2002):

> Carol Brown waited so long for this moment that she forgave herself a few tears.
>
> After 16 terrifying months, her daughter's cancer was gone. "Don't cry," she whispered to 8-year-old Bria at the door of her first-period music class. "Be strong. But let someone know if your leg hurts."
>
> That same morning, Chena Gaines showed the medical-supply delivery men where to set up her daughter Chendarlyn's hospital bed. The apparatus of the on-cology wing was following her home, though she'd vowed that her little girl had seen the last of such things.
>
> Bria Brown lunched on chicken nuggets and Tater Tots, then capped her re-turn to an Opa-locka magnet school by roughhousing in the library.
>
> Nine-year-old Chendarlyn Williams, who hadn't eaten solid food for weeks, sipped morphine and a little Gatorade. She ended another day of pain in Pampers, a hospice nurse smoothing a narcotics patch onto her arm.
>
> As one child resumed her life where cancer had derailed it, her best friend re-treated to a small, darkened room and the intermittent relief of opioid sleep.
>
> It wasn't supposed to happen like this, not in the dreams of two children who thought they were done with bone cancer. Not for their parents, who believed medical science and faith would defeat their daughters' malignancies.
>
> With their high-tech prosthetic thigh bones—Bria's on the left, Chendarlyn's on the right—these two were set to rejoin their everyday worlds. Only surgical scars and slight limps would betray their ordeals.
>
> But cancer is capricious, and their parallel paths diverged. . . . (p. 1A)

There is no doubt about the emotional value in a story about children suffering from cancer. As a writer, you should seek a strong emotional theme in a possible human-interest article. Brecher's story does this by linking the two girls and their friendship with their terribly different fates. These components of stories provide the unifying elements you need to write a good piece. Remember that emotion can be disruptive to your readers. It can be arousing. These reactions link your article to the reader. Emotion is often the difference in an average feature story and an award-winning feature. For example, Dan Luzadder earned a Pulitzer Prize for the *Fort Wayne News-Sentinel* in 1983 for his description of the dreams destroyed by a devastating Indiana flood in spring 1982. The impact of his article comes from the myriad of emotions conveyed to readers who could identify with his description of homes, cars, businesses, and other important possessions under water.

Stories such as this inextricably link the reader and the story. They do so with honesty and clarity. Writers let the emotions do the job and do not have to overwrite the story to make a point. They remain simple because of the double duty that the emotion element carries in the story. Although journalists seldom write the type of "sob story" that was common early in the 20th century, emotion remains the thread to tie together many human-interest stories. They are stories from the heart.

Occasionally, writers encounter stories that have to be told but, for overwhelming reasons, they cannot help but become involved in the story. This sort of reaction is quite normal, writers being people themselves, so it might become an asset if handled well. Compelling stories such as these demand that you write first person or write third person with your own perceptions and reactions becoming a part of the article. It is hard, for example, not to react to a child dying of liver disease who needs a transplant.

Writer Madeleine Blais won the 1980 Pulitzer Prize for feature writing for a 1979 article about a man who was a World War I conscientious objector and who had been given a dishonorable military discharge but who sought to upgrade it to honorable status. Blais (1984), who wrote that article for *The Miami Herald's Tropic* magazine, likes to get very involved with the topics of her articles and the sources themselves.

"Sometimes when I do stories, I can really tell that I've done something that's really worthwhile. I can tell it sort of lives very vividly in my mind while I'm doing it. Even afterwards, I have this level of caring about the people, almost like a kind of friendship forms because of the story. At some point in the research something happens," Blais (1984, n.p.) stated. "Either somebody says something or there's an event that moves me in some way that seems important to me. And then I start feeling this passion about creating through the reader the exact same psychological steps that I went through to get to the point where these people were moving to me—to do that for the reader as well" (Blais, 1984, n.p.).

You need to remember when you do react to such a story, your own journalistic observations can become affected by the experience. If this is not desired, and in some types of feature writing it is not, Rivers (1992) suggested this solution:

When an event makes a writer react emotionally, his or her impressions are especially vulnerable to distortion. You can often resolve this problem by recording your impressions immediately after the event to capture its details and then later, at a more tranquil time, assessing your first account to find and correct for distortion. (p. 141)

## FINDING UNIQUE PEOPLE STORIES

Williamson (1975) stated that most human-interest feature writers are "incurable people lovers." They have to, as he says, "relish the strange, inconsistent antics of the human race and, to a large degree, earn their livelihoods by astutely observing and reporting these antics." Therefore, Williamson observed that if a man bites a dog, it is not news as much as it is a human-interest article. Human-interest stories are often about people down on their luck, the people in society who have been dealt a losing hand, or people who have had a difficult time for no cause of their own.

Individuals with medical problems often fit into this category. Cancer victims and their family members, especially, must cope with the tragedy of a life that ends too soon. A physician who treats cancer patients, David M. Mumford, wrote a first-person human interest article for the *Saturday Evening Post* that provided insight into the process of dying. He recalled a patient that he once treated who was suffering from melanoma. He described the patient's strong will and desire to fight his fate for as long as possible. In addition to this story of a man who did not want to go easily, we learned an important life lesson from the doctor's experience. This is how Mumford concluded his essay written for the magazine's "True Stories from Medicine" department (2002):

> One afternoon I happened to visit while his wife was on an important search—an M&Ms' errand of chocolate mercy. I settled into the chair next to his bed as he turned toward me.
>
> "David," he began, "let me tell you something. I've been imaging how it would be if my coming death were caused by a stroke, heart attack, or some other abrupt ending. When I do, I thank God I have cancer."
>
> He paused a moment and explained. "Without this extra time, I never would have known what love and tenderness are possible between people on this earth."
>
> I knew a profound new question challenged me: Is love the essential marrow of our humanness? I also realized an unknown door in the human spirit—one I could never glimpse through scientific reasoning—had opened to me. Suffering, however difficult, can be a wise parent to personal meaning. One person's verities may unexpectedly differ from another's. And, more enduringly, demonstrations of wisdom and grace by patients can reverberate endlessly in caregivers.
>
> Certainly that happened to me. (p. 32)

For human-interest articles that are based on human suffering, disability, and illness, such as Mumford's article or the *Baltimore Sun* story earlier in the chapter, the ones that seem to touch readers most, you have to proceed with caution. Check medical facts and diagnoses. Be clear about the situation. Medical and legal issues need to be explained carefully and in detail. Some sources may attempt to fool you. Of course, most experiences that are told to you by a source will be true. However, a story occasionally is exaggerated or simply untrue. Not long ago, newspapers and magazines in South Florida were contacted by a woman who was having difficulty getting public assistance for her ill child. She painted a picture of bureaucratic delays that might cost the child its life. A newspaper reporter checked the woman's story and found that most of the facts were true. Yet, because she did not reveal all the facts about the illness, there were missing pieces. The reporter found out from a physician whom he had telephoned for background that the illness was serious, but not as immediate a problem as the woman claimed. In fact, the child could expect to live a number of years before the illness turned serious or fatal. The newspaper decided not to publish the written story in light of the new information. Another newspaper, however, did not check the facts as closely and did run the story.

Children, as you saw in *The Boston Globe* story described earlier in this chapter, make good human-interest subjects regardless of their plight or the location of the story. Although it has been argued that the local human-interest story is preferred, occasionally some stories are so compelling that geography matters little. To find these sorts of stories, feature writers must keep in touch with the world around them and people in that world. Stories are found in many places. For starters, try the local courthouse. Criminal and civil courtrooms are filled with this type of human drama that has, for various reasons, reached the need to be resolved before a judge. Usually the best court cases that make human-interest stories have a broader social issue element within them, McKinney (1986) explained.

Certainly good human-interest articles come out of hospitals and other health care institutions. Similarly, you can expect to find good stories at schools and churches. Government social services offices can often bring you in contact with good stories, too, if you can build dependable sources there. Each of these is a place where people gather and interact. You can expect to learn a lot if you take the time to talk and listen. Established writers know these stories find their way to them. If you are new to a community, it might take some time before people seek you out to tell you their stories, but eventually they do. Certainly neighbors and acquaintances often can lead you to stories. Listen to what they have to say. Remember people you meet and where they live and work. Even other publications can produce good ideas for you if you take time to read the newspapers, magazines, and newsletters in your area carefully. Reading carefully for run-of-the-mill news stories, you might find a missing angle or perhaps the next step that was not taken. Try it and see for yourself.

In searching for that good human-interest article, award-winning Massachusetts feature writer Blais (1984) recommended not heading into the story right away. Give yourself time to look around even when you have a subject before you zero-in on a theme or unifying thread. "My technique—was listening, hanging out, absorbing—a kind of inventory. It seemed ridiculous to be standing here stockpiling every little quote or whatever because I really needed more to get impressions than facts," she explained about her strategy on one assignment (Blais, 1984, n.p.). Blais also suggested looking for the little things in your prospective articles. "I love, as a writer," she said, "to take things that are not readily observable as monumental and try to find the monuments in them" (Blais, 1984, n.p.).

Minnesota freelance writer Perlstein (personal communication, May 3, 1993 and January 15, 1998) added that human-interest article writing often depends on the editor you serve:

> Human-interest is dicier [to freelance] because it is so subjective. What one editor thinks is a great human-interest piece, another thinks is just dumb. I wrote a piece for *Modern Maturity* about Garrison Keillor and how he puts together his radio show every week. That magazine thought it was a wonderful idea and commissioned it almost on the spot, but when I tried to sell it to other markets I got nowhere. The second book I'm working on is going to be 300 solid pages of human-interest—the chronicle of the first year of the Northern League, an independent minor league, which one principal has called "the second chance league." It will be made up of young hopefuls passed up by the big-league organizations and veterans who've been released and are looking for another go-round. It's dripping with emotional potential. (Perlstein, personal communication, May 3, 1993 and January 15, 1998)

## INSPIRATIONAL, MOTIVATIONAL HUMAN-INTEREST

Inspirational features are a type of how-to motivational essay. The purpose of such articles is to arouse and prompt readers to take action of some form to reach an objective or goal, to set an objective or goal and strive for it, to get involved in a social movement, to perform on the job better, to stick to a diet, or to break a bad habit. Inspirational feature writers often offer their successful experiences, or the experiences of others, in describing events that have changed a life or otherwise made life better for an individual or group, or helped some people improve themselves, sell more, or succeed in what they want to do. These are typically short articles with strong personal and human-interest elements.

Inspirational and motivational feature articles are a growing interest area for some magazines. Magazines such as *The American Salesman, Reader's Digest, Home Office Computing, Personal Selling Power,* and *Selling* use them frequently.

One freelance feature writer who specializes in motivational or inspirational human-interest articles is Kansas resident Susanna K. Hutcheson. She uses a very simple formula based on personal experiences for these stories. Here's how she said she does it: "They're quite short really. They're an interesting article to write in that they require no interviews. They're basically an essay based on some experience the author has had that will inspire others. They require excellent writing and an ability to inspire with your words" (Hutcheson, personal communication, April 27, 1993).

Hutcheson said she has a formula that results in two approaches to the articles. She follows one or the other in her work:

> Often I write a very brief outline before I write. But more often than not, I simply start to write and then do a rewrite and then a polish. I have found that the more of these I write, the less work they require. Most of them are from 700 to 1,200 words and take little time. I try to paint a picture for the reader. I first lay out the problem. In one that I did on insurance sales, the problem was making more sales. Then I use a few quotes from prominent people on the subject, put in some facts and figures, and back it all up with personal experiences or experiences of others. I always wrap up my articles with a summary of what I have said at the beginning. I leave the reader feeling good and thinking to him or herself, "I can do that!" (Hutcheson, personal communication, April 27, 1993)

## PERSONALITY-CELEBRITY FEATURES

The international fascination with celebrities of all types is not a new one. We commonly read articles about entertainment, sports, political, social, literary, and religious celebrities. Many general interest newspapers, specialized magazines and newsletters, and online publications have placed a new emphasis on coverage of personalities and newsmakers in film, music, sports, and other entertainment areas. You do not have to look far to find people-oriented columns and sections in your daily newspapers. Many newspapers devote prominent portions of their news sections, as well as larger amounts of feature sections, to personality-celebrity news. Other publications simply edit their wire or bureau news into personality-celebrity roundup columns featuring a half dozen or so items and pictures about well-known people. And some, of course, exist solely to report about celebrities.

However, the point is clear—these items reflect the growing public interest in celebrities and personalities. These features tell us the daily activities of famous people—whom they are seen with, where they are going, their latest work, and their personal lives. And, surely, there are emotional stories that can be told about the famous as well. Although these people may be internationally known, or even just known across their communities, others care about them and what happens to them. When a local radio disk jockey falls ill, if a popular

nightclub singer gets married, or members of a royal family are having problems, the events become human-interest story material. You write about this in
the same manner in which you would handle any other human-interest story.
The ongoing emphasis on people stories, combined with the growing attention
to personality-celebrity news, is a response to the strong demand for personality
human-interest features.

## WRITING HUMAN-INTEREST ARTICLES

You have a number of alternatives in writing a human-interest article. Much of
the time, the material you have collected can dictate the form of the story. Or-
ganizationally, you often choose from these approaches:

1. Suspended interest approach.
2. Storyteller's chronological approach.
3. Narrative approach.

The suspended interest approach is a pyramid organizational strategy. The
lead is only a partial summary of what happened, saving resolution of the human drama for a later point in the article. Most of the time resolution comes at
the ending. The article's body, or main section, is a description of the main
events in chronological order. Finally, the article winds up with its outcome, or
revelation, in the conclusion or climax. This approach has its advantages. It
forces the reader to stay with your story for the big ending or moral to the story.
This plan is not unlike that of the novelist who unveils the murderer on the last
page of the mystery.
     The second strategy for organizing human-interest articles is to approach
writing, as you would tell a story: tell the entire story in chronological order.
This sort of plan is simple and easy to write once you get your facts straight. The
sequence of events does the work for you. This sort of approach does not fit all
human-interest stories. It works well when events culminate with a major action on the part of a principal source in the article.
     Narrative organization is also easy to use and works particularly well for be-
ginning writers. Like the chronological form, this approach is dictated by the information you collect. Your major decision will be how to start a narrative article because you are not necessarily bound to start with the first event in any
sequence. McKinney (1986) said a human-interest narrative article lead should
"lure the reader (and this includes the editor, who will decide whether the
reader gets a chance at it or not) into your story and to capture that person's interest so that he cannot put it down until he learns how it comes out" (p. 27).
     Narrative organization, then, just tells what happened by running from be-
ginning to end. In this case, narrative is different from the suspended interest be-

cause the best material is saved for the end and different from chronological because it does not lead with the first event or end with the last event. You have
the most flexibility with narrative writing by not forcing what becomes the beginning, middle, or end through a chosen structure. You can merge elements of
the story using narrative organization, pulling from two divergent tracks, or
themes, if needed.

Blais likes to use metaphors to structure her articles whenever possible. Blais
(1984) said, "The structure should rise from the material. The way to make it
happen is to make yourself an authority, to know so much about your subject
that you know almost as much about your subject as your subject knows about
himself" (n.p.).

## YOUR BEST SOURCES FOR HUMAN-INTEREST STORIES

People—Interviewing and Observing
Neighbors
Workplace friends, acquaintances
Institutions—Interviewing and Observing
Hospitals
Social services offices
Schools
Churches, synagogues
Funeral homes
Civil courts
Criminal courts
Places—Interviewing and Observing
Parks, playgrounds
Clubhouses
Festivals and celebrations
Senior citizen centers
Missions, centers for homeless
Schools
Churches, synagogues
Halfway houses, rehabilitation centers
Courthouses
Libraries

## GIVING A FEATURE ITS PERSONAL TOUCHES

Maryln Schwartz, former long-time *Dallas Morning News* feature writer and columnist, has won numerous awards over the past 30 years for her work. She ad-

vocates giving a personal touch to her stories (personal communication, September 14, 1988):

> Sometimes writers find it hard to distinguish between a feature and a news story. This is the best way I can explain it: We all know the biblical story of Noah and the Ark. Just before it rained for 40 days and 40 nights, Noah built an ark. He took his family and two of every kind of animal that was then living on earth. Every living creature on the ark was saved from the flood. That is a news story.
>
> If I was writing about that event, I'd want to talk to Mrs. Noah, who was probably having to clean up after all those animals for 40 days and 40 nights. That's a feature story.
>
> When I'm writing my newspaper column, I look for the small details that give the readers a clear view of the big picture. For instance, when Prince Charles visited New Mexico, I wanted to give an example of what it means to be royalty. I didn't want to just write that people were bowing, because we already know that people bow to royalty. So I just watched for a little while. Then I noticed that Prince Charles was the only person at the party who wasn't wearing a nametag. And this wasn't a "B" Party. Cary Grant was there and he wore a nametag.
>
> This is the kind of touch that separates real royalty from mere legend. I did the same thing recently when I was watching the Miss America contestants give their predictable pre-pageant TV interviews. They were all insisting they weren't beauty queens, they had a message to give the world. They didn't want to discuss sex appeal. They wanted to talk about nuclear disarmament. Then I would flip channels to interviews of the presidential candidates. The political analysts kept trying to talk about Michael Dukakis' charisma or George H. Bush's sex appeal. I knew I had my column when I began to realize that politics and beauty pageants have somehow become confused with each other: "Would someone please tell me what's going on? Why is it that Miss Montana can't wait to discuss Manuel Noriega and George Bush only seems to want to discuss his grandchildren?"
>
> To write a good feature story requires as much observing as it does writing. You can have a beautifully crafted story, but no one will really care unless you have something to say. Information is the most important aspect. There will always be an editor who can help you turn a better phrase. But all the editing in the world isn't going to help if your information isn't interesting.
>
> You don't have to have been at a major news event to find a good feature story. And you just have to train yourself to see details that other people overlook. Actress Farrah Fawcett was the most interviewed actress in the country when she was starring in the "Charlie's Angels" TV show. My editor asked me to do a story and to be sure to mention that the actress had been named one of the "10 Most Beautiful" on campus when she attended the University of Texas. The story had been done again and again. I didn't think anyone would even want to read it. Instead, I decided to find out what had happened to the other nine most beautiful. The story went on the wire and was used in about 40 newspapers. I got my information by phone. It took only two days. (Schwartz, personal communication, September 14, 1988)

# CHAPTER EIGHT

# Profiles and Personality Sketches

Following the September 11, 2001, attacks on the World Trade Center in New York, *The New York Times* began publishing special sections devoted to ongoing developments in this major international news story both down the street from the newsroom of the newspaper as well as halfway around the world. Some portions of the coverage focused on the lives of the people who died. The stories were brief profiles and sketches of the more than 3,000 victims. The features were reported and written by *The New York Times* staff writers.

Each sketch of a victim attempted to provide readers with a glimpse into the life of that person. Reporters devoted several hundred words to describing each life that had been cut short, using information obtained during interviews with the victim's friends and family. Each story presented a small bit of insight into what made the person unique. The sketches often used anecdotes, direct quotations from loved ones, friends, and coworkers, detailed physical descriptions as well as a small "mug shot" photograph, key biographical information, and the favorite memories of those who knew the person. Each sketch became compelling reading, but each set of profiles taken together demonstrated just how the much the losses of these individuals meant to their communities, their businesses, their coworkers, and their families. This excerpt of one of the short profiles illustrates the approach taken on each one (Ayers, 2001):

Glenn Kirwin was fit. Triathlon fit.

Over the years, he competed in a number of triathlons, and though he stopped the endurance events after the children arrived, he kept himself in enviable shape. "He was a fitness freak," said his wife, Joan. "He did 50-mile bicycle rides." When they were dating, she tried to keep up, but it was hopeless. "I once did 30 miles with him," she said, "but I couldn't sit for a week."

Mr. Kirwin, 40, lived in Scarsdale, N.Y., and was up at 5:15 in the morning to catch the 6:30 train to New York, where he was the head of product development at the eSpeed division of Cantor Fitzgerald.

It was usually 8 at night when he arrived home. It was his practice, though, to always do something with the children, Miles, 10, and Troy, 7, before they went to bed. He would read them a story or play checkers or engage in a game of Go Fish. Sometimes they would go outside and play catch or shoot baskets. . . .

The series of sketches and profiles were part of the overall coverage of *The New York Times* that earned it the 2002 Pulitzer Prize for Public Service. Some profile writers will tell you that profiles are short, vivid biographies. Profiles such as these are similar to the efforts of portrait painters or sculptors. An artist paints a lifelike portrait of a person with oils or watercolors. A sculptor might use clay or marble to create a bust. As a writer, you can also create a portrait of a person using your command of some very different communication tools—words and language. Still, personality sketches and profiles are a bit different from biographies and different from other portrait art forms. Obviously, a profile for a newspaper, magazine, or newsletter will not be as long as a book-sized biography. Some newspaper, magazine, and newsletter profiles do run thousands of words and some are even occasionally published in installments. And some are excerpts from book-length studies of an individual—biographies. Most, however, are much shorter—in the 750-word to 1,500-word range—and more concentrated and focused.

Magazine writer Tom Callahan (1995) said article profiles are a hard craft to master, but they can be highly rewarding for writers and their readers. "Profile writing is fun," Callahan said. "Where else can an ordinary person like yourself end up interviewing French actresses, powerful politicians and other exciting, beautiful people? Such assignments give you a backstage pass, a ticket to go places few of us would otherwise see and to glimpse lifestyles others only envy" (p. 40).

Williamson (1975) called profiles in-depth stories about an individual designed to capture "the essence of his personality" (p. 151). Profiles have been a part of the nonfiction writer's portfolio for generations. In the early part of this century, magazines in New York, particularly *The New Yorker*, began to publish personality-based stories labeled profiles. *The New Yorker* readers thumb through new issues, looking for profiles to see who's who. Personality sketches and profiles are important feature articles in the overall content mix of newspapers, magazines, and newsletters. Newspapers and wire services use them to introduce new newsmakers to readers on almost a daily basis. Someone receiving a high government appointment at the national level is almost guaranteed to be profiled by the major news organizations. This also occurs at the local level, of course. New government officials, especially appointed individuals, are profiled on page 1. Star athletes having a good year or who have just completed a record effort are highlighted in sports. Award-winning singers and musicians are subjects for the entertainment section. Some magazines regularly present profiles of industry or profession leaders and newsmakers to their readers in sections devoted to highlighting individuals. *Continental*, the Continental Airlines in-flight magazine, was formerly known as *Profiles* and continues to highlight prominent or otherwise interesting persons—such as business executives, entertainers, athletes, and social and political leaders—in each issue. *The New Yorker* has used profiles regularly for decades, and newer magazines have recognized the value of regular profiles.

The usual newsmaker profile focuses on a new appointment or other newsworthy achievement by an individual thrust into the limelight. This is the news peg or nut graf for the profile. Something has happened recently to the individual to justify the attention. In addition to spot news stories about the decision and announcement, these profiles serve as sidebars. Editors use them because they believe their readers want to know more about the individual in the news.

Although most profiles focus on people, profiles do not have to be about people. You will find profiles of cities, companies, sports teams, management teams, musical groups, acting or dance companies, committees, and other subjects. These organizational and institutional profiles are popular in certain sections of newspapers such as business, sports, entertainment, and in similar departments of magazines as well. The ability to produce a profile and personality sketch is a necessary skill for the versatile nonfiction writer. This story form should be a part of your standard writing repertoire. This chapter describes the basics of the profile and personality sketch, and the different approaches to writing these stories. Your first stop is with the basic elements of writing profiles.

## BASIC PROFILE CONTENT AND STRUCTURE

Profiles have common content and generally follow a standard organizational format. You will find variations, of course, but most profiles include certain basic information. The result is a structure that has evolved over the years. When profiling an individual, whether it is for a newspaper, magazine, or newsletter, you should include biographical material offered in a mostly chronological order, an environment or surroundings description, anecdotes or stories by and about the subject, personal information, and family information. It does not have to be presented in this order, of course. A combination of these elements should produce a full, insightful picture of the individual or subject.

Writing the article will be easiest to do if you follow the general format for profiles. After you have done a profile or two, you will probably begin to experiment with other organizational approaches as well as other means of focusing on the individual. A standard profile can have several purposes and forms. A full profile will be a narrative article of considerable length depending on whether the profile is for a newspaper, magazine, or newsletter. Many publications are publishing profiles in capsule form, called thumbnails or sketches by some editors. These are abstracted profiles with only the basic facts presented in a summary or listing format.

---

## THE BASIC PARTS OF PROFILES

A traditional profile formula has five major parts:

1. Lead paragraphs, typically an anecdotal or highly descriptive lead.
2. "News peg" or "nut graf" outlining spot developments of significance.
3. Subject's current successes and accomplishments.
4. Biographical chronology.
5. Ending or conclusion, often connecting to the lead.

---

The lead can be built by using several parts or only one component. Like other articles, it is two or three paragraphs that are interest-arousing for the reader. These can be stirring quotations, a dramatic scene description, or a telling anecdote. The lead should melt into the current accomplishments portion through an effective transition. That is the article's news peg. This is where you tell your reader: This is why you should read about this person. This is the point of the story where you describe the subject's achievements and responsibilities.

Christopher Kelly, Fort Worth *Star–Telegram* film critic, had the opportunity to sit down with award-winning actor Robin Williams. He decided to approach a profile of Williams by stating that movie fans either loved him or hated him, but regardless of their reaction to his films, he always generated some sort of reaction. His portrayal of Williams in a Friday cover feature for the *Star–Telegram's* Weekend Life & Arts section, illuminated the actor's serious side and offered his views about his craft. Here's how Kelly organized the profile, using a basic essay and narrative structure (2002):

> When you talk to Robin Williams in person, he is not the man you'd expect. Or at least he is not entirely that man.
>
> Yes, there is much of his famously discursive, rapid-fire comedy; within one fractured train of thought, he can bounce from an impression of Miss Cleo the television psychic to an extended riff on "wet burka contests."
>
> But once Williams starts talking about his approach to acting—particularly how he tackled his role as the psychotic photo developer Sy Parrish in *One Hour Photo* (opening in wide release today)—he turns focused and very serious.
>
> "His isolation is triggered by pretty horrible abuses as a kid," he says, talking to a group of reporters at the Sundance Film Festival, where *One Hour Photo* premiered in January. "There's a psychological disorder called Asperger's syndrome. You can't deal directly with people, but you're very good with mechanical things, and you relate to people through objects. I used that as a template."
>
> Williams is a famously intense comedian, and he also seems to apply that same intensity to his serious roles. That's precisely what makes his career both fascinating and frustrating. His performance in *One Hour Photo* is one of his most man-

nered and deliberate. It also marks his third film this year—after *Death to Smoochy* and *Insomnia*—in which he plays a bad guy. And this particular cycle of movies follows a series of sentimental dramas in which he played basically the same holy fool over and over again, in *Jakob the Liar*, *What Dreams May Come*, *Bicentennial Man* and *Patch Adams*.

Williams doesn't do anything halfheartedly. He doesn't let you miss his point.

"I'm trying to get different colors going," Williams says, by way of explaining his decision to star in *One Hour Photo*, *Insomnia* and *Death to Smoochy* in the same year.

The question for a lot of people, however, is: Is Williams trying too hard?

"He's got a wonderful career, he's a megastar," says Mark Romanek, the director of *One Hour Photo*. "But like any creative person in any endeavor, he's looking to grow. The guy has made 40 or 50 movies. He's running out of new challenges."

That's the politic answer to why Williams has made such a glaring 180-degree turn from movies like *Patch Adams* to ones like *Insomnia*. For his part, the actor says that the reason he's playing three bad guys back to back is because he wanted to try something new.

"I've never been offered too many chances like this," Williams says. "One was *Dead Again* [1991]. I did *The Secret Agent* [1996], because that was Bob Hoskins' movie, and it was also Joseph Conrad, and it was a great despicable character. But I haven't had a chance to play these characters. So when [my agents] found this film, I thought, this is great."

But why doesn't Williams take the approach of someone like Jim Carrey, an actor who now alternates steadily between broad farce and serious drama. Why, for Williams, is it always aggressively one thing or aggressively the other?

In a scathing critique of the actor in the August issue of *Esquire*, the critic Tom Carson suggests that Williams' defining trait as an actor is a need to overdo things. "[Williams'] fatal flaw . . . is that he's always overcompensating; whenever he gets anxious that our attention is slipping, we've got to brace ourselves for a whole new form of excess. His current pursuit of the charms of villainy is no exception." *Boston Globe* film critic Ty Burr, in his negative review of *One Hour Photo*, postulates that Williams has always been the tearful clown longing for adulation. He writes, "Robin Williams has a raging need for love that fuels his best work as a comedian and his worst work as a film actor."

The irony, of course, is that Williams has never gone without audience adulation, or critical respect, for very long. Tom King, who writes the "Hollywood Journal" column for *The Wall Street Journal*, points out that with a string of $100-million hits (*Mrs. Doubtfire*, *Jumanji*, *Patch Adams*) and Oscar recognition (nominations for *Good Morning, Vietnam*; *Dead Poets Society*; *Awakenings* and *The Fisher King*; the Best Supporting Actor prize for *Good Will Hunting*), Williams didn't need to undertake the sort of radical career makeover he's attempted this year.

"He is not someone whom I think of as being in 'star jail,' " says King.

Williams' recent choices are those of an actor trying to avoid falling into a trap that isn't really there—which ends up being a trap in and of itself. Indeed, this current makeover might not have been necessary at all had Williams not served up four consecutive movies that followed the same grossly sentimental *Patch Adams* model.

There is, to be fair to Williams, the fact that no actor wants to be typecast. Says Charles Lyons, the film reporter for *Variety*, "Robin Williams, like all actors, doesn't like to get straitjacketed into one kind of role. That's what agents and producers try to do with actors, directors, etc., in an environment that has become increasingly corporatized."

But it must also be noted that Williams is partly responsible for his own typecasting. He can play all the Sy Parrishes he wants, but if he shows up to promote those films on talk shows and immediately resorts to his patented, caffeinated routine, audiences aren't ever really going to see him in a different light. More to the point, by making four "nice guy movies," followed by three "bad guy" movies, he shoots himself in the foot—by playing into the carefully defined, know-what-you're-getting-in-advance rules of Hollywood.

Will Williams' bad-guy cycle result in a backlash among both critics and Oscar voters, who likely will see his work not on its individual merit but as part of a calculated stunt? Williams has received generally favorable reviews for *One Hour Photo*, as he did for *Insomnia*. (*Death to Smoochy* was so badly directed and written that it seems unfair to pass judgment on Williams' performance.) But Tom Carson's criticisms of *One Hour Photo* have been echoed in a number of other reviews of the film.

That's a shame, because for all its ostentation (in fact, precisely because of all its ostentation), Williams' work in *One Hour Photo* ranks with his most fascinating. Williams has thought Sy through from top to bottom—the awkward staccato walk, the half-beatific, half-menacing smile, the way he pushes his glasses up against the bridge of his nose whenever he is nervous. Sy turns out to be another of Williams' characters who desperately needs attention. And Williams' shtick becomes the means by which the actor forces us to notice a man most of us would never notice in our everyday life.

Based on its success in limited release thus far, *One Hour Photo* certainly looks like a hit, providing Williams the last laugh. But Tom King says that Williams is ultimately too mercurial—and audiences are too in love with his comic talents—for the actor to remain a bad guy for long.

"I would expect that at some point in the near future, we'll see Robin Williams back in a dress," he says. "That's what the audience wants. And usually studios and agents, and the people in power in Hollywood, are able to convince stars to give them what they want—even if it's not what the star wants to do." (Kelly, 2002, pp. 1E, 7E)

(Reprinted with permission from the Fort Worth *Star-Telegram*)

Following the lead paragraphs, a profile establishes the news value of the story. Kelly (2002) does that effectively in his story by noting that the latest Williams film opened on the day his story appeared. What is the person doing? Why is this individual in the news? The two examples lay out this information early in each lead. This approach also serves as a form of transition from the lead to the middle of the story. With a good transition from the lead, you move to that portion of the article where the personal background on the individual is presented. How did the individual get to where he or she is? This is a biographical section, told most of the time in chronological order from childhood (or beginning of professional career, perhaps) to present. This usually demands the variety of sources necessary in a profile to give a complete picture. But beware—This section can be dull unless it is spiced up with anecdotes and direct quotations, even some storytelling by the subject or others close to the subject. The ending is linked to the rest of the article in several ways. The most common method is to bring the reader back to the present in the chronology, connecting with the points made in the news peg section. Another method is to link up with an anecdote offered in the lead or some other observation made by you, the subject, or another source, near the beginning of the article.

Some profiles use a chronology upon which to build the entire story. *Rolling Stone* Contributing Editor Chris Heath (2002) gave readers a look into the life of actress Jennifer Love Hewitt using a basic chronological plan to organize the story. After a short narrative introduction, his cover story gave readers a look at the 23-year-old by taking them through a day in her life just prior to the debut of a new movie. It starts at home and describes her close relationship with her mother, with whom she still lived at the time the article was published. Readers go to work with her and then to lunch. Heath integrates numerous direct quotations to let Hewitt tell readers about herself and how she views her career. Readers then accompany her to a massage, a media interview, various cell phone interruptions throughout the day, and on to a party with three of her closest friends. The story ends, fittingly, with her taking another cell phone call, this time from her mother.

In a profile about a controversial professor at the University of Chicago, *Chicago Tribune* Sunday magazine writer Julia Keller set up her cover profile by getting to the point in the lead of her lengthy article. Keller (2002) prepared for her profile of the scholar and author by reading books and articles written by the professor. As a writer, Keller said the issues that made the professor controversial also made her appealing material for the article. "What makes her (the professor) controversial is also what makes her interesting. She believes fiercely and passionately in ideas and, frankly, most of us don't. That keeps us out of bitter intellectual feuds, but also keeps us from feeling the intense, world-changing heat of thought," Keller said about the professor and how she approached the assignment (Taylor, 2002, p. 2). Keller, a former television critic for the *Columbus Dispatch* and a Ph.D. in English literature, discussed just what it is that makes the Professor Martha Nussbaum such a hot topic among intellectuals in the academy:

> Martha Nussbaum is smarter than you. Chances are, she's also prettier. Works harder, runs faster, knows lots more about Greek literature.
> If you find the foregoing a bit irksome—perfection being far more annoying to behold than the propensity to screw up, since the latter invites a kind of cozy ruminative sympathy—then join the club.

But there is another club too, a sizable contingent deeply impressed by Nussbaum and her considerable achievements, a group that concurs with time magazine in dubbing her "one of a handful of thinkers coming up with ideas that will change the world" and with *The New York Times* and other publications that routinely refer to her as "the most prominent female philosopher in America."

Few are neutral about Nussbaum. Within academia, that quaint cameo of a world, she is a large and vivid presence, loved or hated but impossible to ignore. A professor at the University of Chicago since 1995 with appointments in the law and divinity schools and the departments of philosophy, classics and South Asia studies ("Every department," says an admiring student, "except pediatrics, I think"), Nussbaum, at 55, is reminiscent of Samuel Taylor Coleridge, the British romantic poet about whom a friend once remarked, "There is no shore of thought upon which he has not touched—and none upon which he has rested."

She is fiercely smart, deeply learned, defiantly opinionated, relentlessly energetic—and just a touch notorious.

She is almost absurdly prolific: book after book, essay after essay, endless scrolls of e-mail exchanges with students and fellow scholars around the works. "The gross flood of works appearing under her name is stunning," writes Geoffrey Harpham, and English professor at Tulane University, in a pointed critique of her work. Nussbaum, Harpham calculates, "has gotten into a rhythm of publishing around seven or eight hundred words a day, 365 days a year; in a good year, of which she has had many, she can double that."

She runs marathons. She travels the world. She muses in print about politics and literature and moral philosophy and child psychology. She establishes foundations. She is fluent in Greek, Latin, French and German. She dates Nobel Prize-winning economists and renowned constitutional scholars. . . . (Keller, 2002, p. 8)

## Using the Q & A Format for Profiles

Some publications prefer to publish profiles in a question and answer (Q & A) format. *Details* magazine, for example, uses the Q & A approach as a regular feature. Recent articles have focused on celebrities such as legendary musician Robert Plant and baseball manager Bobby Valentine. *Interview* magazine also uses Q & A in each issue. *Interview* presents Q & A with a twist, often assigning one celebrity to interview another. The interview is taped, edited, and published and the result is often a very conversational article. For example, a cover interview of actor and television comedian Jimmy Fallon was conducted by rock singer Mick Jagger. Actress Catherine Keener was interviewed by actress Jennifer Anniston in the same issue. However, as will be noted later in this chapter, interview stories and profiles are often similar, but often quite different.

Publications use Q & A as a standard format for a feature or department in each issue. These regular Q & A often are simply an interview article but can also be the basis for a Q & A format profile or personality sketch. Both are quite popular with magazines, newsletters, and online news media, although the approaches are also found from time to time in daily and weekly newspapers.

When published in any printed form, the length varies from a few questions and short answers to lengthy presentations that cover thousands of words.

Typically, Q & A interview articles and profiles have a narrative introduction and then begin the edited questions and answers. Seldom do these articles appear in print unedited. Question content as well as the exact words of the subject of the story are presented as they were recorded during the interview, but some questions and answers may be edited out for length or other editorial reasons. But what appears represents the words of the interviewer and the subject.

For example, *Renaissance Insights* magazine, the in-room publication for the Renaissance Hotels group, profiled long-time NBC News anchor Tom Brokaw using the Q & A format. Editor-in-Chief Sheldon Czapnik sat down with Brokaw and discussed the anchor's new book, the terrorist attacks on September 11, 2001, and changes in network television news. Here is how the narrative introduction and first questions and answers were presented to readers (Czapnik, 2002):

Tom Brokaw, a South Dakota native, joined NBC News in 1966. He was the White House correspondent for NBC News during Watergate, and from 1976 to 1981 anchored Today on NBC. He's been the anchor and managing editor of NBC Nightly News with Tom Brokaw since 1983, and has won every major award in broadcast journalism. *Renaissance Insights* editor-in-chief Sheldon Czapnik interviewed him in mid-July to talk about network news today. The conversation began with the effect of 9/11 on news coverage and the challenge that event is presenting to a new generation of Americans.

**Tom, you've seen so much—Watergate, Vietnam, the Cold War—and you've written several books on World War II. Given that background, was there anything that struck you in a special way about 9/11? What were your thoughts as you watched that unbelievable event?**

I think it was the wholly unexpected character of it and the nature of the attack. We go through cycles of innocence in America. We were in a big economic boom, we felt impervious to terrorism that was happening around the world, including terrorism that was directed at American targets in Tanzania, Kenya, the USS Cole. And then, out of the blue, civilian airliners were converted into guided missiles and there was a terrible human loss, a big psychological blow, obviously. What it did was expose our vulnerabilities; even though we are the most powerful military nation in the world, we had no defense against that. And it caused, I think everyone, to rethink all of those various components. How do we defend ourselves against terrorism, how do we defeat it? What is it about America that makes some radical Muslims think that we're unworthy? I guess what I came away thinking after 9/11, when I had a chance to catch my breath, is that we've never been in a situation like this before, an unconventional war. It comes to us from unexpected places. There are some radical Muslims out there who are determined to do as much damage to us as they possibly can.

**You gave a really excellent commencement speech at Johns Hopkins in May and in one part of it you talked about 9/11 as the beginning of what you**

called the "war of cultures." In other words it's not country against country or NATO versus the Warsaw Pact, all well-defined, but that so called "clash of civilization." How do you cover such a war?

Well, you cover it in a variety of ways; you don't cover it just with your best military correspondents. You also have to make sure that you're covering those aspects of it that I talked about at Johns Hopkins. . . . (p. 34)

*Rolling Stone,* which covers the entertainment world with emphasis on music and film, often publishes celebrity profiles. In addition to narrative style profiles, *Rolling Stone* editors use Q & A format presentations for a regular feature called "The Music Q & A." A recent example prepared by writer Jenny Eliscu focused on long-time singer and songwriter James Taylor (2002):

"I heard that my album was Number One on the Internet," says James Taylor, in a tone that suggests he's unsure whether that's a good thing. There's little doubt, though, that the fifty-four-year-old musician is enjoying a sweet comeback: October Road, his first new record since 1997, debuted on Billboard's albums chart at Number Four, putting him in the company of Eminem, Nelly, Avril Lavigne and Bruce Springsteen. But Taylor can name only one artist on the charts he actually digs: Norah Jones, whose music he calls "intriguing" and "dynamic." Mostly he still listens to the Brazilian blues, classical and folk he's always loved. "I was baked in a time when sensational production techniques weren't so available," he says. "Back when it was about how interesting details were, and it wasn't like getting hit over the head."

**What's your earliest musical memory?**

I remember when I was six or seven, I went away to a summer camp. They put us on a bus to take us somewhere, and the driver was listening to the Coasters' "Searchin' " on the radio. I'd never heard anything like that before. It sounded like people were playing pots and pans or throwing kitchen utensils downstairs. It lit my head on fire.

**What album have you listened to so much you had to stop playing it?**

When I was eighteen and on my own for the first time, living in New York, I had a small record collection, and I listened to those four or five records way too much. One was the Beatles' Revolver. Another was Fantasia on Greensleeve . . . Miles Davis' Sketches of Spain . . . the album with "Girl From Ipanema" on it, with Antonio Carlos Jobim and Astrud Gilberto; I listened to that to distraction. I remember the summer of '67 when I was listening to those. And I remember that apartment at Eighty-fourth and Columbus—in those days used to lie in bed and listen to glass break. It was a rough neighborhood. (Eliscu, 2002, p. 36)

As you may have noticed from the Tom Brokaw and James Taylor examples, the Q & A form has certain advantages. One is brevity. A second is the sense of realism, the feel of listening to the conversation that readers often get from the presentation style. They sense they were there during the interview. A key to success, however, is organization of questions and other information prior to the interview. These interviews do not have to be verbatim, of course, because it would then become a transcription. You have to edit and select material to be used as much as you would in the more traditional format. Because there is a strict Q & A format, the ordering of questions and answers must be as logical as any other sort of writing. There is also the need for some sort of editor's note to introduce the interview. You can write it, of course, for the editor, but this brief introduction needs to explain the who, what, when, where, why, and how of the Q & A.

---

## BASIC PROFILE INFORMATION CHECKLIST

Biographical material:
  Birth date, birthplace
  Schooling
  First job, other positions held
  Family (parents, brothers, sisters)
  Childhood friends

News peg information:
  Promotions, appointments, advancements
  Awards, honors, citations
  Present situation
  Environment and surroundings
  Home, workplace description, decor
  Former living and working environments (for contrast)

Physical characteristics:
  Physical appearance of person
  Mannerisms
  Clothing style
  Hairstyle
  Anecdotes and stories
  Embarrassing moments
  Greatest accomplishment
  Memorable first times

Family:
  Spouse, marriage information
  Previous marriages, commitments, or other relationships
  Children, ages and names
  In-laws
  Pets

Personal:
  General lifestyle, philosophies of living
  Plans for the future
  Personal Web sites
  Dreams and fantasies
  Hobbies, special interests
  Favorite foods and music
  Recreational activities
  Religion
  Military service
  Volunteer work or other civic or community service
  Club memberships
  Major traumas and problems (current or past)

---

This format also has its share of disadvantages. One is a lack of writing creativity. Of course, your editing creativity may substitute for it. There is often a need for precision in question asking and in recording responses. There is temptation to leave extraneous material in such articles, also, to keep them more realistic. But this is a reason to edit carefully and thoroughly. Make certain the answers stick to the questions and do not drift.

Industry and trade publications also use the Q & A format for profiles of prominent individuals in the business, often because of its efficiency in presenting information and its simplicity in organization. *Playboy* magazine's longtime series of interviews by Larry Grobel also effectively uses Q & A format to profile newsmaking individuals, partly because of the lengthy introductions often given to the Q & A interviews, but also because of the actual depth of the interviews and the answers to Grobel's questions as well.

## A Difference in Purpose

Art Spikol (1979), former editor of *Philadelphia* magazine, noted there is a clear distinction between the interview story and the profile. "Even if the terms are occasionally used interchangeably by beginning writers, the fact is that the two types of writing bear little resemblance to one another" (p. 7). Spikol said an interview is just that, a conversation with someone. He added the following:

> A profile is something else: It is an article whose main subject is a particular person, and it is rarely based exclusively on an interview or on interviews with that person. In fact, profiles are probably at their least expository—and writers at their laziest—when written with information supplied by their subjects. After all, no subject—particularly one with some sophistication dealing with the press—will supply information that might be damaging or embarrassing; the only anecdotes the writer will get will be those the subject wishes to share. (p. 7)

## Your Profile's Tone and Writing Approach

Do you have to love your subject? Trash them? Profiles should not be entirely positive or laudatory. Most are neutral or balanced in presentation. In fact, some profiles are written about a person who has been responsible for criminal activity or other socially unacceptable behavior. Your readers are likely interested in these persons as well.

Some profiles seem to write themselves, up to a point. Usually you can tell your readers the news and the past about the person. It is possible, Spikol (1979) said, you might wind up without a good ending. "Profiles are like that. You have swooped down on a subject and caught him at a certain point in time; naturally, you'll have to swoop away and leave him to act out the rest of the script. About all you can do is speculate a little about the subject's future" (p. 10).

Writer Tom Hallman Jr., a member of *The Oregonian* staff in Portland, told the amazing story of a young man with a severe facial disfiguration with a high level of sensitivity through his overall tone and respectful approach to the subject of the story and his family. Hallman spent almost a year working on his story about Sam, "the boy behind the mask," by spending hours with the boy and his family and hours with documents, medical records, family journals and diaries. He spent considerable amounts of time traveling to the East Coast with Sam and his family to see doctors, and hours and hours just hanging out at the family home. He even spent time going to school with Sam. The resulting 4-part series, published over consecutive days, was an emotional and poignant profile of the 14-year-old and his decision to undergo life-threatening surgery to improve his appearance. Hallman, a former police beat reporter for his newspaper, described scenes with exquisite detail, quoted Sam and his family and friends, and witnessed almost all major events during the period leading up to and following the delicate operation. The first installment in the series began this way (Hallman, 2000):

> The boy sits on the living room sofa, lost in his thoughts and stroking the family cat with his fragile hands. His younger brother and sister sit on the floor, chattering and playing cards. But Sam is overcome by an urge to be alone. He lifts the cat off his lap, ignoring a plaintive meow, and silently stands, tottering unsteadily as his thin frame rises in the afternoon light.
>
> He threads his way toward the kitchen, where his mother bends over the sink, washing vegetables for supper. Most 14-year-old boys whirl through a room, slapping door jambs and dodging around furniture like imaginary halfbacks. But this boy, a 5-foot, 83-pound waif, has learned never to draw attention to himself. He moves like smoke.
>
> He stops in the door frame leading to the kitchen and melts into the late-afternoon shadows.
>
> He watches his mother, humming as she runs water over lettuce. The boy clears his throat and says he's not hungry. His mother sighs with worry and turns, not bothering to turn off the water or to dry her hands. The boy knows she's

studying him, running her eyes over his bony arms and the way he wearily props himself against the door frame. She's been watching him like this since he left the hospital a few months before.

"I'm full," he says.

She bends her head toward him, about to speak. He cuts her off.

"Really, Mom. I'm full."

"OK, Sam," she says quietly.

The boy slips behind his mother and steps into a pool of light.

A huge mass of flesh balloons out from the left side of his face. His left ear, purple and misshapen, bulges from the side of his head. His chin juts forward. The main body of tissue, laced with blue veins, swells in a dome that runs from sideburn level to chin. The mass draws his left eye into a slit, warps his mouth into a small, inverted half moon. It looks as though someone has slapped three pounds of wet clay onto his face, where it clings, burying the boy inside.

The series of articles earned Hallman the 2001 Pulitzer Prize for feature writing. The complete series may be read at the Pulitzer Prize Web site (http://www.pulitzer.org/year/2001/feature-writing/works/).

## THE SUBJECT AS THE SOURCE

How do you choose the right person or subject for a profile? People and organizations are chosen for profiles because they are newsworthy. Because of what has happened to them lately, these persons are thrust voluntarily or involuntarily into the public eye and readers want to learn more about them. Judgments about the newsworthiness of a profile of an individual by editors are usually based on recent developments in the person's personal or professional life.

As noted earlier, people are not the only subjects of profiles. Cities, for instance, can be profiled, or institutions, or organizations. Such an article uses the same basic formula described for profiles of people—multiple sources, observations, a chronological summary of the city's recent history, and factual support for generalizations (a university study, among other sources). In choosing a subject, you should consider that a person would be a good candidate to be profiled if the individual is well known. An individual may be popular because of his or her professional activities, or the person may be controversial because of a position on an issue that may divide a profession, community, or even a family.

Another reason to profile someone is because the person has reached a new level in his or her career or personal life. This means there has been a promotion, a new accomplishment, career change, or other step taken recently. You also want to select an individual based on a third reason—leadership. The sort of person to profile is an industry or business leader who serves as a role model.

You should try to select individuals for their talkative nature and fluency of speech. A profile often is, in part, based on the thoughts of the person being highlighted. Someone who is not so glib or garrulous, for example, might not provide you with strong material for your story. Furthermore, it is also helpful for the subject to have a large circle of professional and personal acquaintances that are willing and able to discuss the subject of the article.

However, you do not always have to profile someone because of fame or recent accomplishments. Sometimes, especially for feature treatment, a profile can focus on someone who is not a celebrity. These "common" people, the rank and file, often also make good human-interest stories that are appealing to readers. For example, *The New Yorker* magazine publishes a newsletter as part of its education program. The publication goes to teachers and others who use the magazine as a teaching tool. In one recent issue, the newsletter, named *Talk of the Classroom,* profiled a university teacher who uses the magazine in her classes. The detailed article for the "Classroom Close-Up" department of the newsletter utilized a full page of the 12-page publication. The article told other teachers about the educational successes enjoyed by Professor Owene Weber, including, of course, how she uses *The New Yorker* as a "textbook" in her English composition and literature courses. Although the profile is purely descriptive, without direct quotations, it discusses this teacher's style, manner, and her research focusing on a *New Yorker* writer. The article contains advice of strong practical value for the newsletter's readers (A Classroom Close-Up, 1993).

The idea of profiles that focus on "ordinary people," of course, is to emphasize what makes this individual, who might otherwise be like your readers, a bit unique or successful. The profile of Weber achieves that goal. Spikol (1979) said profiles should be chosen depending on the answers to five questions:

1. Is the person everything he or she seems to be?
2. How did the person get that way?
3. How does the world react to, and perceive, the person?
4. How does the person perceive himself or herself?
5. What can we learn about the person by analyzing his or her environment—the people, places, and things with which he or she surrounds himself or herself?

After deciding the person is right for your attention and effort, you need several things to fall in place. For starters, to do the profile you need cooperation from the person you will be interviewing. A profile will rarely succeed without the person agreeing to be interviewed. Ideally, the person to be profiled will agree to the idea and allow you to interview him or her one or more times. This is not always an easy matter because the type of person you often profile is usually quite busy and in demand by many other people at work, home, and in the news media. Some people, such as those who feel they have been treated poorly by reporters, may resist you. However, most people like to be profiled and will agree to it.

You need a significant block of time with the person to get to know him or her. If possible, request interviews in several different environments. You need to talk with the person in his or her creative or work environment, but it adds a dimension to talk to the person at his or her home in a more relaxed setting. Being at both the work environment and home environment allows you the chance to see the person in distinctly different (most of the time, at least) environments. If possible, find a "neutral" location as well, such as a park where the person likes to jog or a quiet coffee shop, for conversations. The more variety of atmospheres you can use, the more you will learn about the individual.

People who do not want to be profiled or do not have time to talk to you can still be profiled. The job is just harder, requiring you to do more work in your research and in interviewing others who know the person well. For example, Gay Talese's (1966) widely read and reprinted profile of Frank Sinatra that first appeared in *Esquire* in 1963 characterized the entertainer without the author directly interviewing him. Instead, Talese carefully and tediously observed Sinatra and talked to Sinatra's friends and acquaintances to gather his information for the article, "Frank Sinatra Has a Cold." He watched Sinatra during filming of an NBC television program and he watched him with his friends in a Beverly Hills bar. Talese wrote down conversations he heard for passages of dialogue in his article. He noticed what the singer ate and drank. He watched Sinatra's mood changes. Talese incorporated all this research into his profile of a man who was, in Talese's words, "the champ." Here's how his article began, setting a scene and atmosphere displaying Sinatra's unusual mood:

> Frank Sinatra, holding a glass of bourbon in one hand and a cigarette in the other, stood in a dark corner of the bar between two attractive but fading blondes who sat waiting for him to say something. But he said nothing; he had been silent for much of the evening, except now in this private club in Beverly Hills he seemed even more distant, staring out through the smoke and semidarkness into a large room beyond the bar where dozens of young couples sat huddled around small tables or twisted in the center of the floor to the clamorous clang of folk–rock music blaring from the stereo. The two blondes knew, as did Sinatra's four male friends who stood nearby, that it was a bad idea to force conversation upon him when he was in this mood of sullen silence, a mood that had hardly been uncommon during this first week of November, a month before his fiftieth birthday. . . . (Talese, 1966, p. 89)

## ACCESSING AND OBSERVING THE SUBJECT

In the previous section, it was suggested that profile writers take the time to watch the subject of the profile do what he or she does best. Why are you writing about this person? Is he or she a top dress designer in a market? Then try to watch this person creating, designing, or at least, introducing his or her work at a show. For short-term fast profiles, it is difficult to do this, but for deeper profiles such as those used in magazines or other nondaily periodicals, it is essential for the success of the feature. If you are profiling a politician, watch the person interacting with constituents, on the floor of the legislature, and in a political party meeting. Each experience tells you more about the person and helps you write a more complete profile of the individual. This requires access and it is vital to writing a good profile. The person must, ultimately, grant access.

"The key in good profile reporting is access. It has always been access and will always be access," said veteran writer Walt Harrington (1997), who spent many years writing profiles of political leaders, religious leaders, entertainers, other prominent people, and what he called "ordinary people" for *The Washington Post*. "You need to be with your subject. You need to immerse yourself with your subject. You need to find time where you can be with your subject while they are doing what they do. This is classic immersion journalism. In profile writing, you need to be able to integrate that into your reporting" (Harrington, 1997).

The idea is to understand the person and not necessarily the image he or she presents, to understand his or her motivations and what drives the individual. Harrington asked the following:

> What is the hierarchy of values that makes them the person that they are? The techniques for doing pieces on people like that are not unlike the techniques I would use if I were going to do a profile on a typical 13-year-old boy or a fundamentalist family. I try to think in terms of doing profiles on prominent people the same way I think about doing profiles on an ordinary person. I've always had the catch phrase that "you find the extraordinary in the ordinary" and when you do prominent and famous people—you are really going out "to find the ordinary in the extraordinary." (Harrington, 1997)

Detailed observations and thorough understanding of the individual will help you create a better, more complete picture of this person in your mind, and, consequently, in the minds of your readers. Note the person's mannerisms. How does the person deal with other people? Is his or her work behavior with others different from behavior with superiors, with family, and with friends? If so, why? It is also beneficial to your profile to explore the meaning of the details you note—if possible. What do the peculiar office decorations that you noticed mean to the person using the space?

Your job as a profile writer is not only to dig out the facts and lay them out, it is to evoke the world in which that person lives. Evoke that person to make people in some way understand what it is like to be that person. By definition, the finest profile writing is sympathetic to the persons being interviewed in the sense that you are trying to make people understand their world as they see it. You are trying to use a lot of techniques to unravel the person's conception of the world (Harrington, 1997).

You can approach this in two ways. Depending on the individual and his or her activities, you can observe him or her without his or her knowledge you are doing so. This can be in public places, of course, when the individual is performing, speaking, or whatever. You can also, under circumstances where you might not be able to remain anonymous, watch as a known observer to the person. This might be necessary when you watch in a small-group situation for demonstrations or less public forms of work.

Profiles benefit from detail and depth of information. Profiles are about people and what they represent. To accomplish this type of understanding and content, a profile writer must spend time with the person and individuals around the person. For depth profiles, it can require traveling and observing in addition to interviewing. For Auletta (1997), long-time writer for *Esquire* and *The New Yorker* and author of several books that profile prominent business executives, gathering information for a profile means much field research. He advocated a process he calls "access journalism" that involves gaining complete access to his source and source's activities before he begins writing.

For a business executive, for example, this approach includes typical interviews, but also sitting in the office and attending normally private meetings as a "fly on the wall" and observing. In doing this, Auletta (1997) tried to visit the person at home as well as talk to the individual in his or her office. He recently wrote about international media executive Rupert Murdoch. "In Murdoch's case, I asked to go to his home. I had dinner at his home. I always ask them to let me talk to their spouse. In most cases, they allow it, but in Murdoch's case, he could not deliver his wife—she wouldn't see me. She didn't trust—I interviewed his kids, his family, friends. I saw how he lived" (Auletta, 1997).

*The Washington Post's* Harrington (1997) offered an observation trick that adds detail to his profiles (what he calls "nonfiction short stories"). He carries and uses a camera and a large amount of audio taping. At times, when activities are too fast or hectic to note detail he may want to use later, he takes his own photographs as a form of note-taking:

> It helps me evoke scenes and settings. There are times when something is going on too fast and you cannot quite get it. Sometimes in my pieces you might have a description of a look on somebody's face, or the way they are holding their body, or the way that they're pointing to someone's chest while they are talking to them. It is literally the description of a photograph that I have taken that I can build upon. It gives me an image to deal with in my mind—I use a lot of tape. You cannot get detail and precision without a tape recorder—There's too many things going on. (Harrington, 1997)

## OTHER SOURCES THAT MAKE A DIFFERENCE

As with other types of feature articles, one source is not enough to give a full picture of what you are writing for your readers. Even if that source is the subject of the story, you should not stop with just this source. You can be fooled by a good interview or series of interviews with your source into thinking you have everything you need to write; you do not. Good profiles are balanced in their use of sources. You should attempt to give the positive and negative elements of the individual and you usually have to go beyond the person for that. Writer Lou Ann Walker, who has completed numerous profiles for magazines such as her profile of Candice Bergen for *New York Woman*, strongly recommends this approach. "Become friendly with the people who work with the person you're interviewing," Walker (1992, p. 323) suggested.

> Charming a secretary who is snooty can lead to important revelations. One such secretary confided in me that the actress I was interviewing was just breaking up with a man and dating someone new. I would have never have found that out if I hadn't done a little buttering up. (Walker, 1992, p. 323)

So, how many interviews are enough? Seldom do you need to interview as many as 50 people. Some writers do this, but usually that kind of depth is necessary only for a book. Generally, you can get a good sense of the person by talking to a half dozen to a dozen sources. This is no magic range. The real trick is variation in the type of source you use. Too many similar sources will not tell you anything new. You need to try to find a balance of friendly and unfriendly sources, and family and professional sources, for example. There are seven categories of human interview sources you can most often use. Here's a list:

1. Family members such as brothers, sisters, parents, spouses, and children. Former family members such as ex-spouses should be included.
2. Neighbors and former neighbors.
3. Business associates where the person works.
4. Business associates through professional organizations.
5. Competitors and rivals in the workplace.
6. Personal friends.
7. People that work where the person shops and places where the person goes for entertainment.

You want to incorporate as many anecdotes as possible into your article to help generate "insight" into the person's personality. During your interviews, encourage the person and your other sources to tell these stories. These should be informative, amusing, and profound.

There are two other types of research to use in a profile beyond interviews. You should also check clippings of other articles written about the person (this is particularly true of newspaper writers who have access to such libraries). Although magazine writers might not have such resources as easily available, the fact that many newspapers have computerized their libraries and now sell access to the public, research for freelancers and magazine writers without office libraries is not as serious a problem as it was a decade ago. Another form of research to complete in preparing your profile is public records. You may find interesting details about a person by reviewing civil and criminal court files, police records, property records, and other public documents of similar nature. This is especially applied to profiles of individuals in public service such as appointed and elected government officials. It is also an effective strategy to learn more about business executives, entertainers, athletes, and others widely known in your community or region whose activities are on the public record.

## OBSERVING YOUR PROFILE SUBJECT

Some of the best profiles are built on research through first-hand observation. For profiles of public people who lead very public lives, this is not difficult. Go out and watch them do their thing. In you have an assignment to profile an entertainer, go to some of the live performances. If the person is a politician, go to the public meetings and attend some of his or her speeches. If the person is a social leader, try to get invitations or tickets to some of the parties or charitable events this individual supports and attends. Watch them work.

The descriptions of the individual add an entirely different dimension to your work. The information you obtain from an interview or two with the person is critical, no doubt, but observations give you richness in detail that you cannot always find in interviews. You see and, perhaps, hear how the person works. You see the person interact with others in his or her most comfortable milieu.

Walker (1992), who specializes in writing profiles of entertainers and other celebrities, believes this is one of her most useful tactics in creating a profile:

> One of the best tactics is to stay with the person all day, particularly on a movie set. Academy Award winning actress Marlee Matlin allowed me to tag along on a free day, and we had a most illuminating time. I let her drive me all over Los Angeles. (Frankly it was a death-defying stunt. She's so excitable that when she uses her hands to sign, she often takes both of them off the steering wheel.) She took me to visit her elderly grandmother in a nursing home, and I could see the family affection. We went to a Beverly Hills restaurant where she used her TTY—to have a conversation with her boyfriend, an actor on location in Canada. It was these small moments that made our interview memorable. (p. 323)

These moments can also be obtained second-hand, of course, by interviewing others. There is no real substitute for the real thing and being there yourself. Of course, this creates access issues. To be able to spend time with a busy actress such as Matlin requires arrangements well in advance. Access to celebrities, major business executives, political leaders, and other busy individuals in the news and public spotlight, is not often easy to obtain. If access is granted, the additional depth to the story is superior to most other observation. This does not prevent you from spending time watching the individual in public. For some persons, this will not occur often. Reclusive individuals are most difficult. But for some profile subjects, public appearances are part of their lives and therefore easier in your effort to observe them and to profile them.

## SPECIAL PROBLEMS INVOLVING CELEBRITIES

As noted, there are numerous barriers to gaining access to celebrities such as Marlee Matlin. These people are always in demand by writers for stories of all types. These barriers include secretaries and receptionists for business executives; bodyguards, publicists and press agents for entertainers; and public information officers and media relations liaisons for individuals in high levels of public service. Their jobs include "protecting" their employers from people who might want to interrupt or disrupt.

There is a strategy to get to your source for the interviews you need for your article. Your first step is to fully identify yourself and directly ask the celebrity's assistants for their help, explaining what work you are doing and why. Because your work is legitimate and serious, you might get to the person to request the interview. You might also be asked to wait while your request is taken to the person for a response. If you work for a publication, your reputation and your publication's reputation can be an asset. Do not be afraid to use it to help you.

If you are still denied access, then try to work your way around the barriers. One way is to find the person as he or she leaves the workplace, or where the person shops on weekends, or at some other public location where you can introduce yourself and state your purpose. This direct approach often works, although it requires extra effort. There are occasions when a writer, stopped by a person's staff, gets an interview because he or she went to the extra effort to ask directly. It is possible, and often is the case, that the person never got the original request submitted to an intermediary.

Some creative reporters and writers use a different approach. They will write an e-mail message or send a letter to tough-to-reach subjects. This is a way to access busy people, well-known business executives, celebrities, politicians, athletes, and others who have tremendous demands on their time.

You can also use published or broadcast quotations from other sources that you locate in your research. Of course, this means you must attribute the information to its source in your article. You can take these from speeches, press conferences, and similar public events. And it does not harm your article to tell readers that you made attempts to reach the person but were refused for whatever reasons.

## 12 TIPS ON WRITING PROFILES

Here are a dozen tips from David McDaniel (1986, p. 4), business editor of the
Neptune, NJ, *Asbury Park Press*:

1. One of the best ways for writers to portray character is with *anecdotes*. Get
   these from the subject and from people who know the person such as business
   associates, family, and friends. One good anecdote, like a good photo, could
   be worth a thousand words. "What was your most frustrating experience?
   Why did you decide to go into business/politics?" These questions might get
   you a good anecdote.

2. Profile pieces should use some description of *physical characteristics* such as
   mannerisms, appearance, and dress, all of which can be woven into a story or
   dropped in with a paragraph. Don't be afraid to make obvious characteriza-
   tions. Is the subject rugged looking (large build, beard, ruddy complexion)? Is
   he or she well dressed and attractive (well-groomed, neatly pressed suit,
   starched white shirt, neatly combed hair)?

3. Find out as much about the person's *business or job* as you can. For a business
   executive, for example, what are the company's assets, annual sales, main
   products? How many employees, at how many locations? What is unique
   about the business?

4. Include all the usual *biographical material*—age, family, education, service, and
   so on. Much can be tacked on at the end, but it is better to weave this into
   your story.

5. Be sure to include the subject's *tastes and habits*. Does he or she chain-smoke?
   Like classical music? Have an unusual hobby?

6. Find out what the person's *goals* are. Is he or she satisfied with the present situation? Where does this person want to be in ten years—expanding the present
   business or sitting on someone else's board of directors?

7. Ask what *influences* made the subject a success today. Parents? Spouse?
   Teacher? Tragedy?

8. Try to find out the person's *shortcomings*. Use them, if necessary, to give the
   entire picture.

9. Get three times as many *quotes* as you need. Get them from the subject,
   spouse, friends, competitors, and suppliers. Good quotes tell the story best.

10. Ask the subject to give *advice* to others aspiring to the same career and to
    make predictions about the future of the industry.

11. In preparation, *research* the subject by seeking library clips, other articles or ad-
    vertisements by the person's company. Be prepared with good, thought pro-
    voking questions and try to put your subject at ease.

12. Form your lead after the interview, but keep your eyes and ears open for the
    "*peg*" as you gather material.

If you are fortunate enough to get an interview with your subject, then you must, like any other interviewer, get yourself prepared. Grobel (1978), who has interviewed celebrities for *Playboy* magazine, said it helps to have certain expectations for the "star" interview. "Know what you are getting into. Find out in advance if there is a time limit—Good interviews are ones in which the subject is as interested as you are. That's difficult with celebrities, who have to hear the same questions over and over, but that's not impossible" (p. 20).

You may have restrictions other than time. You might be asked to conduct your interview with another writer in a small group setting. You may have a language barrier and need translation, so you actually interview the translator. You may be told that you have to conduct the interview with this busy celebrity in an unusual environment—in a car, backstage, or even at home with the kids screaming and dogs barking.

Prepare your major questions in advance and write them down. You might wind up not needing them, but these serve as a crutch when awkward slow moments occur. And tape your interview for accuracy. For very important interviews, use two tape recorders to guard against mechanical failures. This also lets you participate more in the conversation because you do not have to spend so much effort taking detailed notes. Grobel (1978), *Playboy's* veteran interviewer, also recommended that you should work to keep control of the interview. This means you should be in charge of the direction of the conversation. Change topics if you must do so when a pause or interruption occurs.

## THE NEED FOR FOCUS

You now know that a good profile has focus. When you are beginning to work on a profile, you need to think about what focus it will have. Most people that are worthy of profiles have multiple elements of their personalities and accomplishments that force you to choose a particular direction for the profile. When you are restricted on length, particularly for traditional newspaper or newsletter profiles of 750 to 1,500 words (three or four pages), you cannot afford to drift aimlessly in your description of the individual. You can probably get deeper into an individual in magazine profiles if the luxury of a longer manuscript (5,000 to 10,000 words, or 20 to 40 pages, for example) comes with the assignment. This would permit you the chance to probe several directions. But most profiles do not permit such depth and require more writing discipline through limited focus. Some profile writers call this focus a "theme" for the article. Whatever it is called, the point is the same—give your article some direction. The direction might become apparent in your research before you begin interviewing or writing. Even if it is not after you have completed most of your research, you can still look for the focus during your interviews with the person and others.

Like many of the magazines that frequently publish profiles and personality sketches that are discussed in this chapter, well-edited newspapers use profiles in more than an ordinary manner. One example is the *Dallas Morning News*. The *Dallas Morning News* has published a Sunday edition special feature called "High Profiles" for many years. The profile presents a lengthy look at a community leader and a full page is given to the story and accompanying photographs. A recent High Profile, written by *News* staff writer Dianne Solis (2002), focused on celebrated artist Celia Alvarez Muñoz:

> At the U.S.–Mexico border, where El Paso and Ciudad Juárez meet, there is a 600-acre patch of land known as the Chamizal. There, for a century, the Rio Grande ran through it, frequently changing its course.
>
> Rainstorms, floods and erosion would muddy the border. Mexicans would suddenly find that they were north of the river; on the other occasions, gringos would find that they were south of the Rio.
>
> Celia Alvarez grew up in the '40s and '50s near the Chamizal, and the cultural convulsions left their impression in her memory.
>
> As Mexicans moved into what was the United States, houses erupted in color hues of mango shades of raspberry. Blooming cactus replaced frilly peonies.
>
> The "Chamizalization" of El Paso would eventually become the Chamizalization of all the United States, as Latin migration changed the United States.
>
> And Celia Alvarez would tell its story through her photo-based paintings, elegantly rendered romanticizations of the tension that is universal to immigration as border points across the globe.
>
> "We all know that epochs and places in time are defined by big forces," says the artist, who married and became Celia Alvarez Muñoz.
>
> "Writers and artists are those that interpret it. I am an excavator using social archaeology. All those digs inform you."
>
> The Chamizal boundary fight ended legally in 1963 when President John F. Kennedy moved the border back to its position at the time of the Treaty of Guadalupe in the 1800s. Ms. Muñoz would soon find other tales to tell.
>
> Like any good storyteller, she knows that conflict moves the plot along. Frequently, she accompanies her pieces with text, a means of solidifying the narrative, high-lighting the tension. . . . (p. 3F)

Themes are important to profiles. Professor Edward Yates (1985) suggested that, in searching for that theme, you remain flexible. "If he or she (the writer) has selected a theme from pre-interview research and a more interesting one develops during the questioning, he or she must be ready to switch directions" (p. 210). Yates said themes often concern a person's range or type of experience, personality or character traits, aspirations in life, personal achievements, or philosophy of life.

Like other individuals in the public eye, professional athletes often are good subjects for profiles. These types of profiles often have themes such as conflicts, comebacks, the underdog, and so forth. In the case of the profile written by

Kevin Cook (2002) for *T & L* (*Travel & Leisure*) *Golf* magazine, about Spanish professional golfer Sergio Garcia, the themes are the conflict and intense competition of the international Ryder Cup tournament. Cook profiles Garcia and suggests that he will lead the European team in the latest competition. He sets the scene and theme by focusing on a dramatic moment at a previous cup:

> He heard the roar. After losing his last match he found himself hurrying toward the seventeenth green at The Country Club in Brookline, jostling through throngs of enemy fans. That's when Sergio Garcia heard a huge, joyful noise and knew his team had lost the 1999 Ryder Cup. "The Americans were jumping around," he says. "I was sure it was over." But it wasn't. To his amazement, U.S. players and their wives had danced and jumped on the green while Garcia's countryman Jose Maria Olazabal waited to putt. Olazabal could still tie Justin Leonard, who had just jarred a forty-five-foot putt, but now the green was being trampled and Ollie was clearly distracted. "That moment, it was difficult to watch," Garcia says, looking annoyed. Then his smile reappears. It is never gone for long. He shrugs—a shrug that says whatever is Spanish for "whatever"—and reshapes the memory with positive spin: "The Americans apologized, as they should, and I accept it. And now we try again to beat them!"
>
> Garcia, 22, might be the most appealing professional golfer of all. He might be the most talented (except for Tiger Woods) and could soon be the richest (ditto), perhaps even the one with the most gorgeous girlfriend (no comment). And now we are getting to the heart of the matter, for like every other player he must always be compared to Woods. Unlike most of the rest, however, Garcia invites the comparison. He welcomes the challenge. "I want to beat Tiger," he says. He is smiling, but not joking. (p. 116)

## WRITING PERSONALITY SKETCHES

A personality sketch is not as involved with the subject as a profile must be. Although some personality sketches are as long as some newspaper or magazine profiles, sketches generally are short and to the point. The article is designed to give us a quick look at an individual and to tell us why the person is important. These articles usually lack the depth of profiles and must not waste words with the reader.

Rivers (1992) said a personality sketch is a tough assignment, forcing you to "become a keen observer and recorder of significant details" (p. 254). These articles, Rivers noted, contain imagery created by details that you find in profiles. However, there is just not as much in these shorter pieces. You must show; do not tell. You have to do this in your own sketches. Rivers also suggested that sketches be strengthened by use of anecdotes. These have tremendous value to you as a writer and offer much strength to your sketch. "Anecdotes, by their nature, are not great world-shaping events. They are human looks at something. They have small cores, but radiate ramifications" (p. 260).

## BEST SOURCES FOR WRITING PROFILES

People
Person being profiled
Family
Neighbors
Workplace associates, rivals and competitors
Businesses where person shops
Observations
Person at work
Person at home with family, friends
Person enjoying personal activities
Library research
Resumes, press kits
Public records
Writings by person, if any
Previous newspaper, magazine article clippings
Film and video tape, if available

## WRITING CAPSULE AND THUMBNAIL PROFILES

Brief or capsule profiles, often called thumbnail profiles, are growing in popularity with newspaper and magazine editors. These profiles are quite short, just a few hundred words, and usually follow a standard format developed by the editors of the publication or news service. These formats may even vary within the publication, with different sections or departments offering their own profiles depending on the nature of the subject being profiled.

There is also a trend toward writing profiles of nonhuman subjects such as institutions, corporations, sports teams, network programs, films, and similar subjects. These articles follow a certain content outline, usually set by the individual publication based on a dozen or more categories of information, and are regularly offered. A new company, a successful business, or a new investment category might be profiled by a business magazine, specialized company or industry newsletter, or business section of a newspaper. At the beginning of a new sports season, standardized profiles of teams or leagues might be part of a special section or part of the regular coverage of a top game of the day or week. In the news section during election campaign periods, personality sketches or capsule profiles of all serious candidates are standard fare. In entertainment, profiles of new movies, books, records, and other art forms are commonplace. Each of these serves a purpose for the reader: The capsulized profile is an information digest for quick reading. These capsule profiles can be placed within larger articles on broader subjects as a sidebar or placed beside articles of equal importance.

Some publications ask people to profile themselves by answering a short standard list of questions. This form is an abstracted version of what you might write in a full profile, but without the elaboration. These short profiles are the bare bones. There are no wasted words. They are direct to the point.

## AVOIDING PROFILE PROBLEMS

Can you make mistakes when writing profiles? Yes. You can permit yourself to be overly positive, impressed with the "star" quality of the person you are profiling, or be intimidated, or superficial. These are three major pitfalls of many beginners, especially students. And you can talk too much during the interview, for example. Some interviewers get involved in the interview to the level of talking too much and getting less from the source as a result. Or you can waste valuable time with terrible questions. To avoid mistakes, exert self-control and discipline. Be careful not to depend on only the person you are interviewing. Perhaps worst of all, you can be "steered" by the person to a certain agenda and focus of the person's choosing.

One way to avoid some of these problems is to use numerous sources representing a variety of perspectives. Do your homework, of course. Research for background provides a strong foundation for the story and your interviews. As for writing the story, there are some tips for that part of the profile assignment also.

- Do not write in chronology only. Select a strong focus for your article.
- Do not drift.
- Do not jumble your facts together.
- Use good transitions to connect the pieces.
- Above all, do not forget your nut graf.

John A. Limpert, *The Washingtonian* magazine editor, said beginning profile writers often make poor decisions in approaching their craft. Because they are big part of the magazine writing and editing, Limpert said it is important to avoid these basic mistakes (personal communication, September 29, 1988 and January 21, 1993):

> *Thinking it's an easy payday.* When writers tell me they like to write profiles, it sets off warning bells. Often they mean an easy personality piece from a quickie interview. Best-selling author Judith Viorst was one of our best profile writers. She would first read about the subject, then call the subject and say: "I'd like to do a story on you. I've read a lot about you. Before we talk, can you give me the names of people who know you well, both friends and enemies?" Famed trial

lawyer Edward Bennett Williams said he never asked a question in court he didn't know the answer to; writers should know most of the answers before they start asking the questions of the profile subject.

*Loving the subject too much.* In a variation of the Stockholm Syndrome, in which hostages begin to identify with their captors, some profile writers develop too much empathy with their subjects. When it comes time to write the profile, the writer worries more about the profile subject than the reader. The writer has to make a shift in mindset after the research: When you sit down to write, your loyalty is to the reader. You owe the reader a clear-eyed, professional look at the subject, and you can't worry about pleasing or displeasing the subject.

*Hating the subject too much.* Again, you owe the reader a clear-eyed look even if the subject has been difficult to deal with or runs into one of your biases.

*Trying to be too clever.* Some writers try to cover up weak research or a dull subject with very clever writing. It's harder to fool readers than many writers think. A good editor has a sensitive BS detector and won't let you get away with it. A corollary: Write about sophisticated ideas in simple language, not the other way around.

*Giving up when the subject won't cooperate.* Some of our best profiles were done on people who wouldn't talk to us. It takes a lot of smart reporting to do this kind of piece, and, again, don't let the subject's feelings toward you poison your attitude, but the lack of cooperation allows you more freedom to make judgments and draw conclusions. And we've often found that uncooperative subjects become cooperative when they realize we're going to do a good reporting piece on them whether they talk or not.

*Not thinking enough about how you're going to get the reader into the subject.* Leads—usually a good scene or anecdote—are important, but also think about what kind of headline, art, captions, and pull quotations the story needs. Editors appreciate suggestions (but not demands). If you were the reader, what in the story would interest you the most? Suggest that these points be highlighted. Many readers graze through publications, looking for a picture or caption or headline or pull quote that interests them. Then they may read your story.

*Not protecting your reputation.* Some writers try to build a fast name for themselves by doing what we call "hit" pieces. It's the journalistic equivalent of an assassination. I've seen it work for some writers for brief periods of time, but media subjects are getting more sophisticated. Before they talk to you, the subjects will do some checking: How fair are you? How accurate are you? Is your main goal to leave a lot of blood on the floor? Conversely, some tough profile subjects will talk to you if you send them copies of stories you've done along with a letter explaining what a fair, thorough, knowledgeable writer you are. (Limpert, personal communication, September 29, 1988 and January 21, 1993)

# CHAPTER NINE

# Seasonal Features

When you think of seasons, perhaps you think of the weather, or sports, maybe food, perhaps special clothing, or the holidays, or vacations, or family gatherings. There are many types of seasons and people connect as many different memories, activities, and traditions with them. We often associate vacation camp with summer, for example. In the winter and spring of each year, typically, many daily newspapers and certain magazines devote attention to summer camps. As part of this annual activity, parents and children spend countless winter and spring hours talking about camps and deciding what they will do that upcoming summer. Will they attend the same camp as last year, or something new, or will there be a new specialty or theme for this year's camp? As a seasonal feature doubling in a service role, these articles help such discussions with new information and descriptions.

Journalists often write feature articles about the seasons and seasonal activities such as summer camp. Seasonal articles celebrate the regularity of life—the cycles and rhythms of nature and human life that govern our lives. Traditional seasonal stories, such as one about Christmas or Easter, call your readers' attention to the beginnings and ends of important segments of their lives—such as the shift from winter to spring and summer—to special dates and events that demand our recognition and memory.

Seasons, as a force of nature, transcend all human life. The seasons dictate the parameters of human life: seasons affect plant life, animal life, the world climate, Earth's natural and seemingly unnatural events, migration, hibernation, and the Earth itself. British author Anthony Smith (1970) said quite succinctly that "the complex rhythm of our planet Earth, rotating upon its axis in its orbit around the sun, encircled all the while by its neighbour the moon, provides the basis for the ceaseless rhythm of life itself" (p. 16). The growing concern with man and life rhythms emphasizes the regularity of life. The cycles of life have evolved over thousands of generations to what we now know of it.

In this century, modern writers have provided seasonal articles for their readers to help them prepare for changing natural seasons, for the end-of-year religious holidays such as Christmas and Chanukah, for the beginning of vacation, for the start of a new school year, for graduation, for ethnic celebrations, for national and regional birthdays and anniversaries, for special days for mothers and fathers, and even for the loves of our lives. Few publications overlook marking these events in some fashion each year. For some publications, entire issues may be built on the season or holiday. For others, a brief article may be sufficient. But for most, something in between is preferred.

Mandy Bolen, a reporter and feature writer for the daily *Key West Citizen* in South Florida, told her newspaper's readers what to expect in the month of October with a front-page story about how the change in calendar—a new month—means a series of annual welcome changes for their community. The beginning of the month signals change in the summer weather. The end of the month brings Halloween and a major downtown festival and the beginnings of the high tourist season. Here's what Bolen (2002) wrote:

> The new calendar page, the one usually decorated with pumpkins and orange leaves, slipped quietly into view with almost no one noticing its arrival.
>
> The town has been a little preoccupied. Rent is due this week, and there has been a marked absence of visitors since the bikers roared out of town. The sailors filled the streets for a few days, and Key Westers have been keeping one eye on storms that just won't die.
>
> The wind has been blowing—hard—for what seems like weeks, and the humidity has remained relentless.
>
> But there's light at the end of the tunnel that was September, and the island's dance card is getting full.
>
> The new month brings perennial delights and the promise of cash for thousands of workers who have been living on draft beer and Ramen noodles for the past 30 days.
>
> October brings with it that first comfortably cool breeze of the fall. No one knows when it will drift through town, but its arrival is imminent, its relief immediate, as long as it doesn't have a name.
>
> The autumn month brings earlier sunsets as daylight savings ends on the 27th. It brings a gradual end to necessary air conditioning and signals the return of open windows.
>
> It ushers in a weekend of local reunions in the back yard of Blue Heaven, where friends, classmates and former roommates bump into each other amid curried goat and various kebobs. Petronia Street turns into a happy promenade during Goombay, when costumes are still being planned and beads are just beginning to appear by the thousands.
>
> The small-town character of Goombay is quickly swallowed by the international melee of Fantasy Fest that marches down U.S. 1 and explodes on Old Town streets throughout the week, finally culminating in a dizzying sensory overload of sights, sounds and surrealism.
>
> But as visitors wince against the Sunday daylight on Oct. 27, hundreds of locals bid them farewell and trudge off to Bayview Park because it's the kids' turn to have a good time at Children's Day, where the town once again becomes a small one.
>
> Kids see their teachers dressed in shorts and T-shirts. Little ones fall asleep on picnic blankets. And dad-sized shoulders offer optimal views of the park and its costumed frolickers gearing up for Halloween.

October may have slipped quietly into town, but its departure is always a noisy one.

(Reprinted with permission of the *Key West Citizen*.)

Unusual perspectives are often what it takes to get a reader's attention to a routine seasonal event. A typical fall season story might focus on the change in weather, household chores, or special holidays such as Halloween or Thanksgiving. Since many of us associate seasons with food, *Tulsa World* Living section staff writer Ashley Parrish (2002) decided to write about fall dishes to serve at home. Her article offered a series of fresh ideas for fall seasonal foods, such as apples, and other produce. Here are the lead paragraphs for her article for the *Tulsa World's* food pages to show how she set up the article:

The urge to fill this story with fall dishes was strong.

There must be something instinctual about September, because slow-cooked apples suddenly sounded wonderful and there was an overwhelming desire to simmer something.

Luckily, apples are starting to hit the market. And there's the winter squash, already displayed with Halloween decorations. The weather report is calling for slightly cooler temperatures, so maybe it really is time to start cooking again.

But there are a couple of good weeks of summer produce left. The peaches that took so long to get here this summer are almost over, but the late varieties are very good. So we've got a peach recipe for you. And you might pick up a watermelon before the season runs out.

This first recipe comes from October's *Food and Wine* magazine, which is worth seeking out. It hits a perfect note for this time of year, with a zucchini, basil linguine and other late summer treats and a preview of fall with boeuf bourguignon, braised short ribs and this apple buckle. (Parrish, 2002, p. D7)

Parrish (2002) discussed various special dishes made from apples, watermelon, and peaches. For a beginning feature writer, perhaps one of the more basic features to master is a seasonal feature article, no matter what section of the newspaper or department of the magazine and no matter what time of the year.

Fall is also state fair season in many states. A unique approach to the state fair story was taken by Associated Press writer Edward Perez (2002), who wrote about the unusual state fair treat that had begun to appear along midways around the country. He wrote about deep-fried Twinkies. His story, with its unusual twist, will amuse readers. Here's how he began his story:

LITTLE ROCK, Ark.—In the South, where some joke that the four basic food groups are barbecued, baked, broiled or fried, state fairs are filled with booths that sell everything from corn on a stick to club-like turkey legs.

For dessert, an odd new treat has emerged: fried Twinkies.

Phil Dickson of Hot Springs has sold about 1,000 of the batter-dipped, deep-fried goodies topped with powdered sugar since the Arkansas State Fair opened Friday.

"It's amazing to me," Dickson said Monday. "The response has just been tremendous."

Each Twinkie, at 160 calories and five grams of fat a pop, is impaled on a stick and frozen until firm, then dipped in a batter similar to that used to fry fish.

Deep frying adds more calories and fat, and the powdered-sugar coating apparently complements the Twinkie's altered state.

"The inside creamy part stays cool, while the outside is warm," said Rhonda Yates, a postal worker spending her vacation helping Dickson with the Twinkie booth.

Fairs in Arizona, California, Kansas and Washington also are expected to roll out fried Twinkies this year.

Suzanne Hackett, the general manager of an English restaurant in New York City called The ChipShop, said the fried Twinkie was born in her eatery out of boredom.

"We had a very slow night in the restaurant so we decided to buy a bunch of junk food and deep fry it," Hackett said Monday. "And the Twinkies just tasted so good."

Interstate Brands Corp., the firm that owns Twinkie-maker Hostess, doesn't object to the new creation—it actually promotes the idea—though it doesn't suggest a steady diet of the culinary concoction. . . . (Perez, 2002)

Articles such as the food features by Ashley Parrish (2002) and Edward Perez (2002) show how easy it is to take a normal home activity such as cooking or a fun treat such as state fair junk food and apply it to the unique situation of the fall season. These articles are necessary throughout the year and appear in just about every part of every newspaper, magazine, newsletter, and online news site, and there are ample opportunities to write them.

"Seasonal articles are not particularly hard to write—in fact, I think they are easier than general articles," said veteran seasonal article writer Clinton Parker (1975). "They do require a certain depth of research, however, and absolute historical accuracy. That's why it is best to specialize in a particular event or field. Once you have done the basic reading for the specialty, the articles are much easier to write" (Parker, 1975, p. 44).

Whether or not you specialize in seasonal articles, you will find that much of your feature article writing is controlled by the calendar. Newspapers, magazines, and newsletters run features to highlight special events on the calendar each year. Readers expect it. Seasonal features are not much different from the other types of features. In fact, you will probably mix some of the different elements and types of feature articles when writing a seasonal article. There may be humorous seasonal stories, or highly personalized stories, or stories with great human-interest elements, or a review of traditional holiday season music, food, or dance. This chapter focuses, however, on the context of the article regardless of the approach taken.

## REFLECTING APPROPRIATE TONE

One significant point is that seasonal features should reflect the tone and the theme of the season. Local customs and traditions largely dictate this. A seasonal feature can be ruined with the wrong approach. It would, obviously, be in poor taste to write an irreverent feature about the military for Memorial Day or Veteran's Day. Then again, a newspaper reporter or magazine writer who does not try to be especially creative and tricky on April Fool's Day or Halloween is completely missing the point of those special days.

It is not unusual for newspapers to run several seasonal articles at the beginning and during a major holiday or holiday season. Labor Day is an example. Each fall, newspapers and magazines advance the special weekend and national holiday as well as cover the special events scheduled honoring those who work hard for a living. Paula Kaufman, a writer for the Charleston, WV, *Gazette,* drew an assignment to cover a traditional Labor Day picnic. Her story began with historical context for the holiday and then focused on local activities to celebrate the day. In an area of the country where coal mining is a significant part of the local economy, she wrote about one of her area's largest events. She found a unique and unlikely combination of teens and politicians at the event and tried to show the common interests of the two groups. Her story describes the event's atmosphere, the feelings and opinions expressed by those present, and the sentiments about the mine workers of West Virginia (Kaufman, 2002):

> In 1894, President Grover Cleveland signed a bill making Labor Day (celebrated the first Monday in September) a national holiday. Since that time more than a century ago, the United States has risen to the occasion to celebrate workers' values, organizations, working people and their families in myriad ways.
>
> Wearing caps collected at home, symbolic of miners' struggles over the years, my younger sisters and I followed the beckoning scent of chili dogs, the promise of peanut butter fudge and the sight of iced tea. We were led through the large crowd that gathered in Racine for one of the state's largest Labor Day celebrations. It has been in existence for 64 years.
>
> While I took a seat on the metal bleachers, my sisters grabbed their towels and raced toward the adjacent outdoor pool, which was free on Labor Day.
>
> After listening to country music, the president of the United Mine Workers of America, Cecil Roberts, took the microphone and declared, "Labor Day means freedom for everyone that works and recognizing workers' struggles and accomplishments."
>
> "Over 200,000 workers have either lost their lives in the coal mines or to [black lung disease] to stoke the furnaces in faraway cities and to keep America run-

ning," he said. "These people were your brothers, fathers, sons, grandparents and loved ones."

A nearby Boone County resident could be seen wiping tears from her eyes. She was wearing a shirt that read, "I'm a coal miner's widow." Like many retired coal miners and their families, she was there to celebrate the labor movement.

"The union gave my husband a pension, better health care and Social Security—things our life would have been terrible without," she said.

Besides Roberts, Sen. Jay Rockefeller, D–W.Va., Gov. Bob Wise, Democratic Congressional candidate Jim Humphries, former Boone County Sheriff Johnny Protan, other politicians and people of all ages turned out for the festivities.

Karie Dolphin, a seventh-grader at Sherman Junior High School, said she has come to the Racine County Labor Day picnic many times and has always enjoyed herself.

Thirteen-year-old Sara Workman said, "I come because my granddad's the chairman of this picnic, and I feel it's important for us to keep celebrating this tradition."

While Workman walked around the many vendors' stalls and hot dog stands, other teen-agers had fun watching a wrestling match. "I could have wrestled but decided just to watch my dad instead," said Bo Conrad, a freshman at George Washington High School.

Gov. Wise said Labor Day is significant for young people because it is important for them to realize that Americans have the freedoms we do because of labor and what it stands for.

Backstage, Sen. Rockefeller (who started out in West Virginia as a Boone County poverty worker 38 years ago) talked about how it felt to return to the area.

"It's very emotional for me because this was my beginning, and I worked only a few miles down the road from here."

WSAZ–TV cameraman Phillip Copney commented on the atmosphere of the event. "In this area, you will find the best people you will ever meet, and you can sometimes hear stories from the older generations about picket lines and the mines," he said. (p. 1C)

(Reprinted by permission of the Charleston *Gazette*.)

Although it is more common to publish a major article or feature package of several articles, some newspapers produce entire special sections in recognition of local festivals or holiday periods. Similarly, it is not unusual to find a monthly specialized magazine devote a cover and a majority of its top articles in the issue to a seasonal theme. Food and entertaining magazines often prepare "special holiday issues" featuring new recipes, party and gift ideas, holiday getaways, and, of course, their versions of the ultimate Easter, Thanksgiving, or Christmas feast.

Author Daniel Williamson (1975) said a seasonal feature is "an account of an annual event or an aspect of that annual event which captures its spirit" (p. 170). Think about all the Christmas, Thanksgiving, and other holiday stories you have ever seen; hundreds, no doubt. To make the special season come to life, you have to capture the sights, sounds, smells, tastes, and even feel of the season. These stories lean heavily on your descriptive abilities when you write about events and activities surrounding these special moments in our lives.

## WHY WRITE SEASONAL FEATURE ARTICLES?

There are numerous reasons for writing seasonal articles. First, there's professional opportunity. Although editors generally have enough copy for the routine issues of their newspapers, magazines, and newsletters, there always seems to be a shortage of good seasonal material. This editorial need means seasonal features are an effective way to crack the freelance market and to get an editor to notice your work above and beyond the work of others. Even experienced writers often overlook seasonal article opportunities. These articles, geared to a special time of the year, can also open the door to you for other, nonseasonal opportunities, Parker (1975) explained.

Seasonal features often can focus on the normal and, sometimes, the obvious. Readers are always interested in the most important elements of a season. This is often reassuring and helps present the atmosphere of a holiday season. *Brunswick News* reporter Karen Sloan wrote about Christmas season displays in her holiday feature that was published on a recent Christmas Eve about a growing tradition of extensive light displays and decorations in a small mobile home community near Brunswick.

"I wasn't quite sure what to expect when my editor told me to go up to the small, rural town of Townsend to write about the Christmas displays. I had heard about the lights in passing, but I wasn't really prepared for what I saw when I arrived there," Sloan recalled about the holiday assignment (personal communication, January 18, 2003).

> The small trailer park community had put a rural, Georgia twist on traditional holiday light displays and I wanted to capture the quirkiness in my story. It ran on Christmas Eve, so I just wanted to make it a fun little read about this working class community that takes holiday decorations very seriously. I didn't want to get overly descriptive, because I felt the photos would tell most of the story. I just wanted to let the homeowners tell the story in their own words as much as possible. And, of course, I couldn't resist a few holiday puns. You really only get to use those once a year, so I decided to take full advantage. (Sloan, personal communication, January 18, 2003)

Here's Sloan's (2002) front page story for the southeast Georgia daily newspaper:

I'm dreaming of a . . . bright Christmas?

Bing Crosby might disagree, but the residents of Townsend will take an impressively illuminated Christmas any day over a white one.

With a significant number of families in the small McIntosh County community adorning their homes and yards with extensive light displays and decorations, Townsend is the Christmas must-see of coastal Georgia.

In fact, the light displays on private homes are so popular that lines of cars develop as drivers move slowly along streets illuminated only by the glow of such figures as red-outlined Santa Claus shapes and star-bright white deer figures.

While the history of how Townsend became such a hotbed of Christmas light activity is a bit foggy, resident Brenda Ryals said that homeowners really started investing time and money in their displays in the late 1980s.

"It has gotten bigger and bigger every year since then, and now it's so big I can hardly handle it," said Ryals, with a good natured laugh.

Along with her neighbors on Old Townsend Road, many of whom are family, all of whom are good friends, Ryals has filled her yard with not only lights, but sleighs, reindeer, manger scenes, angels, candy canes, presents and almost every other Christmas image imaginable.

In addition to the more traditional images, Townsend residents have infused a little south Georgia humor into their displays.

Santa Claus stands atop John and Angie Ryals' home with his pants on fire, while Leroy the Redneck Reindeer has proven to be popular with visitors.

Preparation for the holiday displays begins in July, when Brenda Ryals starts making wooden cutouts in her workshop. Homeowners pitch in to help paint the figures.

November is crunch time in Townsend, since residents like to have the bulk of their displays completed by Thanksgiving and lighted until New Year's.

"We try to meet a Thanksgiving night deadline," said Brenda Ryals. "The closer it gets to Thanksgiving, the tempers get shorter and shorter."

Rainy weather delayed some displays this year, but homeowners persevered and got most of the decorations up in time for Thanksgiving.

The work does not end once the lights have been put up, the reindeer have been assembled and the manger set out, however. Maintenance is an ongoing issue for Townsend decorators.

No one knows this better than Gloria and Jerry Braxton, whose yard, just several miles down Highway 57 from Old Townsend Road, is packed with a multitude of different light displays, from Jesus on a cross to Santa in a helicopter.

"It's a constant battle to keep all the lights on," said Jerry Braxton. "We've been doing this for about five years now, and my wife really loves it. She stays out late into the night fixing bulbs and making sure everything works right."

Pesky squirrels, Jerry Braxton said, have been nibbling at insulation on wires of some of his light displays.

There are so many different light displays in his yard that Braxton has lost track of the number. In addition to religious and holiday images, the Braxtons have a lighted carousel, horse-drawn carriage, the American flag, a train and several palm trees.

This holiday display is no small production. The Braxtons order decorative frames from a supplier in Tennessee, then make an annual trip north to pick them up. They attach strings of lights to the frames, leaving them with a panorama of lighted images throughout their yard.

Gloria Braxton even had a frame custom-made to read "Welcome to Townsend."

All of this Christmas cheer does not come cheap, however.

In addition to the cost of the lights and frames, the electric bill for December will come in at about $500, said Jerry Braxton.

Despite the hours of preparation and the costs involved, the Christmas light displays are something that Townsend residents look forward to all year.

"It is a blessing to those of us who live here," said Cheryl Moore. "It's really like a big family, and everybody tries to help each other out."

Not only do the displays bring the community together, but they give Townsend a chance to show off its holiday spirit to outsiders.

According to Brenda Ryals, not only do cars come through for passengers to gawk at the illuminations, but buses, motorcycle clubs and Corvette clubs have made the pilgrimage to see the holiday lights of Townsend.

"It's really worth it when you get done with everything, and you see the cars stopped out in front of the house," said Brenda Ryals. "You see the little faces hanging out the car windows. It's nice to hear the comments and the laughs." (Sloan, 2002, p. 1)

(Reprinted with permission of *The Brunswick News*.)

The importance of seasonal features extends beyond the need to entertain readers by describing the occurrence of holidays, special attractions, annual events, major anniversaries, or even the changing natural weather and growing seasons. Wire service and newspaper articles focusing on weather often look at the seasonal nature of weather. Some features highlight it. In the Northeast and Midwest, the cooling fall means the season to go into the countryside to see nature's colors. In the south, along the Gulf of Mexico, late summer and early fall is the rainy season or, as some call it, the hurricane season.

Seasonal feature articles are also used by newspaper, magazine, and newsletter readers well in advance of the seasons or holidays to help prepare for the celebrations, the changing weather, and any special activities associated with seasonal events. There is a certain functional value to seasonal stories that extends past their pure entertainment value. A well-written seasonal story educates readers about a religious holiday or about a national hero. It teaches our children the value of remembering an important family day such as Mother's Day or even a routine civic activity such as voting. These stories help readers prepare for potential weather disasters such as winter blizzards, spring tornadoes, flooding, or subtropical hurricanes. The articles can teach your readers how to make, prepare for, and understand the meaning of a special meal such as a Passover Seder.

## DEVELOPING SEASONAL IDEAS

To begin generating seasonal article ideas, take a look at any calendar. For starters, there is a list of major annual holidays and seasonal occasions later in this chapter. But you can go well beyond this list because these are only the major national dates you should know. There are, of course, various other national holidays (such as those in Mexico) that are celebrated in the United States. There are also unique regional holidays and state holidays that are peculiar to the regions and states. You can probably think of one or two in your own state that are not on the list included with this chapter.

Many of the local holidays and seasons do not appear on nationally sold calendars and appointment books, so do not depend on these sources for complete lists. Instead, check with local libraries, school systems (for their own calendars), local newspaper files, and even local museums, ethnic groups, and civic–business groups. This will help you especially if you are a newcomer to an area or, for example, you want to write for a publication in another region of the country that you might not live in or be familiar with its customs and history.

However, a serious feature writer—regardless of whether he or she is working for a newspaper or magazine, or is freelancing—is organized about writing seasonal articles. There are many ways to keep up, but the most obvious method is to keep your own calendar for the current year, but also for the next 2 years. This helps you work ahead and in the present. You might be working a day or two or a week or two in advance on seasonal articles for a newspaper, or several months ahead for magazines, and you need to be tuned in to needs far ahead, not today.

Another good place to check for seasonal ideas is an almanac. Most general annual reference books such as *The World Almanac* and *Information Please Almanac* are quite thorough in listing public and religious dates of significance throughout the year. These books are annually updated and often run special events date listings for many years beyond the current year.

Another good source category is theme appointment books. These books come ready-made for persons who wish to specialize in certain subjects such as sculpture or personal computers. They are easy to find on sale in most bookstores. Inside these books, in addition to the regular listings, are special dates such as anniversaries unique to that theme or subject (e.g., when the first personal computer was placed on the market, or Microsoft founder and chairman Bill Gates's birthday). You might have to look a little to find these, but you can usually find them in specialty shops or advertised in specialty publications such as organizational newsletters.

The key to getting the right idea for a seasonal article is anticipating, being able to successfully "guess" what is going to be on your readers' minds when the season nears. You must be thinking about what people will want to know about a holiday or special event long before that event is on the general public's mind. You are trying to anticipate interests: What activities will be interesting? What foods will be tasty? What ceremonies are essential? You must be able to think about seasons that have not yet arrived. Also, you must be able to find a fresh approach to a story that has been told dozens of times before.

Successful seasonal article ideas must be timely. You cannot write stories about Thanksgiving meals that require a week's preparation if they are written or published 2 days before Thanksgiving. You cannot jump the gun too much either because even good ideas are forgotten if they come along too far ahead of the big day. A strong idea draws readers into your story by making them think to themselves as they read your lead: "Yes! This would be fun. I want to find out more."

Good seasonal features also have strong visual potential. Try to select topics that lend themselves to strong photographs or other forms of illustration to help tell the total story. Try to suggest to your editors that they use photographs with your story. Suggest potential photographic content, also. How about proposing a schematic diagram that shows how to make an object, or show how something happens, or perhaps show a boxed set of instructions that include a recipe? For newspapers, magazines, and newsletters, packaging is important with seasonal features and, if you want maximum attention given the article you write, plan to propose strong graphics in addition to your well-written and reported article.

Parker (1975) recommended developing a specialization as a seasonal feature writer, such as becoming an expert on a certain season. What is Parker's specialization? He has been a pastor in Plymouth, MA, so he focuses on the Pilgrims and Thanksgiving. "Much of the trick to selling seasonal material is to stick to a certain holiday or event, mining it for neglected angles," he stated (p. 30). For feature writers, this means you should simply think about the regional activities that are occurring around you, and perhaps one or more of these will develop into a specialization for you that can be sold. He suggested looking not only at the regional calendar but thinking about annual local festivals and fairs for your prospects.

## WRITING IN ADVANCE OF THE SEASON

There is no doubt that much of the seasonal feature article writing is produced in advance. This is particularly true for monthly and less frequently published magazines, but it is also true for newspapers. The major difference is that the lead-time varies. For a newspaper, work on a seasonal piece for a Sunday supplement magazine would be not much different from the deadlines you face for a weekly to monthly magazine or newsletter. Newspaper feature editors like to work as much ahead as possible while keeping their articles as timely as can be done. This assists in production of graphics such as large color illustrations, posed photographs, and so on. Even for the spot seasonal feature, done a day ahead, the advantage goes to the writer who finishes early in the day to permit time for revision and collection of new information as deadline nears.

For a magazine or newsletter published monthly or even less frequently, you have to be particularly conscious of lead time in preparing stories with content sensitive to seasonal changes. Some monthly magazine and newsletter editors work 4 to 6 months ahead of the current calendar. So, if you are reading this in December or January, you should be thinking now about summer vacation, Father's Day, Fourth of July, or graduation stories. Admittedly, this is hard to do when there is snow outside and temperatures do not easily suggest going to the beach or to picnics.

What is the reason for this? It's preparation time. Lead time is that period of time between the decision of a writer to write the article or the decision by an editor to buy it, and the appearance of the article in the publication. Preparation time includes securing rights, assigning photographers and illustrations, editing, fact verification, typesetting, paste-up, proofreading, printing, and even distribution. With all that to be done, it is no wonder that you have to finish writing your Thanksgiving cooking article in May or June to get it into the hands of readers in early November so they can begin thinking of your ideas for their own tables at the end of November.

Jacqueline Shannon (1984), a seasonal feature writer and former magazine editor, said the mastery of timing is critical to your success. Four months, she said, is a dependable industry average for magazines that use color. However, she warned the following:

> If you're submitting on spec[ulation], your lead time is obviously not the same as the publication's lead-time. To give your article time to be considered, you must add "reporting time" to lead-time. Therefore, if the reporting time for your targeted publication is one month, you must submit a seasonal story five months in advance. But don't stop counting yet. There's the possibility that your story will be rejected. So you must also figure in a couple of months to market it elsewhere. That brings us up to a free-lancer's lead-time of six or seven months. In other words, start circulating "Christmas Ornaments from Pine Cones" in May or June. (p. 34)

Shannon (1984) said the same rule applies for queries on seasonal articles. In fact, she observed, many publications will provide minimum lead time for you in listings of market information. Also, she advised, there is such a thing as too much lead time. Up to 1 year, she recommended, is acceptable, but only for important events such as the Olympics, an election, or a major public anniversary. So, she said for the usual material, do not submit more than 7 months in advance. This leaves a golden window of advance work from 4 to 7 months for magazines and some newsletters. You become a calendar juggler, but to be an effective seasonal writer, this is part of the job. Some writers such as Shannon keep a seasonal picture wall calendar, turned 6 months ahead of the present date, on their desks. All this requires a seemingly simple decision: to plan ahead when writing a seasonal article. This means developing an "editorial body clock," as Shannon called it.

It also requires writing alertness and discipline. While you are working in August preparing an article for February readers, you have to keep references to "this year" and "last year" straight in your mind—or readers will be confused for sure. Shannon (1984) also recommended saving a good article idea when the timing is off. As long as the subject is timeless, she said, it can be held a few months in the interest of timeliness when it is submitted to an editor.

Rivers (1992) suggested seasonal feature writers should try thinking like department store managers and advertise their Christmas specials in July. Editors, like store managers, often need additional "stock" to use. "Editors also need stories that are not time-bound, stories that could be published at any time of year without losing their newsworthy qualities" (Rivers, 1992, p. 97).

There are numerous events calendars that have been placed on World Wide Web sites in recent years that may be useful to seasonal feature writers who need to plan ahead. These sites provide lists of major events by date. Some are regional calendars, as well, featuring events from a particular state or community. Some are specialized by subject or type of sponsoring organization.

## FINDING FRESH ANGLES FOR ANNUAL ARTICLES

One thing all newspaper and magazine features editors want to avoid is the same old seasonal story each year. So, it is necessary for writers to work with their editors to come up with a creative, fresh angle for an annual seasonal article. When it is a certainty that you need to write that St. Valentine's Day romance article, and the idea of another local couple's 60th or 70th wedding anniversary story bores you (and probably your regular readers, too), it is time to work on a new approach. Ask yourself, "What's new this coming Valentine's Day?" Check with retailers such as card shops, candy stores, and florists. Check with small companies that offer special services such as breakfast in bed or singing telegrams to find out what unique ideas they are offering for the coming special day. You will find that at times, these businesses come to you with their ideas in hopes for some advance publicity to foster business. Thus, you will find a cooperative source eager to help you with your article. The strategy is to not limit yourself to the traditional story. Why stop short on a seasonal feature when you can give your readers a better story? Why do the same old stories if something stimulating is just waiting to be written?

Parker (1975) said the formula is simple for the new angle: Fresh material plus solid background equals a successful story. Like generating any good story idea, as you remember from the chapter on developing story ideas, a good seasonal feature must be the product of thorough looking around, talking to lots of people, and careful listening. It also takes thinking and an ability to put things together. This approach results in some solid article idea leads that could develop into that story you wanted for this year.

Of course, there are times when a very old idea works for a seasonal article. There are times when an idea or theme has not been used for years, or at least, it has not been used as the basis of an article. More than 20 years ago, what is now a classic seasonal "what-if" feature story idea was generated. Reporters for the *Florida Times–Union* in Jacksonville were sitting in their newsroom at Christmas time, a traditionally slow news period, trying to come up with a good Christmas Day page one feature for their readers. Reporter Jerry Teer (1973) wondered if it might not be fun to see if the true Christmas spirit still existed in Jacksonville. "Do people really believe all this Christmas stuff?" he asked. "And if they do, how deeply do they believe it?" To find this out, he asked the managing editor the following: "What if I wrote a story about what happens when myself and a pregnant woman, apparently my wife, visit inns around the city on Christmas Eve in search of a room?" (p. 24). With his editor's okay, he asked a young female friend to join him as the two went from motel to motel looking for a place to stay for the night. They looked a bit ragged, wearing old clothes and carrying their belongings in a duffel bag. They told innkeepers they had no money and, with the help of a pillow, Teer's friend was dressed to appear pregnant. This modern-day version of the Biblical story of Joseph and Mary on Christmas Eve was a widely read feature in the newspaper the next day. Although he hoped to find one Good Samaritan, Teer and his friend found no free rooms among the 15 "inns" they visited. This angle, far more interesting than a story about left-over Christmas trees, demonstrates what is meant by a fresh angle on an annual season or holiday assignment.

Joshua B. Good (2002), a feature writer for the *Atlanta Journal and Constitution*, offered a fresh idea to Valentine's Day features. In addition to the usual feature coverage about relationships and romance leading up to and on Valentine's Day, Good offered Atlanta area readers advice to keep the romance going after Valentine's Day. His story appeared 10 days following Valentine's Day:

> The flowers are faded. The negligee is already in the bottom of the drawer. That heart-shaped chocolate box is sitting in the trash.
>
> It's only been a week, but already routine has replaced the Valentine's Day romance.
>
> So how to keep love alive the rest of the year? The odds aren't good. About 2.4 million Americans get married each year, but 1.2 million get divorced. In Georgia, the divorce rate is slightly above the national average. About 60,000 people get married each year in Georgia and 36,000 are divorced.
>
> Infidelity and disputes over money and child rearing are the key culprits, says Georgia State University Professor Elisabeth Burgess.
>
> Atlanta is even worse than the rest of the state, Burgess says, because a large part of the population is from somewhere else. Transplanted couples don't have a local family network that supports a marriage or pressures a husband and wife to stay together, she says.

But there are ways to keep that love buzz going, the experts say.

Turn off the TV and talk. Flirt. Make a date, even if you've been married for years.

Here's what else 10 relationship experts say about keeping romance alive all year long:

1. Be thoughtful—Put surprise notes in your lover's briefcase whenever he or she goes on a business trip, says Mimi Doe, author of "Busy But Balanced: Practical and Inspirational Ways to Create a Calmer, Closer Family."

2. Anticipate—"If you have the time, stamina and desire, there's nothing wrong with having sex every day, but if that's your routine, I would also suggest taking a break from time to time. Try to keep your hands off of each other for two or three days and then see if the intensity of your next lovemaking session doesn't make such a wait worthwhile," Dr. Ruth Westheimer advises.

3. Tell the truth—"To keep the spark alive . . . is more about honesty and openness. It's more about telling the truth. It's about risking emotional openness, emotional intimacy. And it's scary because you let yourself be seen in all your nakedness," says Virginia Erhardt, a Decatur sex therapist and psychologist.

4. Take charge—"I look at my husband and I say, 'I want you and I want you right now.' And I take charge," says Laura Corn, author of "101 Nights of Grrreat Sex" and "The Great American Sex Diet."

5. Have fun—"When [my husband] walks out the door in the morning and blows a kiss to me, I say 'No way,' and I pull him back into my arms and give him a real kiss. I love to bite his rear end when he shaves in the morning. Those are the kinds of things that you have to enjoy with each other," says Millie Kagan, 81, of Druid Hills, a retired marriage therapist who has been married to Irving Kagan, 83, for 61 years.

6. Wait on each other—Each morning, Jeff Earle gets his two children ready for school and brings a cup of coffee to his wife in bed. "That's just down-right sexy," Joy Earle says. "Bringing my coffee in the morning may seem like nothing to someone else." The Earles are Christian-based marriage coaches in Alpharetta.

7. Compliment—"Men come to me and say, 'My wife isn't sexy anymore.' And I say, 'Well, you're not doing your job.' "The key is to compliment your wife about how beautiful she is and how lucky you are. Then she feels special and acts sexy," says Doug Rosenau, a sex and marriage counselor in Atlanta.

8. Plan ahead—"You need to plan for sex . . . Scheduling takes away the worry about when it's going to happen. When you plan, you really get more excited. You can get pulled together," says Joan Sughrue, a sex therapist in Woodstock.

9. Surprise—Last year for Valentine's Day, Sally Lehr sent a barbershop quartet to her husband's office. Her advice: Do nice things to break up the routine. "Small things that say 'I'm thinking of you,' " says Lehr, who teaches at Emory University and counsels couples.

10. Laugh!—Have fun," says Bobb Patterson, an Inman Park marriage counselor. "Laughter is usually a sign of safety. When you are laughing with
someone, it is the prime environment for romance. No fun, no romance
. . . Singing to each other is fun. A shaving cream fight is fun. Dancing is
fun." (Good, 2002)
(Reprinted with permission of the Atlanta *Journal-Constitution*.)

## MAJOR HOLIDAY AND SEASONAL ARTICLES CALENDAR

*January*
New Year's Day (1st)
Martin Luther King's birthday (15th, officially, it varies)

*February*
National Freedom Day (1st)
Groundhog Day (2nd)
Constitution Day (Mexico, 5th)
Abraham Lincoln's birthday (12th)
St. Valentine's Day (14th)
Susan B. Anthony birthday, also Women's Liberation Day (15th)
George Washington's birthday (3rd Monday)
Ash Wednesday (varies)
Mardi Gras (varies)

*March*
Baseball training season opens (varies)
St. Patrick's Day (17th)
First day of spring (21st)
Mardi Gras (varies)
Palm Sunday (varies)
Good Friday (varies)
Easter (varies)

*April*
April Fool's Day (1st)
Palm Sunday (varies)
Good Friday (varies)
First day of Passover (varies)
Pan American Day (14th)
National Secretary Week (3rd week)
Easter Sunday (varies)
Easter Monday (Canada, varies)

Arbor Day, Bird Day (last Friday)
Daylight Savings Time begins (varies)

*May*
May Day, also Labor Day (Mexico, 1st)
Loyalty Day (1st)
Mother's Day (2nd Sunday)
Victoria Day (Canada, varies)
End of school year
College, high school graduation (varies)
Armed Forces Day (3rd Saturday)
National Maritime Day (22nd)
Memorial Day (last Monday)
Traditional Memorial Day (30th)

*June*
End of school year (varies)
Summer vacation season begins
College, high school graduation (varies)
National Smile Week (varies)
Flag Day (14th)
Father's Day (3rd Sunday)
First day of summer (21st)

*July*
Canada Day (1st)
U.S. Independence Day (4th)

*August*
Civic holiday (Canada, varies)
Ecology Day (varies)
National Aviation Day (19th)

*September*
Labor Day (U.S., Canada, 1st Monday)
Summer vacation season ends
Start of school year (varies)
Football season opens (varies)
Grandparents Day (11th)
Independence days (Mexico, 15th–16th)
Citizenship Day (17th)
Rosh Hashanah (varies)
Yom Kippur (varies)

First day of autumn (22nd or 23rd)
American Indian Day (4th Friday)

*October*
Child Health Day (1st Monday)
Columbus Day, Discoverer's Day, Pioneer's Day (2nd Monday)
Columbus Day (Mexico, 12th)
World Poetry Day (15th)
Thanksgiving Day (Canada, varies)
United Nations Day (24th)
Daylight Saving Time ends (varies)
Halloween (31st)

*November*
Election Day (1st Tuesday after 1st Monday)
Veterans' Day (11th)
Remembrance Day (Canada, 11th)
Sadie Hawkins Day (1st Saturday after 11th)
Elizabeth Cady Stanton birthday (women's rights, 12th)
Thanksgiving Day (4th Thursday)

*December*
First Day of Chanukah (varies)
Basketball season begins (varies)
Bill of Rights Day (15th)
Forefather's Day (21st)
First Day of winter (21st)
Christmas (25th)
Boxing Day (Canada, 26th)
Kwanzaa (26th–Jan. 1st)

---

Holiday and seasonal features are a lot of work. To find out what is new for the summer vacation season or what is different for Easter this spring, you have to be willing to do some digging. It takes time to find the right travel agents, hotels, or tourist commissions to get that vacation story that comes out in late May or early June, the start of vacation time for many families, in the middle of winter. It might seem early, but this is when the decisions are, or already have been made. The same goes for the religious holidays such as Easter. You should not only contact stores for the commercial side of the story—new candies, stuffed toys, and the like—but also contact churches of the many denominations in your community for the celebrations that are scheduled. Depending on your deadline, you must work ahead and often press individuals for information to make your story timelier when it appears in the newspaper, magazine, newsletter, or online publication.

## USING LOCAL SOURCES FOR SEASONAL FEATURES

The best-read seasonal material is localized. It is interesting to know what people are doing for a holiday 1,000 miles away, but readers really care most about what's interesting in their own neighborhoods and communities. The neighborhood parade for Flag Day might be just the story your newspaper needs. Or a city or regional magazine might want to begin the summer vacation season with an article on nearby vacation destinations. You cannot ignore the activities in your own areas for the highest percentage of sales to newspapers and, if the market permits, magazines.

Local angles are defined in different ways, of course. A magazine looks at localization differently than does a newspaper. Most national magazine editors would consider too much localization a potentially serious flaw in an article. Then again, a local or regional magazine might just be looking for that localized article on coping with winter storms. Newspapers are much the opposite. Most newspapers are edited for their specific communities—a market usually defined by the name of the newspaper. Some major metropolitan newspapers serve multicounty and even statewide markets. A few others, of course, are nationally circulated. In short, know the market and write for it in an appropriate fashion for seasonal articles just as you would any other feature article you write.

Tom Shaw (2000), staff writer for the *Omaha World–Herald*, drew on local specialists and experts for his story about winter holiday season driving. He talked with a local weather expert, an automobile association expert, the airport manager, and spokespersons for the state highway patrol and the state roads department. He also used information from a local safety and health council in his reporting. Recognizing that many Nebraskans travel by car during the Christmas holidays, his article offered drivers advice about preparation for trips. He also offered tips for negotiating often dangerous winter driving conditions on the Great Plains. Snow, ice, and low temperatures can often lead to trouble if drivers are not prepared with proper supplies and they must know what to do. This is how he approached his story:

> It's that time again—bundle up the kids, pack into the car and head off for the holidays.
>
> The good news is it's going to be too cold across the state for freezing rain and sleet.
>
> Anyone with tingling ears and chapped lips knows the bad news.

Temperatures will remain lower than normal, with wind chills that could push the needle below zero.

Snow is expected today, with 2 to 5 inches possible in eastern Nebraska and less than 2 inches in the central and western parts of the state, according to Bryon Miller, a meteorologist with the National Weather Service in Valley, Neb. Wind gusts up to 40 mph are predicted during the afternoon in the east.

Lows are expected to be below zero tonight in northeast Nebraska and around zero or slightly above for the metropolitan area.

But the weather looks clear from Thursday through Sunday, except for the chance of light snow Saturday across the state.

The temperatures Friday morning are expected to be zero to 10 below state-wide, but a small warm-up will occur. During the day on Friday, temperatures could reach the teens in the east to the 30s in the west.

No matter what the conditions, AAA Nebraska is urging people to plan ahead for traveling this holiday season.

"Don't put yourself or your family at risk," said Rose White, public affairs director for AAA Nebraska. "Always be prepared."

Planning ahead is important, especially if emergency help can't get to you right away.

AAA Nebraska has been busy with the recent storms. Since Dec. 11, crews have received 3,961 calls—more than twice the number usually handled during the winter season.

The volume has been so heavy, AAA has been asking people to wait or seek service elsewhere if they are at home or another safe place.

Motorists stranded away from a safe area are a priority.

"We have to get to those people in health hazard situations," White said.

Members who use another service can submit their bill to AAA for reimbursement.

White said travelers should have an emergency kit with them. It would also be a good idea to bring along nonperishable food and antifreeze.

The average gas price in Nebraska is $1.37. The price has dropped 12 cents a gallon in the last five weeks, White said, but it is still 12 cents higher than the same time last year.

She added that some gas stations may close early on Christmas Eve, so it's best to fill up before 6 p.m. Some stations may be closed on Christmas Day, but 24-hour mini marts and 24-hour stations at major interchanges on the Interstate will be available, White said.

The Nebraska State Patrol is planning a special enforcement project for this weekend, said spokeswoman Terri Teuber. The patrol has applied for state grants to fund 400 overtime hours for troopers for Christmas.

Troopers especially will be on the lookout for intoxicated drivers. If the patrol doesn't get its grants, there still will be special enforcement, but it may have to be cut back, Teuber said.

Overall, she said, drivers should leave extra time to get where they're going and shouldn't get frazzled by other drivers.

"Enjoy the white Christmas instead of being frustrated," she said.

Mary Jo Hall, spokeswoman for the Department of Roads, said Interstates and highways are in good shape.

If the weather does take a turn for the worse this weekend, workers will be called in as usual, Hall said.

"There's no holiday for the maintenance crews if bad weather arrives," she said.

Those flying should make sure to get to airports early or call the airline. AAA recommends that people be patient. If possible, pack things such as extra games and treats for children in case of delays.

Don Smithey, executive director of the Omaha Airport Authority, said the outlook is good for Eppley Airfield, but delays could develop if bad weather elsewhere has an impact on major hub cities, including Chicago and Denver.

As for the airlines, Smithey said, there shouldn't be problems from labor disputes.

"Obviously, several of the airlines do have labor negotiations going on, but I won't anticipate any slowdowns or labor problems during the holiday season."

As always, get to the airport early. Also, make sure bags are tagged and that they are always with you.

Car Safety Kit—Cell Phone; Snow shovel; Windshield scraper; Jumper cables; Properly inflated spare tire, wheel wrench, and jack; Sand, cat litter or another abrasive material for traction; Tow chain or strap; Flashlight with fresh batteries; Candles and matches (or lighter); empty 3-pound coffee can (to melt snow for water or put lighted candles in to create a heater); Flares or reflective triangles; Sleeping bags or blankets; High-energy foods such as dried fruits and nuts; First aid kit.

Travel Safety Tips—

Before You Go—Belt and hoses: Check for signs of wear; Motor oil: Use a multiviscosity motor oil. These are identified with a "W"; Antifreeze: Check level and concentration. Most manufacturers recommend a 50/50 mix of antifreeze and water, which provides protection to -34 degrees Fahrenheit. Battery: Have a strong one; Tires: Keep properly inflated. Be sure tread is at least 1/4 of an inch deep.

Winter Driving—Watch bridges and overpasses. They can be slippery. If you get stuck, don't spin your wheels. In heavy snow, push wheels side to side to move snow out of the way. Gentle rocking might get your car loose, but check your owner's manual for the recommended procedure. If you hit an icy spot and start to slide, don't hit the brakes. Take your foot off the gas and turn your wheels in the direction you want to go. If you don't have anti-lock brakes, pump and release the brakes a few times. Do not allow the brakes to lock up because you could lose control. Keep field of vision clear. Scrape and defrost windows. Crack window slightly if needed. Keep headlamps clean. A film of dirt on headlights can reduce their range by up to 10 feet.

If You're Stranded in a Storm—Stay in your vehicle. You are more likely to be found. Keep fresh air in the vehicle. Snow can completely seal the passenger compartment. Beware the gentle killers: carbon monoxide and oxygen starvation. Run the motor and heater sparingly and only with the downwind window open.

Exercise by clapping hands and moving arms and legs vigorously from time to time. Do not stay in one position for long. Turn on dome light at night to make the vehicle visible to work crews. Keep watch. Do not permit all occupants of the vehicle to sleep at once. Source: Safety and Health Council of Greater Omaha, Pennzoil, Pontiac GMC. (Shaw, 2000, p. 17)

(Reprinted with permission of the *Omaha World–Herald*.)

## BEST SOURCES FOR SEASONAL ARTICLES

- Published specialized or theme wall calendars.
- Topical or theme appointment books.
- General almanacs, such as the *World Almanac* or *Information Please Almanac*.
- State travel department calendars.
- City, regional chambers of commerce.
- Holiday festival committees, organizations.
- Historians and history museum curators and directors.
- Encyclopedias and annotated bibliographies.
- Newspaper, magazine, or newsletter files from a year before the annual event.
- Retail store sales managers and clerks.
- Product manufacturers' regional sales representatives.
- Web sites devoted to event calendars, specific subjects, holidays, or seasons.
- Subject experts.

## SEASONAL COLOR ARTICLES

Although you may have already given thought to writing color feature articles, it is important to point out that many successful seasonal articles mix in the elements of strong color and descriptive writing. Writers use seasonal article assignments as a chance to exercise their imagination along with their descriptive writing skills. Description is important to some seasonal features. The event's unique atmosphere is present because of it. Readers sense it. However, use this descriptive and color-laden approach with caution and deliberate skill.

Rivers (1992) said the following:

> The worst flaw in seasonal stories is that the writer tries too hard to be overpoweringly descriptive. Instead, the writer should be content with touches of description: a few visual verbs, an unpredictable adjective or two, an adverb that is al-

lowed to do its work because it's in a crisp sentence rather than in a sentence burdened with other adverbs. (p. 251)

Like other color articles, many times a good seasonal story with a strong dose of color will use anecdotes to open the article. This form of storytelling draws the reader into the article easily, Rivers (1992) said.

## WRITING SEASONAL STORIES FOR MAGAZINES

Doug Jimerson, an editor for *Better Homes and Gardens,* has edited seasonal features for much of his career. He has learned much about preparation of these stories for magazines and recommends that writers be concerned about appropriate timing in preparation of the story:

> Obviously timing is essential when you're freelancing seasonal material. Every publication whether it is a newspaper or magazine has its own lead time that you must take into consideration if you want to successfully market your story ideas. At *Better Homes and Gardens,* for example, we plan our editorial calendar 1-year in advance of publication. This doesn't mean that we wouldn't accept a better story idea closer to deadline, but it does indicate how vital it is to be aware of your target magazine's schedule and plan accordingly.
>
> More important, you should know the editorial content or philosophy of any publication you solicit for freelance work. Nothing is more frustrating to an editor than to receive unsolicited manuscripts about topics that aren't even remotely related to his or her publication. For example, our magazine never publishes poetry, songs, book reviews, celebrity interviews, or first person humor stories like "How I Raised Bumper Crops of Broccoli in My Bathtub." Yet, every week we're inundated with submissions like this from misguided writers across the country, usually with a tag line on the bottom of the page asking us to send payment as soon as possible!
>
> I realize that this all might sound pretty basic, but I can't emphasize enough the importance of research. Always take time to read and critique a few issues from the magazine or newspaper before you charge ahead with your own story ideas. It's also smart to check an up-to-date masthead and read the by-lines of all stories. You need to know the names (correct spellings, please) of the appropriate editors you'll contact later. And remember, don't take notes from mastheads that are over 1 year old. Editors retire, die, get promoted, and move on to other publications. One of my pet peeves is that I'll often receive unsolicited manuscripts that are addressed to the garden editor who was with the magazine in the 1950s. That shows me that the writer hasn't done his or her homework about the direction or scope of our magazine.
>
> In conclusion, I'd also like to suggest that you think about specializing in one or more subject areas. There's nothing wrong with being a good generalist, but if you strive to become an expert in a particular field, such as money management,

electronics, parenting, architecture, food, environment, sports, or even horticul-
ture, you'll have a leg up on the competition when a publication is looking for
someone to write that "special" feature. It's also a smart marketing strategy. If
you can sell yourself as a proficient writer with a strong background in a particular subject area you'll stand out from the rest of the thundering herd. (Jimerson,
personal communication, September 19, 1988)

# CHAPTER TEN

# Entertainment Features
# and Critical Writing

Creative expression is an important part of contemporary society. And with the rapidly growing number of choices given for use of our leisure time, the role of interpreting and reviewing creative expression in the form of arts and entertainment is also increasing in value. Arts writers cover both breaking news and write features about their creative world. They often also take on the role of critical writers, venturing into the world of opinion expression. Today's arts writers and editors seek better ways to take arts and entertainment features beyond the routine and ordinary. Daily newspaper weekend sections have been created or redesigned. New departments in popular magazines focus on entertainment and the arts. These publications have extended how they cover the arts and entertainment by adding more depth and scope. Entertainment journalism is maturing alongside the more-established opinion-based arts reviews and critiques (for more discussion, see Bednarski, 1993; Bunn, 1993; Hellyer, 1993; Titchener, 1998; Vawter, 1993).

Many aspiring nonfiction writers associate writing artistic reviews and criticism as a glamorous career filled with opportunities to mix with both the famous and infamous artists of our time. The work is attractive to beginners in the news media because reviewers and critics are often working at the cutting edge of such creativity as filmmaking, book writing, television program production, music and dance performance, and theater production. Perhaps the lives of those who do reviewing and critical writing are often filled with glitter, bright lights, and black ties for the successful few who are nationally known full-time reviewers or critics of the arts. For most people who do reviewing or criticism, it is a part-time specialization and seldom offers the lifestyles of the rich and famous. Reviewing and critical writing are still two of the most popular forms of feature writing among young writers. With the strong appeal of the performing arts to young adults in particular, it only makes sense that many beginning writers seek to develop talents as reviewers and, ultimately, as critics.

However, it remains difficult for a nonfiction writer to build a career in reviewing and critical journalism. Most newspapers, magazines, newsletters, and online publications—when they publish reviews or critical analyses of the arts on a regular basis—use feature syndication services and part-time or even volunteer writers—such as experts—for their articles. Only the largest of metro-

politan area daily newspapers, news wire services, and features syndicates retain full-time reviewers and critics in the arts. It is not uncommon to find
as many as a half dozen to a dozen persons on a large daily newspaper's arts or
lifestyles section staff. However, small and medium daily newspapers cannot often afford full-time critics or reviewers on staff. They turn to full-time staff

## THE ROLES OF REVIEWERS AND CRITICS

Professor Todd Hunt (1972) listed eight primary functions of reviewers, critics,
and entertainment writers in covering the arts:

1. First, and foremost, the reviewer informs readers about the arts—Readers
   learn about the existence of new works from their favorite publications.
2. Reviewing and criticism help to raise the cultural level of the community,
   the region, and the nation—By setting standards for performance, the cultural community is, in the long run, improved.
3. Reviewers and critics impart personality to the community—By writing
   lively copy, expressing well-supported opinions, and by being a little bit
   different, the reviewer and critic provide a unique personal dimension to
   their feature writing.
4. Reviewers and critics advise readers how to best use their resources—Reviewers and critics help readers decide what films to see, books to read,
   restaurants to visit, and which theaters to attend. With limited entertainment budgets, many readers depend on their local reviewers and critics to
   guide them in making these decisions.
5. Reviewers and critics help artists and performers to fine-tune their
   works—As an educated consumer, a qualified reviewer or critic can make
   suggestions that will help artists and performers to improve their efforts in
   later performances.
6. Reviewers and critics identify the new—Whenever new works are offered
   to the public, and, at times, before these new works are presented for the
   first time, reviewers and critics are able to identify, interpret, and explain
   trends and new developments in the arts to their readers.
7. Reviewers and critics record history—One of the best sources of performing arts history is the review. Reviewers and critics write arts history on a
   daily basis.
8. Reviews and critical writing are also entertaining—As reviewers and
   critics impart personality, they also entertain with timely and interesting
   writing.

members who specialize in other types of reporting and writing or editing, to reviewing as additional work. Many use regular part-time writers to extend their staff coverage. Or, of course, these newspapers also turn to freelance writers.

Magazines and newsletters that publish reviews and criticism of the arts most often use regular part-time, freelance, or volunteer sources. Like newspapers of all sizes, some magazines depend on news services and features syndicates to provide their reviews and criticism. Few magazines or newsletters have full-time critics on staff unless they are highly specialized publications devoted to one or more of these arts. Online publications use a mix of staff and freelance sources, but what an online publication does often depends on how much of its content is original or comes from other sources.

Reviewing and critical writing are quite different from other forms of professional feature writing. Generally, professional feature writers do not cross the line often from fair and objective writing into subjective writing and personal opinion, but reviewers and critics must take this bold step for their work to contain value to readers. That's why reviewers and critics are so widely read and valuable to consumers.

It is difficult to discuss reviewing and criticism without also discussing entertainment reporting. For many arts writers, the job involves regularly writing both reviews or critiques and news from their beats. A good reviewer or critic is a major asset for a publication by covering the arts as important news-based feature material. For example, film reviewers or critics are often called on to write the local story when a film crew goes to a community to shoot on location. Regular book reviewers or critics are assigned to profile a local author who has written a successful new book. There are numerous roles the reviewer and critic play in serving their readers and the region's arts community.

## REVIEWERS AND CRITICS

What does it take to get a job as a reviewer? Much depends on the publication. Some small newspapers and magazines without big budgets cannot afford to pay well and offer opportunities to beginners for little or no financial rewards. Some even use volunteers who write for the clips—that is, to get the experience and published articles known as *clips*—but not for remuneration. Editors of these publications allow their reviewers to "learn" on the job. Most publications are more discriminating and require greater preparation of reviewers and critics. Although your writing skills are probably most important in determining your success as a reviewer, the more educated, the more knowledge you possess about the art form, and the more experience you have as a reviewer, the better chance you have in finding a job. Motivation is also a key to being a reviewer or critic. Hunt (1972) maintained that you must have a profound concern for perpetuation and improvement of the art form. He also said you need the roots of a newsman, that is, a sense for news, on which you build your interests in the arts.

There is a significant difference between a review and critical writing, although some arts writers feel the distinction is an artificial one and not really necessary. However, such matters are substantial and worth noting. Reviews are generally written by less authoritative writers and often take the perspective of the consumer of a particular work. Some critics feel the content of most reviews is less substantial, more like high school or college book reports. These articles tend to summarize the work and its major features, but are not so evaluative. The review describes the work and its genre. It can also discuss the skill of the artist or author, even the quality.

The major distinction between reviewing and criticism is expression of opinion. When a writer begins to include personal opinion in the form of evaluation, he or she leaves the realm of objectivity for subjectivity and his or her assessments of artistic performance are offered. The line into criticism is crossed. This is also a more sophisticated, perhaps worldly, view of the art form.

Critical writing at this level usually requires specialization and higher education. One of the most important differences between reviewers and critics is educational background. Most successful critics are college- or graduate-level educated in the art form they criticize. To be a critic, you must have some form of specialized education, and perhaps even amateur or professional experience as a performing artist yourself. After all, what better credentials to criticize performance or an art form than to have been there yourself? Certainly individuals educated with majors in drama or film are going to be better informed critics about the correct or preferred techniques in theater or movie production than someone who is not. An English major or author will likely be a better book critic than someone who is not. A person who majored in food and nutrition or who has been a professional chef would be better qualified to be a restaurant critic than someone who simply likes food and wants to dine out on an expense account.

The point is rather simple: To be a critic, you must know what standards to apply in assessing professional or amateur performance. You must be able to write what you think about the effort in a skilled manner. You must know what levels represent truly excellent work and which ones do not. In fact, some experts on reviewing and criticism feel that because there are many unqualified reviewers and critics it might be better for news organizations to utilize artists as reviewers and critics.

It is becoming easier for beginning writers to specialize in the arts when in school. In addition to reviewing and criticism, these writers also cover the arts as news. Furthermore, because most newspapers, magazines, and newsletters cannot hire individuals solely for coverage of the arts, general feature writing or news writing and reporting skills are necessary. Universities and colleges with programs in mass communication and the arts are the best locations for academic preparation for careers as reviewers and critics. Schools that offer journalism majors in newspapers and magazines and also provide students with a

chance to double major in an art such as music, drama, or creative writing permit maximum development of talents necessary to be a professional reviewer
and critic in the next decades.

## WRITING ENTERTAINMENT FEATURES

Most reviewers and critics also write entertainment news and features. It is a
natural extension of the specialization to be able to write both news and features, in addition to opinion about the arts. At many publications, it is part of
the beat responsibilities to cover breaking news, to write Sunday features, and
to review or criticize. The work is therefore a mix of objective and subjective
forms of feature writing. However, writing entertainment features is as difficult
as any other type of feature writing. It requires the same reporting and writing
skills. It may demand even more patience and resourcefulness because of the
unique nature of the artistic community. There are many responsibilities and
few people to cover entertainment beats at most publications. Like other forms
of reporting, perhaps the most important ability is source cultivation. Developing sources of information about the entertainment world is your bread
and butter.

Entertainment feature writing is often more nationally focused than other
types of feature writing. Many entertainment stories, especially in metropolitan areas, have national interest and appeal. For television beat writers, for instance, there is a mix of national and local stories, but many of the programs
are national in origin because they air on broadcast or cable networks and
must have national focus. National stories, even if they are about television
programs, have a local impact at the stations that air them and in the homes
where they are watched. At the same time, local television stories must have a
priority because they involve persons and companies in the areas served by local publications.

Entertainment writers also seem to have more autonomy in their work than
most other reporters at mainstream newspapers and magazines. As beat reporters, they are specialists. They are expected to know about activities and events
within their areas of expertise. Although entertainment reporters are specialists,
it is possible to be even more specialized with beats within entertainment such
as television–radio–cable, dance, restaurants, and music. Thus, it is up to the
writer to generate story ideas and complete them. On occasion, editors propose
or assign stories, but, for the most part, entertainment writers are expected to
develop a high degree of enterprise in their work. Some individuals, particularly
beginners who cover entertainment, like the independence, but others prefer
direction because they feel they just cannot come up with good material day in
and day out.

Along with that, many entertainment writers—as well as reviewers and critics—work from locations other than the newspaper newsroom or magazine of-

fice. Many work from offices in their homes. Part of the reason is the nature of their work—it is not in the office and at unusual hours. For example, Fort Lauderdale *Sun–Sentinel* television critic Tom Jicha covers the television and radio industries, as well as regularly writing reviews and criticism about television and radio. He depends on the telephone a great deal. "We [entertainment reporters] are a lot like cops; all reporters are. Without sources, we'd be dead. The way you get those sources is that you cultivate them on the phone. A lot of the time, I'll call people up just to chat, to maintain the lines of communication" (Jicha, 1993).

That, it seems, is the nature of entertainment feature writing: people, chatting, interviewing, information gathering, and story writing. Local newspaper, magazine, and newsletter entertainment feature writers have an advantage over their broadcast and cable counterparts because they can get advance material much more easily. Telephone interviews can build stronger advances for big shows in a community, for example. It is difficult, if not impossible, for local market television entertainment reporters to do this.

Entertainment reporters must use publicists as sources for their feature stories. Some entertainment feature writers are generalists—covering all types of entertainment and the arts—but others are highly specialized. The generalists must cover all aspects of the art world and must be comfortable with a wide range of arts and recreational activities. Specialists are focused on film, television–radio, popular music, and so forth. Some are highly specialized. They do not write just about music, but focus on pop music, classical music, or jazz. And it is more difficult for generalists writing entertainment features to have a depth of sources to call on for stories. But they do have a greater breadth of sources.

Just because the subject matter may be lighter and less complex than most other news beats, it cannot be any less accurate or timely. The effort is seemingly endless for some entertainment reporters. Even covering the glamour events such as the Academy Awards program, the Grammy Awards show, a multimillion-dollar worldwide concert tour, or national megaevents can be exhausting. Getting to a location early, waiting, and then being ready at an instant's notice can be stressful and physically demanding. Often covering events such as the Academy Awards means standing in crowded rooms, waiting long periods, screaming questions at sources that ignore them, being subjected to cattle herd-like instructions of publicists, and other less-appealing situations. In fact, most entertainment reporters at a major awards event never get into the auditorium. They wind up covering the event from an auxiliary room (or adjacent building) set up with a television monitor. When postevent interviewing occurs, it takes place in a press conference forum with a chance for only one question, at best. There is rarely any exclusive interviewing that takes place at such events.

Most entertainment reporting at the local level does not involve such spotlight events. Those assignments might be the reward for a year of covering more routine entertainment news at the local level. These stories focus on shows at the local auditorium or arena, touring artists and performers, an occasional interview with a celebrity who visits or who lives in the area, and a lot of features about amateur productions and artistic effort at neighborhood theaters, local colleges, and perhaps even high schools. The types of stories are often classified as nothing more than previews and reviews, some editors like to say. There is much truth to that, but enterprising entertainment reporters go much further with profiles, human-interest stories, seasonal stories, and a wide array of approaches to their beats. It is up to you and your skills to make the most of being an entertainment reporter.

## Using the Essay Structure

Although entertainment features use a variety of organizational approaches, most reviews and critical articles find their way into an essay structure. This is a simple approach that permits the maximum development of writing. A good lead (or introduction) opens the essay with a statement of what you want to do. The body of the essay is a synthesis of generalizations about the work that are supported by evidence and illustrations that are taken from the work. The conclusion summarizes the points, and all this is done in just a few hundred to a few thousand words. Writer William Ruehlmann (1979) recommended 10 points about the basics of what he calls judgmental features. To reach success as a critic, he said

1. Make yourself an expert—The more you know about writing books such as novels, the more authoritative you will be and the better you can handle your assignment.
2. Don't flaunt your expertise—Do not write over the heads of your readers. Teach, but do not assume too much about what readers know.
3. Do not talk down—Assume your reader is intelligent and can understand what you write.
4. Avoid over-dependence on plot summary—Do not tell your reader everything that happened. Tell the reader how and why something happened, but not what.
5. Explain the work in context of our lives—In other words, he asks, is the work good entertainment? Does it help us better understand ourselves or understand the world around us? If so, it is art.
6. Find a strong lead and ending—Be specific and arresting in your lead. End with a snap.
7. Cite specific examples to support your views—If you say something good or bad about the work, show readers. This gives insight by providing your own reasoning behind the assessment.

8. Write well and write cleverly—Apply the same standards for good style and structure that you expect in the work you are reviewing to your own writing.

9. Take your stand with conviction—Do not be timid. Write with confidence and assurance.

10. Have a little charity—Remember this in particular when you are writing about amateur artists instead of professionals. But even in dealing with seasoned professionals, take into consideration all factors when you decide you love or hate something.

Ruehlmann (1979) said that the structure of a review can be as varied as any other type of feature article. He said you must remain flexible to permit the review to take the form necessary to make your points understandable. He also emphasized the need for readable reviews. This is done, he added, by use of specific examples to support opinion and to enliven the critical writing.

Good writing is what sells your work, regardless of whether you are a staff writer or freelancer. Writing must keep readers interested. Andy Rathbone (personal communication, April 20, 1993 and January 17, 1998), a San Diego-based author, writes both product reviews and restaurant reviews. He believes opinion writing should be stimulating for readers:

> You have to hold the reader's interest by going close to the edge, but not over. Nobody wants to read a boring opinion. However, if you go too far in one direction, you'll be branded as a radical, and lose the reader's respect and, more important, the reader's long-term interest. Walking that edge—being radical enough to be interesting, yet still have that truthful edge that makes people nod their heads—is the key.

Although straight entertainment feature writing is normally in third person, there are two schools of thought about perspective in personal opinion-based writing. One side argues for first person writing. The other advocates third person. There is more to it than just use of personal pronouns, however. Consider what you are saying to a reader by writing in first person. You are saying, "I am important enough to be a major part of this review." It is, of course, convention in professional journalism to write most nonfiction, such as general feature stories, in third person. The rules change in the case of personal opinion, especially reviewing and criticism. Use of first person is more acceptable. Still, many reviewers and critics prefer to write in third person. It is really a matter of each publication's own style of writing or, perhaps, that of the individual writer.

In review writing, the philosophical approaches of reviewers and critics fall into two schools: authoritative and impressionistic. Hunt (1972) defined the impressionistic approach as one that generates an expression of the critic's reaction to the work, exclusive of standards or precedents. The particular work is evaluated in reference to historic models which have been previously judged worthy.

The authoritarian critic must have considerable background preparation and exposure to the art form, and he or she necessarily accepts a set of fixed standards of rules.

Most contemporary reviewers and critics are somewhere in the middle of the two approaches, Hunt (1972) said. Most attempt to take the best of both schools rather than fit into one or the other. "[M]ost feel free to switch into the more comfortable personal essay style, often leading to an 'I-like-it-because' conclusion" (Hunt, 1972, p. 29).

As in all other forms of features, selection of the lead is a big decision. How do you begin? This part of your review sets the tone of the entire article and should be considered carefully before you begin. Perhaps you can open with something startling about the artist. You have decided the work is pretty bad and you want to warn readers at the beginning, so you choose an inverted pyramid approach by getting the "news" about your evaluation at the top.

Whatever you choose to say in the lead, your first several paragraphs need to establish the context of the review or critique. What work is being reviewed or criticized? Who is involved; when and where? As you move into the body of your essay, you tell your readers how and why. Some beginning reviewers are so anxious to get into the opinion, they forget to present the basic facts near the beginning of their essay. You should also avoid clichés associated with reviewing and criticism of a particular art form, especially in a lead. These worn-out statements or phrases only drag down the quality of your own writing and bore the reader. Find new and interesting ways to make your points.

Pressing deadlines may change the approach you take when writing reviews. It is one thing to dwell on a work for several days before committing your ideas to paper. For a debuting new play, film, television program, or touring musician, you might get just one shot and only a few hours to complete your work. For newspaper and weekly magazine reviewers and critics, this is generally the case on all new work. For monthly magazine or newsletter writers, deadlines present a different set of problems—remaining timely when you must produce your feature or review weeks, or even months, before a movie or book debuts. The problem is so severe for some magazines that they simply do not try to review certain types of material unless they can get considerable lead time through previews and advance copies. For some magazines and newsletters, for example, book publishers may provide paperbound galley proofs or special advance reading editions for reviewers or feature writers to use before the book has been hardbound and distributed to bookstores for sale to the public.

A thorough review offers readers comparison and contrast. Readers want to know how a new book compares with the earlier works of a favorite author or how a new album will stand against the earlier efforts of a group. What is similar and what is different? Why? Is it relevant? Similarly, many essay reviews compare and contrast the works of different artists on the same subject or same level in a single review. It is not unusual, for example, to find a set of summer movie reviews packaged together or one review that discusses all the new summer releases at the same time. The technique is also popular with book reviewers who might look at new books on one subject—such as the Olympic Games, a presidential election campaign, or a trio of new competing books about the British royal family—in a single review.

It is also important to provide readers with a summary, highlight, or information summary with a review or critique. These information summaries are often boxed typographically by editors to run within or beside the review. However, it is your responsibility, as the reviewer and critic, to provide the information used in these boxes. As you read about the major forms of reviews and criticism in the following sections, you learn what is commonly needed in the information box for each art form. These inserts in your reviews and critiques focus on the basics, but each publication has its own variation of how it should be done. These are general guidelines, however, and it is essential that you present the facts consistently in the style your publication uses.

## WHO HAS THE RIGHT TO SAY WHAT?

Do readers really care about what you say in your reviews? Do they care about your expressed opinions? Some do and some do not. Some accept what a writer recommends because of the writer's reputation. Some ignore the comments or even laugh at your carefully weighed assessments. A few get very upset if you criticize their favorites. And, it seems, some readers just do not get involved one way or the other. As reviewers or as qualified critics, writers have been given the right to comment on the arts of their town by the editors or publishers of their publication. It is a significant role in the arts community that must be kept in perspective at all times. It is a form of public trust not unlike that of the city hall or statehouse reporters who cover—and assess—government for the public. It must be done responsibly.

What are the limits of writers producing reviews and criticism? Do you, as a reviewer or critic, limit your work to art only? Or do you include the larger arena of entertainment? Certainly the umbrella that covers reviewing and criticism has enlarged. Reviewing and criticism have extended beyond pure art to entertainment.

Another important consideration is the legal limitations of criticism under the First Amendment and the various state constitutions. How far can a reviewer or critic go in expressing opinion before it is unacceptable? In terms of law, a reviewer and critic must be concerned with libel because of the potential for defamation of character of an artist. Because libel law varies from state to state, the limits of criticism also vary according to state libel law. What a critic says might not be considered damaging by a jury in a major city as easily as it would be in a small town in the more conservative regions of the country.

Generally, reviewers and critics are permitted to express their opinions, even if defamatory, on topics that are interesting to the public. This is the conditional privilege of "fair comment," a defense that has been used effectively for more than a century. Mass media law professor Don Pember (2003) explained: "Statements of opinion are often immune to a successful libel action. The courts have said that the rhetorical hyperbole—broad, exaggerated comments about someone or something—are obviously not assertions of fact and cannot stand as the basis for a successful libel suit" (p. 217).

Mass media law professors Dwight Teeter and Don Le Duc (1992) added that common law and state statutes extend to "even scathing criticism of the public work of persons and institutions who offer their work for public judgment: public officials and figures; those whose performance public taste in such realms as music, art, literature, theater, and sports; and institutions whose activities affect the public interest" (p. 227).

However, Pember (2003) said the fair comment defense against libel in a review must be based on certain requirements: (a) the comment must be an opinion; (b) the comment should reflect on the public aspects, not the private, of the person's life; and (c) the comment should have a legitimate public interest. Still, Pember cautioned, the difference between fact and opinion is not that clear. The courts, he said, still wrestle with the distinction. This makes life difficult for aggressive critics and reviewers. Perhaps the best legal advice is that you should be able to back up what you say in the public interest with evidence, and that you should be concerned with context of the statement and the words themselves. This way, Pember said, the public has the ability to develop its own opinion about the performer or the work.

## FILM REVIEWS AND CRITICISM

The names of the best-known film reviewers and critics are household words among moviegoers—Pauline Kael, David Denby, Rex Reed, Gene Siskel, Roger Ebert, Judith Christ, Andrew Sarris, Dwight Macdonald, and Anthony Lane. You can, no doubt, add names of outstanding local and regional film critics. The art of writing film reviews and criticism is perhaps the most visible of any type. Film reviews are usually written when a motion picture makes its commercial debut. When they do write an evaluation, reviewers and critics employ a number of strategies to evaluate a new film. The most common concerns are as follows:

1. Quality of story line (plot), social relevance of the story line, or the original source material.
2. Performance of leading actors and actresses.
3. Performance of the director.
4. Consistency and quality of work of the technical support staff (such as special effects, cinematography, or film editing).

5. Use of conventions such as symbols or color.
6. Audience reaction and the film itself as a social event.

Dwight Macdonald (1969), who criticized film for more than 40 years and influenced many of today's critics and reviewers, said reviewers and critics need to judge film on different standards. He said two rules of thumb include "did it change the way you look at things?" and "Did you find more (or less) in it the second, third, $n^{th}$ time? (Also how did it stand up over the years, after one or more 'periods' of cinematic history?)" (p. xi). To those main points in his book, *Dwight Macdonald on Movies*, he added five other standards by which he judged movies:

1. Are the characters consistent, and in fact are there characters at all?
2. Is it true to life?
3. Is the photography cliché, or is it adapted to the particular film and therefore original?
4. Do the parts go together; do they add up to something; is there a rhythm established so that there is form, shape, climax, building up tension and exploding it?
5. Is there a mind behind it; is there a feeling that a single intelligence has imposed his own view on the material? (p. ix)

It is also common for film reviewers to provide adequate background on key individuals involved in the film. Film scholars who focus on the director as the author of the film emphasize the "auteur theory" of film making (Kael, 1979; Sarris, 1979). Hunt (1972) said, however, a majority of film audience members are just not that interested in the author as a focus of a review. Most, he said, look at importance or relevance of the film.

Film reviewers and critics watch a lot of films. An average week for a full-time reviewer or critic for a major publication includes enough time to view 5 to 10 full-length films. Some are shown in theaters, requiring even more time to travel back and forth, but others, such as classics or new versions of existing films, are available on videotape. Devoted film scholars who review or criticize films see some films much more than just a single time. In fact, dozens of viewings of a single film are not unusual for the very best ones, or for personal favorites of veteran reviewers and critics over a long period of time. There is also the time spent each year at film festivals, industry meetings and conventions, and other special events. Just routine viewings, at 2 hours per film, are quite a time investment for a single workweek. Much of this time is spent in preview screenings. These special private screenings are an important means of getting to see a film before the public does. But they are not always final cuts, either. Smart reviewers or critics will not leave a film early, no matter how badly it may begin.

Viewing advance screenings is essential to the success of the film reviewer and critic, however. To gain access to previews, reviewers and critics work with studio publicists and promotion specialists, as well as their own local theater managers and distributors. These individuals contact reviewers who are associated with publications, but beginning freelancers must find these individuals until the freelancers become known to the industry. Often, these showings will be after hours when theaters are available (some after 12 a.m.). Showings are usually early in the same week a film is scheduled to open (such as a Monday or Tuesday for a typical Friday opening). At other times, reviewers and critics travel to Los Angeles or New York to see special screenings set up by the studio.

Students interested in writing film reviews or film criticism should read the works of the top critics. An excellent source for examples of quality film and other arts reviews is *The New Yorker* magazine. Film fans often see some of the top U.S. and foreign films discussed on its pages. *New Yorker* film critic Anthony Lane, named top reviewer and critic by the American Society of Magazine Editors in 2001, wrote this introduction to his review of a recent French film:

> If you find yourself in need of a tonic in the coming weeks, and discover that a close friend has stolen your copy of "Singin' in the Rain," you could do worse than plan a trip to "8 Women." François Ozon's new picture is a tonic of sorts, but you should be warned that at no time does it taste anything other than most peculiar. Put simply, it is a cocktail: a hot-hued, postmodern, nineteen-fifties murder-mystery musical hen party. You may be left with doubts about Ozon as a director, but one thing is for sure: he'd make a hell of a bartender.
>
> The setting is virginal and unashamedly fake—purest Agatha Christie. The hush of a snowbound country house, where deer nibble foliage on cue, is broken by the small matter of a murder (some male of the species named Marcel, who really doesn't count), and also, more important, by a volcanic irruption: the arrival, from nowhere, of a vast, untamable horde of famous French actresses. Each is playing a part, of course, and the rapport between their various personae will form the emotional clutter of the film, yet we are constantly reminded—it would be a grievous breach of etiquette if we dared to forget—that what we are gazing at is a constellation.
>
> The wise thing, I guess, is to name the stars in alphabetical order, since any other system of ranking would cause one or more of them to explode in a solar flare. . . . (Lane, 2002)

Getting started in film reviewing may involve taking a back-up role to a more established writer. This means you have to have a willingness to review the less-important films that might not even rate preview showings. Other opportunities exist at less mainstream publications such as college newspapers, alternative and entertainment-oriented weeklies, and small regional arts magazines.

Film reviews and criticisms are accompanied by synopses of information about the film. This "information box" commonly used by newspapers and magazines usually contains some, or all, of the following information:

1. Name of film, local theaters screening it, their addresses, and opening date.
2. Director, producer, and production company.
3. Leading actors and actresses in the cast.
4. Screenwriters, cinematographers, and music scorers.
5. Running time.
6. Motion Picture Association of America (MPAA) audience rating.
7. Quality rating by reviewer or critic.

## RADIO AND TELEVISION REVIEWS AND CRITICISM

One of the newest types of reviewing and criticism to evolve is broadcast and cable program reviewing. Newspapers and, to a limited extent, magazines are now covering the broadcast and cable industries and reviewing or criticizing programming at levels like never before. Beginning in the late 1950s and early 1960s, it was sporadic. Through the 1970s and 1980s, this new type of reviewer and critic emerged. Today, these individuals focus on reviewing and criticizing new regular programs, major sports broadcasts, special programs, and other unusual activities of interest to local audiences. Many full-time reviewers believe they have the responsibility to reinforce experiences in common with viewers and listeners. They also feel it is their duty to alert viewers and listeners to worthwhile events, to comment about excellence in programming, and to inform readers on developments with local stations.

Opinion essays are also important contributions of television and radio reviewers. These are not limited to single programs or series, but can become more philosophical about trends, questions, and issues involving the industries and their audiences. Broadcasting Professor Peter Orlik (1988) noted this "contemplative approach" is often taken by magazines because it fits a magazine's production schedule more easily and appeals to more specialized audiences attracted to magazines. They are also different in that they tend to be longer and more thoughtful. "Such think pieces and the issues they raise are seen as mooring masts to which can be anchored the shorter and more transitory personality and audience reaction columns—previews and reviews" (p. 44), Orlik argued.

As film reviewers depend on advance showings for much of their work, so do broadcast reviewers. These showings are usually available on videotape or at the local stations of the community where the reviewers work. Much advance viewing is done with special videotape copies of programs sent to reviewers and critics a few days or a week before the scheduled broadcast. Of course, special opportunities are provided to preview shows in New York and Los Angeles, where many television, radio, and cable networks are headquartered, during tours and special promotional events during the year.

Like other commentary writers, television and radio reviewers and critics must do their homework. It means watching and listening to a large number of programs each week. For Fort Lauderdale *Sun–Sentinel* television critic Jicha (1993), a veteran journalist of three decades, it means receiving and viewing as many as 10 to 20 videotapes a day. He explained how he does his job:

> I'll never review a show without watching the whole thing. But I won't watch a lot of shows at all. I just have to make a decision based on whether I have any interest, or if it is a new program or a mini-series. There are a lot of people who are going to be looking to me—and I know it sounds a little pretentious—for guidance: "Is this worthy of my investment in time?" You have to tell them. But some of the programs that show up on the Discovery Channel, the Learning Channel, or Arts & Entertainment, some of that is the best programming on television, but some of it isn't. You make a judgment at some point that people aren't going to tune in to watch certain programs. So why bother? So I don't watch a lot of the tapes I get. But the ones I do watch, I watch from beginning to end.

Jicha (2002) recently reviewed one of ABC–TV's debuting situation comedies at the beginning of a new television season. He did not like the show and was not bashful in expressing his opinion. Here's how he wrote it:

> Just awful is less than perfect—and Less Than Perfect is just awful. This last of ABC's new comedies to premiere is also the least. It is the kind of show that has made "sitcom" a pejorative to many viewers.
>
> The characters are so broadly drawn they are cartoonish. The set-up and plot twists are devoid of credibility and plausibility. Worst of all, most of the intended punch lines are humorless, yet the laugh track is amped up like the bass on a teenager's first car.
>
> The casting of Sara Rue as the lead is perhaps the only praiseworthy aspect of this show. It's a pleasant departure to see a full-size young actress get a chance to stand in the spotlight. Unfortunately, she still has to endure a torrent of jokes about her weight.
>
> Rue, last seen on Popular, is Claudia Casey, a temp for the past two years at the GBN network. She prefers the term floater to temp, which allows for a predictable, tasteless follow-up joke. Her latest assignment is to fill in as the assistant to vain anchorman Will Butler.
>
> Eric Roberts, who makes his debut as a sitcom star as Will, might have made an important enemy of an ABC VIP in describing his character. "He does not find himself amusing," Roberts said. "He takes himself very seriously. He thinks he's very important and when you're that important, it's not a laughing matter." He said Will is a compilation of many TV news people but "It was more Peter Jennings than anyone else."
>
> Claudia is dismissed as a vagrant from the fourth-floor business department by the self-important twits in the 22nd floor newsroom. Kipp Romano and Lydia West are especially cruel, since Kipp, another of Will's assistants, has promised

Lydia, a researcher, that he would get her the job working with Will. Kipp, of course, has an ulterior motive to getting on Lydia's good side.

Zachary Levi is the unctuous Kipp and Andrea Parker is the career climbing Lydia. Parker is most recognizable from The Pretender but she also has one of the most formidable comedy credits of recent years: She was one of the guest stars in the classic Seinfeld episode The Contest. Her presence in Less Than Perfect does not preclude further Pretender participation, although she suspects the most recent TV movie was the last of the line. "I think it would be difficult at this point to wrangle us all back together. But with that show, you never say never."

Whenever Claudia needs a confidence boost or just to see a friendly face, she can count on her old friends downstairs, Owen and Ramona, played by Andy Dick and Sherri Shepherd. It's becoming apparent Dick is a one-trick pony. Owen is indistinguishable from the fey, sexually ambivalent character Dick played on Newsradio, the same persona he adopts for most of his talk show appearances. He insists, with tongue seemingly firmly in cheek, that his character is not gay.

Shepherd should get a new agent. She was in two of the worst, most quickly canceled comedies of last season, Emeril and Wednesdays 9:30 (8:30 Central). Now Less Than Perfect. The cancellation of Emeril could be seen coming for weeks. Wednesday 9:30 came and went so quickly, she said, "I was looking at myself and the TV cut off."

The only way to avoid a similar disappointment is to tune elsewhere on Tuesday 9:30. Everyone else will. (Jicha, 2002)

Daily newspapers are the dominant outlets for broadcast and cable reviewing because of the timing of publication deadlines. For the same reason, most magazines do not get involved in broadcast and cable reviewing. Some weekly magazines, such as the newsmagazines or TV Guide, are able to do so in advance because of lead time given to them by sources seeking maximum promotional value for a special program or series in a big circulation publication. Similarly, these weekly magazines review or cover the broadcast of programs after the fact if a program has strong impact or if ratings show an unusually large audience.

A review or critique of a television or radio program can actually serve a dual purpose. It may also serve as an advance story, alerting viewers of the coming program. Thus, with a dual purpose, writers have to be careful not to reveal too much that would spoil viewing.

Many of the nation's major television industry beat writers, reviewers, and critics collect information on a 3-week press tour of Southern California each summer. The tour is grinding, with writers beginning their days at 8 or 9 a.m. and going nonstop through 12 a.m. The days are filled with previews of new fall programs, interviews with the new programs' stars, producers, and directors, and other individuals involved in the industry. It is often difficult to find time to write while on the road with such a tight schedule. "It's nineteen straight days of screenings like that," said the Sun–Sentinel's Jicha (1993), who has been taking the tours for more than a decade. "And people think we are having fun. We work hard during those trips."

When stories are written from press tours or other more local sources, information boxes are common in many publications, especially newspapers. The information box (if brief enough, information sometimes runs in a trailer—a paragraph at the end) for a television, radio, or cable program advance or review usually contains some or all of the following information:

1. Name of program, network (if appropriate), and local station(s) broadcasting it.
2. Scheduled air time(s), program length(s), and date(s).
3. Major actors and actresses.
4. Content category (drama, comedy, and so on).
5. Capsule summary of content.

## LIVE MUSIC AND CONCERT REVIEWS

For many younger arts writers, there is no more exciting assignment than to cover a live concert by a well-known band or solo artist. In fact, many reviewers and critics start out reviewing concerts or albums of recorded music. Newspapers, magazines, newsletters, and online publications approach live music and concert reviews differently, mainly because of timing, deadlines, and multimedia capacities. Online publications reviewers, for example, can integrate audio and video links into their written reviews. Traditional print reviewers cannot "excerpt" from performances. For newspapers, there are two types of situations that concern reviewers and create different writing strategies. First, there are musicians who are on tour and may make only one appearance on one date in an area. Second, there are extended concert appearances and dates by musicians in a community. You cannot handle each situation the same way.

For the one-night performance, a review might not be as helpful to readers from a consumer point of view. After all, they cannot use your review to decide to go after the fact. A way around this is to review an earlier performance by the same musicians in a nearby community if possible. Nevertheless, reviews of one-night concerts are part of the coverage of the arts of a community. Certainly, persons who attended want to know how others assessed the show. It is important to note those who did not go are interested in what happened from a critical perspective.

For concerts that are scheduled for more than one day in a community, you have more latitude in what you can do. A regular review serves readers in major ways, such as helping them decide whether to attend. Naturally, it is best to publish the review as quickly as possible after the first performance. Daily newspapers usually publish the next day or, at worst, for a very late evening show on the second day. Most daily newspaper concert reviews stick to the basics because of their deadline constraints. These reviews, like other print media, focus on staging, sound quality, length of performance, audience size and reaction and involvement, names of song performed, special performers present, unusual deviations of the performed music (such as live versions dramatically different from recorded versions on well-known songs), and the effort of the warm-up act.

Justin Davidson is an example of how well prepared a critic must be to write at the highest levels. Davidson (2001a), who was awarded the Pulitzer Prize for criticism in 2002, writes classical music criticism for *Newsday,* the Long Island daily newspaper. A multifaceted man, Davidson loves both music and writing. He is an experienced journalist, first working as a stringer for Associated Press (AP) in Rome before heading down the road to becoming a critic. He majored in music at Harvard University and continued working for AP while in Boston. He studied classical guitar and composition. He earned a year-long fellowship in music in Paris and eventually studied music composition at the doctoral level at Columbia University. At the same time he composed works performed all over Europe, and he wrote about music for Slate and the *Los Angeles Times* as a freelancer. His credentials point to the fact that experience and educational credentials matter and contribute to doing the job well. He became a full-time critic at *Newsday* in 1996 and was a Pulitzer finalist in criticism in 1999. Less than 2 weeks after the 2001 terrorist attacks on New York City, Davidson wrote a critical review of a performance of the New York Philharmonic at the Lincoln Center. The memorial benefit concert, as Davidson wrote in his review, was much more than just an ordinary classical performance:

> There are moments when classical music, by common consent, ceases to be a marginal form of entertainment or the finicky preoccupation of the affluent and few, and becomes an essential source of nourishment. Or perhaps that is wishful thinking: Music now also seems more than ever beside the point, requiring an intensity of focus that few of us can muster. Our attention spans, never long to begin with, have been fractured, our thoughts crowded with looped images of ash and flame and plummeting steel. What room is there for art?
>
> Yet for a beautiful hour Thursday night, Avery Fisher Hall became a haven of concentration. In lieu of a festive opening night gala, the New York Philharmonic offered a benefit performance of Brahms' "Ein Deutsches Requiem" as a balm, and it was reverently accepted. All the signs of distraction that usually accompany a concert here—muttering, shuffling, coughing and snoring—had vanished. Aside from one stray cell phone early on, an attentive silence reigned. At the end of the performance, by request of the orchestra's executive director, Zarin Mehta, the audience held its applause and filed out of the hall in silence, letting the music hang in the air for a few extra minutes.
>
> Had the Philharmonic chosen only to remember the dead, it might have played a program of threnodies, beginning, perhaps with Richard Strauss' "Metamorphosen," a rending meditation on the destruction of World War II. But

Kurt Masur, whose final season as music director began that night, did not choose to dwell on lamentation. . . . (Davidson, 2001a)

As with most reviewers and critics, Davidson (2001b) occasionally encounters music he does not feel is well done. For a variety of reasons, he found fault with a new opera entitled "Lilith" that opened at the Lincoln Center:

> New American operas get staged with such demoralizing infrequency that whenever one makes it to the opening curtain, it can count on an ample fund of good will. On Sunday afternoon, Deborah Drattell's "Lilith" squandered it all in the space of a few lugubrious minutes.
> Allegedly about Adam's apocryphal and dangerously lustful first wife, Drattell's new opera, which New York City Opera gave its world premiere, is actually an impenetrable dance pageant featuring a chorus of men in Hasidic garb and a pair of female protagonists who are barely garbed at all.
> According to Jewish folklore, Lilith is the original femme fatale, sapping the juice out of sleeping men so as to give birth to a race of demons. The combination of biblical and vampiric themes, plus Drattell's long orchestral interludes, gave director Anne Bogart the opportunity to choreograph her SITI dance company in some cabalistic soft-core. Dancers and singers, clad in modest black, do some lethargic faux-Fosse numbers with chairs: "A Stranger Among Us" meets "Cabaret."
> Rarely has a score portended so much and delivered so little. Trombones mutter darkly. Strings shiver in awestruck tremolos. Dark-hallway-at-night chords keep pounding away until they have outlived their ominousness. Eerie vamps resolve into plain old oompahs. Semitic melodies announce their ancestry and then have nothing more to say. The orchestral textures are soupy, and the vocal lines jerk between chant-like monotony and thankless leaps. The mood never deviates from a sacramental fug. . . . (Davidson, 2001b)

Veteran popular music reviewer Deborah Wilker (1993) does not write about classical music. She has a vastly different interest in music and a different background. Wilker worked for more than 10 years as a reporter and columnist for the Knight–Ridder Tribune newspapers and the Fort Lauderdale *Sun–Sentinel* and is known as a leading news analyst of the entertainment industry. She has worked as a reporter for cable's Fox News Channel and covers consumer trends, health, and social issues. Interested in pop music, Wilker works very hard to produce a good concert review. It is not always a fun night out on the town with the sole purpose to find gossip about the performers. "When I am assigned to go to a concert, I am assigned to write a thoughtful, provocative review of what the singer did, what instruments were played, what songs were performed, and more. I'm not there to report on who was in the audience and gossipy things like that," she explained.

Music magazines and newsletters, on the other hand, must take a different look at reviewing live music because of their less frequent publication schedules. Some magazines and newsletters simply do not attempt it because it is not part of what they want to offer to readers. Others do not review music because of their infrequent publication schedule and the months of lead time they require for production. Weekly magazines do so in a manner somewhat different from newspapers. Most weekly magazines, such as the major news magazines, which attempt to write about live music, focus only on major artists and do so by writing a roundup style review of their tour. This type of review is generally more descriptive than critical and incorporates information from several stops on a national or international tour, adds nonperformance highlights, and any other aspects of the events that surround a tour by a world or national caliber musician or group. These articles are part review and part color (or atmosphere) feature and perhaps even a little human-interest feature as well.

Your best source for information about a tour is an artist's public relations representative or the tour's road manager. Often, the management of the concert facility can also provide helpful local information. Press kits and other background information are provided most often by these sources if you make yourself or your publication known to them. The information box for a concert advance or opening night review in either a newspaper or a magazine for a series of performances (not a one-time show) usually contains some or all of the following information:

1. Name of main group or artist.
2. Name of warm-up group or artist.
3. Date(s) and location.
4. Ticket sale dates and times, prices, locations of ticket sales points, and additional remote-site ticket service fees.
5. Reviewer or critic rating of the performance.

Generally, information boxes do not run with concert reviews that are written on performances that are one-time shows in a particular area.

## RECORDED MUSIC REVIEWS AND CRITICISM

Just about all adults and most children listen to recorded music in one form (compact disc [CD], tape, or record) or style (classical, rock, jazz, rap, country, easy listening, and so on). Because recorded music is so popular with the public, demand for qualified reviewers and critics in the mass media is high. Also, the need for information about records has been growing since the middle 1960s (evidenced most prominently by one-time alternative newspaper *Rolling Stone* magazine's 35th birthday in 2002). Popular mass media devote considerable attention, time, and space to recorded music than ever before, a turf once reserved only by specialized publications.

Reviews are more popular than ever before. Because record reviews appear regularly in many newspapers and general interest and news magazines, they are written differently than when they were found only in specialized newspapers, magazines, newsletters, and online publications. There was a time when only the most devoted music listener could interpret the special language of these reviews. But because of the mass interest in CDs, reviewers have to write to be understood by more people. The review, taking on this added educational function, has helped bring up the public's level of knowledge of CDs and musical styles.

Preview copies help record, tape, and CD reviewers do their jobs in a timely fashion. Just as film and broadcast or cable reviewers preview their art, so do CD reviewers. The record companies ship preview copies to reviewers once they get on the company's promotion department mailing lists or to generic addresses, such as "Music Reviewer, Arts Department," at a publication. And there are different levels of lists. Some are more important—that is, perceived by the publicists to be more influential—than others. To get on a promotional mailing list, contact the record companies with a legitimate request to be included. You will have to furnish the name of the publication you work for and its address, and you may be asked to submit some clips of previous work.

In fact, preview copies are one reason many music reviewers work at home. They can listen to the newest CDs on their home systems without distraction. For reviewers and critics for daily newspapers, music and entertainment magazines and newsletters, and online publications, it is not unusual to receive as many as 50 to 60 new recordings a week. That makes a lot of music to consider. Reviewers cannot listen to it all. There is simply not enough time in the day. Wilker (1993) set a limit of 10 CDs a day. If not, she said, it all seems to run together and "you are not doing anyone a service. I wish I could give these people more attention."

There are numerous approaches to writing a CD review. Some writers prefer to read the "liner notes"—the words on the back of a CD case—as they listen to the album. Some listen to the album first without taking any notes, just to get a "feel" for the album. Then they listen a second time for technical purposes and for details to cite in their review. And some reviewers like to turn their stereo system high for full effect while others prefer a headset. You might try a variety of approaches until you find a way that works for you.

Regardless of your approach, your basic purpose is to provide a description of the content of the album. After that, you should evaluate the work and provide as much background on the album content and the artist as space permits. At best, you want to be clear and practical for your readers. At worst, you write solely for other record reviewers in a language only the members of the "club" understand. Of course, you want to avoid that because you are serving no one but yourself.

Classical music and opera provide exceptional opportunities for recorded music reviewing. Much of what has been said in this section relates to popular contemporary music. Hunt (1972) suggested properly that education is a most important function of reviews of classical music and opera. "Because many readers are unfamiliar with all but the best-known works of the major composers, the critic must turn teacher when evaluating performances of music by lesser-known persons," he said (p. 136). Hunt also emphasizes the need to analyze the technique of the artist when considering classical music and opera. This is, of course, applicable to performance of established works. A particular challenge, he said, is new works. Changes in styles, techniques, and even instrumentation are worthy of your attention.

The information box for a record review usually contains some or all of the following information:

1. Name of album and artist or group.
2. Record, tape, and CD label and catalog number.
3. List price of record, tape, and CD.
4. Release date (if appropriate).
5. Reviewer or critic rating of the recording.

## BOOK REVIEWS AND CRITICISM

If you enjoy reading, writing book reviews may be an easy extension of that pleasure. There are a large number of daily newspapers and weekly or monthly magazines and newsletters that regularly publish book reviews. These books are often mass market, or trade, books found in most bookstores. There is wide interest in them. On the other hand, there is also a growing market for specialists who write for more specialized magazines, newsletters, journals, literary reviews, bulletins, quarterlies, and other publications with readers interested in the latest book news and reviews.

There are numerous local outlets for book reviews. The leading ones are Sunday newspaper book sections and magazine book departments. Specialized publications such as business magazines often devote considerable space to reviews of books relating to the industry, so do not ignore this potential market. Smaller publications do not ask as much of their reviewers as do larger publications and are good places to start. For instance, established magazines and larger daily newspapers often use other authors or individuals with advanced academic credentials to write freelance reviews.

Poet, novelist, playwright, and essayist John Updike knows something about writing and, of course, book reviewers and critics. Updike once gave the art of book reviewing some thought in one of his essays, the foreword to *Picked-Up Pieces* (1976). His five rules of book criticism included the following:

1. Try to understand what the author wished to do, and do not blame him or her for not achieving what he or she did not attempt.
2. Give enough direct quotation—at least one extended passage—of the book's prose so that the review's reader can, for his or her own impression, get his or her own taste.
3. Confirm your description of the book with a quotation from the book, if only phrase-long, rather than proceeding by fuzzy precis.
4. Go easy on the plot summary, and do not give away the ending.
5. If the book is judged deficient, cite a successful example along the same lines, from the author's *oeuvre* or elsewhere. Try to understand the failure. Be sure it's his or her failure and not yours. (pp. xvi–xvii)

Updike (1976) also recommended not accepting review assignments you might be predisposed not to like or to like. There are many reasons for either stance. Furthermore, it is important to note that some newspapers, magazines, and newsletters will not solicit or accept reviews of second or subsequent editions of books. These may seem new to the author and the publisher, but most publication editors prefer to use reviews of completely new books. Exceptions are possible, of course, when a major change occurs in the new edition. For the most part, individuals new to book reviewing are best advised to work on first editions unless an editor specifically assigns a later edition. You may discover a similar attitude often accompanies sequels to books. These are more likely to be reviewed than second editions, but they will be less sought after than reviews of the first book in a series.

Book reviewers and critics, like other reviewers and critics, must keep up with new developments in their field. Following the book industry is relatively easy if you look in the right places. Book publishing industry organizations, such as the American Booksellers Association (ABA), or writers' groups, such as the Authors Guild, keep members informed of developments. Their publications are helpful to monitor also. The ABA publishes *American Bookseller* magazine, and the Authors Guild has an extensive newsletter issued regularly to members. Other publications are *Publishers Weekly, The New York Review of Books,* and *The New York Times Book Review,* commonly available to the public by subscription or at newsstands. There are many others of course, both designed for industry insiders and for the book-buying public.

Most of the time, general interest publication book reviews are written by individuals who have a specialization in the subject of the book, not people who specialize in writing book reviews. Editors look for staff and freelance specialists in specific subjects because of the levels of expertise necessary to evaluate a new work. Individuals who write book reviews need to know something about books, the authors, and book publishing. Reviewers for the top-of-the-line national publications are often themselves editors or authors. These individuals are rarely staff members and write their commentaries as freelance reviewers. Their depth of knowledge comes from writing itself, working in the industry, and from sophisticated study such as college and graduate level majors in literature or other specializations.

If you are looking for prospective books to review, Boston freelance book reviewer Mark Leccese (personal communication, January 29, 1998 and May 28, 1993) recommended doing your homework. Leccese, editor of a weekly state politics and government newspaper in Massachusetts, has been a journalist for 18 years. He writes four to six book reviews and book articles a month. He decides what to review based on his publishing industry research. Leccese said the following:

> Get the publishers' seasonal catalogs or *Publishers Weekly's* seasonal preview, pick a few books you would like (and feel qualified) to review, and query book review editors proposing to review a specific book. Freelancers don't get to do the "big" books, so look for high-quality niche books. When you query, make it brief, clear and always send clips. Choose areas of specialty for yourself (fiction, political books, etc.), and tell the editors you're querying. Never miss a deadline, always write to length and, at least when you're starting out, don't argue about money. (Leccese, personal communication, January 29, 1998 and May 28, 1993)

*Boston Globe* book critic Gail Caldwell (2001) has written about books and book publishing for her newspaper for more than a decade. She served as book editor in the mid-1990s. She has a master's degree in American Studies and knows American literature. Her series of commentaries and book reviews for *The Globe* in 2001 were honored with the Pulitzer Prize in criticism. Here is how she began one of the reviews from that collection, a new book by novelist Joy Williams:

> "The Quick and the Dead" is fierce, lively, and shocking, and it possesses a tooth-and-claw beauty as dangerous and breathtaking as a cougar on the move.
>
> Poet of the ironic and damned, Joy Williams delights in turning the world on its head: She can make a sunset into end-of-day carnage and the day's carnage into an act of natural grace.
>
> Few writers choose to inhabit these high crevices, where the pitch is steep. But Williams could scarcely live anyplace else. Her writing is so infused with terrible truths and dark comedy—imagine Cormac McCarthy bumping into Flannery O'Connor—that it's difficult to imagine her on tamer ground.

Williams has applied her considerable intelligence over the years to the short story and novel as well as naturalist nonfiction, and "The Quick and the Dead" is her first novel in more than a decade. Its cast of characters has the familiar Williams stamp of transcendent idiosyncrasy: an eco-warrior teenager who's smarter than most adults; a dog more interesting than his human nemesis; a recently deceased woman who returns as a ghost to torment her husband (and give him stock tips). Together, they form a montage of the more colorful aspects of that great, pulsing monster we call life—which is, for some people, a euphemism for the necessary condition preceding death.

Because really, "The Quick and the Dead" is a death trip writ large in gorgeous calligraphy: perfect scenes and dark intent and uproarious cosmic jokes, usually in search of sacred targets. Its loosely woven garment of a plot concerns three teenage girls, all motherless, who are thrust together by geographical circumstance one summer in the Arizona desert. There's Alice, the aforementioned genius-punk who understands corporate greed and imperialist mayhem better than most teenagers understand the Backstreet Boys. There's Annabel, her dialectical opposite, who thinks the world can be changed only by better nail polish or a daring tan. And finally there is Corvus, the heart of these three Furies: Corvus, who lost both her parents to drowning, takes dire action to purify her own life, then devotes herself to the half-living spirits at a nursing home called the Green Palms—a place we are introduced to as "state-of-the-art End of the Trail." (Caldwell, 2001)

To reach the level of quality evaluation, writing, and commentary that critic Gail Caldwell offers her readers, you must gain experience. Often, beginners seeking a place to start writing about books will simply volunteer as reviewers to establish themselves and get clips. Although there is no money from the effort, it provides necessary experience.

The best literary critics strive to achieve the level of excellence attained by the late Irving Howe, who wrote for many years for *Dissent*, which he founded, but also for *The New York Times Magazine* and other publications. Howe was known as the book critic's critic. Although he wrote his own award-winning books, he was widely known for his thoughtful essays and criticism. He was an independent thinker who avoided trends and trendy writing throughout his 50 years of work. Individuals as successful as Howe, for instance, improve with experience and depth of study. Howe taught university-level English literature. He knew his material.

Even beginners these days must know their material. This is an important step in getting started. To get the review process underway, get to know the book contents, its genre, and the author well. Look through it and then read it. Read the title page, note the publisher, read the acknowledgments, introduction, and foreword. This is where you find out what the author says he or she is trying to do with the book. Skim the table of contents to get an idea of the scope of the book. Then turn to page one and read the book from front to back. Perhaps it may be surprising, but there are reviewers who do not read an entire book, or even parts of it, and try to write a review or even simply interview the author. A review can be written without reading the book, but the quality of the review invariably suffers and, thus, so does the service provided to the author, publisher, and the book-buying public. There are countless stories, and even comedy routines, based on talk show hosts, journalists, and others, about persons who did not prepare their work properly.

## A BOOK REVIEWER'S TIPS

Freelance book reviewer and Boston University adjunct professor Mark Leccese regularly writes about books. He said his book review structure is flexible, depending on who will be reading the review.

"The form, shape, and content of my book reviews depend on the publication's audience, the space I have, and the book itself," Leccese (personal communication, May 28, 1993 and January 29, 1998) said.

A piece about writing about books (or music, or film, or art) falls somewhere, I think, on a continuum: On one end are "reviews," ("It's good/It's fair/It's poor; here's what it's about") and on the other end is "criticism" (which tries to place the work in a larger context: of literature, of works in the field, and so forth). Where I aim on that continuum depends on what the editor (and that means the audience) wants.

I have no formula for a review. The book itself, and what I have to say, will determine the shape and tone of the piece. I do have a few touchstones, though:

Take careful notes as you read. I use the (blank) first page inside the cover to note thoughts and comments I have, page numbers of important parts of the book, notes that outline the structure of the book. I underline, I dog-ear pages, I scribble in the margins. As a reviewer, you have to have something to say.

Write clearly, simply, and directly. There's no excuse for pompous, turgid writing, and too many writers think that's how you're supposed to write about books. It ain't—not if you want readers.

Understand the point of the book, not just the plot. What is the writer (novelist or non-fiction writer) trying to say? Why, in other words, did the author write the book? When you understand, tell your reader.

Quote from the book. Don't just tell the reader about how the author writes and what the author writes about—show the reader. When you make a point, prove it.

If you can, read previous work(s) of the author. This helps put the current work in context.

Some research about the author or authors is also important to understanding the book you are reviewing. At times, the publisher will provide some of this information for you on the flyleaf or on an author page at the end of the book. Some publishers, when sending out review copies to publications in advance of an announced publication release date, will provide a press release or biography of the author. "Advance reader copies" are available as much as 6 months before official publication, but often these are uncorrected proofs with minor flaws and are usually only available in paperbound form. These are extraordinarily helpful in getting an advance look at a book, providing time for you to read the book before actually writing anything about it. There may also be summaries of the plot on the flyleaf or back cover that can be helpful to you in deciding if you want to review it at all.

While reading a review, readers want to know something about the author. Who is he or she? How did he or she come to write this book? A good review will integrate such information about the author and tell readers something about the author's previous works. It also makes sense to read as much of the previous works of an author as you can before you take on the current effort. This gives your review perspective and gives you the chance to compare and contrast within the author's own writing. Certainly, it also helps your readers if you, in your review, compare and contrast the book to others like it that have previously been published. Like record reviews, a thorough book review will summarize content without giving away plots, in addition to educating readers about the author. An information box accompanying a book review usually contains some or all of the following information:

1. Author and title of book.
2. Publisher and location, edition number (if applicable).
3. Book availability in hard or soft cover, prices.
4. Publisher's official release date (if appropriate, this is the date it is usually available in bookstores).
5. Length of book in pages.
6. Special distinguishing features.

## DRAMA AND DANCE REVIEWS AND CRITICISM

Along with film, books, and television, drama is one of the traditional major subjects of reviewing and criticism in the United States. Interest in dance, such as ballet, is growing and becoming an important specialization in the arts for those writing features for the mass media. Although the "national theater" remains centered in New York, most people who write about drama and theater are not in New York. These are the people in the hinterlands and other metropolitan areas writing about regional and local theater productions at the professional and amateur levels.

Theater has spread across the country like wildfire in the past 30 years, resulting in a rather sophisticated system of regional and community theaters and drama companies that are no longer solely focused in Manhattan. There are audience-supported theaters in just about every metropolitan area that offer drama and dance.

As a drama critic, you have the duty to look at all the drama performances in your area, good or bad. Todd Hunt (1972) said the following:

> [T]he critic, who must attend all the plays, sees a theater that includes occasional ineptness and a great number of not-too-near misses. He knows that it is easiest to write a rave notice. . . . But more often he will have to struggle to explain a play's apparent purpose, where it failed its goal, and what rewards remain to be found. . . . What makes it worthwhile, of course, is the occasional evening in the theater when the mind is engaged, the imagination is stretched, the intellect is rewarded. (p. 83)

Like reviewing and criticizing other art forms, you must be well prepared to write a drama or dance review. Some reviewers read plays before seeing them performed—easy to do on established works but not so easy with debut material. Others do not read plays, regardless of whether they are available. What you can do, if possible, is read other material by the same playwright.

It is also important to learn as much as you can about the cast prior to the performance. Learn their names and roles, just as a sports writer learns the numbers of key players in a game before it begins. Also note the producer, director, and the other behind-the-scenes personnel who contribute to the production. You can get some of this background information from the playbill or program, but you can also obtain it from the promotion department of the theater a few days before the performance.

As in book reviewing, be careful not to reveal too much of the story line when reviewing a dramatic performance. Telling too much will spoil the experience for others. The critical elements in a drama review must address the play's plot and its relevance, the performance of major actors singly and as a group, the direction they received, staging and sets, costuming, sound, lighting, audience reaction, and overall assessment of the night's entertainment. Any unusual developments, such as technical problems, should also be addressed if they affected the experience. Of course, reviewers often compare and contrast a current production with earlier versions of the same work by different companies or, in some cases, the same one.

The information box for a theater advance or opening night review for a series of performances (not a one-time show) usually contains some or all of the following information:

1. Name of play, author or choreographer.
2. Major actors and name of the touring company (if any).
3. Date(s) and location.
4. Ticket price scale, locations of ticket sales points.
5. Reviewer or critic rating of the overall performance.

Generally, these information boxes do not run with theater reviews written on performances that are one-time shows in a particular area.

Dance, although not nearly as popular in most areas as dramatic theater, still provides creative opportunities for reviewers and critics. Modern dance companies, many with uncertain support levels, certainly deserve the critical attention of the local media. More traditional dance groups, such as ballet companies, are perhaps more stable and generally receive critical review when new performances are staged. Like classical music reviews, dance reviews must educate the public. Few readers of dance reviews thoroughly understand what they have seen, enough to not want assistance in interpreting what the performance achieved or did not achieve.

What do you concern yourself with in a dance review? The focus must be on two levels: the effort of the dance group as a whole or an entity and the effort of the troupe's star dancers or directors. Because a single performer or director dominates many dance groups, this is an important point of view. Hunt (1972) suggested rereviewing dance companies to measure the degree of growth and change in the company over a season. Because performances are not always the same, this is a helpful strategy if time and space permit it.

Generally, information boxes do not run with dance reviews written on performances that are one-time shows in a particular area. A typical information box for a dance performance advance or opening night review for a series of dance troupe performances contains some or all of the following information:

1. Name of dance troupe and the title of performance or program.
2. Names of the company director or choreographer, lead performer, and other artists, such as musicians, if appropriate.
3. Date(s) and location.
4. Ticket price scale, locations of ticket sales points.
5. Reviewer or critic rating of the performance.

## FOOD AND RESTAURANT REVIEWS AND CRITICISM

Life as a restaurant reviewer or critic is a life of diversity, and, of course, calories. Amid the menus and wine lists are certain ways of handling the job, certain liabilities, and certain deadlines. Most food and restaurant critics are occasionally told how fortunate they are to have their jobs. *Milwaukee* magazine restaurant reviewer William Romantini (1987) said, "Everyone tells me how lucky I am to have the job. . . . But, though eating for free can at times be a lot of fun, it involves some major liabilities" (p. 49). First, he jokes, his friends won't have him over for dinner. More realistically, he says he must endure several bad meals for every good one.

Most restaurant critics want to dine anonymously. If the employees of a restaurant know them, it is possible for a restaurant to give unusual and extraordinary attention in preparing the reviewer's meal. Some restaurants, sensitive to reviewer's power and influence in affecting public opinion, keep pictures of reviewers on the walls of the kitchen for waiters to study. Most restaurants prefer reservations and reviewers should make them. To remain unknown, use a dining partner's name. Of course, the experience of making reservations becomes part of your assessment of the service you receive at the restaurant.

Many restaurant reviewers take a consumer approach to their work. They review the food, not as food authorities, but as consumers. What did you get for your money? Was it worth it? Why? Freelance writer Andy Rathbone (personal communication, April 20, 1993 and January 17, 1998) argued this is the most important part of a restaurant review:

> The most significant element of a food review is the price of the food. Is a gratuity added on to the final bill? Do the "dinner specials" include a drink? After price, the next most important quality is a restaurant's overall experience. For instance, fine food can be marred by bad service. Fine service, an exceptional view, or live entertainment can occasionally make up for mediocre food (as long as that's made clearly understood in the review.) Least important? Perhaps the restaurant's location. Most people are willing to drive out of their way for an extraordinary dining experience.

Robert Hosmon, a nationally syndicated wine and restaurant critic based in Miami, has been commenting on restaurants for more than 20 years. Hosmon, a freelance writer who has worked as restaurant critic for *Miami Metro* magazine and also written about restaurants, food, and wine for *The Miami Herald* (personal communication, October 12, 2002), said he considers five important factors:

1. Food ingredients and preparation—Is the food properly prepared as it is listed on the menu? Are the ingredients fresh? Is the presentation of the food satisfactory? One clue to judging a restaurant's capability is to select those dishes that are identified as specials, often carrying the chef's or the restaurant's name on the menu.
2. Service—Is service efficient and courteous? Does the serving staff hover, creating an awkward situation for diners, or does it disappear, leaving diners to fend for themselves, waiting for more water, waiting for the check?

3. Decor—Is the restaurant, visually, a pleasant place to be? Does it live up to its intentions and diners' expectations?
4. Ambiance—Does the combination of decor, service attitude, size of the dining room, music, lighting, and patronage in the restaurant add up to a pleasant dining experience?
5. Price—Is a visit to the restaurant worth the expense? Are any food items overpriced? Is the wine list prepared with reasonable mark-ups? Is the entire experience worth the price?

*Milwaukee* magazine's Romantini (1987) adds three other areas of concern of the restaurant reviewer. They are as follows:

1. The entrance to the restaurant and the first impressions you get as you enter.
2. The attention you receive as you are seated and the appearance of your table (settings, its preparedness, and so on).
3. Not the least important, the taste of food served, its temperature, and timing of service.

In evaluating food, be concerned with the main dishes, but do not forget the significance of soups, salads, other appetizers, breads, and desserts. Writing the review should be easy if care is taken to note details during the dining experience. It is difficult to write a review from memory, without some sort of notes. Try to obtain a menu. Some restaurants will permit it if you ask. Others will sell you a menu. If you cannot take a menu with you, ask for an itemized check. And, of course, take some descriptive notes while you are at your dinner table. This might give you away, but it does not have to do so. Many business people write notes during a meal. With some practice, you can become inconspicuous in your note taking for your review.

Many reviewers write about their dining experience in chronological order. Romantini (1987) said writing should always be done with concern for the effect of what you say. "[K]eep in mind the effect your opinion will have. Can you look yourself in the eye and honestly write what you feel no matter what the consequences? Remember, it's easy to say nice things about someone, but an abundance of tact is needed if you've got to criticize" (p. 52).

Some publications, because of monthly or even less frequent deadlines, choose to review several restaurants in a single article. These are roundup-style reviews and try to find unifying themes for the selected restaurants. This could be done using a style of food (e.g., Mexican), a neighborhood (e.g., the city's East Side), a category of service (e.g., guaranteed fast business lunches), and so forth. For a national magazine, it could be a city's top restaurants.

The information box for a restaurant review usually contains some or all of the following information:

1. Name of restaurant, address of location, and reservations telephone number.
2. Hours of operation.
3. Type and price range of food served per person.
4. Dress code, if enforced.
5. Reviewer or critic rating of the meal (often categorized by quality of food, price and value, service, and decor).

## ADVICE FROM A RESTAURANT AND WINE CRITIC

Dr. Robert Hosmon's wine column appears in 300 newspapers and other publications each week through the Knight–Ridder Tribune News Service. Hosmon has written about food, restaurants, and wines sold in the United States for nearly two decades. Currently his wine column is based at the *South Florida Sun–Sentinel* in Fort Lauderdale. He also regularly contributes to *The Wine News* and the *Robb Report* as well as other magazines and Web sites. It's a lucrative freelance lifestyle that other writers both admire and envy. Hosmon (personal communication, October 12, 2002) offered these observations about restaurant reviewing:

> Unlike other critics, restaurant reviewers have a unique responsibility to the subjects they review. A negative architectural commentary isn't going to cause the razing of a building. A bad movie review won't drive a theater to bankruptcy. The critic who finds fault with a dance company or symphonic orchestra's performance isn't going to provoke the demise of the company. But a negative review of a restaurant can, and often does, put that restaurant out of business forever. Therefore while restaurant critics serve the public, they must also remember the responsibility they have to the men and women whose future livelihood depends on their opinions.
>
> Standards for a good restaurant critic should include extensive knowledge of food ingredients and preparation, esthetic judgment, and an understanding of how restaurants function as a business. Each of those qualities requires experience, experience that can be developed through study and personal investigation. Conscientious restaurant critics dine out often and in many places. In the process, restaurant critics develop a professional approach to the evaluation process.
>
> The professional restaurant critic will, in the final analysis, consider the intent of a restaurant when making a value judgment. A family-oriented, budget restaurant is not trying to provide the same experience as a gourmet French emporium. But either restaurant can be judged as excellent—or poor—according to how well they succeed in doing what they set out to do. A good restaurant critic is never a causal consumer; he or she is a consummate observer, analyzing every food and every operation within the restaurant. Dining out for a restaurant critic is not a social occasion; it's a job.

## WRITING PRODUCT REVIEWS FOR CONSUMERS

A relatively new subject for reviewing and criticism is the area of consumer products. Although a few specialty publications such as *Consumer Reports* have been doing such reviews and evaluations for a long time, other newspapers, magazines, newsletters, and online publications have begun devoting more space to experts who write product reviews. These individuals know the industry and how the products should be performing. They acquire advance copies of the products through loaner programs or testing services and try them out for a period of time.

The range of products covers the marketplace literally. Automobile writers often review and write about new models of automobiles or other vehicles. Outdoor writers do the same with new boats, motors, or other fishing gear. Computer specialists write about new hardware and software based on their experiences using the products before they go on to the market.

Freelance writers who want to produce product reviews must begin by seeking the market. What is your expertise: children's toys, computers, bicycles, or a musical instrument? What publications regularly publish these product reviews? Some market research will determine these answers. San Diego's Andy Rathbone (personal communication, April 20, 1993 and January 17, 1998), the freelance writer whom you met earlier as a restaurant reviewer, also writes computer product reviews for numerous computer periodicals. Here is how he said he handles a computer product review:

> First, I find the market for the product review. Second, I call the product manufacturer's public relations person and arrange for an editorial loan of product. Then I play with the product for a while, and write what I think about it. Other times, the publication sends me the product, and I review it. The most important element is price. That single issue affects everybody. After that, the review should discuss the product's quality: How it handles the job it purports to accomplish. Then the review should compare how the product stands up against other products making similar claims. The review should also compare the product against other, similarly targeted products, even those from different price ranges. (Rathbone, personal communication, April 20, 1993 and January 17, 1998)

## OTHER SUBJECTS OF REVIEWS AND CRITICISM

There are a wide variety of other reviewing and critical writing specializations that have evolved in recent years or have existed for longer periods in specialty publications. Among them are

1. Live entertainment (ice revues, comedy shows, circuses, and so on).
2. Architecture.

3. Painting.
4. Sculpture.
5. Photography.

Live entertainment reviewing and criticism have many of the same concerns as dramatic reviews and concert reviews. It is difficult to say anything negative about such all-American institutions as ice revues and circuses. These articles tend to be more review and less criticism. There is a limit to how much you can hold back. Judgment based on local standards may be your best guide.

Architecture reviewing has become increasingly important since a Pulitzer Prize for criticism was awarded to *The New York Times* critic Ada Louise Huxtable. Architecture critics such as Paul Gapp of *The Chicago Tribune* are well known in their cities and in the industry. The construction boom in the Sun Belt has illustrated the role of major structures in creating the personality, or face, of a community in the past three decades and it continues. The new cities of this century have been characterized by their architecture, and the role of the critic is becoming more significant. A handful of newspapers and magazines use architecture critics as their cities continue to change. Because there is no second chance in terms of buildings, these critics should be on the inside of what is happening in terms of planning in the community before it happens.

Other arts such as painting, sculpture, and photography are most often presented in galleries and museums in special exhibitions and in standing or permanent exhibitions. These exhibitions often say much about the cultural state of the community that displays them, placing a degree of importance on criticism of these exhibitions. Most written evaluations of these exhibitions are descriptive, as they should be, for persons who might want to see the exhibits.

---

## BEST SOURCES FOR ARTS INFORMATION

Films and Movies:

Local theater managers.
Regional or local film company publicists.
National film company publicists.
Distribution company publicists.
Actors and actresses.
Specialized industry-trade publications such as *American Cinematographer* or scholarly publications such as *Film Comment*.
Producers and directors.
Film credits.
Film company World Wide Web sites.

Broadcast–Cable Television and Radio:

Television and radio network publicists.

Local affiliate publicists and promotion departments.

Radio station publicists.

Syndicated program distributor publicists.

Specialized industry publications such as *Broadcasting and Cable, Electronic Media,* or *Radio & Records.*

Program credits.

Network and production company World Wide Web sites.

Live Music and Concerts:

Recording companies of touring musicians (discussed later).

Road managers.

Tour publicists.

Musicians.

Specialized industry publications such as *Billboard* or *Daily Variety.*

Specialized consumer publications such as *Rolling Stone, Spin,* or *Ray Gun.*

Concert site facility management.

Recording label World Wide Web sites.

Recorded Music:

Recording companies' promotion departments.

Regional or local record company publicists.

Musicians.

Specialized industry publications such as *Billboard, Record World,* or *Radio & Records.*

Specialized consumer publications such as *Rolling Stone, Spin,* or *Ray Gun.*

Jacket information of albums, tapes, and compact discs.

Recording label World Wide Web sites.

Theater and Dance:

Theater playbill night of performance.

Theater managers.

Actors and actresses, dancers.

Specialized industry publications such as *Daily Variety* or *Back Stage Shoot.*

Directors and choreographers.

Theater company World Wide Web sites.

Don McDonagh's book, *The Complete Guide to Modern Dance*.

Walter Terry's book, *The Dance in America*.

Phyllis Hartnoll's *The Concise Oxford Companion to the Theatre*.

Gerald Bordman's *The Concise Oxford Companion to American Theatre*.

Books:

Book jacket or flyleaf.

Introduction, foreword, and acknowledgments of book itself.

Publishers' promotion departments.

Regional or local publishers' publicists and sales representatives.

Specialized industry publications such as *Book Week, Publishers Weekly*, and *American Bookseller*.

Authors.

Publishing house World Wide Web sites.

Food and Restaurants:

Menus.

Restaurant managers, chefs.

Public relations representatives of company.

Local health inspector.

Specialized industry publications such as *Restaurants and Institutions* and specialized consumer publications such as *Bon Appetit*.

Local and state restaurant associations.

Restaurant association and individual restaurant chain World Wide Web sites.

Architecture:

Gallery, museum, or show curator.

Architects.

Contractors, builders.

Specialized industry publications such as *Architecture, Progressive Architecture, Architectural Record*, and *Historic Preservation*.

Financing sources.

Local building inspector.

Local and state architects' groups.
Architecture schools and colleges' World Wide Web sites.

Painting and Sculpture:

Artist or sculptor.
Specialized industry publications such as *Art in America, Arts, Artforum International*, and *Art News*.
Published major exhibition catalogs and books.
Gallery, museum, or show curator.
Gallery and museum World Wide Web sites.

Photography:

Photographers.
Published major exhibition catalogs and books.
Specialized industry publications such as *Popular Photography* and *Aperture*.
Gallery, museum, or show curator.
Gallery, museum, and photographer World Wide Web sites.

Popular Live Entertainment:

Specialized industry publications such as *Daily Variety* and *Back Stage Shoot*.
Theater program on the night of the performance.
Theater managers.
Performers.
Performers' public relations representatives and their World Wide Web sites.
Recording label and broadcast network World Wide Web sites.

---

Often, painting, sculpture, and photography exhibits are housed in a facility together and a single reviewer or critic will be called on to discuss each in a single or perhaps separate review at different times. In these reviews, attention is seldom given to a single item unless it is so dominant that it commands the attention. Showings are also often presented by artist or by group of similar style artists.

## ENTERTAINMENT? NO, IT'S WORK

Michael Larkin (personal communication, October 15, 1988 and January 27, 1993), deputy managing editor for *The Boston Globe,* feels that reviewers and critics have a difficult career—at best. He explains

Most people, readers and other journalists included, view critics and reviewers with bemused envy, seeing only that someone could get paid for watching movies or attending rock concerts, eating dinners or reading some hot new novel. It's hardly work, right?

Consider, though, sitting through a screening of "Rambo XI: Thin Blood" and trying to think of something informed and entertaining to write about Sylvester Stallone's peculiar, enduring artistry. Or how about hunkering down in front of the tube for a night of the new fall season: what to say about "Hocus Focus," a new hour-long drama about magician crime solvers? Perhaps Anne Tyler's new book is out. But, then, you've already been assigned five books for the week and the book editor has given that one to someone else. . . . well, maybe you'll get to it on your vacation (if you've the slightest desire to read anything more involved than the back of a Cheerios box).

It is, I think, the most difficult, underestimated, long-term assignment in journalism: Do for a living what other, normal people do for relaxation and fun. Not only that, do it on deadlines only crazed sports writers live with and do it with the understanding that everything you write will prompt a disagreement with someone—readers who know more (or often less) than you do, even probably your editors who have seen the same performance and are hideously callous in venting their opinions. Consider, too, the artists' responses. A sample: "Bigger jerks than me review books, Nathan," writes Philip Roth in *Zuckerman Unbound.* And above all, don't make a factual error; you're the expert and your performance is as public as any play or TV program.

So how does anyone do it? The critics I know love their work; almost all of them—despite crushing schedules—are trying to figure how to cover one more thing or are panting about some upcoming event. Constantly learning about their specialty, they devote their lives to studying it: reading, seeing even performances they'll never write about, speculating about an entrée's ingredients at a dinner party. They thrill when someone achieves excellence or expands the definition of the form; they are mortified yet enthralled (though they may not write it that way) when they witness an all-too-public flop. Mostly, though, they deeply care about the attempts at creation. It is a caring that stems from a lifelong affection for the art; it is the key element in doing this job.

No one gets to be a respected critic simply because someone gives them the job. Usually, critics gave themselves the assignment when they were young, and have spent most of their lives and education trying to figure out why some books are more moving, some films more exciting, some rock stars rockier. It is this fascination that endures. The best have it as a constant and are able to communicate it. It gives them an understanding of the past, an appreciation for the present and enthusiasm for the future, all essential elements in the confidence necessary to make judgments about the ambitious efforts of others, to review and to criticize with personal vision and voice. Without all this, a critic might as well be going to the theater for fun. (Larkin, personal communication, October 15, 1988 and January 27, 1993)

## ETHICS AND STANDARDS TO CONSIDER

Food critics such as those at *The New York Times* spend tens of thousands of dollars on restaurant meals and other expenses. Although these expenses are quite extraordinary, more organizations are paying for what used to be provided free by restaurants, theaters, or record companies.

Who should pay for the entertainment you review? Should you pay for the free tickets, records, books, or dinner? Students often think it is cool that the tickets and parking are "comped" but they don't think about the ramifications of such treatment. Many publications are no longer accepting "freebies" for reporting about the arts, food, or travel. Most newspapers, magazines, newsletters, and online publications have two sets of rules for this important feature writing issue. For full-time staff members, most major publications will reject free entertainment items unless a legitimate reviewer or critic uses the free ticket or book in the completion of an assignment. Other books, records, and similar items are usually donated to local charities when received from a source. For part-time writers or freelancers, these rules may or may not apply. At some publications, part-timers or freelancers are left to their own decisions about who pays.

Why? Usually there are expectations associated with the gift of free tickets, records, and books. The expectation can range from simple recognition of the new work in print (news space publicity for no or little cost) to positive reviews. There have been a changing mood and set of expectations from such sources in recent years, however, as ethical standards have tightened. They expect less.

Clearly there are certain advantages to the special considerations such as good seat locations, receiving books or records in advance of release dates, and so on. It helps you do your job. But there is a chance of abuse of these special considerations if you are not careful. The price is high, too, in terms of your credibility as a reviewer. Once you are "bought" you can never achieve the same levels of integrity in the business. It is a tough concession to make. There is the problem of dealing with sources. At times, reviewers and critics have the opportunity to become too close to their sources. What is the result? It is the temptation to write unwarranted favorable, or too favorable, reviews. This also diminishes your credibility. The two things a reviewer or critic has from the beginning of his or her career are integrity and credibility. They are worth keeping, regardless of the cost.

CHAPTER ELEVEN

# Aftermath, Follow-Up, and Depth Series Articles

Most Americans remember where they were and what they were doing when the three commercial jet airplanes struck the World Trade Center and Pentagon and the fourth crashed into a field in rural Pennsylvania on the morning of Tuesday, September 11, 2001. It was, as many have observed, a defining moment in American history. The events of that day and the months that followed generated countless news stories and features. Many of these features were follow-up or aftermath stories and performed an important function in the overall coverage of newspapers, magazines, news-based World Wide Web sites, and even many subscription and organization newsletters. Americans and others around the world needed their voracious appetite for information and understanding of what happened to be satisfied.

On the first anniversary of the attacks, most news organizations published articles about what had happened on September 11, 2001, and specific events of the following months. In some of the articles, writers took a moment to assess where we were as a nation, a region or state, or a community a year later. Dick Polman (2002), a staff writer for the *Philadelphia Inquirer,* prepared one of these types of features for his newspaper's Sunday magazine section, *Inquirer.* In his cover feature, Polman described how Americans have refocused themselves on their lives once again. He observed that in many cases, lives have returned to doing what we do as individuals despite the mourning for those who were killed. We cannot, he argued, avoid or change the most fundamental traits of who we are as a nation. Here's how he began his article:

> Remember what it was like when the planes became missiles on a morning of azure blue? We were naturally horrified to learn that malevolent forces could appear, seemingly out of nowhere, to sunder our sense of invulnerability. And in our shock and pain, we were moved to declare that we had lost our innocence, that "everything has changed" in American life.
>
> It certainly seemed that way. Jay Leno and the other wise-guy comics fell silent, social commentators insisted that the age of irony was dead, violent films slated for release were put on the shelf, multimillionaire ballplayers laid down their gloves, people of little faith found solace in prayer—and in Washington, the practitioners of slash-and-burn politics curbed their tongues and cloaked themselves in the Stars and Stripes.

The latter response was predictable. Politicians are experts at sniffing out the public mood, and they're only as human as the rest of us. Still, it was a sight to behold. The political community is wired for partisan combat, yet here was this thunderous silence, smothering our disputatious discourse of the moment: Gary Condit and Chandra Levy, the Social Security "lockbox," the budget surplus (remember that?), stem cells, prescription drugs, HMO reform, immigration reform, the hair on Al Gore's cheeks . . . all swept away in the aftershock, seemingly forever.

Now we know better.

Now we know that, even amid our continued mourning for those who died on Sept. 11, we can't stem the most fundamental traits of our natural character, including our rambunctiousness, our love of argument, our impulse to question authority, our inherent pursuit of happiness—traits essential to the traditional functioning of our democratic disorder.

And sure enough, Washington is now behaving much as it did before. . . . (Polman, 2002, p. 4)

When major news stories—such as the attacks on September 11, 2001—occur and continue to be in the public's mind for several days, weeks, months, and, in some cases even years, eventually a variety of types of articles is written. New developments call for second or third or even further perspectives of the story. Anniversaries, recurrences of the dates when these benchmark events of our lives occur, also signal an appropriate time to revisit and attempt to illuminate and further understand. The passage of time has a way of impacting on these events and new stories are often good reads. Feature articles are often the manner in which we write about these special dates and events.

These feature articles have evolved into three basic types of articles that are becoming more important to depth coverage. Those approaches are "aftermath" articles, "follow-up" articles, and "depth series" articles. What are they, exactly?

- Aftermath feature articles are written in the immediate wake of a major news story, typically an unpleasant or tragic event. These stories are assigned and written in the few days after a big story breaks, giving new insights into what happened and the effects of those events.

- Follow-up feature articles are written after a period of time has passed, such as a few months, a year, or even several years. Follow-up stories often offer new information to shed new light on known events or revisit events to reinterpret them. These stories have a more evaluative, analytical, or interpretive purpose through use of experts, witnesses, and others involved in the story in some manner.

- Depth series feature articles are a collection of articles that take a subject into greater depth and scope than a single story could achieve for a publication. In addition to being published in parts, as the nature of a series would require, the depth series is more highly organized and offers a broader perspective through use of human and written sources of information. Depth feature articles in a series incorporate many of the characteristics of aftermath and follow-up stories, of course.

These three types of feature articles, although each a little different from the other, offer explanation and perspective that were not available when the story first developed. The articles use large amounts of description, extensive direct quotation from interviewing, and narration to tell readers more about the events that are the cause for the story to be written. Accidents, fires, bad weather, natural disasters, famine, rioting, war, and other events that cause high levels of human suffering usually demand additional coverage in the form of aftermath, follow-up, or depth series feature articles. On the other hand, positive events or significant changes that bring happiness and joy to a community are also the occasion for aftermath, follow-up, and depth series features.

*Miami Herald* reporters Ina Cordle and Charles Rabin (2002) provided a very human face to the impact of terrorism on the lives of Americans by looking closely at what had happened to flight attendant Hermis Moutardier in the 8 months since she helped stop a man who was attempting to ignite explosives in his shoe on an American Airlines flight from Paris to Miami. The flight attendant, who lived in Miami, was one of the two people who stopped Richard Reid, who sought to blow up the plane in midair. Here's how they approached the story:

Eight months have passed since American Airlines attendant Hermis Moutardier helped subdue a man on a transatlantic holiday flight who allegedly tried to blow up the plane.

She still has panic attacks, yet continues to fly. She avoids the media, though it constantly knocks on her Little Gables door. Once in awhile, her 10-year-old son gives her a pep talk.

Moutardier and fellow stewardess Cristina Jones are largely credited with stopping alleged shoe-bomber Richard Reid from blowing up American Airlines Flight 63 while it flew from Paris to Miami on Dec. 22. Reid, who prosecutors say has links to al Qaeda, was later indicted by a federal grand jury on eight charges, including attempted murder of 197 passengers and crew members. He is scheduled for trial in November.

Jones still has the teeth marks on her left hand where Reid bit her during the struggle. Moutardier's wounds linger inside.

Reached at home Sunday, Moutardier once again politely declined to talk about her experience.

The French citizen, who has made South Florida her home, had just returned from Paris, where she received a medal of honor for her courage.

"The last eight months have been really hard. I'm just getting back my life. I'm just enjoying life because you never know when you are going to lose your life," she said.

Moutardier is one of the 11 individuals featured in *Time* magazine's 9/11 One Year Later edition, which goes on newsstands today.

In the magazine article, Moutardier talks about how the months since the incident have been difficult for her. When the White House invited her and Jones to be the first lady's guests at the State of the Union speech in January, Moutardier considered not going because it meant flying to Washington.

Both women did attend, but Moutardier didn't fly again until July, when she and son Patrice took the same Paris flight on which she had helped restrain Reid for their annual trip to his summer camp in the south of France.

Moutardier was nervous. Patrice tried to reassure his mother.

"Mom, if you saved 200 people, you'll save me," he told her.

The crew welcomed her warmly, and the flight was smooth. But when she finally arrived at the apartment she and her husband keep outside Paris, Moutardier broke down in tears.

Her family has also suffered. Moutardier's 27-year-old elder son Oscar cried when he heard about the incident, but Patrice tried to act as if nothing had happened. Then his grades plunged from A-plus to F. "Finally, he told me he didn't want to show emotion because he was afraid it wouldn't help me to recover," Moutardier said. "I told him, 'Patrice, it's OK. Mommy cried. You can cry, too.' "

Since the shoe-bomber flight in December, American Airlines has offered a self-defense course; neither Jones nor Moutardier has attended the training. Jones returned to work in March; Moutardier has been on medical leave for injuries to her shoulder suffered in her scuffle with Reid. But she hopes to return to work in October.

The *Time* article chronicles what took place aboard the flight, scheduled for the Saturday before Christmas. Like many holiday flights, Flight 63 was delayed an hour due to luggage problems. But the plane took off and all seemed fine, until a few hours later when passengers reported smelling smoke. Moutardier found Reid trying to light a match.

She thought he was smoking and told him to put it out.

He refused. She looked over and discovered the man was trying to set his shoes on fire—shoes that had wiring sticking out of them.

"He's got the shoe off, between his legs. All I see is the wiring and the match. The match was lit," Moutardier said.

Twice she grabbed him; twice he pushed her away, the second time so hard she fell against an armrest across the aisle. I'm going to die, she thought.

Fearing the match would ignite, Moutardier rushed back and got passengers to pass along and pour bottles of water over Reid.

By then Jones was involved. But in the struggle, Reid had managed to bite Jones' hand and keep it in his mouth as she tried to pull away.

By then other passengers were helping. A doctor force-fed Reid Valium, and passengers tied him up so tightly the FBI had to cut the cords, belts and shoe laces from his body to free him after the plane landed in Boston.

Reid continued to taunt the crew even after he was sedated. Moutardier said whenever he would hear the voice of a crew member, Reid would open his eyes and glare. When a flight attendant offered him water, he bared his teeth.

"At one point, he wanted to get loose; he was rocking and praying. I got real scared," said Moutardier. No one knew if Reid had accomplices on board.

Flight 63 landed in Boston several hours later. It would not make it to Miami until the next day.

Both flight attendants may testify at Reid's trial, which is set to begin in Boston on Nov. 4, but Moutardier says she is determined to leave the incident behind her.

"I'm putting a lot of positive thoughts in my head. I cannot live in fear. I'm stronger. We're all stronger," she said in the *Time* interview.

"I know I was there that day, on that flight, for a reason. Now I need to get back to work because I'm doing what I love." (Cordle & Rabin, 2002, p. 3B)

(Reprinted with permission of *The Miami Herald*.)

By showing the human angle, the story becomes less facts and figures and more "people-ized." It should also have a local perspective. Typically, aftermath articles appear on the 2nd, 3rd, or 4th days after an event. Follow-up features begin to be written in the weeks, months, or annual anniversaries after the event. It is also not unusual to use such follow-up stories years afterward. Some editors use these articles 1 year, 2 years, or more after an event as anniversary features.

These articles are commonly found in daily newspapers and sometimes used in weekly newspapers, but they also appear in magazines. Newsmagazines, for example, use aftermath and follow-up articles often as a device to deal with their once-a-week publishing schedules, especially on an anniversary of an event, and also as an approach to coverage of a major event in the first issue to appear after the event. Although this happens each week, you might recall such recurring coverage in news magazines for recent events such as the terrorists' bombing of the federal building in Oklahoma City or the unexpected death of Princess Diana following a traffic accident in Paris.

When something good happens to a community, such as a national sports championship or a major economic development like the decision to build a new automobile assembly plant nearby, these stories also become highly read items. Although readers are naturally curious about disasters and other public traumas such as the Oklahoma City federal building bombing and the deaths of 168 people, people truly savor the more positive success stories from our communities. Major successes also command thorough coverage, and part of this includes aftermath, follow-up, and series articles.

*Time* magazine devoted most of a special double issue to the 1-year anniversary of the terrorist attacks in 2002. The issue devoted attention to a small group of individuals whose lives changed and continued to change because of the events of that day. Managing Editor Jim Kelly (2002) wrote that it was necessary: "We take the measure of 11 people whose lives continue to be shaped by that day. One is George W. Bush, one is the last person rescued alive from the towers, and one is the daughter of a victim; the rest are people who only after 9/11 found themselves swept up by events." A total of 50 writers and editors around the world worked on the project. *Time* staff writer Nancy Gibbs (2002) wrote an overview story positioned at the beginning of the series of articles that began with the premise that a lot can change in 1 year:

> An anniversary can be sweet or solemn, but either way, it is only the echo, not the cry. From this distance, we can hear whatever we are listening for. We can argue that Sept. 11 changed everything—or nothing.
>
> The country is more united, and less; more fearful and more secure, more serious and more devoted to American Idol. It is like looking at your child's baby pictures. You know exactly who it is: every feature is both different and the same, despite new expressions, and furrows and knowledge.
>
> Holding two contradictory ideas in your head was supposed to be a sign of first-rate intelligence. Now it just feels like a vital sign. To say we have changed feels like rewarding the enemy, but to deny it risks losing the knowledge for which we paid a terrible price—knowledge about who we become under pressure, in public and private. People talked about living on a higher plane, with an intensity of fear and faith and gratitude, when it was easy to salute and hard to sleep and nothing was bland or phony or cheap. But we could not live there forever; it was like the day you graduate from high school or your first child is born or your father dies—days of power and insight that grab you for a moment and, when they let you go, leave marks on your skin.
>
> What marks can we see now? President Bush says great good may come from the evil that struck, but you need a long lens to bring that hope into focus. We resist the idea that we have changed because so much of the change of the past year feels like damage. Lives have been lost or broken. . . . (Gibbs, 2002, p. 20)

Often an event is big enough that it cannot be handled as a single event or single story. Rather it becomes a series of events and dozens or even hundreds of stories over several weeks, months, or even a year. Recent local events of national and international interest in that American Airlines jet over the Atlantic Ocean, in New York City, Washington, DC, rural Pennsylvania, and in Oklahoma City illustrate this. The events surrounding the tragedies of the terrorists' actions called for extensive packages of aftermath features, as well as a lengthy series of follow-up stories in dozens of newspapers in the regions affected by these events. A closer look at the types of stories helps further define and explain the roles of aftermath and follow-up feature articles.

## WRITING AFTERMATH AND FOLLOW-UP FEATURES

*Aftermath* and *follow-up* are terms that are often used interchangeably. However, there is a difference that you may have noticed from the discussion and examples so far. Aftermath articles occur most often in the days immediately after a major event or series of events take place. Follow-up articles return to significant events in a community's life also, but more time has passed and new information comes to the story through that passage of time. These revisit the major stories from time to time and, as a result, are a form of aftermath articles. The follow-up article is written with a stronger news approach and is often based on new or updated information, the facts and additional details that were not available in earlier coverage of the story by a newspaper, magazine, newsletter, or online publication. Many publications still try to "featurize" such reporting when it is published. New developments in a story often lead to these articles in newspapers, magazines, newsletters, and online publications.

There were dozens of aftermath and follow-up articles in the wake of the unexpected deaths of *George* magazine editor John F. Kennedy, Jr., and Great Britain's Princess Diana. News and feature stories focused on their accidents—one by air and one by automobile—and their possible causes, their professional and public lives, their public service and other contributions to various social causes, their relationships with other celebrities, coverage of celebrities by the paparazzi, world reaction to the deaths, and countless other aspects. Each follow-up story shed, in some way, new light into the workings and effects of these tragedies that caught the world's attention. How did these stories do that? They relied on investigations, interviews with relatives or the few survivors, release of information collected by government agencies involved in the cases, and other similar reporting. Slowly, readers learned more about how the accidents occurred.

Newspaper reporter Margarita Martin–Hidalgo (2002) covers the police beat for the daily *Lakeland Ledger* in Central Florida. On a recent assignment, she reported about the tragic murder of a man who operated a convenience store. He was shot and killed early one summer morning by an armed robber. Following up her story about the incident, she attended a memorial service for the man 3 days after the shooting. She tried to capture the mood and sentiment in the highly emotional Hindu funeral service. Here's her complete story:

> LAKELAND—In a solemn, and at times highly emotional, Hindu funeral service, family members and friends paid their last respects to slain convenience store owner Maheshkumar Patel on Thursday afternoon.
>
> Following Hindu custom, Patel was cremated shortly after the ceremony.
>
> Patel, 37, died on Monday after an armed robber shot him as he tried to lock the door to his family-owned convenience store, Del's Go Shop, at 14 Coleman Road. The store owner had run to the entrance to lock the door when he saw the man coming, police said.
>
> Nearly 200 family members, friends, customers and former employees packed the Heath Funeral Chapel at the midday service, which lasted about two hours. Several of Patel's family members came from West Palm Beach and Chicago. Some took time off work to attend the service.
>
> Mourners quietly wept as Patel's cousins, sister-in-law, uncle and other relatives gathered around Patel's casket and prayed.

His widow, Darshna, sat in a daze throughout most of the service and could barely stand on her own. She burst out sobbing several times, leaning into the casket to embrace her dead husband as relatives consoled her.

Many of the women around her also broke down into tears. The couple's two boys, Kunjan, 10, and Jay, who is about 1 1/2, sat nearby.

Dressed in a black suit, Patel, who was known to many as "Mike," lay in a lavender-colored casket with his arms gently laid near his thighs. A necklace-like arrangement of roses and leaves was arranged on his chest.

Dozens of chrysanthemums, carnations, roses and other floral arrangements were placed on the podium behind the casket. Some had cards inserted into them.

The Hindu symbol "om" hung in the back. The om, explained a family friend, has several spiritual meanings, including peace. It is often used in prayer.

Small pots with flowers surrounded the base of the wooden box.

A Hindu priest from the Om Hindu Temple from the Orlando suburb of Casselberry presided at the ceremony.

Following Hindu custom, men and women offered their blessings separately. Most of the men were dressed in white shirts and dark slacks. Most women wore delicate white saris.

Family members, including children, fed Patel small amounts of yogurt and butter as the priest recited several prayers. They sprinkled a powdered mixture of tumeric and sandalwood on his forehead, said a family friend. The priest gently rubbed Patel's lips with holy water.

Relatives placed flowers, mostly chrysanthemums, along his torso. The priest and Patel's eldest son, Kunjan, nestled several corn flour dumplings underneath Patel's hands.

The dead are fed and dressed well out of respect, explained Girish Trivedi, a family friend. Hindus believe the soul should be fully satisfied when it leaves the body, said Trivedi, who owns a convenience store in Lakeland.

Rose petals and sandalwood twigs were strewn on Patel's body and the priest placed coconuts in the four corners of the casket. Sandalwood is considered holy wood and is favored because of its pleasant aroma, Trivedi, 65, said.

Patel later was covered with a white sheet.

Family members and friends addressed the mourners, in English and Gujarati, shortly before Patel was cremated. Maheshkumar Patel was from the Indian state of Gujarat.

Patel, they said, was a gentle, good-natured man who would be sorely missed. Indian community groups sent in written condolences.

"Mike is no longer with us . . . but his spirit" will guide us to peace, said Dr. Jitu Metha, a Lakeland-based psychiatrist.

"Maheshkumar was very kind to everybody . . . he was always there for us," said Jatin Patel, who is married to a sister of Darshna Patel's. Jatin Patel thanked those in attendance for their support.

Afterward, a procession of friends and family followed the casket to the crematory. As called for in Hindu tradition, Maheshkumar Patel's eldest son, 10-year-old Kunjan, turned on the button to initiate the cremation process.

Maheshkumar Patel's funeral was held a day after police charged 22-year-old Harold Blake with killing Patel.

Blake, whose last listed address is in Lakeland, surrendered to police Wednesday afternoon after a two-hour standoff with county deputies and Winter Haven police officers.

Friends and customers have said they are outraged and saddened and hope Blake is punished soon.

"(Patel) didn't deserve it," said former employee Debbie Albritton, 32, who worked for Patel on and off for about three years. "He would have given anybody anything."

"He had this glow about him . . . he was a wonderful man," said Ted Evans, 42, a Polk County volunteer firefighter. Evans is stationed at Jan Phyl firehouse a few blocks away from Maheshkumar Patel's convenience store.

"I feel, personally, (Blake) should be punished in a way so that he does not repeat it, that cruel thing," said Trivedi.

And he should be punished soon, Trivedi said, before people forget what he did. (Martin–Hidalgo, 2002, p. B1)

(Reprinted with permission of *The Lakeland Ledger*.)

## PURPOSE OF AFTERMATH ARTICLES

The aftermath is the result of an event, often an unpleasant result, in fact. Newspapers, magazines, and newsletters continue to tell their readers about a major event in the first days immediately afterward by assigning writers to write aftermath articles. These magnify the focus on a story and remind readers of the importance of the story. Williamson (1975) said aftermath articles are features that give new perspective "to a disaster, tragedy or profound news event that captures the impact and dimensions of the event by humanizing its effect" (p. 179).

Aftermath articles tend to contain more of a people approach than the traditional news follow-up. And although these articles often focus on disasters and tragedies, they also focus on other actions, decisions, and developments in the community. When a river overflows in an unusual spring flood, how does it affect those involved? Readers want to know the basic facts, such as deaths, injuries, daring rescues, and damage amounts, but they also want to know the human element—the reaction to all this. How do people endure? What are their feelings and thoughts? Emotions manifest themselves in many ways. An effective writer tries to capture those displays of emotion to truly tell the story in the article. This is what happened when a severe flood tore through Fort Wayne, IN. The description in writer Dan Luzadder's (1982) column, written on daily deadline for the *Fort Wayne News–Sentinel,* gave his personal reaction to the disaster. He told readers in a compelling way how this event changed the lives of residents of his community on that day and, probably, forever. Because it was a column, it had many personal observations and feelings of the writer instead of the usual variety of nonpersonal sources. Luzadder went to the neighborhoods where the flood hit hardest and talked to many Fort Wayne victims. Still, his generalizations about the community's reactions capture the mood and portray the plight of the victims. There is no one named, no heroes—except the community itself—and no one directly quoted. Although it is a highly personal approach, it still achieves what an aftermath story seeks to do—and Luzadder's column earned him the Pulitzer Prize a year later for local general spot news reporting.

Williamson (1975) said the aftermath articles about such events as floods and building collapses use one or more of four different approaches:

1. The epitome of the victim or the victims—This strategy focuses on the one person or group of people who have endured the disaster such as a plane crash or a hotel fire. There may be only one real victim for the focus of the article, such as a child who becomes trapped in a well and must be rescued before the child dies. You try to focus on these individuals by finding the survivors, who become your key sources. If none is accessible, then friends or relatives may assist in telling the story to readers.

2. The mood piece—These articles employ many of the techniques of color articles and are dependent on description by those on the scene. These articles are often rich in detail and help those who were not present to gain insight into the atmosphere of the site, using witnesses, survivors, photographs, and other means of recreating what happened. Dan Luzadder's (1982) award-winning column described earlier is an example of a mood approach.

3. The hero—In some assignments of this type, the best way to tell the story is to focus on the individual who saved the day. There will be times when this person is accessible and quotable. It creates a much-desired angle for the article because most people love to read about a hero and this form of the great American success story. Numerous hero stories were written in the aftermath of the Oklahoma City bombing and the dangerous floods in North Dakota.

4. The goat—Occasionally, someone, or some organization, unfortunately causes a tragedy such as the driver of the Mercedes who may have caused the accident that killed Princess Diana. Investigations into the cause of her untimely death focused on the driver and whether he was under the influence or drugs or alcohol. Furthermore, there was significant interest in a group of press photographers, the paparazzi, that was following the Mercedes carrying the princess and whether the "chase" nature of the situation contributed to the accident. The story becomes a strong angle if you can tell the story from that person or institution's point of view. Because most people or organizations are understandably reluctant to talk to a reporter if they have caused a death or large amounts of property loss, this is a difficult angle to pursue. Regardless, if it can be told this way, it is a compelling story since it is a human story, one of accidental or intentional human error.

You might not have a choice about which angle to choose in handling your assignment. Much of the time, the course of events determines how you handle the story. But on some stories, you may have the choice of one or two or three approaches.

## WRITING AFTERMATH ARTICLES

You have a number of writing decisions to make when you are working on an aftermath article. You must develop your lead, decide the article's structure, locate sources, select a writing style, and decide the article's mood. Let's look at these in a bit more depth:

1. Aftermath lead—The lead of the article is most important. You set the stage for the entire piece, and your decisions about how you plan to tell the story to readers are revealed. Aftermath leads can be anecdotal, focusing on an individual or an example of the major point of the article. This approach makes specific points to illustrate the larger problem—the suffering of one victim can show what an entire group of survivors has experienced and how they feel.

2. Structural plan—Think through what you are trying to achieve with the aftermath article before you begin to write. How will you organize it? What are the major sections? What are the major points and in what order?

3. Sources—At the same time you think through the organizational plan, consider what sources are necessary for information to make your major points. Will it be victims, their families, official sources such as police and firefighters, other people, reports, or observations?

4. Writing style and mood—Your chosen style and mood for the particular article should reflect the type of event you are covering. In other words, for an article that describes the joy of a small town several days after it has won a state high school basketball championship, an informal, casual and upbeat style might be appropriate. But for a natural disaster, such as a tornado striking that same small town, the style should be more serious and respectful.

It is important in writing aftermath stories to bring in the local angle as much as possible. This is easy enough for local events. It might not be so obvious for events that occur hundreds or thousands of miles away. Williamson (1975) offered four more considerations for writing aftermath articles. Your approach, he said, should stir the imagination of readers by going beyond the basic facts of the event that are found elsewhere, such as other articles in the same issue or earlier issues. Here's what he suggested to strengthen your writing:

1. Play heavily on human emotion—Use descriptions of sorrow, fear, happiness, and other emotions to enhance your article. This comes through di-

rect quotations and observation of what happened and its effects on people and places. Can you accurately convey what people experienced? Exercise your vocabulary for this—accurate word choice makes all the difference.

2. Try to help the reader identify with the victims—Will readers think that it might have happened to them? If so, you have probably succeeded in helping them identify with the victims. Writing with detail permits this to happen in most articles. Be alert, and observe to recapture the situation.

3. Write tersely and briefly—A tightly written article will still get to the point and permits more perspective to get to the reader in the same amount of space your editor has assigned to the article.

4. Concentrate on a fast-moving, strong lead—Good leads set the tone for the article. For aftermath articles, you must write a lead that gets the reader involved and still explains the purpose of the article.

*The Chronicle of Higher Education,* a trade publication serving readers who work at colleges and universities, recently told the story of a college professor who died after long service to his campus. Writer Scott Heller (2000) described the aftermath of his death and the lessons of his lost career. Heller told readers the story of this unheralded history professor and how he played by the rules with little rewards. Heller said the professor worked hard without recognition at the same university for 27 years, but died still worrying that he did not have enough money to make his mortgage payments or pay his other bills. It is a compelling story of what happened once one of his friends and colleagues spoke out about the situation on the South Carolina college campus:

> To honor its dead, Charleston Southern University puts together a slide show. But the colleagues and friends who gathered in Lightsey Chapel last October to remember Harold J. Overton, a linguist who died suddenly of cancer after teaching there for 27 years, had to squint to see the handful of images thrown up on a screen in a corner of the stage. There weren't enough photos in the university's P.R. files to fill the time, so they ran in a repeating loop.
>
> Somehow this was appropriate, for even after so many years, Mr. Overton remained a blurry presence on this Baptist campus. Shy, courtly, and eager to please, he was appreciated for his steady loyalty. Many in the audience didn't know that he was an ordained minister and a one-time missionary, that he was an antiques dealer and had a passion for Norse sagas.
>
> The various speakers praised Mr. Overton for his courtesy and kindness, the endearing way he would make a friend's excitements into his own. "Each time during the years when the university was able to provide an increase in salary," said President Jairy C. Hunter Jr., "Harold would always send me a little note expressing thanks."
>
> And who else, asked Lisette Luton, an assistant professor of French, could—or would—speak so passionately about obscure distinctions in Old French? Only Harold, who wryly described himself as the "tall, skinny, bald guy" when arranging their first meeting at the Charleston airport.

Then, as the event wound down, Robert Rhodes Crout, an associate professor of history, strode to the podium. A fellow Southerner, he had been Mr. Overton's closest friend on campus. If the assembled expected another run-of-the-mill tribute, they were to be sorely disappointed. "Harold Overton was a shy and private man who lived a shy and private life, and wanted his dying days to have that same quiet and private dignity," Mr. Crout began. "I honored that wish." (Heller, 2000)

## BEST SOURCES FOR AFTERMATH AND FOLLOW-UP ARTICLES

Participants, victims.

Friends and relatives of participants, victims.

Neighbors.

Witnesses.

First persons to arrive on the scene afterward.

Spokespersons from investigating federal, state, and local agencies.

Public records and reports as they become available.

Private sources of information released to the public.

World Wide Web sites devoted to the event or emergency and related subjects.

## WRITING FOLLOW-UP FEATURE ARTICLES

The follow-up feature approach is often an appropriate alternative for stories of this type because after a time, readers need background information as well as the new information to remind them of events surrounding the original story. Although traditional in newspapers and the wire services, the 2nd day, or follow-up, approach is also used by some magazines and other specialized publications to cover a major story. Using the follow-up approach is routine for news magazines such as *Newsweek, Time,* and *U.S. News & World Report.* With their one-time-a-week publication schedule, editors and writers at the major news magazines are forced to find new angles in writing featurized follow-up articles that also serve as roundups on the event.

Most newspapers believe in the importance of follow-up stories, especially as new information becomes available on a breaking story. Follow-up articles have wide application in all types of publications. In addition to news coverage, follow-up articles are often used in sports coverage as 2nd- or 3rd-day stories, meaning they give new information such as players', coaches', or fans' reaction to the conclusion of a major sports event. They are common in entertainment sections after events such as the Academy Awards, a major concert or special performance, or other similar events of note and give readers the inside story about an entertainer's reactions, emotions, and explanations for why he or she did or did not succeed.

These types of feature stories, with their new information combined with the already-known information, help readers. Earl Maucker, editor and vice president of the Fort Lauderdale-based South Florida *Sun–Sentinel* (1993), said that his newspaper's research shows that readers want relevance and ability to understand the events of the day from their newspaper's follow-up on major stories. "They want to understand their world," he said. "They want follow-ups on stories. They want those follow-ups to be balanced and fair, to list information, to explain and describe trends, to provide analysis, and to show them, not tell them." Follow-up feature stories, if they are written well, can help readers to understand why something has occurred and to share the reactions other people have to the event. They are, as Maucker explained, essential supplements to coverage of events by newspapers, magazines, newsletters, and online publications.

## THE VALUE OF AFTERMATH AND FOLLOW-UP FEATURES

Mike Foley, journalism professor at the University of Florida and former vice president and executive editor of the *St. Petersburg Times,* believes in the value of aftermath and follow-up features. Foley (personal communication, October 10, 2002) offered this advice:

> The feature story after the big disaster, the crucial vote, the key game or that triple-axe murder is not only real journalism, but it's your time to shine. You'll have the time, space and, probably, a lot of freedom to decide how best to handle the story.
>
> How often do you get an opportunity like that in this business?
>
> But it's also a challenge. Your usual excuses—or, rather, reasons—for a less-than-stirring account won't work. The deadline is farther off than a few hours or minutes. You can talk to more people. You can get the details. You will be able to sort out the confusion. Then, you can sit down and—can you believe it?—write. So, you've got challenge, you've got opportunity. Can the possibility of massive, career-ending failure be far behind? Of course not. So, before you blow it, you might consider a few suggestions:
>
> *Relax.* Take a few deep breaths, a blank piece of paper, a pen or pencil, and figure out what you need to do. This preparation should include reading stuff already written on the topic, and planning other research, including public records, historical documents, books and outside experts. (You'll find later that background information is almost as important as the new reporting you'll do.)
>
> *Talk to your editor.* He or she has either assigned this story, or, at least, has permitted you to pursue it. Only an expert (or a fool) would work on a story without talking it over first with the boss. This also will allow you to find out how much

time and space you'll have. You also should, at this point and throughout the gathering and writing stages, think of other material that will enhance the story—photos, maps, charts, illustrations. Your editor will thank you for any suggestions. Editors like to look good, too.

*Think about what you want to do.* Sound redundant? Maybe it is. But many writers, especially young and beginning ones, forget to set goals. They're after a 'story,' without thinking about what the story might be. Sure, the story will change many times as you gather information. But it helps to start with some idea of where you could be going.

*Don't forget the little things.* The follow stories are the detail stories. What's the dog's name? What did the family eat for dinner? What was the dead guy wearing?

*Conduct a sensual survey.* What music was playing? What scent was in the air? What was everyone drinking? Was it hot? You get the picture. Really, this way you really get the picture.

*Feel it.* Attention, all you aloof, neutral observers: It's time to get real. If you want to write a good story (even gather enough material to fashion a good story), you have to let loose, be a human. Don't take sides or get involved, but use your own emotions to try better to understand what the human in your story might have felt.

*Tell me a story.* Sure it's journalism, but let's not forget what a 'story' is. It's a narrative, with a beginning, middle, and end. Reread your research, study your notes, shut your notebook (and maybe your eyes for a minute) and tell me a story. Step back and tell it whole.

If you have done your job, I'll even read your story, maybe all the way to the end. And that's my ultimate compliment.

## WRITING DEPTH SERIES FEATURES

There are times when routine feature coverage, whether it be an aftermath, follow-up, or other type of feature article, just cannot do the job in a single article. Even longer magazine articles might not be adequate for certain subjects. Major topics, such as a presidential election campaign or a public health issue, often demand more than a single article can accomplish. Usually this occurs because of one or more of these characteristics:

1. Magnitude of the issue—An issue often affects many individuals and communities. Public policy issues, such as taxation or care for the elderly, affect many individuals and often demand depth coverage. Coverage telling how many people are impacted must also tell the human side of the story by illustrating it through the eyes of the people involved.

2. Seriousness of the problem—Certain matters are necessary to cover in depth because of the serious nature of the subject. For example, discovery of contamination of a major source of public water requires thorough attention. Aside from the straight news approach, feature approaches examine the per-

sonal effects such a problem brings to a community by looking at individuals and at the group.

3. Immediacy of the event or issue—Because certain subjects are current now, they cannot wait. Public concern about an issue, such as the potential risks of AIDS or the potential dangers of nuclear power, requires attention in such a fashion that articles serve the community's thirst for information right away. Fear of the unknown often creates problems that compound existing troubles, so educational-instructional articles are a public service. These articles illustrate the situation by humanizing the problem so readers can identify with the subject at their own level. Answering questions such as "How does this affect me?" makes a depth series successful.

4. Broad scope of the story—A depth feature series usually evolves when a subject is broad in scope, encompassing a number of subtopics that must be covered in adequate depth to make sense to readers. Often, a trend is significant enough to justify thorough analysis and illustration through a series of features. The effects of the growth of Vietnamese and other Southeast Asian refugee communities on the West Coast over the past decade, for example, have been covered by a depth feature approach by various publications.

Some inexperienced writers feel writing short articles is easier than writing long ones. Actually, it becomes easier to handle longer material because you have more opportunity to use the information you have collected. It is also easier because of the additional dimension of organization that serialization permits (Rivers, 1992).

The feature series should be a highly organized study of a subject that is neatly and cleanly divided into parts of equal significance. The pieces within each series installment need to be linked together with transitions. The pieces of the series should be presented in logical fashion with linkages as well. Series are often accompanied by editor's notes, sidebar boxes, or other short editorial devices to explain to readers what the purpose of the overall series might be, as well as the role of the individual story that they are reading in an issue.

Each part should be written to stand alone. That is, the individual story should be strong enough and self-explanatory enough to be useful to readers who did not see earlier, or will not see later, parts. The series approach is common in newspapers, magazines, and newsletters, but perhaps it is more frequent in daily or biweekly newspapers and weekly or biweekly newsletters because their publication frequency is conducive to publishing pieces over a short period of time. However, magazines also run depth feature series when a subject justifies the treatment over several issues in succession.

Thomas French (1998), a staff feature writer for the *St. Petersburg Times,* wrote a highly compassionate look at the deaths of a woman and her two daughters on vacation in Florida. The project was entitled "Angels & Demons." French, a reporter and writer at the newspaper for two decades, specializes in project-length features. He writes in narrative style and offers image-creating details and depth of information that are the results of extensive research and interviewing. He uses a technique often called "immersion reporting" in which he spends lengthy periods of time with sources and records to prepare for the writing and storytelling process. French prepares his lengthy features in serialized form. Several of his recent *St. Petersburg Times* projects have led to popular nonfiction books and he was awarded the Pulitzer Prize for feature writing in 1998 for "Angels & Demons." Here's the introduction to that project:

> In their last hours alive, Jo Rogers and her two daughters took a series of snapshots. One showed Michelle inside the motel room, sunburned and staring into the camera.
>
> But it was the very last photo that would be the most haunting. Shot from the motel balcony, it caught the sunlight fading over Tampa Bay. The three women were about to leave to meet someone who had offered to take them for a boat ride on the bay.
>
> On June 4, 1989, the bodies of Jo, Michelle, and Christe were found floating in Tampa Bay. This is the story of the murders and their aftermath, a story of a handful of people who kept faith amid the unthinkable.
>
> One year had gone by since the murders, and then another, and now the investigators were deep into a third. They were working day and night, working weekends, putting off vacations, losing weight, gaining weight, growing pale and pasty and haggard, waking at 3 a.m. with a jolt and scratching notes on pads beside their beds. Their sergeant did not know if they would ever find the answer. As far as he was concerned, the case was not even in their hands.
>
> Ultimately, he believed, it was up to God whether they made an arrest.
>
> A born-again Christian, the sergeant carried a Bible in his briefcase. He had no doubt that both heaven and hell were real. He saw good and evil not as theoretical or philosophical concepts, but as absolute realities walking upright through the world. He believed in the forces of light and darkness. He believed in demonic possession. He took it as a matter of fact that Satan and his cohorts currently reigned over the Earth.
>
> "I believe there are demons all around us," he would say, "just as I believe there are angels all around us." . . . (French, 1998)

## WRITING A FEATURE SERIES FOR NEWSPAPERS

For projects as extensive as the "Angels & Demons" series by Thomas French (1998), organization is a key. Distinct divisions of the subjects within the overall topic are necessary to determine what goes into what story. A writer or editor planning such a series should outline the project first, then refine each story idea as it develops. There should be minimal overlap of the subjects and there should be an editor's note at the beginning or end of the article to inform readers that the article is part of a series and that other articles have been published and will be published on the topic. Subjects are, of course, varied but must be broad enough to permit subdivision.

Newspapers have used the feature series approach for many years. At times, it is a strategy simply to accommodate long stories when large amounts of space are not possible. At other times, editors use a series to attract readers into the newspaper over a period of time. The topics for a newspaper feature series vary as widely as single features. Recently, for example, the Charleston, SC, *Post and Courier* published a series in its business section that focused on the Year 2000 problem facing computer programmers and users. Instead of using a single staff writer or several staff writers, the newspaper invited local experts to contribute articles about different aspects of the problem, which it called the biggest computer bug in history. The articles were explanatory narratives, giving readers background to understand the issues and to see how the problem may or may not impact on their businesses, their work, and their homes and lifestyles.

On some occasions, the length of a depth feature project for a daily newspaper requires it to be presented in installments. In the series called "Justice for Becky," South Bend, IN, *Tribune* Staff Writer Gina Barton prepared a true crime mystery in 19 parts over the same number of days. The special series told the story of a missing girl and efforts by police to figure out what happened to her. Barton (2002) explained in her introduction to the series:

> "Justice for Becky" is the story of a police detective's struggle to solve the mystery of what happened to a missing 15-year-old Niles girl. As Becky Stowe's friends and family assisted the police in the glare of the media spotlight, they learned hard lessons about growing up, friendship and community.
>
> For 19 consecutive days, *The Tribune* is publishing Becky's story in a serial narrative format. The serial narrative has a long history in newspapers, dating back to the work of Charles Dickens in the 19th century and before. In recent years, the form has experienced a revival, meeting with positive feedback from readers across the United States.
>
> Each day, Becky's story unfolds with suspense and drama. Although it is written in the form of a novel, it is all true. The information contained in these scenes and conversations comes from police reports, court files and the recollections of the people involved.
>
> Each chapter is short enough to be read over a cup of coffee, so that you will have time for it each day. . . .
>
> We are devoting this attention to Becky's story because the media frenzy that enveloped her case as it unfolded didn't tell the whole story. Her case changed the way a community viewed its children. The effects of her life and legacy will linger in Michiana for years to come. (n.p.)

Each part in the *Tribune's* series was given a unique title when it was published. These titles reflect the direction of the installment in the series. They were as follows: a call in the night, a community searches, looking for answers, the love of her life, amateur detective work, a mother's desperation, the truth machine, memories and nightmares, the rumor mill, an unhappy birthday, a break in the case, finding Becky, facing the facts, suspicions confirmed, saying goodbye, no chance to grow up, witness for the prosecution, the verdict, and the epilogue: remembering Becky.

The entire series has been placed on the newspaper's World Wide Web site (http://www.southbendtribune.com/beckyindex.htm). Audience reaction to the package, the newspaper told readers, was intense. More than 6,000 telephone calls to listen to dramatic readings of the installments were logged. Another 100 calls and letters came into the newsroom. The effective storytelling drew interest and readership.

## WRITING A FEATURE SERIES FOR MAGAZINES

It may seem unusual for a magazine to run a series, right? With all the space a magazine can give to a major article, why would it need to serialize? It is more common than you might think. Monthly magazines, especially the specialized ones, occasionally run a feature series of two or three or more parts. Usually, this is done not because of a space crunch, but because an editor wants to develop an ongoing readership habit. This is common for new magazines and for those that have a high proportion of newsstand sales instead of subscription sales.

*Men's Health* magazine recently published a 10-part series about workouts. Each of the installments, published one per month between February and December in 2002, focused on exercise workouts and was called the total-body workbook. Individual installments emphasized the shoulders, the chest and back (two articles), the legs and glutes (two articles), the abs and lower back, the arms (two articles), total-body muscle, and total-body fat loss. Each installment featured step-by-step routines and details and narratives about each specific exercise program and was supplemented with numerous color photographs on a foldout page.

Writer Andrew Essex (2002) prepared a recent multipart diary series for the "Dossier" department of *Details* magazine about becoming a father. In his ongoing journal published by the magazine, he told readers of his emotions and experiences as a father-to-be. In one journal entry, he told of his new worries, changes in concerns about his wife's health, and how his relationship with her grew even closer. In another installment, he discussed about how he became prolife. And in still another entry, he told readers about his experiences in childbirth classes. Throughout the series, he described changes in his and his wife's behaviors and their daily habits brought on by the pregnancy. Although his experiences were not uncommon and known to just about any parent, they were appealing because they were told from the man's point of view and led to an interesting reading experience. And, because the journal entries were published in short monthly installments of less than 1,000 words, the diary entries did not take long to read.

Newspapers also publish serialized or excerpted books on some occasions. This can occur when the author is a staff member of the newspaper. Typically, it occurs when major daily newspapers or larger magazines buy rights to new blockbuster books as publishers prepare to release the book. Book publishers like to serialize parts of books to encourage sales of the entire book. It is a marketing "tease" tool. Some newspaper and magazine editors like to run these advance peeks if they feel excitement about an anticipated book is substantial enough to justify it in terms of enhancing readership of their own publications.

The serial approach is also particularly useful for specialized business and industry periodicals, such as magazines and newsletters that must cover issues of a highly technical nature for readers with specialized knowledge. The approach works well for those magazines and newsletters with sophisticated levels of knowledge, but it also works for new or not widely known subjects of common interest of readers of a specialized publication.

# CHAPTER TWELVE

# Travel Writing

Americans are on the go. They spend a lot of money and time going from place to place. Some of the travel, of course, is for business. However, there is considerable travel devoted to pleasure and other personal reasons, such as vacations and weddings. And Americans spend a lot of money on travel. The figure was reported at $582 billion in 2000. Travel and tourism is also the second-largest employer, accounting for 19 million jobs in the United States (Kearney, 2002; Bouncing back, 2001). And international visitors to the United States spent $106.5 billion in 2000 (Bouncing back, 2001). In some parts of the nation, tourism and travel is at the heart of the local economy. In Hawaii and Florida, for example, global-based travel and tourism are dominant factors in the states' economies. In fact, travel and tourism are either first, second, or third-largest industries in 29 states (Bouncing back, 2001). Even in other areas, such as small towns, tourism may be the big story. In Branson, MO, for example, a community of about 5,000 residents, there are more than 7 million visitors each year (Federal Document Clearing House, 2002).

A large number of people travel substantial distances. There were about 150 million U.S. travelers in 2001 and they are served by 200,000 travel agents. An estimated 40 to 60 million Americans traveled during one or more of major holidays. An estimated 60 million Americans, one in five in other words, traveled during Christmas and New Year's Day (Thrasher, 2001). Personal nonbusiness travel activities are not singularly focused. Americans travel to visit families, go shopping, to visit historical places, attend special events such as festivals, to gamble, to enjoy the great outdoors and national or state parks, to enjoy the beach, and to participate in sports such as skiing and golf.

No wonder travel is big business and involves a lot of people. And no wonder there are many publications devoted exclusively, or in part, to travel. The American public is traveling more than ever before, creating a growing market for travel writing. Books, magazines, newspapers, newsletters, other printed material, and online publications are used for guidance in making travel decisions and for getting the most out of travel budgets. For most writers, travel stories are fun assignments. Perhaps one of the most glamorous feature writing assignments is to write about an exotic, faraway land. People are enriching, not escaping, their lives by travel, according to recent surveys of travelers. And those who travel do so frequently. They are interested in cultural and historical locations and places of natural beauty instead of nightlife, luxury, or shopping. A recent national survey found important factors in planning a vacation or other leisure trip included a location with natural beauty, a place where the traveler has never been, freedom to decide what to do during the trip, and the opportunity to experience local culture and history. Less important factors in travel were recreation such as golf, luxury resort areas, nightlife, and shopping. People who consider themselves seasoned travelers take several trips a year, including trips overseas. The leisure traveler is not a young person and may have more time on his or her hands. Market studies show the average leisure travelers to be individuals in their late 40s, female, and living on a household income of about $46,000 (Clarke, 1993).

Much of the travel writing designed to help both leisure and business travelers make decisions about their trips is done by freelance and part-time writers. Most daily newspapers have at least one staff writer or editor assigned to travel, and many larger dailies have a Sunday section filled with color photographs, stories, and information about interesting places. Even the largest daily newspapers have few—one to three full-time persons—who work exclusively as travel editors and writers. Small dailies usually offer a special page or pages once a week and the person handling travel news and features may divide his or her duties with other features or news duties. Most weekly newspapers devote little or no regular space to travel features unless the publication is in a resort area or has a special tie to the travel industry.

Magazine editors depend on articles with travel-oriented features by either staff or freelance writers. Many national and regional lifestyle consumer magazines offer readers travel stories that appear in every issue or with some other regularity. And, of course, there are numerous travel-oriented periodicals, such as *Conde Nast Traveler, National Geographic, National Geographic Traveler, National Geographic Adventure, Travel/Holiday,* and *Travel & Leisure* on the consumer magazine market, dedicated to a person's urge to wander. State and regional publications, such as *Arizona Highways* and *Texas Highways,* also focus on travel in their respective states and regions with similar content.

Leading national travel magazines such as the American Automobile Association's *Home & Away* (3,311,000) and *Going Places* (2,142,000), *Travel & Leisure* (1,004,000), *National Geographic Traveler* (732,000), and *Conde Nast Traveler* (780,000)—their approximate circulations in 2002—publish issues in a large-page full-color format each month. *Conde Nast Traveler* focuses on worldwide destinations of the "in" traveler, the airlines, the cruise industry, luggage, rentals, restaurants, and tips from experienced travelers and travel industry professionals. These magazines generally have five or six main feature articles, including the cover article. There are also regular monthly departments, such as those devoted to letters from readers, food, shopping, personal care, wine, the world weather outlook, books, business travel concerns, upcoming current events in major cities around the world, new travel products, and opinion articles such as columns and editorials. Naturally, this list is just a sprinkling of the possibilities for major travel publications on which to focus. Travel publications make heavy use of color photographs, maps, and other graphics to help readers understand the subjects about which they are reading.

There are also growing magazine and newsletter markets for travel-related manuscripts in industry and trade travel-oriented publications. These include periodicals of travel agents; hotels; convention and tourism organizations; convention planning organizations; tour operators; bus companies; attraction operators; rail lines, cruise lines, and airlines; recreational vehicle businesses; and similar travel-related markets. These publications are geared to individuals who work for businesses associated with the travel industry. Examples of these publications include California's *RV Business,* published for the recreational vehicle (RV) industry, and New York's *Destinations,* published for charter motorcoach tour planners and operators.

Online travel information has also grown in large amounts in the past several years. This has led to demand for new and updated travel features by both freelancers and staff writers. Much of the growth has taken place on the World Wide Web. Not only are there destination sites hosted by travel-based businesses (e.g., hotels, resorts, airlines, rental car companies, and restaurants), chambers of commerce, attractions, and other organizations and commercial enterprises, but there are also travel reference materials, maps, listings, and other information provided by online travel publications. Some traditional print publications produce online Web sites to meet the interests of travelers in their region. For example, the *Knoxville News–Sentinel* in Tennessee provides a free Web site (http://www.gosmokies.com) for information about the busiest national park in America, the Great Smoky Mountains National Park, which is located near Knoxville.

These days, consumers turn to the news media for help in making travel planning decisions. A major purchase, such as a vacation package, requires the traveler to gain the expertise to make the proper decisions. Airline deregulation has made a quagmire of airline routes, service, and ticket prices. Ground travel is no different. Unpredictable weather and often wildly fluctuating gasoline prices constantly affect automobile travelers, for example. Thus, a good travel feature can make a difference as readers turn to their favorite newspapers, magazines, newsletters, or online publications for assistance. Travel writing, then, can include an element of consumer reporting. One distinction, journalism professor and former *Miami Herald* travel editor Alan Prince (personal communication, October 20, 2002) recently noted, is that you must be honest with readers:

> The reader who is stimulated by a travel writer's destination piece doesn't return home with a computer or a television set. Instead, he or she's got an airline ticket stub, photographs, and souvenirs, and, most of all, memories. That's not a lot considering today's cost of travel. The reader should understand that he is paying

money for an experience, not for an appliance. Henry David Thoreau wrote, "It is not worthwhile to go around the world to count the cats in Zanzibar." Both the travel writer and the traveler must understand that.

For some 5,000 years of recorded history, the only way humankind could travel faster than on a horse was to fall out of a tree. And most people stayed close to home. Today, people travel to distant areas in a matter of a few hours—and that means the travel writer faces a credibility standard. The thousands who have visited a place before the travel writer gets there set the standard. The travel writer must realize that in his or her mass audience there are many readers who know more about the place than the travel writer can learn in a brief visit. There's no way the writer can pull the wool over these readers' eyes. He can't fake it and keep his credibility. It's that simple. The other share of your audience—those who haven't been there—might someday go. And if they find the destination to be quite different from what the travel writer has pictured, they will never again believe—or will always be skeptical of—anything that travel writer ever writes.

It's a matter of trust.

Travel writers, especially those who are on newspaper staffs, don't have the luxury of spending weeks in a destination. Two to 4 days are more likely, and that's hardly enough time to get to know the place—especially when you're supposed to be an expert when you leave.

There's no question in my mind that the most important element in competent travel writing is "knowing the place" before you get there. You can accomplish this by reading anything and everything you can get your hands on. A reporter doesn't begin an interview with a celebrity by asking how the celebrity spells his or her name. The reporter already knows that and, one hopes, a lot more about the celebrity. The same principle applies to doing a destination piece. Otherwise, the destination piece is going to be awfully "thin," and that just isn't good travel writing.

Even the short-distance or regional traveler needs information to best use his or her time and resources. Travel writing serves this purpose when done well. Business travelers need guidance on all aspects of their travel (including airlines; ground transportation; hotels, motels, and inns; restaurants; and entertainment), and an entire industry catering to business travelers has evolved in this century. Included in that movement is a subdivision of the travel publication industry that produces magazines and newsletters aimed at veteran travelers.

Simply writing about your recent vacation will not get the job done. Most travel-oriented publications provide a standard fare of information for the traveler, or the person thinking of traveling, or the person simply daydreaming about traveling some day. "Travel writing is an overcrowded field and much of it is poorly written," said Southern California-based freelance travel writer Kit Snedaker (personal communication, April 17–18, 1993 & January 23, 1998). Snedaker writes for *The Robb Report* and for *Westways,* Southern California AAA's magazine. She is a member of the Society of American Travel Writers and believes good travel writing means hard work: It is no vacation.

## THE LEADING TRAVEL PUBLICATIONS

The *Dallas Morning News,* the *Orange County Register,* the *New Orleans Times–Pic-ayune,* and the Arlington Heights, IL, *Daily Herald* were honored for best news-paper travel sections of 2001 and 2002 in the 18th annual Society of American Travel Writers (http://www.satw.org/) Foundation Lowell Thomas Travel Journalism Competition.

The newspaper sections were honored for their current information, origi-nal columns each week, feature packages, travel consumer news, local travel news, for their tips that travelers use to keep informed and alert on the road, and for tips about day trips.

*National Geographic Adventure* was named the best travel magazine and *Yan-kee* won honors for best travel coverage in nontravel magazines. The most out-standing Internet publication or Web site was *National Geographic Traveler On-line* (Abbott, 2002).

---

Too many travelers believe they are travel writers after managing a post card and the rest are in it for the free trips. They write payback stuff. But the best make stories out of it. The biggest fault is what I call the "Summer Vacation" story. "We climbed on board and then we went to—and then—and then—" It's a diary and about as interesting as watching a fly climb up the draperies.

Readers of the travel pages, as well as readers of the business pages of con-temporary publications, are generally erudite. These persons are those in the higher income brackets with the money and time to spend going places. Thus, many of them are likely to be well traveled and informed readers of your sto-ries. And, as some travel editors will tell you, the writing must simultaneously serve two distinct audiences: people who have not been to the place you write about and people who have already been there.

Christopher Baker (1989), an award-winning full-time travel writer and pho-tographer who specializes in adventure travel articles, has published work in most of the nation's major travel magazines. He described what makes a travel manuscript a winner:

> A successful travel article does more than conjure up unforgettable images and lead readers by the hand. It entertains, provides reliable and useful information, and tells the truth. But if you fail to place your reader vicariously on that moun-taintop or on that beach you've described, you will not sell your article in this highly competitive market. (p. 22)

How can you succeed? What do you write about? You write about places to visit. You tell readers about historical places, annual festivals, national parks, cities, resorts, and inns. You tell them about places to stay, restaurants with views, and the easiest and cheapest ways to get there. You convey the richness, the color, the excitement, the fun, the moods, and the atmosphere. You give important information such as admission prices and times for an attraction. But you also relate personal experiences, such as the best place to park in a busy neighborhood—New Orleans' French Quarter or Boston's North End, for example—to make your story complete.

Thus you find the unusual, the unique, the odd, and the entertaining. Writing Professor Shirley Biagi (1981) said, "Visiting Waikiki may have been fascinating for you, but asking a travel editor to buy 6,000 words about 'gorgeous white sand beaches' is an insult. The successful travel writer chooses the offbeat, photographs the unusual, visits the out-of-the-way" (p. 24). Baker (1989) said the unusual is essential, but writers must also "breathe *possibility* into your readers' own travel plans—and make your destinations come alive" (p. 22).

Colorado's Curtis Casewit (1988), author of 12 books on travel, recreation, and photography, believes travel writing requires enthusiasm to succeed. He is right: This is something you have to want to do to do it well. Some people travel because they must; others do it because they love it. "You cannot enjoy being on the road without a genuine enthusiasm. For some of us, travel is almost a physical necessity. It springs from a chronic curiosity and desire to uproot ourselves," Casewit said (p. 6). He also observed that the most successful travel writers have finely developed skills and traits involving observation, accuracy, humor, flexibility, patience, curiosity, and ability to overcome adversity.

Have you ever taken a major trip? Have you ever gone that one step further by writing about it? What would you tell your friends about the trip? This can be the foundation of a good feature. Travel writing requires good reporting because it is much more than going from point A to point B by jet. Most successful writers are experts, too, and know the details of a successful journey from planning to budgeting to itineraries and more.

You need to consider what works for those already in the business. Start out by reading the weekend travel section or page of your local newspaper; also study it. What kinds of stories and photographs are published? Where do they come from? Does the section contain more than basic "destination pieces?" If so, what else? In the stories, what sources do the writers use? What is the writing style? Is it narrative or first person? What supplementary material comes with the stories, photographs, or locator maps?

Whom do you contact and with whom do you work: travel editors, of course. The individuals who review your work have various responsibilities and titles. Most are called travel editors, but some are features editors or Sunday editors at daily newspapers. At many magazines, they are called travel department or features editors, depending on the level of specialization of the publication. These are highly educated, well-traveled individuals. They are also experienced journalists who have earned the coveted position they hold. And they often really love their work.

## CONTEMPORARY TRAVEL WRITING ISSUES

Travel and recreation have emerged in recent years to become major subjects for coverage by magazines and newspapers. Sections and departments have enlarged beyond simple articles on destinations. There are numerous issues facing travel writers and editors in this decade, not the least being ethics and objectivity. Often there are ethical issues related to travel feature writing to be debated.

### Ethics Involving Subsidized and Sponsored Travel

The primary travel writing ethics issue relates to what is called *subsidized* or *sponsored* travel. This means finding sources other than the newspaper or writer to pay for the sometimes high expense of domestic and international travel. Often, travel writers accept free hotel space, complimentary airfare, and free meals while touring an area. But the expenses are paid by interests represented by those areas, such as the resorts, tourism commissions, chambers of commerce, national or regional airlines, restaurants, and other groups with a financial interest in the area. They usually seek news and feature articles providing instant credibility and positive publicity in place of advertising.

Some publications will not accept articles based on subsidized or sponsored travel (Oberlin, 1995). Although larger newspapers and magazines can afford to pay for their staff writers or freelance writers to travel, many smaller publications and most freelance writers cannot do this and also expect to earn a living. And some publications do not reimburse sufficiently for the cost of travel to prepare a feature. The travel writing field, both editors and their freelancers and staff writers, is divided over the issue and no simple solution seems readily available, but an increasing number of publications seem to lean toward disclosure; that is, revealing to readers who paid for trips that are the focus of articles.

### Use of Subjectivity

Although the issue of subsidies is a major topic, so is whether travel writers should take an objective or more subjective approach to their work. Both schools of thought have their supporters. Some editors feel travel writing should be as objectively presented as any other news or features in the newspaper or magazine. Others, however, prefer a more personalized and subjective approach to the presentation with the hope that it will be more appealing to readers.

## Public Policy Issues in Travel and Recreation

There are other concerns based on public issues related to travel and recreation. In addition to the more traditional destination or service piece, there are serious news and feature articles. Topics include public and private travel and recreation issues and controversies, many focusing on public spending, the environment, development matters, and quality of life concerns.

U.S. society seems to be moving in two distinct directions. First, there are individuals who are working more and more hours per week. The percentage of persons working long hours has risen. But second and even more important, the percentage of unemployed and underemployed has also increased. Researcher Thomas Kando (1980) wrote the following: "The point is that those persons who have increasing free time on their hands are involuntarily retired, poor, unskilled, chronically unemployed. Thus, there is a growing category of people condemned to leisure, as well as a growing minority of persons who, of their own volition, work increasingly hard" (p. 13).

Other research tells us people do certain things with their leisure time, including travel, and these studies raise certain issues that travel writers might investigate for their readers. There are six general trends relating to travel and leisure time issues that you should consider in your writing:

1. The idea—What is the general idea of leisure? What constitutes travel and vacationing patterns in your region?
2. Types of leisure—What are the prevailing community types of leisure activities or vacations? What seem to be the different philosophies about leisure time usage in your area?
3. Priorities—How do your readers spend their personal funds on travel and leisure? How do they spend their time? Is it local or on the road? Simply, what do people think, feel, and do about their nonwork time?
4. Development of attitudes—You will not only want to know the characteristics of leisure, but you might benefit from understanding how these priorities have developed. What are the conditions leading to decisions? What does government policy toward travel and recreation or leisure have to do with it? What are the influences of the private sector?
5. Social problems—For a reporter using this approach, you can ask the following: What are the different leisure or travel needs of different sectors of the community or market I serve?
6. Promotion—What are the best ways a community can promote its travel and tourism? What are the roles of government and the private sector?

Economics alone cannot explain leisure and travel activities. It is difficult, if not impossible, to split the economic from the social, political, and technical factors, according to sociologist Max Kaplan (1975).

## WRITING STYLES—FINDING THE BEST APPROACH

The experienced traveler-turned-writer is the travel writer today. Your job as travel writer is to take the reader on destination stories, to give your reader the facts in service stories, and to provide opinion about current travel and tourism industry issues. Most travel writing is narrative. It remains descriptive, however, as writers use their command of the language to paint a mental picture for the reader. Remember, not all travel stories are illustrated with color photographs or graphics, so you must use your vocabulary to convey impressions of the subject through precise adverbs and adjectives.

Travel writers often utilize a more personalized style of writing. Although most features in a newspaper, magazine, or newsletter are written in an objective, third-person style, travel writing allows several different writing style approaches, including a growing emphasis on a first person, personal experience approach. The personal approach puts the author into the story as a principal source of information. It is firsthand experience writing. It is friendly and casual. Use of the first-person pronoun "I" is characteristic of this style. It is storytelling just as if you were telling it to your friends. Your own observations and reactions are important in this approach. Recreation of dialogue using direct quotations of brief conversation is common in this style also. Although first person is not as common in other sections or departments, it is a trend in today's travel writing that makes the story more appealing to readers. Full-time freelance travel writer Arthur Harris, Jr. (1992) said that you must study the newspaper or magazine first to determine what writing styles it prefers for what types of travel articles. "If uncertain what approach a travel section takes, I pop several dollars in an envelope and mail it to the paper's circulation department requesting a recent Sunday paper" (p. 21).

A simple, but successful, formula for travel articles begins with a dramatic or, at the least, interest-arousing lead. You have to sell the story to the reader. There are plenty of travel articles out there. The story must convince the reader this one is worth his or her time. Some writers do this with an anecdotal lead, some use a dramatic moment, some use heavily descriptive openings to create impressive images in the reader's mind, and others try a summary approach that simply creates an atmosphere or mood of the place.

A highly successful writer known for his detailed writing in his nonfiction and his unique settings for his novels, award-winning author Peter Matthiessen (2002) was assigned to write about the endangered Bengal tigers of India for a recent issue of *Outside* magazine. His experience and depth of knowledge are obvious from the first sentences of his first-person feature that is rich with details and vivid imagery of the region:

The heart of wild tiger country in India is the Central Highlands state of Madhya Pradesh, on the Kanha plateau. A remote region of forest and savanna in the

Maikala Range, the plateau was set aside in 1955 as Kanha National Park, where in March 2001, from atop an elephant, among the wistful cadences of forest birds, I observed a male tiger on a gaur kill. The tableau was stirring, since the dark wild ox known as the gaur is the largest of all bovine animals, and the Indian tiger, Panthera tigris tigris, is rivaled only by another subspecies, the Siberian or Amur tiger (P.t. amurensis) as the greatest terrestrial predator on earth.

Unwilling to abandon its unfinished meal to the looming mass of the intruder, the tiger stretched its jaws wide in uneasy yawning, and with those incisors so close, the elephant was restless, too. Checking our beast's skittishness with heel kicks and harsh grunts, the barefoot mahout who piloted the elephant let it shift in place every few moments to distract the tiger from any impulse toward departure. Eventually the fire-colored cat, affecting vast feline indifference, eased away into the trees, losing itself in the leaf shadow and dappled light of the dry woodland.

In the warming sunlight, as the elephant returned to the road, I fairly glowed with exhilaration, feeling fortunate indeed to have seen a tiger at all. As the new millennium begins, this magnificent species, which once prospered all across Asia, from the Caspian Sea to the East Indies, in boreal forest and hot tropical jungle, from saline mangrove estuary on the Bay of Bengal to alpine tundra in the Bhutanese Himalayas—in every habitat, in fact, except dry desert and rock mountain—has been reduced to remnant populations scattered across the Indian subcontinent, Southeast Asia, Indonesia, and southeastern Siberia (where the single sparse population survives in the Sikhote-Alin Mountains).

Of the last tigers left in the wild. . . . (Matthiessen, 2002, p. 136)

After deciding what works best for your story for the lead, set the rest of the story up by providing some sort of thesis or nut graf for the readers. Tell them why they should continue reading. What is the point of the story? Why should they care about the dogwoods blooming in East Tennessee in April, or the side trip you took in Hawaii to that remote waterfall? This portion of the story needs to tell the readers why they should read the article and what is going to follow. Let them know what you are going to do with their time, even if it is only 5 minutes for a shorter piece, and especially so if it is 15 minutes for a much longer magazine-length article.

The remainder of the article must carry out the promises made. Put people and places into the story. Travel writing is about people and places; share that. Let readers travel with you. Baker (1989) recommended strongly that travel writing show, not tell, to be effective. "The ability to share travel experiences with others relies on your skill in painting strong and sensual pictures with words," he said (p. 24). One way to accomplish this, he said, is to rely heavily on similes and metaphors in your writing. Another means to be effective is to use dialogue and recreate conversations of those at the scene. The following example, written by *National Geographic Adventure* Contributing Editor Gretchen Reynolds (2002), details the natural beauty of the red rocks of the West during a trip from Telluride, CO, to Moab, UT. But she does not simply tell readers that the place is beautiful. Her powerful description does it instead. Reynolds, who is based in Santa Fe, NM, made a 215-mile cross-country mountain bike trip along the San Juan Hut System with six friends to gather material for the article. Her use of first person and inclusion of her spouse and friends in the article adds a highly personal dimension to the writing that is common in most travel writing today. Notice how the descriptions that Reynolds uses make a difference:

> The hut becomes visible as we clear a last small green rise. Hidden from the road by scrub oak, ponderosa pine, and a few shimmery aspens, it has the impact of a mirage. We've made it. We can toss aside our mountain bikes, raid the hut's stores of Fritos and little chocolate doughnuts, and fall nervelessly onto the buffalo grass or sink into the shade and stare, unmoving, into the middle distance. It's 11 a.m., and for the past four hours, our group of seven friends has been making its way up a switchbacking dirt road from the hot, chalky low county along

## FIVE BASIC APPROACHES

There are five common types of travel writing today:

1. Destination articles—Destination stories simply tell readers the basics about places they might go on a trip. What's there? What is there to do? What sorts of accommodations are available?
2. Attraction articles—Attraction stories are more specific than destination articles. These tell readers about a particular place, such as a park or historical site.
3. Service articles—The service story explains how to travel better by letting the reader understand the mechanics of traveling. This includes articles about buying airline or cruise line tickets or negotiating customs and other legal hurdles in a country known for its tight import and export and immigration rules.
4. Personal experience articles—Personal experience stories may do the same as any of the three previous approaches, but they interject a personal experience perspective, including such things as emotional responses to the experiences. As personal features, these stories have high levels of anecdotal content.
5. Roundup articles—These stories give readers a summary view of a subject by theme. Two examples might be the "five best-kept secrets of Maui" or "10 bargain deals for this winter's Caribbean cruise season," in which the writer assembles information from different places and summarizes them in listed or other organized formats.

Colorado's Dolores River to this, the cool shadowy forest of Utah's La Sal Mountain. It's been a spectacular climb. "I'm fried," calls Jonathan from somewhere within the deep shade beside the hut. "Me, too," says my husband, Russell, spread-eagled beneath a tree. He sounds content.

"Are there any more doughnuts?" I ask, a slight quaver in my voice. I hope someone will leap up to fetch them. No one does, and I can't summon the strength. So we all sprawl languorously in what, from above, must seem a comical tableau of fallen bodies, as the limpid sunlight filters through the leaves. This, indisputable, is the most desirable shelter on our trip along the San Juan Hut System. Since leaving Telluride, Colorado, six days ago, we've pedaled more than 175 miles on dirt roads through the heart of the high southern Rockies on our way to that cyclists' red-rock dreamland: Moab, Utah. We've glimpsed cowboys, marmots, elk, and other exotica, and spent our nights in one-room wooden huts. All were well stocked (by a private concessionaire) and comfy. But none had quite the setting of this one. (Reynolds, 2002, p. 70)

## WRITING THE TRAVEL ARTICLE

The single most important step in writing a good travel story is preparation. Although taking the trip and writing the story may seem important, these steps cannot be as successful without laying groundwork before leaving home. The biggest reporting assets writers have in travel journalism are the telephone and the fax machine. Use them often. They can offer the basis for a good story and save you a lot of time and trouble in the long run. Do not forget the mail as well. When you need information but are not in a big hurry for it, send a fax or call for background information, such as press kits. Get on mailing lists of public relations firms that represent the travel industry. You will soon have more information than you need.

If you plan to get into travel writing, either for a magazine or newspaper, start a set of reference files. Organize them as you see fit, but try to put information you collect in some system so it can be found quickly when needed. One easy approach is to begin an alphabetic system based on destinations and attractions. You could also begin a set of files on service-related topics that is organized by subject. Keep a telephone number file, too.

To get you thinking about what goes into reporting and writing a travel story, here are some suggestions for a good start:

1. Search the World Wide Web—Most tourist destinations, such as cities and regions, and other travel-oriented places, will have a significant presence on the World Wide Web. There are plenty of organizations geared to travel on the World Wide Web as well. In short, there are tens of thousands of travel-oriented Internet sites. Find these sites that relate to your story idea and read through them before getting on the phone or going anywhere. The sites may contain a lot of commercial hype, but can also offer basic information such as contacts, maps, hours of operation, directions, and prices.

2. Call or e-mail sources ahead of time—When you decide you will do a story, call or e-mail sources at the locations several weeks (if it is domestic) or several months in advance (if it is foreign) to gather advance information. Call or e-mail tourism offices that are usually government-operated and government-sponsored. The best possible help on foreign sources are the domestic offices of government travel bureaus. Many are located in major metropolitan areas and ports of entry such as New York, Chicago, Los Angeles, Miami, and Washington, DC.

3. Contact local business organizations—These include chambers of commerce and convention bureaus. These organizations can provide economic reports to give you a better feel for the area. They can also give you the best information about hotels, motels, restaurants, and transportation. Often they also have information about historical sites, popular places to visit, and more. The best approach is to call or e-mail these organizations.

4. Use visitors' bureaus—Popular vacation and resort locations will have sophisticated visitors' offices and will be eager to help you before your trip. These persons can also arrange tours once you arrive.

5. Use sources at your hotel—Do not forget the hotel or motel where you plan to stay. At higher-end hotels, resorts, and motels, concierges can be very helpful. Many times the management of these places will offer help in advance if you request it.

6. Go to the library—Check out books about the areas you will visit. Review articles from periodicals that have been recently published so you can get a better idea of what might be a "new" angle for your story.

7. Build your own travel library—As you go to a new place, add a book about it. Fodor's series of country and city guides, published in paperback annually by David McKay, is a good example. Arthur Frommer's guides offer a similar perspective. Do not think these two examples are the only ones; they are not. Simply visit the travel section of a good local bookstore and you will see a wide range of travel guides—most written by experienced travel guides and travel editors. There are also a growing number of travel oriented newsletters available by subscription. These vary a great deal in their approach, focus, and price but can be the most up-to-date sources of information available to you as a travel writer. Examples include: *Consumer Reports Travel Letter, ASTA Notes,* and *Entree.*

8. Contact specific site sources—Once you know where you are going and when, start to ask specific questions when you write or call. Contact the individual sites and begin to request information to provide the needed background for your story. But always remember the wide range of possible sources that you have at your disposal. A good travel writer, like any reporter, has multiple types of sources.

9. Use a wide variety of sources—Many good sources serve the travel industry. These sources are individuals working for hotels, airlines, cruise lines, automobile clubs, and specific attractions. Many are in public service, such as city and county tourism commissions, state tourism offices and departments, and regional agencies. Many are in private service, representing businesses such as local and state chambers of commerce, tourism cooperatives, and promotional organizations. However, you must exercise care in dealing with industry sources. These sources have a particular point of view and a positive perspective to represent and may try to influence you toward their way of thinking.

10. Call to confirm appointments and visit dates—Your time is valuable, but so is the time of the person who might be your tour guide or source. But to help your work, be reliable and keep appointments.

Freelance travel writer Barbara Claire Kasselmann (1992) talks to local residents for color and other details when she visits a destination for a travel article. She said, "I always talk to the people in a region to get the flavor of their accents, their interests, and their styles that make that part of the country or the world special. If you make these people come alive in your writing, it will pique the prospective traveler's interest in the destination about which you will be writing" (p. 21). She said these sources also provide local lore and tips on the best places to eat or tour that might be off the beaten path.

Many offices are set up to deal with drop-in visitors such as journalists. However, others are not, so consider the source and determine if the people you need to see will be able to see you at a moment's notice, or if these people need a call ahead of time. It never hurts to call ahead. Use the telephone and fax machine to your advantage.

## USING YOUR OBSERVATIONAL SKILLS

After your research stage is complete, after all the appointments are made, and, after you arrive, your onsite reporting work begins. Remember, your senses will be serving as the senses for your readers when the time comes to write the story. Good observational skills are critical here and these are developed through discipline and practice. A successful travel writer always has an eye or ear open for new possibilities. There are stories that you do not expect that will develop, forcing you to abandon part of or the entire original plan. You cannot be so rigid as to not consider the chance this will occur. If you are fortunate, you could encounter a new angle on a story that you planned to write. This will not only be exciting for you, but it will also excite the readers of your story. You must constantly look at the story with the idea there is something new to this approach.

A good observer will use the senses to the fullest and convey this to the reader. Consider colors, sounds, and smells. Notice textures and tastes. All of these, if written with the right adjectives and adverbs in your story, will take the reader to that special place that you write about each time. Veteran *Washington Post* travel writer L. Peat O'Neil has written freelance travel features for major magazines in addition to her own newspaper. She has also authored a book, *Travel Writing: A Guide to Research, Writing and Selling.* O'Neil (1996) argued that the best tool of a travel writer is a journal kept during a trip:

> Whether you call it a diary, log, notebook or journal, the written record of imme-
> diate impressions is the travel writer's most valuable tool. Sentences and phrases
> reported as they happen or a few hours later are vigorous with the energy of the
> experience, full of fresh detail. With his or her senses alert to surroundings, the
> observant writer jots down colors, sounds, smells, word sketches of people and
> scenes. At this notebook stage, the writer's eye is like a magpie collecting ele-
> ments that shine, cramming the journal page with description. (p. 30)

O'Neil uses a small spiral notebook. However, writers can use a wide range of devices—such as pocketsize notepads, hand-held tape recorders, and even small computers. To keep a journal is to be a disciplined traveler. However, professional traveler writers have this discipline because their livelihood often depends on it. The point is to record the reactions and observations while the memories and moment are still in the mind with all the rich detail you want in your story when you write it days or even weeks later.

Another word about writing: Avoid clichés in travel articles. Most editors de-test them and they can be the kiss of death for an otherwise sound manuscript. There is special temptation to use them to convey impressions. Do not use them because clichés often turn off readers. Work a bit harder to find the words you need to describe what you saw, heard, or felt. It will pay off. A similar warn-ing can be issued about perpetuating stereotypes. This is especially a problem when you are writing about foreign countries and their cultures and peoples. Strive to find fresh and innovative ways to describe the areas you visit and the anecdotes you include in your articles. It is quite possible to write about na-tional or regional customs, beliefs, and other traditions without feeding on ste-reotypes. It might require some work beyond the surface, but it will pay off in the form of more appealing travel features.

Using your observation skills means you can also have fun with an article. *Backpacker* magazine writer Michael Lanza (2002) compiled a series of short descriptive pieces that created an entertaining feature about outdoor toilets or privies with some of the best views in North America. The article listed his and a handful of other writers' descriptions of 10 of the most scenic outhouses available in the great outdoors for readers of *Backpacker*. This is how he began the article:

Let's see, how can we broach this subject delicately? Well, there are moments on any backcountry trip that stir feelings deep inside us of . . . no, no, bad choice of words. The magic of the wilderness is capable of moving us in ways . . . hmmm, better try again. Sometimes the beauty of the mountain or canyon view inspires us to gush forth with . . . uhhh, that might not be the most appealing eye image, either.

Okay, let's face it, there's no polite way to lift the lid on the topic of wilderness privies. This is a story about outhouses. Honey huts. Mud shacks. In the following pages, we'll introduce you to 10 of the most scenically situated seats in North America. These wooden thrones sit upon Mother Nature's most majestic altars, inviting deep thinkers to puzzle—sometimes at great length—over life's great riddles. (Riddle #1: Why is there never paper in these stalls?)

All of the seats lie deep in the backcountry, reached by way of very worthwhile hikes. We're confident your next visit will leave you flush with awe, and feeling lighter and less burdened. Just don't forget to bring a fresh roll . . . of film. Now scat.

1. Boulder Pass campsite, Glacier National Park, Montana. We'd spent the day hiking beneath the crest of the Continental Divide, across hanging valleys populated by mountain goats, and later hoofed up Boulder Peak for an expansive view of the park's jagged mountains. At sunset, I mounted this open-air seat overlooking Kintla and Kinnerly Peaks and the Agassiz Glacier, and watched vivid bands of yellow, orange, and red stack up on the horizon as the sun disappeared. Camp at Boulder Pass on a 5-day, 36.6-mile traverse from the Bowman Lake trailhead to the Kintla Lake trailhead. . . . (Lanza, 2002, p. 64)

## SOUND ADVICE FROM A TRAVEL WRITER

Journalist Lesley Abravanel spends some of her time writing about celebrities, but most of it is devoted to writing travel books and features. She is a former cruise magazine editor and writer. When she's not combing South Beach for celebrity activity for "Velvet Underground," a weekly nightlife column in *The Miami Herald* and *The Street,* she travels the entire state of Florida as author of Frommer's *South Florida* and *Florida* guidebooks. She is a 1994 University of Miami graduate with a B.S. in Journalism and English Literature. She recommended taking a fresh approach to any sort of travel assignment:

As the former managing editor of *Porthole Cruise Magazine,* an international Time–Warner distributed consumer newsstand and subscription publication dedicated to cruise travel, I was faced with the responsibility of making sure that writers I hired did not subscribe to the "What I did on my summer vacation" school of travel writing. And while it's not easy to make countless cruise ship articles sound innovative or interesting, it was necessary to hone in on one or two particularly interesting aspects of each trip. The quirkier, the better. No one wants to read about the hackneyed midnight buffet—unless, of course, there was a rather risqué ice sculpture, a fight between two hungry passengers over the last piece of Baked Alaska, or, perhaps, a chef who happened to sing karaoke songs while serving the food.

The point is that, when it comes to travel writing, you need to bring the reader onto that trip with you. With a careful combination of facts, local color and amusing anecdotes, a travel article can be a whole lot more than a mere brochure. People can get brochures for free. If they are paying to read your article, you better be sure that you're giving them their money's worth. (Abravanel, personal communication, October 15, 2002)

Abravanel also noted that writers should view destination articles with the same attitude:

As far as destination pieces are concerned the same holds true. No one wants to read about how "the people on the island are friendly and accommodating." Tell us what provoked you to make that assessment. Did a local islander give you some of his homemade sunscreen after you suffered a serious burn? Did you happen to talk to any locals who've lived there their entire lives and explained the evolution of the destination from a sleepy spot to a hot spot? Did your cab driver happen to drive Madonna to the Ritz Carlton, but insisted he stop to show her the "real" city? Stories about how you spent hours lounging at the hotel's lovely, lima bean shaped pool are dull with a capital d. We do like the description of the pool as lima bean shaped, however. (Abravanel, personal communication, October 15, 2002)

Abravanel offered these two specific tips for your travel feature:

• Always avoid clichés. "The sunset was breathtaking." "The view from the balcony was awe-inspiring." We want to know why you think so. Capture your observations with color and innovation.

• Depending on what your travel assignment is, it's best to avoid the tourist traps. Explore—after all, you are a reporter. Discover some hidden gem—by the way the term "hidden gem" is as overused, as overexposed, and as insipid as Anna Nicole Smith. Try to discover an undiscovered spot—a small restaurant off the beaten path, a hotel you can only get to by foot or donkey or whatever, a local dive bar in which barflies can tell you the best place in town to get a hamburger. It's all about exploring:

When working on the Frommer guides, I take my own advice. While it is absolutely a must that I cover the Sea Worlds and the Disney Worlds and all those touristy mouse traps, I try to give an offbeat description to make it all sound interesting. Beyond writing about the obvious, I tend to focus on the less obvious, such as an unassuming rib shack, a makeshift tiki hut on the edge of Biscayne Bay serving dollar beers and chunks of smoked fish (and no utensils either!), or a hotel whose exercise equipment is smattered throughout the hallways with a rooftop patio lined with waterbeds. A good quote from a proprietor or even someone who has been to these places always helps illustrate your point, too. In guidebooks, however, space is tight, so use your discretion when it comes to quotes.

The bottom line when it comes to travel writing is to show, not tell. Examples, anecdotes and a keen eye for the unusual will almost guarantee that your article will not resemble a travel brochure. (Abravanel, personal communication, October 15, 2002)

## BEST SOURCES FOR TRAVEL WRITING

On the following pages are several checklists of sources for travel writers. Some of these sources are important to you because of the organizations they represent. Others are going to be important to you because of the positions they hold within an important travel-oriented organization. The best advice for you is to use them often because they will be there to help you before, during, and after your trip (when you are writing about it).

## PUBLIC AND PRIVATE TRAVEL INFORMATION SOURCES

Public Sources:
Neighborhood tourism offices
City, county tourism offices
Multiple area tourism boards
State tourism departments
Parks, recreation offices
Public relations firms
    that serve governments
Local corporations
National tourism offices
Travel, tourism Web sites
Restaurant associations
Travel-oriented Web sites

Private Sources:
Specific tourism attractions
Hotel, motel offices
Development boards
Airline travel desks
Airline public relations offices
Chambers of Commerce
Business associations
Tourism boards
Hotel, motel associations
Attraction Web sites

## WRITING DESTINATION ARTICLES

One of the oldest, and still the most common, forms of travel writing is the destination piece. This type of story is designed to focus on a place that the reader might want to visit or has already visited. It is generally a descriptive story. The

story is designed to tell your reader about the place, whether it is an exotic location such as Honolulu or Singapore, or a more traditional vacation destination
such as Niagara Falls or the Smoky Mountains.

These stories focus on cities or specific attractions. They must be crammed
with facts. The reader is seeking the best information about these locations as
possible destinations for a meeting, vacation, or other purpose. Tell the reader
what he or she should see. Tell what should be avoided and why. Tell your
reader about the major parks and other public facilities. List the historic sites.
Give details of hours of service, costs, and other necessary information. Where
does the reader write for additional information? You should know this and
should tell the reader.

Destination articles should be rich in detail and offer direct quotations from
local authorities to back up generalizations about places of which you have
written. Quote residents and experts. Talk to historians and visit historic sites.
Talk to food critics about the best restaurants. Ask other travelers to comment
about the same things you experience. Then summarize the most important
facts in a special abstracted form known as the facts box. This helps your reader
by providing a fast-reference list while he or she is in the car or plane. An interesting and unusual place is often the subject of a strong destination feature.
*TravelAmerica* magazine writer Ellen Clark (2002) found such an unusual place
when she wrote about Glacier National Park in the mountains of Montana. This
is how she began her article, describing the stunning landscape:

> If I had to pick a single word to describe Glacier National Park, it would be "dra-
> matic." From its towering rock formations, with undulating striations in arrest-
> ing shades of brown and red, to the lush mountain foliage and astounding variety
> of wildlife, the park seems to give rise to the oohs and ahs usually reserved for
> dazzling fireworks displays on the Fourth of July.
>
> Sheer rock faces are mirrored in 27,000 acres of lakes and ponds. Wildlife runs
> the gamut from squirrels and weasels to mountain goats and bears. Named for its
> glacially carved topography, Glacier National Park is a natural wonderland that
> assails the senses.
>
> No trip to Glacier would be complete without a ride along Going-to-the-Sun
> Road. A spectacular ribbon of two-lane, steep and winding roadway, it snakes its
> way for 50 miles from the park's west entrance near the community of West Gla-
> cier to the east entrance of the park at St. Mary.
>
> The road was completed in 1930, placed on the National Register of Historic
> Places in 1983, and designated a National Landmark in 1996. It passes over the
> Continental Divide at 6,646-foot Logan Pass. Besides vistas of looming rock
> walls, plunging gorges, pine forests, lakes, and waterfalls, there's a good chance
> of seeing mountain goats, deer, and even an occasional bear.
>
> While Going-to-the-Sun-Road is a good way to get an overall view of the
> park, the best way to enjoy it up-close and personal is to get out of the car and
> hit one of the 151 hiking trails. There are trails for every ability. . . . (E. Clark,
> 2002)

## POPULAR TRAVEL BOOKS AND PERIODICALS

*Hotel & Travel Index*
*Official Hotel and Travel Guide*
AAA tour books
Arthur Frommer's guides
Fodor's guides
*Travel Research Bibliography*
Steve Birnbaum's guides
*Air Traveler's Handbook*
*Goode's World Atlas*
*The Travel Writer's Handbook*
Curtis Casewit's *How to Make
    Money from Travel Writing*

*National Geographic*
*Signature*
*Frequent Flyer*
*National Geographic Traveler*
*Conde Nast Traveler*
*Official Airline Guide*
*Travel & Leisure*
*Endless Vacation*
*New Departures*
*Family Motor Coaching*
*Travel-Holiday*
*World Traveling*
*Travel Smart*
*Odyssey Hotel & Travel Index*
*ASTA Agency Management*
*The Travel Agent*
*Travel Smart for Business*
*Southern Living*
*Sunset*
AAA magazines such as *Home &
    Away* or *Going Places*

Freelance writer Irene S. Levine (2002) told Texas readers about the "real" Bellagio in her package about the small Italian Alps village on Lake Como for the *Dallas Morning News*. While many of the newspaper's readers may be familiar with the namesake hotel on the Las Vegas Strip, Levine visited the original travel destination and described it:

Bellagio, Italy—Tell anyone that you'll be spending your vacation in Bellagio and they are likely to assume you're talking about the glitzy hotel on the Las Vegas Strip. They might even ask you to place a bet for them at the gaming tables.

That's because the real town of Bellagio (in the Lombardy region of northern Italy) is far less well known, even to many Italians, than its popular American namesake.

The town perches on a remote promontory overlooking Lake Como. Your jaw drops when you first see the panoramic view of the majestic Italian Alps, juxtaposed against the large expanse of blue water in Europe's deepest lake.

With an unspoiled grace and charm, the town of Bellagio offers its guests a rare opportunity to experience a style and pace of life that have remained unchanged for decades. Since 1873, statesmen, royalty, aristocracy and stars of the silver screen—such as Winston Churchill, King Farouk, the Rothschilds, John F. Kennedy, Clark Gable and Al Pacino—have made the Grand Hotel Villa Serbelloni their holiday home. The hotel still serves a well-heeled, but low-key clientele.

For the past three years, my husband, teenage son and I have spent our summer vacations . . . (Levine, 2002, p. 6G)

Levine's (2002) article was well-illustrated. She not only wrote the article, but also provided color photographs that were used as part of the total Sunday travel section package. The newspaper published five of her images in color and provided two additional black and white locator maps showing Bellagio in Italy as well as a more focused map of the Lake Como region.

## DESTINATION ARTICLE FACT BOXES

A popular approach to writing destination features is to include a "facts" or "if you go" typographic box with the story. This information goes beyond what is contained in the main article but also supplements the article with an abstract of key information for your reader who skims the section or who is interested in clipping only the most basic information about this destination. What do you include? Here is a list of the 10 most common categories of information for the box:

1. Directions—How do you get there? What is the address? How do local visitors get there by car, train, boat, bus, or air?
2. Parking—Where do you park? What is the cost? When does the lot open and close?
3. Days and hours of operation—When are the attractions and accompanying facilities open?
4. General information—Whom does a visitor contact for general information, such as advance tickets or brochures?
5. Contact—What is the contact telephone number and address?
6. Lodging—Where can readers stay and what are the price ranges?
7. Food and other facilities—Can you buy food? Can you find restaurants there? What are the price ranges? What other facilities (or the unusual lack of them) are worth mentioning to your reader?
8. Souvenirs—Can you buy anything? Is taking anything (e.g., at a national or state park) illegal?
9. Tours—Are there organized, regular tours? How do you sign up or reserve space?
10. Special upcoming events—What's in store for the current or next season?

*USA Today* staff writer Laura Bly (2002) told her national newspaper's readers about the best places to see the color changes of fall in a feature for a recent weekend edition travel section. Her article included a boxed sidebar that listed, state-by-state, the peak dates, locations, contact telephone numbers, and World Wide Web sites for peak fall foliage viewing. This is how she began the package:

> Before last September's terrorist attacks sparked a flurry of no-shows and acceler-ated a swing to spur-of-the-moment, closer-to-home vacations, snagging a New England stay during fall foliage season often meant planning months in advance.
>
> But this autumn, procrastinating "leaf peepers" are finding more room at the inns—and even some discounts from what are usually the steepest rates of the year.
>
> "Fall foliage in New England used to sell itself, and simply finding a room was difficult," says Marti Mayne of BedandBreakfast.com, an online booking agency. "Now we're starting to see more inns offering midweek specials and other pack-ages that would have been almost unheard of a few years ago."
>
> Case in point: Faced with a 15% to 20% slump in reservations for this fall, the 16-room Tamworth Inn in Tamworth Village, N.H., has dropped its peak-season rates by $10 to $15 a night and axed a two-night minimum-stay requirement.
>
> And though innkeeper Virginia Schrader reports "very limited" weekend availability from mid-September through mid-October, her White Mountains re-treat has enough empty weekday rooms that she launched a first-ever "fall get-aways" package, knocking $150 to $250 off the cost of a four-night stay through November. (More information: 800–642–7352.)
>
> "It's been a very fluid year, with people holding off till the last minute to book," adds Janet Serra of the Litchfield Hills Visitors Bureau in northwestern

---

## LEADING TRAVEL INDUSTRY SOURCES

Human Sources:
Local editors, reporters
Tourism directors, staffs
Hotel staff where you stay
Public information officers
Managers of attractions
Residents of area you visit
Tour guides

Shop merchants
World atlas
History section at a local bookstore
U.S. atlas
Hotel, motel room guest books
Web travel sites
Airline in-flight magazines

Written Sources:
Tour books (annuals)
Local authors' books
Local newspapers' files
National, regional travel magazines
Auto association guide books
Attraction press kits
Telephone directories
   (local information section)
Local authors
Local historians
Local museum directors
Cab and bus drivers

Connecticut, where more than a dozen inns and hotels are offering packages for the first time this season (860–567–4506 or www.litchfieldhills.com)

In Newport, R.I. . . . . (Bly, 2002, p. 7D)

## WRITING SERVICE TRAVEL ARTICLES

One of the most practical types of travel features is the service article. These pieces provide useful and important information to help readers make decisions about an upcoming trip or what to do with their time while on the trip. Service stories also provide another important function because these stories, short or long, offer tips and ideas for simplifying the trip and the means for making the trip. For example, a travel service story helps your readers negotiate a busy major international airport—such as Atlanta's Hartsfield, Chicago's O'Hare, or New York's Kennedy—by offering descriptions of the terminal, concourses, parking, other fees, luggage storage, and security policies. These are stories that tell your readers when and how to book reservations on cruises or at that popular area resort by providing information such as names and addresses, deposit amounts, and deadlines. Service stories also give tips on getting good camera angles when photographing sites such as national parks or historic neighborhoods or buildings.

To tell someone about changes in airline food service, for example, you have to know the in-flight food service standards and you have to talk to the experts. For an article explaining how to negotiate a foreign city's complicated public transportation system, you have to know that destination and its underground rail system inside and out. These stories are strongest when they draw on the experience of the travel writer who has been there. This means you must get out on the road as often as possible to write these types of articles.

It is not impossible, however, for you to write good service articles from where you work. Telephoning to the right source makes a big difference on these types of articles. If you are writing for a market outside of the region where you live, a local story might be appropriate for that market and the story would not necessarily require you to leave the office to do it well.

---

### TRAVEL INDUSTRY AND TRAVEL CONSUMER NEWSLETTERS

| | |
|---|---|
| *Travel Alert Bulletin* | *Travelwriter Marketletter* |
| *Travel Companions* | *Travel Distribution Report* |
| *Travel Matters* | *Travel Smart* |
| *Travel Partners* | *Travel Scoop* |
| *Travelin' Woman* | *Traveling Healthy* |
| *Traveling Times* | *Travelweek Bulletin* |

---

The service article requires good timing to be valuable to your reader. If you want to write the type of story that readers clip and save—sometimes these are called *refrigerator stories* because people clip them to their refrigerators or put them on office bulletin boards—you have to produce the story with sufficient advance timing to get it to the reader when it is needed. Usually this requires months for magazines and weeks for newspapers.

Service articles do not always follow this more conventional approach. A successful service article in a newspaper or magazine does not even have to be in traditional story form. Travel sections and departments provide important travel information in tables, charts, and boxes that stand alone (without a story). These are called *informational graphics* and are a specialization in the news media. Yet it is still the responsibility of the travel writer to gather the information for the graphics artists who compile it with their mastery of art and the computer. For an effective service article, you must know your traveling readers' information needs. This takes research and a thorough knowledge of the traveler and the reader of your particular market. A writer who does not know the market will not have his or her stories read if they are published, and a freelance travel writer will not get the stories published very often.

Service articles most frequently take the form of one-shot feature articles. These stories are designed to stand alone, but there are other forms. Some travel editors and writers produce columns that are functional with service-type information to help consumers make those big decisions about vacations and business trips. And there is the opportunity on certain service subjects to develop a series. What are some ideas? How about highway safety and auto maintenance in preparing the family car before a long trip?

## SERVICE CONTENT ABOUT TRAVEL GOES ONLINE

Service content is also important for online news publications. CNN.com, for example, is one online news publication that places high value on travel service articles. In the travel section of the Web site, editors have compiled an archive of articles that can be helpful to travelers. One recent article, written by CNN's Thurston Hatcher (2002), focused on the easiest ways to acquire a passport for international travel:

> The prospect of getting a new passport typically ranks up there with root canals and an evening with the in-laws.
>
> But it's really not such a huge ordeal these days—or it doesn't have to be if you plan ahead and follow some simple guidelines.
>
> For starters, figure out whether you need a passport for your trip abroad.
>
> If you're a United States citizen, you don't need passports for travel to and from Mexico, Canada and some Caribbean countries, just identification and proof of U.S. citizenship.

If you have a current passport but it will expire soon, you'd be wise to renew before heading abroad. Some countries require that the passport be valid at least six months beyond your travel period.

Once you've decided you need one, the next step is figuring out the easiest way to get one of the more than 6 million U.S. passports issued each year.

If you've never had a passport, your last one was lost or stolen or more than 15 years have passed since you last got one, you'll have to apply in person for a new one.

There are more than 4,500 passport application sites nationwide. . . . (Hatcher, 2002)

Other similar service articles, for example, offered advice for European travelers seeking affordable housing in Paris and how to avoid problems when renting automobiles. The housing article, written by Travel Correspondent Stephanie Oswald, described how to find apartments for short-term use when visiting Paris. The car rental article provided the basics about car rental, such as rate structures, insurance, extras, and the special circumstances of international rentals.

## SPECIAL TRAVEL ARTICLE NEEDS OF MAGAZINES

In the past decade, there has been a boom in the national and regional travel magazine market in the United States. *Conde Nast Traveler* was founded by Conde Nast Publications, its first such publication, in 1987. Other existing travel magazines retooled. Take a look at any freelance writing market book (such as *Writer's Digest's* annual volume entitled *Writer's Market* or *The Writer's* annual *The Writer's Handbook*) and you will get a good idea of what magazines want from freelance travel writers. Most magazines maintain very small in-house staffs of full-time writers. These publications require the services of freelance writers to fill their space.

What do they want from freelance writers? Florida's *Caribbean Travel and Life* magazine is published for an upscale audience. The magazine has a circulation of about 135,000 copies nine times a year and approximately 80% of the articles it publishes are from freelance writers. Editors want material four months in advance, as outlined in a recent edition of *Writer's Market* (Holm, 2001). This is the sort of material *Caribbean Travel and Life* editors seek:

We're always looking for new takes on the oft-visited places we must return to again and again. . . . Our only requirements are that the writing be superb, the subject be something unique and interesting, and the writer know his/her subject. We are NOT interested in stories about the well-known, over-publicized and commonly visited places of the Caribbean. Our readers have likely already "been there, done that." We want to guide them to the new, the unusual and the interesting. . . . (p. 768)

*Travel & Leisure,* one of the leading travel magazines produced by American Express, depends on regular freelancers for material on travel and vacation places, food, wine, shopping, and recreational sports. Nearly all of the articles for this magazine, however, are assigned to experienced and proven writers.

Magazine writer Daisann McLane (2002), a columnist for *National Geographic Traveler* monthly magazine, regularly offers advice to readers about how to be a traveler, not just a tourist. She likes to offer her recommendations in both words and photographs. McLane gives experience-based advice about finding hotels, getting around, and other aspects of travel. In a recent column for the magazine, she explained that getting a good night's sleep in a foreign hotel is only a part of the hotel experience:

> I stood in the arrivals lobby of the airport in Ajaccio, Corsica, and realized that my heart was beating fast—from anxiety, not excitement. There was no obvious reason to be having an attack of travel jitters. The afternoon sky was bright and sunny—a soothing, clear Mediterranean blue—and around me were no shady characters of pushy taxi drivers, only a crowd of several hundred Parisian tourists. My trusty little blue Patagonia duffel suitcase was at my feet, so there was no need to worry about being separated from my toothbrush that night. So why were my palms sweating?
>
> Answer: Because I had come to Corsica impulsively, at the last minute and I had not arranged for a hotel room.
>
> It probably seems strange that a person who travels all the time would get edgy and flustered about not having a hotel reservation. But I obsess about where I am going to sleep more than any other aspect of traveling. Having a comfortable home-away-from-home, I think, makes it possible for me to wing it in other ways: eating when and where the mood strikes, changing itineraries at whim, and accepting with Zen bliss the fact that flights are sometimes grounded and trains sometimes stop for an hour between stations.
>
> But there's another, more important, reason why you'll often find me at midnight, in front of a glowing computer, searching website after website for little hotels that haven't' made it into any of the guidebooks yet.
>
> For me, a hotel is more than a room with a bed; it is my first friend in an unfamiliar place. And I want to do everything I possibly can to make sure my first friend is someone I'll like—and someone who can lead me to the heart of the place that I traveled so far to see. . . . (McLane, 2002, p. 32)

With the additional space often afforded to major features by consumer travel magazines, writers can be more eloquent in their writing about the destinations or services on which their articles focus. These articles often have a storytelling quality to them or are much more descriptive and detailed. Writer

Bette Coomber (2002) told potential cruise passengers what they should wear during the winter Caribbean cruise season. Her article, geared for individuals who have not had the on-board experience and who might not be aware of the function and fashion required at sea, looked at some basics to consider when shopping for clothes for a cruise. This is how her article began:

> Pack easy . . . go easy . . . look terrific all the way. It's a breeze with the fabrics available today. The only homework you have to do is read the labels when you shop. Look for the new blends to simplify the care of your travel clothes.
>
> Old Aunt Poly is alive and well and living in garment priced from moderate to designer lines. Look for the blends of poly with cotton, linen, rayon and acrylic. Also, look for Tencel; it's a hit . . . wears so well, feels comfortable and never creases. Ditto for Lycra which holds the shape of pants and is totally crease resistant.
>
> The first rule of packing is make it multipurpose . . . i.e., flats for daytime double as slippers in the cabin. A big shirt for daywear or a light terry top can go over swimwear on deck, your nightie in the cabin.
>
> Pack with these easy fabrics, and you'll find that separates and dresses roll up so well that they allow you to travel lighter.
>
> You'll want to look your prettiest onboard ship, whether at Bingo or bridge, High Tea or cocktails. The romantic, feminine, almost-the-'30s influence includes blouses with ruffles and tucking on them. Many tops have the poet collar. Embroidered detail, eyelet inserts and nostalgic touches embrace the 2003 look. Jewelry takes its lead from this period, including cameo pins and rings with antique finishes. . . . (Coomber, 2002, p. 22)

Coomber's article was part of a cover package of articles devoted to the issue's cruise season theme. Another service article in the same issue was devoted to a Question and Answer approach to providing information for first-time cruisers. Another article looked at sizes of ships, services and destinations, and value for the cruise dollar. Two additional articles in the issue focused on food and eating and recreational activities offered on board while on cruises. Other articles described cruise industry trends, visiting Caribbean islands, cruise news and informational tidbits, and going to sea on large sailing ships.

The award-winning *National Geographic Traveler* is another example of a magazine that depends on service content. In addition to its destination features, it offers readers trip planning guides and columns such as "Travel Watch," "Local Color," "Real Travel," "48 Hours," and "Trips." The magazine also offers information about special travel package deals. As an online companion, the magazine also offers a searchable events calendar.

*Backpacker* magazine, which focuses on wilderness experiences such as outdoors travel, hiking, and climbing, uses a large volume of service content in each monthly issue. Skills articles focus on fitness, first aid, food, animals and plants, camping, climbing, and hiking. The magazine also uses numerous articles about outdoors destinations and personal experiences in the wilderness, but it places a premium on how-to information related to travel to and during the outdoors experience. One recent article, for example, focused on the necessary gear to take on a day-long dawn-to-dusk wilderness hike and listed 10 essentials for such an adventure.

Another example of a specific magazine travel market to target is airline in-flight consumer magazines. These publications depend on freelance writers and use considerable amounts of both destination and service content. For example, American Airlines produces *American Way,* Delta Airlines publishes *Sky Magazine,* and British Airways has two magazines distributed to passengers, *High Life* and *Business Life,* especially for business travelers. British Airways *High Life* magazine uses a variety of service articles each month. One recent issue offered a list of the free personal cosmetics, lotions, and other personal items offered by many hotels throughout Europe. Another article offered a description and listing of hostels in Great Britain. And in the same issue was a lighthearted look at matchmaking with advice from experts on how to find a mate, including a brief boxed sidebar that focused on six steps to a dream date.

Instead of being subscriber-based, these periodicals are provided to passengers on the airplanes and in waiting areas free of charge. Contract publishing companies produce most airline magazines and these companies often need freelance contributions from serious writers. Airline in-flight magazines are a solid market for travel writers. Often overlooked, especially at the international level, these publications need destination and service articles for their readers. Most airline magazines are monthlies, but some of the smaller airlines have bimonthly or quarterly editions. These publications usually run major features in front, regular departments in the back, perhaps some columns mixed in, and some listings of events, in-flight programming, safety matters, or other useful en route information.

For travel writers, airline magazines are an opportunity to present major features and shorter pieces for the regular departments. Major feature articles need to be tuned to cities and people served by the airlines, of course, and the major activities within those areas. Articles typically highlight upcoming events in destination cities, the best restaurants, sightseeing, recreation, and entertainment, profiles, lifestyle concerns of travelers such as business executives, new technology, and vacation ideas. Specialized columns can cover a wide range of topics but are often written by regularly contributing experts on such subjects as finance and money, business and management, personal health and fitness, and living or lifestyles. Regular departments focus on information about the airline itself, safety features on board the airplanes, movies and music available on the flight, games, quizzes, and puzzles, and other diversions.

To write for travel magazines and newsletters, you must know the precise informational needs of the specific market. Study these travel magazines before you begin to write for them. Each one is a little different in what it likes to publish. Know their particular style of writing and presentation. Know the approaches. Magazines and newsletters are tough markets, but if you can meet the orders of your editors, you will have a widely read article.

## TRAVEL COLUMNS AS FEATURES

Travel columns are permanent fixtures in most newspapers and many travel-oriented magazines. These columns are given a wide variety of titles. The question and answer format is also popular in newspaper travel sections and magazine travel departments. These columns typically answer questions posed by readers and are either answered by experts or by staff writers. One example is *The New York Times*'s Sunday "Q and A" column. This column is compiled and written by members of the travel section staff. Columns and features such as these come in wide varieties of presentation formats, such as single author, multiple author, or just staff credit. Some publications run edited travel columns that list no credited author. Some are weekly and some are monthly. Most run from 600 to 800 words, but some are longer, 1,000 to 1,500 words per article.

Smaller publications often depend on syndicated material and wire services for their travel columns or material that makes up an edited travel column. Magazines usually depend on freelance writers to provide material on a regular basis and editors pay by the item. Syndicated travel columnists cover a variety of subjects. Popular topics for specialized travel columns include camping and other outdoor recreation, cruising, international travel, business travel, bargain and money-saving travel, and solo or senior citizen travel.

Travel columns can be used as a collecting point for shorter items that come to your attention but might not make a publishable story on their own merit. Calendar information—such as upcoming events, hours of operation, and free information by mail—fits neatly into a column. Put together, rewritten into tight form with minimal promotion to the source (such as a commercial enterprise), the information can be practical and go well with the longer features in the section or department.

The column is also a feature in its own right, with the author taking advantage of the regular space and appearance date (weekly or monthly, for example). In this format, writers such as editors of sections present their personal perspectives on subjects. Travel editor Mike Shoup of the *Philadelphia Inquirer* handles his column this way. Many columnists choose this personal approach because of their extensive backgrounds. Although this sort of commentary might be inappropriate in other sections or other articles in the travel section, you can express opinions, reactions, interpretations, and generally comment on current travel industry developments.

## WRITING OTHER FEATURES WHILE TRAVELING

Not every article that you plan to write from a trip out of town has to be based on the trip itself. You can generate other kinds of feature articles while traveling to unusual or faraway destinations. Mix the types of articles you plan to write if necessary to generate the maximum benefits from the trip. If you are a freelance writer, this may be essential to paying your expenses and turning a profit from expensive travel.

Phil Philcox, a New York freelance writer and author of numerous books and articles, recommended writing miniprofiles of businesses while traveling to foreign countries, for example. Philcox (1989) reminded freelancers that there are several thousand trade and business periodicals in the United States that would consider queries or manuscripts about businesses and business practices in foreign nations. "What these [magazine] readers have in common is that they're in business, and all business people want to know how other businesspeople operate," he said. "Would a florist in Cleveland, for example, be interested in how a florist in Munich buys and maintains an inventory?—Almost certainly" (p. 27).

Similarly, other assignments can be generated about people, especially individuals from your region or community who have relocated elsewhere and became successful or otherwise did something newsworthy. For example, a former public schools superintendent in your community may have moved to another state to accept a bigger and better position. How is he or she doing? This story prospect is clearly not a travel feature but might be the ideal freelance assignment, along with other more travel-oriented plans you have.

You are not limited to writing for the travel section of the Sunday newspaper or the travel department of your favorite magazine. You can write about sports on a travel-oriented assignment, or recreation, business, fashion, or health and medicine. Remember, these stories can be marketed as well, but just not as travel features. And it is likely that the fact that you went after the story, sometimes a long distance, cannot hurt. This effort should make the story at least a little more appealing and, at the least, compel an editor to give it a closer look during the query process.

## A TRAVEL EDITOR'S PERSPECTIVE

Mike Shoup, veteran travel editor for the *Philadelphia Inquirer,* believes reporting is at the heart of good travel journalism:

> Travel writing by its very nature tends to be positive, but that doesn't mean it has to be puffery, and it certainly doesn't mean that normal standards of fairness and accuracy can be ignored or compromised. There is simply no substitute for good,

old-fashioned reporting with pen and notebook. If the facts aren't there or they are wrong—and my finding is that this is often the case—the story will simply never get off the ground. My wall is practically papered with the humorous errors of would-be-writers, including no less than 37 wrong spellings of my last name. And my reasoning is this: If the writer can't get the editor's name right, what guarantee is there that any place or name spellings in his story are correct? Travel writing is not simple. I receive from 50 to 100 manuscripts a week in my job and reject 99% of them. Some are inaccurate, some are sophomoric, but most are just plain boring, dull and lifeless. It doesn't have to be that way.

Those who are not brilliant writers (and most of us aren't) should look for the details and nuances that make one part of the globe different from another. It is these same details that breathe life into a narrative and make each story different from the next. Writers should employ concrete examples rather than hyperbole, and be sparing with the use of adjectives.

Most travel stories written for newspapers seem to occur in a vacuum that excludes humanity—there are no people in them. It doesn't hurt any to inject characters into a story, when and if they fit. The best stories, in my opinion, accurately reflect the whole travel experience, whether good or bad. They also reflect preparation and research, and often have a historical or societal perspective. It is difficult, for example, to write a travel story about Mexico City without at least mentioning the air pollution, or the street beggars. This does not mean it is necessary to dwell on such subjects, but mentioning them in passing gives the reader the idea that he is, after all, in the real world and not in some make-believe La-La Land invented by a travel writer whose trip is paid for by the Mexican government.

My final word would be my first: There is no substitute for basic reporting and writing skills. Those intent on travel writing—or any form of writing—will find a year or two of newspaper reporting invaluable. Meanwhile, yes, it is Soup. But with an "H," please. (Mike Shoup, personal communication, November 1, 1988)

# CHAPTER THIRTEEN

# Service Features

For its recent 45th anniversary issue, the fashion and men's lifestyle magazine *GQ* (also known as *Gentlemen's Quarterly*) published a bulky 506-page catalog-sized edition. Amid the countless pages of clothing advertisements, editors published a series of retrospectives that took readers back into the past 5 decades since the magazine first debuted. Some of the features emphasized the usual look at the good life—such as the latest in men's suits—but the magazine also offered a considerable amount of what is known as service content. In this particular edition, *GQ* published a series of lists that focused on the "best of everything" since the magazine was created in 1957. The lists included the 45 best movies, books, regrets (things editors felt readers could have done without), the greatest television show episodes, CDs, biggest moments in sports, villains (people, places, and things we love to hate), charismatics (cool people as social icons), and unforgettable women. The lists were compiled by the editors or by specific experts such as movie or book critics.

*New York* magazine routinely publishes articles about apartment living; tenant–landlord relations; the art of purchasing apartments, townhouses, and condominiums; parking; the social scene and parties; working and the workplace; and self-defense. Like most city and regional magazines, it depends on large amounts of this sort of feature content. Service content such as the *GQ* anniversary issue lists and the lifestyle and living features in *New York* magazine are quite popular with readers today. Readers are discovering publications that serve them by providing practical information to help them solve problems or in other ways to live their lives better. Entire publications are devoted to "service journalism." Many of them are aimed at women, but some recent efforts have been aimed at men as well. And some women's magazines are going through major changes. Readers like the practical value of service articles.

You may know the titles of many national magazines that have strong service components: *Family Circle, Woman's Day, Ladies' Home Journal, Good Housekeeping,* and *Better Homes and Gardens,* to name a few. Although those are geared to women, some men's publications are service oriented also: *Popular Mechanics* and *Popular Science* are sound examples. Many city and regional magazines offer strong service content each month.

Service features should help people live their lives better. "Any subject can become service journalism," writes University of Missouri magazine writing professor Don Ranly (1992). "It's simply a different approach to writing. The one word that best characterizes a service article is the word 'useful' " (p. 18). The articles and other content help readers to make better decisions as consumers, to take better care of themselves, to improve relationships, to make things, and cope with "realities of everyday life, and not matters of cataclysmic importance," said Pamela Fiori (1992), editor of *Town & Country* magazine.

> Service magazines are more apt to be micro than macro; local as opposed to global; practical and directional; a bit flat-footed at the minimum and bordering on gimmicky when they try too hard. But at their best, they can have tremendous impact: They can change the way readers think or act, alter the way they spend time or money, influence style, eating habits, and travel plans, improve relationships, diminish biases. (Fiori, 1992, p. 78)

Many feature articles are written to provide this type of service to readers. They do not have to be a service to all readers all of the time. Many are specialized topics that interest a segment of readers. City and regional magazines often fill their pages with service content. These magazines appeal to readers with their restaurant, club, movie, and theater listings, entertainment-oriented calendars, and sports and concert events schedules. Another important service area has become real estate. City magazines such as *New York* magazine devote space to finding apartments and apartment living. A recent issue of *Chicago* magazine focused on housing. The magazine's annual survey of house prices included 270 towns and neighborhoods in the Chicago metropolitan area. The cover article written by contributing editor Dennis Rodkin (2002) focused on value and what type of home a buyer could find for different amounts of money. This is how he began his article:

> Mario and Diane Palermo had taken a close look at all the $1-million houses on the market in west suburban Wheaton, so they thought they had a pretty good idea of what kind of home they could get there for that much money. Then they happened upon a woman who had listed her house—complete with two fireplaces, a three-car garage, and a backyard pool—at $1.275 million. "We had done our homework," says Diane, "and we knew she couldn't get almost $1.3 million for that house. So we offered her $1 million." At first, the seller said no. But last October, after the place had gone unsold for several months, she finally accepted the Palermos' original offer on the 11-room brick house. . . . "We had looked around enough to know what a million dollars gets you in Wheaton," says Diane. "We just had to wait until she knew, too." That same kind of research can pay off for other people looking to buy into the Chicago area's energetic housing market. Whatever the rest of the economy has been doing for the past year or two, the local real estate market has stayed healthy. . . . But because local house prices are steadily rising, buyers can have a hard time pinning down an accurate answer to that all-important question: How much home can I get for my money?

"You are absolutely getting less and less all the time," says Edwin Mills, the former director of Northwestern University's Guthrie Center for Real Estate at the Kellogg School of Management. Data indicates that house prices "have gone up at two or three times the rate of inflation in the past decade," he says. . . . (Rodkin, 2002, p. 78)

Service journalism such as *Chicago* magazine's special issue on housing has been around for a long time. The earliest efforts were published in the traditional women's publications such as *Ladies' Home Journal* and *Good Housekeeping,* first developed more than 100 years ago. Much of their content was service-oriented information about the home. These articles are not necessarily "spot news" in the sense that we usually talk about news. Although they are very new, online publications have quickly come to use these types of articles as well. This is especially true of online publications that maintain theme Web sites or specializations.

Service feature articles are an important part of any newspaper, magazine, newsletter, and online publication and readers depend on these articles as part of the total package. These articles help readers do something better; they help make life easier. These articles are usually found in four forms: how-to-do-it features, listings, art of living articles, and chronological case histories:

1. The how-to article explains how something is made, built, cooked, protected, purchased, or otherwise accomplished by an expert on the subject. These articles are often found in home and garden sections, food and cooking sections, and increasingly so in consumer-based sections of newspapers and in the similarly named departments of magazines or newsletters. How-to articles are the most frequently published forms of service article. It is certainly a popular story form with editors, according to Alexander (1975). "[I]n a pragmatic nation, Americans look more and more to magazines to advise them and show them how to do the things that are important in their lives" (p. 213).

2. Listings have become more interesting in recent years in newspapers, magazines, and newsletters. Sports sections of newspapers and sports-oriented magazines offer lists of records and interesting trivia as regular features for readers. Business- and finance-oriented publications frequently run lists of top businesses, top salaries of executives, real estate transactions, and so on. Feature sections of newspapers and city and regional magazines have, for many years, listed in calendar form the major events of an upcoming weekend or month and have listed top restaurants and theaters in their circulation areas.

3. Art-of-living articles teach us how to get more out of life. These often are inspirational articles, with readers feeling uplifted after reading about someone else's skill at making his or her life better. Sometimes these articles (and books) are called self-help articles and are simply narratives or essays that affect readers in one way or another and give them ideas about how to improve their lives or

the lives of family members or friends. These articles include subjects such as retirement, love and family relationships, and making tough decisions.

4.  Chronological case histories teach us about something by looking at a particular example in depth. Readers are served by the lesson learned from the case history. These can include descriptions of purchasing a house, curing a medical problem, or resolving a conflict between neighbors.

The four approaches to these articles are not limited to single articles. There are entire magazines that specialize in "how-to" journalism, for example. Books, too, have been written on hundreds of subjects to help readers in the same way—everything from career choices, résumé writing, and job hunting to personal finance, automobile repair, and relationships with the opposite sex.

## BASIC APPROACHES TO WRITING SERVICE ARTICLES

*Town & Country's* Fiori (1992) said service magazines and articles

> help the reader to cope—with aging parents or one's aging self, an alcoholic co-worker, a serious illness, unemployment, change of address or change of life. They might even inspire the reader to contribute to society—by volunteering his or her services, by writing to Congress, by joining a local environmental group. Or, closer to home, by spending more time with the kids. (p. 79)

How do these articles achieve these seemingly lofty goals? Although the service article seems self-explanatory, there is more to it than the topic description indicates. The best service articles provide information, which result in action or behavior change on the part of readers. Often the information gleaned from the article is the sole reason for a reader's use of the article. By providing information, you are offering readers the best advice you can find on the subject. This is done in a readable fashion, but at the same time in the clearest way possible because you are explaining how something works or how something is done. Service feature articles take one or more of these three fundamental reporting and writing approaches:

1.  Writer-as-expert perspective—Individuals who are experts on a subject write how-to articles. As writers, they are able to communicate their expertise to persons who want to know about the subject. Merrill Lynch, the financial services firm, has published numerous editions of its 30-page booklet, "How to Read a Financial Report," since it was first published in 1973. The firm's expertise adds credibility and authority to the effort.

You can often write as an expert from your own personal experiences, thus combining the best elements of a personal experience feature with a service how-to feature. Eugenie McGuire is a freelance multimedia programmer and freelance writer based near San Diego. She specializes in writing about horses and other agricultural animals and produces a large amount of how-to feature material based on her own expertise and experience. "I personally find that if I haven't done it, I cannot write effectively about it," McGuire (personal communication, April 20, 1993 & January 19, 1998) explained:

> For me the practice of actions is a requirement to get the words on paper correctly. My articles start out as blow-by-blow descriptions of the action, almost as if I was looking at a movie of the thing and describing it to someone who was blind. The articles get refined from that point but still retain the first-person feel.

For the publications that she has written for, such as *Southern California Riding Magazine* and *The Hoofprint,* McGuire believes this works well. But she cautioned, "I'm not sure this would be suitable for more mainstream features" (personal communication, April 20, 1993 & January 19, 1998).

2. Someone-else-as-expert perspective—This is the more common approach to how-to service articles. This approach requires you as the writer to find one or more experts on a topic and relate in detail to readers how he or she does the activity. Finding these experts is relatively easy—there are hundreds of them in your own community at colleges and universities, government offices, and in private business. In this story, your task is equal to that of the reporter-as-expert approach by which you must take the approach of the expert and tell readers how he or she does it. Many times, these articles are primarily for enjoyment and not necessarily to be used by the reader to improve his or her lifestyle.

3. Writer as source or generator of informational graphics devices—As the primary organizer for a service article, the writer has the responsibility to gather information for creation of lists, boxes, short sidebars, informational graphics such as "exploded diagrams," calendars, recipes, step-by-step instructions, and so forth. Writers rarely put these in final form for publication, but editors depend on them to produce the raw information for these elements either on the writer's authority or on the authority of expert sources found by the writer.

## CHOOSING THE BEST SERVICE SUBJECTS

Possibly because there are so many subjects and sources available for how-to, lists, and other service articles, some experts feel how-to articles are one of the easiest ways to break into print. Feature writers Schoenfeld and Diegmueller (1982) made that point when discussing service features. Subjects that readers want to learn about tend to make the best service articles. These are day-to-day "how-to-live better" subjects of a rather routine and practical nature. These include subjects on personal health care, fashion, car and home repair and care, home and office decoration, gardening, food preparation, money and finance, shopping, and a variety of arts and crafts subjects. Readers often depend on their hometown newspapers and regularly read magazines and newsletters for advice on living better. *Town & Country's* Fiori (1992) said "readers want intelligent choices and solid judgments delivered in a compelling way" (p. 80).

Minneapolis feature writer Steve Perlstein (personal communication, May 3, 1993 & January 15, 1998) believes how-to articles are important forms of service features that should be mastered by all feature writers:

> There are few better ways to sell a piece to a magazine than to offer a title and topic like "10 Ways to Get Your Kids to Eat Their Veggies" or "How to Make a Killing on Health Care Stocks." Editors love this stuff. These ideas can come from virtually any slice of life you run across. The ideas I get for *Parenting*—things like microwaving baby food and how to know what to believe in newspaper nutrition stories—come from real questions my wife and I have asked ourselves. This way, I can find out the answer and make a lot of money at the same time. I'm writing a how-to book that guides parents through work–family options like family leave, job sharing, telecommuting, compressed workweeks and part-time scheduling. The project stemmed from when I took family leave when our son was born. We wanted to learn more about how to go about taking such a leave, but nobody had written anything; that's where I came in. The old adage goes, "write what you know." With how-to stories that can be adapted to go, "write what you want to know," because somebody else is probably wondering the same thing.

Service article writers should also be concerned about their own attention span in dealing with a subject. For service articles, pick subjects you have interest in and really care about. This makes your efforts much less difficult when you have to spend a large amount of time learning about the subject. What are hot service topics? If you are a good researcher, use your skills to compile unusual idea lists. How-to articles can include a variety of topics beyond home and garden usual ideas, such as how to hang wallpaper or how to grow a bonsai exhibit. Include timely and socially or financially important topics such as how to handle sex in the era of AIDS, how to survive the extreme ups and downs of the stock market, or finding full-time employment during the seemingly wild fluctuations of the job market.

If you are not an expert in such complex stories as AIDS and securities, then you must locate authorities on the subjects to help you do the stories. A problem with these stories is simple enough: some experts make a living from their expert advice and they might be reluctant to share it with a newspaper or magazine writer. A counterargument is publicity. Some reluctant sources may respond if you remind them that publicity can help them build their businesses. You may need to go to several local or national authorities on the same subject to put together your story.

*Writer's Digest* contributor Spikol (1984) said his best advice for how-to writers is to pick the right subject. "The secret of success is to identify a need that isn't being sufficiently filled, and to fill it. In other words, take on a job that nobody else wants" (p. 15). This is the case for service articles, he said. "If you weigh the time you must put into them against the money you earn from them, you have to strain to reach the poverty level. That's the bad news. It's also the good news, because that's one of the reasons that nobody else wants to do them" (p. 15).

Spikol (1984) said service articles should do legwork for readers. You become the reader's helper. If you can select subjects that do this, you will have a successful service article. He pointed out their importance today: "[T]hey sell magazines. They're staples, often staff-written, at many publications. Especially today, when special-interest publications abound" (p. 15). To get assignments from your ideas, Spikol recommended querying editors with a few ideas before investing time and money. This way, if an editor likes an idea but wants a slightly different focus or different sources, you can make the changes early into your work.

## WRITING AUTHORITATIVELY

Novelist and short story writer William Browning Spencer (1992) said that all writers, fiction and nonfiction, need to use the voice of authority. Using authority results in "the impression the author gives that he is in control of his material" (p. 28). This, Spencer said, can be achieved in several ways, but getting the facts right, of course, is most basic of all.

When you have firsthand expertise in a subject, it is easy to speak with authority. Because you experienced it, you know it. For example, a journalism graduate student at the University of Miami combined her interest in magazine feature writing with a specialty interest in exercise to write a profile about a Pittsburgh woman who started her own successful exercise club. Some students double major in college and can use their second major with their journalism major to create a specialization. Regardless of how you obtain it, your expertise should dominate the service article. Without conscious effort, it might become difficult for you to write for readers who do not know the subject as well as you do.

When you know the ins-and-outs of a subject, you know the detail and precision needed for such service writing. But when you do not, and you are a feature writer with no particular specialty or if you are just starting out, then you must be able to give your articles the sense of authoritativeness when you go to other sources for your expert information.

Stern (1993) and McGill (1984), both authors of how-to books, said you can accomplish the same type of firsthand authoritativeness in your writing even if you go to other sources for your how-to article. Stern argued that for freelance writers, "the art of instant expertise is a must" (p. 35). McGill said

Two traits are essential: Curiosity. A willingness to use your inquisitive pick and shovel to unearth information that makes you sound authoritative. I've recently sold articles on how to order clothing from Hong Kong, how to combine various sports in an exercise program, and how to cut the cost of shaving. Before researching these subjects, I knew about as much about them as I do about building submarines. Nothing. (p. 26)

McGill (1984) also recommended that you seek four types of information when doing research:

- Specific descriptions.
- Subject-bound terminology.
- Concrete examples.
- Expert facts.

As Stern (1993) and McGill (1984) said, experts talk shop by using specifics. They just do not generalize. For example, if you are writing about bicycles, you do not just talk bicycles. There are racing bicycles, sport and touring bicycles, all-terrain bicycles, commuter bicycles, women's bicycles, tandems, and children's bicycles. Then you can begin talking about frames, gearing, brake systems, rims, tires, and hubs. Take this specific type of description, combined with correct technical language used by the bicycle industry (terms such as freewheel, derailleur, crankset, or head tube angle), and you can write with the authority of a veteran. Current examples make these terms come to life—discussing whether to get a particular brand's front or rear derailleur on a sport or touring bicycle begins to make sense to readers when applications are made (e.g., a specific brand of bicycle). Facts, such as the number of new products on the market or prices, make the story practical and useful.

Stern's (1993) secret to instant authoritativeness is logical and simple: "There are always experts who can answer your questions, and lead you to new sources" (p. 36). The trick is finding the experts, right? Stern recommended these 12 ways to become an instant expert:

- Brainstorm for sources.
- Find an "angel" or mentor to help you find other sources.
- Let one expert source lead you to another.
- Be wary of self-serving experts.
- Use clip files.
- Ask your editor for suggestions.
- Use trade and professional publications.
- Find a dissenting view.
- Use think tanks and their experts who are paid to study subjects such as the one about which you are writing.

- Use reference experts at the local library.
- Consult public relations directors and public affairs coordinators of companies and organizations.
- Keep a list of experts for future reference, but be wary of "rounding up the usual experts."

As Stern (1993) suggested from his list, multiple sources make a difference in service journalism. When you are writing authoritatively about something that you actually know little about, you must consult as many different sources as possible. The wide variety and diversity gives you insurance against conflicting information and advice. McGill (1984) advised against overuse of the pronoun "you" in how-to articles. Most editors complain about this, he said. Do not rely on it and use it in a limited fashion. McGill warned of two additional concerns:

1. Make certain you are not presenting opinion instead of facts. Multiple sources help filter out opinion.
2. Present the facts and instruction as yours, not someone else's. A number of interviews with different sources lead you to certain conclusions of your own and make this easier to do. You can become authoritative on your own in this way.

Dr. Carin Smith (personal communication, April 26, 1993 & January 25, 1998) is a Leavenworth, WA, veterinarian who loves to write. She has written eight books, in fact, including *Career Choices for Veterinarians* and *101 Training Tips for Your Cat*. Some observers may say she is a writer who loves veterinary medicine. But she is an expert who uses her high levels of specialized knowledge as a basis for her award-winning books and magazine features. "I'm a veterinarian/writer who has been fairly successful selling my how-to articles on a freelance basis," she said. "I write business articles for veterinarians and pet health articles for pet and horse owners." Smith, former contributing editor to *Horse Illustrated* and *Cat Lovers* magazine and author of numerous magazine articles about animal health care, explains her approach to how-to writing:

My best-selling articles are those that answer the questions that I hear everyday. These are the "average" questions, the ones that appear simple on the surface. For instance, an article on flea control will sell much better than one on fancy new methods of brain surgery in dogs. You don't have to pick an obscure or complicated or highly technical subject. To any potential writer, I'd say: Think of what you know the most about—whether it be plumbing or gardening or computing. Then consider the typical conversations you have with friends or co-workers. What questions are you asked most often? About what kinds of things do people ask you for your advice or turn to you for answers? Why are you the one they ask? If you aren't the one, then what do you need to do to increase your knowledge in that area so that you know more than just about anyone you talk to? Once you are in that position, you know enough to write an excellent how-to article.

Assume your readers are very intelligent, but that they know absolutely nothing about your field. That way you avoid talking down to the reader, but you still don't go over their heads with words they don't understand. Explain every technical word, but learn to do so without making a big deal out of it, so the reader isn't offended if he or she already happens to know what the word means." (personal communication, April 26, 1993 & January 25, 1998)

Service features with the voice of authority can be helpful in many different ways. Some can be timely and practical. For example, when the management and financial problems of the enormous Enron Corporation began crashing down on employees, families, and friends in the Houston, TX, area, where its headquarters are located, some very subtle social issues began to emerge. Although these were not comparable to the financial and other problems experienced throughout the region when Enron filed for bankruptcy, these social matters were still a concern. *Houston Chronicle* society writer Shelby Hodge (2002) rolled up his sleeves, checked on what the experts recommended, and tried to resolve the matter of how individuals in the middle of Houston's upper crust social world were supposed to deal with indicted individuals. He went to nationally known authorities on this somewhat unique category etiquette. Here's a portion of his feature:

> Another round of Enron-related indictments is just around the corner, and so are those awkward encounters with the legally encumbered.
>
> The Enron players have left us with a social conundrum that tests our loyalties and social sensibilities. It was difficult enough when the scent of impropriety merely hung in the air like a bad ozone day. But once the legal ax falls, the questions of sociability burn even deeper.
>
> Should we snub Ken Lay as he gregariously works the Coronado Club at lunch or welcome him with affection? Should we offer to buy the troubled Jeff Skilling a drink at his favorite hangout, Zimm's, or move to another table when he sits near? Should we tie yellow ribbons around our trees in support of Andrew Fastow, or ignore the existence of the man whom the Washington Post on Monday called an "American pariah."
>
> In search of an answer, we turn to contemporary etiquette books and discover that they, too, have let us down. The guides to gracious living offer no direction for dealing with the indicted, the criminally charged or the morally suspect.
>
> Where is the chapter on "My friends are going to jail"? Or the sub-chapter "When country club members are indicted"?
>
> Charlotte Ford, author of 21st Century Etiquette (Lyons Press, $24.95), agrees that in the current corporate climate, an addendum to good manners guides is called for. Her book was published last November, before the full tilt of Enron, WorldCom, Tyco, et al., was realized. For those in need of direction, Ford offers a few pointers.

For tarnished corporate leaders, she advises, "Have a very low profile, because it just causes people to talk even more if you go out and are seen socially".... (Hodge, 2002)

---

## TEN TIPS ON SERVICE FEATURE BOXES

Pamela Fiori (1992) has been editor of *Town & Country* magazine since 1993 and is former executive vice president and editorial director of American Express Publishing Corporation. She developed this checklist of 10 tips for preparing service items such as lists and boxes:

1. Keep it simple—Give great information, not great literature.
2. Make it lively—Material should be inviting.
3. Be kind to the reader—Graphics should be legible.
4. Display the material prominently—Don't diminish material by burying it.
5. Be accurate—Fact check because it is essential. You can't risk losing trust of readers.
6. Avoid giving the reader too much—Be selective. You can do too much.
7. Stick to one style—Develop and use a standard format for presentation.
8. Coordinate with the art department—They produce the artwork.
9. Exercise restraint—Too much irritates and confuses readers.
10. Don't fake it—There should be a legitimate reason for the box or list.

---

## WRITING HOW-TO ARTICLES

Perhaps the major type of service article focuses on how to do something: how to cook a particular dish, how to make a piece of furniture, how to repair a broken appliance, how to set up a computer, or how to buy a car. These are the bread-and-butter articles of service feature writing and a form that all feature writers should master early in their careers. Some freelance experts say the how-to article is freelance writing's biggest single market. How-to articles accommodate a lot of approaches and related forms of approaches. If you can write "how-to" articles, then you should also be able to write "what is," "where is," "when is," and "why is" features also. They each have a common element of authority and expertise that makes these articles appealing to readers needing information about a subject.

These articles are not usually the exciting, award-winning forms of journalism you might have aspired to produce when you first became interested in writing nonfiction. However, these are the practical types of articles that help freelancers make a living and help staff writers keep their editors happy. "[F]ew literary reputations have been built upon, and no Pulitzer awarded for, how-to tomes," wrote Colorado full-time freelance writer David Petersen (1992, p. 38). "I write how-to because freelancing helps pay my bills, and how-tos probably comprise the largest single slice of today's freelance market. Instructional nonfiction is where the assignments are, and where the money is" (1992, p. 38).

Petersen (1992), who has written several hundred how-to features in more than 20 years, uses a basic formula. Like most articles any feature writer would outline, his how-to articles have three major parts: the beginning, middle, and end. Each has an important role, as he explained: "An old journalistic truism— you've no doubt heard it—holds that every article should have a beginning, a middle, and an end. Well, in how-to writing, it's more than a truism, it's a mandate. And none of those three distinct parts is more important than the opening hook" (p. 38):

1. Lead—The "hook" as Petersen (1992) labeled it, is the first few paragraphs where you get readers interested and entertain them at the same time. This is the portion of the article where the stage is set. The introduction tells what the story accomplishes. It contains a paragraph that is a statement of purpose. It helps the reader so he or she does not have to struggle with your article to figure out what will be gained from reading it. McGill (1984) recommended "letting readers know you will teach them something valuable" (p. 28). State the benefits of your advice, he said. Tell readers you are going to help them solve a problem, if that is the point of your article. At the end of the beginning there should be a transition to the middle of the article.

2. Middle—Petersen (1992) recommended outlining the middle of how-to articles during the writing process to keep them highly organized. Start with decisions about the main points and purpose of the article. What are you trying to do? How do you accomplish that? Generally, the step-by-step portion of your article follows. Take readers through the process to get to their goal. This is detailed and should leave no guessing. You must be careful to explain all steps with the assumption that your reader does not know certain basic points about the process. McGill (1984) said readers expect information in how-to articles in a "cadence" approach. This means writing the instructional portions of the article in a cookbook style. For example, you might write in four quick and short sentences: "collect tools: drill, bits, ruler, pencil, dry wall mount. Measure location of picture. Drill hole. Screw mount into wall. "Readers expect to receive how-to information in such a cadence," McGill said (p. 28).

3. Closing or ending—This portion of the article "weaves it all together," Petersen (1992) explained. You have previewed, explained, and now you are recapping. Some repetition is important here, especially on the most significant points. The conclusion can also offer a bit of final advice for your readers. These tips might hint at trouble-shooting, setup, or maintenance, for example.

Spikol (1984) urged that you also create a chart to help keep organized when producing service articles. "List everything you want to know about whatever it is you are investigating," he said (p. 16). "In constructing such a chart, you might begin by listing the names, addresses, and phone numbers" (p. 16) of your primary sources, along with other essential information about the sources. In short, a key to success is being organized when gathering facts. This should also benefit you when you begin to write the article itself. Your urge to keep the article brief might have to be quelled in the interest of clarity in service features. Additional words, used in the right places, might make the difference in a positive direction in this type of feature writing.

A good way to double-check your approach is to write a rough draft and then ask someone who knows absolutely nothing about the subject to read it to see if the article makes sense. This way you spot unclear passages before it goes to your editor. You want to be certain to eliminate ambiguous or vague content that would lead to guessing on the part of readers. Because you are so familiar with the material, it is easy to lose sight of a detail that someone else unfamiliar with the process will easily spot. On the other hand, if you are unfamiliar with the material, you might have the same problem spotting problems with details. Even after you have checked your article, your newspaper or magazine will also give it a thorough once-over. For example, many major publications test new food recipes and review other how-to food articles in their own kitchens or in the kitchens of experts. Editors of how-to publications, such as *Popular Mechanics,* check potential how-to articles by building the furniture or equipment or by testing repair hints in labs or workshops before articles are published. In a recent issue, writer Thomas Klenck (2002) told *Popular Mechanics* readers how to maintain and tune up their garage doors:

If your garage door seems a little heavier than it used to, it could be that you're just out of shape. On the other hand, it may be that your garage isn't doing its part. An overhead sectional door can weigh several hundred pounds, and without a little mechanical help it might as well be locked shut.

Garage doors that roll away overhead use springs to counterbalance their weight. The spring system is either a torsion assembly mounted over the top edge of the door, or a pair of springs, each running along the garage ceiling next to a horizontal length of door track. When the springs get weary after years of use, the door gets harder to lift.

While new springs are a sure way to lighten the load, they won't do much to improve your mood as you pull into your driveway on a stormy night. For the ultimate in convenience, there's only one solution—an electric garage door opener. Fortunately, installing new springs and a door opener are straightforward jobs requiring only basic tools and a free weekend or two.

For our project, we'll focus on garage doors with extension springs—coil springs that are near and parallel to the horizontal sections of door track that hold each side of the door when it's open.

To remove the old extension springs, first fully raise the door so the springs are completely relaxed. Then, lock the door in this upright position by installing C-clamps or locking pliers on the door tracks under the bottom rollers (see above illustration). . . . (Klenck, 2002)

There are thousands of how-to articles such as how to tune up a garage door that are published each year. Some publications exist for the sole purpose of publishing how-to service articles. Students can write them for other students. These are good "training ground" features, in fact. Here's an example: A major university's student employment office newsletter recently published a helpful article that focused on controlling stress. Written and edited by undergraduates, the newsletter often uses articles of this type to help student employees cope with life on campus a little more easily. A recent article discussed stress caused by exams, term papers, campus jobs, and other conflicts. The article gave "helpful hints" from experts about coping at the end of a semester.

Columnist Heloise—daughter of the original Heloise—offers an entire column based on helpful hints for housekeeping and home life subjects. Heloise is a contributing editor–columnist for *Good Housekeeping* and her long-running national King Features column appears in 500 newspapers. The column is a question and answer format feature that solicits questions and suggestions or tips from readers. There are numerous other similar columns written at the local, regional, and national levels that have been popular with newspaper and magazine readers for generations.

---

## A RECIPE FOR HOW-TO FOOD WRITING

*Contributed by Nanette Blanchard, freelance writer*

Root vegetables, recipe software, the history of corn, low-fat ice cream and vegetarian cookbooks are some of the subjects I've written about as a freelance food writer. Getting paid to test chocolate recipes or try out new restaurants may not seem like writing, but it is. Food writing is one of the most enjoyable and versatile types of freelance writing.

You can get ideas for food articles anywhere and everywhere. Start paying more attention to what people are eating. Listen when friends start talking about a new restaurant. Read cooking magazines and the food section of your newspaper. Even television can help you with ideas for food articles. Check your local television listing for daily food and cooking shows. CNN's weekly show *On the Menu* is a particularly helpful program for food writers with information on food trends and news in the world of cooking. For instance, one recent show discussed how apple sauce and prune butter can be easily substituted for the oil or butter to lower the fat content of cookie, cake, or muffin recipes.

Seasonal topics are always in demand by food editors. Because many magazines work 6 months in advance, keep a calendar near your desk when sending food article queries to editors. I keep a spiral notebook and write in pertinent information for each month of the year. That way, I can quickly glance through my notebook and find out that blueberries are in season in July or that March is National Peanut Month.

Don't limit your article topics to national holidays that are traditionally associated with food like Christmas or Thanksgiving. *Cooking Light* ran an article on President's Day with recipes inspired by U.S. presidents such as Brown Rice Pilaf with Peanuts (in honor of Jimmy Carter) and Jelly Bean Cookies (in honor of Ronald Reagan). Many magazines run low-calorie and spa food recipes in their January issue for all the after-the-holidays dieters.

I usually come up with some recipe ideas before I query the publication and offer a sample recipe list. I then look through cookbooks and my extensive recipe files for some preparation ideas and ingredient suggestions. I try to use simple, descriptive recipe titles. I often include some type of short introduction with each recipe such as, "This recipe is a family favorite and I adapted it using brown instead of white rice." If your recipe can be prepared in a different manner or prepared ahead, this information should be included in the recipe's preface.

The style of the recipe varies. Many food magazines send recipe guidelines to freelance writers at the time an article is assigned and some of these recipe guidelines are quite complex. Check each magazine you're writing for and follow the recipe style exactly. Some magazines spell out Tablespoon, some just use T. or Tbsp. Always list all ingredients in the order used in the recipe.

I find that including an ingredient's weight as well as number is often helpful. A recipe that includes two potatoes in its list of ingredients is less scientific than one that states two potatoes, about one-half pound each. Also, include information on how to test for doneness in addition to cooking or baking times. Rather than just stating "Bake about 20 minutes or until done," write "Bake about 20 minutes or until toothpick inserted in center comes out clean."

When testing a recipe for an article, always make it twice. This can help you discover any problems or be certain that the ingredient amounts were correct as written. Save your grocery receipts as the magazines may pay your recipe-testing expenses. The directions of a recipe can be copyrighted although the ingredients can not. If your recipe closely resembles another published recipe, with only a few minor changes, it is always smart to mention the original author and the inspiration for the recipe.

Almost every magazine published today can be queried with a food-related article idea. Don't limit yourself to food magazines. Travel magazines, women's magazines, men's magazines, children's magazines, health magazines, airline magazines, and even romance and confessions magazines all publish food articles. You can write about the history of wheat for *Smithsonian* magazine, famous food scenes in movies for *Premiere*, 15 ways to disguise broccoli for your kids in *Parents* or that wonderful farmer's market in Provence for *Travel & Leisure*. Study several back issues of each magazine you wish to query and you can narrow down a food or cooking topic for every one.

Food writing is an always-fascinating field of writing and you don't have to be a Cordon Bleu chef to get published. With a little study of the food markets and a lot of enthusiasm, anyone with a love of leeks or a yen for yams can be a successful food writer. (Blanchard, personal communication, April 28, 1993 & February 1, 1998. Reprinted with permission of the author.)

## USING ILLUSTRATIONS WITH YOUR ARTICLE

One way to strengthen your service article by making it clearer to readers is to use analogies. This helps you look more authoritative and readers understand the material far better. If you have the chance and space to use them, illustrations, such as photographs, drawings, or charts, make things even clearer. Many how-to articles are presented with illustrations to help describe the process, a critical step, or even the final product. Artwork includes such tools as statistical tables, charts, maps, diagrams, graphs, "exploded" diagrams in which things are taken apart slightly, labeled photographs, "staged" photo illustrations, and tables.

## SELF-HELP NONFICTION THAT SELLS

San Francisco Bay area writer and psychotherapist Eric Maisel (1993) recommended an 11-step self-help program to writing self-help articles and books. These are his suggestions:

Getting Ready:
1. Identify a workable and compelling issue.
2. Frame appropriate questions to give focus to the project.
3. Serve the reader as a mapmaker, not an expert.
4. Reframe problems as challenges for motivational purposes.

Building the Book or Article:
5. Decide on the structure of the project in terms of general information, individual stories, and self-help strategies.

Writing the Book or Article:
6. Provide examples, vignettes, and illustrations.
7. Use available research.
8. Create classification schemes to help convey concepts.
9. Offer workable strategies to readers.
10. Describe available resources and support services.
11. Look to the future to tell readers where they can go from here.

Charts and tables can provide such information as summaries of steps necessary in a process such as cooking, outlined one at a time. Another example for an article might be a rundown of costs for a repair or renovation project or the different options available in a major purchase. Graphs, maps, and diagrams can show how steps or stages in a procedure tie together. As an expert on the subject, you should work closely with artists to make certain such graphs are correct to every detail.

Photographs known as photo illustrations can also do the trick. Photographers will pose the subject matter as an illustration and it is presented with your article. You should attempt to tie these in with references to such illustrations in the text of your article. An alternative is to label parts of the photograph through the cutlines or legends under the photographs or to identify parts of the subject of the photograph with identifications using lines or arrows. Collaborating with copy editors, graphic artists, informational graphics editors, photographers, and page designers makes the total package work better. The tasks of writing and preparing artwork for how-to or other service features should be team efforts if possible. Most editors and artists appreciate, but often simply require, the advice and assistance.

## POPULARITY OF SERVICE ARTICLES AND BOOKS

There are countless how-to books on the market, many that have grown out of original newspaper or magazine articles. A quick look at the *Writer's Market* shows a large number and wide variety of publishers involved in producing these specialty books. The 2003 edition (Brogan, 2002) presents nearly a full-page containing hundreds of listings of both major and minor publishers who consider how-to manuscripts.

Specifically, another popular magazine, newsletter, and online publication category in recent years has been self-help or self-improvement. The *Writer's Market* also contains a section listing publications such as the bimonthly magazine *Psychology Today. Psychology Today* seeks manuscripts on psychology and self-improvement because it defines itself as a hybrid of science, psychology, and self-help content. Another self-help and improvement example is *Personal Journaling Magazine,* which focuses on journal writing. The publication seeks self-help nonfiction articles as well as first-person accounts of how journaling has affected the writer.

The psychology and self-help section of *Writer's Market* describes the demand from magazine editors for these articles: "These publications focus on psychological topics, how and why readers can improve their own outlooks, and how to understand people in general. Many General Interest, Men's and Women's publications also publish articles in these areas" (Brogan, 2002, p. 605).

How-to audiotapes, videotapes, CDs, and DVDs are also popular, with these evolving from articles and books on personal development subjects (exercise and stress management), sports subjects (golf and tennis), and personal finance (real estate and stock market investments).

## DEVELOPING LISTS AS SERVICE FEATURES

It is not unusual to find stand-alone lists such as those described in *GQ* at the beginning of the chapter. Lists are common in contemporary newspapers, magazines, newsletters, and online publications. You can enhance your service feature by combining the best of the narrative article and a listing. The listing thus becomes a sidebar or remains a major portion or purpose for the article. These approaches are often given titles such as "10 Richest Women in the State" or "Five Steps to Losing Weight Overnight." Newspapers such as *USA Today* have capitalized on the curiosity aroused in readers by such lists. Combining the *USA Today* staff talent for inviting graphics, these lists often are provided as a visual feature for readers. Magazines also use lists with regularity. Travel magazines often run lists of 10 best amusement parks, 10 ways to save money on airplane tickets or car rentals, the top business hotels in a city, the best resorts or museums, or the top restaurants. Personal computer magazines run lists of tips for users or the top products in a certain category.

To be successful at listings, you have to have a creative energy for research. Compiling lists often requires multiple sources in different locations. At other times, information may be found in one place. Listings must also be current and timely. To provide the service to readers, they must be given the most recent and current information available from the most authoritative sources. Therefore, your list is also the most accurate.

Newspapers, magazines, newsletters, and online publications that publish listings are often considered authoritative sources on their own and find their published lists cited and reproduced elsewhere. Here are some examples:

• *Real Simple* magazine recently told readers about techniques for talking with aging parents about important matters such as finances, health care, and even their final wishes. After a short narrative introduction, the list of 10 questions was presented with two- and three-paragraph elaborations and explanations. The article also included a list of "talking points," a list of resources such as books, Web sites, and organizations that offer assistance, and a list of critical information (e.g., insurance, credit card information, and banking information) that grown children need to obtain from their aging parents.

• *Chicago* magazine publishes its Chicago Guides that offer listings of places to go and things to do as well as the best restaurants and brief staff reviews in the area.

- *Health* magazine published a list of the top 10 medical advances for a recent year that helped readers understand what editors called the secrets to a long and healthy life. The narrative article was a compilation and simply organized item by item and included several hundred words to describe and discuss each advance. Each item was offered by a different staff writer, who had worked together to poll medical experts.

- *Nashville Parent* magazine, a free distribution monthly publication serving Middle Tennessee, recently published writer Laurel Schmidt's narrative list of seven hints for parents who help their children with homework. Schmidt, a veteran teacher and principal, provided several hundred words to introduce the subject and then her article listed each suggestion with a paragraph or two of elaboration.

- American Airlines' in-flight magazine, *American Way,* recently gave readers a series of tips to help parents with school-aged children who are taking mandatory standardized tests. Freelance writer Helen Bond, who specializes in health and parenting, provided short answers to questions about the tests and tips for moms and dads. She also provided a sidebar boxed list of five World Wide Web sites concerned with standardized testing and a summary of the content of each site.

- In the Up Front section of *BusinessWeek* magazine, editors offer an item called "The List" that provides readers information about a wide range of topics that vary from week to week. One recent issue listed ways that some airlines, hotels, and transit companies were responding to the special needs of women executives on the road. Another issue offered a list of salaries and total compensation packages for a sampling of chief financial officers of major U.S. corporations.

List information is used in many different ways. Readers like to keep them, turning them into "refrigerator features" that are clipped and stuck on the refrigerator door with a magnet or piece of tape. Some lists can become publicity sources for the publication, too. For example, many morning drive-time radio program announcers like to pick unusual listed feature information out of their local newspaper or news magazine to read to their audiences (e.g., David Letterman lists, best- or worst-dressed lists, and top-attended movies of the past weekend).

Most stand-alone lists are short and to the point. These are usually a top 10 or top 12. Too much information is usually not retained or read in listed form. Thus, a brief list of the top 10 busiest airports might be appealing, but a top 100 becomes useless and overly thorough unless it is part of a major project or a complete list of all the elements in a group and the detail is necessary. Most published lists are presented in tabular form. Tables are quick and easy to read. Paragraphed information of the same kind is just not as easily skimmed and understood.

## ART-OF-LIVING ARTICLES

Articles such as self-help or self-improvement are part of a broader category of service articles called art-of-living articles. These have been made popular by their regularity in widely read publications such as *Reader's Digest*. Art-of-living articles can be an easy market for beginning feature writers, said *Reader's Digest* senior staff editor Philip Barry Osborne (1987). These articles include features that are inspirational narratives and essays, inspirational essays on faith and religion, and self-help articles. Inspirational and motivational features are also a type of human-interest feature and were discussed at some length in chapter 6.

As you may recall, inspirational narratives and essays tell stories with a message to readers. The main difference is in approach. Narratives are chronological, whereas essays are in essence dealing with philosophy and "feel." These are "good" stories about people that make readers feel better after finishing them. Inspirational essays on faith and religion are not always sermons; these are, instead, articles on worship, personal revelation, prayer and meditation, and love. As Osborne pointed out, these can vary greatly in length as much as in topic.

Osborne (1987) offered five tips for art-of-living articles:

1. Guard against overwriting—Do not get too ornamental or exquisite in your writing. "[T]hink more in terms of creating a small, delicate watercolor, rather than a giant oil painting," he advised (p. 22).
2. Steep yourself in what you're writing about—Simple themes, he said, require much more than simple or superficial research.
3. Pinpoint your lesson or message—This is a fundamental requirement, so give the article what *Reader's Digest* editors call a "takeaway"—some theme that readers can take with them on finishing the article.
4. Sharpen your eye for the telling anecdote—These articles are about people, so use anecdotes. In fact, anecdotes can become the entire basis for an article.
5. Don't be afraid of ghosting—Writing under someone else's name is acceptable at *Reader's Digest* because art-of-living stories are best told in first person. Thus, write for experts who cannot do it themselves, he said.

*Yoga Journal,* a 280,000-circulation bimonthly magazine devoted to yoga and improvement of the mind, body, and spirit, recently published an inspirational article describing how a successful clothing company founder improved the quality of her life by using yoga and transcendental meditation following life-threatening surgery to remove a brain tumor. Writer Susan Cohen (2000) started the story of Annette Dale this way:

Annette Dale, the founder of Yoga-stone, a line of yoga apparel, is a busy entrepreneur living in the Berkshires in Massachusetts. If you met her today, you would never know that eight years ago, she underwent risky neurosurgery to remove a brain tumor.

In the spring of 1989, Dale landed her dream job in Los Angeles as a skiwear designer and was as passionate about her career as her exercise program. At the same time, she was beginning to feel unwell. She suffered severe insomnia, vertigo, panic attacks, and a host of other symptoms, including hearing loss, mental fuzziness, and digestive problems. Because she loved her job, Dale kept her health problems to herself. Yet she suffered constantly, fighting her fatigue during meetings and business trips.

Dale sought advice from more than 40 health care professionals, including allopathic and alternative practitioners. Yet no one was able to diagnose her condition, and many doctors said it was psychological. But Dale instinctively knew that her body was not functioning correctly and felt that she would die unless she soon found the proper diagnosis and treatment. After discussing her problems with a dermatologist, she received the recommendation that would save her life: to visit an ear–nose–throat physician, who discovered her brain tumor with an MRI. Doctors scheduled Dale for a high-risk removal procedure which could result in stroke, loss of speech, and the need for a permanent gastrointestinal tube. Dale opted to have the tumor removed, and following the operation, half of her face, throat, and digestive tract were paralyzed; she could not speak or eat.

Dale began incorporating Transcendental Meditation into her rehabilitation process. After just one session of meditation, she felt movement for the very first time in her face. She continued to meditate. . . . (Cohen, 2000)

## CHRONOLOGICAL CASE HISTORIES

You can often learn easiest from example. This is where chronological case histories—some writers also call them "case summaries"—enter the category of service feature writing. Just as how-to articles, listings, and art-of-living articles teach readers, so do chronological case histories. A good case history can hit home for your readers. A patient who has had heart trouble and has made it through major surgery to repair the problem has a story to tell. Other patients and their friends and families benefit from the story.

A chronological case history outlines the case of the patient for readers in a moment-by-moment, day-by-day approach. Many times, in fact, these articles are organized by date and time. In telling the story of the heart patient, no detail should be spared. And in concluding it, resolution must be achieved. Tell readers whether the efforts of doctors and nurses paid off—did the problem get solved? Did the patient live? Are there breakthroughs in health care to result from this?

How can this type of service article be prepared? Let's look at an example from the monthly *Health* magazine. In a series of case histories packaged together and published in a recent issue of *Health*, freelance writer and frequent contributor Karin Evans (2001) tells the stories of women who changed their own lives through "journeys of the spirit." She prepared the article focusing on the lives of a small group of women and used the premise that today's complex lives not only create stress, they distract and change focus away from what is truly important to individuals (Evans, 2001). Evans and two other writers, who provided additional reporting, wrote narratives describing these women and the events in their lives that led to the need for change. Then each portrait looked at how the woman built a higher level of spiritual meaning in their lives.

## CAUTION MAY BE REQUIRED

It is quite possible to get so enthusiastic about how-to articles that you can forget potential dangers. As a writer, you must emphasize safety at all times. Especially dangerous, or potentially dangerous, subjects, such as those involving poisons (in gardening) or electricity (installations), might need an extra dimension of safety written into them. As a writer, you do not want to de-emphasize the possibility of risk in the stories you write—if it exists. On the other hand, stories that involve other kinds of risk, such as investments, should be written just as carefully and thoughtfully for readers. You cannot write enough cautions and safety reminders into these types of articles.

One particular area of concern is the subject matter itself. Although it might have been interesting and entertaining reading, quite a controversy arose when the *Progressive* magazine published a now-famous article 2 decades ago about how to make a hydrogen bomb. On a more practical level, there is still concern about how much you tell readers, even if you personally know or if an expert is willing to discuss it, on certain subjects.

The ethical considerations on stories about crime such as auto theft, for example, are many. Do you write an article about how parking lot car thefts occur? How much do you tell? Is it right to have a former thief as your source—and is it proper for him or her to describe, in detail, how to produce tools to break in and steal a car? Or, if your community has a problem with arson in a particular neighborhood, should you write a how-to article about how an arsonist does the job?

One recent newspaper feature highlighted a one-woman crime wave. This woman, the article related, broke into countless homes of wealthy individuals by dressing the part of a well-to-do visitor—including wearing fancy clothing and driving a luxury rental car. Too much information about how this woman managed her 300 to 500 burglaries might suggest the idea to someone else. However, it can also alert persons to a potential thief in their neighborhood. A fine line of judgment must govern content of such articles. In another case, three Florida teenagers were once arrested for making an incendiary device—napalm—after reading how to do it in a book, *The Anarchist Cookbook,* written nearly 20 years earlier. They were mixing the substance in their kitchen when local authorities discovered them. Even the newspaper reports of the arrest described in detail the ingredients the boys were using. Would you write that article for publication?

---

## BEST SOURCES FOR SERVICE ARTICLES

There are a number of individuals who will be your best sources for service articles. Here is a list of major categories:

How-to Articles:

| | |
|---|---|
| Craftsmen and women | Builders and contractors |
| Mechanics | Carpenters and electricians |
| Artists | Gardeners and horticulturists |
| Technicians | Chefs and culinary experts |
| Authors of books | Consumer advocates |
| Inventors | Scientists |
| Investors | Decorators |
| Government World Wide Web sites | |

Lists and Listings:

| | |
|---|---|
| Historians | Statisticians |
| Reference librarians | Museum curators |
| Government studies | Census data |
| Government World Wide Web sites | |

Art of Living Articles and Case Histories:

| | |
|---|---|
| Ministers | Physicians |
| Lawyers | Psychologists and counselors |
| Psychiatrists | Financial advisors |
| Chronological case histories | Social workers |
| Physicians | Psychologists |
| Psychiatrists | Teachers |
| Police officers | Sociologists |
| Historians | |

---

## WRITING HOW-TO SERVICE FEATURES

One magazine editor who has nailed down the concepts of how-to and service features content is Joe Oldham. He is the long-time editor of Hearst's *Popular Mechanics* in New York. He gave this advice about service features (Oldham, personal communication, May 12, 1993):

If I had the opportunity to say only one thing to a young writer who was interested in making a living as a feature writer for magazines, newspapers, or any other medium for that matter, it would be this: Write the way you speak. Be natural. Write the words as if you were having a conversation with someone. Imagine that you're telling the reader a story or giving the reader some new information. This is especially true of service-oriented and/or how-to articles. Here, it's essential that you get the interest of the reader with the lead, then hold his interest by transmitting information in an easy, accessible style. For most of us, that means, again, writing the way you speak.

Just about everyone can speak to another person and transmit a thought. That's really all nonfiction, feature writing is. There's nothing mysterious, nothing magical about it. It's just transmitting a thought. Then another. And another. Until finally, you've written an article that transmits many thoughts in a logical sequence.

"Talking" to another person on paper should give your article a conversational tone. Unless you're writing a formal paper or treatise, you want that conversational tone in all your feature writing. That means speaking (on paper) clearly, using common language, and just being you. For instance, most of us speak in contractions. We say "You're going," not "You are going." So write that way. Your sentences will flow a lot better.

Most of us speak in the vernacular. It's true that we all have several different vocabularies, and that our writing and speaking vocabularies are not the same. Still, good writers don't differ much in the way they write and the way they speak. An easy, conversational tone is always the end result—and with it, a well written article. It always amazes me when someone I know as a regular guy writes something in a pompous, affected style that is totally unlike his natural manner and normal speech pattern. Somehow, when some people sit down at the computer, they feel that they have to become more formal or stodgy or achieve a so-called higher tone than they usually operate in as a person.

Wrong. Just the opposite is true. Good writers are who they are all the time. They don't take on a different personality when they sit down to write. Instead, they extend their own personality right into the words and sentences and paragraphs they're writing. They never step out of character. Good nonfiction writers also write to one person at a time, no matter what the circulation of their publication. Each month, *Popular Mechanics* staffers write for over 9 million readers—one at a time. Especially in nonfiction, service, how-to and the like, you've got to talk to that one person out there reading your stuff. When you reach him, you've reached them all. Use the word "you" a lot. Not the word "I." You should do this. You shouldn't do that. You should buy this. But don't buy that. Sometimes the "you" is implied. But it should always be there. Be yourself. Be natural. Relax. Write the way you speak. Then you'll be a good writer. (Oldham, personal communication, May 12, 1993)

# CHAPTER FOURTEEN

# Personal Experience Articles

*USA Today* staff reporter Olivia Barker (2002) wanted to learn about the Miss America pageant from the inside. So, she did the only thing she could do to get the story. Barker, a staff reporter who was 28 years old at the time she worked on the assignment, persuaded officials to allow her to become a participant in the annual contest. Of course, she was not an official contestant, but she was given permission by pageant organizers to take part in two of the nights of preliminary events as a competitor. She was on stage for the talent and evening wear portions of the pageant. She performed a dramatic monologue and was introduced to the audience as a representative of the newspaper. She did not participate in other preliminary events, but she was interviewed by pageant judges. None of her activities were televised, but she was scored by judges like the other 51 women that participated. And, expectedly, she did not do as well as the other women.

Barker's (2002) reporting about her unusual experience appeared in the newspaper during the pageant week, getting top billing as the "cover story" on the front page of the *USA Today* weekend edition on the day before the finals were internationally televised. She even appeared on NBC's "The Today Show" to discuss her experiences on the same day that her feature article was published. "I thought there is so much mystery around this pageant. . . . But no one's ever really sensed, you know, how much stamina, how many—how much intelligence it takes to get through this," she said on NBC (Lauer, 2002). "And I thought it would really require stepping into that role and getting a feel for it. And I think I got at least an inkling" (Lauer, 2002).

Barker (2002) was also highlighted in a photo package that was published with her first-person story about her moments on the runway and backstage. The images were published in another section of the same edition. Her story was an insightful read for pageant followers and entertaining even for those who aren't fans of the annual event. This is how she began the *USA Today* article:

ATLANTIC CITY—My dark brown hair is rolled, teased and pinned into what can only be described as a hood ornament, a lacquered bouffant that's part Lady Bird Johnson, part Bride of Frankenstein.

I've grown several inches since this morning, and I have yet to strap on my high heels. I can't stop marveling at my updo, as glossy and spongy as meringue.

"It's not Olivia," says my stylist, Bonnie Lampe–Florence, smiling into the mirror.

I'm taking that as a compliment. After 3½ days of pretending to be a Miss America contestant, perhaps I'm finally starting the metamorphosis.

The Miss America Organization offered to take me between the seams of the institution, to let me step into the hose and heels and beaded gowns as the hypothetical 52nd contestant in the Miss America 2002 pageant.

The assignment intrigued me. Talk of the pageant's increasing irrelevancy has swirled for so long that it has become a cliché. Here was my chance to not only go behind the crinoline curtain, but also to stand in front of it, center stage.

Considering Britney's belly and J. Lo's booty, Miss America looks positively quaint up there in her pink bikini and 5-inch heels. Those who covet the crown come here with names like Misty and Casey and hail from towns called Eden Prairie and Pearl City. They go to church. They don't swear (at least in public). This year's Miss Kentucky likens her family to the von Trapps of *The Sound of Music* fame. . . . (Barker, 2002, p. 1A)

Insightful writing is one goal of personal experience feature writing. Writer Olivia Barker (2002) gave readers considerable insights into the beauty pageant world with her personal experiences. A personal experience feature article allows you to do much more than the usual feature article because you, as a writer, can become highly involved in the storytelling. Most beginning writers have been encouraged to take themselves out of the story—to de-personalize the article—as much as possible. However, personal experience feature writing offers something unique in journalism—the chance to become part of a personalized story.

Writers are involved in interesting activities and write about them with amazing regularity. Travel writing, as noted in another chapter, is often first-person and personal experience oriented. Human interest articles also often offer a personal perspective. And often personal experience articles simply give readers the story from a unique point of view that results in greater understanding of a situation. Take a look at these recent examples:

• *Las Vegas Review–Journal* boxing writer Royce Feour was on assignment covering an upcoming Oscar De La Hoya fight at his training camp. But when the small passenger airplane he was traveling in crashed during a landing and caught fire in California, he had more to write about than just a professional boxing event. The private plane was carrying a group of fight promoters and journalists for a media day event when the accident occurred. A few days after he and all the other passengers and crew survived the life-threatening incident, he wrote about surviving the crash and the efforts to get everyone out of the burning plane.

• A recent book compiled by the Washington-based Newseum (an interactive news museum) published 1 year after the terrorist attacks on September 11,

2001, *Running Toward Danger: Stories Behind the Breaking News of 9/11* tells first-person stories by 100 journalists who covered the story of their lifetime in New York and Washington. There are a number of well-known journalists who contributed to the work, but it is the story of the events of that day told by rank-and-file reporters, photographers, and producers who seldom are known to the news-consuming public.

• The *Charleston Daily Mail* asked the Rev. Karl Ruttan, rector of a local Episcopal Church, to write about his experiences during the attacks on the World Trade Center in New York 1 year after it occurred. He was, by chance, in New York at Trinity Church, near the site of the attacks, attending a lecture. He wrote in depth—about 1,800 words—about how the events unfolding before them that morning caused those in the church to question their values and their future. His compelling narrative recalls the emotions and confusion, the terror, and the horrifying moments when the group left Lower Manhattan to move to the safer Midtown area. He detailed how he found strength in talking to his wife by telephone and in his faith and, in the year that passed, the lessons about life and humanity that he has learned.

• *Fresno Bee* staff writer Sheila Mulrooney Eldred wrote a recent summertime feature for the Sunday edition of her newspaper. She rode her bicycle 100 miles for the story. Her tale was a first-person account of riding her bicycle with a group of 58 people, including a *Fresno Bee* staff photographer, her husband, and two friends, across 100 miles of California flatland and farms, then foothills and, eventually, even mountains. Her story utilizes details and description, but also a good dose of comments and other direct quotations from members of the group. Although the event was a cross-country race, winning didn't matter to her. She told her readers that she felt good just to finish it.

• *The Miami Herald* uses several writers on a regular basis to give readers personal experience perspectives about life in South Florida. Annie Vazquez writes first-person features about the unusual and extraordinary things she does. She has recently learned to cook with a top chef, wrestled an alligator, learned skateboarding, taken horseback riding lessons, learned trapeze techniques, volunteered at a children's hospital, ridden in an aerobatic airplane, and gone rock climbing. Her column in the newspaper's Neighbors section is called "The Annie Files." Taking a different approach, college student Romina Garber recently wrote a series of weekly columns titled "College She Wrote" that told first-person stories about her freshman year at Harvard University that was published in the Tropical Life section of the Sunday edition. She wrote about living in the dorms, being away from home the first time, making friends, roommates, and other typical experiences of a student away from home for the first time.

Regardless of whether you are telling a story from your own experiences or shaping someone else's personal experiences for publication, these are stories people seem to love to read. Most nonfiction writers have experienced events in their lives that would make good foundations for personal experience feature articles. One enterprising college student writer jumped out of an airplane (with a parachute) to write a feature about skydiving for her biweekly campus newspaper. Without that frightening experience, she might not have had the right mood, the touch of drama and fear, and the right words for her first-person feature article about skydiving.

Photojournalist David Handschuh (2002) was getting ready to go to work in Lower Manhattan on the morning of September 11, 2001, when he first saw the smoke coming from the World Trade Center. He grabbed his camera gear and headed to the scene. In the next several hours the drama that occurred during the collapse of the two towers nearly took his life as he took photographs to document the moment. He survived the smoke and dark cloud of debris that covered him on the street by ducking into a delicatessen and gasping for breath. He later wrote about the experience for the International Press Institute's *IPI Global Journalist* publication. It was a moving and emotional story to tell and to preserve. There's no doubt many journalists and emergency workers that day had similar close-call experiences. After setting up his story for a chronological approach to the events of that morning and the rest of the day, he outlines in detail his experiences. Here is a brief passage from early into the narrative about his realization of the serious nature of the event, before and during the instant that the second airplane struck the second tower:

> As I turned my camera lens on the flaming tower, I realized that not all the debris falling to the street was glass and metal. I can't begin to describe the picture as some chose to jump to their deaths rather than be burned alive. Many photographers recorded images that morning worse than any nightmare we can have.
>
> West Street was littered with debris—office papers, broken glass and body parts. These are sights that I never want to see and photographs I will never show anyone again. I walked south to the corner of Liberty Street to take pictures of people exiting the towers. There were few, yet the smoke and flames continues to spread and grow.
>
> People were fleeing the Marriott hotel, carrying their high heels so they could run faster and covering their heads with serving trays as they fled. Others were helping others avoid the blizzard.
>
> New York's financial district resembled World War II scenes. Cars and vans were burning. Long, shiny limos had three-foot long pieces of airplane parts through their hoods.
>
> And then came the noise, a loud high-pitched roar that seemed to come from everywhere but nowhere. The second tower had exploded. In just seconds, it became amazingly obvious that what originally had appeared to be accidental was really an overt act of intentional hostility.
>
> I didn't see the second plane although I was looking at the tower at the time it hit. I have no recollection of taking the picture—a photograph taken milliseconds after the plane hit the second tower—that appeared on page two of the *Daily News* the next day. . . . (Handschuh, 2002, p. 23)

When you become part of your story as Handschuh (2002) did, your readers become closer to you because they find they can identify with you. Readers can become part of the story because the writer has shared his or her observations and experiences as well as their thoughts and emotions. You gain detail in your writing from close-up observation. This type of personalized feature article can be as simple as spending a shift at work with someone—getting involved personally. Personal writing is a broad-based approach to your craft. Your own point of view makes a difference in any story, but on these types of assignments, you can let it become part of the story itself.

## TWO BASIC APPROACHES

Generally, there are two basic approaches to personal experience articles:

1. Personal experiences of others about which you write—These articles describe in detail the unusual and appealing experiences of individuals in a highly personal approach but are not written in first person. These are your descriptions as a writer who uses the experiences of another person for the basis of the article.

2. Personal experiences of your own—These are commonly called first-person articles. These articles draw on your own experiences for primary material for the article. These articles are often stories of medical problems, trips, crime incidents, life or death accident situations, human relationships, family experiences, and countless other similar events. You are the reporter, storyteller, and the central source—or one of the major sources—in the article. These can be everyday occurrences, but the articles that receive the most attention are unusual, adventurous, frustrating, or dramatic.

*Ladies' Home Journal* senior editor Shana Aborn (1995) asks four questions about possible personal experience stories before she decides they are marketable. First, she wants to know if the experience is dramatic. Second, she asks if it is timely. Third, she checks to see how involved the author is in the action. And fourth, she checks to see if there was an ending or resolution to the experience. She also strongly advises new personal experience writers to stick to the facts, do interviews with experts and witnesses, begin the story with impact, and organize it well so the chronology is clear. Furthermore, Aborn recommends using direct quotations in the storytelling, develop the people involved as you would do characters, avoid too much detail and personal emotion, and keep an eye on the tone of the piece.

Feature writer and teacher Nancy Kelton (1988) said personal experience articles should look at the world as honestly as possible, "seeing the truths—both the dark and the light—within our experiences so that we can share them with other people who will nod and say, 'Yes, that's how it is. I've been there, too' " (p. 24).

There are times when magazines will publish personal experience features written by well-known individuals. Many magazine readers would know the name Heather Mills. She's a British model, television star, public speaker, and activist. She runs a charitable trust. When she met and eventually married former Beatle Paul McCartney, her life story and interests became worldwide news. *Vanity Fair* magazine editors worked out an arrangement with the publisher of Mills's new autobiography, *A Single Step,* to run an excerpt. The book tells her own story of her modeling and television careers, a serious motorcycle accident in London that cost the lower half of one of her legs, the work of her charities, and how she came to be the bride of one of the world's best known musicians. *Vanity Fair* published a portion of Mills's (2002) own story that described how she met McCartney:

> Since 1995, with my TV career and charity work for the Heather Mills Health Trust, which supported refugees and land-mine survivors, running flat out, my personal life had been more or less on hold. I'd had a couple of relationships, but ended up being quite badly hurt in both of them. So when, on May 20, 1999, I attended the *Daily Mirror* Pride of Britain awards ceremony, meeting the love of my life was not remotely on my agenda. Fate, however, had her own plans.
>
> My job that afternoon was to present a bravery award to Helen Smith, a young Ph.D. student who had recently lost both legs, an arm, and a hand to meningitis. She'd been studying to be a biochemist and had also been a very good pianist, so her whole life had been devastated. Helen had had trouble getting the right treatment because of the National Health Service's funding crises, so I had encouraged her to make a nuisance of herself to the authorities who were treating her as if she didn't deserve anything better. It didn't win either of us any Brownie points from the N.H.S., but the publicity did pay off. Today, Helen has state-of-the-art, natural-looking arms that respond to pulses sent when she flexes her remaining upper arm muscles. Her new fingers open and close so well that she can even apply her own makeup. Not only that: she has a flourishing career as a presenter for Anglia Television. Helen Smith's story was well known in Britain, and when she came onto the stage in her wheelchair to give her acceptance speech, many people were crying. What happened next was so typical of what disabled people have to put up with that it might have been planned. The microphone was fixed at head height for a standing person, so when Helen started to speak, no one could here a word. I was so cross, I just yanked the microphone out of the lectern and pulled it down to her. She gave a lovely speech, and I glanced down at the front row V.I.P. guests to see Virgin tycoon Richard Branson, Piers Morgan, the editor of the *Mirror,* Queen Noor of Jordan, and Sir Paul McCartney. . . . (Mills, 2002, p. 328)

## COMPONENTS OF PERSONAL EXPERIENCE FEATURES

A personal experience article must provide readers with an unusual story, an adventure, or a real-life drama. A personal experience article should also attempt to put that story in context. Often, the context is current trends in the community or society such as those affecting medical care or employment. Yet it could add the dimension of historical context as well. There are three major components of personal experience articles, according to Kelton (1988), a specialist in personal experience article writing:

1. A point of view—What is the unique way in which you can present the situation? How are you or your source involved? What perspective do you offer? An inside view will generally be preferred. Usually, Kelton (1988) said, this fares better than filling the article with descriptive details of the actions of others at the expense of personal reactions and opinions. You have to tell how it felt, what it meant, and how you grew as a person during and after the experience. This, she said, is the best way to write a personal experience article.

2. Arrival at some basic truth—After you have made your trip, been released from the hospital, survived the criminal assault, or floated to the ground after parachuting from an airplane, you should be able to reach a conclusion about what you have learned. "[S]omething should become clear to you," Kelton (1988) said. "You should reach a new level of understanding that you convey to your readers" (p. 22).

3. Emotional involvement—It helps readers to share your experience if you can place them in the middle of your emotional reaction to the situation. You cannot afford to hide your feelings in writing such an article. You have to offer a complete description of what you felt. Write in such a manner that you can put your reader next to you, watching the experience all over again.

Putting these three main components to work is the key to a successful article, Kelton (1988) said. Here's how she does it:

1. Pick an experience you care about deeply—Some writers, Kelton (1988) related, like to say that subjects pick writers, not vice versa. Although you do not have control over the events that you might use for an article, you can control your selection of those about which you feel most strongly. These are the ones to use for your articles.

2. Don't make publication your primary goal—Your primary objective should be to discover how you feel about an experience by writing about it. Afterward, in writing, you also try to publish the article, and you have an added benefit. "Your initial satisfaction should come from the writing and the discoveries you make in the process," Kelton said (1988, p. 22). Her new experiences

with motherhood, which she eventually wrote about, were her reasons for thinking about and trying to understand these new emotions she felt.

3. Don't write a personal experience article to vent anger, indignation, or other negative emotions—Sometimes you experience things that make you angry. It might be bad service at a garage or an annoying neighbor's lifestyle. Personal experience articles should not be used to vent these feelings.

4. Have the courage to reveal yourself honestly—You must convey feelings by opening yourself to others, perhaps thousands of others. That takes nerve, Kelton (1988) said, and is not for everyone. These feelings are not always positive and bright. "You must be courageous enough to reveal yourself honestly," Kelton said (p. 22).

5. Don't tell what you went through—show it—To show it means to dramatize it. Reset the scene and put yourself and the reader there together. Often this means telling the story in chronological fashion. This is a simple step-by-step process that takes readers from beginning to end.

6. Don't show everything—don't write about the mundane details of the experience—Much of the time, too many details drag the story down. The clutter can get in your way. Is the detail relevant to the story? If so, include it. If not, forget it.

## IDENTIFYING INTERESTING EXPERIENCES

What have you done that makes interesting reading for others? From some of the examples discussed so far, you are aware of successful personal experience articles. Much of it is simple good or bad luck—depending on the nature of the event. Massachusetts-based freelance writer Howard Scott believes feature writers often overlook their own experiences. "In the search for subjects, many writers ignore an obvious possibility: their own personal experiences," he said (1992, p. 359). "Although these events do need some drama, tension, and a resolution (or solution), they don't have to be earth-shattering or catastrophic. Most of us have such experiences, and writers can make them come alive on paper" (Scott, 1992, p. 359).

A writer may find himself or herself in a place to develop a story by sheer coincidence. Your sound news sense is often a good guide. The elements that make a good feature become even stronger if you are personally involved in that topic or event. So, instead of a routine story about the problems that people have settling with insurance companies after a break-in, an automobile accident, or natural disaster, the story takes on more meaning if you have had the misfortune to experience such an event yourself and can write about it. Scott (1992), who has written personal experience features for magazines and newspapers, feels you should consider several things when thinking about your own experiences as potential material for features:

> Think of a personal experience as a series of events that happened to you, and might be worth sharing with others. What else constitutes a personal experience? Have you ever spent time with a famous person, lived through a medical crisis, lived in or visited an exotic place, taken up any strange hobbies? Have you had a close brush with death—an accident or a sickness, recovered from a disabling addiction, attempted and accomplished a difficult feat? (p. 359)

Sometimes the routine at home makes good material. Many columnists do this. They are not at all hesitant to discuss topics such as sex education by using their own families as the example for others. Writing in first person, such writers even mention husbands, wives, and children by name in relating stories to readers when making their points in their regular features.

Freelance writer Sarah Mahoney (2002) wrote about major changes in her routine at work and at home in a personal experience feature for a recent issue of *Reader's Digest*. Mahoney was the former editor of *Fitness* magazine, a major women's publication in New York City. She wrote about her life-changing decision to walk away from that job. Her goal was to spend more time with her children. At age 41, it was not an easy decision for a professional journalist, she told readers using a first-person voice. She had commitments to her career, yet she made the decision to become a full-time freelance writer, leave New York, and move to Maine. She told readers how she did it.

Unusual adventures that most people cannot experience are the focus of many appealing personal experience articles. Writer George Plimpton (1990) has made a career of trying unusual sports and other activities and writing magazine articles and books about the experiences. He has been an athlete as well as a jet fighter pilot. In one article prepared for *Popular Mechanics,* Plimpton wrote about his experiences flying an $18 million F–18 Hornet at Mach 2 speed above the Atlantic Ocean.

Writers can write about exceptional activities such as a flight in a jet fighter or more down-to-earth and ordinary activities, such as shopping. Writer Alice Garbarini Hurley (2002) tells a first-person story for *Good Housekeeping* magazine about her love of shopping for jewelry, finding a piece she likes, and purchasing it. Here's how she began her "confessions of a jewelry junkie:"

> I have fallen in love at first sight many times. With jewelry. My pulse quickens, my palms get sweaty, my heart pounds. I'm starry-eyed, swayed by delicate jingling crystals, a sexy slender chain, a fiery sparkle. I have to have it. And once the deal is sealed, the treasure in the bag, I never look back. I'm walking on air.
>
> You know how it goes. You're minding your own business, shopping around, when you catch a glimmer out of the corner of your eye. And then the craving comes on, as strong as if you were a chocoholic in Hershey, Pa. Look at that set-

ting . . . the way it reflects the light . . . the statement it makes . . . imagine how it
will play off the simple lines of a black dress or snug white tee.

This could be mine, I think, as the saleswoman lifts the bauble off its velvet
bed. What's stopping me? This will change my life, and make me feel pretty.
Even my hair will look better if I wear this tomorrow. A sweater or a pair of shoes
can't do that. And so what if I promised myself no more fashion treats until my
next paycheck? . . . . (Hurley, 2002)

Writer Tim Rogers (2002) wrote a light-hearted, yet serious look at water
conservation in the Dallas, TX, area at a time when a drought was forcing city
water officials to restrict use of water. He portrayed himself as a "water vigilante" as he rode around the city with a water code compliance officer for an
article for *D Magazine,* an award-winning monthly city and regional format
magazine serving the Dallas metropolitan market. Here's how he began his
first-person story on water patrol:

> If you violate the city's new conservation code, I will be your judge, jury, and exe-
> cutioner.
>
> I took a ride the other day with a redhead in her 1991 Chevy Caprice. Her
> name was Patricia Stark, and she's a code compliance inspector for the city of
> Dallas. As one of two city employees who enforce the new water conservation
> ordinance, she spends the majority of her day driving around, looking for pud-
> dles. I wanted to tag along because I thought I was a concerned citizen. Patricia
> let me because her boss made her.
>
> In preparation for my ride-along, I studied up on the city code, section
> 49–21.1, "Conservation Measures Relating to Lawn and Landscape Irrigation." I
> found it to be fascinating stuff. Who knew it was even possible to "recklessly irri-
> gate" a lawn? Basically the code states that, from June 1 through September 30,
> you can't water your yard between 10 am and 6 pm, and you can't water while
> it's raining (or snowing or sleeting) no matter what time of the day it is or what
> day of the year. Also, you can't water the sidewalk. Plus, you can't take your gar-
> den hose, fill a 60-gallon trashcan halfway up, lean it against your neighbor's front
> door, then ring the doorbell. This offense, committed by yours truly in the Pres-
> ton Hollow area in 1984, when I was a high school knave, is covered by a differ-
> ent section of the code entirely. (Rogers, 2002)

Obviously, more serious subjects than jewelry shopping or going on a water
usage patrol, such as life-or-death situations, public safety, and health, make
compelling personal experience stories. A first-person approach to modern
health issues is illustrated by the case of a student journalist who was once a co-
caine addict. Her experiences gave a critical dimension to her story about the
impact of drugs on a middle class coed that she could not achieve as meaningfully from a source in an interview. If the student can bring herself to write
about this trying part of her life and others learn from it, then the story has had
impact. Her story, which was written for a university newspaper's monthly

magazine, chronologically told how her increasing dependency on drugs cost her a promising career, her marriage, and an entire lifestyle. Her article described how she eventually managed to win the battle with drugs and told the high price she paid. From this writer's rare personal situation, we learned that a peek into someone else's life can teach us much about one woman's highs and lows and how she put herself back on the road to a productive life.

Ideally, personal experience stories should relate to broader community concerns, if possible. Although some incidents can be interesting as isolated happenings, an experience takes on more value if it is placed in a more meaningful big picture. The final test is to determine if the experience is "writable:" Can you tell this story to someone else? Would someone else want to know about what you experienced? If so, then you might have a good story idea.

## FINDING THE BEST STORYTELLERS

In every community there are entertaining storytellers. You might have occasion to tell your own personal experience stories from time to time, but much of your grist will be from other sources, people known as the local storytellers. Who are they? They take many roles—minister, Boy or Girl Scout leader, historian, police officer, and social worker. People who are involved with other people on a regular basis often have the best experiences to tell. If you can find one or more of these persons, you will have rich potential for a story.

Where do you find them? Some storytellers put on performances to make a living or just for fun. These individuals can be found at community centers or at schools. They appear from time to time at local bookstores entertaining children and their parents. They may give tours of unique nearby neighborhoods or your area's historic districts. Some teach adult classes or volunteer at museums or historic places. Many storytellers are often found in areas where tourists or other visitors gather. These individuals can be found just about anywhere, but look for places where they have a chance to share what they know with others and you might just connect with someone with a good personal experience or two on which to build a feature story.

Research, as you are often reminded, makes a difference even in personal experience storytelling. You might be aware of events that can be the basis of a good personal experience story. By searching records and newspaper clippings, you can often get the names of persons who were witnesses, victims, or otherwise involved in the event. These are also some of your best storytellers.

## TELLING A MEANINGFUL STORY

Some personal experience feature articles can be called factual short stories. This might help you to remember a good approach to writing a meaningful story—write and organize it as you might handle a short story, but just be sure to keep the content factual. Accomplishing this is easier than it seems. It helps a great deal if you use the same storytelling techniques of short-story writers:

- Dialogue—Use an ample number of direct quotations and reconstructed conversations between key individuals.
- Description—Bring in plenty of rich descriptive words and detail. This includes using active verbs and adverbs and impression-filled adjectives.
- Plot—If your story permits, try to organize it so it has a plot or story line. Make it suspenseful if appropriate. Give the story a moral. You should introduce the plot or story line early in the article and stick with it throughout.
- Facts—Stick to the facts. Do not embellish or falsify to enhance the story line. Use real names of those involved, real places, actual dates and times, and other factual details. The reality adds a truly valuable dimension to the article that cannot come from any other type of writing device or technique.

There can be problems with telling a story. One of the most serious ones is selective or failing memory. On some personal experience story assignments, you might depend on memories of events that occurred months or years ago. Your memory gets hazy. There may be no written record of events, either. Fading memory filters out certain details over time. If this happens to you, it can happen to your sources, too. You must be prepared to go to extra lengths for details that might be forgotten. For example, you may be able to use yearbooks, photo albums, and other records to stimulate detailed recollections. Many writers, when faced with missing information, are better off admitting to readers that they cannot recall some detail or piece of the puzzle. Do not guess. This openness and honesty are personal touches that make the article even more appealing to readers.

## USING YOUR OWN EXPERIENCES

Has anything extraordinary ever occurred to you? Would it make an appealing story? Can others learn from your experiences? There are unusual events and circumstances that occur in your life that could generate an article. Newspaper reporters and magazine writers experience the full range of human experiences and you should be prepared to write about the unusual events that you experience. Of course, the ordinary activities in your life might make good feature article material, too.

    *Washington Post* reporter George Lardner, Jr., may have taken on the most difficult assignment of his career when he decided to write an article about the death of his 21-year-old art student daughter, Kristin. Lardner's article was a description of how the criminal justice system failed in protecting his daughter from a jilted boyfriend who stalked and murdered the woman in Boston in 1992 (Kurtz, 1993; Lardner, 1992). Lardner, a 30-year veteran of the *Post* staff, was normally an investigative reporter. He had written about the assassination of Robert Kennedy in 1968, the Chappaquiddick incident involving Ted Kennedy, the Watergate coverup trial, and the Iran-Contra scandal. But he turned to a very different writing style—a much more personalized feature approach in telling the story of his daughter's death and her murderer's suicide. His article, "The Stalking of Kristin: The Law Made It Easy for My Daughter's Killer," was published in the newspaper's Outlook section. In first-person style, he described what he wanted to achieve with the article: "This was a crime that could have and should have been prevented. I write about it as a sort of cautionary tale, in anger at a system of justice that failed to protect my daughter, a system that is addicted to looking the other way, especially at the evil done to women" (Lardner, 1992, p. C1). Lardner (1992) said his work on the story began when he spoke with a Brookline, MA, police officer. Lardner discovered, after talking with the officer, how little he really knew about what had happened to his daughter. In his efforts to find out the truth about Kristin's case and her death, he collected enough information that would grow into his article, which won the 1993 Pulitzer Prize for feature writing. This is how Lardner began his lengthy article:

> The phone was ringing insistently, hurrying me back to my desk. My daughter Helen was on the line, sobbing so hard she could barely catch her breath.
> "Dad," she shouted. "Come home! Right away!"
> I was stunned. I had never heard her like this before. "What's wrong?" I asked. "What happened?"
> "It's–it's Kristin. She's been shot—and killed."
> Kristin? My Kristin? Our Kristin? I'd talked to her the afternoon before. Her last words to me were, "I love you Dad." Suddenly I had trouble breathing myself.
> It was 7:30 p.m. on Saturday, May 30. In Boston, where Kristin Lardner was an art student, police were cordoning off an apartment building a couple of blocks from the busy, sunlit sidewalk where she'd been killed 90 minutes earlier. She had been shot in the head and face by an ex-boyfriend who was under court order to stay away from her. When police burst into his apartment, they found him sprawled on his bed, dead from a final act of self-pity.
> This was a crime that could and should have been prevented. I write about it as a sort of cautionary tale, in anger at a system of justice that failed to protect my daughter, a system that is addicted to looking the other way, especially at the evil done to women.
> But first let me tell you about my daughter.
> She was, at 21, the youngest of our five children, born in D.C. and educated in the city's public schools, where not much harm befell her unless you count her taste for rock music, lots of jewelry, and funky clothes from Value Village. She

loved books, went trick-or-treating dressed as Greta Garbo, played one of the witches in "Macbeth" and had a grand time in tap-dancing class even in her sneakers. She made life sparkle. (Lardner, 1992, p. C1)

Lardner (1992) told the story chronologically after setting it up with this lead. Following the description of his daughter, he traced the history of the relationship—how Kristin met the man who would stalk and kill her and himself. Lardner gave readers detailed biographical material about Cartier, her murderer. As he did, the story became more third person in voice. Lardner quoted friends of his daughter and persons who knew Cartier, a man with psychological problems. The detail of Lardner's writing included numerous incidents and anecdotes recounted by persons who knew the couple. He also used his investigative reporting skills in locating and reviewing public records involving his daughter's murderer. His eye for detail is evident in this paragraph midway through the story:

Left in her bedroom at her death was a turntable with Stravinsky's "Rites of Spring" on it and a tape player with a punk tune by Suicidal Tendencies. Her books, paperbacks mostly, included Alice Walker's "The Color Purple" and Margaret Atwood's "The Handmaid's Tale," along with favorites by Sinclair Lewis, Dickens and E.B. White and a book about upper- and middle-caste women in Hindu families in Calcutta.

Her essays for school, lucid and well-written, showed a great deal of thought about art, religion and the relationship between men and women. She saw her art as an expression of parts of her hidden deep inside, waiting to be pulled out, but still to be guarded closely: "Art could be such a selfish thing. Everything she made, she made for herself and not one bit of it could she bear to be parted with. Whether she loved it, despised it or was painfully ashamed of it—she couldn't stand the thought of these little parts of her being taken away and put into someone else's possession." (Lardner, 1992, p. C1)

Still another insightful passage utilized another writing technique. Lardner (1992) recreated dialogue in this portion:

What did she see in him? It's a question her parents keep asking themselves. But some things are fairly obvious. He reminded her of Jason, her friend from New Zealand. He could be charming. "People felt a great deal of empathy for him," said Octavia Ossola, director of the child care center at the home where Cartier grew up, "because it was reasonably easy to want things to be better for him." At the Harbor School, said executive director Art DiMauro, "he was quite endearing. The staff felt warmly about Michael."

So, at first, did Kristin. "She called me up, really excited and happy," said Christian Dupre, a friend since childhood. "She said 'I met this good guy, he's really nice.'"

Kristin told her oldest sister, Helen, and her youngest brother, Charlie, too. But Helen paused when Kristin told her that Cartier was a bouncer at Bunratty's and had a tattoo.

"Well, ah, is he nice?" Helen asked.

"Well, he's nice to me," Kristin said.

Charlie, who had just entered college after a few years of blue-collar jobs, was not impressed. "Get rid of him," he advised his sister. "He's a zero."

Her friends say they got along well at first. He told Kristin he'd been in jail for hitting a girlfriend, but called it a bum rap. She did not know he'd attacked Rose Ryan with a scissors, that he had a rap sheet three pages long.

Kristin, friends say, often made excuses for his behavior. But they soon started to argue. Cartier was irrationally jealous, accusing her of going out with men who stopped by just to talk. During one argument, apparently over her art, Cartier hit her, then did his "usual thing" and started crying. (Lardner, 1992, p. C1)

Lardner (1992) completed the article with a continuation of the chronology of his daughter's relationship, her and Cartier's breakup, the stalking, and the final days of her life. In great detail, he reconstructed what happened in her life for the 3 or so months leading up to the day of the murder. He also reviewed events that occurred following her death: his efforts to trace the weapon used in the murder–suicide and detailed descriptions from public records of his daughter's efforts to stop the stalking and harassment after she had ended the relationship with the man. The final portion of the article is devoted to explaining how the judicial system failed to protect her. This section alone is a startling lesson to readers. He questioned, "How many—[people] should have known she was in grave danger?" (p. C1). But his concluding paragraph summarized in an effective manner just how little the judicial system worked: "The system is so mindless that when the dead Cartier failed to show up in Boston Municipal Court as scheduled on June 19, a warrant was issued for his arrest. It is still outstanding" (p. C1).

Writer Nan Robertson (1982) told another amazing personal story for *The New York Times Magazine* that explained to readers her battle against a medical condition known as "toxic shock syndrome." The article, appealing because of the very personal story it told, earned her the Pulitzer Prize the following year for feature writing. Robertson wrote in rich, precise detail about her experience with the rare medical problem. Structurally, she took a chronological approach, beginning just hours before she was stricken. She took readers through her near-fatal attack, the ride to the hospital, diagnosis, and treatment. Her article used direct quotations of recalled dialogue during her attack and treatment. She also depended on family members and friends to remember details and quotations, and she used a diary one friend kept for her during her hospitalization. After setting the scene—her trip to the hospital in Illinois—readers are told the following:

This is the story of how, almost miraculously and with brilliant care, I survived and prevailed over that grisly and still mysterious disease. Almost every major organ of my body, including my heart, lungs and liver, was deeply poisoned. This is also the story of how—with luck and expertise—this life-threatening disease can be avoided, detected, monitored, treated and destroyed before it reaches the acute stage. (Robertson, 1982, p. 30)

Robertson's (1982) article, written in first person, is understandable even when she discussed the medical reasons for the disease. Readers are able to share the experience of her personal fears, her suffering and her pain, and her joy in winning the battle. Yet, she also incorporated into her article considerable discussion about the disease by experts from the Centers for Disease Control and other medical research centers. Woven into her own experiences, this made the article instructional as well as entertaining.

These examples illustrate how reporters with a variety of experiences that appeal to readers can use their own lives as the basis for their articles. Clearly, neither Lardner (1992) nor Robertson (1982) would have wanted to go through their experiences. But they did and eventually turned them into learning experiences for themselves as well as others. Although one writer chose to use her own amusing family experiences as material for lifestyles features and a parenting column, the other two turned dangerous, even fatal, situations into valuable stories from which others are able to learn.

## ORGANIZING NARRATIVE ARTICLES

Personal experience features require care in organizing the sometimes-large amounts of material. Because you, or someone you are working with, have experienced the subject firsthand, writing about the experience can become difficult because you or your source is so close to it. Many features rise or fall because of their organizational structure. A strong personal experience story depends on organization also. Because many personal experience stories are not written in the traditional inverted pyramid—with the most important facts first—a strong lead makes a difference. This lead is the first step in the organizational effort. It must capture the flavor of the article by hinting at its essence without giving away the outcome or moral. The lead must arouse readers by piquing their curiosity, teasing them, and even raising their eyebrows in reaction to what they have read. Writer Gerard F. Baumbach (2002) accomplished this with his simple, but effective lead for an article he wrote for the 350,000-circulation monthly Catholic magazine, *St. Anthony Messenger,* on the 1-year-anniversary of the terrorist attacks on New York. Here's how he started his article about finding his son during the attacks:

I wept when I heard the news that my youngest son had escaped the World Trade Center, alive but injured. Then I learned a lesson about life.

My usual routine places me on a 7:02 a.m. train from Long Island to Manhattan, which I catch after morning Mass in my parish. But on September 11, 2001, I had slept late, having arrived home shortly before midnight the night before, after speaking at a Connecticut parish. So on a beautiful, sparkling morning, I boarded the 9:05 train.

The train had just left the station when the conductor announced that a plane had struck the World Trade Center. I remembered my youngest son, Dan, saying good-bye to me as he left earlier that morning for his office on the 80th floor of the World Trade Center.

I gingerly asked the conductor where the plane had struck. His response left me sunken in my seat: The upper floors of the North Tower had been hit. I was horrified.

I tried calling my wife, Elaine, from my cell phone but could not get through. She is the librarian at a Catholic school.

When we finally made contact, we stammered our way through mutual fear and unmentionable possibilities: "Where was Danny? Was he O.K.? In which tower did he work?" . . . . (G. F. Baumbach, 2002)

As the chronological account of the morning and his search for his son continued, G. F. Baumbach (2002) reached the point when he learned about the fate of his son:

Finally, after some fellow New Yorkers ushered me to the head of the line at a public telephone, I reached my wife. I forget what I had prepared to say to her, but it did not take long for me to hear the best news of my life: Dan was alive!

I learned that a friend of Dan's had tried to call him repeatedly from the time of the first attack. He finally reached our son shortly after Dan had made his way through the darkness onto a local street.

Exhausted and dazed, Dan had collapsed at Canal Street. He did not have to wait long for assistance. Hands of kindness aided him, flagging down an ambulance, enabling EMS workers to do what they do with such care.

As he lay in the ambulance, Dan received a call from Karen, who quickly shared the news of his survival with Elaine.

The news was simple yet profound: Alive! Alive! Alive!

I wept as I held the phone. I remember asking Elaine to repeat what she was saying. . . . (G. F. Baumbach, 2002)

Most personal experience articles are organized as essays written in chronological order, simply recounting a series of events that will interest readers. Articles often follow a loose chronological structure with some small departures. An essay requires a basic organizational structure also—a beginning or introduction, body, and ending. Chronological stories must be told in a time-based order of events—often including the times to help the reader understand the sequencing. It is essential that you stick to the topic—that is, remain focused—in your article. Because it is often a personal story you are telling, the temptation can be great to drift away from the real focus.

You must also keep the story moving. Doing this requires pacing and a skilled use of transitions. You can tell each single episode that contributes to the entire experience an item at a time, but you must constantly try to tie each item together with good transitions that remind the reader of the links. For example, using times of the day or days of the week in a chronological piece aids readers a great deal. Helter-skelter movement around a series of events confuses readers and can lose them.

Like travel writing, personal experience features are often written in first person. When you are telling a story that you have experienced yourself, it is often easier to write it in first person. You should also remember that when writing a personal experience story from someone else's experience, the best writing approach is third person. Taking a first-person approach is only confusing to the reader if your byline is on the article and someone else is really telling the story.

---

## SOURCE IDEAS FOR PERSONAL EXPERIENCE ARTICLES

These are some of the most commonly used sources to write about the personal experiences of others and the personal experiences of your own:

Researching the experiences of others.
Other newspapers, magazines, newsletters, and online publications.
Civil and criminal court files.
Radio and television talk shows.
Neighbors and friends.
History books.
Local museums and schools.
Specialized World Wide Web sites.
Your own experiences.
Family albums.
School yearbooks.
Observation.
Notebooks, diaries, or logbooks.
Home movies and videotapes.
Conversations with family and friends.

---

## SERVICE FEATURES: THE CORE OF MAGAZINES

John Mack Carter, former editor of *Good Housekeeping* and president of Hearst Magazine Enterprises, feels that personal experience features are the heart of what magazines do best. Carter (personal communication, October 6, 1988 & May 23, 1993) explained

> To my way of thinking, the personal experience feature is the core of magazine journalism, one of the hallmarks that sets us apart from the news media. In one form or another—the first person article, the case history, anecdotes, nostalgia—I consider personal experience the most important part of the mix of features in *Good Housekeeping*.
>
> In *Good Housekeeping*, these articles may take any of ten different formats:
>
> 1. *The exclusive celebrity interview*. Two examples of this type of article that we've run in *GH*: "My 12 Years with Prince Charles" by Stephen Barry and "Diana's Life as a Wife, Princess and Mother."
>
> 2. *Crime and suspense*. Two examples: "Shattered Night," the trial of the wife of a famous heart surgeon who, after suffering years of physical and psychological abuse, shot and killed her husband. "Who Killed Patricia Gilmore?" This young woman was killed by her former boyfriend after the authorities failed to take his threats seriously.
>
> 3. *Weight loss stories*. We look for new but sound breakthroughs on weight-loss products, techniques, or diets. An example: "I Lost 100 Pounds Through Hypnosis."
>
> 4. *A miracle or legal first*. Two examples: "A New Life for My Joi." This is the story of the first pancreas transplant as a treatment for severe diabetes. "The 14 Million Dollar Woman." Story of Dorothy Thompson, who initiated and won a landmark antidiscrimination suit against the U.S. government.
>
> 5. *A woman's personal courage triumphs over a difficult challenge*. Example: "Alice Williams' Impossible Dream." Inspiring story of how a sharecropper's daughter, the only one among her siblings to graduate high school, managed to put her own 11 children through college.
>
> 6. *A provocative issue*. Examples: "Doctors and Rape." The trial of a young nurse who accused three doctors of raping her. "Malpractice." A doctor and expert witness opens his casebook on malpractice suits, some of which have made medical and legal history.
>
> 7. *Personal stories of medical oddities*. Examples: "I Froze to Death—But Lived." A young girl, caught in a Minnesota blizzard, was frozen literally as stiff as a board—but much to her doctor's amazement, she recovered fully. "My Heart Stopped While My Baby Was Being Born." Doctors thought there was a high probability that neither Laura Spitler nor her baby would survive—but they both beat the odds.
>
> 8. *Unique family lifestyle*. Examples: "A Very Different Kind of Family." A fascinating glimpse into what it was like growing up in a polygamous Mormon household with 47 brothers and sisters. "His, Mine—Ours." What hap-

pened when a mother of two married a widower with four—and got his former mother-in-law as well.

9. *The brief, personal, nostalgic essay.* Examples: "A Spoonful of Love." The precious gifts passed down from mother to daughter. "Watch Out, Great Grandma is Coming—" An anecdotal tale of multigenerational life.

10. *A woman's problem and how she solves it.* Examples: "My Husband Was a Tightwad" and "I Fell in Love With My Doctor."

# CHAPTER FIFTEEN

# Writing Humor in Feature Articles

What is funny to you or to someone else? Is there a difference? One dictionary said humor is a person's disposition or temperament, sort of a state of mind. *Webster's New World Dictionary* (1966) defined humor as whim or fancy. Then it added, well into the definition, "the quality that makes something seem funny, amusing, or ludicrous; comicality—the ability to perceive, appreciate, or express what is funny" (p. 708).

Scholars have been studying humor since the days of the Greek philosophers. Humor takes many different forms. As a writer, your humor can be jokes, brief fillers, quips, or sketches, essays, columns, or even a more traditional feature article. Humor remains an elusive concept and there still is no agreement on how humor should be defined. The bottom line is simple enough—what is humorous is different to each individual. Humor historians Walter Blair and Hamlin Hill (1978) put it this way: "[L]aughter is a highly subjective response. So writers who are foolhardy enough to discuss the humor which does or doesn't produce it are an endangered species" (p. vii).

J. Kevin Wolfe, a producer for radio personality Gary Burbank in Cincinnati, OH, said there are two keys to good humor. He argued that people laugh at two different things: surprises and misfortune of others. "We laugh in *surprise* at the union of two things that don't fit together, such as the Pope skateboarding. Surprise humor leads you in one direction and then takes a sharp turn," Wolfe (1990, p. 19) noted. "We also laugh at people's *misfortunes:* of the rich and famous, of the poor and ethnic, of living where you do, of being yourself. This type of humor has a butt. Think of jokes you've heard recently. Who did they slam?" (Wolfe, 1990, p. 19). Another point Wolfe made is that humorists often combine surprise and misfortune. Surprise can be a misfortune and misfortune can be a surprise. Many comedy performers, cartoonists, and humor writers employ this strategy, he observed.

The market for high quality humorous prose is always strong. A truly funny and creative writer can just about fill in the blanks on his or her own paycheck for full-time work or freelance assignments. Some publications specialize in humor, but most simply use it along with other content. Some magazines and newspapers use humor as spot features; others use it as a regular item in columns or departments. Still others use humor only as fill material. Regardless, if you have an eye and ear for funny stories, and if you have an ability to express things in a humorous way, humor might be a potential specialization for you. To be successful as a humorist—people such as Dave Barry, Calvin Trillin, Garrison Keillor, Ian Frazier, Alice Kahn, Patrick McManus, Roy Blount Jr., Al Franken, Art Buchwald, or James Lileks—requires a combination of keen wit, observation skills, knowledge of human nature, basic hard work, and a little luck. These are some of America's best contemporary humorists:

- *The Miami Herald's* Dave Barry, winner of a Pulitzer Prize for his satirical commentary, is syndicated by Tribune Media Services and Knight–Ridder/Tribune News Service and is the author of numerous best-selling humor books about working, traveling, children, and health. His unusual, distinctive approach to ordinary topics is part of what has made him popular. He has also recently begun to write offbeat fiction.
- Garrison Keillor, perhaps best known for his work on National Public Radio (NPR), began as a writer for *The New Yorker*. His stories for the "Prairie Home Companion" have entertained both theater audiences and radio audiences for many years. His books and occasional magazine features focus on the life and values of people living in mythical Lake Wobegon in Minnesota.
- Calvin Trillin is a humorist, novelist, poet, travel writer, and short story author who frequently writes for publications such as *The New Yorker, Time,* and *The Nation.* He lectures and has even performed one-man humor shows in New York. His essays are filled with commentary about the American scene. He is known for his success in highly diverse forms of writing.
- Ian Frazier, regular humor columnist for *The New Yorker,* has been honored with the Thurber Prize for American humor. He is author of *Coyote v. Acme,* a collection of his essays that earned him the prize.
- Phoenix humorist Laurie Notaro wrote a weekly humor column for the *Arizona Republic* for about 10 years before a collection of her best essays, *The Idiot Girls' Action-Adventure Club,* was published in 2002 and quickly made the best-seller list. No longer writing the newspaper column, she has several new "Idiot Girls" books underway. Her success as a humorist is based on storytelling about her own life, which she says is often embarrassing, really stupid, and out of control.
- Roy Blount Jr. may be best known for his long list of books, including novels, but he is a frequent magazine writer whose work has been featured in *The Atlantic Monthly, Playboy,* and *The New Yorker.* Blount, who might be described as a jack-of-all-writing-trades, often combines humor with sports and contributes to *Sports Illustrated.* However, he is also a poet, lecturer, performer, sportswriter, and dramatist.
- Art Buchwald has authored numerous best-selling books and newspaper columns satirizing politics over a long and distinguished career that includes a

Pulitzer Prize for commentary. He authors a *Los Angeles Times* syndicate column from his home base in Washington, DC.

- James Lileks is a humor writer and novelist. He is author of four books and writes a weekly column for the Newhouse News Service. Based in Minneapolis, Lileks is a columnist for the *Minneapolis Star Tribune* and Star Tribune Online. He focuses on politics and U.S. culture and writes an interactive humor column on the newspaper's Web site called "Backfence."

- San Francisco Bay area humorist Alice Kahn writes sarcastic and biting commentary about life on the West Coast. The Berkeley-based writer creates entertaining newspaper columns and books that take off-beat looks at relationships, social trends, and how we live our lives.

Most writing experts say that writing humor is among the toughest types of writing to master. Because humor writing has this reputation, few people try it and, of course, even fewer succeed. Such success requires basic hard work. Yes, you have to have something funny to say, but you must also have the wide-ranging experiences and unique perspective to make it work. Hollywood writer Larry Wilde (1976) said humor writers are "hypersensitive, indulgent, indefatigable, disciplined, sentimental, highly intelligent, and well-educated individuals. Their influence on society is immeasurable. They are the word-picture painters, word coiners, phrase makers, colloquial-expression designers of our times" (p. 6).

Among periodical and book publishers, humor can be big business, too. There is intense competition for the truly successful humor writers and editors, and publishers are constantly searching for new voices with talent. Some of the most popular humor writers are also stand-up comedians or cartoonists. Look at the humor section of any local bookstore and you see names like Tim Allen, David Letterman, Chris Rock, Ellen DeGeneres, Cathy Guisewite, Matt Groening, and Scott Adams. Many humor writers who are not comedians or cartoonists develop the writing skills with small publications and work up to major newspapers and magazines and then to book authoring. However, some humor writers begin their careers as stand-up comics and then try their hand at writing. U.S. writing has a rich tradition of writers with an ability to entertain and make readers laugh. "From Artemus Ward and Mark Twain to James Thurber and Peter De Vries, American popular literature has been plentifully supplied with humorists," wrote *Publishers Weekly's* Robert A. Carter (1990, p. 24). "And in publishing there's no doubt that humor is a serious business" (Carter, 1990, p. 24). Much of the success of both a writer and the publisher depends on luck and timing, many experts say (Dahlin, 1992). "More than any other genre, humor is a fragile contraption. Tricked out in cartoons, amusing essays, or cheeky one-liners, what's funny to one person is stupid, offensive or utterly mystifying to another," Robert Dahlin (1992, p. 23) wrote in *Publishers Weekly*. The author, however, not the subject, ultimately sells humor, Dahlin rightly observed.

This chapter cannot describe everything about humor writing. In fact, entire books are devoted to this subject (for example, see Gene Perret's *How to Write and Sell (Your Sense of) Humor,* Writer's Digest Books, 1984). However, this chapter shows you the basic elements of writing funny stories, columns, and other material. Although humor can be both fiction and nonfiction, spoken or written, this chapter's focus is on written nonfiction. This chapter discusses formulas that make writers such as internationally syndicated newspaper and magazine humorists Dave Barry and Art Buchwald so successful. Although you might not become the next Dave Barry or Art Buchwald, this chapter discusses writing humorous feature articles, briefs, and brights. It demonstrates how proven humorists have built their reputations—one funny word at a time.

## DRAWING HUMOROUS IDEAS FROM REAL LIFE

Some of the funniest stories we find in features are not fiction. When we hear or read one, it might seem as if some very creative person just thought it up, but the best is what happens on a daily basis. Just keep yourself on alert for the possibilities. *Austin American-Statesman* humorist John Kelso writes about the odd and ordinary things happening in his part of Texas. Political humorist Mark Russell, perhaps best known for his television performances for the Public Broadcasting System network and live performances around the nation, also writes a syndicated humor column and occasional magazine articles. His political humor is based entirely on what is happening in Washington, DC, and other power centers of the nation. Although he lives in Buffalo, NY, Russell said he reads *The New York Times, The Washington Post,* and *The Wall Street Journal* to keep up with current events and to find ideas for his material. "It's almost too easy, when you've got Congress, the White House and both political parties writing the material," Russell explained (Belcher, 1988, p. 1F).

Texas journalist Molly Ivins approaches her political commentary in a similar manner. She feels that politicians are the easiest material to use for humorous political commentary. She focuses on politics at both the regional and national levels. An author of books and syndicated as a columnist through the Creators Syndicate, her work appears in newspapers and magazines across the country. Often taking a humorous approach to her commentary, she utilizes satire and colloquialism to comment on issues involving our national and regional leaders, the Congress, the White House, and other political institutions. She's known as a storyteller and is in demand as a public speaker.

*The American-Statesman's* John Kelso (2002) recently wrote about his trip to the annual University of Texas and University of Oklahoma football game at the Cotton Bowl on the Texas State Fairgrounds in downtown Dallas. By any standard, it is a big sports and social event. He focused his column on his friends, the thousands of football fans, the pregame fun at the state fair, and a strange character named Okie Pokie who went along for the ride, but didn't manage to get into the game:

DALLAS—No, my friends and I did not take Okie Pokie into the Cotton Bowl to see the Texas–OU football game Saturday.

We didn't figure we should spend $60 for a ticket for a 5-foot 9-inch Sooner running man sculpture made out of Oklahoma cow pies.

Besides, you don't want to spend 3 1/2 to 4 hours listening to people holler, "Down in front!"

On the other hand, Okie Pokie did attend a couple of tailgate parties in Dallas, and we did take him into the State Fair, where he got his picture taken in front of Big Tex.

Okie Pokie had to stand in the security line for about 15 minutes with the other fans to get into the fairgrounds.

The security people were wanding everybody, but they were not wanding Okie Pokie. One security guy took a look at Okie Pokie, broke into a smile and said, "I ain't even checking that (stuff)." Then he hollered over to the guy working next to him, "Rashad, it's your turn."

For the most part, Okie Pokie was very well-received. On Friday and Saturday, he had his picture taken more times than Britney Spears. He even got his picture taken with a couple of UT cheerleaders.

"It's impressive," said Buck Dossey, a UT cheerleader who met up with Okie Pokie at a tailgate party Friday night in the Quadrangle area of Dallas. "The (Sooner) hat takes it over the top. My professor said something about it in a class, and he wanted to see it, but I didn't expect to see it here."

Even some Oklahoma fans seemed to enjoy the sculpture.

"I've seen things hung in effigy; I've seen a lot of things," said Bill Kerr, an investment banker from Oklahoma City. "But one made out of the proverbial substance, that's very unique. It's absolutely something that fits with rivalry, but I can't go along with agreeing with it 100 percent."

Sometimes these gags are more work than you would think.

The logistics of parading Okie Pokie all over Dallas were difficult, to say the least. We had to bring him up Interstate 35 in the back of a pickup covered with a tarp so he wouldn't blow out the back.

Every time we wanted to display Okie Pokie, we had to find a place to park, then drag him—all 30 or so cow chips glued to a piece of plywood—out the back of the truck. Then we had to put him on his truck dolly so we could wheel him around.

We had to affix Okie Pokie to the dolly by tightening down the wing nuts. We had to roll him up curbs and then down curbs. Fortunately, a lot of people seemed to appreciate our efforts.

But the really good news is that I've expense-accounted the $28.34 worth of cow chips from Beaver, Okla., to the newspaper, which should get me in the expense account Hall of Fame.

"That's just wonderful," said Heidi Bloch, an Austin lawyer. "That's the best use of cow (chips) I've ever seen."

Some Texas fans even seemed to think that Okie Pokie looked eerily like their Sooner rivals.

"It's awesome," Bucky Couch of Austin said. "It looks like the people who are staying at our hotel." (Kelso, 2002)

(Reprinted with the permission of the *Austin American-Statesman*.)

Like Mark Russell, syndicated columnist Art Buchwald uses the daily newspaper for most of his ideas. A new Buchwald column, usually about 600 words, begins when he reads the newspaper. Often he sees something he will file away for later use. Then he looks for the news peg for whatever idea he has filed away—in other words a reason for writing about that subject. Then he writes. He repeats this process 3 times a week.

Syndicated humor columnist James Lileks commented about politics. He jokingly said, "I love the opportunity to be one of the more incoherent political voices out there" (Lamb, 1993, p. 35). Lileks grew up in South Dakota and went to school at the University of Minnesota. He began writing for an alternative weekly and then moved to the *St. Paul Pioneer Press* before moving to Newhouse News Service and his current base at the *Minneapolis Star Tribune*. He characterizes himself as an essayist, and he frequently uses satire to make his point.

*New Orleans Times–Picayune* humor columnist Angus Lind (2002) also uses real stories, but has even asked readers to send along their humorous stories. His strategy works because his readers call—even long distance—to tell him of their experiences. Lind uses the best material for his column. He recently wrote a column looking at the unexpected success of the local professional football team (the team was in 1st place with one of the league's best records at the time the column was published):

"I'm having this recurring dream and I'm having trouble dealing with it," the man lying on the couch was telling the shrink.

"Every Sunday I sit in front of my TV set and the Saints keep winning and winning. It's terrible."

"Go on," the man in the white coat said.

"Then on Sunday night I watch the late sportscasts on TV and all I see are happy locker rooms and players smiling and laughing. On Monday I open up The *Times–Picayune* sports section and they've won again! Pete Finney says the Saints played their best game of the season against the best team they've played so far this year. I buy *USA Today* and there are more stories about the Saints than any other NFL team. I tell ya, I can't take it."

"Continue, please," the doc said.

"It gets worse. Monday afternoon I take a break from work and ESPN's Len Pasquarelli says, "The Big Easy Bandwagon might need to be retrofitted for those heavy-duty shock absorbers, so crowded has it become in recent days." The New York Times' NFL computer power ratings have the Saints the top-ranked team in the NFL—that's the whole league! I can't cope with this."

"Please, keep going."

"I'm driving home and Buddy D says his wife, Peggy, wants to help him pick out what dress he'll wear when the Saints go to the Super Bowl. And Buddy's not laughing about the possibility anymore. Then I go to my bar to relax and have a few beers and gather my senses and guess what happens?"

"What?" asks the psychiatrist.

"Jim Henderson comes on with his weekly sports commentary. You know what his message to Saints fans is?"

"Please tell me."

"He says, 'If you care to throw caution to the wind, be my guest. The magic of 2000 is back. If there was ever a time to dream the impossible dream, this is it.' I tell you, doc, this is sheer agony. The next thing you know, we'll be on the cover of Sports Illustrated. It'll be torture."

"Why do you say that?"

"Because it can't last."

"Why can't it last?"

"You're new in town, aren't you?"

"Yes, I moved here from San Francisco."

"Don't say that word."

"But you beat them."

"That was this time. What about the next time?"

And so it goes as the city of New Orleans collectively tries to cope with its negative mentality on a voyage into infrequently chartered waters—a fast start with wins over some of the NFL's elite, a ton of promise, talent-wise, and incredible national media attention.

Coping with success isn't an art Saints fans have had many chances to perfect. We are experts at dealing with disappointment, but that other stuff is as rare as, well, a 22-point fourth quarter. Right now, while everything is copacetic, the fans—like the team—are week-to-week, cautiously optimistic. It's fun to look down the road and think, "What if?" But it's also scary. It's intimidating.

"There's definitely an uneasiness," said Fred Koenig, professor emeritus of sociology at Tulane University and a man who knows quite a bit about crowd behavior. "You can sense it."

There are a lot of ways to look at what's happening before our very eyes, Koenig said. "In a lot of ways it's like the stock market when it was going up and up and you knew it couldn't last but how long would it? We've been through this before but this time I'm not sure what's going on. I left before the fourth quarter and at that time we couldn't stop anything the 49ers were running and Deuce McAllister was gaining about a yard a carry."

The fourth quarter, however, in no way resembled the third. "I'm thinking that this time it might be the real deal," he said. "This is such a contrast to last year—the morale of the team, the relationship between the players and the coach is different, this is a winning team and there don't seem to be any prima donnas or conflicts."

So?

"It's kind of like fear of heights. When you're on a pinnacle and you're looking down from farther up than you've been before . . . well, it's easy to be apprehensive. We've never been to the Super Bowl and the playoff record is not good . . ."

So?

"We don't want to get hurt all over again. We're still bruised from past years," he said.

So?

"So you could look at this whole phenomenon like the fear of flying. We're all up in the air about this. Pick your own metaphor."

Any other thoughts?

"Yes. How in the world did we lose to Detroit?" (Lind, 2002)

(Reprinted by permission of The Times–Picayune Publishing Corporation. All rights reserved.)

New York humorist and college professor David Blum (1990) depends on his friends for writing ideas. He wrote this light-hearted description of the process:

> One way I come up with ideas for columns is to bribe my friends. The arrangement I have worked out is this: If a friend comes up with a fully formed notion for a column that meets with my editor's approval, he (or she) gets a steak lunch at Sparks. The only restriction is that he may not make me feel bad by using witty euphemisms throughout the lunch, like "That was a tasty piece of cow flesh" or "I'm in the mood to do the horizontal hula." If a friend's idea leads me to a column but isn't an idea in itself, then he does not get the lunch. If the friend says something funny that I use in a column as my own joke, then I tell him I will buy him lunch, but when the check comes, I tell him that I'd had the same idea myself. (p. 30)

Funny writing often takes advantage of unusual and ordinary experiences that come from a variety of directions. Biagi (1981) said humor writing depends on a writer's ability to form images and word pictures, along with the surprise or unexpected finish or resolution of the story. The strategy keys on building up to the end by taking a small step at a time to tell the story, allowing momentum to grow. By using a combination of little jokes, she said, you can then break the punch line.

Wolfe (1990) suggested there are four elements in telling humorous stories used by humorists ranging from Mark Twain to Dave Barry. These elements are a funny opening, colorful narration, colorful characters, and a concise plot. Tom Ladwig (1987), writing for the daily *Columbia Missourian*, simply told a funny story and let situations in the story do the job. The story was based on a series of incidents involving a Missouri couple who took a trip filled with strange, but true incidents and coincidences. As Ladwig tells the story, it builds increasingly funny from the first step to the conclusion. And it is quite entertaining reading. His eye for a good story and his ability to retell it won Ladwig first place in the humorous column category of the National Newspaper Association writing contest. This is Ladwig's story:

> This story is intended for those among us who think we've had a bad day.
> It doesn't seem to have one whit of historical significance, but it is a story that probably will be told and retold.

Adam (not his real name) is a man of the cloth. He and his wife were missionaries for many years, and he now teaches in a bible college in southeast Missouri.

For the first time in many years, they have weekends free. To enjoy them more, Adam purchased a small pickup and had a camper shell installed. They explore the Ozarks and occasionally help a fellow minister when he needs a Sunday off.

They filled in for a colleague one Sunday last summer. They started home early Monday and passed one of those tourist attractions where you see all sorts of wild animals in a pseudo-natural setting.

It was early, and it seemed like fun so they drove in. After buying their tickets they saw all the animals they wanted to see from the safety of their pickup camper.

As they neared the end of the road, they found a huge elephant standing in the middle. Adam, a calm man, edged the truck closer. The elephant didn't budge. Adam edged closer.

Possibly patience and prayer would have worked better, but Adam honked. The elephant did move. It sat down, right on the hood of the truck.

The rear end of the camper went into the air and Adam, now in desperation, honked and honked. The proprietors came and sent the elephant keeper who finally convinced his charge to leave.

Of course the management arranged for the damage to be repaired and left Adam their business card with the insurance firm's telephone number. The motor still ran and Adam decided to limp home.

They had driven about 20 miles on the four-lane when they passed a wrecked car. Seeing there were other travelers assisting they drove on.

Four miles down the road, a highway patrol car approached and as it came abeam, wheeled across the median and flagged them down with siren and lights.

The trooper approached and told Adam he was investigating a hit-and-run accident a few miles back and asked Adam how his truck came to be damaged.

Adam said: "Officer, you're not going to believe this. An elephant sat on my hood." The trooper said: "You're right, I don't believe it. Get out."

It took a while for Adam's story to check out. The trooper, a 20-year veteran, still shaking his head in disbelief, told them they were free to go.

By this time Adam's head ached. He asked his wife to drive while he rested in the camper. They made good progress. Adam's wife made a rest stop at a service station. Adam awakened and decided this was a good idea.

When Adam returned he found the camper gone, his wife obviously thinking him still asleep in the camper. He walked to the highway and sat on the curb to plot his next move. While there, the same patrolman drove by. Seeing Adam, he stopped and asked: "What now?"

Adam explained. The trooper said he was going toward Adam's hometown and could drop him off. They took off and somehow arrived before Adam's wife and the pickup camper.

It was still daylight, and Adam, the keys to the house still in the truck, thanked the trooper and said he would just sit and wait.

It wasn't but a few minutes before Mrs. A turned into the drive.

As she approached the house, she caught sight of Adam waving from the porch. She jerked her head violently back toward the camper. And while in the position, her battered pickup slammed through the garage door.

Fortunately, Adam's wife was not injured. And nothing unusual happened to Adam and his wife for the remainder of that day. Or since for that matter. (Ladwig, 1987, p. 20)

(Reprinted with the permission of the *Columbia Missourian*.)

## THE BEST HUMOR WRITING TECHNIQUES

The market for humor is ready and waiting for copy such as Ladwig's story because it is entertaining and an escape for readers from their day-to-day concerns. The pay for humor writing is not so bad, either—some magazines pay $100 to $400 per item for brights and more for longer pieces. Topically, however, most publications do not want off-color or sexist humor. Taking shots at others, such as telling ethnic jokes, is not welcomed much by contemporary mainstream publications, either. So, a smart professional humor writer stays away from these out-of-favor subjects and approaches.

Humorist Patrick McManus (Finley, 1988), author of books and articles, offered four major tips for writing short (up to 1,500 words) humor. First, he said the idea should be covered by a single theme. Second, develop the characters in the story. Third, list the bits of humor—the jokes, in other words—you can fit into your prescribed length in words. And fourth, start writing and rewrite frequently. Concentrate on the lead because it is often the hardest part. However, McManus said you should make it funny to alert readers that the piece is funny.

The best humor writers employ a number of different tools when writing humor. These are most often in the form of satire, parody, exaggeration, contrast, understatement, asides, irony, grammatical and typographic emphasis, puns, and logic-internal consistency. These assist humor writers in achieving their goal of entertaining readers.

### Satire

Writers often ridicule a subject's vices, excesses, abuses, follies, or stupidities. This is satire. This form of criticism is perhaps one of the most widely used in contemporary humor writing. When someone prominent is caught in the act, perhaps drinking a little too much, using an illegal drug, or otherwise breaking the rules, and the story is reported in a serious way, it does not take long before humorists take the poor victim's mistakes as fair material for their writing. Satire often becomes the approach used to criticize a gun-toting leading citizen who takes a position for gun control, for example. Portraying the individual as using his weapon to protect himself against overly aggressive children who want their weekly allowances might get the point across.

Dave Barry often uses satire in his column. One recent example made fun of a recent literary trend. He poked fun at novels written by lawyers, such as those by John Grisham and Scott Turow, and the amazing popularity such "block-buster legal thrillers" enjoy. Barry not only satirizes the mystery genre, but he also takes shots at the people who read such books. His article was actually a mininovel satire structured as Grisham might write one of his books. Ultimately, Barry takes all attorneys to task for their inability to communicate effectively in writing. Barry (1993) produced his own "blockbuster legal thriller" for his loyal readers. Here is how it began:

> "Ohhhhhhh," she cried out. "OOOHMIGOD."
> "I'm sorry," I said, "but that's my standard hourly fee."
> Like most people, I can always use an extra $7 or $8 million, which is why today I have decided to write a blockbuster legal thriller.
> Americans buy legal thrillers by the ton. I was in many airports over the past few months, and I got the impression that aviation authorities were making this announcement over the public-address system: "FEDERAL REGULATIONS PROHIBIT YOU FROM BOARDING A PLANE UNLESS YOU ARE CARRYING THE CLIENT BY JOHN GRISHAM." I mean, everybody had this book. ("This is the captain speaking. We'll be landing in Seattle instead of Detroit because I want to finish The Client.")
> The ironic thing is that best-selling legal thrillers generally are written by lawyers, who are not famous for written communication. I cite as Exhibit A my own attorney, Joseph DiGiacinto, who is constantly providing me with shrewd advice that I cannot understand because Joe has taken the legal precaution of translating it into Martian. (Barry, 1993, p. 27)

Barry also uses satire in his account of a lunch date with Sophia Loren. It is a classic Barry treatment that his readers love so much. Barry got to take this peek at the world of the rich and famous and, of course, told his readers about it in his unique style. He uses satire—he makes fun of himself by writing that he was "working" when he lunched with the movie star (and a lot of other people). He satirizes the lifestyle of the luxury residential complex that the luncheon event and the actress promoted. He pokes fun at the free food and champagne, the high prices of the exclusive apartments, the press kit descriptions, and even the eager and fawning press itself. When it comes time for him to ask the legendary actress a question, he asks her about cockroaches in her own luxury apartment at the complex. Here's Barry's (1986) article:

> My original plan was not to have lunch with Sophia Loren. My original plan was to eat a chicken salad sandwich, then go pick up my son at kindergarten. In fact, I had actually purchased the chicken salad sandwich at *The Miami Herald* cafeteria when a person in the Business Section asked me if I wanted to have lunch with Sophia Loren. "Sure," I said. This kind of thing happens all the time in the news game.
> So I called my wife. "Could you pick up Robby?" I asked. "I'm going to go have lunch with Sophia Loren."

"Sure," she said, in a sweet and kind and totally understanding voice. She will get even.

The reason I was invited to lunch with Sophia Loren was that she was promoting something. Somebody is always promoting something in the news business, and it is our job, as communications professionals, to go and find out what it is, even if this means eating a lot of free food. In this case, Sophia Loren was promoting something up in North Dade called "Williams Island," which, according to the press packet, is "a luxury, 80-acre island resort residence community on protected waters just off the Intracoastal Waterway." It's very nice. I would recommend Williams Island as a potential residence for anybody, whether he had $250 million or just $245 million.

No, seriously, the brochure says they have "residential offerings" there starting at a very affordable $180,000, which I bet you could round up just by walking around and picking up the money that blows off the balconies of the nicer units. One of those units is occupied, when she's in town, by world-famous raving-beauty movie actress Sophia Loren, who also does promotional work for them in exchange for money. (Yes! Even Sophia Loren!)

We had lunch at the restaurant on Williams Island, the Island Club. They have a new kind of Very Trendy food there called "tapas," which also was being promoted. According to Richard Lamondin, director of marketing and sales for Williams Island, "The Tapas Experience is now one of the North American rages."

So we media people all sat down at our assigned tables and had the Tapas Experience, which consists of eating things off little plates. I thought they were great, except this one plate that I swear to God had a small dead octopus on it. Probably it was a prank. Probably back in the kitchen, they said: "Look what Lester found in the protected waters just off the Intracoastal Waterway! Yuck! Let's see if the news media will eat it, because it's free food!"

After the Tapas Experience, they served us lamb chops, during which Sophia Loren herself came over to our table and sat down to chat with us personally. You ladies have heard, of course, that Sophia Loren is very, very beautiful, especially for a woman of 51, but let me tell you something: When she is up close, when you really get a look at her, she is Beyond Perfect. I'm sorry, ladies, but there you have it. Genetics. If it makes you feel any better, there is probably some area in which you are superior to Sophia Loren, such as playing the accordion.

So after we had just looked at her for a minute, we asked her some questions. This is where I would hate to be a famous movie actress, because she got asked, for example: "Is there any message you would want to give to the women of the world?" Think about that. There you are, trying to eat your lamb chop, and you have to come up with a message for the women of the world. I know if it was me, I'd blow it. I'd say something like, "Well, they should floss their teeth." But Sophia Loren, she was very poised. She said she felt the women of the world should be Generous. She came up with that right off the top of her head.

I had given careful thought to what question I would ask her. I wanted it to be the kind of question you, my readers, would want to ask in the astoundingly unlikely event you ever had a personal lunch with Sophia Loren.

"Have you found any large insects in your apartment?" I asked.

"Insects?" she said.

"Cockroaches," I said. "They get huge down here." I held my hands about a foot apart so she'd get the idea.

"Not yet," she said.

So there you have it: an exclusive interview with the lovely Miss Sophia Loren at her South Florida residence, the luxurious and cockroach-free Williams Island. If you want my opinion, you all should head over there as soon as possible and try the tapas and maybe purchase yourself a residence offering. And I don't say this just because they gave me a lot of free food. I say this because they also gave me champagne. (Barry, 1986 p. 1B)

(Reprinted with permission of Dave Barry.)

## HOW HUMOR COLUMNISTS MAKE HUMOR WORK

Bowling Green State University journalism professor F. Dennis Hale (1999) has analyzed the techniques of the nation's most successful humor columnists. Hale determined that there are 10 primary devices and techniques:

1. Exaggeration.
2. Understatement.
3. Long lists.
4. Short lists.
5. Surprise.
6. Life's little problems.
7. Humor in the news.
8. Constructing a comic reality.
9. Attractive beginnings and endings.
10. Puns and word play.

### Parody

Parody is another one of the trendy humor approaches today. Subjects vary widely, but parodies are popular with contemporary readers. Parody is the best approach for some humor. At times, there is an opportunity to imitate the style of an individual, place, object, or institution. This is basic parody. To do parody well, you must study the subject about which you plan to write. Popular subjects in recent years have been preppies, yuppies, entire publications such as magazines, and various ethnic groups. Once you have mastered the characteristic style of the subject, you take a nonsensical approach to it. This works best with serious subjects such as political leaders or revered institutions. For example, a local humor columnist might use parody to write about a local public official that made a bad political decision or squandered public resources. *National Lampoon* and *Mad* magazines have used parodies for many years with great success.

*Ocean Drive* magazine staff writer Suzy Buckley (2002) took a fun approach to parody the 20-somethings' search for the perfect mate in a recent article about the stereotypical men and women found along the famed Ocean Drive and Washington Avenue in Miami Beach's South Beach area. She highlighted six types—the never-good-enough girl, the mooching man, the M.I.P. (made in Prada) girl, the hayseed model, the go-go boy, and the Latin playboy. Her piece, timed for around Valentine's Day, was a tongue-in-cheek guide for readers to identify and connect with "the perfect Miami mate." Buckley said the trendy magazine's readers reacted very positively to the how-to piece that was published with color illustrations and listed descriptions of each type of person. "I had the best response from that article," Buckley (personal communication, September 4, 2002) recalled. "People still come up to me to tell me that they liked it. . . . It is one of my favorite articles." Here's how she started her article:

> Tossing friends, neighbors and innocent bystanders into a handful of clichéd categories is nothing but a cheap shot. It's rude, shallow, insensitive—and so much fun! The city's average citizen is nowhere near as unique, special and one-in-a-million as you, so learn to spot a South Beach stereotype before you date one. But remember, you can't go around labeling people—unless they deserve it.
>
> THE NEVER-GOOD-ENOUGH GIRL
>
> Mommy and Daddy subsidize the rent on her hip, overpriced luxury apartment, which explains all those $900 handbags and $350 haircuts. She'll have you know she's an otherwise entirely self-sustained professional with an Ivy League-*ish* education, an important family business back in New York, and every pair of fashionably significant Jimmy Choos since 1996. She could have stayed in Manhattan, if that problematic male–female ratio hadn't thwarted the game plan. See, it wasn't going to be like this. She was never supposed to have to actually *take* the bar exam after law school: Those exciting postgraduate months were originally set aside for wedding planning and world travels, not hunting for a one-bedroom condo and an 8-to-6 job. Help Never-Good-Enough Girl get her nice little life back on track: If you're into fine dining ("When you said Hiro's, you meant Nobu, right?"), fabulous vacations ("St. Barth is a little proximal, don't' you think? This year is all about the Seychelles" and hobbies such as retailing, remodeling and ring-shopping, then this one's for you.
>
> THE MOOCH MAN
>
> Why make a proper dinner reservation when you can make a beeline to the open bar and free hors d'oeuvres? This makes sense to Mooch Man. . . . (Buckley, 2002, p. 252)

## Exaggeration

In telling funny stories, a useful technique is exaggeration—to enlarge, distort, and overemphasize to make a point. Although the size of the cockroach on your kitchen table might not be quite equal to that of your Irish Setter, it makes the point better when you stretch the fact a little. This emphasizes your perspective and conveys to readers that the insect in your kitchen really did scare you into jumping onto a chair and causing you to cry out for help. Remember that when you make a point using a technique like exaggeration, you make a promise with readers to have a reason for it. Exaggeration and overstatement for nothing more than the purpose of overstating often do not work.

Connie Willis writes humor as an award-winning science fiction author. It might sound like an odd combination, but she uses the same techniques as nonfiction humor writers. One of her favorite tools is exaggeration, a tool she calls "the cornerstone of comedy" (Willis, 1996, p. 32). She said to use exaggeration, writers must start with the truth. "You must know when to stop, because bigger and wilder and more ridiculous aren't necessarily funnier," Willis wrote (1996, p. 33).

Exaggeration can be used on yourself as a subject also. Writer William P. Holton (1993) took himself to task for his bad work habits. He amusingly described in a column for *Writer's Digest* how he made up answers "that stretch the truth" when his wife would call him from her job to ask how his writing at his home office was going (p. 6). Rather than tell her the truth about his writer's block, how he had not managed to finish (or even start) his household chores, and how he had nothing to show for a day's effort, he made his effort seem like more than it was. He used a "What I say" and "What I'm actually doing" approach. Here are three examples of his technique:

> What I say: *I'm cleaning up a few odds and ends.*
> What I'm actually doing: *Disassembling my five-box paper-clip chain because I want to try my hand at the tricky, tri-clip braid.*
> What I say: *I'm conducting some research.*
> What I'm actually doing: *Flipping the dial between* Donahue, Oprah, *and* Geraldo.
> What I say: *I'm just finishing up a chapter.*
> What I'm actually doing: *I'm three quarters of the way through the latest Stephen King opus.* (Holton, 1993, p. 6)

*Minneapolis Star Tribune* humor columnist James Lileks (2002) uses a variety of techniques in his humor columns for the newspaper and for the online editions of the column. He calls his space the "Backfence." He also moderates a talk corner for the online edition of the newspaper. He recently wrote about his role as a father and his experiences with his young daughter in a portion of one of his online columns. Other parts are entertaining dialogues with readers. Exaggeration takes a significant role in the essay:

> Blurgghh. (Cough)
> I'll explain.
> First, an apology. Sorry about that long Fenceless interlude; couldn't be helped. My wife was out of town on business, so I stayed at home with Little Miss

Adorable. She's in the whatzdat phase, where Daddy is expected to identify every object in the world. Eventually you realize she's just pointing out the car window at random and testing you, so you're free to improvise.

Daddee whas dat? That's a proton. Daddee whas dat? It's a Bolshevik, honey. Daddee whas dat? It's a store that sells beer, sweetheart. Cold, pure, lovely, beer. Daddy is going to have one when you go to sleep. If you go to sleep. Ever. Daddee whas dat? That's Jasper Dog, honey. You know Jasper. He has an itchy butt. Yes, he does. Thas funny. Whas dat on Teevee? That's a North Korean auto-crat. Oh. Why? Because he has nuclear weapons. Why? Because humankind is sinful and wracked with fatal ambitions, dear. Watch Elmo? Sure.

Six days of that, 13 hours a day. Wouldn't trade it for the world. While I'd love to say I spent the last week trading Backfence duties for a vacation in some exotic locale, I was doing my best to fulfill the parental prime directive: When the other parent returns from a long trip away, the child should be in good working condi-tion, and should have all extremities intact.

So now what? Don't ask me. I'm sick. I woke up at 5 a.m. in a fever dream, shouting something about Iranian plastic vegetables. The KIND YOU CAN CUT IN HALF! The fever has abated, but I still have a head full of dryer lint, and there are strange aches running up and down my legs and back, as though I am being tortured by some extremely timid interrogators. Oh, you refuse to talk? I will add another C-cell to the prod, then, and wave it in a threatening fashion over your knees! This is the flu, and it's the flu that everyone at *Star Tribune* World HQ seems to have. If tomorrow your paper says WHATEVER for all the headlines, and the stories read "Sniper, blah, blah, police stumped, blah, the end," you'll know why; this place is full of wheezing zombies a half-step from the morgue slab. The guy a few desks over sounds as if he's coughing up loofahs.

## Contrast

Contrast can also be described as incongruity. In using contrast, you establish a lack of harmony with the world; you show unreasonable and unsuitable situa-tions. There are times when something that is expected and routine becomes something completely unexpected and nonroutine. For example, a story about a business trip that was well planned with hotel and rental car reservations, air-line bookings, and other details turns into a series of humorous situations when the realities of the trip begin. These include an airline strike, a rental car break-down, hotel reservations denied by a clerk, and just plain bad timing (for exam-ple, you finally arrive at the hotel at 11:15 p.m., hungry and tired, but find out that room service closed at 11 p.m.).

## Understatement

Just like exaggeration, understatement works to create emphasis and reaction on the part of the reader. An intentional, softer comment will draw attention when it is contrasted with the expected. If, for example, you were referring to the real summer heat that the local readers know was 98°F with 80% humidity by saying, "It was a little warm outside yesterday," then you have understated the case dramatically and no doubt drawn a reaction from your reader.

Novelist Connie Willis feels understatement is as important as exaggeration in creating humor. And you can use them together, she believes. "Don't get the idea you must choose one or the other," Willis (1996, p. 33) wrote. "Humor is not a decision between More or Less. (Mark) Twain often uses understatement and exaggeration in the same sentence" (Willis, 1996, p. 33). The concern of writers, she noted, is when to use one or the other. Every author, she observed, seems to use them differently. "Things are already funny; you're simply using exaggeration and understatement and whatever else to bring out the humor that was already there" (Willis, 1996, p. 33).

## Asides

Many humor writers like to use asides—short messages in parentheses or other form—to communicate with readers on a quasi-private level. This is a technique often used in acting that permits the actor to communicate only with the audience. In writing, humorists who use asides are attempting the same technique as if to privately communicate with you (and not the book's editor). Did you notice? The previous sentence contained an aside. You don't have to use parentheses all the time. Some writers prefer dashes "—" or other typographic devices to accomplish the same thing. Some writers will even use footnotes for the same effect. Dave Barry is one contemporary humorist who likes to use asides in his writing.

## Irony

Similar to contrast, irony is a technique that employs contradictions through writing tone and subject. Irony focuses on the direct opposite of what is usual or expected. The outcome of the story is different from what is expected by readers. The distance between what happened and what should have happened or what is said and what is intended is irony. Writers using irony set up the story by leading the reader to expect one type of finish through a combination of circumstances or steps involving the principals of the story. Then the reader is stunned by the opposite or inappropriate conclusion of the episode. This technique is used often in writing short humorous items known as brights.

## Grammatical and Typographic Emphasis

Some writers make points in their humor writing by intentionally overusing and abusing English grammar or typography. One such technique is overuse of exclamation marks (e.g., multiple exclamation marks after a word in the middle of a sentence or a string of typographic symbols such as "*@!©!#$%&!!@" to represent bad or strong language). Another is capitalizing improper nouns (e.g., a term such as Campaign Trail) used in generic references rather than specific contexts. These tricks draw reader attention to certain words and terms in an extreme fashion and help place focus where the writer wants it. Other humor writers intentionally invent words or new usages of existing words when they cannot find the right word to express their feelings or actions (e.g., the seemingly endless different ways that the characters in the film "Wayne's World" referred to what doctors commonly call "regurgitation"). These diversions from the ordinary uses of grammar are functional and help the writer as he or she tells the story.

## Puns

For many centuries, humor writers have used puns for a good laugh from readers. In recent years, it seems, puns have gained a bad reputation. It seems that some writers (and readers, too) feel puns are categorically bad. However, this is not the case; the use of puns may be the problem. Much of the value of the pun is in its use. A pun is a writer's device that uses plays on words to provide double meaning. One common use of puns by some contemporary humorists is in references to sex. No doubt you can think of countless puns you encounter in everyday conversation, reading, and your own writing.

## Logic and Consistency

Logic is the science of correct reasoning and valid thought. Logic involves correct reasoning through induction or deduction. Some successful humor is based on its internal logic. Crazy behavior and absurd conduct by people make up much of modern American humor. But after everything else, the humorous story must maintain its internal logic. One way to do this is to begin a story with an absurd premise and keep that premise throughout the story as it is told. Related to that is internal consistency. Changing the focus in the middle of a story will often hurt it more than help it. Wolfe (1990) called internal logic and consistency two of the major building blocks of humor writing.

*Other Humor Writing Techniques.*    There are other techniques that humor writers use. For example, Art Buchwald likes to use dialogue in his columns, creating fictitious conversations that might have occurred. Dave Barry also uses conversations frequently. In fact, most humorists find dialogue to be an essential device for their writing and use it often.

Screenwriter and film director Noah Baumbach (2002) recently wrote an amusing essay for *The New Yorker* about his relationships with women in the form of a series of brief reviews of Manhattan restaurants. Taking the reader through each restaurant, he tells us about how each one is best-suited for a particular stage of a relationship. Here's how he began his piece:

AASE'S Bring a "first date" to this "postage stamp"-size bistro. Tables are so close you're practically "sitting in the laps" of the couple next to you, but the lush décor is "the color of love." Discuss your respective "dysfunctional families" and tell her one of your "fail-safe" stories about your father's "cheapness" and you're certain to "get a laugh." After the "to die for" soufflés, expect a good-night kiss, but don't push for more, because if you play your cards right there's a second date "right around the corner."

BRASSERIE PENELOPE "Ambience and then some" at this Jamaican–Norwegian hybrid. Service might be a "tad cool," but the warmth you feel when you gaze into her baby blues will more than compensate for it. Conversation is "spicier than the jerk chicken," and before you know it you'll be back at her one-bedroom in the East Village, quite possibly "getting lucky."

THE CHICK & HEN Perfect for breakfast "after sleeping together," with "killer coffee" that will "help cure your seven-beer/three-aquavit hangover." Not that you need it—your "amplified high spirits" after having had sex for the first time in "eight months" should do the trick.

DESARCINA'S So what if she thought the movie was "pretentious and contrived" and you felt it was a "masterpiece" and are dying to inform her that "she doesn't know what she's talking about"? Remember, you were looking for a woman who wouldn't "yes" you all the time. And after one bite of chef Leonard Desarcina's "duck manqué" and a sip of the "generous" gin Margaritas you'll start to see that she might have a point. . . . (N. Baumbach, 2002, p. 74)

## BRIGHTS, QUIPS, AND OTHER SHORT ITEMS

Much humor published in U.S. newspapers, magazines, and newsletters takes the form of short, brief stories that fit in various places throughout the publication. Some newspapers like to run front-page one-line chuckles or quips and editorial page one-paragraph funny stories. Other publications incorporate such short humorous material into regular news or columns. These are collectively referred to as brights.

Some publications simply use these funny feature articles as fill material when it is needed to complete a page or fill a specific space. Magazines, such as *Reader's Digest,* use regular humor features that are collections of brights about different aspects of daily life. And they're very popular. Research at *Reader's Digest* shows these sections are among the most popular in the entire magazine. They can be lucrative also; *Reader's Digest* pays up to $300 for brights and other published short articles. These brights are typically amusing stories that offer, as Williamson (1975) defined them, "a humorous and unusual quirk" (p. 117). These items can come from reporters on the police beat, the courts, meetings, or from callers.

Alexander (1975) said the main purpose of a bright is "to change the pace and tone of the newspaper, the magazine, or the broadcast. Being so short, a bright makes fine filler, fits anywhere to complete a page, round out the makeup of a section or fill out a broadcast. And in this process, brights accomplish their main purpose: they provide variety" (p. 30).

Quips are similar, just shorter. Quips use word play, such as puns, to get attention and reader reaction. Selma Glasser (1990), a freelance writer and book author who has published many shorter humorous items in national publications such as *Reader's Digest* and *Good Housekeeping,* said quips are an easy way to get published. "I give simple words or phrases new sparkle, variety, energy, and meaning. Timely subjects act as dynamic idea generators, recognizable because of their relevance to topics of the day. Just being alert and observant can pay off" (p. 16). Here's an example: Glasser sold the three-word line "Need anything colorized?" to "Dennis the Menace" cartoonist Hank Ketchum, who produced a cartoon showing the boy with his crayons asking that question of his mother. Quips and brights can be a gold mine for writers, Glasser (1992) believed. "The only qualifications are alertness, perseverance, and adaptability. The words are all in the dictionary. It's how we choose to 'doctor them up' that counts" (Glasser, 1992, p. 19). "Be alert and ready to jot down inspirations. You can add your own touches, a new title, or interpretations later" (Glasser, 1992, p. 19).

Author and comedy writer Gene Perret (1987) said writing these short humorous anecdotes is easy and takes little time. It is quick writing, it is fun and a challenge, he argued. Brights are particularly popular with the news services, which use them for both the newspaper wires and the broadcast wires. They are then used by editors, radio announcers, or television anchors as counterpoints to the day's usually serious news. The writing style dictates that these items remain brief, using the most concise writing. People and places cannot be thoroughly described or themes developed in detail. The usual bright is a couple of sentences to a couple of paragraphs in length. Usually, this means fewer than 50 words, but no more than 300 words.

With such short, funny items, structure is important. Brief and to the point leads work best for brights. They must be terse. They should be fast moving and skeleton-like. Many briefs are written in inverted pyramid form, but some stories lend themselves to chronological writing. A strong lead and an even-stronger ending dominate the structure. The best material goes last. There should be an unexpected outcome, a surprise finish. If readers expect one sort of resolution, the bright strikes them as funny because it does the opposite.

### Submitting Brights for Publication

Perret (1984), who has written humor for Bob Hope and Carol Burnett, recommended three rules for submitting short humorous anecdotes, quips, and other similar material for publication:

1. Send your submissions in batches–No less than five should be in each envelope you send, although you can submit as many as a dozen each time. Giving the editor a few to read through each time helps your percentages.
2. Send each anecdote on a separate page–On each sheet, include your name, address, phone number and Social Security number (the last will help speed payment).
3. Neatly prepare all submissions–Don't cut corners because it's "only" an anecdote. Be professional. Buyers don't want to read through handwritten or messy submissions. Make sure your printer has a new ribbon and double-space submissions for easier editing. The usual SASE [self-addressed, stamped envelope] is not required because most periodicals don't acknowledge these submissions except when and if they send an acceptance check.

Brights have a "twist," as some humor writers explain them. This twist is the uncommon point of the story, the writer's statement about human nature. Alexander (1975) described the main characteristics of brights:

1. They make fun of human nature and human errors.
2. They must have a news peg (be about someone and be recent).
3. The situation should be unusual.
4. They must be cleverly written.
5. The item should end with a punch line.
6. There should be good transition elements.

Some brights do not have a punch line finish. Brights without a punch line must leave readers wondering why something happened, who was involved, or simply what happened. This is usually a finish forced on writers because no resolution is available. For example, did the man ever get his keys out of the car? Did the child get the ink off her face? Did the student pay the overdue book fine?

Finding brights is easy, Perret (1987) said. His advice is to review your own personal stories, to trade stories at gatherings, read a great deal and remember what you read, stay aware of what is going on in your community, and be alert of what is happening around you. Brights, it should be added, should not be written with the solution in the lead. This spoils the effect for readers and destroys the value of the item. A well thought-out bright holds its best for last. In addition, Alexander (1975) recommended avoiding the inverted pyramid structure in writing briefs. You write a brief much like you tell a joke. Not all brights have to be funny. If brights are not going to bring a laugh, they should draw out sympathy or another emotion. They can draw their reaction from the reader's intellect. Brights are not always time-bound. Some editors compile them for use in columns and other regular features. The entertainment value of brights is more important than the time element, yet a timely bright is even more valuable when it is available.

Perret (1987) recommended another approach—writing the bright backwards. Begin with the ending when you write, then build toward that ending and be compact. The beginning, he advised, should be "a short explanation of why you're telling this story" (p. 29). The good bright writer is also a good reporter. The funny story, as tempting as it may be, cannot invent facts or even stretch them for the effect the stretching might bring. Stick to the facts; good reporting helps get the facts right.

*Reader's Digest,* founded in 1921, was the third-largest magazine in the United States with a circulation of 12.2 million copies a month in 2002. Editors publish several dozen brights each month. In *Reader's Digest,* potential contributors are invited to submit material for sections such as "Humor in Uniform," "All in a Day's Work," "Life in These United States," and "Laughter, the Best Medicine." Some contributions are purely descriptive–narrative form and others are narrative with dialog woven into it. The magazine also accepts contributions through its Web site. Here is a sample from "Life in These United States":

> A buddy of mine, Mike, had season tickets to the Detroit Lions football games. Last year they had such a miserable record that he couldn't give away two tickets to a game he wasn't able to attend. While parking at a mall, he decided to leave his tickets under a windshield wiper.
>
> "And that worked?" I asked.
>
> "Not exactly," said Mike. "I returned to find six more tickets to the same game." (Fromm, 2002, p. 214)

Here is another sample from "Humor in Uniform:"

> When my father was in boot camp, the troops were instructed to put their belongings in their footlockers, write their last names and first initials on the containers, and report back for inspection.
>
> A few minutes later the commanding officer, having seen my father's locker emblazoned with his last name "Locke" followed by his first initial "R," furiously bellowed, "Okay, who's the wise guy?" (Locke, 2002, p. 62)

> Everyone's got a funny story. Just send us yours, and if we publish it in *Reader's Digest,* you'll be laughing all the way to the bank. Here's how it works: We pay $300 for true, never-before-published stories we publish in Life in These United States, All in a Day's Work, or Humor in Uniform. We pay $100 for the first submission of a previously published or original item we print in Laughter, the Best Medicine; in Quotable Quotes; or as a short item used at the end of an article (Go Ahead: Make Us Laugh, 2002, p. 12)

Readers are also advised in each issue what editors look for because many contributors are magazine readers as well as professional feature writers. The maximum length is 100 words.

Does the bright about the football tickets achieve its goals? Structurally, yes. It sets the situation up and then delivers a surprise ending that may bring a smile to a reader's face. It contains description, but not overwritten description. The scene is set in a very few concise, but clear sentences. What about the locker bright? Did you get the joke? It is more subtle, but still saves the catch-line for the ending statement. Both work well and should bring a smile to a reader's face.

## HUMOR COLUMNS

Humor columns are regular efforts and a challenge to any writer. The requirements of columns force writers to prepare for standard length (800 to 1,000 words, typically) and regular frequency (some are weekly, some twice a week, and so forth). Truly creative people can be funny on demand, but the challenge of humor columns is to be able to draw on that point of view and talent consistently. A number of people have done this successfully and have attracted large national and international followings.

Dave Barry is one humor writing success story. The Coral Gables, FL-based writer is the source of weekly columns distributed by Tribune Media Services. Barry has been on the staff of *The Miami Herald* since 1983, when he moved from a small daily in West Chester, PA, to join the staff of *The Herald's* Sunday *Tropic* magazine and the lifestyles and features department. Although he continues to write on assignments for the newspaper, he devotes much of his time and attention to his humor column. His numerous humor books fill a library or bookstore shelf and he has recently begun to write humorous fiction. His success is based on real-life humor and a writing style that is unique and entertaining. For some writers, winning a Pulitzer Prize for commentary may be a zenith of a long career, but not for Dave Barry. When he was awarded the prize in 1988, he simply used it as a platform on which to explore new subjects, writing approaches, and even writing forms. He has found new opportunities with his entry into writing a series of humorous novels that began with *Big Trouble*. He writes about politics when his newspaper assigns him to cover the national political conventions or political campaigns. He writes sports when his newspaper sends him to a Final Four or an Olympics Games. He is not afraid to take on the conventional and the unconventional. And he occasionally writes serious and contemplative content for his newspaper, exemplified by a somber 1-year anniversary essay about the heroes on the jet airliner that crashed into a field in Pennsylvania on September 11, 2001. Barry is also in demand as a speaker and entertainer. He sees his work as purely entertainment and often makes appearances on television, radio, and the corporate and campus lecture circuits.

Art Buchwald's 40 years of political satire columns are examples of success at humor column writing. Buchwald's humor focuses on big government but is not inappropriate for family consumption. The column on frequent flyer programs is just one example of this approach. Buchwald writes a regular column 3 days a week. Buchwald's ability to regularly produce amusing material is rare. What is funny varies, depending on the reader, so Buchwald said he writes to please himself. He said he likes to laugh at his own material and tries not to think whether a reader will think it is funny. Although many humorists are syndicated and write from an independent base—such as Buchwald—major newspapers and magazines often have a humor columnist on staff. The most popular humorists have become syndicated and their followings have grown from regional to the national and even an international level.

For almost 7 years, William Geist wrote real-life humor for *The New York Times*. Before that, he wrote a column for *The Chicago Tribune*. Although he has moved on to write books and to write and produce humorous segments for the *CBS News Sunday Morning* program, he still writes about the people, the environment, the scenery around him, and the most commonplace activities he experiences. He looks for ideas in his own neighborhood. Geist explained he finds material for his regular regimen of writing in this manner: "I always look for a story where there's a conflicting sense of values or ethnic groups, or anything where something doesn't fit, is out of whack, in order to get insights on what people are really like" (Spielmann, 1988, p. 30). Here is an example: Geist focused on class conflict when he wrote about "driveway dress codes" in suburbia—all brought about by a New Jersey community's ordinance preventing certain vehicles (e.g., service trucks) from being parked in driveways overnight (Spielmann, 1988, p. 30).

## THE DIFFICULTIES OF HUMOR WRITING

It is worthwhile to remind you that humor writing is not easy. Most professional humorists agree and are often frustrated to even attempt to describe how they do it or how you should do it. Some say it cannot be taught. Here's how *Writer's Digest* columnist Spikol (1986c) summed up writing humor:

> It's hard to write humor. I can teach any half-decent writer to write a salable magazine article, but I can't teach anyone to write funny. That ability really comes from an inner voice, and that inner voice may not necessarily be there when you need it. After a few years of developing the muscle, you'll be able to flex it at will—but you'll never get that far if you're not somebody who thinks funny to begin with. (p. 18)

Spikol is right. You need that certain unusual perspective on life to write quality humor. And you need a mind for it, as well—you must know your market and what makes it tick. If you write for a general audience, as most newspaper writers do, then you have a different humor challenge from those who write for specialized magazines. Those who write humor for specialized magazines know the "inside" issues and concerns in which inside jokes can be built. Humor is not, as Spikol said, written in a vacuum.

There is no substitute for grand creativity. A very imaginative individual has an edge in writing humor. Former *Miami Herald* reporter Stephen Doig's inspired April Fool's Day hoax displays this sort of approach. His story told readers that pigeon and snipe hunters had found a cache of weapons in the Everglades area west of Miami. The story was laced with hints, such as trick names and deliberate typographic errors (such as FBI spelled FIB), that it was a joke and sharp-eyed readers saw them. This was his lead:

> A couple of serious hunters who spotted a light flashing Morse code in the Everglades early this morning stumbled onto a cache of arms worth at least $411,987, according to puzzled authorities. (Doig, 1987, p. 1B)

The suggestion that pigeons and snipe were involved should have tipped off some readers. Another hint is in the amount of money. Did you notice that it is really the date? Topically, the hoax was perfect for South Florida readers at the time because the ruse involved possible drug smuggling, weapons, and the mysterious, swampy Everglades. The subject and presentation as a "straight" news story on the front of the local section misdirected readers into thinking the story was serious news. For those who read the story but did not catch on, the newspaper ran a second story the following day that explained the little April Fool's joke (Every fool, 1987). Doig's (1987) genius in creating this article with its numerous tricks and other devices made the article a success. It was amusing, entertaining, and clever. Readers appreciate such efforts and respond.

Although well-known humor writers get the best publication breaks, it is not impossible for you. You might want to start at a low-pressure level by writing humor when you are inspired to be funny. By writing infrequently and thinking small in the beginning, you gain confidence one step at a time. Small newspapers, such as your community or neighborhood weeklies, and small magazines or newsletters are easier markets to crack. Dave Barry and Art Buchwald did not become successful overnight. Their careers developed slowly and methodically from local levels into national superstar levels.

Once success as a humor writer is achieved, it must be maintained through hard work. Inspiration, as Dave Barry told *Writer's Digest* writer Marshall Cook (1987), is not enough if you make a living off the writing. "I write seven days a week," Barry said (Cook, 1987, p. 29). "If I don't write, I feel guilty. There's real work out there, and I'm not doing it. The least I can do is write" (Cook, 1987, p. 29).

## A HUMORIST'S VIEW OF FEATURE WRITING

San Francisco Bay area humorist Alice Kahn (personal communication, October 17, 1988) likes to joke around when it comes to writing humor. She has written numerous books and newspaper columns based on her sarcastic views of daily life on California's West Coast. She is a highly quotable and memorable writer. But as she does, she has lots of sound advice:

I am often asked: "Alice, how can I join the exciting and glamorous world of article writing and hardly work at all and make tons of money?" There are several foolproof methods of achieving this goal. The most common are the sleaze dig, the trend invention and the integrity-ectomy. Let me give you an example of each.

Recently a young woman called me and asked if she could interview me for a paper she was writing for her journalism class. It was a profile of John Raeside, editor of the *East Bay Express*, the paper where I got my break. She asked me many probing and interesting questions about the influence of Raeside on my *oeuvre*. I was only too happy to go on at length about how much my old editor had encouraged me, how lucky I have been to work with supportive editors, the importance of including the writer in the editing process, etc. Obviously, time had glossed over whatever battles we had had, because I couldn't recall a single fault in my former editor other than his being born with the genetic defect of frugality.

After she asked me about Raeside's particular qualities, we got to the hidden agenda. "How long have you known him?" she asked. "About six years," I answered.

And, lifting her shovel for the sleaze dig, she said, "And did you have what we might call a personal relationship?" "Are you asking if I slept with him?" "Just trying to dig something up," she said.

Now, I could understand, if she were interviewing me in person, how she might think a swell-looking babe like me would have no other way of succeeding than by sleeping with editors. But this was a phone interview. I don't know what they're teaching them in journalism schools these days, but they'd better get one thing straight: "Bay Area Writer Sleeps with Editor" is not going to have the same market potential as "Liz Taylor Found in Pat Robertson's Love Nest."

Within hours of my conversation with the student journalist, I got a call from an experienced writer who is on the staff of a major metropolitan newspaper. She asked me if I could give her some "quotes" for a story she was doing. You see, she was on deadline, so she didn't want to have a discussion. Just gimme some quotes and keep your stinkin' ideas to yourself. She said she was writing something about yuppie despair. She had a major trend going. That is, she had three yuppies that were willing to be desperate—on the record. Now she needed something from me as an expert on yuppies. I had written three articles on yuppies. I was an expert. I said three things. Those became three quotes. A trend was born.

When the final call of the day came, I realized I needn't write any more. I could just fill requests. The person wanted to know what I thought of something or other. He was writing an article that consisted of nothing more than calling up other people and asking them what they think of something or other. He didn't even have the integrity to dream up a trend or fantasize someone's weird sex life.

Now, we here at The Alice Kahn Column consider ourselves a full-service agency. We are only too happy to oblige the readers by providing them with further information about the important subjects covered in this column. But I am serving notice on all writers of articles in search of a point that if you want me to pop open your idea, it's gonna cost you. Henceforth, a 10% surcharge will be added to your bill for intellectual corkage. (Kahn, personal communication, October 17, 1988)

# CHAPTER SIXTEEN

# Writing Science and
# Technical Features

Feature writers who focus their work on science and technology have the opportunity to write about some of the most exciting times in world history, but they also face the challenge of making difficult subject matter understandable. Each year, there are stunning advances in science and technology. Think about the newest developments in medicine. Cloning, once a dream of science fiction writers, is now a daily reality in animal science research. Its impact on agriculture and other areas of our lives grows daily. Exploration of space still seems exotic, but people other than astronauts are now entering space and routine life on Earth changes regularly in subtle ways because of space exploration. Examples such as these increase in number each year.

There are many stories to be written that will help the "gee-whiz" world of science and technology make sense. The stories must be accurate, but also informative, interesting, and entertaining. The national Council for the Advancement of Science Writing (2003) noted the importance of this type of writing:

> Science writers not only must meet daily challenges of accurately translating the often arcane and complex news of such discoveries into lay language. In many cases, their reporting must also attempt to objectively put those discoveries into historical, personal, political, economic, and social context. For example, while science writers have traditionally been faced with balancing the conflicting opinions of scientific experts, they must now include the influence of potential financial implications of scientific discoveries in their reporting equations, especially in biotechnology.
>
> Reporting new developments in science and medicine to the general public can be one of the most exciting and fascinating "beats" on any newspaper, radio or television station. Unlike reporters on other assignments, the science reporter seldom writes the same story twice. Just as each scientific development is a discovery of something the scientists had not known before, each science story is about something neither the reporter nor his/her reader knew before. Science reporters cover some of the most momentous events in human history. Science reporters were the first to tell the public of the splitting of the uranium atom and of the consequent explosion of the first atomic bomb.
>
> Science reporters also covered the discovery of antibiotic "wonder drugs," the first human heart transplant, the launchings of the first artificial satellites, the dis-

covery of the structure of DNA, the first unmanned explorations of other planets, the first genetic engineering experiments, the identification of all human genes, the first cloning of an animal, the discoveries of neutron stars, pulsars and black holes, and the man landings on the moon that helped unravel the history of the solar system, to name just a few of the major science stories of the 20th century. (Council for the Advancement of Science Writing, 2003)

Writing about science and other technical subjects such as medicine and health can be doubly rewarding. You can provide an educational service to readers who learn about the latest medical or engineering developments. This, in turn, helps readers to live more complete, enjoyable, and fulfilling lives. Increasingly, this is a major role of the science feature writer in our society. But for some reason, there has been a science phobia among most feature writers (Dahir, 1995).

The topics are often daunting for many feature writers, and the science is frequently difficult to sort out. Concern about AIDS, with the ongoing mixture of rumor and fact, left the public confused over the truth about this disease. Governments around the world turned to the news media to help to disseminate the known facts about AIDS and to educate the public about how to avoid the fatal epidemic. These public health information campaigns depended in part on science writers and medical writers for their success. Citizens are generally better informed about AIDS today, but still turn to the news media for the latest developments in the prevention and treatment of the disease. The public's dependence on the news media for such valuable information underlines the significance of science and health feature writing. Through news stories, and through feature articles about discoveries dealing with AIDS and other medical problems as well, the public is educated and better served.

There is equal concern today about the environment. Environmental reporting and writing has become its own specialization. Numerous publications have full-time staff writers who cover the environment and many publications today use freelance articles on the subject. For many communities, the environment is a critical part of their lifestyles and economies. Consider the importance of the Rocky Mountains region to states like Colorado and Utah, which have enormous resources devoted to skiing and other outdoor recreation. Or consider the value of a stable and safe environment to the marine life and the residents of the Florida Keys, the chain of islands and fragile coral reefs south and west of Miami. Reporters, feature writers, photographers, graphic artists, and editors at the *Times–Picayune* in New Orleans understand the importance of the natural environment surrounding their city, the rest of Louisiana, and the Gulf Coast. The newspaper's team of journalists began to look into the diminishing quality and supply of fish in their region. The result was an 8-day series of 40 news and feature stories that was titled "Oceans of Trouble." The stories told readers about how a way of life that developed over several generations had been endangered by careless treatment of the ocean. Overfished waters, polluted spaces, commercial and sport fishing, industry, business and residential development, and other forms of human intervention, they wrote, had broken an ancient rhythm of the seas. The package of stories looked at the entire Gulf of Mexico region, from Texas to South Florida. The staff earned the prestigious Pulitzer Prize for Public Service for this important science feature series.

## DEFINING SCIENCE AND TECHNICAL WRITING

English Professor Robert Gannon (1991) described confusion involving science writing, technical writing, and scientific writing. These are each different types of communication about science, he noted, explaining the following:

> Science writing is often confused with technical writing and scientific writing. It is neither. The difference lies mostly in the audience. The technical writer prepares "technical" material—reports, memos, and brochures—for a captive audience that needs data: a client, a colleague, an organization. A scientific writer, preparing scientific papers, writes for readers who want the information—many of whom are in the discipline and must keep abreast of what's happening. But the science writer (or science journalist) addresses the lay public. This job is much more complicated. The science writer must make complex theories and systems clear to a large, diverse readership, and must do so with the utmost clarity, accuracy, and excitement. (p. v)

Science writers, at least as a group, have worked in a recognized specialty since 1934. That was the year the National Association of Science Writers (http://www.nasw.org) was founded in New York. There are numerous other specialty professional writers' groups who concern themselves with scientific and technical material—groups such as the American Medical Writers Association (http://www.amwa.org) and the Aviation–Space Writers Association. There are also groups such as the Nature and Environmental Writers—College and University Educators (http://www.new-cue.org) that work to assist writers who focus on environmental issues. There are courses on the subject at many universities and colleges offered through journalism programs or science departments. It is a growing specialization in feature and news writing.

Many newspapers and news magazines have reporters assigned to specific science and technology beats. Among the most common beats are health and medicine, the environment, aviation and transportation, and energy. With the growing interest in science and high technology, many major newspapers have science and technology sections or pages on a regular basis.

Some consumer magazines, with their well-defined markets, specialize in scientific content. Some are generally about science. They include top 100 publications such as *Smithsonian, Discover, National Geographic Magazine, and Popular Science.* Other popular science periodicals include *Nature, Scientific American,*

*Archaeology, Audubon,* and *Science,* the official publication of the American Association for the Advancement of Science. Although these consumer magazines are devoted to general science, there are other major consumer magazines devoted to health, personal care, and medicine. These include four of the top 100 magazines in the country, such as *Prevention, Men's Health, Shape,* and *Health.* Technology magazines are popular as well. *PC Magazine* and *Popular Mechanics* are among the top 100 magazines. Many other magazines have departments devoted to medicine and health, space, engineering, the environment, and new technology. Thus, you have probably deduced by now, science and technical writing is subdivided into numerous specializations. Some writers are able to handle the general science assignment as it comes up, but most try to develop their own specialties within the science because of the difficulty of the subject matter.

Basic feature writing and reporting skills are no different in science and technical writing than in other forms of feature writing. However, the growth in information and interest in science requires it be treated as a specialization of newspaper and magazine feature writing. Beyond the basics in writing and reporting, there is one critical difference. You must be able to gather this usually complex scientific information, digest and understand it, and then translate it into understandable information for the general public. This requires a feature writer willing to accept this challenge and able to overcome it. You must often cope with a technical language unique to a specific science. You must be able to write along a fine line that keeps well-educated readers interested without losing the less-sophisticated ones. It is always a difficult assignment.

You must also be able to define and explain. It is critical to maintain accuracy in use of unique scientific and technical terminology. Consider an article about DNA, for example. What is it and how does it impact on our daily lives? What are genes? Such words must be explained in your article; you must take the time and effort to define terms and then use them in precise fashion in your article. What does the subject mean to the average person? How will the information in the article affect his or her life, or the lives of succeeding generations? This determination of meaning often is the most difficult challenge of all science and technical writing.

Although you are faced with the challenge of writing about new scientific and technical developments that affect our lives, there is still another challenge. You must also be able to write about subjects that readers already know about in a manner that is appealing and new. This may be more difficult for a writer than a story dealing with new developments. Making the old and familiar seem new is a tough assignment.

## DEMAND FOR SCIENCE AND TECHNOLOGY NEWS

Recently, these articles have appeared in the following monthly magazines:

- *American Scientist*—Managing the legacy of nuclear weapons production and the origin of solar wind.
- *Popular Science*—Boeing's new top-secret Bird of Prey aircraft debuts and why NHL players select a particular hockey stick.
- *Time*—A special report issue devoted to "How to Save the Earth" and a discussion of climate change, new technologies, and other environmental issues.
- *Smithsonian*—The contents of the sunken and raised USS Monitor, giant river otters, and varieties of apples.
- *Scientific American*—Global pollution and the Mediterranean Basin and hackers launching a major assault to bring down the World Wide Web.
- *Discover*—The voyage of Christopher Columbus to the New World and remapping history, the taboo of marriage among first cousins, plastics and shapes, HIV drug therapies and treatments, and using tomato extracts to repel mosquitos.
- *Reader's Digest*—controversial therapy for individuals suffering from Parkinson's disease and radical surgery and weight loss for overweight people.

We are all part of a new generation of serious science and high technology. They pervade all aspects of life as these examples indicate. The same applies to magazine, newspaper, newsletter, and online publication readers. There are vital issues involving contemporary science that never existed before. Most, in fact, were not even in the minds of our best scientists a generation or two ago. Few people could have anticipated a medical problem such as AIDS, for example. The first mainframe computer was developed 50 years ago and desktop personal computers are still less than a generation old. Manned aviation itself is less than 100 years old. It would have been hard for most scientists in the early 1940s to imagine an energy source that could be as inexpensive or as dangerous as nuclear power. The list of these types of recent major scientific developments is endless.

It is one of the news media's most important duties to provide the latest science and technology information to those who live in our communities. Certainly, reporting about new developments that are lifesaving techniques, or simply just time savings, can be particularly satisfying for science feature writers. "Writing technical articles is not only easy, but surprisingly enjoyable," noted high tech freelance writer Angela D. Mitchell (1997, p. 37). "Your market is huge—you'll be able to submit your pieces to magazines on the local, regional, and national level, and you'll sometimes get a look at products far before most consumers will. You'll develop an enhanced appreciation for the ever-changing world of technological innovations" (Mitchell, 1997, p. 37).

Staff writer Mike Toner (1992) of the *Atlanta Constitution* wrote a startling six-part "occasional" series about the diminishing effects of pesticides and antibiotics entitled "When Bugs Fight Back." Explaining how insects develop resistance to chemicals in the human effort to eradicate them, Toner was able to teach readers about the science behind such work by making a complicated topic involving chemistry and biology easy to understand. He interviewed dozens of scientists and other experts. Toner illustrated the problem with numerous actual medical cases and examples. He discussed the problem by reviewing its history and development. Toner's efforts earned him the Pulitzer Prize for explanatory journalism and the JC Penney–University of Missouri Newspaper Feature Writing Awards certificate of merit for a series. This is the first part, a 3,300-word installment, in Toner's highly enlightening series:

Editor's Note: The bugs are fighting back. And they are getting very good at it. The world's simplest creatures—bacteria, viruses, insects and weeds—are unraveling the chemical security blanket that has nurtured a half-century of progress in both public health and agriculture. First in an occasional series, "When Bugs Fight Back."

The death certificate attributed the 58-year-old heart patient's demise to "complications" following bypass surgery. The real reason made even his doctors cringe. Antibiotics didn't work anymore.

For four months, doctors at the University of Michigan Medical Center had struggled to control a bacterial infection that had invaded the man's chest cavity. The germs, however, were resistant to every available drug.

In the end, the bugs triumphed—and doctors at one of the country's premier medical institutions were as powerless to prevent it as doctors were 50 years ago, in the days before penicillin.

"If he hadn't had such a resistant strain, he would have made it," says Dennis Schaberg, professor of medicine at the University of Michigan medical school in Ann Arbor.

"I hate to sound like Chicken Little, but with certain micro-organisms, we are back to a point in time where we have no options left. It's tough to explain something like that to the family of the patient. Very tough."

A growing number of patients—and their families—are discovering a grim new reality of medicine in the 1990s. Antibiotics, those too-good-to-be-true compounds that have provided mankind with mastery over infectious disease, don't work like they used to.

The bugs are fighting back. And they are getting very good at it.

On city streets, in remote jungle clinics, on the farm and in back yards, the world's simplest creatures—bacteria, viruses, insects and weeds—are unraveling the chemical security blanket that has nurtured a half-century of progress in both public health and agriculture.

Whether we are conscious of it or not, the ability of these mindless creatures to adapt to the chemical warfare we wage on them has become a significant force in our daily lives. Look closely at any infectious disease for which there is a cure and you'll find bugs with a cure for the cure.

Have a child with an ear infection that won't go away? Deep in the recesses of your toddler's middle ear, there is probably a resistant bug to blame.

Having trouble getting rid of Fido's fleas or the cockroaches under your sink? Chances are, they're resistant too.

Did your stomach tie itself in knots after your last trip to a restaurant salad bar? If it was food poisoning, chances are one in three that the bug you took home with you was resistant.

Like the villains in a late-night horror show, resistant strains of mankind's oldest enemies are finding ways to sabotage our most sophisticated technology. And even the malevolent microbes of "The Andromeda Strain" or the angry hordes of "Killer Bees" aren't as scary as the real-life "superbugs" that are now emerging throughout the world.

In U.S. hospitals, where most people go to get well, 2 million people a year get sick after they check in—and the Centers for Disease Control (CDC) estimates that 60 percent of those infections are now resistant to at least one antibiotic. Because drug-resistant germs are twice as likely to be fatal, they contribute to 50,000 hospital deaths a year. And because they take twice as long to cure, they add as much as $30 billion a year to the cost of hospital care.

The toll in hospitals, however, is only the most documented facet of an insidious trend. Resistant strains of some of man's oldest enemies—malaria, tuberculosis, gonorrhea, food poisoning, pneumonia, even leprosy—are undermining public health throughout the world.

Some new strains of tuberculosis, resurgent after 30 years of decline in the United States and Europe, have become resistant to so many drugs that they are virtually as untreatable as they were before the discovery of antibiotics.

Malaria, which claims at least 1 million lives a year in the tropics, is on the comeback trail too, bolstered by the malaria parasite's growing resistance to drugs, and pesticide resistance of the mosquitoes that carry it.

Even that familiar nemesis we call pneumonia, which claims more than 3.5 million lives a year worldwide—up to 50,000 of them in the United States—is becoming steadily more resistant to penicillin, which has controlled it for nearly 50 years.

Almost every human infection—from drug-resistant "superclap," which has become a worldwide problem, to stubborn staph infections that linger in nursing homes for years—is now resistant to at least one major class of antibiotics.

## TRACTOR-TOWED BLOWTORCHES

Among the insects, things are no better. On Long Island, where the Colorado potato beetle is now resistant to every major class of pesticides, potato farmers use tractor-towed blowtorches to kill the insects—one of at least 17 "superbugs" that are now resistant to all pesticides.

Weeds are getting tougher too. More than 100 species are now resistant to at least one herbicide, and wheat growers in Australia and the United Kingdom are encountering the first multiply-resistant "mega-weeds," which scientists say could threaten the world's wheat supply.

Farmers' problems, of course, quickly become consumers' problems.

The clouds of pesticide-resistant sweet potato whiteflies that devastated last winter's vegetable crops in California, Texas and Florida triggered supermarket sticker shock that gave us $3.50 cantaloupe and $2-a-pound tomatoes.

There is no great mystery about what is happening. The bugs, whether single-celled microorganisms or the six-legged variety, are doing what comes naturally. They're surviving.

Bacteria have been on the Earth for at least 3 billion years; insects for at last 850 million years. Like all living things, they are constantly mutating, testing new traits that may give them an edge in a hostile environment.

With a new generation of bacteria every 20 minutes, trial and error can be a powerful survival tool. And when one bug finds something that works, it passes it on, sometimes even to other species.

With eons to adapt, bacteria have learned to live in the Earth's most hostile environments—from superheated deep-sea vents to the frozen slopes of Mount Everest. The few thousand antibiotics and pesticides that mankind has thrown at them have been, by comparison, a minor challenge.

The bugs' subversion of man-made chemicals has been unwittingly aided by the industries that market them, by "experts" who overuse them, and by ordinary people who treat them as technological "no-brainers" that promise, for a time, to change the course of evolution.

"The problem is not chemicals; it's the irresponsible way they are used," says University of Illinois entomologist Robert Metcalf. "Our shortsighted and irresponsible use of antibiotics and pesticides is producing strains of monster bugs resistant to nearly everything in our arsenal. The outlook is dismal. And it is getting worse."

The benefits of the 20th century's chemical "miracles" are indisputable. In the decade after the introduction of antibiotics, U.S. death rates from pneumonia, TB and influenza dropped 50 percent. Worldwide, penicillin is thought to have added 10 years to life expectancy. And the heavy chemical use that fueled the Green Revolution has helped feed a burgeoning population.

Resistance is not a new phenomenon. The emergence in the 1940s of penicillin-resistant staph infections in hospitals and DDT-resistant houseflies proved that bugs could fight back.

Until recently, however, human ingenuity always pulled some new solution from technology's seemingly inexhaustible bag of tricks. Now, like an audience that has seen the magician's act before, the bugs are getting harder to fool.

In recent years, resistance has become so pervasive that some experts now fear medicine and agriculture are on the verge of regressing into the technological dark ages that preceded the era of antibiotics and pesticides.

## THE ULTIMATE NIGHTMARE

For most people, for most illnesses, antibiotics still work. But in a growing number of cases, like the 58-year-old Michigan heart patient who died of mediastinitis caused by a hard-to-treat strain of enterococcal bacteria, the bugs' ability to accumulate resistance swiftly to several drugs at one time conjures up the ultimate nightmare.

"For some infections, we are very close to the end of the road," says Fred C. Tenover, the head of antimicrobics investigations for the CDC. "The worst-case scenario is almost here. We are very, very close to having bacteria resistant to every significant antibiotic ever developed. Only this time, there are no new drugs coming down the pike."

No aspect of the problem has dramatized the predicament more than the resurgence of tuberculosis—a disease that was once thought to have been vanquished by antibiotics. Although the numbers are relatively low—26,283 cases in the United States last year, 909 in Georgia—the upward trend and the growing prevalence of resistant TB worry many experts. A 50 percent increase in cases in Atlanta last year left the city with the highest TB rate in the country.

"TB is out of control," says Dixie Snider, who heads the CDC's tuberculosis control division. "These outbreaks we have seen in the last year may be just the beginning."

But while tuberculosis gets the headlines, resistant strains of other diseases have been spreading almost unnoticed. Salmonella infections, which cause up to 4 million cases of food poisoning a year in the United States, have been rising steadily for 15 years—and antibiotic-resistant strains now make up one-third of all cases.

Health officials say the spread of resistant food-borne germs, which often acquire resistance genes from exposure to antibiotics used to treat farm animals, will mean larger outbreaks of food poisoning in the future—like a 1985 case of contaminated milk that sickened 180,000 in the Midwest.

New strains of resistant bugs are spreading globally. In Georgia, soaring rates of penicillin-and tetracycline-resistant gonorrhea—once unknown outside of Southeast Asia—have rendered obsolete drugs that controlled the disease for three decades. In five years, drug-resistant gonorrhea has increased tenfold in Georgia, enough to give the state the highest rate in the country.

Several antibiotics are still effective against gonorrhea, but pockets of resistance to these "last resort" drugs are already emerging in other countries.

"There is a global movement of these gonococcal strains, so it is probably only a matter of time before we have them in the United States," says Joan Knapp, an epidemiologist with the CDC's division of sexually transmitted diseases. "We are standing at the edge of a crisis. Every new antibiotic we have thrown at this bug has ended up making it more resistant."

Old enemies aren't the only ones learning new tricks. The AIDS virus is already resistant to the first three drugs approved to treat it.

Development of two other AIDS drugs was curtailed this year after researchers discovered that the virus had developed resistance after only 12 weeks of treatment.

## INVASION OF THE WHITEFLIES

Insects are proving every bit as adept at chemical countermeasures as the microscopic "bugs" that cause human disease.

When Rachel Carson warned in 1962—two decades after the introduction of DDT—that repeated pesticide use would create a crisis in which "only the strong and fit remain to defy our efforts to control them," 137 insects were resistant to at least one pesticide.

Today, resistance has been documented in 504 species of insects and mites, 273 weeds, 150 fungi and other plant pathogens, and five kinds of rats—and there are at least 17 insects that are resistant to all major classes of pesticides.

When pesticides fail, the consequences can assume almost biblical proportions—as they did during last year's invasion of sweet potato whiteflies in California, Texas and Florida.

"We had fields that were completely devastated," says Nick Toscano, an entomologist at the University of California at Riverside. "It was like the plagues of locusts and grasshoppers that they have in the Middle East and Africa. At times, the clouds of whiteflies were so thick, it looked like a dust storm. If you drove through one of the clouds, you had to stop and scrape off your blackened windshield so you could see."

The U.S. Department of Agriculture has launched a five-year research program to seek new solutions to the problem.

But "Invasion of the Sweetpotato Whitefly II," the sequel, may be only months away—and experts say the insects, which thrive on cotton and peanuts, could soon become a major headache in Georgia, Mississippi and New Mexico, too.

"Control may not be impossible, but it's going to be very expensive," says Gary Herzog, research entomologist at the University of Georgia's Coastal Plain Experiment Station in Tifton. "I had to tell a farmer the other day to expect a couple of years of serious hardship before we come up with a solution."

The rising tide of resistance is by no means an unbroken trend. The boll weevil, which almost instantly became resistant to DDT, is as susceptible to parathion as the day in 1949 when it was first sprayed on Southern cotton fields. Penicillin is still as effective against syphilis as it was when GIs were treated with it during World War II.

At other times, compounds that took years to develop have sometimes been rendered ineffective within months of their introduction.

Sometimes the bugs leapfrog ahead of technology. Farmers, using a class of chemicals called pyrethroids for the first time, have discovered insects that were already resistant. The same gene the bugs used to beat DDT also works against pyrethroids—and the trait has persisted even though DDT hasn't been used in the United States for 20 years.

Man-made chemicals of all kinds apply the same kind of "selective pressure" that Charles Darwin first described more than a century ago.

But the unrelenting use of antibiotics and pesticides has, in effect, thrown the evolution of resistance into fast forward.

In 50 years, bacteria have evolved more than 100 resistance factors to survive the onslaught of antibiotics. The same 50 years have seen the evolution of at least 1,640 combinations of insect–insecticide resistance.

## "RACE BETWEEN MAN AND BUGS"

From the bugs' point of view, the pressure to succeed is enormous.

Americans use 700 million pounds of pesticides and herbicides and 30 million pounds of antibiotics each year to treat everything from acne and gum disease to farmed catfish and feedlot cattle. Worldwide use of antibiotics and pesticides is three to five times that of the United States.

In the long run, the effects of this chemical blitz are not all for the better. Even though U.S. farmers use 33 times more pesticides than they did in the 1940s, pests now destroy 37 percent of the annual harvest, about what they did in medieval Europe, where farmers lost "one of every three grains grown."

The record on antibiotics is no more encouraging. Doctors write 220 million prescriptions for oral antibiotics a year, one for nearly every person in the country. But surveys show that about half are unnecessary or incorrectly prescribed. In addition to wasting billions of dollars a year, the misuse encourages the spread of resistant infections.

"The widespread, often inappropriate use of antibiotics ensures their phased obsolescence as new resistant organisms emerge," says Calvin Kunin, professor of medicine at Ohio State University, who has studied doctors' prescribing practices for more than a decade.

"Too many people think antibiotics are harmless," says Thomas F. O'Brien, a specialist in infectious diseases at Brigham and Women's Hospital in Boston. "We need to start persuading them that resistant bacteria can be just as dangerous as high blood pressure or cholesterol. You don't want it—and the way to avoid it is not to take antibiotics unnecessarily."

Although experts in infectious disease and agriculture seldom discuss their problems with each other, they think remarkably alike on one point. As bugs of all shapes and sizes grow more resistant, urgent efforts are needed to preserve the weapons that still work. That means abandoning the quick-fix mentality that has shaped the use of these chemicals for 50 years, and adding an ingredient that often has been missing—common sense.

Some farmers are discovering that simple biological control—insects eating insects—works better than chemicals. Others believe advanced technology will ride to the rescue. Scientists, for instance, are already engineering insecticidal traits and herbicide resistance into hundreds of crops—a generation of plants that could reduce the need for chemical pesticides.

Some insects, however, have already developed resistance to these biological pesticides, and some experts worry that widespread use of such plants could actually promote resistance.

"History is repeating itself," says Marvin K. Harris, an entomologist at Texas A&M University. "Every time we come up with a new class of chemicals, we think we are finally home free. In every instance we have been wrong. There's no reason to think we won't be wrong again."

Advances in genetic engineering also promise a new generation of anti-infective drugs and vaccines, as well as speedier diagnosis of resistant microbes. But if hope springs eternal, it no longer flows with the optimism that greeted the introduction of penicillin a half-century ago.

"This is a race between man and bugs," says Colin Marchant, associate professor of pediatrics at the Tufts University School of Medicine. "The bugs have been very clever about finding ways to evade the drugs we make. So far we have been very clever about devising new ones, but I don't know how much longer we will be able to." (Toner, 1992, p. A1; © 1992 Atlanta Newspapers Inc. Reprinted with permission of Atlanta Newspapers Inc.)

Toner (1992), a graduate of the University of Iowa and Northwestern University, also developed a chart focusing on the "do's and don'ts of antibiotic use" for the first installment of the series. His other stories discussed global spread of resistance, "tougher" germs in hospitals, how doctors and drug companies encourage resistance, the growing difficulty in controlling weeds and insects, and the dwindling supply of "magic bullets."

The excellence in former *Baltimore Evening Sun* feature writer Jon Franklin's two stories about a new brain surgery procedure is built through detailed description of the complex operation on a 57-year-old woman. Franklin used an approach he calls the nonfiction short story. This approach, applied to writing about science and other technical subjects, makes the material more appealing to readers. "The principal difference between the short story of old and the nonfiction short story of today is that in its modern form, the story is true," Franklin wrote (1986, p. 27). The effort won Franklin his first of two Pulitzer Prizes, this one in 1979 for feature writing. Franklin began the short story-like article about the complicated surgical attempt to untangle and remove a knot of abnormal blood vessels in a woman's skull. He set up the dramatic conflict between the surgeon and what the patient called the "monster" internal growth that was slowly killing her:

In the cold hours of a winter morning Dr. Thomas Barbee Ducker, chief brain surgeon at the University of Maryland Hospital, rises before dawn. His wife serves him waffles but no coffee. Coffee makes his hands shake.

In downtown Baltimore, on the 12th floor of University Hospital, Edna Kelly's husband tells her goodbye. For 57 years, Mrs. Kelly shared her skull with the monster: No more. Today she is frightened but determined.

It is 6:30 a.m.

"I'm not afraid to die," she said as this day approached. "I've lost part of my eyesight. I've gone through all the hemorrhages. A couple of years ago I lost my sense of smell, my taste. I started having seizures. I smell a strange odor and then I start strangling. It started affecting my legs, and I'm partially paralyzed.

"Three years ago a doctor told me all I had to look forward to was blindness, paralysis and a remote chance of death. Now I have aneurysms; this monster is causing that. I'm scared to death—but there isn't a day that goes by that I'm not in pain, and I'm tired of it. I can't bear the pain. I wouldn't want to live like this much longer."

As Dr. Ducker leaves for work, Mrs. Ducker hands him a paper bag containing a peanut butter sandwich, a banana and two fig newtons.

Downtown, in Mrs. Kelly's brain, a sedative takes effect.

Mrs. Kelly was born with a tangled knot of abnormal blood vessels. (Franklin, 1978, p. C–1)

Franklin (1978) proceeds to tell this dramatic story with a chronological approach. Yet, readers do not find out what happened until the struggle ended 7 hours later on the operating room table. With detailed description, Franklin puts readers in the operating room as observers. He lays out Mrs. Kelly's story as a fiction writer might write a short story. As this real-life drama builds in his story, the condition of the patient is left hanging. At the same time, a very difficult medical procedure becomes understandable and meaningful to readers. It is not until the last sentence of the article that Franklin reveals what happened to Mrs. Kelly. "The monster won," Franklin simply wrote in that final sentence (p. C–1).

Why did these writers succeed? Why did each win such high-level recognition? Each one has mastered science feature writing. Although the topics were different and the author approached each in a somewhat different manner, each told his or her story in a manner understandable by readers. This chapter outlines the basics of writing science, technical, medical and health, and other specialized features. Toner and Franklin succeeded because of their abilities to take complicated subjects and write them in an accurate manner that could be understood by readers without medical backgrounds. For example, Franklin's (1978) article displays the uncertainty and tension surrounding any surgical procedure that risks human life, particularly the drama of a revolutionary technique. The story is even more effective because of the humane approach to the article—readers get to know the patient and the neurosurgeons because Franklin develops their roles in the story beyond just name and identification. This type of science and technical writing is sensitive and dramatic through its narrative description. It is a good read. That is what writing about complicated subjects should do—allow readers to learn from, and enjoy, the subject.

## DESCRIBING SCIENCE AND TECHNICAL FEATURES

Science and technical feature topics literally cover the universe. Some of the hot topics include personal health and fitness, medicine, computers, astronomy and space travel, psychology and psychiatry, nutrition and diet, sports and exercise science, geography and oceanography, meteorology, and biology. Any of these topics can be broken down into numerous subdivisions that are important topics themselves. In medicine for example, focus continues to be on drug abuse, AIDS, cancer, paralysis, burns, heart disease, children and childbirth, sleep, and sex.

It seems there are more subjects in science, technical, and medical and health writing than there are sciences. It is up to you as a writer to determine which of those subjects are marketable and appealing to readers. You can be certain that subjects such as those already mentioned appeal across the board. Increasingly, newspapers, consumer magazines, and newsletters are devoting portions of their content to personal health and fitness subjects, for instance.

What does it take to be a science or technical feature writer? First, it takes some interest in a scientific subject such as the environment, medicine, space, or computers. Second, it takes some education in the sciences. It is not necessary to be a science major, but some general science education, especially at college, is very helpful. Third, it makes a difference if you specialize. This focuses your "learning curve" in a particular area.

Bill Steele (personal communication, May 24, 1993), a Cornell University graduate working near the school in Ithaca, NY, began college as a physics major but wound up in psychology. He said he was more interested in people than things. Steele, who has written numerous articles as a freelance writer for national general interest magazines such as *Family Circle, Working Mother, National Wildlife, Popular Electronics,* and *Health,* as well as trade and business publications, specializes in medicine, computers, and more general science writing. He explained how his education has helped him:

> In my work as a science writer, I drew mostly on the basic courses I took in the first couple of years. Today, I draw much more heavily on what I've learned since college. For example, when I was an undergraduate, there was no such thing as molecular genetics, yet today that's a subject I write about far more often than physics. I've made a point of becoming informed about it, and probably know more about it now than I know about physics. Or psychology. A good scientific education teaches you how to *do* science. To write about it, you need to know the basics, and the vocabulary, so you can understand what a scientist or engineer is telling you. You also need to be up on the state of the art, so you know what's news. After that you use the same interviewing and story-telling skills you use to report on business, law, sports or anything else: Here's the expert who knows what's going on and you have to find out what that is and ask questions or do research until you can explain it to your audience in terms they can understand.
>
> The work of most science and technical writers is difficult to generalize about. Newspaper writers who specialize in science and technical writing many times have other duties. While a science writer for a small daily newspaper might focus on the medical beat, he or she might also have assignments to cover schools or city hall. Many science and technical writers for smaller consumer magazines work freelance and must be able to generate assignments on their own initiative and enterprise. This effort requires paying attention to developments by reading and talking to the leading information sources in the area. (Steele, personal communication, May 24, 2003)

Research about science and technical writing has determined that there are four factors that affect reader interest in science and technical subjects, according to Michael Shapiro, a science writing researcher. Two concepts do influence a person's interest in science articles, but two others seem less likely (Shapiro, 1988). The two that certainly affect interest are as follows:

1. Relevance of the subject—You must, as a writer, find a way to help readers see how the subject is important to them. If you do, this enhances readership.
2. Entertainment value of the article—The article must be prepared in such a manner that it satisfies the readers' need for stimulation if you want a widely read article.

The two concepts that have traditionally been associated with readership now seem less likely to influence interest, the study reported:

1. Ease or difficulty of the subject material—Although it seems that difficult subjects would be less inviting to readers, there is little evidence that interest in science articles is related to subject difficulty.
2. Topic familiarity—Although many writers believe that people turn to material that they already know, this is true only for actively sought material. For casually encountered articles in newspapers, magazines, newsletters, and online publications, familiarity has little affect on interest.

## WRITING FOR THE RIGHT AUDIENCE

You have an assignment. You must write about unhealthy levels of asbestos found in local public elementary school classrooms. How much does your publication's average reader know about the complicated subject? How much do you have to explain and define as you write this article? You must make these types of decisions before you write one word. Your science and technical writing approaches will vary considerably—depending on whether you write for a general audience or a specialized audience.

### The General Audience

Much of the science and technical writing you do in consumer publications is oriented to the general public. The wide range of educational levels puts a special demand on you to write in an interesting fashion for the reader with a professional degree as well as the reader who did not finish high school. But you must know as much as you can about this general audience because it might have special interests. For the general audience, it is best to err on the side of stating the obvious and too much explanation. You should remember that part of your work is educational, too.

Writing for the general audience is not automatic. Translating complicated information into understandable form requires effort on the part of the writer. Freelance writer and editor Wendy M. Grossman (personal communication, May 20, 1993 & January 15, 1998), who specializes in computers and paranormal science from her home near London, said writers who deal with complicated subjects benefit from talking to everyday people:

> Stay in touch with real people. This is a problem you see often among computer journalists—they know too much and the result is they don't understand what's difficult for anyone else. The other thing is to maintain some detachment from your subject—in my case, I'm a writer who happens to be writing about computers and science. If you're a little more focused the other way—a computer junkie who happens to be writing about them (instead of selling them or making them), it will be much harder for you to write for a general audience. (Grossman, personal communication, May 20, 1993 & January 15, 1998)

## The Specialized Audience

Some science and technical writing you may do is designed for a specialized audience of high sophistication. Feature writers for business and industry periodicals, for example, prepare articles for those with high interest levels in a subject and, it is likely, high knowledge levels as well. Most specialized audience readers have some experience with the subject themselves, either through their work or education. This expertise on the part of readers requires that you have an even greater awareness of audience when you write. You do not want to make the mistake of assuming too little, and thus bore the reader. And you do not want to assume the audience knows too much and turn it off by leaving too many vague explanations or unanswered questions. Some preliminary research about your readers may help solve this problem.

"A good science article is an easy read; it carries the readers along effortlessly, with fascination," said Gannon (1991, p. vi). "And when readers are finished, they are often surprised (if they think about it) at just how much highly technical material they have picked up along the way" (Gannon, 1991, p. vi).

Most newspaper and magazine editors have a particular audience and subject range in mind for each article they accept. For example, *Writer's Market* (Brogan, 2002) reported that the editors of the 1.5 million circulation *Popular Science* seek applied science feature writing for their unique market:

> *Popular Science* is devoted to exploring (and explaining) to a nontechnical, but knowledgeable, readership the technical world around us. We cover all of the sciences, engineering and technology, and above all, products. We are largely a "thing"-oriented publication: things that fly or travel down a turnpike, or go on or under the sea, or cut wood, or reproduce music, or build buildings, or make pictures. We are especially focused on the new, the ingenious, and the useful.

Contributors should be alert to the possibility of selling us pictures and short features as they are to major articles. Freelancers should study the magazine to see what we want and avoid irrelevant submissions. (p. 660)

---

## NEED SOURCES? TRY THESE "SCIENTISTS ON DEMAND"

Need a scientist as a source?

The Media Resource Service hotline is a science writer's "911" number that is operated by the Scientists' Institute for Public Information. Established in 1980, the hotline helps when science-based stories break in the United States and elsewhere. Such major stories as new AIDS developments and natural disasters create a need for fast, authoritative information.

Feature writers can call the service toll free by dialing 800–223–1730. The service refers writers to experts who can help them. Callers will be given names and telephone numbers of potential sources. The line is monitored for fast response even during nonbusiness hours such as evenings, weekends, and holidays.

---

## KEY SOURCES FOR ARTICLES

There are dozens of categories of sources to be used in science and technical feature writing. Many times, reporters and writers will need to work with organizations and institutions and their representatives. This often means working with an intermediary such as a public relations practitioner. Often, in government or other public sector roles, these are called public information officers (PIOs). PIOs can help locate the best individuals and help you obtain access to them.

There is also a growing set of experts' directories available to journalists in either online or printed formats. Typically, World Wide Web sites maintained by journalism organizations such as press clubs or professional groups are the most reliable. For example, the National Press Club in Washington, DC maintains a useful source-finding service on its Web site (http://npc.press.org/newssources/index.cfm) that can be searched by subject or name. However, there are a number of others developed by commercial enterprises that may be useful. One example of a commercial expert-finder service that has gone online is known as ProfNet (http://www1.profnet.com/). ProfNet, operated by PR Newswire, provides sources of all types; its base is a link to information officers at universities, colleges, research institutes, and think tanks and that opens the door to scientists of a wide range of specializations. ProfNet, a subsidiary of PR Newswire, may also be reached at 800–776–3638.

## BEST SCIENCE AND TECHNOLOGY SOURCES CHECK LIST

Organizations, such as professional or trade associations.

Resource books prepared for the news media.

Professional associations and trade group conventions and exhibitions.

Professional meetings.

Professional journals and newsletters.

Bibliographic indexes and abstracts.

Online access bibliographic database services.

Business and industry publications.

Universities and colleges.

Research and technical institutes.

Research groups and foundations.

Museums and libraries.

Commercial research organizations.

Information hotlines and World Wide Web sites.

---

Specialized publications can be a good starting point. Familiarize yourself with those in the subject areas that interest you. There are numerous special handbooks, guidebooks, and directories available for reference. Specialists in a field write many specifically for reporters and writers. The International Food Information Council Foundation in Washington, DC, recently prepared a 12-page booklet titled "How to Understand and Interpret Food and Health-Related Scientific Studies" for writers who cover the food and health industries (Survey indicates, 1997). Journalists also prepare some of these resources for other journalists. For example, science journalist Edward Edelson (1985), wrote *The Journalist's Guide to Nuclear Energy* for the Atomic Industrial Forum, a collective of organizations involved in peaceful use of nuclear energy. This book and ones like it contain explanations, definitions, diagrams, and other helpful resources for writers.

Veteran freelance feature writer Bill Steele (personal communication, May 24, 1993) uses research to find the human sources he needs. He said he goes wherever the needed information can be found. He uses both experts and principals involved in events about which he is writing:

Sometimes on small jobs, it's just the library. Mostly I prefer going to live people who are the principals in the event or the experts in the subject. Library research will give you clues as to who and where these people are, as well as telling you what's already been covered. But writing entirely from what's already been covered isn't journalism; it's more like writing a paper for school. You sometimes have to go through PR people to get to the primary sources, and they can send you literature, but they're not worth much as sources themselves; again, what they tell you is what's already been covered, by them. In writing about science I always follow up references to technical journals, but don't find them very useful except for getting precise numbers and names of things right. They usually cover one narrow research event, and seldom put it in context. (Steele, personal communication, May 24, 1993)

Another freelance science and cyberspace writer, Grossman (personal communication, May 20, 1993 & January 15, 1998), uses computer databases and networks of people for her reporting. She explained the following:

> I use the magazine databases on CompuServe a fair bit. When I'm reviewing products, I also like to look in the vendor forums and see what people are complaining about. For the paranormal stuff, I use the network of skeptics; for computers, a lot of what I do is asking PR people to come up with appropriate contacts. I rarely read computer magazines. *Science News* was recommended to me as a good source of science coverage, but in fact I'm finding *Business Week* more useful, and I now have a subscription—it covers technology companies very well. One unfortunate thing is that most editors here won't let me quote from other magazines, which I think is unfair if the magazines have uncovered really useful material.
>
> A lot of journalists complain about PR people, but to a freelancer they can be enormously helpful: Arranging loan and review equipment, supplying information about their clients, finding someone for you to talk to and making sure that person actually follows through with the interview, and so on. We're pampered far more here than journalists are in the U.S., partly because most of the magazines are so underfinanced. You have to watch it, of course, because obviously PR people are paid to put the best face on the company they can, but nonetheless they can save you a lot of time chasing people. As I have increasingly specialized in reporting about cyberspace, I find PR people and material are less and less useful except in introducing me to people from the many companies inventing Internet-related technology. Most of the subjects I write about—junk mail, censorship, privacy issues, and social and cultural stuff—are subjects I research directly on the Web or Usenet. Also, the presence on the Web of most technology companies means that UK-based journalists, who typically used to be fed press releases several months after their American colleagues, now have access to the original U.S. launch material—and since all of us read technology headlines on the Web, we all know what the news is. (Grossman, personal communication, May 20, 1993 & January 15, 1998)

Many organizations and events are buffered by the public relations specialists or other media liaisons whose job it is to provide writers with access to scientists and technicians who have the expertise needed for your article. With this in mind, let us look at these major categories of science and technical sources in more detail:

## Scientific Journals and Other Publications

The literature of a particular discipline or field is the best place to seek out story ideas. Most science and technical writers who specialize in a subject (medicine or environment, for example) read the major publications. When possible, it is advisable to subscribe to these publications. In medicine, two of the leading publications are the *Journal of the American Medical Association* and *The New England Journal of Medicine.* Yet, there are dozens of more highly specialized medical journals, magazines, and newsletters. General science and official organizational technical publications, such as *Science,* are also good for story prospects. These journals also have a presence on the World Wide Web.

## Professional and Technical Organizations

In science and technical subjects, professional organizations exist for exchange of new knowledge and for continuing education. Most leading researchers participate in these organizations in one way or another. Examples include the American Psychological Association, the American Chemical Society, and the American Institute of Architects. These groups hold regional, national, and international gatherings on an annual basis and they provide a perfect forum for story ideas. They have World Wide Web sites for members and for the general public. Most scientific organizations also produce newsletters for members, or produce their own journals and magazines. These publications can be excellent sources.

## Conventions and Meetings

In addition to regular organizational meetings, industry- and profession-wide conventions or symposia are regularly scheduled—generally once a year—to permit leading experts to gather and discuss the latest developments. Often, the latest research findings are discussed at these meetings and the leading authorities on topics gather to discuss trends, plan research, and share findings. These meetings transcend individual and institutional interests and provide even better opportunities for writers to develop story prospects and sources. Many groups that hold national and international annual sessions have subdivisions by specialization and interests (for example, cardiologists within the American Medical Association) and regional subgroups (for instance, by state or county). Often these meetings may be previewed simply by checking the group's Web site. Groups frequently post schedules, speaker information, and other details that are easy to access.

## Universities and Colleges

You probably have one nearby. Major universities and colleges that have research missions (usually the larger state and private 4-year schools) provide a ready, and usually willing, series of sources for new information on just about any subject. This is particularly true about universities with medical and other professional schools and centers. A look at a current catalogue will let you know what programs exist at the university and, from that, what types of research are being conducted. For more specific information, check the institution's Web site or contact individual departments or the public relations offices. In addition to these sources, some universities and colleges have begun to offer science and technical writing programs. One such program, at Lehigh University in Pennsylvania, allows students to specialize in science writing.

## Institutes, Centers, and Research Groups

Perhaps the best-known organization that supports science and technical development is the National Science Foundation. This is not only a national funding source for research, but it is also a source of information about the research that it is funding. Other sources exist at independent institutes, centers, and groups that can provide the latest information on topics of current concern and these research organizations often post basic information on the World Wide Web for writers to use for background and for generating story ideas.

## SCIENCE AND TECHNICAL WRITING TROUBLE SPOTS

Writing about science and technology, even with the best sources available, can have its trying moments. As a feature writer involved in writing about complicated information, you must be able to discern fact from opinion. One way this can be done is by using multiple expert sources. Diversity of authoritative sources is often necessary when writing about scientific research and similar work at the cutting edge of a subject, where the lines between scientific opinion and fact are frequently blurred. Scientists frequently disagree about matters, especially new developments and theories.

Science writers also have the occasional opportunity to write about what some authorities call *maverick* science. This involves writing about very unorthodox or unusual scientific theories such as those that would predict earthquakes or propose miracle cures or treatments for major diseases. The least-preferred—but perhaps most tempting—approach to this, conventional journalistic practices dictate, is to tell readers what to think about these maverick theories. Traditions of objectivity and fairness do not support this approach, however. Most science writers feel they should be more critical of maverick explanations and the individuals who advocate them than they would be of more conventional sources with more credible explanations. Research at Michigan State University suggests that because science writers already depend on authority figures for the content of stories about scientific controversies involving maverick theories, they should also depend on these expert sources for interpretation of the context of the controversy (Dearing & Kazmierczak, 1992).

Science and technical feature writing runs the risk of being incomplete as well. At times, sources may be unwilling to discuss all aspects of their work. Incomplete reporting causes confusion and uncertainty, and this results in lack of clarity. At times, sources are unprepared to talk with reporters, or they cannot adequately explain their work to you. If this occurs, how can you expect to make sense of things for your readers? Nevertheless, scientists can be skeptical about you and your effort to communicate their work to the world. You must make a concerted effort to gain their confidence and trust.

Science and technical writers can get involuntarily involved in the politics of the scientific community as well—especially when hard-to-get funding is at stake from public and private sources. Writers must be able to cut through the competitive nature and hype of some scientists and technicians to get at the heart of a matter. Cures and solutions to difficult scientific problems must be viewed with skepticism on your part, too. At times, announcements of study results can be premature and create unjustified optimism in readers. Writers must be careful not to overdramatize the importance of results of studies they report.

Still another caution about science sources involves the illegitimate source. You will occasionally encounter sources that attempt to provide evidence about new discoveries that is faked or artificially enhanced. There are individuals who try to gain attention through tricks and hoaxes played on the news media. To avoid being duped by a hoax, it is important not to depend too much on the information provided by a single source. Science writers should go beyond press releases and research reports in collecting information. These sources are only starting points and should be supplemented by interviews and other written sources where possible.

Public relations staffers for companies involved in research and development of new products can be helpful to you, but they can also be an obstacle. These individuals can stop you in your tracks from getting important information that they see as negative for their clients. They often have different ideas about how to use new information. It is up to you to get around these barriers by talking to the scientists and managers directly whenever possible.

On occasion, it might be appropriate for you to double-check your story's first draft, or parts of it, with your primary sources. This is done solely in the interest of accuracy. Although this is not normal procedure in most feature writing, it is sometimes necessary when writing on highly scientific and technical subjects.

It is also important to discuss sensationalism in science and technical writing. Despite your impressions about the value of the story and the enthusiasm of your sources, be careful about "hyping" the story. Because science writing is not often glamorous and does not often command page 1 or cover story levels, there is a temptation to overwrite an article and exaggerate its importance to gain an editor's attention. For example, Jim Sibbison (1988), a U.S.-based correspondent for *The Lancet,* a British medical journal, said too many reporters are drawn into the magic of "breakthrough" medical reporting:

> Medical scientists often criticize the news media for proclaiming major break-throughs on the strength of what are, in fact, no more than tentative findings.— But the scientists can't rightfully unload all the blame on the media. Some of them can, on occasion, be found egging on the press with exaggerations of their own. (p. 36)

Sibbison (1988) added an observation that seems to be central to the whole problem: good medical articles that are properly qualified tend to be of low news value. "Stories that say a salve performs miracles are more attractive than ones that say there may be flies in this particular ointment," he wrote (p. 39). He said there is a simple test that can be a solution to this problem. He advised the following: "If [your] story includes words or phrases such as 'for the first time,' 'cancer-causing peanut butter sandwiches,' 'dawn of a new age,' 'milestone,' 'or breakthrough,' a second scientist's opinion may be in order" (p. 39).

In science and technical article writing there is a vast, rich lode of sources to mine. These include professional and trade associations, professional and trade groups' conventions and exhibitions, regular local and national professional meetings, articles in professional journals and business and industry publications, researchers at local and state universities and colleges, area research and technical institutes and centers, research groups and foundations, scientists on staffs of museums, and commercial research organizations.

---

## MAJOR ISSUES IN SCIENCE JOURNALISM

Contributed by Robert Logan (personal communication, November 10, 2002), associate dean for Undergraduate Studies and professor, School of Journalism, University of Missouri.

> The significant problems in science, environmental and medical reporting today seem to revolve around innumeracy (Paulos, 1988; Levi, 2001) and the need for reporters to independently evaluate the empirical information supplied to them

by government, public interest groups, universities, independent institutions & foundations and corporations.

At the foundation of accuracy and contextual problems is a widespread journalistic inability to evaluate scientific data coupled with little reportorial understanding of relative risk.

Although there are notable exceptions, some reporters, editors and producers in U.S. print and broadcast newsrooms are unable to judge whether a scientific or environmental report is highly professional, moderately professional or unprofessional and are unable to gauge the veracity of health risks assertions.

In addition, even sophisticated reporters are sometimes blocked by editors to explain whether a finding represents textbook research or is at science's frontiers. Textbook science is well-established research with high scientific credibility and credence. Although frontier science (such as recent allegations that link cell phone use to brain cancer) often is provocative and newsworthy, assertions even from articles in peer review journals represent preliminary or equivocal evidence.

In a 1996 book, Marcia Angell, M.D., former Executive Editor of the *New England Journal of Medicine,* noted some of the social consequences of innumeracy. Angell (1996) explained that in the early to mid-1990s the news media frequently reported that silicone gel-filled breast implants were harmful to women's health. Angell finds the collective reporting created an impression that the manufacture, sale, distribution, clinical recommendation or use of silicone breast implants was medically irresponsible. Angell reports the publicity helped plaintiffs in class action litigation against breast implant manufacturers and distributors as well as a few clinicians who recommended the procedure to patients. However, Angell notes that from the outset there was a dearth of empirical evidence to buttress the claim that silicone breast implants were unhealthy for women.

In short, Angell asserts that a women's health crisis was contrived with the press as inadvertent participants. Angell challenges journalists (as well as attorneys, public interest groups and physicians) to avoid hyperbole in asserting health risks and she underscores the degree that public opinion can be erroneously manipulated.

Similar discrepancies between the public's impression of a looming health risk and actual evidence occurred in reporting about Alar, a chemical preservative in apples in 1989, and in more recent reporting about electromagnetic fields.

Earlier in the 1990s, negative publicity about health risks from exposure to electromagnetic fields (EMFs) appeared in newspapers, magazines and on radio and television news across the US. EMFs caused by power lines outside one's home, school or office, and given off by home and work appliances, were allegedly associated with a variety of health problems, including children's leukemias. The publicity helped galvanize public opinion and resulted in protective legislation in several states. But in 1996, an independent review board of the National Academy of Sciences reported that an EMF-health risk link was not supported by current, international scientific evidence (Logan, Fears and Wilson, 1997).

Press critics asked two challenging questions: how did public opinion and state legislation ever get ahead of scientific evidence? What was the press' role in creating the public's impression of health dangers? (Logan, Fears and Wilson, 1997).

In the Alar case, the news media in the US and Great Britain reported (in February 1989) that Alar, a chemical preservative for apples, had potentially inimical affects on children's health. Alar's negative publicity was orchestrated by the National Resources Defense Council (NRDC), which was critical of governmental stewardship over the preservative's manufacturers.

Reporters naturally trusted the NRDC; they won the Nobel Prize in recent memory before the Alar news conference. The environmental records of multinational conglomerates (plus the U.S., British governments) have merited widespread criticism and skepticism for the past 45 years. But there were almost zero challenges from journalists about the data the NRDC found—and it was internationally reported as a highly credible assertion.

Millions of persons worldwide were told by the news media that apples and apple products contained dangerous carcinogens and unsuspecting children were especially at risk. Sales plummeted, jobs were lost in apple growing areas of the Pacific Northwest and Great Britain, and the public confidence in the food supply was jolted with equivocal evidence—as most reporters later discovered and today acknowledge (Nelkin, 1995).

But unlike the EMF and breast implant cases, Alar and similar reporting about meat and vegetable safety created a backlash within the food industry, which fostered a new journalistic vulnerability to libel and other litigation. In the late 1990s, some branches of the vegetable and meat industry received special libel or legal protection from assertions of health risks in several states. It was one of these new state laws that landed television host Oprah Winfrey in a Texas courtroom for allegedly libeling the beef industry in winter, 1998. Ms. Winfrey was acquitted.

Returning to how journalists might approach these issues in the future, some serious problems could be avoided if more reporters, editors and broadcast producers received basic statistical training. Journalists should be able to look at data and immediately judge weak statistical associations, methodological flaws and poor sampling techniques that would not pass peer review in serious scientific publications, or represent preliminary evidence.

As the Alar and other examples demonstrate, journalists should cover epidemiological data regarding environmental issues with a solid, working knowledge of sample sizes, generalizeability from a sample to a larger audience, if demographics are comparable to a larger population; methodological flaws in research designs; if appropriate controls such as a control group are used in the study; and if basic nonparametric and parametric statistical tests are used appropriately. Reporters and their editors need to be grounded in epidemiology and risk assessment in the same way many journalists care about grammar, sentence structure and placement graphics.

The bottom line to understand scientific, biomedical and environmental issues is to adjudicate the evidence independently—this enables a reporter to evaluate the honesty and reliability of a scientific source. If journalists cannot do this—particularly when public health, or epidemiological questions are raised—then, it is unsurprising that serious mistakes are made in newspapers, magazines and broadcast newsrooms with emerging consequences for the profession and society.

A second, related issue is a lack of comparative perspective about relative risks and journalistic reluctance to point out inconsistencies between what persons take for granted and what frightens them. Perhaps these issues were best pointed out by biochemist Bruce Ames, University of California–Berkeley. Ames asked persistently in the late 1980s why is it that natural carcinogens in natural fruits and vegetables are seen as benign while lower traces of man-made pesticides in foods are seen as significant risk to public health (that demands public policy action?) (Ames and Gold, 1989) Why don't reporters, as part of their basic training, frequently point out relative risks in news stories (Friedman, Dunwoody and Rogers, 1999)?

A third problem is the intervention of public relations firms that seek to heighten publicity for a client engaged in litigation against large corporations for negligence usually linked to an expensive illness, or disease. In personal injury litigation, it is to an attorney's advantage to obtain favorable publicity about the pain and suffering of a client who is hypothetically alleged to have contracted cancer because of a toxic waste site near his or her property. Although there is rarely a question that the client is seriously ill, the epidemiology that links cancers to many environmental factors (or silicone breast implants to illness) is less direct than most persons realize. The fact a cluster of persons become ill does not mean there is an environmental cause, and it reflects a profound, but common misunderstanding of statistics and reality to assert otherwise (Logan, Fears and Wilson, 1997).

Under some of these circumstances, the press can be manipulated to obtain a more favorable verdict for a client. In most other judicial activities, journalists would not intervene on a side—so why is this behavior accepted in reporting about cancer clusters and alleged environmental malpractice (Gorney, 1993)?

In fairness, a major barrier for concerned journalists to remedy these problems is the inconsistency among many press critics whether the news media should evaluate information and confer legitimacy on one scientist or another.

For example, most food chemists want journalists to independently assess the epidemiology of a pesticide. But many food chemists do not want a journalist to assess global warming evidence; a food chemist would rather see the charges and counter charges with little press intervention.

In a scientific or biomedical subdiscipline, or arenas of expertise, experts are consistently yelling at journalists to become more literate, better informed and make distinctions about who are legitimate sources, who has the best evidence,—and they ask reporters to actively discredit, or ignore persons with less evidence to advance scientific claims. But as soon as experts move outside their discipline their message to the news media is the reverse: just publish what you find and let us make up our mind.

In science and environmental coverage, the scientific community is sending a flawed, mixed message to journalists. While the press is asked to decipher and elucidate evidence part of the time, most of the public can't make up their minds whether reporters are the first line guardians/gatekeepers of scientific credibility.

For the news media to make progress, it is important for the scientific/biomedical community and the public to decide what role they want journalists to serve and send a consistent message.

The most desirable scenario would be for readers and viewers to insist that reporters and their editors receive statistical/epidemiological/risk assessment training and use their judgment to ascertain if claims are based on grounded evidence—and support news organizations when they take the brave stand to report what the science yields—and no more. News organizations also might inform readers when assertions (of public health risks) are based in "frontier" science, which is often too preliminary to merit a scientific consensus or public policy conclusions.

In closing, there needs to be additional leadership from scientists and journalists to support news organizations that place health risks in context, publish "frontier science" warnings and publish only what the data assert. Some pioneering efforts by veteran journalists such as the late Victor Cohn (1990; Cohn & Cope, 2001) have been followed by important initiatives sponsored by journalism organizations to overcome innumeracy. Among the organizations that now provide novice to advanced training for journalists are: the Association of Health Care Journalists, the National Institute for Computer Assisted Research, Investigative Reporters and Editors, the Society of Environmental Journalists and the National Association of Science Writers. Their collective efforts and influence are an important step in the right direction.

Web sites of important science, environmental, medical and investigative journalism organizations:

National Association of Science Writers, http://www.nasw.org

Society of Environmental Journalists, http://www.sej.org

Association of Health Care Journalists, http://www.ahcj.umn.edu

Investigative Reporters and Editors, http://www.ire.org

National Institute for Computer-Assisted Reporting, http://www.nicar.org

---

## HOW TO READ A SCIENTIFIC JOURNAL

Most scientific journals that report the findings of new studies in a discipline follow the same general model for publication of articles. Some sections are more important than others for nonexpert readers. Here is a list of those main sections and their value to science and technical feature article writers:

1. Introduction and literature review—This section can be skimmed but usually has minimal value to you. In it, you find out about the problem being studied, what has previously been done by other researchers on the subject, and justification for the present study.

2. Statement of hypotheses or research questions—This part is more important because it tells you the particular focus of the study. What does the researcher want to find and, in the case of hypotheses, expect to find?

3. Method—Almost all research reports should have a section devoted to study procedures. What materials and methods were used in the study?

What type of study (survey, experiment, and so on) was it? This section is valuable to reporters only if the procedures used are controversial, revolutionary, or otherwise noteworthy.

4. Findings—The findings are far more valuable than the previously noted sections. Usually these are reported as text, but findings may also be placed in tables for quantitative studies. What did the study determine? The article should tell you in this section. What do you think of the findings?

5. Discussion—Interpretation and conclusions may be as important to you as the findings. Much of their value depends on the quality of this section, but this is the place where the researcher tries to make sense of the findings. The key point here is for the researcher to describe the meaning of the findings and simply not retell them.

Other common parts of research journal articles include the abstract, the author's identification and acknowledgments, data tables and graphics, and, of course, appendixes.

## COPING WITH QUANTITATIVE INFORMATION

One reason some writers shy away from science and technical writing is their aversion to anything involving numbers. This is especially true if the numbers are so small or so large most people cannot comprehend them. Readers often have the same aversion to statistics. Science and technical articles with many numbers or articles burdened with statistics simply turn off certain readers. It is up to you to judge the right amount of quantitative information in your articles.

Hart, writing coach for *The Oregonian,* said we must be prepared to deal with numbers because there is no way of avoiding them. "The march of science and the computerization of government means that counting things becomes more and more fundamental to the process of daily life," Hart said (1991c, p. 1). "We must not only get numbers right, we must keep stories that contain them interesting and meaningful" (Hart, 1991c, p. 1). Hart proposed that writers do the arithmetic for readers. Check how a number was computed and its accuracy before the story is published. He said it helps to visualize what the numbers represent. He also advised writers to use comparable forms of numbers (e.g., percentages or fractions) when using more than one statistic in a sentence or paragraph and to make the numbers meaningful by putting them in terms average readers understand.

It is also beneficial to use only the numbers you need and eliminate others. Minimize numerical density and avoid excessive detail, Hart (1991c) said, by not packing too many numbers into a single paragraph. Often, making numbers in science and technical articles reader-friendly means finding ways to sugarcoat the statistical medicine for readers. The information may be critical to the article and you must use it. Being creative helps retain readership. Here are some additional tips to beat the technical game:

1. Use informational graphics, a subject that is discussed in more detail later.
2. Round off or shorten the detail of certain numbers. Although you cannot do this on all statistics, it can be done on very large or small numbers.
3. Put numbers in a meaningful context for readers with examples. If you have statistics for an entire state or country, reduce them to a level that makes more sense.
4. Interpret unusual statistics. Tell readers what they mean. Is a statistic good or bad, high or low?

## A BASIC STRUCTURE FOR WRITING

When you sit down to write a science or technology article, the usual rules for writing and organization apply. Because of the unusual nature of the material involved, a little extra effort makes a difference. Regardless of the organizational plan you choose, if you accomplish these four goals in the article, you will probably succeed:

1. Get the reader's attention—Using whatever lead you choose, draw the readers into the article. Make them want to read it. Create drama. Use tension. No matter what you do, do not lose your potential readers with a slow, unimaginative start.
2. Get the reader personally involved—After you have the reader's attention, show the reader how this subject affects him or her. What does it mean to the reader? Can you help him or her identify with the subject? Have you written it in a personal way so that it appeals on an individual level? How can your reader benefit from the article's content?
3. Illustrate your points—If you achieve this goal, you are showing readers about what you are writing. Give examples and case studies. But try to provide situations that can be understood at the level of your reader— whether the general public or the sophisticated specialist.
4. Explain the meaning—Tell readers what this development means. Do not leave your reader with the feeling, "so what?" when he or she puts down your article. This is the major point of your article, so be certain you have made this assessment at some point. Many writers recommend the "so what?" be placed near the end as part of the conclusion.

## WRITING ABOUT TECHNOLOGY

Darrel Raynor (personal communication, May 26, 1993 & February 5, 1998), a management and information systems manager, project manager, and independent computer consultant who writes freelance technical articles about management, computer hardware, and software, lives in suburban Dallas, TX. He offers a cookbook approach to writing technical feature articles:

> First, I identify a hot topic I think will be of interest to specific readers. Then I spend about a half hour finding out if there is enough interesting research material. Then I hone a three-to-four sentence description I can pitch to editors–publishers as I talk to them. If approved in writing, unless I have a long relationship with the editor–publisher, I start gathering research material immediately and keep at it! My averages are 1 hour pure research time per 500 words, if I already know a lot about the topic, and about 1 hour research per 250 words if I am less familiar with the topic (if I have the lead time to gather materials at my convenience, otherwise double the times). Then I outline the piece to find out if fill-in research, quotes, or interviews are required.
>
> I start writing 1 day ahead of deadline for every 100 words in the piece. This is my rule of thumb to avoid deadline fever and 3 a.m. mistakes. I then get an unsuspecting friend and at least one person knowledgeable in the subject to edit. I pay attention to what they say and finish in time to let the manuscript rest at least 2 days for final edit and review. I send in at least 2 days before deadline, preferably via e-mail." (Raynor, personal communication, May 26, 1993 & February 5, 1998)

## TECHNICAL AND TRADE PUBLICATIONS

Although technical and trade publications might be an excellent source for some of your feature writing ideas, have you ever considered these publications as possible markets for your features? If you have an interest in science and technology writing, then you should consider these publications as outlets for your work, especially if you want to be a freelance writer. If you want full-time employment as a science and technical feature writer, then these publications might be your new home. These publications are highly specialized and require that you have extensive knowledge of the subject as well. Alert students should consider a second major in addition to journalism that might create that specialization. For example, if you have an interest in transportation, an engineering second major would be useful.

For writers getting into the profession after their college experience, think about your undergraduate major as a possible specialization. Write about what you know. It is not uncommon to have a "previous life" before an interest in journalism, and this experience can often be the ticket to a specialization in these highly defined publications. There are many business and industry, or trade, publications in the United States. Thousands of such trade periodicals mean thousands of opportunities for a writer. *Writer's Digest* columnist Art Spikol (1987) summed up opportunities with these publications:

> [I]t's hard for me to think of any field of human endeavor for which a trade publication doesn't exist. And since many of you do something else with your time when you are not writing—like holding down full-time jobs—chances are you already know enough about something to come up with some articles you can sell to the trades themselves. (p. 18)

Some trade magazines and newsletters are in-house publications. That is, they represent and are published by institutions, organizations, corporations, and other businesses—each with special interests. The nature of these publications reflects the sponsor or source, of course. In many cases, however, these publications are produced for the technical community of the organization and are often no different in subject matter approach from non-in-house, or consumer, publications that frequently use scientific and technical articles.

Spikol (1986b) said there are some differences, however, that you must remember if you consider writing for such a publication:

> Of course, corporate publications are *supposed* to be different from consumer publications. What makes them different, are, among other things, the selling of advertising, the advocacy position (the corporate publication is supposed to enhance the corporation), the captive audience, the clearances required, the free distribution. (p. 16)

## ILLUSTRATIONS HELP TELL THE STORY

Visual communication techniques such as informational graphics help tell the science and technology story that contains complicated statistics, numbers, or other quantitative information. However, that is only one important use of graphics and illustrations in science and technical writing. Newspapers, magazines, and newsletters have found new artistic and computational means to create visual tools such as info-graphics to help explain complex issues. These illustrations combine factual information with visual techniques such as graphs, charts, maps, or exploded diagrams to tell a story.

With more and more publications using color, the value of these visual packages in explaining complicated science, medicine, or technical subjects is growing. Because computers, informational graphics software, and photocopies are aiding in the rapid preparation of these images as well, they can be prepared more easily on shorter notice to art departments. At times, photographs can be the answer. Posed photographs that serve as illustrations make the point also.

Art, such as drawings, maps, and graphs, can show the interrelationships of parts, procedures, and plans to clearly explain it. In many cases, it is appropriate and necessary for you as the writer to take the lead in suggesting visual applications for an article. These techniques are particularly helpful for science and technical writers. For example, in explaining how the space shuttle disaster occurred, many publications used color graphics to supplement features that were written weeks and months after the accident.

The principle is no different from certain types of service articles such as the how-to article. To make information more understandable—something as routine as bypass surgery or as unusual as a nuclear reactor fire and explosion—illustrations such as informational graphics are necessary to tell the story.

## ENTICING PEOPLE TO READ ABOUT SCIENCE

Patrice Adcroft (personal communication, August 16, 1988), a veteran magazine journalist and former editor of the recently closed science-based *Omni* magazine, said it is a challenge to entice readers into science and technical material:

> Nobody but nobody wants to read technical writing. It does nothing that good writing ought to do: inform, entertain, and move the reader in some way. Expose an idea to the air, convert a nonbeliever. Instill a sense of wonderment. Let the reader in on a universal truth.
>
> What science writing should be is really up to you, the writer. Every piece should carry with it some kind of agenda: a determination to arrive at something greater than just a set of facts. I can tell you what good science writing—good journalism—should not do: it should never intimidate, pontificate, or confuse. Even the most complex scientific breakthrough can be described in ordinary terms. Writers who rely on jargon are either befuddled or snobs. I wouldn't want my readers to have to put up with either of these.
>
> Telling a good story is fundamental to good writing. Don't forget to leave a trail that guides the reader from lead to end. Just be sure that the trail consists of something more substantive than breadcrumbs. The trail should be clearly marked, with a few resting-places along the way where a reader can stop and catch his breath and reflect on what's been said. I really care about the way an article sounds. If one of my editors is having trouble with an article, I'll tell him to read the piece aloud. Then he gets an idea of how it will sound in the reader's head. If a sentence just clunks along, or you can't get its meaning from one reading, there's a problem.
>
> Science writers should know how to interview professionals. That means getting them to talk on the average person's level. If you don't understand a concept or formula, neither will the reader. I have something I call the amazing dumb animal question. When there's something terribly complex to grasp, the theory of chaos, for example, or automata, I preface my questions with: "OK. This may sound like a dumb animal question, but . . ." I've asked bioengineers to compare

artificial organs to washing machines, neurologists to compare the central nervous system to the New York subway lines (the article was going in a publication geared for New Yorkers). Always ask your source to compare whatever he's talking about to an everyday item. Seek out an image the reader can hang on to. This will make the item, concept, equation, live.

A few words about the best science-technology stories I've published: All contained some human element (a maverick scientist's struggle with a staid institution, for example); all were clear, but not simple-minded; all took the reader on a journey which left him more aware of himself and the world around him. Many were cleverly packaged—an article on the future of films appeared as movie treatments, actually written by famous directors who were told to pretend that they had the most futuristic technology at their fingertips. Good science writing doesn't just report on a breakthrough and leave it at that; it investigates the consequences of the discovery or breakthrough.

# PART THREE

# THE COLLEGIATE AND PROFESSIONAL WRITER

# CHAPTER SEVENTEEN

# Writing Feature Articles
# on Campus

If you take a few minutes and browse some of the college newspapers, magazines, newsletters, and online publications available on the World Wide Web, you will discover that the diversity of subjects and approaches to feature articles is not much different than those of professional publications. Campus publications such as 27,000-circulation *The Daily Texan* at the University of Texas at Austin (http://www.tsp.utexas.edu), the 16,000-circulation *UW Daily* at the University of Washington (http://thedaily.washington.edu), or the 17,000-circulation *Indiana Daily Student* at Indiana University at Bloomington (http://idsnews.com) offer real world feature writing opportunities and experiences for students on campus. Campus publications are excellent places to get a start as a feature writer.

Student feature writers produce stories about campus leaders, celebrations, campus tragedies, unusual research studies, film festivals, new CDs, and even the weather. Some of these are challenging stories and require a level of subject expertise or writing and reporting experience to be done effectively. Others are straightforward and perfect opportunities for a beginning feature writer.

Your first feature story assignment may not involve a complicated story; it may be produced for a beginning writing class or for one of the student publications on your campus. You receive the assignment and get started. It is probably a very good opportunity to get your first story into print or online. Student publications serve a noble purpose for their campuses—they are the primary mass communication means at many schools—and their feature content is an important part of those publications. Not only do these publications provide a forum for development of student journalistic skills, they also inform students, faculty, and staff. Campus publications are important voices where there may not be many other options.

Feature articles are a significant part of student publications because so many student publications are produced on nondaily deadlines. The infrequency of publication often dictates a more feature-oriented approach to writing breaking news, which usually would be treated as a news story rather than a feature. Some major campus newspapers are dailies with a larger proportion of breaking or spot news, but most campus publications are not. Student newspapers that publish once or twice a week have even larger percentages of feature content because of their infrequency of publication. It is one of the ways these publications strive to keep stories fresh and appealing. Similarly, campus magazines and newsletters, which may publish only monthly or less often, have large proportions of major and minor feature articles in their content mix.

This means there are numerous feature-writing opportunities for a beginning college-level writer. In fact, these opportunities are the best places for you to build confidence in your work and to show others that you can master feature writing. Large colleges and universities may have a dozen or more university-sponsored, student-funded, and independent student-oriented publications. In addition to the more conventional campus newspapers, you may find laboratory newspapers produced occasionally by news-editorial or journalism programs or by specific journalism or English Department classes. There may be other special newspapers produced from time to time by organizations such as student affairs, the athletic department, various academic units, administrative offices such as admissions and enrollments, and the alumni associations. There are similar opportunities with campus magazines. Most major universities and colleges have one or more regularly published magazines. Some are only once- or twice-a-year specialized magazines, such as literary or greek organization publications, but others are issued on a much more frequent basis.

Student journalists should not overlook newsletters as an outlet for their work. Most student organizations have a need to communicate with their members or potential members and newsletters are frequently used. There are opportunities for beginners looking for their first byline in all of these publications right on your campus.

Feature stories are probably among the easiest types of articles to develop on a campus for beginning writers. You are writing about a place that is familiar to you and using sources that are reasonably easy to contact and develop. There is also the convenience of geographic proximity and easy-to-get background information that helps beginners as well. These experiences not only build confidence, they also give novices their first experiences in working with editors. You have a chance to try out the techniques and approaches you have read about and discussed in class. These may be the least difficult markets for beginners to crack. Sometimes, beginning college-level writers are able to sell their work to local newspapers or magazines, but this is rare. It may not take long for a strong and talented writer to develop the skills necessary to make the jump from college publications to more professional ones, but the place for most students to start is on campus.

## WORKING AND LEARNING WITH OTHER STUDENTS

The opportunities you have to write feature articles while you are a student at a college or university are important ones in your development as a professional feature writer. This experience is very valuable. It is your opportunity to learn.

It is also a chance to experiment with new writing and reporting approaches and styles. In an educational environment, there is more room for making mistakes from which you can grow. There is the chance to work closely with professors, publication advisors, and other more experienced writing coaches who may not be as readily available to you once you leave school.

Working with student editors is also an opportunity for student writers to learn the interpersonal skills needed to function as a professional. The give and take between an editor and writer is not all that different on a college campus. The concerns and basics of the relationships are the same.

Perhaps the major reason campus feature writing is different is that it is a learning experience. Although you do not want to make mistakes, you can. Although you do not want to leave problems with editors or sources unsolved, you might. Although you do not want to use bad judgment, you could. In essence, opportunities with student publications are the time to learn by doing. Try the theory from class discussions and textbooks. Put it into practice. We learn from experiences, and the journalistic opportunities you have on campus enhance your writing. This is the time to experiment with your writing—try things you might not have the chance to try once your career begins. It is the time to stretch yourself and see what might be your real potential.

Most colleges and universities produce publications for students, faculty, staff, and alumni. Although these are written and edited by professional staffs, students often are given opportunities to take assignments as part of classes, for part-time employment, and for other purposes.

How do you get started? At most student publications, it is as simple as walking into the office and asking to meet with an editor. Introduce yourself and tell him or her that you want to write. An application might be completed along the way, but the big step is asking for, and accepting, that first assignment. Some publications give you a specific story to begin. Others are willing to take your own suggestions for stories. Because you may be asked to propose something, be prepared to suggest a strong feature story idea.

## WORKING WITH STUDENT EDITORS

Most of the editors you work with on campus are also students. Although some may be graduate students, the vast majority are undergraduates. This means that most student editors have limited experience and are learning as they work. Although the editors might have more experience as a staff writer or news reporter than you, they do not have that much more experience. This means there has to be a lot of flexibility in the relationship between student writers and editors. Mistakes will be made on both ends. Questionable decisions are made. Tempers may get out of control. But you, as a feature writer, need to take as much as you can from the relationship by gaining additional experience and learning from your editor.

Student editors, as individuals also learning their jobs, might not be as well organized as they should be. You may find the direction of your assignment changes in midstream. Some editors might not be as specific on the focus needed for an assignment. They might forget details you need or they might not be able to suggest sources as effectively as a more seasoned professional. These individuals have earned their positions by paying some dues and usually have learned something from that experience. You can benefit from it, too. In fact, some students argue that they learn more from their student editors and their experiences writing for these peer "bosses" than they do in writing and other journalism classes because there is no pressure of grades. The practical value of the experience is not to be doubted.

Perhaps the most important part of the student editor–feature writer relationship is for you as the writer to earn trust in your work. This is done through meticulous attention to detail. The story must be complete, but it must also be accurate. Student editors are exactly like their professional counterparts in this regard, of course. If you go into a publication office with a hastily prepared, poorly written article with no direct quotations, you are in trouble right away. An error-prone feature article does not impress any editor, so do not expect to get a second chance. There are few student editors working in newsrooms around the country who do not experience receiving copy like that on a regular basis. On the other hand, if that feature story is thoughtfully done with clever writing, sound organization, attention-getting description, and personality-filled direct quotations, your story will not only be published, but probably you will be asked to take on more assignments for upcoming issues. In other words, be prepared. Make a strong first impression even if it is for a student publication. Put time into the effort. It will pay you back in countless ways, but the most significant one will be in the number of opportunities you develop for yourself.

## CAMPUS NEWSPAPERS

As in the commercial world, college newspapers come in all shapes and sizes. Some are broadsheet (or traditional full size) whereas others are tabloids (rotated half-size pages). Some campus newspapers publish as seldom as 2 or 3 times a month, others as often as 5 to 7 days a week when school is in session. Some have summer editions whereas others do not. In terms of management, some campus newspapers are independent of the school's central administration, but many are not. Regardless of the type of newspaper on your campus, it is likely that your school has some sort of newspaper and perhaps even more than one.

Depending on the school and its size, opportunities to write features for campus newspapers vary. Some campus newspapers, even the highest quality publications, can never seem to recruit enough news and feature writers. Others, most likely ones published at major state universities and other big schools, have much more competitive situations and any staff writing positions are difficult to secure.

Two of the most popular feature-oriented sections are typically entertainment and sports. A third section embraces student lifestyles and extracurricular activities. These are subjects in which college students often seem to feel most comfortable and are great places to start. However, remember that there are other sections needing help, too. Opinion section editors are always looking for insightful and interesting columnists with a fresh look at current events or with something to say about the issues. Student activities—how students spend their time both on and off campus—never cease to be potential feature material.

Activities, entertainment, and campus events that are a part of student lifestyles are also reasons to write news features for campus publications. And it is newsworthy when proposals are put forth to change policies or laws that affect the activities and interests of students. Thus, when a local law is proposed that might keep students from participating in a favorite leisure activity, a strong feature would look at how students feel about the proposal.

News sections also use features to balance the routine spot coverage of the day. These features often offer unique perspectives and sometimes can set a seasonal tone for readers. This was the case for one writer for the University of Florida's daily student newspaper. Keith Herrel (1989), who was a student feature writer for *The Independent Alligator* in Gainesville (http://www.alligator.org), wrote an entertaining Thanksgiving seasonal feature. In the story headlined, "The Lord Provides It, and We Cook It," he tells a warm personal story about a rural family that lives near the university and how it prepares its highly unusual holiday feast in true communal style. Note how the story is enriched by Herrel's use of strong and revealing direct quotations. He allows his sources to tell their story. This is Herrel's engaging story:

> It's easy to find Thelma Markham at Thanksgiving. Just pull up next to the Grove Park store on Highway 20 east of Gainesville, roll down the window and ask for "T.J." One of the many locals who gather around the picnic table will point east and say, "Just follow your nose."
>
> The brief directions are explicit indeed. If Thelma is home and the wind is blowing the right way, the delectable scent of roasting wild meat will mingle with the aroma of fresh vegetables and attract hungry visitors from all over town.
>
> Down the pitted dirt road that leads to Thelma's place, the modern world temporarily ceases to exist. On both sides of the road, amid the trees draped with Spanish moss, stand multi-colored houses arranged helter-skelter like handfuls of tin-roofed dice thrown down by some impetuous gambler.
>
> It's easy to distinguish Thelma's house from the rest. The laughter there is louder, the crowd larger and the welcome heartier.
>
> "Pick up a plate and sit down," is a favorite greeting of Cheristine, Thelma's sister. She will tell you in a friendly bluffness to go into the dining room and fill up your dish.

The food will be in a horseshoe-shaped arrangement in the rustic dining room. But filling your plate may not be an easy task; at any time there might be 40 or more of Thelma's friends and relatives vying for the steaming foods in the compact room. If this is the case, then it is a perfect time to visit the cook.

Thelma, 26, will be in her small kitchen, adjacent to the dining room. She will greet you with a smile and talk to you as she skillfully prepares some of her specialties, ranging from cooter to 'coon and gator to gravy. Some opossums will be in the pot and turkeys in the oven as she wipes her hands with a towel and carries a casserole dish heaped with swamp cabbage into the awaiting holiday throng.

Thelma, who is single and has no children of her own, is the uncontested culinary master of her family. She has been for years.

But exactly how long ago she took command of the kitchen is uncertain.

"She was about 8 years old when she started," Thelma's uncle Johnny Mack, 40, said. Sitting on one of the two living room couches, wearing a gray Fedora and sipping a cold Old Milwaukee, Johnny reminisced about Thelma's earliest meals.

"I started cooking at least 18 years ago," Thelma said.

"She was 11. And the first thing she cooked was a red velvet cake," said Zennie Sheffield, Thelma's 80-year-old great-grandmother.

Although her family disagrees about when Thelma began her cooking, everyone agrees that her food is excellent.

"They better tell me my food is good. 'Cause if they don't, they won't be eating here anymore," Thelma said with determination.

For Thelma's family, having her in the kitchen means having a cornucopia on the table. But exactly how big is Thelma's family?

"I got so many grand, great-grand and greater-grandchildren that if they were all hogs, I'd be rich," Mrs. Sheffield said. "I came down here from Georgia about 45 years ago with my father and my five children. Now I have close to 100 relatives living around here."

Mrs. Sheffield lives in the house next to Thelma's. The two houses, along with the yard that separates and surrounds them, have a personality all their own. The yard is frequented and fertilized by an array of animals, domestic and wild.

Red and yellow hens and roosters, pecking and cock-a-doodling at whim, strut around the amber grass and green shrubs. Armadillo and wild turkeys sometimes venture on the grounds and usually find themselves on Thelma's table. Bunky the cat scampers around, evading the eight or nine dogs that wait not so patiently for a generous handout from Thelma. A black pig named Arnold rounds out the cast.

The cacophony created by those animals sometimes competes with other noises made by various children screaming and groups of men shooting their shotguns in preparation for the day's hunt.

"You should have been here this past Super Bowl," Johnny Mack said. "I brought home a 10-point deer." He spread his arms wide to show the breadth of the animal's antlers with the 10 horns. "It fed about 15 people."

Thelma opened up one of her family's five full-length freezers. It was as full as a supermarket's meat case. She started pulling out the frozen bundles to try and tell what each one contained. After scraping ice off of the basketball-sized chunks of meat, she began to tell what was in each plastic-wrapped package.

"This is some of that wild boar. This is rabbit. This is probably 'coon. I think this is some of that wild turkey. Hmmmmmm. I don't know what this is."

"All of our freezers are like that," Cheristine said as she sat at the table eating some of Thelma's fried opossum and sweet potatoes, garnished with red peppers. "We're prepared for anything—hurricanes, tornadoes, water flows, fire, you name it.

The hundreds of pounds of meat and vegetables tucked away in Thelma's freezers probably could feed the whole family every day for one month before the supply ran out. But the freezers are unlikely to become barren, because everybody constantly adds either animals or vegetables to the stockpile.

"My cousin, he's the one who gets me the swamp cabbage," Thelma said. "He goes down by the trestle where the fishing water is, and there are these pell-mell plants.

He gets a machete and cuts away at the bark to the middle. Then he brings it to me. You have to cook it longer than regular cabbage though, just like you're cooking a pot of greens.

"Now my granddaddy, he has a garden with red peppers, greens, iced potatoes—just about all the vegetables we eat come from his garden. He's about 68 or 69 years old, and brother, he could sure get around. He's also cheaper on your pockets. All you have to do is go down there and bring him a six-pack, and he'll give you whatever you want."

With bartering like this, Thelma's table is seldom lacking in food, and this fact is never more obvious than at Thanksgiving.

The heat from the wood-burning stove banished the autumn cold and gave the house an old-world scent as Thelma sat at the dining-room table and told how she prepares her holiday banquets.

"In the evening, I start cooking. I'll cook until about five o'clock in the morning, and then I'll go take a nap.

"When I get up, I'll start putting out the food. It will be spread over that dresser, that dresser and this table." She made a sweeping motion with her hand around the room, showing the extent of the banquet area.

"Everybody starts at one end and works their way around. If they don't get enough the first time, they just have to go through the line again. Most people will come with their Tupperware dishes and take the food to go because there wouldn't be enough room for everybody if they stayed here."

The more than 40 guests who Thelma fed last Thanksgiving, however, found ample dining area in the yard and an overabundance of food on the table.

"I had ham, two turkeys, deer, opossum, 'coon. Let's see. Oh, yeah, I had a duck too. My nephew got it. My granddaddy gave us mustard and collard greens, string beans, potatoes, peas in the shell and okra. And we had swamp cabbage, too."

As if trying to establish the logic of it all, she said, "You see, you just can't have one or two meats at Thanksgiving or Christmas."

Her words came almost as an echo of her great-grandmother.

"If the children eat all that's there, there wasn't enough," Mrs. Sheffield said. "I brought them up that way."

To feed squadrons of hungry guests in the hearty manner that Thelma does, one would expect to pay dearly at the neighborhood supermarket.

"I gave my mother $50 to get some eggs, salt, pepper, milk and macaroni from the store," Thelma said. "Altogether I paid less than $40 for the Thanksgiving meal that lasted two days. The rest of the food was all natural. It came from out there." She pointed toward the dense woodland that sprawled behind her backyard.

Thelma's natural, robust personality is mirrored in the way she cooks her food. She abides by a no-frills code when preparing her meals. She has no need for exotic spices or arcane herbs. And she finds no need for a pencil and paper.

"A lot of people come along with a recipe book, and still their food don't taste good," Thelma said.

She went into the kitchen and came out with a one-quarter teaspoon silver measuring spoon. Then she dipped it into an imaginary canister, showing her spicing technique.

"I take a little spoon like this and I estimate. I judge a little bit. At times, I'll use parsley, bay leave, paprika, seasoned salt, celery or oregano. I put whatever I want to put in."

She put down the spoon and picked up a three-inch bone from a plate.

"Could you tell this was once a opossum?" she asked smiling. "Let me tell you about opossum. First, you can't go reachin' in the trap and grab one out or you'll get bit. Then you'll have to make sure they aren't foamin' at the mouth or you'll get sick. Then you swivel them over an open flame to get the hair off of them. After that you wash them down with washing powder and let them sit in salted water for a while to get the burnt taste out."

Thelma has a similar technique for wild turkey. She also has tricks on how to take the wild out of wild rabbit and ways to tenderize even the most sinewy meats. Yet there remains some secrets she won't reveal.

"I don't go giving away all my recipes," she said.

Even if some of her recipes are sacrosanct, most of the pleasure is in the palate, not in the preparation. Except maybe for Thelma.

"Cooking is a wonderful experience," Thelma said with an air of satisfaction. "I enjoy cooking and knowing that everybody knows where they are going to eat. It's just like the Waltons. They say grace, hold hands, and especially bless the cook." She halted, and with arms akimbo, said, "If they don't they'll get sick!"

Enthusiastically, Thelma went on to tell about her aspirations for a special kind of restaurant.

"I'm gonna have some of everything. I'll be open for breakfast, lunch and dinner and have two bodyguards because of the crime and stuff. And I'm gonna call it, 'The Soul Food and Wildlife Restaurant.' "

If only a fraction of Thelma's friends and family dine at her prospective restaurant, it will become a bonanza. But until then, her intimate clientele will continue its feasting and festivities at her home, realizing how good life can be.

"We do it good in the woods," Cheristine said as she enjoyed a piece of Thelma's wild rabbit. "The Lord provides it, and we cook it." (Herrel, 1989, p. 8)

(Reprinted with the permission of the *Independent Alligator*, University of Florida, Gainesville.)

## CAMPUS MAGAZINES

Campus magazines come in several forms. Some magazines are affiliated with campus newspapers and distributed as part of the newspaper, but many are independent publications that are not tied to the newspaper in any manner.

---

## THE CREAM OF THE CAMPUS CROP

Some of the nation's best campus publications were recently honored in the Associated Collegiate Press "Best of Show" competition at the National College Media Convention, in fall 2002 in Orlando, FL. The winners included the following:

Newspapers: 4-year daily broadsheet—*Indiana Daily Student*, University of Indiana, Bloomington.

Newspapers: 4-year daily tabloid—*The Daily Mississippian*, University of Mississippi, University.

Newspapers: 4-year weekly broadsheet—*Index*, Truman State University, Kirksville, MO.

Newspapers: 4-year weekly tabloid—*The Central Florida Future*, University of Central Florida, Orlando.

Newspapers: 4-year less frequently than weekly—*The Arkansas Traveler*, University of Arkansas, Fayetteville.

Newspapers: 2-year tabloid—*El Don*, Santa Ana College, Santa Ana, CA.

Newspapers: 2-year broadsheet—*The Advocate*, Contra Costa College, San Pablo, CA.

Newspaper Special Edition: 4-year daily—*Indiana Daily Student*, Indiana University, Bloomington.

Newspaper Special Edition: 4-year nondaily—*FS View and Florida Flambeau*, Florida State University, Tallahassee.

Newspaper Special Edition: 2-year—*The Advocate*, Contra Costa College, San Pablo, CA.

Feature Magazines—*MPJ*, Syracuse University, Syracuse, NY.

Literary Magazines—*Pandora*, Centenary College, Shreveport, LA.

Yearbooks: fewer than 300 pages—*Kanza*, Pittsburg State University, Pittsburg, KS.

Yearbooks: 300 or more pages—*Royal Purple*, Kansas State University, Manhattan.

Newspaper-published magazines are campus versions of Sunday magazine sections found in metropolitan newspapers. These publications can be weekly, monthly, or perhaps once-a-semester periodicals. They can be routinely organized, or formatted, to offer longer features, listings, columns, and other content. Or they can be publications devoted to special topics such as spring break, job hunting and careers, a season preview of a varsity sport, or a special annual event on campus such as homecoming. Some magazines are special reports in tabloid format published as part of the student newspaper or independently by classes. In recent years, some online campus magazines have appeared also. These may or may not be tied to existing printed publications. Some are organizational in nature, whereas others serve the entire campus. Although most publish on a regular basis when school is in session, some campus magazines and special reports are published as infrequently as once a year.

Campus magazines that are not associated with campus newspapers are often specialized publications. Some are published for distribution on campus by magazine programs and others are published for sale in the neighboring community or region. Still other student-written and student-edited magazines represent the interests of student organizations, academic departments, or other units of the institution. Commonly found in English departments, for instance, are student literary magazines containing a mixture of fiction and nonfiction articles. These magazines often use nonfiction feature articles and essays in addition to short stories, poetry, and other creative writing.

## COLLEGE AND UNIVERSITY YEARBOOKS

Most universities and colleges have yearbooks. After a generation of absence or downsizing on some campuses and experimentation with video formats, traditional yearbooks have made a comeback. Although these publications are annually issued, they afford opportunities for student feature writers interested in specialized forms of writing that are not time bound and are more people oriented. Yearbooks are usually dominated by their photographic content, but most yearbook editors seek some sort of balance with a collection of student-written articles that focus on all aspects of student life.

Usually a yearbook has a single editor in charge of the whole book; he or she delegates responsibilities for specific assignments to section editors. Students find articles about organizations, major unusual events on campus, new facilities, student leaders, annual major activities each year, outstanding administrators, and the best faculty members on campus. Some yearbooks run extended feature articles much like a magazine, using text and photographs. The main distinction is the perspective the articles take—keeping in mind that yearbook features are frequently explanatory (why or how) or retrospective features. The focus is on people (who) and activities (what) from the past year. Many yearbooks also run short, but informative, features discussing the purposes and accomplishments of active individuals and organizations during the past year.

Photographs, artwork, and other graphics dominate yearbooks, so articles usually do not run as long as those found in magazines or newspapers. Because yearbooks are often published each spring or summer, the articles have to take an overview or general approach to the subject. Feature articles include profiles of student leaders and administrators and features about athletic teams and academic departments. Also common are feature articles about benchmark events on campus such as graduation day, the day one of the athletic teams won a big championship, homecoming, or a visit by a dignitary such as a politician, internationally popular entertainer, or renowned scholar. Other features may be aftermath or follow-up articles that combine a series of related campus events into a single story.

Student writers interested in contributing to the yearbook should study the most recent two or three editions, but each one is a bit different. These are usually kept in the main library and the yearbook office. It is also a good idea to look at "exchange" yearbooks, ones that your school's yearbook staff receives from other schools in trade.

## CAMPUS NEWSLETTERS

There are thousands of student organizations on campuses across the country. There may be hundreds on your own campus. With low-cost computer-based publishing technology and fast, inexpensive printing and photocopying available near campuses, it is no longer financially difficult for these usually impoverished organizations to produce readable printed newsletters. Some have become electronic editions, using the World Wide Web or electronic mail for distribution. Many are published locally on college and university campuses by student, faculty, staff, and alumni organizations and are known to few people outside the members of the organizations they serve. Some, however, are produced on a national or regional level for college-level readers, and command wide attention.

These newsletters may be as small as two pages of text or as professional appearing as a slick, full-color, magazine format. These newsletters are also excellent places to gain feature writing experience. Why is this? First, chances are good that you know something about the organization and the special interests it represents. Even if you do not know much about the group or its mission, the organization may be small and probably needs assistance in producing its newsletter. This makes editorial access relatively easy. You can probably select the assignments yourself—if not in the beginning, not long after you "prove" yourself. You probably will not get paid for working on a campus newsletter, but you will get your writing published. For a beginner, this is important.

## FAVORITE CAMPUS SOURCES

With thousands of persons on a college or university campus, there are many choices for reliable sources for feature assignments. Here is a list of some of the most used sources on campuses:

Administration:
    President's office and staff.
    Academic provosts, chancellors, and staff.
    Vice president of student affairs and staff.
    Deans, department chairs, and staff.
    University counsel and other attorneys on staff.
    University relations and public relations office staff.
    University "official" Web site maintained by school officials.

Faculty:
    Research grant holders.
    Faculty authors.
    Distinguished faculty chair holders.
    Long-term faculty veterans.
    Outstanding teacher or outstanding researcher award winners.
    Academic advisors.
    Individual faculty course and research Web sites.
    Community service programs supervised by faculty.

Students:
    Independent, greek, and other social organizations' leaders.
    Student organization Web sites.
    Student government officers and government Web sites.
    Academic organizations leaders.
    Professional societies' leaders.
    Graduate students involved in research or teaching.
    Undergraduate and graduate student research award winners.
    Varsity athletics and sports information office.
    Individual student Web sites.

Support staff:
  Residence halls advisors.
  University center director and staff.
  Health center director and staff.
  Employment and placement director and staff.
  Dining service director and staff.
  Recreation and intramurals director and staff.
  Campus public security and parking officers.
  Physical plant director and maintenance staff.
  Administrative support offices' Web sites.
  College and university printed and electronic publications for employees.

---

Who is interested in reading about a college or university? That would be faculty, staff, students, parents of students, alumni, supporters, and even campus neighbors. Editors of these publications often seek part-time student writing assistance. This is for several practical reasons. First, these publications want to provide the opportunities for students to learn. Second, established professionals charge a heftier fee than students charge. An editor in this situation is willing to trade off one-on-one teaching to get the needed staff assistance when the publication's budget is strained. Advanced reporting courses, practicum classes, internships, college work-study programs, and other opportunities are available for beginning feature writers to help create regular part-time or temporary clerical or writing positions at these publications. Most of the time, assignments are given by professional editors or teachers, but a feature writer with initiative—displaying enterprise with strong story ideas—can make his or her own break.

One example of this type of publication is the *Tennessee Alumnus,* published quarterly by the University of Tennessee National Alumni Association in Knoxville. The magazine is distributed to supporters of the large state university and alumni who attended any of the four campuses across the state. The magazine typically offers a dozen or more feature articles in each issue in addition to occasional feature items in the magazine's regular editorial departments (such as "UTopics" and University of Tennessee people in the national news). Features highlight the activities of faculty, alumni, the administration, and current students. Articles often focus on the school's programs, facilities, and activities, but are always strongly focused on university people. Issues in education are also addressed. A recent issue included articles that looked at the Oak Ridge National Laboratory, genome research, molecular research, and the school. Articles also highlight developments in medicine and the physical and social sciences. Articles about research conducted by faculty members that solve social needs and problems are common. The publication's editors will frequently highlight successful alumni from around the world. The *Tennessee Alumnus*, printed in full-color, has a circulation of about 66,000 copies.

Similar campus magazines aimed at alumni, donors, and others connected to universities and colleges include *Brown Alumni Magazine*, *Syracuse University Magazine*, *Harvard Magazine*, *Miami*, *Notre Dame Magazine*, *Oregon Quarterly*, *The Penn Stater*, *The Purdue Alumnus*, *Ripon College Magazine*, and *Rutgers Magazine*. These publications, according to the *Writer's Market*, use from 10% to 75% freelance material (Brogan, 2002).

Many colleges and universities produce professional-quality newsletters for general or specialized consumption. Some of these are distributed free, but others are subscription-based or tied to membership in organizations that are hosted by the university or college. There are literally thousands of such publications that have specialized orientations. These are often disciplinary in nature, focusing on a particular academic interest.

The Center for Peace and Conflict Studies at Wayne State University in Detroit, MI, produces a small newsletter, for example. Wellesley College's Center for Research on Women publishes a small semiannual newsletter. The Division of Agriculture at the University of Arkansas in Fayetteville publishes the bimonthly *Vision*. This newsletter, established in the mid 1970s, is distributed free. Often student writing assistance is sought for newsletters such as these because these newsletters are produced on shoestring budgets. Students may find funding available for these positions as well, often provided through College Work–Study program grants and other similar government programs.

## LIFE AS A CAMPUS STAFF FEATURE WRITER

The rigor of working for a campus newspaper, magazine, newsletter, or Web site will help you determine how committed you are to feature writing. There is a never-ending demand for effort by staff members on most student publications. The work never seems finished. For campus newspapers, the hours are often long and late. Most campus newspapers are morning publications, and the hours leading to publication of an issue are frequently worked in the middle of the night and on weekends. This often means sacrificing social activities and other extracurricular interests to get an assignment completed.

Student magazines, newsletters, and yearbooks have more laid-back staff work styles because there are less-frequent publication schedules and deadlines to meet. For students writing features for these publications, the hours can also be long and frequently late. Staffs for these publications are often much smaller than those of campus newspapers and the degree of interaction among staff members and editors is also high. The commitment to work on these publications is equally serious and costly, too, in terms of other extracurricular activities.

## OTHER CAMPUS FEATURE WRITING OPPORTUNITIES

There is a wide range of other options for campus feature writing for students. Perhaps the fastest growing are publications and information sites on the World Wide Web. In the past several years, educational institutions and their respective subdivisions have recognized the value of information on the Internet. This has created a wide range of possibilities for individuals who can write feature and other types of information for these institutions. Furthermore, a number of special online publications hosted by institutions have been created.

Within academic units and extracurricular programs, numerous traditional publications are also produced. Departmental, college, and university publications are among them. Numerous colleges and universities also offer feature writing opportunities. Students in the School of Communication at the University of Miami regularly write features for local newspapers through its Miami News Service. Undergraduates also contribute features such as profiles of outstanding alumni to the school's magazine-style *Communique*. Students also write features for the daily *Key West Citizen*. For more than a decade, students have produced special feature publications published both for tourists and for Monroe County residents. Undergraduate student writer Rachel Luhta (2003) took a fresh look at camping in the Florida Keys by making the requisite telephone calls, looking at Web sites, and then visiting several campgrounds, looking around, and talking with campers and campground managers. She then wrote this story for a 2003 special section:

> Camper Debbie Pursell was up early Saturday morning, but her husband was up even earlier.
>
> By 9:30 a.m., he was long gone—out fishing—and she was exploring the marina area just beyond their campground site with their kids in tow, all bundled in jackets and sweaters to stave off the morning chill, weaving their bicycles in frenzied paths around their mother, who was walking on foot.
>
> The Pursells, residents of Sunrise, decided to camp for two nights at John Pennekamp Coral Reef State Park for its location near family friends and cost—only $19 per night.
>
> Debbie Pursell said she frequents state and national parks with her family.
>
> "They're beautiful and a good price. They're not out to make a profit. I never camp at those other [commercial] parks," Pursell said.
>
> While ideal camping conditions for some include only the bare minimum: tent, campfire and secluded, rustic location under the stars, others prefer camping with the amenities of home only a few steps away: heated pool, game room, washer and dryer.
>
> Such camping areas dot the Florida Keys in the form of public parks and commercial sites, stretching from Key Largo past Key West to the Dry Tortugas National Park.
>
> Hardy, adventure-minded visitors may opt for an overnight national or state park stay, while less rugged campers may find commercial facilities more closely fulfill their needs.

Both possess similar safety precautionary measures with nighttime gate lock-downs, passable only with a specific code given to each camping party. Commercial areas and parks also offer both RV and tent sites, and often even small cabins. Differences arise, however, when comparing prices, amenities and scenic surroundings.

John Pennekamp Coral Reef State Park, located at MM 102.5 in Key Largo, is the nation's first underwater park.

Mangrove swamps, tropical hardwood hammocks and coral reefs are preserved for visitors to enjoy by hiking nature trails, snorkeling, scuba diving and canoeing. Glass bottom boat tours are offered, as are scuba certification lessons and snorkeling tours, where visitors can see the renowned "Christ of the Abyss" statue.

The park's central visitor center showcases a 30,000 gallon saltwater aquarium featuring fish indigenous to the area, such as grouper, yellow snapper, grunt and Queen Angelfish.

"It's a nice campground, convenient to a lot of things with full marina, boat rentals, etcetera—in Key Largo," Eric P. Kiefer, park manager, said.

Kiefer, Pennekamp manager since July, said that despite problems with campsite availability, 39,000 visitors stayed overnight last year. He urged campers to book sites "as far ahead of time as they can," especially during the peak season after December.

Of all the Pennekamp amenities, the campsites are nearest to the marina, circling the edge of a creek. The 47 sites crowded together are fairly void of barrier vegetation, allowing for little privacy. Bathroom and shower facilities are at each end of the campground and a new central facility is in the construction stages.

Park entrance fees are $2.50 for one person or $5 for two with 50 cents added for each additional person. Overnight camping is $19 per night. For more information, call 305–451–1202.

One mile south of Pennekamp lays Key Largo Kampground, a commercial facility mainly catering to RV campers, but it also offers tent sites. Tent sites with electricity hookup are $24.50 daily.

The campground provides its customers with laundry areas, a central recreation/meeting hall, heated swimming pool, marina and boat ramp, and a location one block away from Publix and K-Mart. Certain RV sites are situated on the campground's channel to the ocean and possess their own private dock and thatched "tiki hut." For more information, call 305–451–1431.

"With all businesses, location is primary. Our location here is ideal. Location, location, location," Pat Larcomb, Fiesta Key KOA employee, said.

At MM 70, campers can stay at Fiesta Key KOA Kampground, where tent site prices range from $40 to $55. A KOA Value Kard may be purchased for discounted rates at KOA locations across the country.

Gulf-front camping areas are available, as are RV sites and 20 motel rooms. Pool, hot tub, sauna, game room, playground, restaurant and pub are on location for the KOA camper's convenience. Cable TV and internet hookup services are provided.

According to Larcomb, a KOA employee for 12 years, more than 85 percent of Fiesta Key's campers are repeat customers. For more information, call 305–664–4922.

Further south, at Long Key State Park at MM 67.5, each campsite offered is oceanfront. Secluded and serene, most campers choose to relax on their private—if only for a few days and a nominal fee—beach, reading, swimming or conversing with neighbors. Except for the faint hum of U.S. 1 traffic, the grounds are quiet and peaceful.

"No [loud] kids, no [loud] dogs. At other places, people don't seem to take care of their animals," camper Ray Heath said, adding cost as another factor that persuaded him to return to Long Key with his wife.

This was the Heaths' second visit to Long Key. Their first stay was a year earlier. So pleased with their experience, they decided to drive from their home in New Smyrna to stay for another nine days and nights.

Heath sat at his site's picnic table, on the bench opposite the blue, calm waters, alternately skimming a magazine article and gazing at the ocean. His wife, Joan, lounged a few feet away reading a novel under the bright, midday sun. Three sites over, an impromptu guitar lesson was taking place among three visitors and nearby, a neighboring family began pitching their tent.

Activities aren't as plentiful at Long Key as at Pennekamp, but do include hiking, swimming, canoeing and picnicking. A winding boardwalk, flanked on each side by covered picnic areas, cuts through the tropical vegetation of mangroves and other shrubbery. This clean, litter-free area is on the other end of the Key. An observation tower rises at the beginning of the wooden-planked trail.

"We preserve the natural and cultural aspects of Florida while providing outdoor based recreation," Kim Crouch, assistant park manager, said.

Campsites are $17 a night, not including the park entrance fee and other minimal costs. For more information about Long Key State Park, call 305-664-4815.

Only 12 miles south of Marathon is Bahia Honda State Park, the southernmost state park in the nation at MM 37.

"It's the best spot in all the Keys. The entire Key is the state park," visitor Bryant Edmonson said.

Home for Edmonson is nearby Grassy Key. Formerly a part-time resident of Alaska, he was at Bahia Honda visiting vacationing Alaskan friends. Their Buttonwood area campsite faced the Gulf of Mexico and the massive overseas U.S. 1 bridge to Key West. Nearing sunset, the friends were relaxing outside their RV as other campers settled in for the night around them.

Campers must pay $19 a night to stay at one of Bahia Honda's three campgrounds: Buttonwood (48 sites), Bay side (eight sites) and Sandspur (24 sites, though temporarily closed). Gary McKee, park manager, said more than 500,000 people visit each year, producing annual revenues of approximately $1.5 million.

Bahia Honda is most noted for its natural sand beaches—Calusa, on the Gulf, and Logger Head and Sandspur, which overlook the Atlantic Ocean—although it offers amenities such as kayaking and snorkeling tours, as well as dive shop and bicycle rentals. The Looe Key National Marine Sanctuary is close for further exploration. Key West is only a 45-minute drive away.

According to McKee, state park camping offers more advantages than camping at commercial facilities.

"Number one, it's cheaper, and number two, the park is managed for recreation and resource," McKee said.

McKee recommended prospective campers book their reservations 11 months in advance. For more information, call 305–872–2353.

Big Pine Key Fishing Lodge, at MM 33, offers campground, room and mobile home rentals for daily, weekly and monthly fees. It resembles more of a hotel than a rustic, natural area. A camping site with full electric hookup is $37 per day. For more information, call 305–872–2351.

With only 13 sites, no water, no showers, no deposit areas for trash and a $3 per person nightly fee, Garden Key campground at Dry Tortugas National Park is usually yet another option for the Keys camper. Reachable only by seaplane or boat, the campground is about 70 miles west of Key West, on the same island as Fort Jefferson.

The campground, however, is temporarily closed until further notice due to a septic system failure after unusually heavy mid-June rains. For more information, call 305–242–7700.

Florida state parks are open from 8 a.m. to sunset each day of the year. Camping or cabin reservations may be made online at http://www.reserveamerica.com or by calling 800–326–3521. (Luhta, 2003, pp. 16–18)

(Reprinted with permission of Rachel Luhta and the Key West *Citizen*.)

Alumni publications, such as magazines, newsletters, and Web site content, offer still more campus writing opportunities. Although many of these publications are university-wide, others are designed to serve specific units, such as a college, school, or department. Sometimes positions on these publications can be obtained through part-time employment or through more formal internship programs.

Athletic department publications offer still other options. At National Collegiate Athletic Association Division I–A colleges and universities—which operate the major athletic programs in the nation—numerous publications are issued for the news media, alumni, students, and for season-ticket holders and supporter clubs and associations. *Inside Indiana* magazine, for example, focuses on Indiana University varsity sports.

## MARKETING CAMPUS STORIES OFF CAMPUS

As mentioned earlier, you may have a chance on some occasions to write a feature story that has interest far beyond your campus publications. The story may originate as an idea of your own or as an assignment from a campus publication editor. Originally, you might complete the assignment for your school's newspaper or magazine. As you began to research the story, conduct interviews, and write it, you may discover that the real potential for the story goes beyond campus. For example, your story about migraine headache research at your university's medical school could interest many people in your community.

Therefore, you need to look at the feature assignments you complete for campus publications to determine their prospects to be sold elsewhere as well.

Most student publications encourage it. There's nothing wrong with selling two or more articles from the same research. Campus publications, especially, have limited circulation and do not directly compete with commercial publications. In some cases, this might be a conflict, but for the most part, it is not a problem. If you consider this option, as a courtesy, you should discuss with the editor of the publication the possibility of taking your story elsewhere to make certain there are no legal reasons, such as copyright, that would prevent you from doing so.

There is a strong chance you will have to modify or rewrite substantial portions of the original story. It may have to be rewritten in a major way, changing the focus of the topic and the range of sources used. A fresher lead may be necessary, also. But with a minimal amount of work, you might be able to take a story originally written for a campus publication and turn it into a strong story for a local weekly or regional daily newspaper or a regional magazine.

## Off-Campus Publications

Students should never overlook writing opportunities off campus even while they are on campus. Local and regional newspapers, magazines, newsletters, and online publications—especially Web sites—are routinely seeking part-time assistance and freelance contributions. As a student, you should investigate these opportunities as your writing skills mature. If you are not sure if you are ready, ask one of your professors for advice.

The number and quality of these off-campus opportunities are often a function of the size of the community in which you live. Larger cities often offer more chances, but there could also be more people, some with better qualifications than yours, competing for those assignments. Weekly newspapers and newsletters are particularly good places to investigate because their staffs are ordinarily quite small and they often welcome help. Specialized magazines, such as trade publications, may also need help but could require some advanced knowledge of the subject.

Stringing, a form of freelance writing involving a regular relationship with a publication, is another option. The local newspapers and major regional newspaper in the area that your school serves might be an option for feature writing opportunities. Similarly, there may be magazines and newsletters in your community that need student staff assistance. These assignments can come on a single-story basis, on a more ongoing basis as a regular part-timer or stringer, or as an intern. To look into these opportunities, check with your journalism or writing professors or contact the publications directly. Stringing for newspapers in other cities and states is a possibility for college students. Some students interested in sports cover their school's varsity teams for out-of-town newspapers. There may be opportunities to write features about successful students for their hometown newspapers. Another category of feature story prospects are significant faculty research being conducted on campus. Inquiries by telephone or letter may be all that is needed to set up an ongoing relationship with a newspaper or other publication. One thing is certain: these opportunities rarely seek you. You must find them.

### News Services Oriented to Campuses

There are several news services at the national level that cater to the interests of student publications. One example is U-Wire (http://www.uwire.com). U-Wire, founded in 1994, serves college and professional news media and distributes hundreds of student-produced stories to member publications each day through a password-protected Web site. Most stories focus on news, opinion, sports, and entertainment. In addition to written content, the wire also distributes photos and other graphics.

### Publications Oriented to Students and Campus Life

There is a growing number of national publications geared to supplement and serve college markets. Among them is *U* (http://www.colleges.com/Umagazine/), a magazine that focuses on the college and university market. Numerous publishers have oriented their magazines and newsletters to national, regional, or statewide campus markets.

Some publications are aimed at particular segments of that market, in fact. One example is *The Black Collegian* (http://www.black-collegian.com), which serves African–American college students and recent graduates seeking career and job information. *First Opportunity* (http://www.neli.net/neli/publications_fo.html), another such publication, is aimed at African–American and Hispanic students. *Equal Opportunity* (http://www.eop.com/eo.html), issued 3 times a year, publishes articles on a wide range of topics ranging from careers to travel to profiles of role models.

*Florida Leader* (http://www.floridaleader.com), published 4 times a year and distributed on campuses at private and state universities and colleges in Florida, is another example. This publication encourages student writers to submit how-to, profile, and humorous features about events, interests, and issues related to campus life. A separate *Florida Leader* is published for high school students.

## STUDENTS MUST EARN THEIR CREDIBILITY

Nancy Beth Jackson (personal communication, July 27, 1993) is a freelance feature writer and professor at the School of Continuing and Professional Studies at New York University. Jackson, a former professor at the University of Missouri, knows the value of getting information right and she has made that point with emphasis in her classes:

Students at the University of Missouri, the nation's first school of journalism, find it easy enough to master the basics of the reporter's trade: inverted pyramids, feature leads, interviewing techniques, sourcing, stylebook rules, libel, and infographics. What's tough to add to the tool box is *credibility*.

Sure, all reporters must strive for facts, but accuracy and sensitivity are even more essential for feature writers, who literally walk into the lives and living rooms of strangers and walk out with stories that will be read by hundreds or thousands of people. A cityside reporter covering a council meeting or press conference can always rely on a more experienced journalist to ask just the right questions. A feature writer does one-on-one with the subject. Failing to establish rapport, the reporter will have to sweat to pull off the tale.

If you are working for a major daily like *The New York Times,* you can tap into the credibility of the institution. For starters, people return your calls. But in Columbia, Missouri, students at both the *Maneater* campus weekly and the *Missourian* city daily produced by the J-school, suffer the sins of their predecessors. The joke goes that in this overly reported town with two dailies, three college newspapers, and high school publications, every man, woman and child over the age of three has been interviewed at least once. Many refuse a second or third go around because they feel the first reporter was unprofessional. The problem is not unique to the University of Missouri.

Since reporters don't have time to build up byline or personal reputations with readers, students must strive for instant credibility. How? The answer is both institutional and personal. Establish a publication policy for checking quotations with sources before a story is printed. Both *Maneater* and *Missourian* reporters are required to call back to verify all direct quotations even if it means missing a deadline. The two newspapers also require multiple sources on all stories, including features, and put a share of the credibility burden on the copy desk, pointing out that errors in grammar, spelling, and details like street addresses can also turn off readers.

On the personal side, student journalists must be—like actors—costumed for their roles. Sweats and sneakers may get the story for you when interviewing contemporaries, but university administrators, city officials and other nonstudents sources may see sloppy dress as a reflection of a sloppy mind. Tee shirts, ripped jeans, hair out to there, and nose rings might be the current campus fashion, but they generally are inappropriate for the job. Appearance is only part of a professional demeanor. Prepare for the interview—even more than an established professional does.

Whether your subject is a novice at being interviewed or someone swamped by the media, you increase your credibility by letting them know you have done your homework. But your own youth and inexperience can work for you with many subjects. Make them like you. Then they'll talk. (Personal communication, July 27, 1993)

# CHAPTER EIGHTEEN

# Freelance Writing
# and Marketing

Ready to write freelance feature articles for pay? Many freelance feature writers, especially those just starting out, write part-time while they also do something else for a living. Some become successful enough that they build a lucrative full-time career as freelance feature writers. To be realistic, it is not a safe bet that you will find your full-time career in freelance feature writing—at least, not in the beginning. It takes time. If you follow the path of most feature writers, especially those writing for magazines, you become a part-time writer who has a full-time career in another, perhaps related, field. This is frequently the case for magazines and newsletters, which usually maintain small writing staffs. An increasing number of daily and weekly newspapers are using freelance writers for feature and other news material as well. Numerous new online markets have opened for writers in recent years as well. Writers will find opportunities writing for online publications such as newspapers and magazines.

Work as a freelance feature writer is tough and demanding. You are your own boss. This puts you in charge of generating ideas, preparing the articles, marketing and selling them, and, of course, submitting the work. No one does any of this for you. Some people thrive in this sort of environment—they are attracted to the freedom and flexibility. Others cannot handle it well and prefer less independent staff positions. You have to decide what is best for you.

Some professional writers feel there is no better time than today to be a freelance feature writer. There are more magazines, therefore more markets, than ever before. There is greater specialization than the magazine industry has ever known. Although there may be fewer newspapers, there are more editions of the major dailies caused by zoning, or segmentation, of neighborhood coverage. Online feature writing opportunities are available that did not exist a decade ago. Yet, other writers say full-time freelance writing has never been so tough. Pay rates are consumed by inflation, some larger fee magazines have closed, and larger numbers of writers make the work more competitive. Are you ready for that? Freelancing is not an easy endeavor for beginners, especially younger writers who may lack savvy business skills.

Whether freelance writing becomes a good or bad experience, a full-time or part-time career, or a short-term or long-term commitment, is up to you. Now that you know the basics of writing features, this chapter focuses on how to get your work published. This is where you turn to a professional writing life. This chapter discusses the basics of marketing and selling—to be your own agent. You learn about query letters and article proposals, preparation of manuscripts, cover letters, photographs and other graphics, and developing multiple articles from a single research effort.

## MARKETING YOUR WORK

As a freelance writer, you must be aggressive about marketing your ideas and articles. This means identifying the right market for your work. It means researching markets. It means knowing where to find the opportunities to sell your writing. Effective freelance writers use all forms of mass media—newspapers, magazines, newsletters, online publications—to market their work. Writers must use all locations, from local to international, also. Marketing requires knowing the guidelines for submission, how to communicate with editors about your ideas, and how to complete a professional quality submission. You must sell yourself on an individual level to people you know and to strangers. You must promote yourself in the same manner a public relations specialist serves a client. Some freelance writers today, for example, even take advantage of the World Wide Web and use Web sites to promote their work (Outing, 2000).

## FINDING THE RIGHT MARKET

The ultimate freelance writing problem is matching the right subject with the right writer and the right publication. How do you do that? In recent years, a number of freelance writing market directories and listings have been published to assist writers in finding the best markets for their work. Some have gone online and are available on the World Wide Web. It is up to you to find the right market. Any freelancer should look at one or more of these market directories.

At the top of the list is the annual *Writer's Market* (Brogan, 2002), the number one source for nonfiction freelance writers. This 1,000-plus page volume is published each fall and lists more than 3,800 publication markets for articles and publishers for books. The company's Web site (http://writersmarket.com) includes another 1,400 listings.

*The Writer's Handbook* (Abbe, 2002), published by *The Writer* magazine and The Writer, Inc., notes more than 3,000 markets for manuscripts in its 1,056 pages. Another popular resource is Gale's *Directory of Publications and Broadcast Media*. Listings of magazines and newspapers also are published annually by *Folio:* and *Editor & Publisher*. Special issues of these two publications, and others such as *Writer's Digest, ByLine,* and *The Writer,* list syndicates, new markets, and other reference books.

---

## BEST SOURCES FOR FREELANCE WRITING MARKETS

Books:

Gale Directory of Publications and Broadcast Media, Gale Research, Detroit, MI.

Guide to Literary Agents, Writer's Digest Books, Cincinnati, OH.

Literary Market Place (agents), R. R. Bowker, New York.

Local telephone book yellow pages (under "publishers").

Newsletters in Print, Gale Research, Detroit, MI.

Newsletter and Electronic Publishers Association Directory of Members and Industry Suppliers, Newsletter Publishers Association, Arlington, VA.

O'Dwyer's Directory of Public Relations Executives, J. R. O'Dwyer, New York.

Oxbridge Directory of Newsletters, Oxbridge Communications, New York.

Reader's Guide to Periodical Literature, H. W. Wilson, Minneapolis, MN.

Working Press of the Nation (volumes I, II), Farrell, New York.

Writer's Market, Writer's Digest Books, Cincinnati, OH.

Writer's Handbook, The Writer, Inc., Boston.

Periodicals:

Business Periodicals Index, H. W. Wilson Co., New York.

Humanities Index, H. W. Wilson Co., New York.

Reader's Guide to Periodical Literature, H. W. Wilson Co., New York.

Social Sciences Index, H. W. Wilson Co., New York.

The Writer, The Writer, Inc., Boston.

Writer's Digest, Writer's Digest Books, Cincinnati, OH.

Newsletters:

American Society of Journalists and Authors—Newsletter.

Communication News.

EFA Newsletter (Editorial Freelancers Association).

Newsletter on Newsletters (Newsletter Clearing House).

On Second Thought.

Writers Connection—Newsletter.

Writers Guild of America (East)—Newsletter.

Writers Guild of America (West)—Newsletter.

---

Gale's Newsletters in Print is an annual directory that lists more than 11,500 subscription, membership, and free newsletters, bulletins, digests, and other smaller publications in the United States and Canada. It describes newsletters in a variety of formats published in business, industry, family and lifestyles, communications-information, agriculture, life sciences, community affairs, world affairs, science and technology, and liberal arts. It also includes newsletter indexes. Similarly, *The Oxbridge Directory of Newsletters* lists in its 1,300-page volume more than 21,000 newsletters on subjects similar to those in the Gale directory. Both directories are comprehensive.

A beginning writer in or near a metropolitan area really needs to go no further than the "publishers" section of the local telephone directory yellow pages for a starting point. This listing tells you which newspapers, magazines, and newsletters maintain offices in your area. Even if you do not have such telephone directories, you can go to a nearby library that should have the directories or microfiche available to use. However, you cannot depend just on directories to find markets. You must set up a network by developing your own contacts in the profession. The more people—especially editors—you know, the better. Attend professional meetings, for example, to make such contacts.

"Editors have one goal that overrides all others," said author and freelance writer Gordon Burgett (1997, p. 7), "to fill their pages with copy and artwork so good that it will leave the reader begging for more (and, where appropriate, asking to renew and extend their subscriptions). To achieve this, they look for tight, well-crafted, accurate articles that fill their particular needs."

To meet those needs, you must be patient. You must be organized enough to market several ideas and work on several assignments at once. Sometimes you develop an idea and just cannot find the right market at the beginning of the project. Put the topic on hold for a while, if you can. While you are working on other writing projects that have more easily found markets, your solution to the tough one might come along.

"Don't be afraid to start at the bottom by writing for free. And don't ever say, 'I'd love to be a writer, but I just don't have time.' Writers make time. They don't spend time playing with friends on weekends. They neglect their families more than they should. They don't have time for anything else but writing," said successful Southern California freelance writer Andy Rathbone (personal communication, April 20, 1993 & January 17, 1998). "Writers must be able to keep writing, even when the spark's not there. You've got to get some clay on the table; you can always go back and shape it later. Finally, I'll spit out the old cliché: People don't choose writing as a career; writing chooses them" (Rathbone, personal communication, April 20, 1993 & January 17, 1998).

If all else fails, try to locate people who work or are interested in the subject you have chosen for an article. Ask them what they read. Find out their favorite publications. Their answers could give you an idea for new markets. This boils down to persistence. If you keep trying, eventually the effort might be rewarded with an acceptance letter and, later, a tearsheet and check.

## BEGINNING WITH NEWSPAPER MARKETS

Many freelance writers start out building a relationship with newspapers in their communities. Some start with weeklies and small dailies. Others break right in with the major daily newspapers in nearby metropolitan markets. Finding full-time positions with newspapers is more difficult than it was a decade earlier. Certainly, freelance opportunities are out there at newspapers for beginning writers, even if less full-time work can be found. Stringers, as editors like to call freelance writers, are a long-standing newspaper tradition. Almost all newspapers need and use them. "Smaller suburban dailies are likely to be receptive to new writers, but the larger dailies usually demand journalism experience," said Pennsylvania freelance feature writer Johanna S. Billings (1992, p. 24). "The best way to sell your work to newspapers is to sell yourself first. Once you have chosen a newspaper, find out who the editor is, and then send a cover letter, including a résumé highlighting your writing credits and 'clips' if you have any" (Billings, 1992, p. 24).

Most newspaper editors like to establish a regular relationship with their freelancers. They want to be able to find a writer for fast response on assignments they initiate. They do not want to wait for stories to come to them in many cases, although they most always consider unsolicited submissions. "Because most editors are not looking to buy just one article, they seldom want query letters. Instead, they want to cultivate a working relationship with stringers to whom they can give assignments regularly," Billings (1992, p. 24) wrote. "As a stringer, you will be doing both 'hard news' and 'features' " (Billings, 1992, p. 24).

## MASTERING MAGAZINE AND NEWSLETTER MARKETS

The number of magazines and newsletters being published sometimes may seem overwhelming. It is quite an effort to keep track of the many opportunities that exist for freelance feature writers. With thousands of magazines in the United States and Canada and thousands more outside North America, there are many different magazine markets for freelance writers.

First, there are the most visible consumer magazines. There are also thousands of trade, technical, and professional publications. Freelance writers should always consider the opportunities available outside the mainstream publications. Although many freelancers may dream of writing for the big fees paid by *The New Yorker, Esquire, National Geographic, TV Guide,* or *Reader's Digest,* it is not realistic for most beginners to shoot so high. Instead, it is wise to look at less competitive markets. Many freelance writers begin their magazine and newsletter writing careers by publishing in smaller magazines or newsletters or those with specializations with which they are familiar. The fees are much lower, generally, and there is great variation in how much they pay. You do not have to be a specialist, but if you have some expertise, use it. This is especially beneficial to beginners looking for that first break.

Denver freelance writer Henry Pratt believes that the thousands of trade publications are a strong option that is "often overlooked" by feature writers (Pratt, 1992, p. 10). There seem to be trade periodicals for just about any imaginable subject. Trade publications—those technical periodicals serving business and industry with articles about news, trends, people, new technology, and research in a particular field—often open up to new writers more easily than consumer publications, Pratt (1992) said. He added:

> Writing articles for trade journals is fun and profitable, if you take the time to know your customer—the publication, its audience, and the industry. [T]rade journals offer writers greater security. Such trades tend to be more stable, and they're not bought or sold as often as some consumer publications. You'll find trade journals are hungry for articles, practical columns, charts, graphs, and photos. Since most have small staffs, the editors depend heavily on freelancers for much of their prose and visuals. (p. 10)

Pratt (1992) suggested trade features should focus on manufacturing processes, histories and chronologies, and successful elements of businesses such as sales, production, finance, and the future.

Magazine writer Eric Friedman (1997) listed seven important parts of a magazine that a writer should check when deciding about a submission. He recommended looking at the following:

- Masthead (the fewer names, the better for freelancers).
- Bionotes (what do they tell you about the writers the publication uses?).
- Table of contents (look at the article types and topics).
- Text (read it and note slant, length, tone, and style).
- Timeliness (are news pegs part of these articles?).
- Artwork (what accompanies the articles?).
- Audience (check the advertising and letters to the editor for hints).

Other small magazines offer good publishing opportunities also. There are a growing number of magazines of limited regional or local circulation that remain options for beginning writers, argued freelance writer Eric Mathews (1991). "In terms of eccentricities, anomalies, and just generally strange publishing practices, these publications, often 'seat-of-the-pants' operations, can be the ultimate test of a writer's patience and professionalism," he said (p. 23). Finding these magazines may be a challenge, but they are often listed in magazine market directories and writers' magazines such as *Writer's Digest* and *The Writer*.

With very small staffs, some only one-person operations, these publications also need contributors.

A growing magazine market in recent years has been regional parenting magazines and newsletters. Ohio writer Mark Haverstock (1993) noted that there may be as many as 140 of these in North America and Australia. "This is a wide-open market for writers, because most of these parenting publications rely heavily on freelance submissions," Haverstock said (p. 6). These publications seek practical feature articles about local activities, places to get help, and advice about childcare. *Atlanta Parent, Chicago Parent,* and *Seattle's Child* are just three examples.

Regardless of the size or type of the publication, study it and learn as much about it and the market as you can before approaching it. "Target your material to the proper market; know the magazine you want to write for. Magazines are much like people. Each is different, with a distinctive personality and special needs. It's folly to dash off a piece and then frenetically search for a suitable market for it," said New York freelancer John Bohannon (1993, p. 22). "One of the most common complaints editors have about free lancers—and it is a justifiable one—is that they're unfamiliar with the market," agreed Oklahoma full-time freelance writer Charlotte Anne Smith (1993, p. 16).

## WORKING IN ONLINE MARKETS

Throughout this volume, the point has been made—as gently as possible—that there are numerous new opportunities with online periodicals. Print publications that have been transformed into online formats as well as publications that are solely available online offer markets for writers. These publications seek new material, but not always the same things you might prepare for print feature-oriented publications. More and more, online publications are seeking multimedia content. This means a written feature article, but also supporting digital photographs, and other graphics such as maps or original illustrations. This is a minimum. Sophisticated online publications seek audio and video clips, such as portions of interviews with key individuals, also. Using the power of hypertext links, editors want related Web links to other related sites and other ways to enhance the interactive experience of reading the article. Thus, the feature writer, either staffer or freelancer, who produces content for an online publication must have multiple talents—or have them available to use. Shooting still digital photographs and video, recording audio clips, and creating graphics may become a routine part of the assignment for an online publication.

"It's a mistake to assume—that editors of Web-based media want the same material you'd produce for that quaint wood-pulp-based medium—," advised Professor Michael Ray Taylor (1998, pp. 18–19). "The Web is still in its infancy; so far no one has figured out exactly what message its audience wants. But what has become increasingly clear is that the online audience doesn't want to read traditional magazine articles thrown across a computer screen" (Taylor, 1998, pp. 18–19).

## OPPORTUNITIES IN INTERNATIONAL MARKETS

A final piece of advice on freelance opportunities should focus on international freelance markets. Clearly, Canadian publications are among the most logical places to begin. Not only are the language and culture similar, some of the U.S. media with which you are already familiar are part of the market. Although Canadian cultural content laws try to keep Canada "Canadian," writers can still sell material across the border if the articles are what the publications need.

United Kingdom publications and other English-language countries offer additional freelance markets, especially in the areas of travel, entertainment, sports, and science and health, for example. Metropolitan London-based freelance writer Wendy Grossman (personal communication, May 20, 1993 & January 15, 1998) described opportunities in the British market for her specialties, computers and science writing:

> The U.K. market is much, much smaller than the U.S. one, and so is the pool of talent. I think it makes it easier to break in—anyone who's good and professional stands a reasonable chance of making some kind of living. Probably science and technology writers have an easier time than some others—the explosion of computer magazines means there's a fair market for that sort of stuff, and there are an awful lot of journalists in London who are too terrified of technology to write about it even for magazines in other fields.

In non-English-language nations, opportunities also exist. Many publications, if they are interested in the proposed article, will translate it into the native language. There is clearly interest in what is happening in the United States. Some personality-oriented publications in Europe and Latin America, for instance, are a steady market for Hollywood-based writers who focus on the motion picture industry. Some U.S. freelance travel writers, for example, regularly sell articles to publishers of in-flight magazines for foreign airlines that have routes touching the United States. Although it may take considerable effort to become established in such a market, it is worthwhile.

## USING SUBMISSION GUIDELINES

When you have identified a publication that might be right for your work, contact the editor, acquisitions editor, or articles editor to obtain a set of submission guidelines. Although newspapers rarely develop printed guidelines, many magazines have posted these guidelines on their Web sites or they will send them by mail or facsimile machine to freelancers on request. One of the most popular outdoors magazines in Pennsylvania, *Pennsylvania Angler and Boater,* uses guidelines. These are included in Appendix B. Contributor guidelines for *Vermont Life,* a small regional magazine, and *Operations & Fulfillment* magazine, a trade magazine, are also included.

These guidelines can be general, but are often very specific. *Operations & Fulfillment* is a monthly trade publication for individuals and businesses in the World Wide Web and catalog mail order, or direct-to-customer operations, industry. Award-winning *Operations & Fulfillment* editor Rama Ramaswami strongly urges potential contributors to familiarize themselves with the magazine and to read the guidelines: "Please read the following guidelines carefully before submitting material for publication. Your article stands a far greater chance of being accepted if you adhere to these requirements," Ramaswami (2002) tells her writers.

## USING ELECTRONIC MAIL TO QUERY

In recent years, the number of electronic queries at magazines and other publications has grown whereas the number of mail queries has declined. Communication with the editors and their assistants is in transition. The reason is the growth in use of electronic mail, the World Wide Web, and the Internet. Most publications today have become part of the networked world. Their presence on the Internet includes Web sites and electronic mail addresses. This includes access to editors and their staffs through e-mail. Editors are using e-mail for submissions, for contact with regular contributors, and for contact with new writers.

This creates a communication quandary for freelance writers. Do writers submit query letters and proposals through electronic mail? Or do writers use more conventional printed documents and "snail" mail approaches? The answers to those questions will depend on the individual editor and the policies of the publication. Some editors prefer to use e-mail because it is faster and less formal. This enables them to reply more quickly than through traditional methods. One way to find the answer for a particular publication is to check its submission guidelines and follow the instructions.

The safest approach is to use conventional submission approaches when no other advice or guidelines are available. However, it is worthwhile to check to see if a particular publication has upgraded to electronic queries and submissions because of the time and, perhaps, money saved. Often a telephone call will get the information needed—such as a name and e-mail address for the editor in charge of queries.

Magazine editor Greg Daugherty (2001) said that using e-mail properly will win assignments for freelance writers, but can also be costly if handled poorly. "I've seen beginning writers send in lively queries that won them assignments—practically by return e-mail," Daugherty, editor of Reader's Digest's *New Choices* magazine, wrote (p. 28). "I've also seen otherwise terrific writers flub it by making mistakes they would have never made in conventional paper queries" (Daugherty, 2001, p. 28).

If a writer does use e-mail, remember to use some of the best rules often used for contacting editors with the telephone: First, use an e-mail address that can be accessed for a response. Second, monitor that e-mail address regularly for responses. Daugherty (2001) also recommended these 11 important tips:

- Confirm that the publication accepts e-mail queries.
- Query with a strong idea.
- Use a formal voice, not the informal or casual voice often used in e-mail.
- Spell check the message before sending it.
- Use the subject line to include the word "query."
- Provide your contact information such as telephone and fax numbers.
- Offer writing samples, but only send them if requested.
- Offer your resume, but only send it if requested.
- Send queries one at a time; don't use multiple addresses for a single query.
- Be patient about response time; wait about 2 weeks.
- Save your sent queries for reference.

## WRITING QUERY LETTERS AND ARTICLE PROPOSALS

One of the most important aspects of selling articles to publications is how you conduct yourself as a professional writer. Writers should maintain a professional attitude in how they work with editors. This involves knowing the standards of the profession for preparing and submitting freelance work. Following general market and specific publication research, it is time to make contact with the publication. Being professional is an attitude, but it is also performing at a high level when this first contact is made (Smith, 1993).

Former *Writer's Digest* editor Thomas Clark (1995) emphasized that an effective inquiry to a magazine, regardless of the form it takes, is the single most important sales tool that writers can use. "A successful query letter gets the client to say *yes*," Clark said (p. 22). "And that's the only real goal of any sales tool" (Clark, 1995, p. 22). Clark said writers should include five essential ingredients in each query: a working title, a projected length, the idea's role within the publication's departments, reference to previous articles, and the results of some of the initial research done for the article.

The right attitude about rejection is also important in freelance writing. Writers must learn to live with rejection. It happens to every writer. A publication's decision not to use a submitted manuscript or idea proposal does not always mean it is a bad one. It could mean that there were other reasons for not using it. However, many inexperienced writers do not contemplate the reason offered for a rejection, if it is specific, and give up on the idea. Freelance feature writer Richard Matthews (1991), like many other successful and persistent writers, explained the next step is not giving up, but revising, refocusing, and resubmitting to "another publication that might be receptive to the same general idea tailored to its editorial content" (p. 22). "Restructuring an idea with a different set of readers in mind often meets with success the second time around," he said (p. 22). A distinction between an amateur freelancer and a real professional, Matthews said, is how you handle the rejection pile. The worst thing to do is to let an idea sit around, he said.

Kevin Robinson (1993), a veteran freelance writer, agreed that rejection is part of the business, but it should be taken personally. "To be a good writer, you must be human; you must see and feel what those around you see and feel. More importantly, you must see and feel what *you* see and feel," he explained (p. 27). If you do that as a writer, he maintained, you react personally to rejection. And, he said, that's perfectly okay. His own rejection rate is about 80%. "I decided long ago that there's nothing particularly noble about suffering in silence or pretending that being rejected isn't painful. But I don't get mad either" (Robinson, 1993, p. 27). His solution, like that of so many other professionals, is persistence. The lesson is this: Do not give up on an idea until all options are exhausted.

There are numerous reasons editors reject or substantially revise accepted ideas and manuscripts. Veteran Southern California freelance writer John M. Wilson (1990) identified at least nine reasons for failure. Manuscripts with flaws, he said, are just unfinished works in progress. Rejected writers simply need to work more to solve the problems. He has created a presubmission checklist that can be helpful in preventing such errors the first time around:

- Angle and focus of the article.
- Appropriate viewpoint and voice.
- Vivid description.
- Logical organization.
- Style in writing.
- Lead that attracts and a distinct, impressive ending.
- Appealing direct quotations.
- Manuscript must reflect what editor assigned.
- Edit and proofread thoroughly.

As a writer seeking a publisher, you must go further than discovering a subject for an article. A subject is simply not enough in the highly competitive writing world. The American Society of Journalists and Authors, Inc. (ASJA) argued that the idea is one step toward the finished product (Bloom, Bedell, Olds, Moldafsky, & Schultz, 1992). An idea is a subject combined with an approach, ASJA said. This is your property, even if you do not have the article written yet. Once you get a good article idea, you have to decide when and where it is best to market it.

Writers should not query a publication by telephone. Most professionals prepare a query letter or e-mail message or they will submit an article idea proposal. Some freelance writers combine a letter and proposal into a single document but, for your purposes as a novice, you should consider them separate steps. A query letter is briefer, less detailed, and an abstract of a fuller proposal. If you have refined the idea, then develop a separate proposal running 500 to 750 words that summarizes what you plan to do. Your basic strategy is to develop the idea—to describe to an editor what you will do, or have done—without writing or sending the entire article. This is a more detailed outline of the article you plan to write. Editors find these helpful in determining whether your work would fit their plans for an upcoming issue.

Perlstein (personal communication, May 3, 1993), a freelance writer and author in Minneapolis, sold his first freelance article to *The New York Times*. Now he writes for a variety of newspapers and magazines. He recommends human-interest features as a type of article that may increase your chances for success:

> When pitching human interest pieces, writers have to tailor their queries to particular markets; editors scan through query letters very quickly, and, unless a human interest piece pegs their niche exactly, they'll drop a preprinted rejection slip in the SASE [self-addressed, stamped envelope] and be done with it. When I'm on a hot streak I get maybe one hit in 20 or 30 queries, many of them human interest pieces. (Perlstein, personal communication, May 3, 1993)

San Diego freelancer Andy Rathbone (personal communication, April 20, 1993 & January 17, 1998) pitches his ideas to editors this way:

> First, get the publication's proper name, address, and writer's guidelines. Usually the weary receptionist will recite these over the phone. Next, grab as many back issues as you can find at local thrift shops or a condominium's magazine-swap-pile. Your story must fit into a magazine's specific area, or the editor won't take it. Next, write a query letter with a grabbing first graph, followed by a short description of the story, as well as the reason why *you* are the best person to write it. Rules? Make sure it all fits on one page. If you can't sum it up in one page, you haven't found a decent angle for the story. If they haven't followed up in a month, send a follow-up letter. After 45 days, I'll give them a phone call. Don'ts?

Don't call the publication unless it's to get their address and current editor's name. Editors don't like being bugged over the phone. And for crying out loud, don't spell anything wrong, either! Editors don't want to work and if they see any misspellings, they know they're in for some serious revisions on the manuscript.

Another veteran freelance feature writer, Bill Steele (personal communication, May 24, 1993), writes about medicine, computers, chemicals, and drugs. Steele, from Ithaca, NY, advocates being prepared when entering the query process. This is especially true of "cold" queries:

> My basic rule in querying is to do a lot of homework beforehand. When an editor who knows you calls up and gives you an assignment, it's usually just an idea the editor had: How are lawn-care pesticides affecting the squirrels, or whatever. And you can approach an editor with whom you work regularly with something like that. But when you're querying *cold,* you have to have the work about half finished; do enough research so that you can show the editor there really is a story there and you know more about it than any other writer they might hire to cover it. 'According to a study published in the *New England Journal of Veterinary Medicine,* squirrels in the northeast have experienced severe depression after eating nuts sprayed with weed killer, and have been known to carry off small children. I plan to travel to Wallingford, Connecticut and interview Mrs. Ida Klumph, the distraught mother who, after innocently killing a few weeds—' The last paragraph of a query letter is always a brief resume listing publications in which I've been published. At the beginning I made up stuff, or at least exaggerated its importance. (Steele, personal communication, May 24, 1993)

Although most articles need proposals or queries to precede them, some articles do not. Publication editors work in different ways. You just have to know the market. This is how writer Wendy Grossman (personal communication, May 20, 1993 & January 15, 1998) described the process in the United Kingdom:

> I don't query publications, except very rarely. The first article I ever got paid for writing was a query, to the Women's Page editor of *The Guardian* newspaper. It was a piece about the 20th anniversary of the Irish Family Planning Association, an organization which had been illegal for the first 10 years of its existence, and which was celebrating its 20th birthday by being prosecuted for selling condoms at a Dublin record store. She asked to see clippings, so I sent her a piece from an American humanist magazine on a related subject (church and state in Ireland), and told her I would write the piece on spec. I did, and she bought it. Because she answers letters, the once or twice since I've had ideas to suggest, I've written to her.
>
> But editors in London really work on the telephone, so mostly I phone them. I try to avoid days when I know specific editors are trying to put their pages to bed. Everything in London is personal contacts, anyway, and now that I've been around for a few years sometimes people call me and offer me work through rec-

ommendations. Also, in the computer world, all the editors and freelancers use the same conferencing system; many of the magazines have conferences on there, too. So the other route I use a lot is E-mail. But I'm actually also fortunate in that there are at least two magazines I write for every month, and then it's a question of what I'm going to write, not whether. I also write almost every week for the specialist technology supplement for *The Daily Telegraph*.

But I can't count on this continuing forever, so I do try to think about other markets. It's important to remember that whatever your ideals may be, you're running a business. It's very easy here, for example, to spend all your time going to press conferences or whatever; if you want to make it as a freelancer, you have to have respect for what your time is worth, and decide how you spend it accordingly.

I find contacting people I don't know much easier by E-mail, and therefore, I find it all easier since more editors have gotten online. I got into *Scientific American's* Cyberview column by E-mailing the editor cold; in that case, I got lucky because he'd read and liked something I'd written and was interested in hearing ideas from me. I've done three pieces for him now.

For editorials, humorous anecdotes and briefs, and most other articles less than 1,000 words, a query is not as useful as the finished piece, literary agent Linda Collier Cool (1985a) said. Cool also stressed that query letters must be convincing. "[B]efore you begin writing your query letter, think your article idea through carefully. Imagine you are describing the article to a friend. Could you get the point across in just a few words?" she asked (p. 24).

Some editors prefer only query letters on first contact. If their initial response to your letter is positive, you might be asked to produce a proposal. The problem with many query letters, veteran freelancer Lorene Hanley Duquin (1987) said, is that the letter writers do not know what they are really proposing. If so, how can you expect an editor to know?

Some editors like to see clippings of a writer's previously published articles on related subjects. In other words, highlight your qualifications. Previous experience as a writer means a lot to an editor. This is an effective way to establish your credibility as a serious freelance writer. If you have some copies of articles that you have already had published, you may want to include two or three as examples of what you are capable of achieving. In fact, this has happened to numerous writers: some editors wind up offering to buy the articles in the photocopied clippings instead of the article that you have proposed. As long as you have the rights to the article, you might make an unexpected sale.

Ideally, a query letter also includes the proposal. Or, if you prefer to be more highly organized, send a proposal with a covering query letter that introduces yourself to the editor by describing your qualifications and recent articles you have written. This more personal approach establishes your credibility as a serious professional writer. Duquin (1987) said a proposal is the result of a four-step system:

1. Capture the idea—When an idea strikes you, write it down to save it. When the time comes, it is there for you to take to the next step.
2. Develop the idea—Get more information. Think about the idea. Some preliminary research helps. Get the basic facts. Conduct some interviews.
3. Tailor the idea—Shape the proposal to the audience that you are trying to reach. Decide who would be interested, and devise a writing and reporting strategy that takes you to that goal.
4. Test the idea—Ask yourself these questions: Do you really want to do this article now? Are you capable? What is the cost (in time and money)? Can you find other uses for the material?

## SUCCESS IN THE SUBMISSION GAME

David A. Fryxell (2000a), magazine editorial director for F&W Publications, said the format of a submission does not matter as much as what the submission says. He argued that editors are more concerned about the lead, the focus, grammar, and overall quality of the work. The submission, whether it is on paper or in electronic form, should be clean and readable. His tips follow:

- Content matters more than format.
- Most editors want an electronic version of your manuscript.
- Send disks in PC format because Macs can also read PC formats.
- E-mail attachments may be infected with viruses, so check all files and make sure the publication will take it.
- Sending the manuscript as e-mail text will usually eliminate formatting, but can be received by most everyone.
- Send manuscripts in readable formats (such as rich text format, or RTF, and text, or TXT).

Read and study the publication you plan to query before you prepare the proposal. Call the magazine to get the name (and correct spelling) of the proper editor (they do change from time to time and you cannot completely depend on annual directories to be up-to-date). Duquin (1987) said well prepared and researched proposals get the best attention:

If you've done your homework, you should have all the elements of a good query. Most editors recognize the time and preparation I put into my proposals and they respond personally. More often than not the editor will like the idea, but sees potential trouble spots. Since my proposal is well-developed, the editor can point to those spots and give me the guidance I need to research and write an article that will fit perfectly into the magazine's format. (p. 40)

*Southern* magazine editor James Morgan (1986) said salesmanship in freelance writing is most important for success. He pointed to the timing of being in the right place at the right time with the right product in the right presentation. You control the last "right" but cannot always control the first three, he said. In saying this, he advised writers to avoid gimmicks, sloppy presentations, and dry formality.

Cover letters and accompanying proposals must provide certain basics, regardless of how you organize the information. Here's a list of information to include in a query letter:

1. How to contact you (address and telephone).
2. Your background as a writer, freelancer. (Do not reveal that you are a student or novice. Act professionally and you will be treated as a professional.)
3. Your unique qualifications to write about this subject or idea.
4. Your availability and prospects for completion of the assignment if you get it.
5. A request for a response.

Most query letters are written in traditional business letter format. An appealing, curiosity-arousing opening gets an editor to read more. Letters with dull starts are often not completely read. If you are writing a separate query or cover letter with a proposal, then the letter should be short and to the point.

Article proposals should also have at least seven elements:

1. Summary of the idea and the approximate word length.
2. Examples or cases to illustrate your focus.
3. Primary expert sources you plan to interview.
4. Facts and statistics from authoritative sources.
5. Time factors affecting freshness of material.
6. Outline of article and tentative title (if possible).
7. Availability of photographs and other graphics.

A proposal should be prepared much like a manuscript. This means it should be typed, double-spaced, and free of errors. The depth of your proposal depends on the publication. In essence, then, you have several options in querying. Some proposals are contained in detailed query letters. Some take the form of two-to-four-page essays. Others may be detailed outlines with other supplemental materials such as letters and descriptive essays.

Veteran Oregon freelance writer Gary C. King (personal communication, May 19, 1993) recalled his first sale was made quickly once he decided to become a freelance writer:

> My first story took me 6 weeks to write, and it sold immediately. But remember that you can't make any money if it takes you 6 weeks to write every story. Now, after nearly 13 years in the business, I can write a 5,000 to 6,000 word story (25 to 30 pages, double-spaced) in about 10 hours. Similarly, I can write a 100,000 word crime book in 3 to 6 months and, again in retrospect, I only wish I had started writing books much sooner. My advice to beginners and college students is to break in with the magazines, but don't wait 10 years to go for the book market. The book market's tougher, to be sure, but if you spend 2 or 3 years carving yourself a niche in the magazine markets, the book markets suddenly begin to open up.

King (personal communication, May 19, 1993) also feels querying and proposing ideas require sophistication and the attitude of an experienced freelancer, even if you are not yet one. He explained the following:

> Never admit to being a novice. Write your query letters with an authoritative ring, and convince the editors that you know what you're doing and can do the job. They'll spot the fact that you're a novice when they read your work; so there's no sense in pointing it out to them up front, unless you're looking to make a large file of rejections. And stay away from creative writing classes; you'll only get hurt (journalism classes are okay, even encouraged; but creative writing classes, if I may borrow a phrase from Spiro Agnew, bring out the "effete impudent snobs" who don't know good writing when it reaches out and bites them).

## WRITING A QUERY LETTER: A LOOK AT EXAMPLES

There are many approaches to writing an eye-catching query letter. To show you how it can be done, take a look at a successful magazine query letter written by Susanna K. Hutcheson, a freelance writer living in Wichita, KS. She sold an article to *Entrepreneur* magazine with a brief, but to the point, query letter to the editor. *Entrepreneur,* a California-based monthly, depends on freelancers for about 60% of its content, or about 10 to 20 purchased manuscripts a year (Brogan, 2002). Hutcheson wasted no words in the single-page letter. She described the purpose of the article and its focus. She gave a little flavor of the individual and the woman's company that is the subject of the article. The magazine publishes a lot of "how-to" articles for those interested in running their own businesses, so Hutcheson focused her article on those elements of the Tennessee bakery. She explained the following:

This short query brought me an assignment in *Entrepreneur*. The idea for it came from a short article in *The Wall Street Journal*. As soon as I read it, I wrote this query and got it off. When the editor called me with the assignment, I phoned the *Journal* and asked where I might contact Ms. Smith. I then had two phone interviews with her. The assignment was for a short article, so I had to really get to the meat in a few words. Note how I get right to the subject in the query. I want to catch the editor just like I would my readers—instantly. I wrote the letter like a terse news story. Then, at the end, I told the editor who I am and why I should get the assignment. (Hutcheson, personal communication, April 27, 1993)

Hutcheson's (personal communication, April 27, 1993) query is also effective because she describes to the editor how her article will benefit the readers of the magazine. "You, the writer, are selling something," she explained. "As a salesperson, you have to sell benefits. The editor, like the buyer, wants to know what this article will do for readers." Here's her letter to *Entrepreneur:*

SUSANNA K. HUTCHESON
ADDRESS
TELEPHONE NUMBER
DATE

Rieva Lesonsky, editor
*Entrepreneur Magazine*
2392 Morse Avenue
P.O. Box 19787
Irvine, CA 92713–6234

Dear Ms. Lesonsky:

Dot Smith owns a tiny bakery in Tennessee called The Pepper Patch, Inc. Three years ago she took on the state's powerful liquor wholesalers and won the right to buy Jack Daniel's whiskey directly from the distiller rather than retailers. She challenged a state law governing liquor purchases and, by doing so, saved her company tens of thousands of dollars a year.

Now, she is again taking on a giant, this time larger. She is showing that a small businessperson can fight for rights just like anyone else. In fact, she thinks they should.

Lawyers for Campbell Soup Co. sent Smith a letter demanding that she stop packaging her whiskey-laced Tennessee Truffles in a small gold box that they said resembled the containers used by Campbell's Godiva Chocolatier Inc. unit.

Some people would be scared off by a letter from a huge and powerful company's attorney. But not Smith. She sued Campbell before they could sue her, enabling her to fight in her own state. The battle has lasted three years so far. Pepper Patch still packages Tennessee Truffles in little gold boxes.

Your readers may have occasion to fight a giant business. I propose an article profiling Ms. Smith and her business, one that will give encouragement and empowerment to others.

I'm a professional writer but have no major national credits. I do, however,

have an article coming out in Home Office Computing, a national magazine. I'm
enclosing a couple of clips. I could furnish you with a photo of Smith and her
business. The article would run about 1,000 to 1,500 words. Interested? Your
readers will be.

Sincerely,
Susanna K. Hutcheson


Susanna Hutcheson's final draft of her article as it was submitted to *Entrepreneur* looked like this:


When is a gold box just a gold box and when does it belong to Campbell Soup
Company? That's the question that's gotten a small Tennessee gourmet food
company and its tenacious owner in an onerous legal battle. It isn't, however, the
first giant corporation she has successfully fought on behalf of her tiny company.

Dot Smith, 54, started Pepper Patch, Inc. 17 years ago in Nashville. Smith
wanted her own identity, credit in her own name, and she didn't want to be
bored like so many of her friends.

"This is what has been the driving force behind this business," she says of her
need to eliminate boredom from her life.

Success, however, has not come easily for her. She and her tennis partner each
put up $1,000 to start the company. Then they needed to borrow another $1,000
to buy a stove. Since they had only been in business one week and had no credit it
was no simple matter. But they did get the money after convincing the banker
they were a good risk. Smith has now gone from doing business in the branch
bank to the corporate lending department in the main bank. She also went from
making her products in a cow barn to manufacturing them in three locations. She
eventually bought out her partner and is now sole owner.

The Pepper Patch makes 38 products that include pepper jelly and Smith's famous Tennessee Tipsy Cakes.

It was the Tipsy Cakes that pitted Smith against her first giant obstacle, the
powerful Tennessee liquor wholesalers. Three years ago Smith challenged a state
law governing liquor purchases and was awarded the right to buy Jack Daniel's
whiskey directly from the distiller rather than from retailers. The spirits are used
in the Tipsy Cakes and other specialties. Her efforts saved Pepper Patch tens of
thousands of dollars a year.

Then, another giant stood in her way and again Smith challenged the big guys.
She got a letter in May 1989 from Campbell Soup Co. demanding that Pepper
Patch stop packaging its whiskey-laced Tennessee Truffles in a small gold box
that looked like the containers that Campbell's Godiva Chocolatier Inc. unit use.

Rather than let them sue her in another state, Smith sued them in Tennessee,
saving her the cost of fighting the battle elsewhere. While neither side can claim
victory yet, Pepper Patch still uses the gold boxes.

Pepper Patch employs 25 people and has gone from a first year gross income
of $29,000 to $1.2 million last year. Although besieged by battles, Dot Smith loves
being in business for herself. "If you're enthusiastic about what you're doing it

makes all the difference in the world," she says. That just may be why she is making a difference in her world. (Hutcheson, personal communication, April 27, 1993)

(Reprinted with the permission of Susanna K. Hutcheson.)

## DRAFTING A PROPOSAL FOR AN ARTICLE: AN EXAMPLE

California freelance writer Kit Snedaker sells articles about a wide range of travel and food subjects to many different markets. Some article proposals can be miniarticles themselves, ranging up to four or five double-spaced pages to give the full flavor of the proposed article, possible sources, and so forth. "My proposals are always accompanied by a covering letter telling what this is about, describing the enclosed clips and resume," Snedaker (personal communication, April 17, 1993, April 18, 1993, & January 23, 1998) explained. She said she believes in keeping the proposal short for editors who have a lot to review in the mail each day. The following article proposal is one that Snedaker wrote about traditional Christmas in Germany and foods from the Old World holiday season:

KIT SNEDAKER
ADDRESS
TELEPHONE NUMBER
NAME
ADDRESS
PHONE
FAX
DATE

Nobody celebrates Christmas as enthusiastically as Germans. Christmas trees started there, so did Yule logs, Christmas stockings, Advent calendars, Christmas gingerbread, and "Silent Night."

Best of all, though, are the outdoor Christmas markets which open on November 30 and close December 24. Besides toys (many handmade), tree ornaments and gifts, the markets are dotted with food stalls selling Christmas marzipan, gingerbread, Dresden Stollen and Baumkuchen or tree cake.

Originally, it was baked on a spit, batter applied in layers. As each one browned, another was added. When the cake was cut, the edges of the brown layers looked like growth rings of a tree. A version of this, called Spettekka, is found in a small area of southern Sweden. Lithuanians also make a "tree cake" and the Basques in northern Spain bake a cake on a spit, too. Whatever it's called, this cake-baked-in-front-of-the-open-fire predates ovens and has to be the oldest, most interesting pastry in the world.

Doing a roundup of German Kriskindlemarkts and German Christmas food recently, I watched baumkuchen being made on electrified spits and learned how to do this crown jewel of German baking in a springform pan in my kitchen.

Along the way, I visited Berlin's 150-year-old market on the Kurfurstendamm, small, but festive. I saw the biggest Christmas market in Nuremberg, the oldest in Munich (creches are a tradition there), and the most sophisticated in Frankfurt.

Not only markets, but entire towns, street cars, subways, airports, everything is covered with Christmas decorations. It looks as though the holiday was invented there and, in many ways, it was.

If you would like to see a story about: A German Christmas or German Christmas food, Christmas markets in Germany, or Baumkuchen, a story with a Christmas spirit that's older than Scrooge and Tiny Tim, check off the enclosed postcard. (Snedaker, personal communication, April 17, 1993, April 18, 1993, & January 23, 1998)

(Reprinted with permission.)

## PREPARING YOUR SUBMISSION

Once the article has been queried or proposed, assigned, and written, you prepare it in final form for submission to the editor. There is an art to preparing your manuscript in a professional manner. Because you have already been invited to submit the finished manuscript for full review, you have good reason to do this job well. How well you prepare the manuscript and package is a strong indicator of the professional or unprofessional caliber of your work. If you are sending the finished manuscript on speculation ("on spec"), that is, without any prior correspondence with the publication, you have an even better reason to attend to the details of mailing your manuscript with professional care.

Generally, follow whatever guidelines you have been given by the publisher. If you have none, there are some general standards. First, a cover letter is an important part of the final package you mail or e-mail to the publication. It should be business-like and stick to the point. It can sell the manuscript that you send on speculation. It should make life easier for the editor handling your correspondence. This means you must remember to help editors. You should be as detailed as possible with descriptions or summaries of earlier correspondence (include correspondence dates). "How you handle these [speculation and sale] and similar situations in a cover letter can help build the impression in the editor's mind that you are a professional who understands at least some of the ins and outs of publishing and the author–editor relationship," said editors George Scithers and Sanford Meschkow (1985b, p. 43).

What exactly do you send? Here's a list:

1. Cover letter—This should describe what is enclosed and why. Remember that not many editors will remember the details of your project. Help them. This letter should also serve as a memorandum that explains any particulars of the work you have submitted. If e-mail is used, it should list any and all file attachments and their contents.

2. Manuscript—This should be clean (error-free), typed, and double-spaced. Final copies should always be printed on plain white paper, 8½ × 11 inches, and most editors prefer laser, letter quality, or near-letter quality printers for the manuscript. If e-mail is used, an attachment for e-mail should be provided in a commonly used word processor—if the publication accepts such submissions.

3. Artwork—This includes any visual elements of your story, such as photographs (or negatives), tables, charts, illustrations and drawings, maps, and diagrams. No marking should be included on any visual materials that may be reproduced with your article. It is also best not to write on the back of any artwork. Clip explanatory notes if needed, but do not damage the art. If artwork is in digital form and is submitted as an e-mail attachment, name the files in a specific manner to make it clear what each file contains.

4. Protective covering—If you mail fragile materials such as original photographs or drawings, protect them with cardboard or padding. Specially made shipping containers can be purchased at most office supply stores.

5. Return envelope and postage—If you are submitting editorial material on speculation by traditional mail, you should include a self-addressed, stamped envelope (SASE) for return of materials. Some editors will not return your manuscript and artwork if you do not include the envelope with sufficient postage. A SASE is not needed when the article has already been accepted for publication. Use a large enough envelope to mail the set of materials so they will not be damaged. This means a minimum size 9 × 12 inch manila envelope, but if you have a large amount of material, an 11 × 14 inch envelope works better.

Editor David Fryxell (2001) advised checking to make sure the same idea has not already been done in a recent issue. Although it may seem obvious to experienced writers, it is also important to get the editor's name and spell it right. Brief and simple queries work best, he advised. He also tells beginners not to worry about details, such as length or deadline, until an idea is accepted and then work out finer points with the editor. Maintaining a professional demeanor is also important, he said, and it is simply not wise to be rude or unprofessional to an editor. Fryxell (2000b) also recommended five steps to increasing success with a submission. First, he said a freelance writer should study the publication of interest and copy its formula. Second, he advised freelancers not to ask editors to take chances on ideas. Propose ideas that fit the publication. Third, he said writers must sell themselves to the editors they contact. Show editors why you are qualified and have the right idea. Fourth, Fryxell said you need a professional approach. Writers must meet deadlines and other specifications as well as finishing the work with quality. And finally, he said writers who are successful must deliver. This means getting the work done as promised.

## TRACKING YOUR SUBMISSIONS

Most writers have a system for keeping track of their submissions. As you get more and more into your freelance writing, you will have a growing list of pending submissions in the marketplace at one time. You need to become organized to track these through the lengthy process of receipt, review, decision, publication scheduling, payment, and even receipt of tearsheets or copies of the articles.

A simple chart permits such an effort, but more sophisticated resources are also available. Some software companies sell project tracking software and a number of personal organizer software programs include tools to keep track of projects and to develop project "to-do" lists. Some writing-oriented Web sites offer the service for free or for a minimal monthly use fee. *Writer's Market,* for example, offers its "Submission Tracker" service to subscribers at its Web site (http://writersmarket.com). This tool manages manuscripts that are in development, the submissions, and the status of queries and assignments.

You can easily keep your records in a word processor file, in a spreadsheet file, or on a hard copy chart. Snedaker (personal communication, April 17, 1993, April 18, 1993, & January 23, 1998) charts the following items on a sheet for every single article—she can list up to 14 article submissions on one page—she submits:

1. The market (note overlapping readership).
2. Name of the editor and contact information.
3. Date the query was sent.
4. The reply given to the query.
5. The submission date.
6. Acceptance or rejection decision.
7. Photographs or other graphics submitted.
8. Publication date.
9. Payments received (dates and amounts).
10. Tearsheet or clipping received.
11. Photos returned.

Another way to organize such information is to keep separate file folders for correspondence and other documents generated with a submission. The master guide can be an index of the folders, of course, and make finding information easier if needed at a moment's notice (such as an unexpected telephone call from an editor).

## WORKING ON ASSIGNMENTS WITH EDITORS

Every writer, whether he or she is a staff writer or freelancer, must work with an editor at some point in the writing and publishing process. The relationship is very close at some publications. At others, it seems nonexistent. Most editors are extremely helpful and can even teach their writers new tricks in the process of working with them. They are often willing to spend some time with you and give more precise direction on an assignment. They can communicate what they want and do it in an organized manner. Some editors are impossible to work with, on the other hand. These misguided souls are capable of losing manuscripts, failing to issue contracts, forgetting to pay writers, denying payment for legitimate expenses, reneging on promises, and even introducing errors into articles during the editing process. Some have less personal integrity, too. This means some editors steal ideas, change their minds about accepting and using a manuscript, and even accept a manuscript, pay for it, and then never publish it.

Freelance writer and editor Wendy Grossman advocates respect for the responsibilities of editors and a professional attitude:

> I think the main thing with editors is to remember that they're busy people, and that they and you are, or should be, professionals. Be honest: Don't say you can do things if you can't, because it will only lead to more problems later. Make your deadlines; don't take their comments personally; don't expect them to do stuff to bolster your confidence—you'll have to do that yourself. (personal communication, May 20, 1993 & January 15, 1998)

Grossman (personal communication, May 20, 1993 & January 15, 1998) also suggested that you learn early when to give up your "hold" on a manuscript. It is a mistake to try to work it through the editorial system unless you are specifically asked to assist:

> My personal rule is that when the copy leaves my hands I'm finished with it unless the editor asks for a rewrite. I don't get involved with what the copy editors change, or the headlines, or the choice of pictures. I may request things. I often am asked to supply pictures, either my own or other people's—but once I've handed the stuff over, my job is finished, and it's important to me not to try to do other people's work (or I'll have temper tantrums).

Relations with editors can become strained, but you cannot let it get to you, Grossman (personal communication, May 20, 1993 & January 15, 1998) tells beginners:

> However badly an editor treats you—and, as one friend of mine said, "Sooner or later you will come across an editor who doesn't care about you"—it's better not to pick fights with him/her. If there is a disagreement, handle it in a business-like manner; decide what's important to you and ask for it, firmly, but politely. That junior prick that just shafted you is nonetheless in a position to badmouth you all over the profession. Most editors want to behave decently, in any case.

New York freelance writer Bill Steele (personal communication, May 24, 1993), who worked as editor of a small newspaper before turning full time to writing, described the writer–editor relationship from his perspective. He explained

> As an editor on a small newspaper (very different from being an editor at a magazine), I was most pleased when people brought me stuff I could use without a lot of rewriting. I was least pleased when people came into the office or called on the phone and took up my time explaining why I should run their stories. So as a writer, I seldom phone editors unless I have something that they need to decide on right away. I will phone, however, if I don't get a reply to a mailed query in a reasonable time. Sometimes that makes them feel guilty and they give me the assignment.

Steele (personal communication, May 24, 1993) has a formula for treating his editors with a fine hand. He explained

> I think one of the reasons editors come back to me with assignments after I've sold them something is that I give them copy they can use—neat, correct grammar, rhetoric and spelling, and maybe even a little style. My impression is that there are a lot of working writers who don't do that, but who can get the information, so the editors buy their work and clean it up; but they'd prefer not to have to. After they've bought your work and start "editing" though, it's important that a writer accept the editor's role and respect his or her expertise. Sometimes you meet editors whose idea of editing is to rewrite the article the way they would have written it, but most are just making adjustments to fit the style of the magazine, space needs, etc. I try to understand this and accept what the editor does as part of my job. After all, they're paying your salary, and you don't argue too much with the boss.

Professor Peter Jacobi (1991) recommended a helpful, easy-to-remember checklist of one dozen writing characteristics, all beginning with the letter "C," which should gain greater success with editors during the submission process. He recommended being correct, clear, concise, cohesive, complete, constructive, consistent, concrete, credible, conversational, comfortable, and captivating. A writer who can accomplish all of these goals will certainly make friends with editors and readers.

## AN EDITOR'S VIEWS OF WORKING WITH FREELANCE WRITERS

Rama Ramaswami (personal communication, October 17, 2002) edits *Operations & Fulfillment,* a trade magazine based near New York City in suburban Connecticut. A veteran journalist, she has elevated the editorial quality of her magazine and won national awards for its excellence. She depends on freelance writers and enjoys her professional relationships with them:

When I took over as editor of *Operations & Fulfillment* in 1997, the magazine was a "mom and pop" operation that relied on consultants and shop-floor engineers to supply articles, which were allowed to run without much modification. The magazine also reprinted presentations from NCOF, the conference that it sponsored. As a non-technical journalist, my goal was to introduce a lively, colloquial voice; use professional freelance writers; break up the copy into smaller chunks; cover a wider variety of topics; and bring more human interest into the magazine through interviews and profiles—in other words, to make *O&F* an edgy, sophisticated business magazine. At present, paid freelance journalists write 50% of the magazine; non-paid consultants, practitioners, or academics write 25% (with heavy rewrites by our staff); and we, the editors, write 25%.

Our approach to finding and hiring freelancers is different from that of most trade magazines. We look for top-notch professional journalists—people who write for the likes of *The New York Times, Forbes, Fortune,* or *The Economist.* Sometimes they find us, through *Writer's Market* or word-of-mouth; sometimes we find them, through referrals or by looking through magazines and newspapers. We prefer writers who haven't written for other logistics or retail magazines; they bring a fresh approach to the subject, are not afraid to be controversial, and haven't been contaminated by the jargon.

Many of our best writers have come to us quite by chance: One of them, for instance, was working at *The Economist* after I had left, heard about me from someone there, and called me here at Primedia to ask about freelance opportunities. Today, he's the writer we turn to when we want something so close to perfect that it needs virtually no editing.

We're also unusual among trade books in that we pay exceedingly well: $1 a word, sometimes more. With most of our articles running 2,000 words plus, the money is enough to attract the best. The same goes for photography and illustration. Our creative director hires artists who work for *Wired, Fast Company, The New York Times Magazine,* and other leading publications.

The professional writers need little or no handholding. Typically, we describe the topic, discuss some of the issues they might want to explore, and provide a basic list of contacts. Most of the time, they can take it from there. The consultants and industry experts are much more time-consuming—their work invariably needs extensive rewriting, plus additional research and interviews, all done by our staff. We send the consultants copies of our writers' guidelines (developed for them, actually, rather than for professional journalists), but they don't pay them much attention.

We use standard contracts (attached) that all writers are required to sign and return to us, whether they're working for pay or not. (Ramaswami, personal communication, October 17, 2002)

## PROVIDING PHOTOGRAPHS AND OTHER GRAPHICS

Although you might fancy yourself as a writer, you might find yourself in a position to be a photographer or graphic artist, or to work in some other form of visual communication. This happens frequently when a publication does not, or cannot, provide a photographer. To strengthen your position to make a sale, you should consider whether photographs or other artwork will make a difference. Most publications today prefer digital graphics. With the decreasing cost and convenience of use of quality digital cameras, photography becomes a viable option for some freelance writers. If you can take your own professional-quality digital photographs, it will strengthen your submission effort. If you cannot, it is best not to submit below-par photographs with strong writing.

What you can often do to assist an editor is suggest visual elements of the total package. You know the material best and are able to propose photograph subjects, graphs or tables, charts, maps, and diagrams that a professional artist can prepare. You should not have to pay for this service, but you should suggest it to an editor at the time of the query. It strengthens your position if you can propose visual approaches to telling the story. A freelance travel story is not as enticing without photographs of the palm-lined beach or snow-capped mountain range. A how-to article or science article is far more understandable with diagrams.

You may be interested in doing your own photographic or informational graphics work. It takes skill development, just like writing. Another solution is to team with a freelance photographer and graphic artist. As you begin to increase the frequency of your freelance work, you may get acquainted with freelance photographers and artists in your area. Teaming up with these individuals can create a strong offering to an editor that might lead to more good opportunities for everyone involved.

Do not forget that you may be expected to write the first drafts of the cutlines, or captions, of the artwork you submit. These can be short, simple, left-to-right identifications of people in the photographs, or they can be more thorough explanations of procedures and other subjects of the artwork. Your newspaper or magazine's style dictates how you handle the cutlines—short or long, tight or descriptive, general or detailed—so be sure to familiarize yourself with the way the editor handles these important elements. Always be sure to provide sources of photographs and other graphics for appropriate publication credit if you did not produce them yourself.

## PRODUCING MULTIPLE ARTICLES FROM RESEARCH

A wise and efficient freelance feature writer is able to develop more than one distinct manuscript from research and interviews on a subject. If you can, you will get more income from your investment in time and resources. This is the result of organization and planning. If you are going to make a 500-mile trip for one manuscript—and spend $500 to $1,000—try to develop a second article prospect for the same trip. Often it is no additional expense to add a second or even a third project; all you give up is additional time. "Full-time writers have to get maximum mileage from each article they produce," said author and free-lance writer Dennis Hensley (1993, p. 32). "That means selling each piece as many times as possible. I do this by marketing from the smallest local publications to the largest circulation periodicals. Most editors don't mind buying a feature that you've already sold elsewhere" (Hensley, 1993, p. 32). Hensley said multiple sales are acceptable if the previous appearance does not overlap readership, if different artwork can be provided, if the article is rewritten in the style of the second publication, and if new items, such as examples or cases, relevant to readers of the second publication, are inserted into the article.

It is smart to consider different markets. "When I realized I'd grossed about 5 cents an hour on my first big writing assignment, I knew I had to mend my ways," wrote freelancer Valerie Zehl (1998, p. 24). What was her solution? She began to take research done for one article and apply it to other articles. "I turned an idea on its head and shook out a few other ideas" (Zehl, 1998, p. 24). And she sold them. Zehl said the technique of reslanting, reselling, and recycling work gets more revenue from it. "Recycling an idea into many reslants and resales is a profitable use of a writer's time and research. With a little imagination and energy, the recycling—and the generating of additional income—from one body of research can go on and on" (Zehl, 1998, p. 25).

As Zehl (1998) suggested, there are several ways to focus on a subject, as you know from earlier discussions. Each may represent an article prospect. Focus on both general markets and specialized markets. A general market approach for an article on personal finance varies a great deal from the specific market approach that a banking magazine would take. Furthermore, consider proposing longer articles in parts. In this way, you are selling two separate, perhaps shorter, articles instead of one longer one. You might earn more for such a sale, but this depends on the rate structure of a publication.

## GOING FULL-TIME AS A FREELANCE WRITER

Sally-Jo Bowman (1996), a freelance writer and regular contributor to *Writer's Digest,* has given a lot of thought to full-time freelance work. That is how she makes a living, so it is quite important to her. She lists four steps to going full-time: put together a mission statement for your career, start it part-time and gain experience, examine the financial side of the matter, and weigh the pros and cons. Here is a list of some pros and cons to consider:

| Pros: | Cons: |
|---|---|
| No commutes. | You must pay your own benefits, insurance. |
| Family nearby. | You generate all revenue. |
| No one to ask for time off. | There may be no checks in the mail. |
| Lower clothing expenses. | There are some tax disadvantages. |
| Work at odd, quiet hours. | There is no maintenance or supply to help. |
| Tax breaks for home offices. | Unfinished work, deadlines are always near. |
| Weather is no factor in going to work. | No paid vacations or sick pay. |
| No one knows if you are in a bad mood. | The work can be lonely. |
| Large checks sometimes come in the mail. | People think you aren't working, interrupt. |
| Master of your own fate. | Feast or famine in terms of income. |

Steve Perlstein (personal communication, May 3, 1993 & January 15, 1998), a Minneapolis, MN, freelance writer, dealt with many of these issues when he made the big jump from full-time newspaper reporting to freelance writing on a full-time basis several years ago. He said you have to be aggressive to make it happen:

It doesn't have all that much to do with talent. If I do away with all modesty, I can say I'm as good a writer and reporter as anybody who gets $10,000 a pop writing overly long features for *Esquire*. But my optimistic side tells me that I'll be there someday as well, for four simple reasons: I make my deadlines, I write to length, I give editors what they ask for, and I sell myself.

If I sat around waiting for the work to come in, or if I shot off a few queries every once in a while, I might make a little money. But I'm in the unusual situation of supporting my wife, two kids, and a mortgage on my freelance income. That presents special challenges (like it's nearly impossible), but it also is an impressive incentive to get me downstairs to my office every morning, working hard. I started small—I took a lot of low-paying local work, I wrote for a dizzying array of trade magazines and I scratched up national assignments where I could find them. Usually I couldn't find them. My credo was, "Never turn down an assignment." I still try to hold to that as much as possible, and that is what has kept food on the table and has enabled me to keep my promise to myself that I would not resort to public relations work to earn a living.

Since then, my level of work has remained steady. But instead of averaging around $200 per assignment, as I did when I started, I'm now somewhere around $400. I've done that through a combination of local freelancing of increasing visibility—including wrestling monthly retainers from two of the Twin Cities' best (and best-paying) freelance markets—and through dogged pursuit of national markets until I wedged my foot in the door somewhere. I sent query after query after query—hundreds in all—before *Entrepreneur* magazine called last summer to commission a 400-word piece on a local businesswoman. At fifty cents a word, I only make $200 (and though the piece is long since finished and paid for, it is warehoused and hasn't run yet), but that one assignment opened the floodgates. I was able to put in my query letters, "I have written for *Entrepreneur* magazine, and more than a dozen others." It worked. Shortly after that I had a long feature assignment from *Entrepreneur,* as well as assignments from *Parenting; Sky,* the Delta Airlines in-flight magazine; *Events USA;* and the nation's largest magazine, *Modern Maturity.*

Still, I constantly have to pitch myself and my ideas to editors. Nobody calls me up begging for my services. There are far too many freelancers around for that to happen. So everywhere I go, everything I do and everyone I meet is a potential story. I got my *Modern Maturity* piece about Garrison Keillor's American Radio Company after I attended one of his shows and found it to be charming. I searched until I found a magazine that agreed with me. My wife and I wondered about how safe it was to microwave baby food; that wound up in *Parenting,* with my byline. There is virtually nothing on this earth that can't be crafted to the proper angle and sold to an editor. The key is always to be thinking of what your next story is going to be. It could be something innocuous like the merger of several natural foods cooperatives or it could be something exciting like a travelogue of one of the Clinton/Gore campaign bus trips (both stories I have done).

I can't imagine a freelancer—unless he or she is a renowned expert on a given topic or named Roger Angell and writing about baseball—who can specialize and make a living. I enjoy how-to and human interest stories, and I write many of them, but I also write a lot about business, politics, health care, parenting, sports and even banner fabrics, if you can believe it. Freelancers with a large inheritance or a wealthy spouse can pick a topic and write only that; those of us who have to hustle for a living need to diversify. (Perlstein, personal communication, May 3, 1993)

# CHAPTER NINETEEN

# Surviving in the Freelance Business

For many students and other beginning nonfiction writers, chances are good that you have never been paid for your work. That will happen. For some of you, it may happen before you finish college. For others, it might take a while to find the match between a publication that needs an article on a particular subject and your original treatment of that subject.

Freelance writers work on two levels. The first is full-time writing. The second is "moonlighting," or part-time writing. This chapter focuses on many important professional concerns of both approaches. The chapter discussion begins with the basics of getting paid. The legal and ethical concerns of freelance writers are outlined, too. You learn about professional writers' organizations, continuing educational opportunities beyond college, and contests and awards for quality work.

Freelance writers earn varying amounts of money for their efforts. As you start writing for pay, you will notice very different degrees of how you are paid, how much you are paid, and even how fast you are paid. Checks are the standard, of course, although a few freelance writers may trade or barter for their services. Checks are issued to freelancers at various times in the publishing process, but most often after the article is completed, submitted, and accepted for publication. Some publications pay only after the article is printed. On major projects that involve long periods of time, writers should seek an advance or a partial payment in the middle of the project. You have to ask for this because most editors will not usually offer such a convenience.

Most professional freelancers include an invoice with their final manuscripts when they are submitted. You need to keep track of such matters because you will likely have several projects going simultaneously and may lose track of who has paid for what after a period of time has passed. Setting up a ledger, spreadsheet, or a card file system will help you to do this. Sending written reminders to be paid are not out of line after a grace period. You should be patient for at least 30 days. After that, send a reminder by mailing a copy of the original invoice to your editor. Editors get busy and occasionally forget to submit payment requests to the publication's business department. Writer Tana Reiff (1987a, 1987b) said freelance writing businesses are no different from any other one-person businesses. You should operate with this philosophy. Be your own accountant and practice the basics of good accounting. It will save you money in the long run.

Veteran freelancer Kit Snedaker (personal communication, April 17, 1993, April 18, 1993, & January 23, 1998) specializes in food, wine, luxury travel, and folk art. Based in Santa Monica, CA, she has traveled all over the world. Snedaker is a former daily newspaper staff writer who made the move to full-time freelance writing a few years ago. She has contributed articles to major publications in the United States and in international markets. Snedaker is a contributing writer for *The Robb Report,* a monthly magazine with circulation around 400,000 per issue and writes regularly for *Westways,* the American Automobile Association magazine in Southern California. She writes food features, reviews of restaurants in cities outside the United States, and prepares travel features as well. She has written several books about cooking, outstanding Southern California restaurants, and the city of Los Angeles. Snedaker has had her travel and food articles published by *Bon Appetit, Food and Wine, Cuisine, Harper's Bazaar, Los Angeles* magazine, Copley News Service, numerous metropolitan daily newspapers, and a long list of travel publications. She works in a home office that includes a PC and modem, a fax machine, and other tools of the freelance writer's trade. She holds memberships in several professional groups, including the Society of American Travel Writers. Snedaker has won awards for her feature writing from several groups and has served as a guest editor for *Mademoiselle.* Snedaker grew up in the Midwest and graduated from Duke University. She has lived in Europe, Japan, and the West Coast (Snedaker, personal communication, April 17, 1993, April 18, 1993, & January 23, 1998). By all standards, Snedaker is a successful freelance writer. However, if you have not detected how she did it quite yet, she has done well because of hard work, discipline, organization, and attention for detail.

## SETTING RATES FOR YOUR WORK

Serious freelance writers should set financial goals for their work. This simply means figuring out any out-of-pocket expenses in reporting and writing the story and deciding how much your time is worth. "Profit is revenues minus expenses. Revenues should cover expenses . . . and leave a little over for profit. Work smarter, not harder. Get paid your due," advised freelance writer and author Jeffery D. Zbar (2002, p. 52). "In small business America, including the professional writing community, the same is true. It is essential to sell your product at a fee that guarantees your expenses will be covered and that you will have something left over to save or enjoy" (Zbar, 2002, p. 52).

Many beginning freelance writers are paid whatever their editors decide is the going rate. They never question or negotiate fees. This works well enough if you are primarily interested in obtaining clips and, especially, if you have an alternative means of support. There comes a time when most freelancers begin to take fees as serious business.

Writers should weigh whether to bargain for bigger fees, veteran national magazine freelance writer Linda Berkhoudt O'Connor (1996) suggested. Negotiating with editors can bring better arrangements than simply accepting what is offered, she stated. Negotiations do not have to be about the fee. It can include expenses, deadlines, and even the direction of the content. But most important, O'Connor said, she has upped her fees income by 50% by speaking up at the time of reaching an agreement with an editor. Houston, TX, freelance writer Connie Steitz Fox agreed: "[W]hen the rent is due or you want to work at a higher level of professionalism, you need a more assertive approach" (1993, p. 6).

Gregg Levoy (1991), a veteran freelance magazine writer, said you need to constantly review what you get paid for your work and ask for more as you gain more experience. Negotiating is essential to getting paid what you are worth, he argued. "When breaking into a magazine—writers *should* take whatever terms are offered," Levoy wrote (p. 26). "Continuing this practice after breaking in, however, is like turning down raises" (Levoy, 1991, p. 26). In his years as a freelancer, Levoy has learned three important lessons about negotiating fees: (a) it is surprising what you can get if you ask; (b) the worst an editor can do is say no; and (c) everything is negotiable, even editing. However, Levoy said, a freelance writer's position in negotiating is affected by performance record, quality of first impression and presentation, level of professionalism, degree of polish brought to the effort, and degree of personal contact with the individuals on the editorial side.

Freelancers must be willing to negotiate for their time and creativity. Editors of most publications set fees for a lot of reasons. For example, they have budgets for freelancers and can spend only so much, or they pay depending on a writer's level of experience. They may have still other reasons. Fox (1993, p. 6) said there are several factors to remember when setting freelance fees:

> Consider these factors: What is the market value of your product or service? What is your cost of doing business? What would constitute a fair profit? How much training do you have? How many years of experience? How much natural ability? Do you have expertise in related fields? Can you help to further your client's business goals, including *their* goal of increased profits?

Tom Yates (1995), a freelance writer with 20 years of experience with daily newspapers and national magazines, offered three rules about fees. First, set the rates in advance. Second, include any income taxes you might expect to pay in the fee. And third, set aside the tax portion of the fee and save it for the day you pay your income tax bills. These recommendations are given with the assumption that expenses are not part of the fee. If they are, he said, you must estimate the costs of anything that might be used and money spent in pursuit of the article—business costs such as office space and overhead, telephone and postage, and travel, but also personal expenses such as food and housing.

There are four ways of being paid for freelance work. Each one is different and, if you have a choice in the matter, requires that you consider which works best in your own situation. Here are your choices:

1. You can agree to a flat fee for completion of a particular writing project. This is perhaps the most common way to handle freelance assignments. For instance, you write an article of certain agreed-on specifications and you get paid $75, $150, or whatever amount is established. This does not always take into consideration how much time it takes you to complete the assignment. You are paid the same amount regardless of the amount of time you need to finish the work. You do, however, have the option of renegotiating the fee if you and your editor discover the assignment will take more time and effort than originally anticipated.

2. You can work by the hour on the assignment. This may be the preferred method from the writer's point of view because it may not be certain how much time is needed to finish an assignment. This is the smart strategy for large projects because it is seldom possible to anticipate how much effort is required. This approach also requires you to decide how much your time is worth per hour or per day on the open market. This can range from minimum wage to the hundreds of dollars a day that high-powered consultants command. Typical rates for beginning freelancers are most likely in the $8 per hour to $15 per hour range. Veteran freelancers receive more, in the $25 per hour to $50 per hour range, depending on the cost of living in a particular region of the country, the size of the publication, and the experience of the writer. Some specialists may be paid even more. Freelance technical writers, for instance, earn $30 per hour to $60 per hour, according to some published reports. This rate may be the hardest to determine unless you have been in the market. It may be easier after you have completed a few assignments and understand how much you were paid and how much time you used to finish the assignment. On the first few assignments, an "hours worked" log would be very useful for that purpose.

3. You can be paid by the word or by the column inch. Some publications stick to the old-fashioned newspaper stringer method of paying by the published length of an article. This can run from one cent to $1 or more per word. This does not mean that you are encouraged to write long. Instead, the amount per word is set in negotiation with the editor, and the maximum length of the article is also set by agreement.

4. You can be placed on a retainer to write for a publication. This is similar to how some attorneys or consultants work for preferred clients. This involves being paid a set minimal amount per week or per month, regardless of the work assigned and completed. The maximum amount is often determined by agreement, either by the hour or by the project. This method is not used as

often as the others and is used when a writer has become a regular contributor for a publication.

You may also want to charge for special conditions of assignments. Dangerous situations, holiday work, overtime hours, rush work, "no-compete" or "exclusivity" clauses that prevent you from writing on the same subject for other publications, and such extraordinary circumstances may call for higher fees or bonuses beyond the going rates. Also keep in mind that, no matter which of the four options are used to pay you for your work, your expenses are a separate issue. However, many editors build in ordinary expenses, such as long distance telephone calls or automobile transportation, into the flat fee paid for the assignment. Additional expenses or extraordinary costs, such as airfare or equipment rentals, must be negotiated to be paid separately.

You are entitled to the money you have earned: it is that simple. Payment should occur within a reasonable period of time. Yet, some careless editors and publishers do not quite see it that way. They delay or simply do not pay writers in a professional manner. Thus, a first step in establishing a payment arrangement is to determine the normal period for the publication. You can ask about this when an agreement to publish your article has been reached. Then you wait.

It is also important to establish a guarantee or a "kill" fee before the work is submitted or even written. If an editor changes his or her mind about your article for whatever reasons, you should be compensated for the work you were assigned to put into it. If a completed assignment is not acceptable due to no fault of yours as the writer, some professional organizations such as the American Society of Journalists and Authors (ASJA) feel, you should be paid a guarantee up to the full amount reflecting the effort put into the article before the decision to "kill" it was made (Bloom et al., 1992). Most professionals agree, also, that you should be paid within 1 month of delivery. This varies from publication to publication and the cycle within which the publication's accounting department or business office works. Some process checks only on a monthly basis.

ASJA also recommends in its code of ethics and fair practices that "no article payment, or portion thereof, should ever be subject to publication" (Bloom et al., 1992, p. 51). If a publisher does not pay and you feel you are entitled to your fee, writer Dean R. Lambe (1986) suggested several potential actions to take:

- Write a politely worded inquiry letter to the editor.
- Next, write the publisher (if different from the editor).
- See a lawyer and have him or her write an inquiry letter.
- Take legal action through your lawyer.
- If a bankruptcy has occurred, file a claim so you can get a share when assets are sold.
- Share your grief with other writers through professional groups.

## KEEPING TRACK OF YOUR EXPENSES

Freelance writers are paid for two types of expenses. One is the time spent writing and researching the manuscript. The other type involves the cost of getting the story. Besides your time, you encounter certain operating expenses when working on an article. As a freelancer, you must arrange to get these costs paid by the publication that accepts your article or else the cost will come from your agreed fee.

If you have proposed an article, you should estimate expenses and include the estimate in your total fee, especially if the cost is excessive. At worst, expenses can consume your "profits" from the assignment. At best, your employer should reimburse expenses. Typical writer's expenses include automobile mileage, plane travel, parking, lodging, food, admissions, express mail and overnight delivery services, long-distance telephone tolls, film, photo processing, and photocopying. You should expect your publication to pay reasonable expenses, but you should check these details when an assignment is made or when your proposal is accepted. Normal business expenses such as printer ribbons, printer paper, routine postage, or computer disks are rarely paid as expenses. Overhead costs such as electricity, office space rental, and local phone costs are rarely covered as specific expenses, also.

Professional writers always keep expense logs and receipts, even for costs that are not directly billable to employers. There are two basic reasons for this. First, you must have a record if you expect someone else to pay for your expenses. Second, if you do not get them reimbursed, you can still claim certain business expenses as deductions on your federal and state income taxes—if they are documented. Because tax laws change on a somewhat regular basis, it is best to check with a tax expert on these matters.

Always discuss payment of expenses with your editor in advance, especially if a major expense such as out-of-town travel is involved. The editor set a ceiling for expenses for an assignment and you are expected to keep within the limit. For example, if you need to make a large number of lengthy long-distance telephone calls, an editor may budget $100 for that particular expense. Yet, if you foresee going over the limit, ask about it first. Otherwise, you may find the expenses chipping away your income when the editor refuses, after the fact, to pay them.

Tracking expenses for editors or for your income taxes is fairly easy. It requires a little discipline and a pen and paper. Or it is even easier to do using readily available financial software such as Quicken, Money, or Excel.

## PERMISSIONS AND OTHER LEGAL MATTERS

You cannot exist in a legal vacuum as a freelance writer. In addition to the general concerns all journalists must have about libel, privacy, copyright, open records, and open meetings, you must also consider other legal issues related to freelance writing. This means knowing the details of obtaining permissions, payment for work particulars, reprint and other second sales rights, contracts, general letters of agreement, and author copyright.

Furthermore, the era of computer networks and the World Wide Web and Internet has brought a new set of concerns. Development of online publications has brought issues involving writer's fees and copyright, among other things. There is increased risk that a writer's work will be used without permission or fees paid if it is a part of a computer network, Boston intellectual rights attorney Howard Zaharoff (1996a, 1996b) observed. Many freelance and staff feature writers do not recognize their rights in the networked computer world and often do not protect them. Zaharoff said the only way to do this is to know the laws.

As a writer, you are concerned with expressing your words. Publishers who want to publish your words, however, are concerned with your rights to them—that is, your copyrights. To protect yourself as you sell your words, you must know what copyrights are, how they are created, transferred and protected, and how such key concepts as "work made for hire" and "fair use" fit into the process (Zaharoff, 1996a, p. 24).

As a writer and reporter, you must be concerned with the laws in your state involving libel, privacy, fraud, copyright, and access to information. There are numerous high caliber discussions of these subjects in other books and they are not discussed in depth here. *Mass Communication Law: Cases and Comment*, by Donald Gillmor, Jerome Barron, Todd Simon, and Herbert Terry (1990), for example, is one of several general treatises of concerns affecting all types of feature writers and reporters.

The recent legal problems of one freelance feature writer may be an illustration of the need to know both state and federal laws dealing with his line of work. A Southern California man pleaded guilty to selling phony celebrity stories to supermarket tabloids and was sentenced to federal prison and then home confinement. He admitted to 21 counts of mail fraud and tax evasion for using fictitious sources to sell story ideas and stories to those publications. The judge in the case felt the writer was encouraged to do the work by the publications, but the publications encouraged him, the federal judge said, to protect themselves from libel and other civil action against them. The writer, a former daily newspaper reporter in Los Angeles, agreed in court to assist in investigations into the professional ethics of the publications (Free-lance writer, 1993).

There are times, in preparing an article, when you will wish to use a substantial passage from another published and copyrighted work. This occurs when quoting other authors, composers, and artists. You must get permission from the source, or rights holder, when you want to do this. Generally, there are four steps to getting permission: find the copyright owner, write a permission request letter to the owner, act on the reply to your request letter (for example, pay a fee or provide a copy of the article), and credit the copyright holder in your article. For short passages, usually up to 250 words or a paragraph, you do not need formal permission. However, writers are asking for trouble if they fail to get permission for use of longer quotations.

## OBTAINING AND KEEPING AUTHOR COPYRIGHT

Copyright law in the United States is designed to protect creative works by authors. Such law is almost as old as the nation itself, dating back to 1790. A recent modification in the law—and it has been changed many times over the past 200-plus years—focuses protection on the author. As a freelance writer, you need to know who owns your manuscript once it is published. This should be stipulated in letters of agreement or contracts. Most such arrangements leave ownership—that is, the copyright—with the author. Thus, unless you give up those rights in writing, ownership of the work remains with you as author, according to U.S. copyright law.

For staff writers producing feature articles in their regular employment role, the work they create belongs to their employers. There can be exceptions to this, but they are rare. Some staff writers, such as extremely popular columnists, negotiate rights to their works when they have become established because they want to publish them elsewhere (e.g., volumes of their collected works). For freelancers, or for full-time staffers doing articles outside of normal work, the work belongs to the author. If there is doubt, discuss it before you get too deeply into your assignment. Whatever is decided about rights should be placed in writing, also.

Under the revised copyright law, authors are protected when the work reaches final form in any tangible medium. This includes not only computer versions of manuscripts, but also photographs, informational graphics, and other works of freelance authors. The law protects authors against unauthorized sale and distribution of their work. Although authors do not have to register their work with the U.S. Copyright Office within the Library of Congress (Washington, DC 20559, 202–707–3000), it is recommended because any legal action that may occur cannot begin until registration is completed. The process is simple and inexpensive ($20). Authors are also advised to use a copyright notice symbol ©, the word "Copyright," or the abbreviation "Copr." with the name of the holder and date on all works, although this is not required for protection. Doing so may reduce what is called innocent infringement (Gillmor et al., 1990).

Traditionally, freelance writers have sold only the one-time publication rights of their work. Reprint fees should be yours as author, ASJA (Bloom et al., 1992) suggests to its members. The publication that prints your article should refer inquiries to you, as well, unless you waive these rights. You hold the copyright unless you grant it in writing to the publication. Any other rights are yours, ASJA says, and it strongly urges writers not to sign any documents that transfer those rights to a publisher. Reprints can be profitable for freelance writers if you retain your reprint rights and then aggressively use them (James-Enger, 2002).

## GET THE DEAL IN WRITING? MAYBE!

Some freelance writers work regularly with none of the terms of their assignments in writing. Any agreements are informal, casually set in telephone conversations. Although this is admirable, it is also potentially troublesome. It is not smart business practice these days. Perhaps the only occasion when this arrangement between a writer and an editor makes sense is when the relationship is an established one and both parties know the terms and details from repeated experiences. In all other cases, it is wisest to get a memorandum, letter, or even a formal contract from the editor responsible for the newspaper, magazine, newsletter, or online publication that made the assignment. In some situations, such as lengthy or complicated assignments involving international travel or dangerous situations, even more formalized contracts may be required to cover all contingencies.

### Working with a Publisher's Contract

Contracts can be beneficial to writers and editors. If done properly, a contract sets down terms of an agreement between the writer and the editor. Most of the time, the contract is some kind of standard fill-in-the-blank legal form used for all freelance employment. If you have been offered a contract with a publication, read it thoroughly before you sign it and return it. Contracts specify certain arrangements between the author and publisher. You may find terms in the document that do not apply to your situation and these should be deleted. Similarly, there may be peculiar aspects of your situation not covered in the document that must be appended. This can be done without significant delays in most cases.

As a writer, you need to look for certain elements of a contract regardless of whether it involves a nonfiction article or something as complex as an entire book. The major concerns about these kinds of contracts, said literary agent Lisa Collier Cool (1985b), include the following: publication fee, kill fee (a guarantee if the article is not used), assigned manuscript length (usually in words), payment of expenses (or limitations), payment schedule, manuscript deadlines, payment of advances, author bylines or credits in the publication, serial rights, book publication rights (usually for collected sets of articles by popular and experienced feature writers), dramatic rights, commercial rights, online database retrieval rights, translations (from English to another language), and frequency of use by the publication (some editors will republish an article from time to time).

Glenda Tennant Neff (1992), assistant managing editor at Writer's Digest Books, advises any writer looking at a contractual arrangement to consider his or her own writing goals:

> As you evaluate a document, consider what you want from your writing. Did you have another sale in mind that selling all rights the first time will negate? Does the agreement here provide the publisher with a number of add-ons (advertising rights, reprint rights, etc.) for which they won't have to pay you again? Contracts are rarely take-it-or-leave-it propositions. Sometimes they are, and the editor will let you know. At that point you will have to decide how important the assignment is to you. But most editors are open to negotiation, and you should learn to compromise on points that don't matter to you while maintaining your stand on things that do. (p. 47)

## Using Letters of Agreement

Often it is a good idea to work with a letter of agreement instead of a contract. As the writer, you can originate the letter of agreement if the editor does not offer one. This is a suitable compromise to no written agreement at all and the other extreme of a detailed contract. A letter of agreement, like a contract, should state the terms of the relationship between the writer and the publication. Like the contract, it should list fees to be paid and when, who is responsible for expenses, the topic of the assignment, the length of the manuscript, the deadline, the person responsible for artwork, and other pertinent details.

Some editors like to work with letters of agreement instead of contracts. These letters function as contracts because they have certain details prescribed in them. *National Geographic Traveler* issues its assignments in writing after discussing the terms of the assignment with the freelancer on the telephone. Senior Articles Editor Carol Lutyk (personal communication, July 15, 1993) works that way. Her letters of agreement represent the magazine and the publisher, the National Geographic Society in Washington, DC. Her letters outline the topic, length, due date, fees to be paid if used or if killed, and any rights that the magazine retains. Some publications, such as *National Geographic Traveler,* even specify that similar work cannot be done for certain competing publications. Lutyk also asks writers on assignment to agree to certain ethical standards such as acceptance of discounts or free goods and services. The agreements often also stipulate that a writer cannot give the work to someone else to do on his or her behalf. A copy of Lutyk's *National Geographic Traveler* agreement letter for a restaurant review assignment and a copy of her generic letter used for travel feature article assignments are located in Appendix G. Two other examples in Appendix G provide a look at agreements used by trade-industry publications. The two letters offer fee-based and non-fee-based agreements used by *Operations & Fulfillment,* a PRIMEDIA Inc. magazine that serves the mail order industry and is based in Connecticut.

## LAWSUITS AND OTHER LEGAL PROBLEMS

Lawsuits can arise from just about anything in a written work. The main causes are claims for libel, defamation, or invasion of privacy, especially in articles that break new ground or are about controversial subjects. You must be concerned with the possibility, whether the cases are legitimate or not. If your work is accurate, then you will have little about which to worry. Truth, of course, is the best defense against libel actions. Writer and journalism professor Bruce Henderson (1984) recommended nine ways to "bulletproof" a manuscript:

1. The idea—Check whether the story idea is a new one. Be certain you are not copying or plagiarizing a work. Check your own motivations for doing the article. If your work involves revenge or venting anger, forget it.
2. The assignment contract—Honor the commitments you make in writing and otherwise. Know what you are liable for, such as legal fees, according to the contract terms.
3. Research—Use written sources if possible to guard against legal claims. Keep accurate records about where you find the factual information you use.
4. Interviews—Select qualified sources. Be sure sources have no grudges against your subject. Get second sources to verify. Identify sources, whenever possible, in the article. Conduct important interviews in person and tape-record them.
5. Note taking—Be thorough in taking notes. Organize the notes after an interview or a records search. When you can, note negative results—that you could not find something.
6. Writing—Tell only what you know. Do not guess or make up information to fill in holes. If you are not certain of a fact, then avoid using it.
7. Editing and fact-checking—Do not change information in a story, even if an editor asks you to do so, unless the change is true and accurate. Be ready for a fact-checker from the publication to verify information in your story. This may mean calling your sources, too.
8. Final checks—Have a lawyer read your final manuscript if you think it might be troublesome. Seeking legal advice before publication is smart and safe.
9. Lawsuit—If you ever find yourself served with a suit, contact the publication immediately. The publisher will be directly involved also. Plan to work together.

## ETHICS AND FREELANCE WRITING

Another important topic for freelancer writers to consider is ethics. Ethics is the set of principles of professional conduct. Although certain practices in journalism are legal, they may not be ethical. In other words, the practices may not be accepted behavior among most professional writers and editors. For instance, there is much concern today about invasion of individual privacy.

There are numerous codes of professional standards in journalism. Among them are the codes of the Society of Professional Journalists (SPJ) and the ASJA. The codes are included in Appendixes H and I. There are other codes, of course, but they have a similar purpose: to set forward an acceptable standard to work as a professional journalist. The SPJ code sets general standards for all journalists and is a good overall model to study. ASJA's code focuses on ethical and economic issues that are the fundamental concerns of writers.

What professional standards should we be concerned about? Ethics codes list more than 24 different issues pertaining to the relation of writers to sources, editors, readers, and even other writers. Most general codes, such as the SPJ code, focus on responsibilities to the public, need for accuracy, need for freedom of the press, need for fairness, elimination of conflicts of interest and acceptance of gifts in exchange for favors, and the desire to achieve honesty and objectivity. Specific writers' codes, such as the one endorsed by ASJA, are more detailed and propose fair practices in the relationship of writers and editors. ASJA's code, for example, addresses nearly 24 separate situations ranging from subjects similar to those in the SPJ code such as accuracy and conflicts of interest to specific details of writers' publication and payment rights and their expenses.

One mark of a professional is the level of his or her ethical conduct. Familiarity with the accepted performance standards in your profession only helps in the long run. Because these are evolving standards, they are constantly changing. It is up to you to keep up with them as your professional career expands.

## MOVING TOWARD FULL-TIME FREELANCE WRITING

Most beginning freelance writers are moonlighting. Their primary means of support comes from another form of employment. There will come a time for writers who are successful at moonlighting to consider quitting their primary job to open up more time for writing. Two of the hardest decisions a part-time freelance writer faces are (a) whether to switch to full-time and, if the decision to switch is made, (b) when is the right time to make the change. Besides giving up an existing career, it is a decision that may mean giving up a regular, steady income. It is one that should be made only after thoughtful deliberation and discussion with family and colleagues.

The main *"real* difference" in a moonlighting freelance writer and a full-time one is the number of hours per week that are devoted to writing, said author Robert Bly (1992). Once they begin to work, moonlighters and full-timers operate the same way, he said. Michael A. Banks (1985), an author who quit a factory job to become a full-time freelance writer, described advantages and disadvantages to making the big switch:

• Advantages—First, there is more time to plan and write. You can take on larger projects, such as booklets and even books. You work as much as you want because you control your time. There is no need for the physical and psychological transition time to go from job one to job two. Also, Banks (1985) said, the full-time writing effort gives you a boost in self-esteem by being in control of your own career and business.

• Disadvantages—You may be the primary wage earner for you and your family. Some economic losses by giving up a steady income are severe and must be considered. You must be able to manage money that comes in uneven surges. You must also endure the operating expenses of being a writer on your own. This means the costs of travel, telephone, equipment, and even ordinary office supplies. You may have to pressure yourself to be productive. Failure can take on a greater significance. There is no supervisory pressure in most cases and you must be self-disciplined. Furthermore, do not forget that you lose all nonpaycheck benefits that come along with a full-time salaried job (e.g., health insurance, pensions and retirement, social security contributions made by your employer [now you must make them], paid vacations, bonuses, sick days, and overtime).

The decision to go full-time must be an economic one. Can you afford it? What is your current part-time income? What would it be full time if you project it to the amount of time you gain by quitting the full-time job? Is that realistic? Can you find that much freelance work? What are your basic normal living expenses? Will you cover them? Can you make sacrifices of other things for a while?

Oregon freelance writer Gary King (personal communication, May 19, 1993) specializes in "true crime" and mystery writing. He has written three books about serial killers and other crime in addition to his numerous articles for publications such as *True Detective* and *Official Detective*. He said he found writing to be addictive. He could not get enough of it as a part-timer. Here's how he said he decided to make the shift:

> When I first broke into crime writing, I was naturally thrilled that anyone would buy my work and in fact wanted more. That was in December 1980. Almost immediately I asked my editor, Art Crockett, if I should give up my job and go full time. His response: "Forget free-lancing on a full-time basis unless you marry a

rich widow—or until you become a best-selling author and have editors clamoring for your work." I took his advice, but only for a while. By 1984 I was free-lancing full time and putting my family through hell. In retrospect, free-lancing is not something I would recommend to anyone who wants to keep the bills paid on time and food on the table. It's very difficult. Appealing as the prospect of being on your own can be, there's still nothing like a steady paycheck.

Freelancer Tana Reiff (1987a) recommends diversification of your writing. The more you can write about different specialties, the more you will bring in fees, she believes. She also recommends diversity in the types of projects. Taking on both short and long assignments can keep a steadier supply of income in the mail, she said.

Prepare for the switch by planning ahead. Put aside extra money for the expected slow period at the beginning. Also, save some good writing ideas for slow idea periods, Banks (1985) recommended. These will help you through tough times. He advised to not "burn your bridges" at your primary job. Try to leave yourself an option to return if things do not work out. Test your career change first by taking a 3- to 6-month leave, if this is available. Sometimes, accumulated vacation time can be taken in one big block for a trial run at full-time freelance writing.

## TIPS FOR SURVIVING A TOUGH ECONOMY

David A. Fryxell (2002), editor-in-chief of F&W Publications and nonfiction columnist for *Writer's Digest,* recommends keeping four tips in mind when the economy is tight and freelance writing opportunities are not as abundant as you'd like:

- Look for time-consuming jobs that magazine staff writers and editors do not have the chance to complete.
- Watch for stories in your region that publications may want to cover, but cannot afford to send writers from their staffs.
- Think of ways to save editors money in their tight budgets.
- Visit local publications and offer to assist.

## SETTING UP A "WRITING ZONE" AT HOME

Writers need a comfortable and familiar space in which to work. Some may be able to write anywhere at any time, but just like at home, there is a psychological advantage to being in a particularly creative place, or zone, reserved just for writing. Robert Bly, author of more than 100 magazine articles and 24 books during his freelance career, said the place you write affects your productivity. "I believe a comfortable writing environment increases productivity, but space and solitude also help," Bly (1996, p. 22) explained.

Freelancer Norman Schreiber, writing in *Writer's Digest,* suggests careful decisions be made about creating a personal workspace, because they help change a hobby into a business. These are Schreiber's (1991) components of a home office:

1. A clearly defined workspace (an extra bedroom, basement, or heated garage) and a large work surface devoted just to writing.
2. A comfortable and healthy chair. Remember, you will spend a lot of time in it.
3. Something to write with, preferably a personal computer and printer.
4. Lighting of some kind, preferably task-specific lighting rather than general overhead lighting.
5. Paper storage space such as file folders and cabinet systems.
6. Shelving and drawer storage for writer's tools.
7. Telephone, preferably a separate line for business use, if needed.
8. Office machines such as a fax and photocopier system.
9. Extras such as bulletin boards, wall calendars, and other personal decorations.

Brett Harvey is Eastern Regional Grievance Officer of the National Writers Union (NWU) based in the New York City area. She regularly deals with problems between writers who are members of the NWU and their employers and has compiled a list of guidelines that should be particularly helpful for beginning freelance writers. Her guidelines are reprinted in Appendix J. Harvey (personal communication, May 24, 1993) said: "These are especially hard times for freelancers, in case you hadn't noticed. Magazines are going belly-up nearly every month, and the ones that are left are cutting every possible corner—which means fewer pieces assigned, lower fees, more and lower kill fees, slower payment, and more all rights-contracts." As she advised, guidelines such as hers will not guarantee solution or elimination of problems, but they should minimize the chance for problems to occur.

## ORGANIZATIONS, CONFERENCES, AND SEMINARS

After your formal education is concluded, the best way to continue developing yourself as a freelance writer is to become involved in professional organizations, attend workshops and conferences about writing, and interact often with other professional writers. Writing groups and special events have numerous benefits that far outweigh any disadvantages such as expenditure of money or time.

## Professional Organizations

Professional organizations exist at the national, regional, state, and local levels. It should be easy to find one or more of these to meet your needs. Professional organizations offer writers the chance to meet other writers, as well as editors and publishers. These groups, such as the SPJ, may offer special professional development programs that provide continuing professional education. SPJ's membership includes staff and freelance journalists, as well as rank-and-file journalists and management.

Other groups focus more on the economic and legal needs of independent writers, not staff writers or editors. Concerns include such matters as fair levels of compensation, health and other insurance benefits, taxation, freedom of expression, uniform standards in contracts, and protection of copyright. Among the best-known writers' organizations are the NWU, ASJA, the Authors Guild, the Authors League of America, and the Writers Guild of America. Membership in these groups often requires meeting certain qualifications. Ordinarily, this means you have to be established as a writer. The NWU, for example, requires publication of a book, a play, three articles, or other works.

There are also numerous specialized writers' groups at the national level, each reflecting particular interests. Some specialized groups are divisions of larger organizations. Others are more specific in their interests but independent also. Groups that may interest freelance feature writers include the American Medical Writers Association, the Aviation and Space Writers Association, the Computer Press Association, the Editorial Freelancers Association, the Jazz Journalists Association, the National Association of Science Writers, the Outdoor Writers Association of America, and the Society of American Travel Writers.

Membership in a professional group might not seem important to you now, particularly if you are still in school, but it is increasingly important as time passes beyond graduation. However, these national organizations do offer guidance through regular contact with members, officers, and staff experts. This comes through publications and local and national meetings. Many beginning writers, especially freelancers, find the contacts made at these organizational meetings helpful for story ideas and opportunities to meet editors and other writers. Local press clubs in major cities such as New York or Washington are also gathering and meeting places for professional writers.

Most professional memberships are not overly expensive but may seem so to beginning writers. Most require national dues of less than $100 a year—the average seems to be between $50 and $100 annually—and some require additional minimal local chapter dues as well. These business expenses are tax deductible, of course, and are sometimes paid by employers. Regional and local professional organizations are usually less expensive and offer greater interaction among members. Most of the national professional organizations, in fact, offer regional gatherings and local chapters for more frequent interaction among members.

Less formalized writers' clubs and associations are another alternative. These often organize in a community with the goal to further members' careers. These groups can be useful for a freelance writer if the groups offer speakers, writing critique sessions, readings of works, field trips, and professional contact opportunities. Some offer service to the community, such as helping local schools, as well. Many are organized by towns or neighborhoods. Some have grown as large as statewide groups and have subdivided.

The Independent Writers of Southern California (http://iwosc.org), based in Los Angeles, serves writers and editors from Los Angeles to San Diego. This group provides numerous benefits for self-employed writers such as group insurance, a credit union, membership program meetings, a monthly newsletter, a grievance committee for disputes, and subgroups that represent specific counties in the region. Washington Independent Writers (http://www.washwriter.org) in Washington, DC, is the largest regional writers' organization in the country with several thousand members. The Washington group also organizes and hosts conferences, publishes a newsletter, maintains a Web site, and provides other services for its members. It was founded in 1975. Similar local and regional writing groups to those described above exist around the country.

Author Dennis Hensley (1986) recommends that you be selective about these clubs so you can find one that will emphasize writing development over social activities. "Manuscript evaluating is one of the great services a writers club or critique group can provide—if it is done correctly. Too often members offer routine praise to each other and shy away from seriously analyzing one another's manuscripts," Hensley warned (p. 38).

## PROFESSIONAL DEVELOPMENT OPPORTUNITIES

Some writers prefer not to join organizations. Some journalists are just not "joiners." Others work in rural areas where local membership is not possible or not very convenient. Nevertheless, there are other options for continuing professional education. These come in the form of writers' classes, conferences, seminars, and workshops. *Writer's Digest* annually compiles and lists the major gatherings of writers. There are hundreds of such events scheduled in the United States.

Such events offer hands-on writing practice and learning, lectures, opportunities to learn from, and meet, established writers, and the chance to learn new techniques. Most events such as these last only a few days and are often sponsored by schools or writers' groups. The chance to interact with other writers during these events may be the best experience—it gives you a chance to exchange ideas, offer critiques, and help one another in social and working sessions.

Writers should try at least one such conference to see if the experience is beneficial. A little preparation before attending (e.g., reading about speakers, reading the works of speakers, or reviewing the program to choose what you will do) will make the experience more fruitful. Such events afford excellent opportunities to talk to other writers, both beginners and veterans, about their work and about your work. Sessions with speakers are learning situations also, so note-taking and tape-recording are recommended. Usually there is a chance to ask speakers questions during a session or afterward and it is wise to take advantage. Many speakers at these conferences, especially smaller ones, are willing to talk with participants afterward. There is also a chance to make contacts for assignments or collaborative efforts, so be prepared to discuss such options.

## PUBLICATIONS AIMED AT FREELANCE WRITERS

Membership in a freelance writing or other professional organization normally includes subscriptions to one or more publications. Most common are small magazines or newsletters issued on a monthly or less frequent basis. In recent years, several new newsletters aimed at experienced freelance writers have begun publication also. These new publications are not associated with organizations and require paid subscriptions. Although they may not be entirely devoted to freelance work, many of the monthly writing-oriented magazines also have regular departments or sections devoted to freelance writing. Leading publications such as *Writer's Digest, The Writer,* and *ByLine* offer regular doses of professional advice and the latest information about new writing markets.

## BENEFITS OF CONTESTS AND AWARDS

Some writers love to enter contests and apply for awards; other writers detest such things. The idea of competition and the thought of recognition for excellence often appeal to writers who want to receive systematic professional feedback on their work beyond the fact of whether they made a sale. Winning some contests can be financially rewarding, but other contests simply offer recognition for quality work. Most contests are offered on an annual basis and are specialized by subject. The 2003 *Writer's Market* listed about 80 contests for nonfiction writers and listed even more for general writing and for newspaper and magazine journalism (Brogan, 2002). *Editor & Publisher* also publishes an annual directory of awards.

Contests can provide opportunities for beginning writers. Winning recognition in a contest means greater professional visibility. It means new opportunities. It is a way to be discovered within your specialization. However, winning an award is not the solution to all your professional problems. It is only a sign that you may have taken the step to the next highest level of excellence in your writing. The key to entering contests is to know about these competitions well in advance of deadlines. By doing your homework ahead of time, you have the chance to prepare an appropriate entry with your best professional presentation. Meeting the deadline with a clean entry that follows entry rules carefully is a must for contest participants. Many organizations sponsoring contests and award programs publish the entry specifications and provide them at no charge if you request them in advance of the deadline. You must always take the time to check your eligibility as well. This should be outlined in the contest rules, but if you are not sure, contact the sponsors.

## PARTING ADVICE FROM A REAL PRO

Long-time editor and writer Art Spikol, a regular contributor to *Writer's Digest*, has a distinguished career as an author, magazine editor, and freelancer. Spikol (personal communication, May 10, 1993) offered this list of advice to beginning freelance writers:

- *"Don't talk your stories.* If you let it come out of your mouth, chances are it won't come out of your fingertips."
- *"Develop a sales approach.* Not a canned pitch, but an effective demeanor for dealing with editors. That demeanor may end up in a query letter or a phone call or a personal visit, but never lose sight of the goal: to sound responsible and competent. If you want success, you can't be just a writer. The biggest cause of failure among would-be-writers is not wanting to deal with the business issues. For instance, a businessperson doesn't write something first and worry about where to sell it afterwards."
- "To be businesslike, ask yourself what kind of magazine you want to sell to. Then what kind of articles that magazine uses. And then make sure that the publication hasn't recently printed an article like yours. And then convince an editor that you're the person to write it. Time is money; don't squander yours."
- "You'll have to sound not just like somebody who can write a good article, but somebody an editor wouldn't mind putting on witness stand someday. Because of litigious times, it may come to that."
- "If you don't make the sale, don't blame the editor. Editors know what to buy, and they know what their readers want. If you don't sell the article, it (or you) wasn't right for the publication."

- *"Do your job like a pro.* If you were a race car driver, neurosurgeon, or astronaut, a mistake could be disastrous. The same applies to writing: misspell a word, punctuate incorrectly, fail to meet a deadline—and your credibility goes up in smoke. Ultimately, your career will follow it."
- *"Take charge of your business.* If, for instance, you wait 10 weeks to get a yes or no from a publication, it's your fault, not the publication's. Take the idea elsewhere—maybe to two or three other markets. If you were trying to sell your car, would you offer it to one person at a time?"
- *"Don't quit your job.* Sure, you want to be a freelancer, but don't give up what you have. It will create too much financial pressure to enable you to succeed. Instead, first see if you have the discipline to spend one hour a day writing. If you can do that on a sustained basis, stretch it to two. See what happens—are you selling? Making contacts? Nothing magical happens when you quit your job—except that your income disappears."
- *"Don't use best-case scenarios as a guide.* You can earn about $25,000 to $35,000 a year if you write for magazines and hit the best of them every month at their highest rates. Or you can earn $8,000 a year, which is far more likely. Prepare for the worst."
- *"Diversify.* If you want to make a lot more than the above figures, take your writing talent down some more financially rewarding paths. Write newsletters, brochures, annual reports. Write advertising, film scripts, books. They all pay better—for less work—than magazine articles."
- *"Finally, love writing.* Practically everybody I meet would like to be a writer, but not many actually want to write. The hard work is sitting down and putting the words on paper. Now, close this book and do it. May your fingers have wings."

# Appendix A

## World Wide Web Resources

Growth of the Internet and the World Wide Web in recent years has led to creation of a large number of Web sites that are helpful to feature writers. Some of these sites relate to writing whereas others relate to specific subjects.

Among the hundreds of useful Web sites are these locations:

Directories and Books:

Amazon Books—http://www.amazon.com

Barnes & Noble—http://www.bn.com

Borders Books—http://www.borders.com

Internet Encyclopedia—http://www.cam-info.net/enc.html

U.S. Postal Service Zip Code lookup—http://www.usps.gov/zip4

People, People-Finding:

555-1212.com—http://www.555-1212.com

ANyWho—http://www.anywho.com

AT&T Toll-Free Directory—http://www.anywho.com/tf.html

Big Foot—http://www.bigfoot.com

411—http://www.411.com

InfoSpace—http://www.infospace.com

Internet Address Finder—http://www.iaf.net

Info USA—http://www.infousa.com

Noble Experts Directories—http://www.experts.com

Phonebooke People Finder—http://www.phonebooke.com

ProfNet—http://www.profnet.com

Public Relations Newswire—http://www.prnewswire.com

SEARCH.COM—http://search.com

Switchboard—http://www.switchboard.com

West Legal Directory Lawyer Finder—http://directory.findlaw.com

WhoWhere—http://www.whowhere.com

World Pages—http://www.worldpages.com

Yahoo!—http://people.yahoo.com

Yearbook Experts Directory—http://www.expertclick.com

Writing Tools:

Bartlett's Familiar Quotations—http://www.bartleby.com

Merriam–Webster Dictionary—http://www.m-w.com

Purdue University Writer's Grammar site—http://owl.english.purdue.edu

Roget's Internet Thesaurus—http://www.thesaurus.com

Miscellaneous Resources:

A Journalist's Guide to the Internet—http://reporter.umd.edu

CIO Guide to Electronic and Print Resources for Journalists—www.cio.com/central/journalism.html

Deadline Online—http://www.deadlineonline.com

FACSNET—http://www.facsnet.org

Gallup Poll—http://www.gallup.com

Internet Public Library—http://www.ipl.org

The Journalist's Toolbox—www.journaliststoolbox.com

KnowX, Public Records Searches—http://www.knowx.com

Library sites on the World Wide Web—http://sunsite.berkeley.edu/Libweb/

Maps On Us—http://www.mapsonus.com

Martindale's Calculator/Converter—http://www.sci.lib.uci.edu/~martindale/RefCalculators1.html

Power Reporting—www.powerreporting.com

Reporter's Desktop—http://www.reporter.org/desktop

Reporter's Network—http://www.reporters.net

Tapping Officials' Secrets, Reporter's Committee for Freedom of the Press—http://www.rcfp.org/tapping/

# Appendix B

***Pennsylvania Angler & Boater*** **Guidelines for Contributors**

*Pennsylvania Angler & Boater* (*PA&B*), published bimonthly, is the official fishing and boating magazine of the Pennsylvania Fish and Boat Commission, and in turn, the voice of the Commonwealth in matters relating to fishing, boating, and to protecting, conserving and enhancing the state's water resources. *PA&B* is a 64-page four-color self-cover with no advertising. About 75 percent of the magazine is freelance-written. Every year we buy 70 to 100 article/photo packages and dozens of color slides.

**Subjects.** The best way to determine our needs is to read and study past issues. If you send us a 9 × 12 envelope affixed with first-class postage for nine ounces, we'll send you a sample copy.

*PA&B's* mainstays have been where-to and how-to articles. We'll continue to publish these kinds of articles, but we seek to widen the variety of material in the magazine to encompass all aspects of the Commission and its functions. The Commission's mission is to provide fishing and boating opportunities through the protection and management of aquatic resources. Our goal is to mirror the entire Commission in *PA&B*. For this reason, we are constantly looking for fresh ideas on subjects we haven't covered recently, and new takes on subjects we've previously covered.

Here is a partial list of our needs:

- Where-to articles that include details on how to fish specific Pennsylvania waterways (or several waterways), times of day best for action, and technically accurate how-to information. These kinds of articles should include hand-drawn maps showing accesses, main roads, landmarks, parking and hotspots.
- How-to articles on fishing in Pennsylvania. We do not publish product information or puffery.
- Boating articles. How-to, where-to, repair, maintenance, trailering and technical.

- "New" subjects. We like to publish articles that inform readers on the latest fishing and boating methods and trends. We consider only "Pennsylvania-ized" subjects. We do not publish pieces about using a specific product.
- Articles that show the benefits of fisheries management applications of research results and studies.
- Shorts. We use articles of 600 to 800 words with two or three photos for published one-pagers. Subjects include fresh, sharply focused ideas on all aspects of the Commission and its mission, and other angling and boating topics.
- Fish and Boat Commission activities across the state.
- Nostalgia, humor and "think" pieces. These articles must be strongly slanted to Pennsylvania. We also publish historical articles, Pennsylvania-based fiction ("me and Joe" articles) and first-person accounts.
- We do not solicit product reviews and roundups, cartoons, poetry, games, puzzles and tournament coverage.
- We rarely publish articles that have appeared elsewhere.

*Writing Style, Submitting.*   Articles are occasionally aimed at novice anglers and boaters, and some material is directed toward the most skilled fishermen and boaters. Most articles cater to people between these extremes. Most material we publish is 500 to 2,000 words.

We encourage diskette and electronic submission. With hard copy we ask contributors to send a diskette with their manuscripts, or to e-mail text attached to messages. We work in Microsoft Word, but we also accept material prepared in other word-processing programs and Mac-based programs.

*Photographs.*   We prefer transparencies submitted with and without manuscripts. We prefer Kodachrome 64 slides (35mm and larger), or the close Agfa and Fuji equivalents with film speeds no higher than ISO 100. We also accept color prints no larger than 8 × 10. We require all photo submissions to be originals. Complete captions are required for all slides and photos. In most cases, anglers in photographs should display a Pennsylvania fishing license. Contact the editor for details on submitting digital photographs.

*Boating Photograph Requirements.*   These requirements refer to photographs that illustrate points about boats and boating, and fishing from a boat. Everyone aboard boats must be wearing PFDs. PFDs should fit properly and be zipped or fastened while underway. PFDs worn should be suitable to the activity depicted. Persons on docks, and those boarding and leaving boats, should also be wearing PFDs.

Boats and equipment should be in optimal condition. This includes proper numbering and documentation. Boats should be equipped according to all federal and Pennsylvania requirements.

Safety equipment should be visible and accessible.

Show safe body positions for operators and for passengers. Persons should sit in seats properly. They should not be shown sitting on seat backs or on the gunwale. If the boat is to be operated at high speed (above 45 mph), appropriate safety equipment should be worn.

Show boats operated safely. Boats should be shown accelerating at a safe rate so they don't create a dangerous wake or throw riders around the boat.

Show generic products whenever possible. To avoid unfair product representation or inference of endorsement, use generic products. If brand names are shown, avoid "showcasing" or concentrating on labels.

Alcohol should not be shown aboard boats.

We prefer that photos of boats show current Pennsylvania registrations. We prefer photographs taken in Pennsylvania, but we accept photographs taken elsewhere. We do not use pictures with obviously non-Pennsylvania backgrounds—snow-capped peaks, saltwater settings, desert backgrounds, palm trees, and so forth.

**Deadlines.**    Submit seasonal material six months in advance. For instance, an article on ice fishing for the January/February issue must be submitted in July.

We prefer queries to completed manuscripts, but completed manuscripts are also welcomed, especially for material of 1,000 words or less. Query at least eight months ahead of an anticipated issue date.

Written queries are welcome, as are e-mailed and faxed queries. Please include a SASE with correspondence.

**Payment, Rights.**    Rights purchased vary. For most material we prefer to buy first rights, one-time rights, second rights and electronic rights. If the material you're submitting has appeared elsewhere, tell us when you submit it. Payment for article/photograph packages varies from $50 to $275. This payment is based on value to the Commission, quality of the material, research required to complete the piece, length of the copy, the photographic support submitted with the article, and how badly we want the story. Payment for articles submitted without usable photographs is less than payment for articles submitted with top-quality, usable photographs.

When photographs are submitted with an article, the price for the article includes payment for the pictures. The front cover pays up to $400, depending on rights purchased. Inside pictures purchased separately earn $30 to $100 per slide or print. This payment is based on the published size of the photograph. Rights purchased for covers include the right to publish the material as it's depicted on the magazine cover on the Commission's World Wide Web homepage.

Please include your social security number with your manuscript or photo submission. We need the number to process payment.

*PA&B* does not accept simultaneous submissions.

**Correspondence.** All materials—queries, manuscripts and artwork—are reviewed on speculation. We report on queries within six weeks, and on manuscripts within four to eight weeks.

*PA&B* is not responsible for unsolicited materials.

# Appendix C

## *Vermont Life* Magazine Writers' Guidelines

Welcome to *Vermont Life Magazine* online. Whether you're a Vermonter or simply want to learn more about the Green Mountain State, *Vermont Life* is your insider's guide to the secret places and special character of this uniquely beautiful place.

In addition to sample content from our Magazine, this site offers a variety of Vermont-related information, including local events, travel ideas, products and a selection of interesting Vermont Links. The Postboy, our official mascot, will help guide you through our site.

*Author's Guidelines, June 2002.* *Vermont Life* is interested in any article, query, story idea, photograph or photo essay that has to do with Vermont. As the state magazine, we are most interested in pieces that present positive aspects of life within the state's borders. We have no rules, however, about avoiding controversy when the presentation of the controversial subject can illustrate some aspect of Vermont's unique character. With most ideas, we prefer written queries first. No phone queries, please.

Articles are seldom planned for inclusion in *Vermont Life* before they have been accepted and received in this office. We often work as much as a year in advance in preparing articles for publication, a fact that contributors should bear in mind.

Our text rates for feature articles range between $350 and $800 depending on the length and research involved in preparing the manuscript. Most articles run approximately 1,800 words and the average fee is $450. We usually pay by the word—25 cents per word is our basic rate. We buy first North American Serial Rights to the article (more detailed information is in the assignment contract). The copyright normally reverts to the author after *Vermont Life* publishes the article. We normally do not publish poetry.

When submitting articles, please send them to us on a 3.5-inch computer disk with a hard copy of the story or by e-mail (jpowell@life.state.vt.us). We use Microsoft Word for Macintosh, but can translate almost any other format.

*Photographer's Guidelines, June 2002.* *Vermont Life* uses original color transparencies (35mm slides and medium or larger format transparencies) and black and white prints. We do not accept color prints or transparencies made from prints or negatives. Photographs should be current—taken within the last five years.

In each issue of the magazine, a number of pages are set aside for purely scenic photography, ranging from landscapes to activities in a Vermont setting. Submissions for this section can be made on:

June 1 for winter

September 1 for spring

December 1 for summer

March 1 for autumn

Submissions for the *Vermont Life* Explorer travel publication as well as calendar submissions can be made on September 1.

Please limit your submission to one per project with no more than 200 transparencies. Enclose your self-addressed stamped envelope or a check for return postage with your submission. Transparencies are returned by certified mail only if appropriate postage is included. We take no responsibility for unsolicited materials. Be sure your name and the location of the photo are on each transparency, and enclose transparencies in a plastic sleeve for convenience of viewing as well as protection. Location information can be submitted on a separate sheet, if necessary. Transparencies not selected will be returned as soon as a decision is made. We will pay first class postage for return of transparencies used in the magazine or calendars upon publication. Because we are part of a state agency with limited resources, we cannot accept transparencies with a delivery memo stating specific dollar valuations, holding fees, arbitration agreements or the like. We do, however, take the utmost care of each transparency.

Transparencies selected for use in the magazine are bought for one-time use only for $75 to $500. Occasionally we will seek permission for a second use in calendars or other products, for which there is additional remuneration. Please refer to the payment schedule below for our current stock photo payment rates. Payment for any photographs selected for use by *Vermont Life* includes the possible reproduction of those photographs in connection with the advertising and promotion of *Vermont Life,* and at the *Vermont Life* Web site.

The photographic rate is $250 per day on assignment, plus film and processing expenses. Expenses for assignments must be pre-approved. We pay for scenics on publication and assignments on acceptance.

For more information please contact us at:

Submission Guidelines
*Vermont Life* Magazine
6 Baldwin St.
Montpelier, VT 05602–2100
or e-mail Judy Powell (jpowell@lif.state.vt.us)

(From *Vermont Life* Online (at http://www.vtlife.com/), reprinted with permission.)

# Appendix D

*Operations & Fulfillment* Magazine Writer's Guidelines—
October 2002

Welcome to *Operations & Fulfillment* (*O&F*), a monthly publication that offers practical solutions for direct-to-customer operations management. Please read the following guidelines carefully before submitting material for publication. Your article stands a far greater chance of being accepted if you adhere to these requirements. For your convenience, we've supplied a checklist that itemizes the elements your story should include.

## WHO READS *O&F*?

Our readers are operations executives who work for

- business-to-business and consumer catalogs
- direct-response companies
- shop-at-home networks
- infomercial marketers
- book, record, and tape clubs
- continuity clubs
- Internet/electronic marketers
- manufacturers who sell directly to customers

We estimate our total per-copy readership at about 35,000. Sample job titles of our readers include CEO; CFO; senior vice president of operations/logistics; director of distribution; director of fulfillment; IT director; human resources director; operations manager; call center/customer service manager; and warehouse manager. Our readers include executives at such leading direct-commerce companies as Lands' End, L.L. Bean, Williams–Sonoma, The Borders Group, and Avon Products Inc.

The magazine covers the following critical areas:

- material handling
- bar coding
- facility planning
- transportation
- order processing
- shipping
- call centers
- payment processing
- warehouse management
- information systems
- packaging
- customer service
- security
- online fulfillment
- human resources

We feature what's newest, best, and most cost-effective, with the ultimate goal of helping our readers improve efficiency and profitability.

## POLICIES

*O&F* does not accept articles submitted by public relations professionals.

We reserve the right to edit features for style and space availability. However, we do work closely with authors to resolve questions and discuss cuts or revisions. Please feel free to suggest headlines, decks, and pull quotes, but the final decision on these rests with the editors.

We do not publish articles that can be perceived as self-promotional.

A word on "recycling" articles: We're all busy, and obviously it's convenient to reuse information that you've gathered for other purposes. But if you send us articles that you've already published elsewhere, you not only put us in a legal quandary but also ruin your credibility with our readers. *O&F* subscribers turn to the magazine for highly specialized information. We would be doing a great disservice to our readers if we published a "generic" article that appears in four or five other trade magazines.

## GENERAL GUIDELINES

We strongly urge you to read the enclosed sample articles and, if possible, several issues of the magazine before sending us your contribution. *O&F* is a business magazine, not a scholarly journal. An article titled "A Conceptual Framework for Operational Excellence" wouldn't be appropriate for us, but one on "How Four Catalog Companies Cut Order Picking Costs" would. We look for the practical, the specific, the concrete, the how-to.

Our features are typically about 2,500 words long, although they may be edited to fit available space. In addition to the main article, you MUST include the following:

(1) At least one sidebar of about 400 words that contains a detailed example or case study of how a direct-commerce company implements or benefits from the process you're writing about. If you can't identify the company, call it "Company A" or, for instance, "a mid-size apparel cataloger."

(2) A checklist or set of practical guidelines (e.g., "Twelve Ways to Ship Smarter") that describe how to implement what you suggest in the article. Again, these must be applicable to mail order companies.

(3) Supporting materials such as photographs, tables, diagrams, illustrations, and flow charts. These must be clearly labeled and footnoted. For information on how to submit these materials, please see "Submission Requirements" below.

(4) An author biography of no more than 75 words.

## Submission Requirements

### Articles

The simpler your document format, the better. Your best bet is to send us a Word or text file. We use Microsoft Word software for the Apple Macintosh, but we can convert most files done on IBM compatibles.

Please do not use formatting options such as tabs, boldface, italics, bullets, borders, tables, or ornaments. We delete all this anyway, since we use our own desktop publishing software to produce the magazine.

Please do not embed graphics, illustrations, diagrams, charts, or files formatted in any other programs (Excel, PowerPoint, PhotoShop, Illustrator, etc.) in the Word text.

We prefer that you submit your article via e-mail to: rramaswami@primediabusiness.com

If you do not have access to e-mail, please submit a 3-1/2" diskette or a CD with a hard copy (faxed or mailed) of your article to: Rama Ramaswami, Editor, *Operations & Fulfillment,* 11 River Bend Drive South, Stamford, CT 06907; fax: 203–358–5836.

### Art

ALL ART ITEMS MUST BE SUBMITTED AS HARD COPY. Please do not attempt to e-mail diagrams, tables, or charts to us! We assign these projects to professional artists to re-create. Just send us a hard copy (fax or mail) to show what the illustration should look like—even hand-drawn is fine—and indicate all numbers clearly and where the art is to be placed in the text. For graphs, please give us the data and we'll create them. If you'd like to use a screen capture, give us the URL and we'll do it. As for photos, color prints or slides only, please. Photos can be e-mailed, but please call us first at 203–358–4208 to get the specs.

NOTE: We've often had to use outside production houses to convert incompatible files and illustrations sent in esoteric programs. Please note that if you choose to submit articles and illustrations in formats other than those noted above, you're liable to be billed for conversion and/or formatting expenses.

## Deadlines

*O&F* deadlines are not negotiable except under extraordinary circumstances. We can arrange for an extension of up to a week if you request it well in advance of your article's due date. Otherwise, we'd be happy to consider your contribution for a later issue.

(Reprinted with permission of *Operations & Fulfillment* Magazine.)

# Appendix E

**Operations & Fulfillment Magazine Content and Style
Guidelines—October 2002**

When considering articles for publication in *O&F*, we look for these important content and style elements:

Research. As practitioners, our readers expect much more than basic overviews of bar coding, slotting, or other operational functions. The more you can support your article with hard data, examples, and other background information, the more credible and useful your story is. As far as possible, use primary sources—e.g., an original survey rather than a report about it. Please cite your sources (e.g., "Source: XYZ Company, Inc., 1993") and provide detailed explanations and footnotes for all graphs, charts, diagrams, and other illustrations.

Organization. Pay attention to this up front, and it'll save you—and us—many hours of rewriting later on. We place a lot of emphasis on structure, because a well-organized story highlights crucial information quickly and effectively. There are dozens of formulas for arranging stories, and you may find it useful to make up your own personal "templates" for the types of articles you tend to write most often. The best stories for us follow a "circular" pattern, with the end pointing the reader back to the beginning.

Here's one way you might organize your article:

1. Read and note all relevant material from your background information, interview transcripts, and so forth.
2. List the key points you're going to make (you shouldn't have more than three or four for an average *O&F* feature), based on your research; then list the elements you're going to use to support each point. For instance:

| Point | Supporting facts |
| --- | --- |
| When return rates soar, you must expand inventory. | (1) Statistics on common mail order merchandise return rates |
| | (2) Catalog company example |
| | (3) Chart illustrating how to calculate correct inventory |

And so on.

3. Now arrange each point (along with its set of supporting facts) in descending order of importance.

Organizing your story like this will help it flow logically from one point to another.

Focus. Don't lose it. It's the point you're making. Stick with it throughout because it's critical to the story's construction. If your point is that call center reps function best when rewarded frequently, everything else in the story, from beginning to end, should relate to that point.

"Slant." Don't merely describe a topic; offer a take on it. Analyze it to give the reader some added value. Pick up on a trend, offer a forecast, highlight significant results of a survey. Tell the reader how what you have to say will affect his or her operation. How will it improve productivity/efficiency? Cut costs?

Detail. Can't do without it in a "service" magazine like ours. Describe equipment. Provide the prices, measurements, and sizes of things. A $100 scanner, a $1,500 headset, an 8' × 4' concrete slab. Provide sample forms, spec sheets, checklists. "Walk" the reader through a process, especially if it's highly technical. Offer a detailed example of how a system works. Show how a retailer would work out an inventory calculation formula and apply it to, say, 1,000 units.

Benefits. Our readers already know how a pick-to-light system works. But if you can tell them about new ways to use it, or about how XYZ Company used it and improved productivity 50%, they'll want to read your article.

Philosophy. While we welcome practical advice and guidelines, please make sure that your article isn't just a laundry list of bulleted or numbered "tips" strung together. There must be an underlying philosophy and approach to the subject.

Point of view. A mere recitation of facts is wimpy and makes for dull reading. For livelier writing, adopt a point of view—make sure you bolster it with facts—and stick to it. Be careful not to editorialize, however. For our purposes, a point of view is the part of the story that you've chosen to highlight, the key argument that you've decided to emphasize and that you're going to substantiate. It's not the same as personal opinion.

Clarity. As far as possible, avoid using vague generalities such as "many," "most," "some," "in the future," and so on. How many? When? Also avoid gobbledygook like "combining the synergy of a group of expanded initiatives" or "clarifying core competencies and fiscal objectives." Similarly, steer clear of passive sentence constructions. For instance, instead of writing "Totes are placed on a conveyor" you could try "Pickers place totes on a conveyor."

Simplicity. Even if you're confident that our readers will know what you're referring to, if you use jargon or technical terms, always explain what they mean and illustrate with an example. Be informal and straightforward—but without "talking down."

Before you send us your article, please use the attached story evaluation checklist to see if it meets all applicable criteria.

(Reprinted with permission of *Operations & Fulfillment* Magazine.)

# Appendix F

*Operations & Fulfillment* **Magazine Story Evaluation**
**Checklist—October 2002**

### Content

1. How does the content fit the focus of *Operations & Fulfillment* as a whole? Is it something our readers would be interested in?
2. How does the specific issue you're writing about affect direct-to-customer retailers?
3. Is your story timely? Why are you writing about this issue now?
4. Does the story have a clear focus? Can you state the theme in 25 words or less?
5. Have you stuck to this theme throughout?
6. Does your story have a coherent, logical structure?
7. Have you included the essential who, what, when, where, why, and how?
8. Have you double-checked all that information? For example: Are productivity figures correct? Are measurements and prices accurate? How about spellings, titles, locations, and dates?
9. If you're presenting the results of a survey, have you included all relevant statistics? Do percentages and figures add up?
10. Have you cited all your sources?
11. Is the story as complete as it needs to be for the topic you're writing about? Can they really get there in ten steps?
12. From your research and notes, have you selected the material that's most useful to the reader for this particular topic?
13. Have you arranged and presented the information in the most useful, logical way?
14. Have you included opposing points of view?
15. Have you included sidebars with real-life examples?
16. Have you included step-by-step guidelines or checklists?
17. Do the facts you've chosen to present support your conclusion?

18. Have you included hard data from a variety of sources—e.g., the government, trade groups, financial analysts, industry consultants?
19. Have you used/included original source material?

### Readability

20. Is your writing clear and easy to understand?
21. Have you defined and explained all technical terms and jargon?
22. Have you used effective transitions?
23. Have you grouped your thoughts so the story moves logically from one point or topic to another?

### Art and Charts

24. Does the art you've chosen reinforce the point of the story?
25. If you're using charts, do they support what you're saying?
26. Do your heads, decks, art, article, and captions all tell the same story?
27. Do all your illustrations have detailed footnotes?
28. Have you cited the source of your illustrations?

(Reprinted with permission of *Operations & Fulfillment* Magazine.)

# Appendix G

**Freelance Letters of Agreement**

*Restaurant Review*

> *NATIONAL GEOGRAPHIC TRAVELER*
> Date
> Mr. or Ms. So-and-so
> Address TK [to come]
> City TK, State TK, Zip TK
>
> Dear So-and-so:
> We are delighted that you can write a feature story for us on Place TK.
> Here are the particulars. (Details about focus, tone, emphasis, and so forth, depending on the nature of the story—national park, museum, city, region, scenic drive, activity).
> Here are a few points to keep in mind. Include present-day voices—quotes from interpreters, curators, and/or fellow visitors—as well as voices from the past. Be sure the reader knows where things are, and where you are, as you move through the story; an overall geographical orientation near the beginning would be helpful.
> If you encounter any negative aspects that you feel should be passed on to readers, please include them. A realistic assessment of negatives (as opposed to potshots and personal gripes) is a valuable service to readers. Just be sure the overall tone of the piece remains invitational.
> Plan on spending TK days in TK PLACE in TK MONTH. You can request an advance on expenses. If, afterward, you think the story should take on a different approach from the above, please give me a ring right away to discuss it.
> The story should run about TK words. Our payment will be $TK,000, upon acceptance. The manuscript will be due one month after you complete your fieldwork (no later than Date TK). In the unlikely event that the first draft does not succeed, we will expect you to make revisions if we think they will make the text publishable. If, after that, the story still is not publishable, we will pay you a kill fee of $TK,000.

Our travel office will be glad to arrange for and furnish you with airline tickets, hotel reservations, and car rentals, where required. Please phone them at least 30 days in advance at Phone TK, so they can get the best rates possible. We can arrange a reasonable advance against expenses, to include fees for accommodations. Please heed the word "reasonable," and be conscious of the fact that we do not have unlimited funds for travel expenses; we will be grateful to you for spending only what's necessary to be comfortable and to do your job professionally.

Expenses must be supported by proper vouchers and receipts. Expense-account guidelines are located in the enclosed National Geographic Expense Account booklet and in the Travel and Expense book from the Controller's Office; the Society follows the IRS Travel and Entertainment Regulations. Within two weeks of your return home, upon completion of the assignment, you will be required to file a final report of your expense account and to settle with the Society by returning all unused cash and traveler's checks, according to your records. Final payment for your manuscript will not be made until all travel advances are accounted for and all Society credit cards have been returned.

You are undertaking this assignment as an independent contractor. The Society assumes no responsibility for your health, safety, or property, or that of any person accompanying or assisting you. While on assignment in the field, you will be covered by the Society's accident insurance policy, which provides a payment of $TK,000 to you in the event of total disability or to your beneficiary, specified below, in the event of death, and lesser coverage for other injuries. The policy also provides up to $TK,000 in excess medical coverage, i.e., for costs beyond those covered by your personal accident and health coverages. The above coverage is restricted to you alone.

While working on this assignment, you will carefully avoid doing similar work for publications that *Traveler* would consider to be editorially competitive with it. You will advise *Traveler* promptly of any possible conflict of interest that may develop. You will also take care not to grant any prepublication interviews or assist in any way in the preparation of any prepublication articles or other press coverage in any medium that would reveal the subject matter, editorial content, or the scheduling of an assignment, article, or story for *Traveler*. You will not accept discounts or gratuities of any kind from any person or organization providing information or services to you.

Your manuscript is a specially commissioned work for hire for use in *National Geographic Traveler,* and accordingly all rights (including copyright) in the story shall vest exclusively in the National Geographic Society. You hereby represent and warrant that you have the full right and authority to sell the manuscript and that you have not previously granted, sold, hypothecated, or encumbered these rights. You hereby further represent and warrant the originality of the manuscript, that it will contain nothing of a libelous nature, and that its publication will not infringe any copyright, right of privacy, or other legal right of any other party.

You hereby grant to the Society without additional charge the right to use your name, likeness, biographical material, and any of your textual material for promotional and advertising purposes.

You or your agent will not sell any of your material from this assignment to: *Revista de Geografica Universal* (Mexico), *Revista Geografica Universal* (Brazil), *Airone* (Italy), or *Bunte* (Germany).

Our articles are intensively checked before publication. A condition of assignment is that you turn over all source materials collected during the course of the assignment once the manuscript has been accepted. (Books and pamphlets bought on expense account belong to the Society; those bought with your own funds will be returned at your request.) You are to furnish a marked copy of your manuscript keying facts, quotes, and other information to a separate list of publications, addresses, and phone numbers of people and institutions mentioned in the text, as well as any other sources of information.

This agreement may not be assigned by you. It constitutes the entire agreement between you and the Society and its terms cannot be altered except by an instrument in writing signed by both parties. If its terms are acceptable to you, please sign this letter and return it to me. The copy is for your files.

So-and-so, I'm looking forward to working with you. If you have any questions, please don't hesitate to call me at 202–857–7352. Have a great trip! I'm looking forward to reading about it.

Best wishes,
Carol B. Lutyk
Senior Articles Editor
For the National Geographic Society

_____

Richard Busch

P.S. If you use a computer for word processing, please submit a disk (with a note attached to the disk of the file name containing the manuscript), along with a hard copy of your manuscript and source list. Please indicate below the model of your computer and the name and version of your software.

Model of computer _____

Name and version of software _____

Signature _____

Social Security Number _____

Telephone Numbers _____

Date _____

Insurance Beneficiary _____

Address _____

Please write a brief bio about yourself for publication with this article.

(Reprinted with permission of Carol B. Lutyk, National Geographic Society.)

### *Industry-Trade Magazine Non Fiction Writer Agreement (for Specified Fee)*

Date: _____

Author Name: _____

Author Address: _____

City: _____ State: _____ Zip: _____

Phone Number: _____

E-mail Address: _____

Provisional Title of Work: _____

Word Count: _____

Assigning Editor: _____

Deadline: _____

Subject to the terms and conditions set forth herein, the **Author** and OPERATIONS & FULFILLMENT hereby agree this Agreement shall be applicable to any article or articles created in the past or to be created for or on behalf of OPERATIONS & FULFILLMENT in the future. This Agreement shall be applicable to all past and future articles created by **Author** for OPERATIONS & FULFILLMENT.

*Articles.* The **Author** agrees to create the article as described above (the "Article"). The Article will be approximately 2,000 words in length for publication in OPERATIONS & FULFILLMENT. **Author** shall use his/her best efforts to submit the Article requested on or before the specified deadline in a form reasonably satisfactory for publication in OPERATIONS & FULFILLMENT.

*Editing.* The submission of an Article by **Author** grants to OPERATIONS & FULFILLMENT, in its sole discretion, the right to publish, produce, use, adapt, edit and/or modify the Article in any way and in any and all media, without limitation and without additional compensation to the **Author**. The **Author** agrees to make such changes in the Works as OPERATIONS & FULFILLMENT may from time to time reasonably request prior to publication.

*Consideration/Expenses.* (a) For good and valuable consideration, receipt of which is hereby acknowledged, OPERATIONS & FULFILLMENT shall pay to **Author** $1,500 (the "Fee") payable upon acceptance of the Article.

(b) Notwithstanding the foregoing, in the event that OPERATIONS & FULFILLMENT does not publish the Article, OPERATIONS & FULFILLMENT agrees to pay to **Author** a kill fee of twenty-five percent (25%) of the Fee due to **Author**.

(c) **Author** acknowledges that he/she is an independent consultant and as such no amounts in respect of taxes shall be deducted from amounts paid to **Author** hereunder. As such, **Author** shall be responsible for the payment of all taxes owing in connection with any amounts paid hereunder including, without limitation, federal and state income taxes and Social Security.

*Rights in the Works.* **Author** grants to OPERATIONS & FULFILLMENT the following rights in each Article and the Works:

(a) the exclusive right to publish the Article in any issue of OPERATIONS & FULFILLMENT before it is published in any other form by any other party. For one year after publication in OPERATIONS & FULFILLMENT, OPERATIONS & FULFILLMENT has the exclusive right to publish or reprint the Article in any other media;

(b) the right to authorize syndication of the Article in all media throughout the world directly or through a syndication company;

(c) the right to authorize publication of the Article in any foreign edition of OPERATIONS & FULFILLMENT and the right to authorize translation of the Article into the appropriate language for a foreign edition of OPERATIONS & FULFILLMENT;

(d) the exclusive right to reprint, republish, transmit or reproduce the Article or Work in whole or in part one or more times on or by means of any electronic, computer-based, digital or online media, methods or means now known or hereafter invented, including the Internet, World Wide Web, any method of electronic storage and retrieval and CD-ROM disks; and

(e) the right to publish and use the Article in any special interest publication or book of OPERATIONS & FULFILLMENT, or in any other magazine or other publication published or distributed, in print or online, by PRIMEDIA Inc.

*Author's Obligations.* **Author** agrees to the following:

(a) No Article or Work will be libelous or obscene or infringe the copyright, or violate the right of privacy, publicity or any third party. **Author** represents that he/she is the sole **Author** of each Article or Work, the Article or Work is original and that no Article or Work has been previously published in any form;

(b) **Author** agrees to fully cooperate with the editorial staff at OPERATIONS & FULFILLMENT in connection with requested rewrites, revisions, and additional reporting if necessary;

(c) OPERATIONS & FULFILLMENT shall have the right to use the **Author's** name, biography, and likeness in connection with the publication and promotion of both the Article and OPERATIONS & FULFILLMENT magazine;

(d) **Author** agrees to provide all fact-checking and research materials as requested relating to all non-fiction Articles; and

(e) **Author** acknowledges and agrees that any and all interview transcripts and audio tapes become the exclusive property of OPERATIONS & FULFILLMENT.

*Miscellaneous.* (a) This Agreement shall be governed and interpreted and enforced in accordance with the laws of the State of New York applicable to agreements made and to be performed in the State of New York. Any claim or litigation arising out of this Agreement or its performance may be maintained only in courts physically located in New York County, New York, and **Author** and OPERATIONS & FULFILLMENT hereby consent to the personal jurisdiction of such courts. This Agreement constitutes our entire agreement with respect to the Work/Article, and supersedes any prior agreements. It may not be modified without the prior written consent of each party hereto.

(b) If this Agreement is executed by an **Agent** on **Author's** behalf, that **Agent** warrants that he/she has full **Author**ity from the **Author** to grant the rights and to make the representations set forth above.

If the foregoing correctly sets forth our understanding please indicate your acceptance by signing in the space provided below. Upon execution by both parties, the contract shall be effective immediately as provided for herein.

Magazine: OPERATIONS & FULFILLMENT
By: _____
Name: Rama Ramaswami
Title: Editorial Director
AGREED TO AND ACCEPTED
AS OF THE DATE FIRST ABOVE WRITTEN:

_____

Signature of **Author**

(Reprinted with permission of *Operations & Fulfillment* Magazine.)


### Industry-Trade Magazine Non Fiction Writer Agreement (Contributed with No Fee)

Date: _____
Author Name: _____
Author Address: _____
City: _____ State: _____ Zip: _____
Phone Number: _____
E-mail Address: _____
Provisional Title of Work: _____
Word Count: _____
Assigning Editor: _____
Deadline: _____

Subject to the terms and conditions set forth herein, the **Author** and OPERATIONS & FULFILLMENT hereby agree this Agreement shall be applicable to any article or articles created in the past or to be created for or on behalf of OPERATIONS & FULFILLMENT in the future. This Agreement shall be applicable to all past and future articles created by **Author** for OPERATIONS & FULFILLMENT.

*Articles.* The **Author** agrees to create the article as described above (the "Article"). The Article will be approximately 2,000 words in length for publication in OPERATIONS & FULFILLMENT. **Author** shall use his/her best efforts to submit the Article requested on or before the specified deadline in a form reasonably satisfactory for publication in OPERATIONS & FULFILLMENT.

*Editing.* The submission of an Article by **Author** grants to OPERATIONS & FULFILLMENT, in its sole discretion, the right to publish, produce, use, adapt, edit and/or modify the Article in any way and in any and all media, without limitation and without additional compensation to the **Author**. The **Author** agrees to make such changes in the Works as OPERATIONS & FULFILLMENT may from time to time reasonably request prior to publication.

*Rights in the Works.* **Author** grants to OPERATIONS & FULFILLMENT the following rights in each Article and the Works:

(a) the exclusive right to publish the Article in any issue of OPERATIONS & FULFILLMENT before it is published in any other form by any other party. For one year after publication in OPERATIONS & FULFILLMENT, OPERATIONS & FULFILLMENT has the exclusive right to publish or reprint the Article in any other media;

(b) the right to authorize syndication of the Article in all media throughout the world directly or through a syndication company;

(c) the right to authorize publication of the Article in any foreign edition of OPERATIONS & FULFILLMENT and the right to authorize translation of the Article into the appropriate language for a foreign edition of OPERATIONS & FULFILLMENT;

(d) the exclusive right to reprint, republish, transmit or reproduce the Article or Work in whole or in part one or more times on or by means of any electronic, computer-based, digital or online media, methods or means now known or hereafter invented, including the Internet, World Wide Web, any method of electronic storage and retrieval and CD-ROM disks; and

(e) the right to publish and use the Article in any special interest publication or book of OPERATIONS & FULFILLMENT, or in any other magazine or other publication published or distributed, in print or online, by PRIMEDIA Inc.

*Author's Obligations.* **Author** agrees to the following:

(a) No Article or Work will be libelous or obscene or infringe the copyright, or violate the right of privacy, publicity or any third party. **Author** represents that he / she is the sole **Author** of each Article or Work, the Article or Work is original and that no Article or Work has been previously published in any form;

(b) **Author** agrees to fully cooperate with the editorial staff at OPERATIONS & FULFILLMENT in connection with requested rewrites, revisions, and additional reporting if necessary;

(c) OPERATIONS & FULFILLMENT shall have the right to use the **Author's** name, biography, and likeness in connection with the publication and promotion of both the Article and OPERATIONS & FULFILLMENT magazine;

(d) **Author** agrees to provide all fact-checking and research materials as requested relating to all non-fiction Articles; and

(e) **Author** acknowledges and agrees that any and all interview transcripts and audio tapes become the exclusive property of OPERATIONS & FULFILLMENT.

*Miscellaneous.* (a) This Agreement shall be governed and interpreted and enforced in accordance with the laws of the State of New York applicable to agreements made and to be performed in the State of New York. Any claim or litigation arising out of this Agreement or its performance may be maintained only in courts physically located in New York County, New York, and **Author** and OPERATIONS & FULFILLMENT hereby consent to the personal jurisdiction of such courts. This Agreement constitutes our entire agreement with respect to the Work / Article, and supersedes any prior agreements. It may not be modified without the prior written consent of each party hereto.

(b) If this Agreement is executed by an **Agent** on **Author's** behalf, that **Agent** warrants that he / she has full **Authority** from the **Author** to grant the rights and to make the representations set forth above.

If the foregoing correctly sets forth our understanding please indicate your acceptance by signing in the space provided below. Upon execution by both parties, the contract shall be effective immediately as provided for herein.

Magazine: OPERATIONS & FULFILLMENT
By: _____
Name: Rama Ramaswami
Title: Editorial Director
AGREED TO AND ACCEPTED
AS OF THE DATE FIRST ABOVE WRITTEN:

_____

Signature of **Author**

(Reprinted with permission of *Operations & Fulfillment* Magazine.)

# Appendix H

**Code of Ethics of the Society of Professional Journalists**
*(Adopted by the 1996 national convention, Washington, DC)*

*Preamble*

Members of the Society of Professional Journalists believe that public enlightenment is the forerunner of justice and the foundation of democracy. The duty of the journalist is to further those ends by seeking truth and providing a fair and comprehensive account of events and issues. Conscientious journalists from all media and specialties strive to serve the public with thoroughness and honesty. Professional integrity is the cornerstone of a journalist's credibility.

Members of the Society share a dedication to ethical behavior and adopt this code to declare the Society's principles and standards of practice.

*Seek Truth and Report It*

Journalists should be honest, fair and courageous in gathering, reporting and interpreting information.

Journalists should:

- Test the accuracy of information from all sources and exercise care to avoid inadvertent error. Deliberate distortion is never permissible.
- Diligently seek out subjects of news stories to give them the opportunity to respond to allegations of wrongdoing.
- Identify sources whenever feasible. The public is entitled to as much information as possible on sources' reliability.
- Always question sources' motives before promising anonymity. Clarify conditions attached to any promise made in exchange for information. Keep promises.
- Make certain the headlines, news teases and promotional material, photos, video, audio, graphics, sound bites and quotations do not misrepresent. They should not oversimplify or highlight incidents out of context.

- Never distort the content of news photos or video. Image enhancement for technical clarity is always permissible. Label montages and photo illustrations.
- Avoid misleading re-enactments or staged news events. If re-enactment is necessary to tell a story, label it.
- Avoid undercover or other surreptitious methods of gathering information except when traditional open methods will not yield information vital to the public. Use of such methods should be explained as part of the story.
- Never plagiarize.
- Tell the story of the diversity and magnitude of the human experience boldly, even when it is unpopular to do so.
- Examine their own cultural values and avoid imposing those values on others.
- Avoid stereotyping by race, gender, age, religion, ethnicity, geography, sexual orientation, disability, physical appearance or social status.
- Support the open exchange of views they find repugnant.
- Give voice to the voiceless; official and unofficial sources of information can be equally valid.
- Distinguish between advocacy and news reporting. Analysis and commentary should be labeled and not misrepresent fact or context.
- Distinguish news from advertising and shun hybrids that blur the lines between the two.
- Recognize a special obligation to ensure that the public's business is conducted in the open and that government records are open to inspection.

*Minimize Harm*

Ethical journalists treat sources, subjects and colleagues as human beings deserving of respect.

Journalists should:

- Show compassion for those who may be affected adversely by news coverage. Use special sensitivity when dealing with children and inexperienced sources or subjects.
- Be sensitive when seeking or using interviews or photographs of those affected by tragedy or grief.
- Recognize that gathering and reporting information may cause harm or discomfort. Pursuit of the news is not a license for arrogance.
- Recognize that private people have a greater right to control information about themselves than do public officials and others who seek power, influence or attention. Only an overriding public need can justify intrusion into anyone's privacy.

- Show good taste. Avoid pandering to lurid curiosity.
- Be cautious about identifying juvenile suspects or victims of sex crimes.
- Be judicious about naming criminal suspects before the formal filing of charges.
- Balance a criminal suspect's fair trial rights with the public's right to be informed.

## Act Independently

Journalists should be free of obligation to any interest other than the public's right to know.
Journalists should:

- Avoid conflicts of interest, real or perceived.
- Remain free of associations or activities that may compromise integrity or damage credibility.
- Refuse gifts, favors, fees, free travel and special treatment, and shun secondary employment, political involvement, public office and service in community organizations if they compromise journalistic integrity.
- Disclose unavoidable conflicts.
- Be vigilant and courageous about holding those with power accountable.
- Deny favored treatment to advertisers and special interests and resist their pressure to influence news coverage.
- Be wary of sources offering information for favors or money, avoid bidding for news.

## Be Accountable

Journalists are accountable to their readers, listeners, viewers and each other.
Journalists should:

- Clarify and explain news coverage and invite dialogue with the public over journalistic conduct.
- Encourage the public to voice grievances against the news media.
- Admit mistakes and correct them promptly.
- Expose unethical practices of journalists and the news media.
- Abide by the same high standards to which they hold others.

(Reprinted with the permission of the Society of Professional Journalists.)

# Appendix I

**American Society of Journalists and Authors**
**Code of Ethics and Fair Practices**
*(Revised September 1997, New York)*

*Preamble*

Over the years, an unwritten code governing editor–writer relationships has arisen. The American Society of Journalists and Authors has compiled the major principles and practices of that code that are generally recognized as fair and equitable.

The ASJA has also established a Committee on Editor–Writer Relations to investigate and mediate disagreements brought before it, either by members or by editors. In its activity this committee shall rely on the following guidelines.

1. Truthfulness, Accuracy, Editing

The writer shall at all times perform professionally and to the best of his or her ability, assuming primary responsibility for truth and accuracy. No writer shall deliberately write into an article a dishonest, distorted, or inaccurate statement.

Editors may correct or delete copy for purposes of style, grammar, conciseness, or arrangement, but may not change the intent or sense without the writer's permission.

2. Sources

A writer shall be prepared to support all statements made in his or her manuscripts, if requested. It is understood, however, that the publisher shall respect any and all promises of confidentiality made by the writer in obtaining information.

3. Ideas and Proposals

An idea shall be defined not as a subject alone but as a subject combined with an approach.

A proposal of an idea ("query") by a professional writer shall receive a personal response within three weeks. If such a communication is in writing, it is properly viewed and treated as business correspondence, with no return postage or other materials required for reply.

A writer shall be considered to have a proprietary right to an idea suggested to an editor.

### 4. Acceptance of an Assignment

A request from an editor that the writer proceeds with an idea, however worded and whether oral or written, shall be considered an assignment. (The word "assignment" here is understood to mean a definite order for an article.) It shall be the obligation of the writer to proceed as rapidly as possible toward the completion of an assignment, to meet a deadline mutually agreed upon, and not to agree to unreasonable deadlines.

### 5. Conflict of Interest

The writer shall reveal to the editor, before acceptance of an assignment, any actual or potential conflict of interest, including but not limited to any financial interest in any product, firm, or commercial venture relating to the subject of the article.

### 6. Report on Assignment

If in the course of research or during the writing of the article, the writer concludes that the assignment will not result in a satisfactory article, he or she shall be obliged to so inform the editor.

### 7. Withdrawal

Should a disagreement arise between the editor and writer as to the merit or handling of an assignment, the editor may remove the writer on payment of mutually satisfactory compensation for the effort already expended, or the writer may withdraw without compensation and, if the idea for the assignment originated with the writer, may take the idea elsewhere without penalty.

### 8. Agreements

The practice of written confirmation of all agreements between editors and writers is strongly recommended, and such confirmation may originate with the editor, the writer, or an agent. Such a memorandum of confirmation should list all aspects of the assignment including subject, approach, length, special instructions, payments, deadline, and guarantee (if any). Failing prompt contradictory response to such a memorandum, both parties are entitled to assume that the terms set forth therein are binding.

### 9. Rewriting

No writer's work shall be rewritten without his or her advance consent. If an editor requests a writer to rewrite a manuscript, the writer shall be obliged to do so but shall alternatively be entitled to withdraw the manuscript and offer it elsewhere.

### 10. Bylines

Lacking any stipulation to the contrary, a byline is the author's unquestioned right. All advertisements of the article should also carry the author's name. If an author's byline is omitted from the published article, no matter what the cause or reason, the publisher shall be liable to compensate the author financially for the omission.

## 11. Updating

If delay in publication necessitates extensive updating of an article, such updating shall be done by the author, to whom additional compensation shall be paid.

## 12. Reversion of Rights

Reasonable and good-faith efforts should be made to schedule an article within six months and publish it within twelve months. In the event that circumstances prevent such timely publication, the writer should be informed within twelve months as to the publication's continued interest in the article and plans to publish it. If publication is unlikely, the manuscript and all rights therein should revert to the author without penalty or cost to the author.

## 13. Payment for Assignments

An assignment presumes an obligation upon the publisher to pay for the writer's work upon satisfactory completion of the assignment, according to the agreed terms. Should a manuscript that has been accepted, orally or in writing, by a publisher or any representative or employee of the publisher, later be deemed unacceptable, the publisher shall nevertheless be obliged to pay the writer in full according to the agreed terms.

If an editor withdraws or terminates an assignment, due to no fault of the writer, after work has begun but prior to completion of the manuscript, the writer is entitled to compensation for work already put in; such compensation shall be negotiated between editor and author and shall be commensurate with the amount of work already completed. If a completed assignment is not accepted, due to no fault of the writer, the writer is still entitled to full payment.

## 14. Time of Payments

The writer is entitled to payment for an accepted article within 30 days of delivery. No article payment, or any portion thereof, should ever be subject to publication or to scheduling for publication.

## 15. Expenses

Unless otherwise stipulated by the editor at the time of an assignment, a writer shall assume that normal, out-of-pocket expenses will be reimbursed by the publisher. Any extraordinary expenses anticipated by the writer shall be discussed with the editor prior to incurring them.

## 16. Insurance

A magazine that gives a writer an assignment involving any extraordinary hazard shall insure the writer against death or disability during the course of travel or the hazard, or, failing that, shall honor the cost of such temporary insurance as an expense account item.

17. Loss of Personal Belongings

If, as a result of circumstances or events directly connected with a perilous assignment and due to no fault of the writer, a writer suffers loss of personal belongings or professional equipment or incurs bodily injury, the publisher shall compensate the writer in full.

18. Copyright, Additional Rights

It shall be understood, unless otherwise stipulated in writing, that sale of an article manuscript entitles the purchaser to first North American rights only, and that all other rights are retained by the author. Under no circumstances shall an independent writer be required to sign a so-called "all rights transferred" or "work made for hire" agreement as a condition of assignment, of payment, or of publication.

19. Reprints

All revenues from reprints shall revert to the author exclusively, and it is incumbent upon a publication to refer all requests for reprint to the author. The author has a right to charge for such reprints and must request that the original publication be credited.

20. Agents

In the absence of any agreement to the contrary, a writer shall not be obliged to pay an agent a fee on work negotiated, accomplished and paid for without the assistance of the agent. An agent should not charge a client a separate fee covering "legal" review of a contract for a book or other project.

21. TV and Radio Promotion

The writer is entitled to be paid for personal participation in TV or radio programs promoting periodicals in which the writer's work appears.

22. Indemnity

No writer should be obliged to indemnify any magazine or book publisher against any claim, actions, or proceedings arising from an article or book, except where there are valid claims of plagiarism or copyright violation.

23. Proofs

The editor shall submit edited proofs of the author's work to the author for approval, sufficiently in advance of publication that any errors may be brought to the editor's attention. If for any reason a publication is unable to so deliver or transmit proofs to the author, the author is entitled to review the proofs in the publication's office.

Source: American Society of Journalists and Authors, Inc., Suite 302, 1501 Broadway, New York, NY 10036; (212) 997–0947. Revised September 1997. © 1997 American Society of Journalists and Authors.

(Reprinted with the permission of the American Society of Journalists and Authors.)

# Appendix J

**Protecting Yourself in the Magazine Recession (Or Any Other Time)**

Brett Harvey
*Eastern Regional Grievance Officer*
*National Writers Union*

These are especially hard times for freelancers, in case you hadn't noticed. Magazines are going belly-up nearly every month, and the ones that are left are cutting every possible corner—which means fewer pieces assigned, lower fees, more and lower kill fees, slower payment, and more all rights-contracts. The guidelines that follow come directly from my grievance files. Following them doesn't mean you won't get stiffed; it just means you will have done everything you as a *writer* can do to minimize the possibility.

1. *Get it in writing.* These days, with the advent of the mighty fax machine, there's no longer any excuse for working without a contract. If you're a member of the National Writer's Union, use its Standard Journalism Contract, which will give you the best and fairest possible terms. If you must use the publisher's contract, try to amend it to include payment "on submission" (best) or "on acceptance" (second best), and "First North American print rights only." If the publisher declines to use a contract, think hard about if it's worth it to work for someone who doesn't want to use contracts. If the answer is yes, prepare your own assignment letter spelling out exactly what you and the editor have agreed to, including: (1) how many words; (2) when the piece is due; (3) how much you'll be paid; (4) *when* you'll be paid; (5) the fact that you're selling only first North American print rights; and (6) as much detail as possible about the content of the piece. Verbal contracts are admissible in court, but a paper trail will help a great deal if you have to bring a grievance, and will be invaluable if you have to go to Small Claims court. Plus, it establishes you as a professional.

2. *Start billing immediately.* Having established when you can expect to be paid ahead of time, include an invoice when you turn in the piece and start pressing for payment immediately. *Don't* let weeks or months (would you be-

lieve years?) go by before they hear from you. It's unprofessional and it supports their delusion you don't need the money. And, most important of all, *they may be out of business by the time you get around to collecting!* My files are full of these cases.

3. *Don't wait to file an action if you haven't been paid.* If you're an NWU member and haven't been paid within a reasonable time from when they promised (I'd say three weeks), write them a letter threatening to bring a grievance and carbon copy your local grievance officer. If that doesn't work, bring a grievance. Promptly. If you are not a Union member, threaten with Small Claims Court action. If you wait until they've folded, you'll never see a penny of your fee.

4. *Don't keep writing for publications that haven't paid you.* If they haven't paid you for one piece, think twice before doing a second. I know this is hard to resist. It's flattering to be asked to write again. But think about it: If they really want you to write for them, shouldn't they be willing to pay for the first piece before you go to work on the second? Chances are very good that by the time you've done the third piece for no pay, you'll find out they're out of business.

5. *Don't sign away all rights unless you absolutely have to.* This should go without saying. However, due to the explosion in electronic publishing, many publications have changed their boiler-plate contract from the standard "first North American rights" to "all rights." If you receive such a contract, cross out "all rights" and write in "first North American print only." Do not be afraid to do this. In many instances, they're just trying to get away with something. They hope the writers are inexperienced enough or scared enough to just sign on the dotted line (and, regrettably, many are!).

This doesn't mean you shouldn't sell the publisher other rights (for example, electronic rights). Just don't *give* them away, which is what you are doing if you sign an "all rights" contract. Make them negotiate those rights separately. *Remember: they will not blackball you if you protest work-for-hire.* The worst they can do is to insist you sign away all rights.

(Reprinted with the permission of Brett Harvey, personal communication, May 24, 1993.)

# References

A classroom close-up. (1993). *Talk of the classroom, 5,* 6.

Abbe, E. (2002). *The Writer's Handbook* 2003 (67th ed.). Boston: The Writer.

Abbott, M. L. (2002, October 30). Lowell Thomas travel journalism winners honored at Society of American Travel Writers convention. Retrieved January 11, 2003, from http://www.satw.org/ltpressreleases.asp

Aborn, S. (1995, August). Writing first-person dramas. *Writer's Digest, 75,* 27–29.

About the Magazine (2002). *Operations & Fulfillment.* Retrieved September 21, 2002, from http://www.opsandfulfillment.com/rp/about/index.htm

Alexander, L. (1975). *Beyond the facts: A guide to the art of feature writing.* Houston, TX: Gulf Publishing.

Ames, B., & Gold, L. S. (1989). Misconceptions regarding environmental pollution and cancer causation. In M. Moore (Ed.), *Health risk and the press: Perspectives on media coverage of risk assessment and health.* Washington, DC: The Media Institute.

Angell, M. (1996). *Science on trial: The clash of medical evidence.* New York: Norton.

Auletta, K. (1997, June). *Great writers on writing.* Paper presented at the Investigative Reporters and Editors annual convention, Phoenix, AZ.

Ayers, Jr., B. D. et al. (2001, December 9). A nation challenged: Portraits of grief: An old-fashioned man, a pair of loving brothers, and a jolly snowboarder. *New York Times.* Retrieved September 1, 2002, from http://www.pulitzer.org/year/2002/public-service/works/portraitsofgrief.html

Baker, C. P. (1989, June). How to travel the lucrative road of travel writing. *Writer's Digest, 69,* 22–26.

Balmaseda, L. (1992, June 4). Neither poverty nor politics can extinguish people's hope. *The Miami Herald,* p. 1A.

Banks, M. (1985, February). Breaking away! *Writer's Digest, 65,* 22–26.

Barker, O. (2002, September 20–22). Miss America and me, the 52nd contestant. *USA Today,* pp. 1A–2A.

Barry, D. (1986, September 12). Dave to Sophia: "Chow, bella." *The Miami Herald,* p. 1B.

Barry, D. (1993, June 20). Courtroom confessions. *The Miami Herald,* p. 27.

Bartel, P. (1992, November). Quick and clean interviewing. *Writer's Digest, 72,* 36–37.

Barton, G. (2002, May 5). Justice for Becky. *South Bend Tribune.* Retrieved September 1, 2002, from http://www.southbendtribune.com/beckyindex.htm

Barzun, J. (1992). *The press and the prose* (Occasional paper No. 10). Freedom Forum Media Studies Center, Columbia University, New York.

Baumbach, G. F. (2002, September). September 11 in Manhattan: Finding my son alive. *St. Anthony Messenger.* Retrieved October 19, 2002, from http://www.americancatholic.org/Messenger/Sep2002/Feature1.asp

Baumbach, N. (2002, September 30). The Zagat history of my last relationship. *The New Yorker,* p. 74.

Bednarski, P. J. (1993, January/February). Creating a new section in less than two weeks in Chicago. *ASNE Bulletin, 747,* 17.

Belcher, W. (1988, August 30). Poking fun at politics. *Tampa Tribune,* pp. 1F, 6F.

Belleville, B. (2002). Florida's deep blue destiny. *Florida Humanities Council Forum, 25,* pp. 8–13.

Bertagnoli, L. (2002). When a man needs a woman. *Chicago, 51,* 28.

Biagi, S. (1981). *How to write and sell magazine articles.* Englewood Cliffs, NJ: Prentice Hall.

Biagi, S. (1986). *Interviews that work: A practical guide for journalists.* Belmont, CA: Wadsworth.

Billings, J. S. (1992, December). Writing and selling in the newspaper market. *The Writer, 105,* 24–25.

Blair, W., & Hill, H. (1978). *America's humor: From Poor Richard to Doonesbury.* New York: Oxford University Press.

Blais, M. (1984). *Writer's writing: Before the first word* [Television broadcast]. Produced by Learning Designs, Inc., and Educational Broadcasting Corp., WNET–TV, New York, and funded by The Annenberg/CPB Project, Public Broadcasting Service, Alexandria, VA.

Bleyer, W. G. (1913). *Newspaper writing and editing.* Boston: Houghton Mifflin.

Bloom, M. T., Bedell, T., Olds, S. W., Moldafsky, A., & Schultz, D. (Eds.). (1992). *The ASJA handbook: A writers' guide to ethical and economic issues* (2nd ed.). New York: American Society of Journalists and Authors, Inc.

Blum, D., (1990, August 20). Laugh track. *New York, 23,* 30.

Bly, L. (2002, September 13). Falling rates are colorful change for leaf peepers. *USA Today,* p. 7D.

Bly, R. W. (1992, January). Writing by the light of the moon. *Writer's Digest, 72,* 22–25.

Bly, R. W. (1996, February). To sell more, write more. *Writer's Digest, 76,* 22–25, 52.

Bohannon, J. (1993, February). Successful article writing. *The Writer, 106,* 20–22.

Bolen, M. (2002, October 3). October glides into Key West quietly, but leaves with a roar. *Key West Citizen.* Retrieved October 3, 2002, from http://keysnews.com/286257666339414.bsp.htm

Boles, P. D. (1985, April). The elements of your personal writing style. *Writer's Digest, 65,* 24–28.

Bonner, S. (1995, August). Hard facts on fact checking. *Writer's Digest, 75,* 37–39.

Bottomly, T. (1991, January). Interview strategies. *Second Takes* [*The Oregonian* newsroom newsletter], 3–4.

Bouncing back may require 'breather.' (2001, October 15). *USA Today,* p. 3B.

Bowman, S. J. (1990, November). How to write irresistibly. *Writer's Digest, 70,* 38–41.

Bowman, S. J. (1996, November). How to weigh your options: Free-lancing full time. *Writer's Digest, 76,* 22–25.

Bowman, S. J. (1997, May). How to study a market. *Writer's Digest, 77,* 22–24.

Bragg, R. (1995a, August 13). All she has, $150,000, is going to a university. *New York Times.* Retrieved September 1, 2002, from http://www.pulitzer.org/year/1996/feature-writing/works/oseola.html

Bragg, R. (1995b, November 1). Where Alabama inmates fade into old age. *New York Times.* Retrieved September 24, 2002, from http://www.pulitzer.org/year/1996/feature-writing/works/prison.html

Bragg, R. (1998, September 23). Mourners pay respects to gentler George Wallace. *New Orleans Times–Picayune,* p. A20.

Brecher, E. (2002, August 30). Different prognoses: Girls' paths diverge in cancer battle. *The Miami Herald,* p. 1A.

Brill, D. (1992, September). Setting the right tone. *Writer's Digest, 72,* 32–36.

Briskin, J. (1979, February). Research is a snap. *Writer's Digest, 59,* 26–28.

Broeske, P. H. (1996, July). 12 tactics for inquiring writers. *Writer's Digest, 76,* 22–25.

Brogan, K. S. (2002). *2003 writer's market: 3,100+ book and magazine editors who buy what you write.* Cincinnati, OH: Writer's Digest Books.

Buckley, S. (2002, February). How to score a South Beach valentine. *Ocean Drive,* 252–255.

Bugeja, M. J. (1996, September). What's online for you? *Writer's Digest, 76,* 18–22.

Bull, C., & Erman, S., (Eds.). (2002). *At Ground Zero: Young reporters who were there tell their stories.* New York: Thunder's Mouth Press.

Bunn, T. D. (1993, January/February). "hj" turns Syracuse paper into a key youth news source. *ASNE Bulletin, 747,* 20.

Burgett, G. (1997). *Sell and resell your magazine articles.* Cincinnati, OH: Writer's Digest Books.

Caldwell, G. (2001, October 1). Joy Williams tries to build a novel around ideas—And around three wisecracking young furies. *The Boston Globe.* Retrieved September 18, 2002, from http://www.pulitzer.org/year/2001/criticism/works/caldwell100100.html

Callahan, T. (1995). Part 5: How to write the profile. *Writer's Digest 75,* 40–42, 66.

Campbell, J. (1993, March 15). The interview: Giving to get. *Folio, 22,* 31–32.

Carter, R. A. (1990, October 12). Tickling the funnybone. *Publishers Weekly, 237,* 24–26.

Casewit, C. (1988). *How to make money from travel writing.* Chester, CT: Globe Pequot Press.

Clark, E. (2002, March/April). Glacier National Park: Eye-popping scenery and classic lodges bring nature lovers to northwest Montana. Retrieved October 13, 2002, from http://www.findarticles.com/cf_0/m0FCQ/5_17/83552485/p1/article.jhtml?term=glacier+national+park+buses

Clark, R. (2002). A letter from the editor. *Rosebud.* Retrieved September 21, 2002, from http://www.rsbd.net/pages/introduc.htm

Clark, T. (1990, December). How to get started as a writer. *Writer's Digest, 70,* 24–27.

Clark, T. (1995, August). How to write assignment-winning query letters. *Writer's Digest, 75,* 22–26.

Clarke, J. (1993, January 17). Traveler's headache No. 1: Answer survey questions. *The Miami Herald,* p. 12F.

Clutton-Brock, T. (2002, September). Juma's story: Growing from pup to patriarch. *National Geographic, 202,* 68–72.

Cohen, S. (2000, July/August). Diagnosis: Brain tumor: Yoga and transcendental mediation help entrepreneur Annette Dale heal after brain surgery. *Yoga Journal.* Retrieved October 17, 2002, from http://www.yogajournal.com/views/310.cfm

Cook, K. (2002, September/October). Sergio takes center stage. *T&L Golf,* 116–120, 146–148.

Cook, M. (1986, March). Training your muse: Seven steps to harnessing your creativity. *Writer's Digest, 66,* 26–30.

Cook, M. (1987, June). Dave Barry claws his way to the top. *Writer's Digest, 67,* 28–30.

Cook, M. (1991, March). Ten roads to better article openings. *Writer's Digest, 71,* 28–31.

Cool, L. C. (1985a, June). How to write irresistible query letters. *Writer's Digest, 65,* 24–27.

Cool, L. C. (1985b, November). Making contract. *Writer's Digest, 65,* 39–41.

Coomber, B. (2002, September / October). What should we wear? Make waves in fashion at sea. *AAA Going Places, 26,* 22–23.

Cordle, I., & Rabin, C. (2002, September 2). Flight attendant tries to get back to her life. *The Miami Herald,* p. 3B.

Council for the Advancement of Science Writing. (2003). *Careers in science writing.* Retrieved January 12, 2002, from http://www.nasw.org/users/casw/careers.htm

Czapnik, S. (2002, August). An interview with Tom Brokaw. *Renaissance Insights,* 34–39.

Dahir, M. S. (1995, November). Writing science & medical nonfiction: It's easier than you think. *Writer's Digest, 75,* 29–31.

Dahlin, R. (1992, March 9). Take my book—Please! *Publishers Weekly, 239,* 23–27.

Daugherty, G. (2001, September). E-query etiquette. *Writer's Digest, 81,* 28–29.

Davidson, J. (2001a, September 22). Philharmonic benefits its audience, too. *Newsday.* Retrieved September 30, 2002, from http://www.pulitzer.org/year/2002/criticism/works/092201.html

Davidson, J. (2001b, October 30). This femme fatale fails to seduce. *Newsday.* Retrieved September 30, 2002, from http://www.pulitzer.org/year/2002/criticism/works/111301.html

Davidson, M. (1990). *A guide for newspaper stringers.* Hillsdale, NJ: Lawrence Erlbaum Associates, Inc.

Dearing, J. W., & Kazmierczak, J. (1992, August). *Newspaper coverage of maverick science: Balancing the unbalanced controversy.* Paper presented at the annual meeting of the Association for Education in Journalism and Mass Communication, Montreal, Canada.

Decker, D. (2002, September 15). Behind the veils: Islamic women reveal cultural pride and a generational divide. *Dallas Morning News,* pp. 1J, 6J.

DeSilva, B. (1990, September). Secrets of storytelling. *Second Takes* [*The Oregonian* newsroom newsletter], *2*, 3–4.

Dickson, F. A. (1980, April). Thinking ahead: 34 article ideas for fall and winter. *Writer's Digest, 60*, 33–35.

Doig, S. K. (1987, April 1). Coded message. *The Miami Herald,* p. 1B.

Dunn, D. (2002, October). The new standard of business travel. *Condè Nast Traveler,* pp. 51–59.

Duquin, L. H. (1987, January). Shaping your article ideas to sell. *Writer's Digest, 67*, 37–40.

Eddy, B. (1979, February). Spelling: The curse of the working journalist. *The Quill, 67*, 15–17.

Edelson, E. (1985). *The journalist's guide to nuclear energy.* Bethesda, MD: Atomic Industrial Forum.

Eliscu, J. (2002, October 3). The music Q&A: James Taylor. *Rolling Stone,* p. 36.

Essex, A. (2002, September). He's having a baby, part IV, Vol. 20(10), p. 134.

Evans, K. (2001, April). Journeys of the spirit. *Health,* pp. 118–123, 178–179.

Every fool has his day; this is yours. (1987, April 2). *The Miami Herald,* p. 1B.

Federal Document Clearing House. (2002). *Chairman holds hearing on tourism after 9/11 (FDHC Transcripts).* Washington, DC: Author.

Finley, M. (1988, July). Patrick F. McManus and the funny four. *Writer's Digest, 68*, 33–34.

Fiori, P. (1992, May). Celebrating service magazines. *Folio, 21*, 78–80.

Fischer, C. (1990). Newsletter journalists find their jobs interesting, rewarding and fast-paced. *Newsletter Career Guide* (p. 2). Arlington, VA: Newsletter Publishers Association.

Flesch, R. (1946). *The art of plain talk.* New York: Harper & Brothers.

Flesch, R. (1949). *The art of readable writing.* New York: Harper & Brothers.

Fox, C. S. (1993, January). How to set your freelance fees. *ByLine, 152*, 6–7.

Franklin, J. (1978, December 12). Tales from the grey frontier. *Baltimore Evening Sun,* p. C–1.

Franklin, J. (1986). *Writing for story: Craft secrets of dramatic nonfiction by a two-time Pulitzer Prize winner.* New York: Mentor.

Free-lance writer sentenced for selling phony stories. (1993, April 24). *Editor & Publisher, 126*, 72.

French, T. (1998). Angels & demons. *St. Petersburg Times.* Retrieved September 1, 2002, from http://www.pulitzer.org/year/1998/feature-writing/works/

Friedman, E. (1997, May). How to dissect a magazine. *Writer's Digest, 77*, 24.

Friedman, S., Dunwoody, S., & Rogers, C. (Eds.). (1999). *Communicating Uncertainty.* Mahwah, NJ: Lawrence Erlbaum Associates, Inc.

Fromm, J. L. (2002, October). Life in these united states. *Reader's Digest,* 214.

Fry, P. (1997, January). Looking for a few good ideas? *Writer's Digest, 77*, 38–40.

Fryxell, D. A. (1990, March). Getting organized. *Writer's Digest, 70*, 42–44.

Fryxell, D. A. (2000a, May). Sending it off right. *Writer's Digest, 80*, 16–18.

Fryxell, D. A. (2000b, July). Avoiding the editorial "Dear John." *Writer's Digest, 80*, 14–16.

Fryxell, D. A. (2001, July). Bulletproof queries. *Writer's Digest, 81*, 16–19.

Fryxell, D. A. (2002, January). Looking for the silver lining. *Writer's Digest, 82*, 17–18, 54.

Gagné, L. (Ed.). (1997). *Newsletters in print, 1998* (10th ed.). Detroit, MI: Gale Research Inc.

Gannon, R. (Ed.). (1991). *Best science writing: Readings and insights.* Phoenix, AZ: Oryx Press.

Garrison, B. (1990). *Professional news writing.* Hillsdale, NJ: Lawrence Erlbaum Associates, Inc.

Gates, B. (1995). *The road ahead.* New York: Viking.

Gibbs, N. (2002, September 11). What a difference a year makes. *Time, 160*, 20–22.

Gilder, J. (1981, April). Creators on creating: Tom Wolfe. *Saturday Review, 8*, 40–44.

Gillmor, D. M., Barron, J. A., Simon, T. F., & Terry, H. A. (1990). *Mass communication law: Cases and comment* (5th ed.). St. Paul, MN: West.

Glaberson, W. (1993, May 3). Press: Newspaper publishers consider a heretical new gospel: Just how outdated their products are. *The New York Times*, p. D7.

Glancey, J. (2002, September 9). Architecture: Everything ship-shape: Jonathan Glancey is thrilled with Cornwall's new maritime museum. *The Guardian* [London], Features, p. 12.

Glasser, S. (1990, October). Read my quips! *The Writer, 103*, 16–18.

Glasser, S. (1992, July). Write shorts that sell. *The Writer, 105*, 19–20, 45.

Go Ahead: Make Us Laugh. (2002, October). *Reader's Digest*, 12.

Good, J. B. (2002, February 22). Fun, surprises keep the love bug buzzing. *Atlanta Journal and Constitution*, p. 5E.

Gorney, C. (1993, February 12). Litigation journalism is a scourge. *The New York Times*, p. 22A.

Goss, F. D. (1988). *Success in newsletter publishing: A practical guide* (3rd ed.). Arlington, VA: Newsletter Publishers Association.

Greenberg, H. (Ed.). (1992). *Oxbridge directory of newsletters*. New York: Oxbridge Communications.

Grobel, L. (1978, January). A star interview is born. *Writer's Digest, 58*, 19–23.

Gunning, R. (1968). *The technique of clear writing*. New York: McGraw-Hill.

Hale, F. D. (1999, March). *Analysis of techniques used by humor columnists*. Paper presented to the Newspaper Division, Southeast Colloquium, Association for Education in Journalism and Mass Communication, Lexington, KY.

Handschuh, D. (2002, Fourth Quarter). Trapped twice in the rubble: A photojournalist who almost lost his life learns to hug everyone he loves. *IPI Global Journalist*, 23–25.

Harrington, W. (1997, June 13). *Investigative profiles*. Paper presented at the annual convention of the Investigative Reporters and Editors, Phoenix, AZ.

Harris, A. S., Jr. (1992, February). Writing the newspaper travel article. *The Writer, 105*, 21–23, 44.

Hart, J. (1989, October). Cutting fine figures. *Second Takes* [*The Oregonian* newsroom newsletter], *1*, 1, 5.

Hart, J. (1990a). Dripping with color. *Second Takes* [*The Oregonian* newsroom newsletter], *2*, 3.

Hart, J. (1990b). In the reader's shoes. *Second Takes* [*The Oregonian* newsroom newsletter], *1*, 1, 3–4.

Hart, J. (1990c). Seizing the action. *Second Takes* [*The Oregonian* newsroom newsletter], *1*, 1, 3.

Hart, J. (1990d). Telling terms. *Second Takes* [*The Oregonian* newsroom newsletter], *2*, 1, 8.

Hart, J. (1990e). Writing to be read. *Second Takes* [*The Oregonian* newsroom newsletter], *1*, 1, 3.

Hart, J. (1991a). Building character. *Second Takes* [*The Oregonian* newsroom newsletter], *3*, 1, 4–5, 8.

Hart, J. (1991b). Building character II. *Second Takes* [*The Oregonian* newsroom newsletter], *3*, 1, 4–5.

Hart, J. (1991c). News by the numbers. *Second Takes* [*The Oregonian* newsroom newsletter], *2*, 1, 3, 5.

Hart, J. (1991d). Storytelling. *Second Takes* [*The Oregonian* newsroom newsletter], *3*, 1, 3, 5, 7–8.

Hart, J. (1991e). The ladder of abstraction. *Second Takes* [*The Oregonian* newsroom newsletter], *3*, 1, 4–5.

Hart, J. (1992, March). High tension. *Second Takes* [*The Oregonian* newsroom newsletter], *3*, 1, 4–5.

Hart, J. (1995, September). Stories in the news. *Writer's Digest, 75*(9), 29–33.

Hatcher, T. (2002, September 1). *Don't go around the world and back to get a passport*. Retrieved September 1, 2002, from http://www.cnn.com/TRAVEL/ADVISOR/passport.adviser/index.html

Haverstock, M. (1993, March). Writing for regional parenting publications. *ByLine, 154*, 6–7, 21.

Heath, C. (2002, October 3). Jennifer Love Hewitt. *Rolling Stone, 906*, 45–50.

Heller, S. (2000, May 26). The lessons of a lost career, how one unsung professor played by the rules, worked hard at the same university for 27 years, and died worrying that he couldn't pay his bills. *The Chronicle of Higher Education*. Retrieved September 1, 2002, from http://www.chronicle.com/free/v46/i38/38a01801.htm

Hellyer, K. (1993, January/February). Three ways to satisfy the hunger for useful entertainment news. *ASNE Bulletin, 747*, 16.

Henderson, B. (1984, April). How to "bulletproof" your manuscripts. *Writer's Digest, 64*, 28–32.

Hensley, D. E. (1979, May). Pumping the profs. *Writer's Digest, 59*, 34.

Hensley, D. E. (1986, January). Getting the most out of your writers club. *Writer's Digest, 66*, 36–38.

Hensley, D. E. (1993, August). 7 simple steps to multiple marketing. *Writer's Digest, 73*, 32–33.

Herrel, K. (1989, November 22). The Lord provides it, and we cook it. *The Independent Alligator* [University of Florida], p. 8.

Higgins, J. (2000, July 14). Staying afloat on WEBLOGS: Sites are water wings for surfers sinking in sea of cybermadness. *Journal–Sentinel*. Retrieved August 21, 2002, from http://www.jsonline.com/enter/netlife/jul00/weblogs16071400.asp

Hodge, S. (2002, October 1). Etiquette guides silent about those indicted. *Houston Chronicle*. Retrieved October 2, 2002, from http://www.chron.com/cs/CDA/story.hts/features/1599040

Holm, K. C. (2001). *2002 Writer's Market: Where & how to sell what you write*. Cincinnati, OH: Writer's Digest Books.

Holton, W. P. (1993, March). A free-lancer's phrase book. *Writer's Digest, 73*(3), 6.

Hunt, T. (1972). *Reviewing for the mass media*. Radnor, PA: Chilton.

Hurley, A. G. (2002, October). Confessions of a jewelry junkie. *Good Housekeeping*. Retrieved October 19, 2002, from http://magazines.ivillage.com/goodhousekeeping/consumer/shopping/articles/0,12873,404905_290201,00.html

Hynds, E. C. (1998, March). City magazines meeting new challenges, offering variety of services for readers. Paper presented to the Southeast Colloquium, Magazine Division, Association for Education in Journalism and Mass Communication, New Orleans, LA.

Jacobi, P. (1991, December). 12 ways to win readers (and editors). *Writer's Digest, 71*, 34–37.

James–Enger, K. (2002, March). Cash in with reprints. *Writer's Digest, 82*, 27, 56.

Jicha, T. (1993, April 8). *Why should we take entertainment reporting seriously?* Paper presented at the Society of Professional Journalists program at the University of Miami, Coral Gables, FL.

Jicha, T. (2002, October 1). Less than perfect is all that, and less. *Sun-Sentinel*. Retrieved October 2, 2002, from http://www.sun-sentinel.com/entertainment/tv/sfl-tvtjlessoct01,0,6582733.column

Kael, P. (1979). Circles and squares. In G. Mast & M. Cohen (Eds.), *Film theory and criticism* (2nd ed., pp. 666–679). New York: Oxford University Press.

Kando, T. (1980). *Leisure and popular culture in transition* (2nd ed.). St. Louis, MO: Mosby.

Kaplan, M. (1975). *Leisure: Theory and policy*. New York: Wiley.

Kasselmann, B. C. (1992, May). You don't have to go to Spain to write travel articles. *The Writer, 105*, 21–24.

Kaufman, P. (2002, September 14). Picnic with a purpose: Teens, politicians mix at annual Labor Day event. *Charleston Gazette*, p. 1C.

Kearney, S. (2002, September 8). One year later, tourism is still . . . up in the air. *Houston Chronicle*, p. 1.

Keller, J. (2002, September 29). The Martha show. *Chicago Tribune Magazine*, pp. 8–14, 28–33.

Kelly, C. (2002, September 13). Robin Williams, seriously. *Fort Worth Star–Telegram*, 1E, 7E.

Kelly, J. (2002, September 11). Covering the story. *Time, 160*, p. 8.

Kelso, J. (2002, October 11). Okie Pokie is developing a fan club. *Austin American-Statesman*. Retrieved October 25, 2002, from http://www.austin360.com/aas/metro/kelso/1002/101302.html

Kelton, N. (1988, January). How to write personal experience articles. *Writer's Digest, 68*, 22–24.

Kilpatrick, J. J. (1985). *The art and the craft*. The Red Smith lecture in journalism, Department of American Studies, University of Notre Dame, South Bend, IN.

Klenck, T. (2002, October). Garage door tuneup. *Popular Mechanics*. Retrieved October 17, 2002, from http://www.popularmechanics.com/home_improvement/home_improvement/2002/10/garage_door_tuneup/

Knight–Ridder, Inc. (1986). *The 1986 Pulitzer Prize winners*. Miami, FL: Knight–Ridder.

Krol, J. (Ed.). (1992). *Newsletters in print, 1993–94* (6th ed.). Detroit, MI: Gale Research Inc.

Kubis, P., & Howland, R. (1985). *The complete guide to writing fiction, nonfiction, and publishing*. Reston, VA: Reston.

Kurtz, H. (1993, April 14). Post wins three Pulitzer Prizes; national reporting, feature writing, book criticism honored. *The Washington Post*, p. A1.

Ladwig, T. (1987, October 5). The baddest of bad days gives a couple a good story. *Columbia Missourian*, reprinted in *Publisher's Auxiliary, 123,* 12.

Lamb, C. (1993, June 5). Humorist holds his own in newspapers. *Editor & Publisher, 126,* 34–35.

Lambe, D. R. (1986, April). What to do when the publisher won't pay. *Writer's Digest, 66,* 36–38.

Land, M. E. (1993). *Writing for magazines* (2nd ed.). Englewood Cliffs, NJ: Prentice Hall.

Lane, A. (2002, September 9). Femme fatales. *The New Yorker.* Retrieved September 10, 2002, from http://www.newyorker.com/printable/?critics/020916crci_cinema

Lanza, M. (2002, September). Best seats in the house. *Backpacker, 30,* 64–68.

Lardner, G. (1992, November 22). The stalking of Kristin: The law made it easy for my daughter's killer. *The Washington Post,* p. C1.

Lauer, M. (2002, September 20). Olivia Barker of *USA Today* discusses taking part in the Miss America Pageant for an article, "The Today Show," NBC News Transcripts, NBC, Lexis–Nexis, accessed September 22, 2002.

Levi, R. (2001). *Medical journalism: Exposing fact, fiction, fraud.* Ames: Iowa State University Press.

Levine, I. S. (2002, September 15). The real Bellagio. *Dallas Morning News,* pp. 6G, 9G.

Levoy, G. (1991, July). The art of negotiation. *Writer's Digest, 71,* 26–29.

Lileks, J. (2002, October 24). Backfence: Everything . . . that is the question. *Minneapolis Star Tribune.* Retrieved October 25, 2002, from http://www.startribune.com/stories/804/3383526.html

Lind, A. (2002, October 25). The strange smell of success: All this talk of the Saints and the Super Bowl is making fans nervous. *New Orleans Times-Picayune.* Retrieved October 25, 2002, from http://www.nola.com/living/t-p/lind/index.ssf?/livingstory/lind25.html

Locke, T. (2002, October). Humor in uniform. *Reader's Digest, 62.*

Logan, R. A., Fears, L., & Wilson, N. (1997). *Social responsibility and science news: Four case studies.* Washington, DC: The Media Institute.

Luhta, R. (2003, January 29). Camping in paradise, exploring the Keys 2003. *Key West Citizen,* pp. 16–18.

Luzadder, D. (1982, March 15). A fitful night for those whose dreams lie under the river. Fort Wayne, Indiana, *News-Sentinel.*

Macdonald, D. (1969). *Dwight Macdonald on movies.* Englewood Cliffs, NJ: Prentice Hall.

Magazine Publishers of America. (2003, January). Fact sheet. Retrieved January 10, 2003, from http://www.magazine.org/resources/fact_sheets.html

Mahoney, S. (2002, October). Trading places. *Reader's Digest,* pp. 49–52.

Maisel, E. (1993, May). The 11-step program for writing self-help nonfiction: Rejection dependent no more! *Writer's Digest, 73,* 27–29.

Martin–Hidalgo, M. (2002, August 16). Store owner mourned: Emotional Hindu service pays last respects to a man slain on Monday. *Lakeland Ledger,* p. B1.

Mathews, E. (1991, March). Writing for the "little" magazines. *The Writer, 104,* 23–24.

Matthews, R. (1991, January). How to increase your rate of acceptance. *The Writer, 104,* 22–23, 47.

Matthiessen, P. (2002, October). Burning bright. *Outside, 27,* 134–145.

Maucker, E. (1993, June 11). *In search of readers.* Paper presented at the convention of the Florida Press Association and Florida Society of Newspaper Editors, Coral Gables, FL.

McDaniel, D. (1986, December). 12 tips on profiles. *The Editors' Exchange, American Society of Newspaper Editors, 9,* 4.

McGill, L. (1984, August). Give your how-to articles the voice of authority. *Writer's Digest, 64,* 26–28.

McKinney, D. (1986, January). How to write true-life dramas. *Writer's Digest, 66,* 24–28.

McLane, D. (2002, September). Hotel room reflections: A good night's sleep? That's only part of the story. *National Geographic Traveler, 19,* 32–35.

McManus, K. (1992, November). If you absolutely, positively *have* to talk to real people. *ASNE Bulletin, 745,* 18–19.

Meredith, S. (1987). *Writing to sell* (3rd rev. ed.). New York: Harper & Row.

Mills, H. (2002, October). When Heather met Paul. *Vanity Fair, 506,* 328, 369.

Mitchell, A. D. (1997, March). 10 hot tips for writing high tech. *Writer's Digest, 77,* 36–37.

Morgan, J. (1986, July). The secrets of superlative salesmanship. *Writer's Digest, 66,* 30–33.

Mumford, D. M. (2002, September/October). True stories from medicine: A chance to say good-bye. *The Saturday Evening Post, 274,* pp. 32, 91–92.

Neff, G. T. (1992). The business of writing. In M. Kissling (Ed.), *1993 writer's market: Where & how to sell what you write.* Cincinnati, OH: Writer's Digest Books.

Nelkin, D. (1995). *Selling science: How the press covers science and technology.* New York: Freeman.

Nelson, D., & Danis, J. M. (1995). *A national survey of newsletter publishing firms.* Evanston, IL: Northwestern University and Newsletter Publishers Foundation.

Newsletter and Electronic Publishers Foundation (NEPF). (2002). *Newsletter career guide.* Arlington, VA: Author.

Newspaper Association of America (NAA). (2002). *Circulation and readership.* Retrieved August 29, 2002, from http://www.naa.org

Nielsen, J. (2002, April 15). *Statistics for traffic referred by search engines and navigation directories to Useit.* Retrieved September 17, 2002, from http://www.useit.com/about/searchreferrals.htm

Nuwer, H. (1992, July). You can paraphrase me on that. *Writer's Digest, 72,* 28–30.

Oberlin, L. H. (1995, October). Write your way to a paid vacation. *Writer's Digest, 75,* 40–41.

O'Connor, L. B. (1996, January). How to bargain a bigger paycheck. *Writer's Digest, 76,* 25–27.

O'Neill, J. (2002, Summer). USA Today. *News Library News, 24,* 1, 14.

O'Neil, L. P. (1996, May). The travel writer's most valuable writing tool. *Writer's Digest, 76,* 30–33.

Orlik, P. B. (1988). *Critiquing radio and television content.* Boston: Allyn & Bacon.

Osborne, P. B. (1987, April). Writing the "art-of-living" article. *Writer's Digest, 67,* 20–25.

Outing, S. (2000, July). Market your work in virtual places. *Writer's Digest, 80,* 44–45.

Paré, M. A. (Ed.). (2001). *Newsletters in print* (14th ed.). Detroit, MI: Gale Group Inc.

Parker, C. E. (1975, December). 'Tis the season for seasonal articles. *Writer's Digest, 55,* 30–31, 44–45.

Parrish, A. (2002, September 11). Start the stove! It's September. *Tulsa World,* p. D7.

Patterson, B. R. (1986). *Write to be read: A practical guide to feature writing.* Ames: Iowa State University Press.

Paulos, J. A. (1988). *Innumeracy: Mathematical illiteracy and its consequences.* New York: Hill and Wang.

Pember, D. R. (2003). *Mass media law* (2003/2004 ed.). Boston: McGraw-Hill.

Perez, E. R. (2002, October 15). Deep-fried Twinkies emerging as new taste treat. *Fort Lauderdale Sun-Sentinel.* Retrieved October 15, 2002, from http://www.sun-sentinel.com/news/local/southflorida/sfl-1015twinkies.asp

Perret, G. (1984, July). How to build humor, one chuckle at a time. *Writer's Digest, 64,* 30–32.

Perret, G. (1987, September). Short investments, sweet returns. *Writer's Digest, 67,* 27–29.

Peters, E. (1992). Where do you get your ideas? In S. K. Burak (Ed.), *The writer's handbook.* Boston: The Writer.

Petersen, D. (1992, March). How to write the how-to article. *Writer's Digest, 72,* 38–40.

Philcox, P. (1989, June). Fare-paying assignments. *Writer's Digest, 69,* 27–28.

Plimpton, G. (1990). *The Best of Plimpton.* New York: Atlantic Monthly Press.

Polman, D. (2002, September 8). Our old selves. *Philadelphia Inquirer Magazine,* pp. 4–7.

Pollak, L. (1996, December 29). The umpire's sons. *Baltimore Sun,* p. 1–J.

Postman, N. (1985). *Amusing ourselves to death: Public discourse in the age of show business.* New York: Viking.

Pratt, H. J. (1992, November). Writing features for the trades. *ByLine, 150,* 10–11.

Press, S. (1996a). What's online for you? *Writer's Digest, 76,* 32–34.

Press, S. (1996b). Working the Web. *Writer's Digest, 76,* 39–41.

Quindlen, A. (1984). *Writer's writing: Before the first word*. Produced by Learning Designs, Inc., and Educational Broadcasting Corp., WNET–TV, New York, and funded by The Annenberg/CPB Project, Public Broadcasting System.

Ramaswami, R. (2002, October). *Writer's Guidelines*. Stamford, CT: Operations & Fulfillment.

Ranly, D. (1992, June). There's a market for service articles! *The Writer, 105*, 18–20.

Rauch, J. (2002, August). *Hands-on communication: The rituals limitations of Web publishing in the alternative zine community*. Paper presented to the Association for Education in Journalism and Mass Communication, Miami Beach, FL.

Reidy, C. (1992, May 12). A lapse and a "miracle." *The Boston Globe*, pp. 1, 18.

Reiff, T. (1987a). How to keep the money coming. *Writer's Digest, 67*, 22–26.

Reiff, T. (1987b). How to keep the money coming, part II. *Writer's Digest, 67*, 40–42.

Reynolds, G. (2002, October). 200 miles to Moab. *National Geographic Adventure, 4*(8), 70–78.

Ritz, D. (1993, March). Inside interviewing. *The Writer, 106*, 15–17.

Rivers, W. L. (1992). *Free-lancer and staff writer: Newspaper features and magazine articles* (5th ed.). Belmont, CA: Wadsworth.

Rivers, W. L., & Harrington, S. L. (1988). *Finding facts: Research writing across the curriculum*, 2E. Englewood Cliffs, NJ: Prentice Hall.

Robertson, N. (1982, September 19). Toxic shock. *The New York Times Magazine*, pp. 30–34.

Robinson, K. (1993, June). End piece. *ByLine, 157*, 27.

Rodkin, D. (2002, October). What your money can buy. *Chicago, 51*, 78–91.

Romantini, W. (1987, May). So you wanna' be a food critic? *Milwaukee, 12*, 49–52.

Rogers, T. (2002, August). First person: Water vigilante. *D Magazine*. Retrieved October 19, 2002, from http://www.dmagazine.com/august02/person0802.shtml

Ross, J. F. (2002, September). No exit: An illegal pet industry in Indonesia is pushing orangutans to the brink of extinction in the wild. *Smithsonian, 33*, 62–69.

Ruehlmann, W. (1979). *Stalking the feature story*. New York: Vintage.

Ryan, J. (1997, June 13). *Great writers on writing*. Paper presented at the annual convention of the Investigative Reporters and Editors, Phoenix, AZ.

Salant, N. (1993, May 6). *Jury election completed in New Yorker libel trial*. United Press International West wire, 6:13 p.m.

Sarris, A. (1979). Notes on the auteur theory in 1962. In G. Mast & M. Cohen (Eds.), *Film theory and criticism* (2nd ed., pp. 650–665). New York: Oxford University Press.

Schoenfeld, A. C., & Diegmueller, K. S. (1982). *Effective feature writing*. New York: Holt, Rinehart & Winston.

Schreiber, N. (1991, December). Home is where the office is. *Writer's Digest, 71*, 41–45.

Scithers, G., & Meschkow, S. (1985b, September). Under cover. *Writer's Digest, 65*, 42–43.

Scott, H. (1992). Writing the personal experience article. In S. K. Burack (Ed.), *The writer's handbook*. Boston: The Writer.

Seemuth, M. (2002, August 12). The changing magazine world. *The Miami Herald* (Business Monday), pp. 22–25.

Seibel, M. (1991, July 22). On reporting: Getting to Fidel. *The Bay View* [*Miami Herald* newsroom weekly newsletter], *29*, 1.

Shannon, J. (1984, November). Typewriter as time machine: The secrets of selling seasonal material. *Writer's Digest, 64*, 33–34.

Shapiro, M. A. (1988, July). *Components of interest in television science stories*. Paper presented at the annual convention of the Theory and Methodology Division, Association for Education in Journalism and Mass Communication, Portland, OR.

Shaw, T. (2000, December 20). Weathering winter journeys: Plan ahead for holiday travel. *Omaha World–Herald*, p. 17.

Sibbison, J. (1988, July/August). Covering medical "breakthroughs." *Columbia Journalism Review, 27*, 36–39.

Siegel, B. (2001, December 30). A father's pain, a judge's duty, and a justice beyond their reach. *Los Angeles Times*. Retrieved September 1, 2002, from http://www.pulitzer.org/year/2002/feature-writing/works/

Sloan, K. (2002, December 24). Displays keep on growing. *The Brunswick News*, p. 1.

Smith, A. (1970). *The seasons: Life and its rhythms*. New York: Harcourt Brace.

Smith, C. A. (1993, April). Breaking into magazine article writing. *The Writer, 106*, 15–17.

Smith, S., & Davis, M. (1997, December 4). Evolution of alternatives. *Nashville Tennessean*. Final edition, p. ARC.

Solis, D. (2002, September 15). A subtle social critic. *Dallas Morning News*, p. 3F.

Sorrels, R. (1986, March). The sensuous writer. *Writer's Digest, 66*, 38–41.

Spencer, W. B. (1992, August). The voice of authority. *Writer's Digest, 72*, 28–29.

Spielmann, P. (1988, January). The real-life, stranger-than-fiction humor of William Geist. *Writer's Digest, 68*, 28–31.

Spikol, A. (1979, March). Nonfiction: Profiles with punch. *Writer's Digest, 59*, 7–10.

Spikol, A. (1984, October). Non fiction: Service please. *Writer's Digest, 64*, 15–16.

Spikol, A. (1986b, September). Non fiction: Different worlds. *Writer's Digest, 66*, 16–18.

Spikol, A. (1986c, January). Non fiction: Make me laugh. *Writer's Digest, 66*, 16–19.

Spikol, A. (1987, March). Trading in on trade journals. *Writer's Digest, 67*, 16, 18.

Spikol, A. (1993, July). Non fiction: "May I quote you on that?" *Writer's Digest, 73*, 54–55.

Steinberg, S. (2002, September 15). Can't sleep? Here's some news you can snooze to: Zzzzzzzzzz zz does it. *The Dallas Morning News*, pp. 1F, 11F.

Stern, G. (1993, June). Become an instant expert. *Writer's Digest, 73*, 35–37.

Strunk, W., & White, E. B. (1979). *The elements of style* (3rd ed.). New York: Macmillan.

Survey indicates business and personal travel is up 5 percent since last year. (1997, December 10). *Columbus Ledger–Enquirer*, p. A7.

Swanson, M. (1979, May). Covering the campuses. *Writer's Digest, 59*, 33, 35.

Sweeney, J. (1993, March). Pay attention to the process of writing. *ASNE Bulletin, 748*, 27.

Talese, G. (1966, April). Frank Sinatra has a cold. *Esquire, 65*, 89–98, 152.

Taylor, E. (2002, September 29). About this issue. *Chicago Tribune Magazine*, section 10, p. 2.

Taylor, M. R. (1998, February). Write for the Web and sell! *Writer's Digest, 78*, 18–24.

Teer, J. (1973, January 20). Florida newsman discovers Samaritans still hard to find. *Editor & Publisher, 106*, 24.

Teeter, D. L., & Le Duc, D. R. (1992). *Law of mass communications* (7th ed.). Westbury, NY: Foundation Press.

Thibodeaux, R. (2001, July 15). Good home-cooking serves as catalyst for good times: Supper club livens up small-town social life. *New Orleans Times–Picayune*. Retrieved January 10, 2002, from http://www.nola.com/news/

Thrasher, P. C. (2001, November 11). Voice of Atlanta panel: Most say yes to travel for holidays. *The Atlanta Journal and Constitution*, p. 1A.

Titchener, C. B. (1998). *Reviewing the Arts* (2nd ed.). Mahwah, NJ: Lawrence Erlbaum Associates, Inc.

Toner, M. (1992, August 23). When bugs fight back. *Atlanta Constitution*, p. A/1.

Updike, J. (1976). *Picked-up pieces*. New York: Knopf.

Vawter, V. (1993, January/February). Taking "detours" to reach new markets in Knoxville, Tenn. *ASNE Bulletin, 747*, 18.

Vitez, M. (1996, November 17). Families in agony on when to let go. *The Philadelphia Inquirer*, p. 1A.

Vitez, M. (1998, January 1). *Explanatory journalism: Biography*. Retrieved April 9, 2003, from http://www.pulitzer.org/year/1997/explanatory-journalism/bio

Walker, L. A. (1992). How to write a profile. In S. K. Burack (Ed.), *The writer's handbook* Boston: The Writer.

Walker, L. (2001, June 21). *Moving from logs to blogs: Technology and you.* Retrieved September 6, 2002, from http://www.spokesmanreview.com/sections/sports/stateb/2002/stateb.asp?ID=2002\blog\blog-primer

Wardlow, E. (Ed.). (1985). *Effective writing and editing: A guidebook for newspapers.* Reston, VA: American Press Institute.

*Webster's new world dictionary of the English language.* (1966). Cleveland, OH: World Publishing.

Wiesenfeld, L. P. (Ed.). (2002). *The world almanac and book of facts 2002* (134th ed.). New York: Press Publishing Co.

Wilde, L. (1976). *How the great comedy writers create laughter.* Chicago: Nelson-Hall.

Wilker, D. (1993, April 8). *Why should we take entertainment reporting seriously?* Paper presented at the meeting of the Society of Professional Journalists, University of Miami, Coral Gables, FL.

Williams, G. (1996, March). How to interview celebrities. *Writer's Digest, 76,* 34–36.

Williamson, D. R. (1975). *Feature writing for newspapers.* New York: Hastings House.

Willis, C. (1996, March). The more and less of writing humorous fiction. *Writer's Digest, 76,* 32–33.

Wilson, J. M. (1990, October). How to give an editor nothing to do (except buy your article). *Writer's Digest, 70,* 33–35.

Wilson, J. M. (1996, February). Successful interviewing: It's all in the preparation. *Writer's Digest, 76,* 35–37.

Winship, F. M. (2002, September 6). African art market thrives in storage unit. United Press International wire service, Entertainment, n.p.

Wolfe, J. K. (1990, June). The six basics of writing humorously. *Writer's Digest, 70,* 18–22.

Wolfe, T. (1966). *The kandy-kolored tangerine-flake streamline baby.* New York: Pocket Books.

Wolk, M. (1991, January 20). Another victim of magazine slump dies. *The Miami Herald,* p. 2G.

Wood, M. (1997, August). What's online for you? *Writer's Digest, 77,* 28–29.

Wood, T. (1993, March). Getting tough interviews. *Writer's Digest, 73,* 28–31.

Wysocki, P. M. (1999). *The ultimate guide to newsletter publishing.* Arlington, VA: Newsletter Publishers Association.

Yates, E. D. (1985). *The writing craft* (2nd ed.). Raleigh, NC: Contemporary Publishing.

Yates, T. (1995, June). How to set your rates. *Writer's Digest, 75,* 31–33.

Zaharoff, H. G. (1996a, May). Questions and answers about copyright. *Writer's Digest, 76,* 24–26, 57.

Zaharoff, H. G. (1996b, June). Showdown on the electronic frontier. *Writer's Digest, 76,* 36–38.

Zbar, J. D. (2002, September). Setting goals for making more money. *Writer's Digest, 82,* 52–54.

Zehl, V. (1998, January). Turn one sale into a dozen or more. *Writer's Digest, 78,* 22–25.

Zinsser, W. (1980). *On writing well* (2nd ed.). New York: Harper & Row.

# Index